Best wishes to you and your family now and in the future. Your contributions in the past are greatly appreciated.

Larry J. O'Daniel

9/27/05

Trails
of
Deceit

by
Larry J. O'Daniel

author
Missing in Action:
Trail of Deceit

 **Golden Coast™ Publishing**

Trails of Deceit

First Edition

Grateful appreciation to Mrs. Fran Masterson for her kind approval of the use on the front cover of the likeness of her husband, LTC Michael J. "Bat" Masterson, lost on 1/10/68 in Laos, whose status may have acutally been that of a POW.

Author Larry J. O'Daniel with his wife, Yun, and Congressman Robert K. Dornan at CPAC 1981 where much of the story you will read about developed, especially the part about the attempt by President Ronald W. Reagan to bring back prisoners from a camp in Laos.

ISBN 0-9701341-0-X
Library of Congress Cataloguing Applied for

Introduction

All warfare is based upon deception. This maxim, popularized by the Chinese tactician Sun Tzu, is the key element to this book. When I first wrote the book, **Missing in Action: Trail of Deceit** in 1979, I knew the maxim well. I had been trained in it through my indoctrination in tactical cover and deception. I assisted the staff at the Army Electronic Warfare School, Tactical Deception Department, in researching the whole range of combat deception. My research took me from the simple put a twig in the helmet type of cover to the grand strategy of deception as practiced by the United States, the Soviet Union, China, and their respective allies. I introduced into the curriculum the Soviet use of disinformation. Being schooled in both EW and TC&D (earning the E prefix to my formal MOS of tactical intelligence staff officer - E standing for both Electronic Warfare and Tactical Cover and Deception trained) today helps lead to the unraveling of the mystery of the fate of Prisoners of War and Missing in Action from several wars.

The book is the product of a concept I learned in Vietnam, the Phoenix concept. That is bringing together information from as many sources as possible for evaluation. From this evaluation process, a picture emerges. The image depicted is ugly. I maintain, for the record, that this Phoenix concept is a model for how our intelligence agencies should operate at the National level. While imperfect, it is leagues above what we have now, a politicized morass in which honorable men feel they must lie to national leaders in order to hold true to a national purpose, even if the cover story is totally implausible.

Before presenting the ugly image which has been uncovered, I want to show the way of this story. In September 1996, Congressman Robert K. Dornan, a friend and the writer of the forward to my first book, stated the problem with this issue: "There has never been a systematic methodology, as I begged for 20 years, since I first ... met with CIA Director Stansfield Turner... a methodology by fearless Sherlock Holmes type investigators to build upon the successes and the mistakes of our historical record .... Instead, we ... see ...where cynics are able to reign supreme with a simple line: 'That's hearsay. Get it out of my face....'"

At the same hearing, Commander William G. "Chip" Beck, a special operations operative put another perspective by testifying, "... most of what I heard falls into the pattern that I think is perfectly logical ... from what I consider to be a clandestine operation directed against us since World War II. ... the deception. When we spend a lot of time looking for bones ... to the exclusion of the strategic importance of what happened to our men ... we lose a lot of, I think, the substance and the importance of what we should be doing."

What is this clandestine operation? It falls into several areas, I believe. The first is most logically, the POW story. The story of brave men lost in combat as either a prisoner of war or missing in action. This was how I approached my first book because of a lack of concrete information about the rest of the story.

Always missing has been the answer to the nagging question; Why would another nation hold onto the men? What is to be gained? After many feeble attempts to answer that question, I believe I now have a logical, systematic, response. It is based upon thirty years of research beginning when I was an intelligence officer in Vietnam, assigned to the Phoenix Program and ending with this book.

The answer is the ugly dilemma alluded to.

To many, this book reads like fiction. However, it is a true account of men who were sacrificed for political expediency. Some were murdered by corrupt communist warlords planning to take over the world. Some were tortured in subhuman environments ranging from Hanoi to the reaches of the U-Minh Forest. Some were exploited through drug and chemical interrogation to satiate the communist desire for information necessary to overcome the technological prowess of the American juggernaut knocking out the best missile defenses Moscow and Beijing could supply to Hanoi.

The prisoners of the Vietnam War were officially "all released" by the middle of 1973. Hanoi said so. Our State Department agreed. The plan was to declare dead all who did not return within one year. No one would object and no one would care! However, the plan got disrupted. Family members, many of whom were military themselves, objected loudly. They were aided by current and former intelligence operatives who knew men were left behind. Men still held in the stark "second tier" of prisons. Oloeving the truth became the cause of a loose coalition exchanging information, crossing enemy borders, and penetrating the vaults of America's intelligence agencies. Sacrificing political careers to help were numerous politicians who gave the coalition public forums to arouse public opinion.

Thirty years after I began my search for POWs, the fight still rages. The endless trails of deceit have been explored. The numerous questions about how and why this happened are now answered for the first time. From start to finish, **Trails of Deceit** relates the story of three generations of war veterans sacrificed because unnamed bureaucrats withheld from their superiors vital information, which if known, would lead to international confrontations of staggering proportions.

In World War II, tens of thousands of men disappeared into the Soviet Gulags. In Korea, the exact number probably ranges in the low thousands. Vietnam sent 4400 men into the dark recesses of Nazi-like experimentation. The one lone person "known" to have emerged was politically sacrificed as a "traitor" by those who more fittingly were worthy of that title.

The coalition, of which I am a proud member, combed the "declassified" records of three wars. Friends on the inside leaked what was not "declassified" to those capable of interpreting what they revealed. Active duty "spooks," frustrated by the roadblocks, risked ridicule and censure to help their "active duty" comrades still in captivity. An academic researcher in the failed Soviet Union discovered the "Rosetta Stone" providing proof from the classified vaults of the Hanoi communists. As a final gesture before his untimely death, a former high ranking communist official who oversaw decades of Russian, Chinese, and Vietnamese duplicity once more related his electrifying charges almost three decades after the CIA "deep-sixed" his original account.

Everyone wanted a simple answer to a complex problem. Even Vietnamese GEN Tran Van Quang never covered those men who were transferred to the Soviet Union and China or those still being held in Laos. He never covered those men because he was part of another deception, so secret that even members of his Politburo were not cleared to know, with few exceptions.

There were prisoners of war, not only from Vietnam, but Korea and World War II and probably before and after, who have disappeared into the deep recesses of clandestine warfare or those actions that "never occurred." Our government will not acknowledge that these actions were taken against our armed forces, because the inevitable question would be did we engage in similar types of activities? The deception on the part of our government, however forms one of the many trails of deceit that will be investigated in this interrelated mystery.

Presented for the first time is the accumulation of intelligence, secret White House and DOD files, eyewitness accounts, and government investigations which tell the astounding story of sacrifice, duty, and duplicity. The sacrifice of the men; the duty of the coalition; and the duplicity of the diplomat and politician.

What I am charging, backed by the brave testimony of warriors of the dark side of military operations, and an eyewitness from the armed forces of our adversaries, the late General Major Jan Sejna, is that many of our prisoners of war and missing in action from several wars were used in Nazi style medical experiments that are leading directly to a dilemma faced by this country even as I am writing this forward. Failure to react to this information will cause untold harm to the national interests of this country. When a country first builds a deception story without thinking of the consequences of it unraveling ten, twenty, or more years down the line, then the chips will fall in untold directions.

From the viewpoint of the enemies, Vietnam, Russia, and China plus their associated allies, there was no expectation that this trail of deceit would ever be uncovered. Who, in 1951, expected the Iron Curtain to fall? Who expected the foreign policy of Ronald Wilson Reagan to cause the fall of communism in most of the world? Who ever expected that hundreds of families would persevere for decades to find out the fate of their men? Little did I expect in 1969 to be finishing in 2000 a book as far ranging, yet tightly compartmentalized, as this one. Who expected a little known governor from a corrupt administration in Arkansas to become President of the United States with a record of being a draft evader and demonstrator against his own government in wartime? To become Commander in Chief of the Armed Forces?

What is his role? He took over the role of President at the time several other trails of deceit came together. These trails were corruption in obtaining campaign money from enemy foreign sources; the "1205" document previously alluded to; and the testimony in 1996; also previously alluded to. Added to that is the knowledge that the campaign money may enable the communist Chinese and Koreans, plus other adversaries, to accurately launch missiles towards the United States carrying chemical and biological weapons made as a result of the torture and experimentation upon our own men held hostage in two wars. Our own security may be threatened by a president too weak to fight but all too willing to send other men into war. A president all too willing to seek power through the help of our sworn enemies and yet will not lift a finger to bring back men held in captivity. William Jefferson Clinton embarked upon a policy of appeasing the enemies of our country; Vietnam and China in particular, by giving away precious diplomatic "chips" and leaving in the lurch the fate of brave men still in captivity and those whose fate can now reasonably be accounted for.

Much has been learned in the 30 years since I first became a Phoenix operative charged with the responsibility of finding and neutralizing the political apparatus of the Hanoi lead, Moscow and Beijing funded, Viet Cong Infrastructure (VCI). One collateral job was to find, identify, and rescue American and allied POWs. Now, thirty years later, working with the coalition, often in the background,

I've put together this startling story of a Byzantine road of duplicity. This story reads like fiction. It is all too real. Others have been threatened, intimidated, ridiculed, lied about, and had their rights trammeled. I've taken up the call with this "final" book and added my own unique brand of investigation.

There are other trails of deceit including the very real probability that men were returned to this country using clandestine means. There is the very real possibility that corrupt methods were used to obtain intelligence, the price we are just beginning to realize. Then there is the trail that shows that many investigators were quietly discredited, even though their work is backed by other eyewitness and documentary proof. This trail of deceit leads right back to our own agencies. Persons have been convicted of crimes on less evidence than will be presented in this book. Circumstantial evidence, plus first hand evidence will be used. Both are valid in courts of law.

The ultimate challenge is I've been told that "no one cares;" "it's old news;" and "get a life." Well, on October 20, 1999, NBC Nightly News confirmed the biological warfare story of General Sejna, minus the part the POWs played. They showed the world, after a Congressional testimony from another Russian defector, the Top Secret labs where the weapons were made. Once again, the role of POW "rats" was ignored or covered up. So, I decline the kind offers to "quit."

This story will be provocative, exciting, and totally unnecessary, if the government had done it's job properly. It could not have been told earlier because the facts were not all known earlier. Now, using the Phoenix method of intelligence coordination, this record of "deceit," "duplicity," and "mindset to debunk" will be put together by the "connect the dots" to get the "whole picture" method.

I thank the late LTG Eugene Tighe, the late Dermot Foley, the late COL Nick Rowe, the late Marian Shelton, and those organizations whose help is acknowledged as the book unfolds. No single person could do this story himself. The fact that my findings dovetail with other professional personnel in DIA, CIA, NSA, and other secret agencies is not coincidental. Whatever stance I take in this book, regardless of the sources or material used, is mine alone.

Some, like former POW Senator John McCain, refuse to confront the reality of what the staff the POW Committee said; the POWs of Vietnam were alive through the hearings of 1992. His own father, the late Admiral John McCain, knew they had been abandoned and so testified.

I wish to acknowledge the help of tens of families who have shared their innermost secrets about their lost men with me. Returned POWs have been instrumental in acting as sounding boards for some of my theories. Their criticisms have been pointed, objective, critical, and demanding. Unnamed, still on active duty, are many in the deep recesses of government with seemingly "hostile" attitudes to the families. Your help is also appreciated and will be rewarded.

To the public, heed this "call to arms" and look for the "choice" of action rather than the "echo" of past failed policies.

Larry J. O'Daniel
Arizona, January, 2000

Chapter 1: The EC-47Q Case

Chapter 2: The Broken Promises 16

Chapter 3: Trail to Captivity 30

Chapter 4: Are they still alive? 41

Contents

Contents

Contents

Contents

L:TG John Wilson "Iron Mike" O'Daniel, first MAAG Advisor to and true friend of the Republic of Vietnam - said - who pays, rules -

Vietnam President Nguyen Van Thieu was threatened with assassination like his predecessor, President Ngo Dinh Diem

Possible E & E Photo found in the Thomas Hart Affair - a 1573 or 1973 and TH - in Laos

President Ngo Dinh Diem, was assassinated for his refusal to bow to liberal Democratic policies - CIA inspired - like that of Project Cherry - attempt to assassinate Norodom Sihanouk

LTG Eugene Tighe, Director of DIA, bravely testified his conscience on the POWs left behind and stood his guns against the "revisionists."

EC-47 Case: A Study in Deceit

January 27, 1973. The war was over. Secretary of State Henry Kissinger and President Richard Nixon concluded a long, divisive war, declaring "Peace with Honor" in Vietnam. In Thailand, crews flying covert missions into Laos and Cambodia knew better. Their missions continued. Their necessary combat support operations lay in that "gray area" of diplomacy. These fliers were knowingly not covered under the Peace Accords.

Casualties occurred in these flights. Some men were declared killed in action (KIA); some were Missing in Action (MIA); and many were Prisoners of War (POWs). These casualties caused problems as the acknowledged POWs in Vietnam were being released. The missions in Laos were hidden. This case gives a reason why MIA families do not take seriously any pledge, statement, or promise, not backed by firm action.

The Secrecy Begins

The EC-47Q shoot-down occurred in 1973. It was partially uncovered in 1978. It has been examined twice in court cases. Relatively new information was uncovered in early 1994. I've worked on it since 1978, ending with a confrontation with DOD in April, 1997. If the words "cover-up" and "deceit" have any meaning, they are synonymous with "EC-47Q."

On February 4, 1973, an EC-47Q airplane (call sign Baron 52) took off from Ubon Airfield, Thailand. Aboard were eight men, four officers and four enlisted men. They were CPT Arthur Bollinger, CPT George Spitz, LT Robert Bernhardt, LT Severo Primm, SGT Peter Cressman, SGT Joseph Matejov, SGT Dale Brandenburg, and SGT Todd Melton. Their mission was to conduct aerial electronic surveillance and reconnaissance. What did their mission encompass? An October 24, 1989 classified oral history gives the true story from some participants.

Mr. Willard Ellerson, a chronicler, asked:. "Was this mission at night?" CMSGT Ronald L. Schofield, formerly a SGT replied, "Yes Sir." LTC Lionel Blau, formerly the OPs Officer added "Our Smoker missions were at night."

Smoker Missions? Schofield said, "That one was going in after the tanks. Where they put the sensors, (Project Igloo White) they had indications that there were a lot of tank movement on that trail. Our role ... was to identify and locate the tanks. The problems with the tanks, though, (material censored) But that's what we were out there for." Blau added, "We were flying those every night. That was just part of our routine schedule."

Mr. Ellerson read for the record, "the reports show there were 300 - 500 tanks moving through area 11. The next night, there was a report ... of up to 11 tanks in the area. So there was heavy tank movement ..."

The EC-47 was no ordinary plane. It was a converted C-47 "Gooney Bird" loaded with sophisticated electronic equipment. Often called a "Flying Pueblo," one official description said that it was so loaded with equipment the crew did not wear their parachutes. In 1992, Robert DeStatte, a senior analyst with DIA, testified to the configuration. "... I know the aircraft, it is particularly tight ... it is very difficult to move and when you are in your position, you were kind of there."

Secrecy surrounds both the EC-47 and the AC-47 in Vietnam. The basic plane body is the same. Their insides, however, differ. Little is known about the EC-47. In many standard books on Vietnam era planes, the EC-47 is noticeably absent.

The last flight of this EC-47Q started routinely. At 1:25 AM (Laos Time) on February 5, the command center received a message that the EC-47 was observing ground fire. They either evaded or were receiving hostile "radar controlled" anti-aircraft ground fire. Five minutes later, the crew signaled everything was normal. Radar plotted their location. Communications ceased. Their last radar plot occurred at 1:40 AM.

At 2:00 AM, Baron 52 failed to call a scheduled "Operations Normal Report." A communications and electronics search began for the presumed downed plane. At dawn, a search and rescue mission was mounted. Baron 52 failed to respond either through secure or normal channels.

It took two days to find the wreckage of the plane and two more days to get a para-rescue team to examine the crash site. One official description of the search said the team was allowed to probe for an undisturbed forty minutes. Those with a first hand knowledge, however, said "the area was hot" and the search was hasty and sometimes under fire.

One official report described the scene as indicating that the plane had come in, landed hard, skidding for several hundred yards. Another official report said that there were no skid marks; the plane had impacted upside down. The fuselage was gutted by an extremely intense fire with everything reduced to ashes or melted. DeStatte testified to the Senate POW Committee that "an absence of skid marks, indicated the aircraft had plunged in nearly vertically to earth, bounced once, and landed upside down and burned."

Unofficial reports speculate that stress on the wings caused them to snap and possibly caused the plane to flip. The converted C-47s used in Vietnam were old with service records prior to Korea. One "scathing report" on their maintenance was referred to in the Oral History.

LTC Blau examined the crash site photos because of his PI (photo interpretation) training. Blau correctly identified this crash site as being "new," the Baron 52 site, while others identified it as an old one. This non-recognition of the crash location was partially responsible for the long time in getting people to the locale. Blau explained what he found in the photos.

"One of the points that I always like to point out ... is that this does not show the way the aircraft came into the crash site. When you look at the film... it was very obvious that the aircraft had hit up on top of the hill and came directly in and impacted upside down. The wings were knocked off, and part of the aircraft ... a tail section, was up on the hill," said Blau.

Ellerson asked how far away was the hill. Blau replied that about 400 yards or so, adding, "The thing that I think is important ... to note where that tail section was ... up on the hill ... relative ... with the nose ... is that in determining that the individuals were KIA, COL Francis Humphries, ... the ...Wing Commander ... said would cause him to say they were KIA was that if the aircraft was spinning, no one could get out of the aircraft. I pointed out ... that the aircraft hit straight ahead. It was not spinning ... He totally disregarded that, as well as **other (censored) messages.**" (**Emphasis added**)

Ellerson added, "You mean an airborne evacuation as opposed to on the ground,

... so any survivors would have had to bailout. Is that a correct assumption?" Schofield said "Absolutely sir, and **there was an intel report...**" (**Emphasis added**) No survivors were found at the crash site. At this point, the official version of the crash becomes strained.

Found on the ground.

The official version had the para-rescue team on the ground for an unmolested forty minutes with members unable to bring back a single dog-tag, ID card, or any other piece of identification save the partial remains of one man, Robert Bernhardt. This lead to speculation that the real mission of the rescue team was the destruction of the highly sophisticated secret equipment aboard the plane.

Three or four bodies were found strapped to their seats coinciding with EC-47 emergency Standard Operating Procedures (SOP). The enlisted personnel were expected to bail out with the crew riding the plane into the ground. The remains found were in the front, where the officers were. Schofield said "We found the aircraft was on its back. ... it had a full fuel load which accounts for the intensity of fire. **All I was there for was to make sure there was no classified still available.** When we got there, one of the PJs (para-rescue personnel) set up a perimeter, and the other one and myself were looking for bodies. We only found three bodies (all officers) The back-end ... was burned, and the Colonel (Blau) and I have talked about it. These aircraft flew with the doors on. If that aircraft had crashed with the door on, there would have been a little bit of it left at the top. There was absolutely nothing. ... It looked like it had been kicked off." Ellerson asked, "Kicked off? You mean... The door had been ejected?" (**Emphasis supplied**)

Schofield answered, "Pulled the handle ... people bailed out. Because there was about 12 - 14 inches of the aircraft left and where the door was, the top of the door was open. ... it was not there. But everything else had burned. And also the front-end — nomex flight suits were good ... you could recognize the pilot, the copilot, and third pilot, and there should have been some remains of the back-enders in the fire, but there wasn't anything.... The three bodies were right where they should have been. There should have been some remains in the back-end, but there was absolutely nothing."

Ellerson asked about the possibility the enlisted men had been cremated. Schofield replied, "I thought so originally. ... whatever I said, had a direct impact on the decisions made. No, I've given it a lot of thought and I've talked to the Colonel (Blau) about that, and the absence of the top of the door, **the intel report about the four fliers,** shock, which indicates ... suffering from burns, which they probably would have... **I felt in my own mind that they had, ... been captured and ... interrogated.**" (**Emphasis supplied**)

Blau added, "One of the typical things on a smoker, if you were being shot at, you had on your parachute harness and, if they had chest packs, ... And I know for a fact that those guys could slap the chest packs on and be out the door in 1 1/2 minutes, ... they had more than ample time ... I've had a hard time accepting that they were killed in a crash, ... those guys would have been out long before they would have gone down with the aircraft."

Schofield said, "We really couldn't spend that much time on the ground. We had some intruders ... We called in some A-7s.... and they made some passes, but nothing happened. And then we got an IFE (in-flight emergency) on the chopper that we were on, so we made the decision ... to try to recover one of the bodies. The one that was in the best position was the third pilot. ... it separated at the waist and we were only able to bring up the upper torso. ... We probably should have spent some more time there, but because of the area, they didn't want to put us back in."

Ellerson made a point — "So there were five unaccounted for in the back-end. One officer and the four enlisted..."

Classified Intelligence Report

On February 22, 1973, all eight men were declared KIA. The case lay dormant until columnist Jack Anderson and the *Atlanta Journal* broke a story in mid 1978 showing a cover-up on this case from day one. At the request of the late Dermot Foley, the legal counsel for the National League of Families (The League), I was doing the same with a reporter for the *Philadelphia Inquirer*. Anderson and the *Journal* reported at least four crewmen survived and were captured.

They reported that on February 5, the day of the loss, our intelligence forces intercepted enemy radio communications showing the movement of "air pirates" about 65 kilometers from the crash site, or about 40 miles. A unit of either Vietnamese or Laotian troops {the nationality was not then determined due to censorship} moved them from point 44 to point 93 {presumably mile markers} and, "They were having difficulties moving along the road."

A second intercept on February 5, stated this "group is holding four pilots captive and the group is requesting orders concerning what to do with them." A third intercept occurred on February 17 stating: "All ... units are to fire at enemy aircraft during the new season." It continued, "The people involved in the South Laotian campaign have shot down one aircraft and captured the pilot/pilots."

This last message ended, look for aircraft parts, "this is to be done immediately, you are to report back on the 19th. That is all the time you have to report. It has to be reported by the 19th." The EC-47 was the only plane lost in this period.

The official version of the loss, released in 1978, stated, "Shortly after the loss of this aircraft, an intelligence source, that may not be further identified, reported that enemy forces were transporting four captured men, who may have been American pilots, about 65 kilometers from the crash site. However, no identity or nationality was specified." The consistent government stance is they cannot be sure that these men were Americans. In February 1981, Mr. & Mrs. Robert Cressman received a letter from Admiral Jerry Tuttle of the Defense Intelligence Agency (DIA). This letter responded to information provided by the Cressmans. This letter, dated February 25, said, "The DIA has completed a review of your son's case, including the material you provided... However, based upon our review, the information, ... is correct in that no identity or nationality of the reported prisoners was specified, and that there was no certainty that these people were American or that the information was connected to the crash of your son's aircraft."

In the strictest literal sense, Admiral Tuttle was correct. Nothing in the public realm proved the intercepts were 1) real, 2) pertinent to the EC-47, or 3) even about Americans. Admiral Tuttle did not reveal classified material.

More Classified Material

Another document emerged. It was a May 1973 analysis of "all available information concerning the four fliers." This document added: "Two (censored) persons were to be contacted concerning movement of the POWs and if problems were encountered, high (censored) was to be notified to supply ways and means (references to trucks) to move the fliers." "Sufficient water was to be given to the fliers. There has been some difficulties in transporting the fliers and (censored) asked (censored) to see if these problems had been resolved so movement could continue... (censored) ... also asked that he be notified of their ... departure ... he was waiting for them."

The document continued "although the initial location given is some 65 kilometers from the crash site, it is possible ... part of the crew were able to bail out ... been closer to this point than the crash site when they were captured... since vehicle transportation was indicated, rapid movement is reasonable. **It is possible that the 4 fliers were part of the crew of the EC-47**" **(Emphasis supplied)**

DIA decided to regroup. It did a re-analysis of the intercepts. For the first time in years, it decided that they did not pertain to the EC-47 case. DeStatte testified in 1992, "Over the years, there has grown the impression that we had evidence that some of the members of that crew survived. In fact, a careful analysis of the information ... reveals that the information did not pertain to that crew. There never has been any evidence that any members of that crew survived...four sets of Intelligence Reports, portions of which were declassified ... led others to speculate that four electronics specialists could have survived. Two of the documents were dated 5 February, 1973, and another 17 February, 1973 ... and the fourth 2 May, 1973....Through long-standing misinterpretation of these sanitized documents, an erroneous impression of survivors was preserved.... the four reports do not relate to the loss of the EC-47... following the loss of Baron 52, none of its crew-members were ever seen alive and **there is no intelligence** whatsoever which would indicate any of the crew survived the incident of loss." **(Emphasis supplied)**

Since I was one of the first non-family members to look at the EC-47 case, providing DeStatte's "misinterpretation," I take umbrage to his interpretation of what I did. The tone for the rest of the book is set by examining both sides, carefully, to see who has the strongest case. First, we'll examine some background.

First Court Examination

Before the 1978 public release of the material in the EC-47 crash, a court case, *Hopper v. Carter*, was in progress. This case was an attempt to keep MIAs from being declared dead without evidence. Former Assistant Secretary of Defense Roger Shields was deposed under oath. Part of his deposition relates to the EC-47 case. I helped Foley with some evidence he presented in *Hopper* and the EC-47 case. In the following material, **(F)** is for Foley and **(S)** is for Shields.

F: Is it not a fact that there were some provisions for some of the planes ... that the sensitive equipment on those planes would not fall into the hands of the other side, even if there were a casualty?

S: I think that extreme measures would have been taken.

F: Were they not, in fact taken?

S: I would say, yes... The C-47 is a very old aircraft. You could put a lot of sophisticated equipment....

Elaine Buck (government attorney — **EB**): Excuse me, what is the purpose of this line of questioning?

F: He knows where I am going....

F: What measures were taken to see to it that the equipment didn't fall into enemy hands?

EB: I object....I see no relevance.

F: I think he knows what I am after...

F: ... there is information that relates to the necessity of protecting the information that a man had which also relates to his chances of survival which his family has not been told...

S: Could I break for a few minutes, and could I caucus with my friendly counsel, with the government's counsel? (A recess was taken)....

F: ... there was a question you wanted to clarify, ... whether there were some details related to the sensitivity of the equipment ...

S: What you ought to do is ask me another question.

F: Let's ask that question in just that form....

S: Can I go off record for just a second? ...

F: ... We make a distinction between missions before and after January 27, 1973, ... there were casualties and combat missions after that date?

S: Yes, there were....

F: ... After the 27th of January, 1973, what do you know about non-disclosure of information ... of combat missions ...

S: ... certain kinds of missions, ... had more secrecy to them ... and I know a couple of times I questioned in my own mind decisions ... about a change of status (from MIA to KIA).

F: ... were there reasons to believe that after the crash, **interceptions and other intelligence sources** indicated that the other side had the man captured or that he was alive?... (**Emphasis added**)

F: ... After January 27, 1973, whether there are specific instances ... that **there were intercepts or other sources of intelligence that showed that he had in fact been captured?** (**Emphasis added**) You have three answers: That there was, or wasn't, or you can't go into it because it was classified....

S: Well, I would prefer to rely on the last answer....

Shields, at this point, made a phone call to the Department of Defense (DOD) to get a ruling on what he could or could not discuss. He talked to Florence Madden, DOD counsel.

S: Mrs. Madden said that if there were elements of the case that were classified, ... not to comment on the specifics. So for my own protection, -

F: For you protection, over my protest ... this information, ... is declined, because of the possibility that it is classified. Is that right?

S: Right. **I do not want to go to jail.** (**Emphasis supplied**)

Shields' deposition ended. Less than three months later, the declassified intercepts were made public. This testimony of Dr. Shields is also important because it contains some key elements of deceit (though not from Shields) that had not become totally clear until mid-1989.

After the 1978 release of information, the families fought for another three years to get a picture of the crash site. The government insisted it did not exist. I examined the Cressman's material and found messages referring to the pictures. Using those messages, they finally got the pictures.

The government still maintains there is no connection between the intercepts and the crash of the EC-47. I wrote previously, they were connected. My writings were hampered by security considerations. I walked a tight line between discussing the information and revealing classified information, but I could not cross it.

Insider documents reveal how the government arrived at their official releases. On July 24, 1978, Mrs. Madden, in an internal draft statement for Jack Anderson, wrote, "Shortly after the loss of the aircraft, a sensitive intelligence source reported that **Laotian forces** were transporting four captured pirates about 65 kilometers from the crash site. No identity or nationality was given, although the term 'pirates' was usually used to describe Americans..." (**Emphasis supplied**) The official release read "...an intelligence source that may not be further identified, reported that enemy forces were transporting four captured men who may have been American pilots...However, no identity or nationality was specified...."

Why wasn't the commander notified? The draft answer said, "It was highly classified ... higher than the field commander had access to. Even in unclassified form, it was not available until after the men had been declared dead." And the families? **"It was the belief of DOD ... that after the repatriation of POWs, the communists no longer held any of our men alive."** (Emphasis supplied)

That is where the matter stood until January 1986.

The Dam Breaks

In January 1986, Jerry Mooney, a former cryptanalyst for the Air Force, filed an affidavit in a Federal Court Case called *Smith-McIntire* for short. This affidavit referred specifically to the EC-47 case based upon his own personal knowledge. He stated that an analysis of enemy messages showed the Vietnamese exhibited an inordinate amount of interest in capturing crews of intelligence planes such as the EC-47, RF-4, and pilots of the F-4 laser bomb equipped aircraft. "It was clear from the intelligence collected that the North Vietnamese were ... interested in capturing the crews or pilots ... alive. They were considered very important prisoners."

He further swore that in February 1973, "my section received, analyzed, evaluated, and formally reported the shoot-down of an EC-47Q aircraft in Laos. Based upon the enemy messages ... there were at least five to seven survivors ... identified as Americans and as being transported to North Vietnam....This information was formally reported to interested consumers with an add-on of White House."

"I personally wrote the message," Mooney said, "that these men had been captured alive, that they were Americans, and had been transported to North Vietnam. In secure phone conversations with the DIA, we were in total agreement that these were the crew members of the downed EC-47Q."

Mooney swore the Feb. 1981 Cressman letter was false in some of its assertions. He showed that a February 26, 1980, DIA roll of MIAs listed the crew of the EC-47Q as a "category 1," meaning we knew the enemy had verified knowledge of the fate of the crew. (*Categories explained later*)

On January 22, 1992, Mooney testified before the Senate POW Committee. He was asked about the DIA analysis of the case. "It stinks sir." When asked for specifics, he said "DIA says that it's four unknown POWs up in the Vinh area. My position is simply this: it reflects the activity and the movement of the four surviving members from the EC-47Q. The DIA position is impossible... Cryptographically, it does not fit.... the code systems that were used were isolated to the southern area. ... Atmospherically, it doesn't fit. The first collector at Phu Bai could not reach that far into the Vinh area. This was all checked out by a database specialist."

We have two diametrically opposed viewpoints. DIA says that the crew members are dead. Others state the evidence shows that the men were captive. At issue is "intelligence information."

What is intelligence information?

A look at what intelligence is will show how a "sure bet" can be analyzed as "the facts don't support that conclusion."

In a letter to then Congressman Henson Moore, coincidentally, the Congressman for an EC-47Q family, dated 24 December 1981, LTG James A. Williams, then DIA chief, wrote concerning what differentiates between knowledge and presumptive proof. "Thus, regardless of the methodology or techniques utilized to verify a source's report, in the end, it is the analyst who weighs the information obtained and provides the human equation. ... the evaluation of the sources information is a subjective procedure based upon ... the judgment of the analyst ..."

Remember the words "judgment" and "subjective procedure." They play a key role over the years. To gain a further insight into the importance of the EC-47 intercepts; we need to examine communications intelligence.

What is Communications Intelligence?

Briefly, communications intelligence is analyzing the conversations of the enemy. It gives us an uncensored look at the thinking and actions of the enemy camp. A civilian equivalent would be the FBI tapping the lines of enemy agents.

Let's look at the messages with recent releases helping. On February 12, 1973, the USAF 6994th Security Squadron in Thailand asked the National Security Agency (NSA) for more information on Baron 52. The cable said, "Believe the terms 'fliers' vice 'pilots' may be significant. Presumably NVA units know allied pilots are officers. Use of the term 'fliers' may indicate that they are enlisted...." The analysis dealt with wind drift and reasons why a bailout plus transportation would have put the crew members closer to Mile marker 44 than originally thought.

A significant question was asked. "Would the NVA be expected to be transporting prisoners, held for a long period in Laos, north at this time? ... with present prisoner repatriation, this is a possibility, however, ... believe that this might indicate that the 'fliers' were recent captives."

NSA wrote back saying, "Find your speculation very interesting and agree that the crew could have bailed out at a point closer to KM 44 (censored) than the crash site. Considering the time factor of approximately four and one half hours between time of last contact with the aircraft and time of (censored) concerning the four prisoners, and considering that vehicle transportation for the prisoners was indicated, (censored) it is possible that they are crew of the EC-47... the fliers were to be transferred from '44' a probable reference to kilometer marking 44 on route 914 ... to '93', a probable reference to kilometer marking 93 on Route 1032 ... and are apparently en route to the Binh Tram 9 area, west of the DMZ in Laos."

On May 24, 1973, an internal memorandum for Dr. Shields stated, "A short time after the shoot-down of the EC-47, a sensitive intercept of communication between North Vietnamese Army Commands in Laos and the DRV indicated that four Americans had been captured in an area some 40 miles from the crash site... there is some reason to believe that the four may actually have been captured."

These conversations were the moving of "air pirates," a favorite term for American fliers, only forty miles from the crash site of the EC-47. It was consistent with an early bailout, if 1:25 AM was close to the shoot-down. The number of people moved was consistent with the number of people on the plane minus those accounted for. The only exception being the new information of a fifth person being unaccounted for on the plane.

The bailing out of four (or five) men would be consistent with the S.O.P. of the plane. The later communications indicated that indeed the men were pilots or crew members of a plane. The later communications identified it as a plane shot down in the area of the EC-47 crash. A listing of POWs-MIAs from my POW computer data lists shows that the EC-47 was the only plane lost in that area at that time.

The context of the messages shows specific jobs being done; a report on the capture of enemy soldiers and requests for instructions of their disposition. All of this is consistent with known enemy communications patterns. They were being moved from Laos to a point still inside Laos. This is nowhere near Vinh, as indicated by DIA. The government gave no data backing its Vinh assertion.

On February 23, 1987, DeStatte stated in an "exhaustive analysis," "The initial February 5 report originated in the area of Vinh, North Vietnam...In that report...a North Vietnamese unit near Vinh is said to be holding four prisoners who are not further identified." DeStatte said, "DIA's review of the evidence shows that the analyst who prepared the 2 May report made a number of arbitrary ... erroneous assumptions ... speculative assertions ... to infer that the 5 February information originated from a location much closer to the EC-47Q crash-site and that some of the crew survived..... It is further emphasized that following the loss of Baron 52, none of its crew was ever seen alive, and **there is no intelligence** whatsoever ... indicate any of the crew survived the incident loss." (**Emphasis supplied**)

The Air Force personnel replied in their 1989 classified briefing: **Ellerson** — "If they were transporting fliers, ... from Laos for consolidation with other fliers or prisoners of war for repatriation ... I would think any debrief of POWs as to where they came from ... there would be substantiating collateral that would refute the repatriation theory (censored). "

Blau — "(Name — possibly DeStatte) told me that the (censored) that he had been able to find, indicated that the (censored) actually was about fliers over in Vietnam along the coast that were going North, but that didn't hold water as far as I was concerned. But, that's what he said ... "

Ellerson — "The (censored) the four fliers ... coordinates and different routes that they were taking, so there were geographic coordinates (censored) that would have placed them at the location."

DeStatte ignored the 1978 memo of Madden which said, "Shortly after the loss of the aircraft, a sensitive intelligence source reported that **Laotian forces** were transporting four captured pirates about 65 kilometers from the crash site." Laotian forces were not stationed near Vinh.

Terry Minarcin (an NSA specialist) also testified before the Senate POW panel concerning the intercepts and where they originated from. He said, answering Senator John Kerry's question, "What are you suggesting with respect to the intercepts on the Baron 52?" Minarcin answered "I'm not suggesting anything. It's what the Vietnamese said, that they had shot it down and that they had captured ... they were transporting three individuals from the crash site area up to Tchepone, Laos, cross into Khe Sanh and then up to Vinh...There were several reports that we saw in Vietnamese communications the morning of the shoot-down, where four of them were seen in a truck being taken up the road."

Kerry asked "You personally saw it?" Minarcin answered "I'm the one that actually personally recorded the one of the three, and the term that they use is 'giac lai my,' which means American bandit pilots, request for transportation of those three from the Saravane Province area ... up to Tchepone, from Tchepone across to Khe Sanh, from Khe Sanh up to Vinh." Kerry again asked, "You saw the actual messages, or you heard the messages yourself?" Minarcin again answered "I saw the actual traffic, sir."

In 1989, I found out that the intercepts released to the families in 1978 (the same ones used in this book) were "sanitized" versions of the originals. If the "censored" words were restored, they were still sanitized so that the receiving party was cleared to read the intercepts. I would tend to trust NSA, on the spot, analysis of the intercepts, rather than a 14 year old "re-analysis" done by DIA. Besides, the original sender of the messages told me the intercepts belonged to the EC-47 crew.

Air Force experts agree with Mooney and Minarcin. Schofield said, "Where the fliers were picked up ... with the wind direction and everything they plotted out; and it was about the right area where they were captured." Ellerson said "Yes, it indicates that, from the apparent flight profile at the time, it's hard to read, but I think it says, 55 kilometers away. Prevailing winds would have caused them to be floating in that area, and that there were four fliers captured and being transported in ground transport."

Schofield added "Yes sir, and they were suffering from shock, or being treated for shock ...." To which Ellerson replied "Okay, I couldn't find that in this highly garbled message." Schofield answered "That was one of the things that came out, that they were in shock or being treated for shock." (Remember I said that there had been two sanitations of the messages.)

The Air Force Historian's focus goes to specific words being used, which is important in communications intelligence. Captain Ronald Ribellia, formerly assigned to another detachment of the 6994, said, "In reference to pilots, they would refer to officers as pilots, and anytime the referred to enlisted types, it was fliers. I remember seeing that (censored)."

Ellerson said "Okay, I was trying to figure out (censored) from the way they were describing this. From some special source, I take it." Ribellia said, "I never knew the source." To which Ellerson replied "It might have been one of the (censored) type of operations that were going on in the area at that time." Ribellia continued, "The point ... was that they referred to fliers, versus, in the past, they always used pilots when referring to..." In 1992, Minarcin, an NSA analyst reminded the Senate POW Committee, "... the term that they use is 'giac lai my,' which means American bandit pilots..." Part of the EC-47Q crew had been captured.

Further intelligence reports disappear

In 1989, I learned at least one agent reported seeing men alive and on the ground with descriptions consistent with the EC-47Q crew; confirming what both Foley and myself knew in 1978. This was the reason for questions by Foley in Shields' deposition about "other intelligence reports."

Schofield said (in answer to a question about whether or not the back-enders had bailed out) "Absolutely sir, and **there was an intel report.**" Remember the wording "intel report" versus what Blau had said just before that "other (censored) messages." In addition, LTC (Ret) Stephen Matejov and his wife "were made privy" to the "visual sighting" and "radio intercept" reports in question near March 29, 1979.

On June 15, 1989, Robert Wilhelm, an analyst stationed at Ubon, who formerly debriefed Baron 52 crews, wrote a family member:

"Our squadron ... was privy to all kinds of classified information...a few days after the plane was lost, I saw a short message ... a 'normally reliable source' in Laos ... had reported seeing 3 or 4 Americans, clean shaven, and in flight suits, being led through the jungle. Our plane (Baron 52) was the only one lost in that period, so, if true, they would have been our people because if they had been down for a long time, they would not be clean-shaven and they would not have been dressed in their flight suits..."

On January 10, 1993, Jack Melton, who was assigned to Ubon "right after the Baron 52 tragedy" wrote to a brother of one of the missing men, "While at Ubon, I read a shoot-down report, hopefully now unclassified, which reported an 'indigenous person' as stating that he saw a number of 'fliers' being loaded onto a truck in the vicinity of the crash."

DeStatte had testified under oath that there was "there was no intelligence whatsoever" to indicate that the men survived.

What happened to the intelligence reports that Foley, Melton, Wilhelm, Matejov, and Shields knew about? Did they disappear as being "uncorrelated" or "unconfirmed." Get used to this logic. It'll appear often in the book. On February 4, 1993, Charles Trowbridge of DIA wrote to Senator Smith of the Senate POW Committee concerning the original February 1973, NSA messages, and other possible reports:

"We have reviewed out database, and we can find no live-sighting or hearsay reports acquired in 1973 **which were ever correlated** to the unaccounted for crewmembers of the EC-47Q." (**Emphasis supplied**)

I have no doubt that DIA is telling a literal truth. **What?** After arguing about the men surviving, why adopt this stance? Remember, this chapter sets the tone for the rest of the book. So let's do a logical question and see what answer pops up.

Why no Repatriation?

The proposal is that a conscious decision was made to write these men off in 1973. That decision was possibly made to protect returning POWs. Since the fighting in Laos and Cambodia was raging, they could have been an unwanted embarrassment as POWs emerging from an "After the Accords" incident. Evidence supports the supposition the men were written off early. I had a conversation with Mrs. Mary Matejov, mother of SGT. Matejov, concerning a talk she had with Dr. Shields. He told her yes, he did believe the men had been captured. He had been ordered to declare the men dead after previously protesting to the acting Secretary of Defense, Bill Clements, in that 1973 period, that no, these men were alive.

He was told to take the men off the Paris Peace Talks negotiating list and have them declared as KIA. That, he finally did. He told Mrs. Matejov that the reply to him, as an order, was to list the men as KIA.

No doubt the conversation between her and Dr. Shields took place as elements of Dr. Shields method of speaking that she would not be aware of were told to me. In addition, the 1978 deposition of Dr. Shields shows there was "a couple of times I questioned ... the decisions that were made about a change in status." Finally, he testified under oath, that despite the DIA re-analysis and the passage of time, he still felt that the men might have bailed out and been captured.

On April 28, 1983, Shields and former Congressman Bill Hendon met. According to the notes taken by Hendon, Shields said "There was one incident, I can't remember the name of it...this was a C-47 shot down in February,...we had a radio intercept where they (the NVA) were talking about having crew, some of the crew, as prisoners. 4 or 5 were killed, and the rest were captured...we knew it and negotiated it away. I tried to tell William Clements and I almost lost my job. He said they were all dead. I told him we had no evidence of that and we couldn't say that. He said, you didn't hear me, you didn't hear what I said — they're all dead."

Contemporaneous with the Senate POW hearings, the *Washington Post* carried two stories relevant to this issue. On September 22, 1992, Winston Lord, a former Senior Aide to Kissinger, was quoted as saying that President Nixon decided "not to scuttle" the Agreements over POWs, adding, "it was a very tough decision." The next day, the *Post* reported that Brent Scowcroft, former National Security Advisor to President Bush and aide to Kissinger, had worked up on April 10, 1973, "talking points" for President Nixon prior to an April 11 meeting with Shields. Scowcroft denied the Congress access to that memorandum citing executive privilege. On April 12, Shields, held a press conference announcing there were no "indications that there are Americans alive" and on April 13, a DOD spokesman said they were all dead.

Let's go back to the "literal truth" I referred to earlier. To correlate something, in DIA terms, means a particular report was determined to belong to a particular person or persons. Once the decision had been made to declare all the men dead, all further correlations of reports would be made to men already returned or a report would be found to be faulty in some way and then discarded as "uncorrelated" or "unreliable." Thus, DIA was "literally" telling the truth, by their standards.

The Russian connection

In early 1991, I was contacted by Terry Minarcin who told me that he traced POWs through intercepts. He also told me that some intercepts suggested the crew of the EC-47 was taken from Hanoi to Moscow in 1978. He further told me that there existed in the North Vietnamese prison system a "hidden system" or a shadow system in which American POWs were held, isolated, and interrogated by the Soviets, most notably the KGB. (Later in the book, we'll look at one of these prisons in the "hidden system.")

Minarcin made some of his accusations public. He also received some backing from the KGB itself. In late 1991 and early 1992, a Russian KGB official, General Oleg Kalugin, came forward and said that yes, the Soviets did interrogate American POWs and yes, some were interrogated after 1973 - 75. He has not made much of the knowledge public or specific. The government has down-played or denied most of what he said.

In other areas of the book, I will show some of these connections. These status changes were made after intercepts or other intelligence made it clear the men were alive. When an attempt was made for more specific information, Shields refused, adding that he "did not want to go to jail."

In October 1987, Congressman John Rowland (R-CN) added light to the case. He secured the names of men listed in a category known as "confirmed knowledge" or "category 1" men. These were men that the Vietnamese knew for sure what happened to them. They were also men for whom Dr. Kissinger did not negotiate a release for, as Shields told Hendon.

Some of the men on the list were known to have been captured; some died in captivity. Of the one hundred eight men on the list, in the confirmed knowledge status, seven are the EC-47Q crew. The 1980 DIA summary with this list had, next to each EC-47 crewman's name: "KIA-3, poss capt(ured) (4)." (I personally have the computer list)

Two other pieces of information support the hypothesis of deliberate write off. One was found in the May 23, 1991 study "An examination of U.S. Policy toward POW/MIAs," done by the Senate Committee on Foreign Relations Republican Staff. On page 5-4 of the study is a statement: (study herein after called **SFR**)

"Two weeks into this stalemate over the repatriation of U. S. POWs held by the Pathet Lao, between the Pathet Lao and the North Vietnamese on one side, and the United States on the other, the United States announced that: 'There are no more prisoners in Southeast Asia. They are all dead.'"

A declassified message from the Embassy in Saigon to the Secretary of State, dated 11 June 1973 said:

"NVA rallier/defector Nguyen Thanh Son was surfaced by GVN to press June 8 in Saigon. In follow on interview with *AP*, *UPI*, and *NBC* American correspondents, questions elicited information that he had seen six prisoners, ... believed to be Americans, who had not yet been released.

American officer present at interview requested news services to play down details. *AP* mention was consistent with embargo request, while *UPI* and *NBC*, after talk with Embassy Press Officer, omitted item entirely from their stories." Further details were being provided through "Bright Light" channels.

This censoring of news stories began with an April 14, 1973 request of a "United States government spokesman," quoted in an *UPI* dispatch saying "Rumors that there were hundreds of US servicemen held in Laotian prison camps, does the families (of the missing) a disservice."

Producing intelligence

In the EC-47 case, NSA determined that the four fliers were "located on 5 February in the general area north of Muong Nong in the Binh Tram 33 area" in Laos. In 1989, they said their coordinates on the intercepts and the movements were in Laos. DeStatte and DIA, are the only persons saying that the intercepts do not belong to the EC-47 crew.

DeStatte wrote on February 23, 1987, "The initial February 5 report originated in the area of Vinh, North Vietnam...In that report...a North Vietnamese unit near Vinh is said to be holding four prisoners who are not further identified." Ellerson, of USAFSS, said the "different routes" being used, "geographic coordinates" being used, placed them at the location NSA said. In 1978, Madden said the men were being held by Laotian forces.

When the men were declared dead, the commander said that "we did employ a certain amount of conjecture to visualize the events ... However, we made logical assumptions based on all the available ... information." He added, "Conclusive evidence of death is not required for a commander to arrive at such a decision."

The Air Force, preparing to answer Jack Anderson, wrote a draft statement reading, "... **the intelligence report in question apparently fell by the wayside** and no attempt was ever made to declassify it until recently...everything ... including investigations by a House Select Committee and a Presidential Commission lead us to the conclusion that no one is left alive." (**Emphasis supplied**)

Is there a cover-up? Roger Shields was asked that on April 10, 1979, in a House Asian and Pacific Affairs Subcommittee meeting. Mr. Fountain (D-FL) asked "You made a reference to one case in which information was withheld. ... tell us the circumstances in connection with that case?"

Shields replied, "The one case ... in which **there was not ... simply an oversight** ... three men may have been captured..." and then he went on to describe other materials we have previously looked at. (**Emphasis supplied**)

The Air Force disagreed in a letter to LTC Matejov on May 3, 1979, saying, "I do not believe that sworn statements or an investigation are necessary. With respect to the release of the **sighting reports** to you, ... There was no 'cover-up' or intentional withholding of information." (**Emphasis supplied**)

DIA, in an internal message entitled "Background Information for Congressional Response," dated 11 September, 1986, stated, "Intent of the directive was not to pass families classified information...apparently, ... information was not declassified until 1978."

Another section read, "They were told that there were no photos of the crash site ... Cannot explain why families were told there were no crash site photos. Photos were originally classified."

Who's not telling the truth? I believe the government is withholding pertinent information. The exercise you just finished, reading the pages just above, gave you a conclusion in your own mind. That is how "intelligence" is produced.

Let's look at one other aspect. If five men jumped out of the plane, and four were traced, what happened to number 5? It is not conclusive but, let's look at some information developed in 1989 and passed on to me in 1994. It relates to a rescue mission (discussed in another chapter later in the book).

Schofield said "... there have been indications with the 52." Blau replied, "There was a photo ... in the Jack Anderson column, that showed (censored), a POW area, and it appeared that next to the POW area, in an open field, a 52 was stamped out in the grass like someone had walked it."

Ellerson asked "Couldn't that have been a B-52?" Blau came back, "Normally you would not go with that (censored)."

What they are referring to (and I have knowledge of this aspect of the case also) is the possibility that the 52 or B-52 stamped into the ground at Nhom Marrot could have been an authenticator symbol (classified) or in 1981 (8 years after a shoot-down) a desperation symbol (not classified) that said, "There is a person here whose call sign is Baron 52 — B-52 and come and get me." For years the meaning of the B-52 escaped everyone. I believe that this interpretation, made for some reason by these men, is as valid as any other, perhaps more so.

The EC-47 case is not finished. Search personnel on the ground in Laos determined in early 1993 that "all men were dead." On what basis? They found one partial molar, parachute rings, a piece of a hair comb, several pieces of at least two flight suits, a dog tag with the name Joseph Matejov, three identification tags (2-Cressman and 1 Melton), some personal stuff, and 21 parachute "V" rings. That last items were interpreted to "suggest" that at least 7 parachutes were still on board at the time of the crash. That is it. No other information. The last comments said, "All recoverable remains of case — were discovered, No further field work on case — is recommended." In April 1997, DOD told me they were unaware of the AFSS classified debriefing.

Nothing found on the ground contradicts the 1973 findings of men captured shortly after the crash. They found no remains, other than 3. They found nothing contradicting that the back-enders and one navigator left the plane before crashing. As demonstrated, the crash site actually showed that the men probably did parachute before crashing.

Deceit, deception, and cover-up. Baron 52 is probably one of the most substantial cases proving this.

Colonel Millard A. Peck, former chief of the Special Office for Prisoners of War and Missing in Action (POW-MIA) for the DIA wrote in his 12 February 1991 request for relief from duty from his job, "The entire charade does not appear to be an honest effort, and may never have been.... it appears that any soldier left in Vietnam, ... was, in fact, abandoned years ago, and that the farce ... being played is no more than political legerdemain ... 'smoke and mirrors,' to stall the issue until it dies a natural death."

In other parts of the book, we'll examine promises made and broken; historical background to the Vietnam conflict as it affects POWs-MIAs; and examples of POWs being held captive. We'll also show the government is trying to discredit activists working to end the POW/MIA saga. In addition, we'll examine in detail known transfers to the Soviet Union for military information the men had and for more insidious reasons.

The widely heralded "searches" on the ground for POW information are purely an exercise to close the POW / MIA books regardless of the truth of any individual situation. Those searches were cited by the Clinton Administration and Senator John McCain, as a reason for the recognition of Vietnam in 1995. There's money to be made, oil to be discovered, political contributions to be had and butts to be covered. They have other secrets to hide. The foremost one is a major premise of the book. In September 1972, a Vietnamese General, Tran Van Quang, told the Vietnamese Politburo that Vietnam held not the 591 POWs that came home, but a total of 1205 American POWs. What happened to those men is what this book is about.

Unlike many political controversies, this one has several "smoking guns" aimed at administration officials. If the premise of the book is correct, then several courses of action are plausible to end the last chapter of the Vietnam War. All are aimed do what is legally correct to bring the men home or convene war crime trials to force the issue. Unfortunately, Clinton has already dodged the impeachment issue. Vietnam lingers on much too long, but a nation which forgets those who fought to make the country free deserves the trauma such alternatives would bring.

Before one can assume deceit, there has to be promises of action broken. The next chapter will deal with those promises.

The Broken Promises

"The policy people manipulating the affair have ... remained hidden in the shadows, while using the Office as a 'toxic waste dump' to bury the whole 'mess' out of sight and mind to a facility with the limited access to public scrutiny."
        Colonel Millard Peck, Feb. 12,1991

Today, Americans are being as POWs or detainees in various parts of the world.. Elements of the Nixon, Ford, Carter, Reagan, Bush, and Clinton administrations were aware of this. However, these prisoners were all declared dead. The official policy was to ignore evidence of them in captivity. This policy left their captors with a quandary. A "dead" person was not the same as "missing" to them. The distinction is critical. The Vietnamese interpreted the Vietnam Peace Accords literally. They were bound to account only for those men considered to be MIA. Also, it left them nowhere to return live POWs.

One policy, first enunciated by President Johnson, was to keep the issue quiet and declare the men dead as quickly as possible. Past wars, Korea and World War II, elicited little concern over thousands of MIAs failing to return. Until Watergate, the consensus was the government did not lie about things like this.

Why my emphatic statement? The government says all MIAs are dead. The evidence of thousands of reports from refugees, defectors, agents, communication intercepts, satellite photographs, eyewitnesses, and communist documents, say Americans are prisoners. The United States government ignores these reports and their associated analyses, hiding behind "National Security." Despite the clear testimony of experts from our own intelligence agencies, the deception continues.

Our government is deceitful in dealing with the families of the missing men. Intelligence reports are suppressed, destroyed, and discredited. One reason for the deceitfulness is the embarrassment to politicians and bureaucrats if it were revealed that POWs were being detained. Under President Johnson, families were instructed to tell no one about the circumstances of their man's loss. The explanation was that sensitive negotiations were underway concerning the well-being of the men. A public outcry would seriously undermine those efforts. For a while, that explanation satisfied the families.

The war continued. The numbers of missing and captured mounted. The families formed a united front, joining millions of concerned citizens. On October 16, 1972, President Nixon, made this promise: "We shall under no circumstances abandon our POWs or MIAs ... leave their fate to the goodwill of the enemy."

On January 23, 1973, the President expressed his concern over the plight of the missing men: "Throughout ... negotiations, we have insisted on peace with honor.... conditions that ... have been met. *Within 60 days ..., all Americans held prisoners of war throughout Indochina will be released. There will be the fullest possible accounting for those who are missing in action....."* (**Emphasis added**)

The next day, Dr. Henry Kissinger said: "Chapter III (of the accords) deals with the return of captured military personnel ... *within South Vietnam.... The return of American personnel and the accounting of missing in action is unconditional and will take place ...*" {**Emphasis added.**} (within that 60 day period)

This official end to the fighting brought no relief to the families. Only 591 men returned from prison cells in Asia. Not returning were hundreds expected and thousands of remains. Note the difference between "Indochina" and South Vietnam in the statements of Kissinger and Nixon.

Over 27 years have gone by since the official end to fighting. During this time, Presidents Ford, Carter, Reagan, Bush and Clinton have issued statements of concern over the fate of the missing and unreturned POWs. The return of prisoners and accounting for the missing was a "high" or the "highest" national priority. There is a denial of what I believe happened (more on that later).

There has been a systematic attempt to hide from the American people sighting and intelligence reports about prisoners left behind. Through the efforts of the League (when they functioned as useful watchdogs), and groups like The Forget - Me - Nots, Task Force Omega, Operation Baron 52, the American Defense Institute, Project Phuong Hoang Hai, Homecoming II, the National Vietnam Veterans Coalition, and others, reports have emerged.

The Ngo Phi Hung Story

A 48 year old refugee named Ngo Phi Hung gave this startling testimony before the Subcommittee on Asian and Pacific Affairs on August 9, 1978.

Hung previously operated a transportation company hauling war materiel for the Saigon government. In April 1975, he realized his activity would cause him difficulty with the new regime. He also joined a resistance movement called the Interdenomination Resistance Movement.

Hung registered with the new authorities. A boyhood friend procured a license for truck and river transportation; the new regime being short of everything. Hung secured a government contract moving goods and equipment North. This required much travel and the government provided him with a special travel permit. All this was done under an assumed name.

On June 5, 1975, Hung was ordered to the former USAID compound in Saigon. He was to pick up the contents of the office. The compound was guarded. Hung presented his documents and was permitted to pass and come close to the compound. There, he heard voices speaking in English. Hung does not speak or read the language, but he did recognize it as such.

Hung sees the Americans

Hung inquired who was speaking. The guards told him they were American POWs! About this time, the captain in charge came, telling him to move beyond the guards. Hung presented his documents. The captain told him to stay away from the compound, troops would move the material out.

Hung reported to the resistance. He received orders to insinuate himself into the situation and keep the resistance informed. He was further told to develop a close relationship with the person in charge to gather information concerning the Americans. Hung was supplied with gifts to bribe the commander, Captain Huynh Van Tao, communists not being immune to such bourgeois blandishment.

The Resistance Movement obtained for Hung a letter of introduction, signed by a Senior Colonel, stating he was a cadre of much merit in the service of the revolution. Untrue, but it impressed the captain. Hung gained access to the prison compound. About June 12, 1975, Hung first saw the American prisoners.

Due to the letter and the "gifts," Hung became a friend of Captain Tao. Hung sometimes had access to the prison office containing a roster of the names and details about the forty-nine American prisoners. The group consisted of seventeen Air Force Officers, twenty-six Army Officers, three civilians, and three Air Force enlisted men. Whenever he had a chance, Hung looked at the roster, and memorized facts from it. He would then find an excuse to go to the bathroom or other such places and make notes. He later reported to the Resistance Movement.

The names on the roster were in English; other details were in Vietnamese. On September 6, 1975, the POWs were moved from Saigon in three trucks. This time, the number was forty-six POWs. One Air Force officer, a lieutenant colonel, had committed suicide; and two Army captains died as a result of illness.

This first move took the men about five kilometers northeast of Tayninh City. Because of the special travel permit and his continuing friendship with Tao, Hung was able to keep track of the men. He also kept the Resistance informed.

The POWs were next moved to Ban Me Thuot, where they were kept until May 1976. They next moved west of Nha Trang City and finally in January 1977 they arrived at the big cave at Huynh Thuc Khang Mountain, fifteen kilometers east of Quang Ngai City. Hung last saw the POWs about April 19, 1977.

Hung is found out

About this time, Hung received an urgent message telling him the government found him out. An arrest order was about to be issued. Fearing the worst, Hung fled with his family. Some Hoa Hao involved in the Resistance Movement gave him shelter. New papers were issued establishing him as a fisherman. He bribed a local official and bought a fishing boat. During the next ten months, he gradually moved himself and his family across country awaiting an opportunity to escape.

In February 1978, Hung and thirty-one others escaped in the fishing boat. Once, the boat broke down and drifted for eleven days. Near The Three Islands, about half way between Songkla and Bangkok, the refugees were set upon by pirates, robbing Hung of a briefcase containing about 175 ounces of gold and a quantity of jewels. Also in the briefcase was a roster of the prisoners and other documents.

Two months after arriving in Thailand, Hung began writing all details that he could remember. He could not remember the names in English. He could remember other details and the notebook containing those details were given to the House Subcommittee on Asian and Pacific Affairs.

The official reaction to Hung's story was absolute panic. When the story first emerged on July 15, 1978, Frank Sieverts, then a Coordinator for POW/MIA Matters, was at the Annual League meeting delivering his recurring there was no reason to believe that any Americans were still prisoner in Indochina. That was before Ngo Phi Hung made his appearance in the middle of Sieverts' speech. When Hung finished his story, there was elation among the families, described as being the most joyous since the end of the fighting and the release of prisoners.

The government harasses Hung

A neutral observer could safely say Sieverts was outraged. He charged the podium, pointing his finger, making the accusation the families were grandstanding. His performance cooled with television cameras focused on him. Sieverts announced he would interview Hung to determine the veracity of his story. Between this appearance and Hung's Congressional testimony, however, Sieverts kept himself busy telling newsmen Hung was not telling the truth.

On August 4, 1978, Hung opened his apartment door and was confronted by two men identifying themselves as "investigators" from "military headquarters." They were, in reality, DIA interrogators. His New York Attorney's office was closed due to the time difference between California and New York. The DIA interrogators were sent to question Hung despite an agreement between Foley, his attorney, and Sieverts that Hung was to be left alone before his congressional testimony.

Put yourself in the shoes of Hung. He flees a dictatorship, is attacked by pirates, and now faces two "investigators from military headquarters." In spite of this violation of his privacy, Hung still agrees to testify.

After testifying, Hung underwent several days of severe cross-examination by members of the congressional subcommittee and legitimate questioners from DIA. His story survived. DIA challenged some details but never sought to clarify any discrepancies found in their examination. Only after DIA itself was challenged by a former POW, Foley, and the League, did it agree to an effort to reconcile the discrepancies in early 1980. By this time, Hung had been ridiculed, harassed, and had his privacy invaded. Not surprisingly, he declined further cooperation. Because a discrepancy exists between two accounts, it does not mean either lied. It could mean both saw something from a different angle and were telling the truth.

Hung's full story is unbroken. Either he is an expert liar or he is telling the truth. He's never been charged with perjury. During his questioning, Hung was asked if he could remember the names of any of the men. He said that he would prefer to wait. He wanted to be absolutely sure of any positive identifications that he made. Hung knew that he was being scrutinized by every government official questioning him.

Hung and Bott

One incident bears repeating. Hung recognized some facial and other features in the picture of one MIA, Russell Bott. Hung asked if Bott was in the habit of exercising and using weights. The answer to both questions, was yes. Hung refused, however to make a positive ID. AFTER this exchange took place, Bott's case came up for a status review. The new information was known to the review board. Prior to Hung's testimony, the review board already had information that Bott possibly survived. Despite this new information, the board recommended that Bott be presumed dead.

When Hung testified, in attendance were Sieverts and State Department consultant Douglas Pike. Pike told members of the audience that there was nothing to Hung's story. Pike had never met the man. During a break, Sieverts met with some family members after telling newsmen that Hung's testimony was unreliable. Sieverts told us that if Americans were behind, it would warrant military action to get them out. Of course, Sieverts never contemplated such action.

Sieverts was asked an additional question. Did he personally think any MIAs were alive? He looked each of us square in the eye saying the only way he would believe any Americans were still alive was if one of them walked up to him, said I'm so and so, and handed a piece of paper with that POWs own fingerprints on it. This Janus-faced policy hurts the family members deeply.

As shocking as Hung's story is, another amply illustrates deceit and broken promises on MIAs. The "Phou Pha Thi Case" has been reclassified Top Secret. Except where noted, the following is from that "Top Secret" CHECO report.

Site 85 - Phou Pha Thi - Channel 97

In North Vietnam, bombing was used to interdict supply routes, disrupt lines of communications, and hit strategic military targets. Off-shore shelling was previously attempted. Short of military invasion, however, bombing was the feasible alternative. Weather and politics played a key role in the bombing campaigns with politicians making the decision to limit targets regardless of the military outcome. Weather limited visibility on targets led to radar bombing, itself limited by terrain and distance. A decision was made to position a TSQ radar in Laos to guide the bombing of North Vietnam, its interdiction routes, and Laos. This decision was one of the few times that military necessity won over politics.

The TSQ radar was located on important friendly guerrilla base, site 85, in Northern Laos. Guerrilla bases, radar sites, and airfields in Laos were known by numbers. The TACAN number (next paragraph) was Channel 97. Site 85 was on a 5500 foot ridge called Phou Pha Thi, located about twenty-five kilometers from the Lao/North Vietnam Border and about forty-five kilometers west of Sam Neua, Pathet Lao headquarters. The Air Force already had a Tactical Aid to Navigation (TACAN) facility there. It was also a CIA safe site and guerrilla base.

Site 85 was sensitive for several reasons. First, it was in Laos. Second, Site 85 was the only one that could direct operations against both Northern Laos and Hanoi. Finally, the Air Force Technicians operating the military base were under a civilian cover (called sheep-dipping). Instructions from Site 85 were relayed to a C-135 over the Gulf of Tonkin who then relayed it to the strike aircraft, operation code named MOTEL. (**Air Power in Three Wars** pg. 179 hereafter called **AP**).

The Embassy in Laos controlled all military operations. (**AP pg. 85**) LTC (RET) Al Shinkle, an early air attaché in Laos, charged Ambassador William Sullivan, loved that arrangement. (*US Veteran & News Report,* Aug. 1990, pg. 5 — herein after called *USV*) At the time of the defense of site 85, many targets could not be cleared because Sullivan and the CIA were never sure of Meo Commander General Vang Pao's troop locations along strategic routes. To avoid hitting friendly intelligence assets and villages, certain areas could not be targeted. (**AP** pg. 85-6)

Vang Pao's troops, under the command of the CIA and the Embassy, provided the primary defense force at Site 85. Emergency evacuation plans called for removing all TSQ personnel and destroying the equipment thereby keeping politically sensitive evidence out of enemy hands. Those plans were never fully implemented.

A TOP-SECRET CIA briefing in September 1967 listed site 85 as one "secure" area in Laos that Vang Pao's Meo tribesmen had orders to defend. (**CHECO pg. 2**) Other sites were "contested" and changed hands frequently. The Air Force personnel were insufficient in numbers to defend Site 85. The CIA personnel, involved in covert operations, were not sufficient in number either. The 1962 Laotian Accords said American troops could not defend vital installations.

The TSQ site became operational in October 1967. It guided an increasing number of strikes in Laos and North Vietnam. TSQ bombing of North Vietnam targeted area wide facilities including railroad marshaling yards, Thai Nguyen Steel Mill, depots, barracks, and transshipment areas (**AP pg. 179**). The technique, however, required a smooth steady run leaving the attacking aircraft vulnerable to Surface to Air Missiles (SAMs) and Anti-Aircraft (AA) fire. (**AP pg. 179**) The resulting casualties caused it to become less prominent in the highly defended areas.

TSQ bombing in Northern Laos was code-named "Barrel Roll." These strikes were against lines of communications (LOCs). Later it would be of a self-defense nature against the North Vietnamese forces poised against Site 85. The TSQ radar used pre-selected target data for all-weather self-defense air strikes. In the four months of operation, 23% of the total strikes against North Vietnam and 28% of the strikes into "Barrel Roll" were directed from Site 85, called "Commando Club."

Site 85 was a major resupply point for Meo guerrilla operations in Northeastern Laos. This covert operation utilized a six hundred foot runway and other buildings on site. The CIA headquarters were about a thousand feet from the TACAN (channel 97) site, at a lower level. It was also in the midst of the best poppy fields in Laos. (**Kiss the Boys Goodbye** (herein after called **KTB**) pgs. 145 - 150)

The Embassy considered Site 85 to be "impregnable;" the sheer cliffs unclimbable. The self-defense mechanism of the TSQ together with the Meo intelligence network was considered sufficient to hold off all but the most determined attacks. Yet, a top-level political decision said under the appropriate conditions, the site would be abandoned, personnel evacuated, and equipment destroyed.

NVA Plans

In December 1967, a CIA representative outlined the NVA plans. The enemy was entering trucks into Laos at an alarming rate. At a minimum, the NVA proposed taking five Meo sites along the road network. This pressure was designed to keep Vang Pao from Sam Neua. All the objectives were close to Phou Pha Thi. The CIA informants said Site 85 was a prime target, pre-"Tet Offensive."

The value the Vietnamese placed upon eliminating USAF sites in Laos was underscored in December 1967 when TACAN site 61 was overrun. An evaluation of security at the three remaining TACAN sites concluded, "reasonable security exists ... adequate warning will be provided in case of evacuation ... An emergency plan for evacuation exists."

One question remains unanswered. Since the United States denied being in Laos and the NVA denied being in Laos, why didn't the United States provide adequate security for essential military assets such as Site 85? The U.S. had adequate warning that Site 85 was targeted. On January 12, 1968, two Soviet built AN-2 Colt aircraft rocketed, strafed, and bombed the top of the mountain. Four Meos were killed and two were wounded in this attack. The attacking planes were shot down and burned. (An interesting footnote to this attack was that the bodies from one air craft were identified. The report on this was labeled Secret-No Foreign Dissemination. This is unusual unless the bodies themselves were unusual — like perhaps Soviets? The answer provided to me by persons familiar with other more highly classified reports, was that yes, the Soviets were involved in this attack. They needed pictures of the TSQ radar. It was similar in design to those guiding our bombers on an attack of Moscow if such an attack was ordered.)

An all intelligence assessment determined the attack would be on the ground. (This all-intelligence assessment included agents, captured documents, other intelligence assets, and radio interceptions.) That assessment judged correctly. Days after the air attack, several hundred Pathet Lao troops, along with their NVA allies, started to overrun friendly LIMA (guerrilla and other allied) sites near Phou Pha Thi. They also brought in mortar and artillery pieces to begin circling the TSQ site.

The Defense plans

The defense of Phou Pha Thi depended upon the Meos keeping a twelve km "defense radius." A 105 mm howitzer was added to recently acquired foreign made anti-aircraft guns. Guerrilla patrols were beefed up to provide intelligence for aircraft strikes as the TSQ went into a self-defense mode.

On 7-8 February 1968, HQ 7th Air Force asked the Air Attaché (DIA) about the security of Site 85. He maintained if the twelve kilometer perimeter was secure, "Do not believe site 85 can be taken...If the enemy concentrates ... (four battalions) ... Phou Pha Thi could be taken." He also said that the buildup should give adequate notice to affect "site destruction and evacuation."

On January 30, enemy patrols exploded defensive mines on the southern edge of Phou Pha Thi. They followed with a thirty minute mortar attack. By Mid-February, CIA agents reported that Phou Pha Thi was the ultimate target. On February 18, detailed plans of that attack came from off an NVA officer, killed in an ambush. Those plans showed, "The enemy used the word 'TACAN' as it appears in English and was aware of its exact location." Security forces were beefed up with mortars and an additional howitzer. The Ambassador authorized more air-strikes in support of the defense. Despite mounting threats, politics still ruled.

What to do?

Beginning 21 February, Sullivan, authorized the Laotian Commander to allow "Commando Club" strikes within the twelve kilometer radius with restrictions. No target could be struck within five hundred meters of the nineteen active villages on the order. Authorization could come only over a secure network and radio relay.

The CIA, on February 15, just three days before the enemy documents were captured, stated, "... the enemy's penetrating the 12 kilometer radius ... represents an imminent threat... while making arrangements for his final assault in three or four battalions." With air-strikes continuing, the enemy would be delayed in his plans. However, "It is not possible to predict... the state of security ... beyond 10 March, because of the enemy's willingness to continue to escalate ..."

Sullivan, on February 26, made it clear that no forces, other than Meos, would defend the site. "... we could not guarantee a static defense... the moment of truth may be approaching for this site... In the final analysis it seems doubtful that the sites can be held in the face of consistent enemy determination."

An evacuation plan was arranged with the final decision reserved for Sullivan. The Air Force wanted helicopters to remain at site 85 while Sullivan ordered them to remain at site 98, nearby. A study note said, "Weather also may have disrupted the rescue flight from site 98..." Helicopters designated as overnight stays were Air America or CIA. Air Force helicopters remained in Thailand. The plan presupposed a daylight evacuation and had very limited nighttime capability.

Phou Pha Thi becomes surrounded

By 9 March, Phou Pha Thi was surrounded. The enemy made steady advances to the mountain base. The Air Force was conceded greater latitude in striking enemy positions. Cluster bombs units (CBUs) were used. Around the clock bombing dictated five more Americans be added to Phou Pha Thi. The total rose to nineteen.

The contradiction of politics versus military necessity is noted in a 5 March message to the Pacific Command: "... the desirability of maintaining air presence over North Vietnam during ... inclement weather period, site 85 probably would not be evacuated until capture appeared imminent. The fact that complete security could not be assured in original plan is noted..."

By 9 March, CIA representatives determined that the end was near. Attacking forces were dispersed. It was difficult to fix their positions for concentrated air strikes. For evacuation, CIA and Air Force personnel were to either **a)** descend to the CIA location or **b)** stay at the TSQ site if the trail to the CIA location was blocked. No other plans were discussed.

The final attack began on the evening of 10 March. Mortar, artillery, and rocket rounds destroyed the 105 mm howitzer and damaged the living quarters of the TSQ technicians. This two hour barrage preceded a lull of two hours. Then, heavy fighting broke out only one mile south of the TSQ site. Fifteen minutes later, fighting was only a half hour walk away.

Air Force headquarters considered an evacuation "as a last resort if the situation became untenable." Mortar shelling began about 12:15 AM. Sullivan decided to partially evacuate at 0815.

The Meos held their defensive positions. Quiet returned shortly after the renewed mortaring. Some technicians returned to the radar. Others went to the edge of the TSQ perimeter where slings run over the sheer cliff to a ledge lower down. With their sleeping quarters partially destroyed, here, they attempted to sleep. This quiet period lasted until 0300.

The loss of Site 85

Either automatic weapons fire or shelling caused the technicians to abandon the TSQ building. Automatic weapons fire at close range killed three outright. A specialized force of about twenty men made it to the top and systematically destroyed the buildings with grenades. They were familiar with the layout of the site.

At 0315, the CIA representative saw the TACAN site go "up in smoke." His location was under heavy mortar and small arms fire. The elite forces on the top of the mountain also pinned down the Americans on the slings.

The Embassy was informed of the fighting by the Senior CIA commander. The fate of the TSQ site was unknown. Radio communications were cut off. At 0515, Sullivan decided to fully evacuate Site 85 at 0715. At 0540, the CIA reported the "outer positions will hold, ... place untenable as operating radar site... Steps ... taken to destroy all remaining equipment prior to evacuation."

Just prior to 0700, the shelling ceased. Rescue helicopters drew fire from the TSQ site. The CIA representative and ten Meos reconned the TSQ site. He found no one at the TACAN site. At the west end of the complex, he and the Meos exchanged fire with the NVA/Pathet Lao infiltrators. Determining that the TSQ site was in unfriendly hands, he directed an A1E attack on the hill. This attack caused one enemy soldier to go down the side of the hill where he found the slings. In a fire-fight with the Americans already on the ledge, one American was killed.

The helicopters came in. Seven Americans were extracted. Inexplicably, the first message from Vientiane to DIA stated eleven men were missing. Return flights recovered some American bodies and removed more Laotian defenders. A delay in trying to recapture site 85 was accomplished so that a "maximum effort could be exerted to try to recover the remaining US personnel and friendly forces."

MIA or POW?

CHECO said, "After the evacuation of the Americans and friendly forces ... on ... 11 March, only tasks remained to be performed (were): missing Americans had to be accounted for, ... recovering them as they still evaded capture ... recovering their bodies and establishing their deaths..."

The Embassy, on 12 March, reported, "Of the 19 Americans ... sixteen had been site technicians, two were CAS representatives (CIA), and ... one attaché office FAC... The CAS representative and the FAC were rescued. The senior CAS representative had been slightly wounded .... Of the sixteen, five were extracted (one died en route), eight were known to have been dead ... the possibility ... the missing three might have fallen from the ledge, ... a sheer drop of almost 2000 feet... Presuming those ... not evacuated ... 11 March were dead, a fairly concentrated air effort was launched ... to destroy the technical and personal equipment left behind on Site 85." This occurred on 11, 15, 19, 22, and 28 March. A Bull-Pup missile was used on March 22. On 13 March, napalm was used.

Thus ended the saga of Site 85. *Or did it?*

Recurring reports show one to six men survived. CHECO has been reclassified. Ann Holland, wife of one of the men lost on site 85, received intelligence reports her husband survived. (**KTB pg. 334-335**) Colonel Gerald Clayton, former commander of Site 85 forces, told Monika Jensen Stevenson about the dope they had to walk through to get to LIMA site 85. (**KTB** pg. 147) I do not intend to get into that problem here. It was fairly documented in **Kiss the Boys Goodbye** (Dutton, 1990). The subject probably provides a partial key to the secrecy of Site 85. I am convinced that *National Security* does not provide all the answers.

New answers from the enemy camp

A Thai sergeant in charge of the indigenous guerrilla force guarding site 85 "told (Senate Foreign Relations) Committee Staff that three ... technicians at the TACAN site were taken prisoner by ... attacking forces. He gave this information to American intelligence officers in 1968." (**SFR pg. 7-2**)

In September 1990, an Air Force Captain in Laos conducting research for his doctoral study interviewed Pathet Lao General Singkapo who claimed to have taken part in the March 10-11 assault on Site 85. He asserted "three US Air Force technicians survived ... and were turned over to North Vietnamese troops for further transport to North Vietnam." (**Ibid. 7-4**)

Further, "A review of POW live sighting documents... contain reports that three American prisoners were brought to a village near Phou Pha Thi by North Vietnamese troops about the time of the attack on Phou Pha Thi. Documents from these files also refer to Americans held in the caves near Phou Pha Thi, while other caves in Sam Neua were used by Pathet Lao, North Vietnamese, and advisers from the People's Republic of China." (**Ibid. pg. 7-3**)

In 1994, Garnett "Bill" Bell, a retired POW / MIA government researcher wrote a letter to Mr. Geoff Stephens, *NBC* News, on the Site 85 attack. He took *NBC* to task for their stance that no one survived. His letter asserted:

"For example, the testimony of the American ... (FAC) who successfully descended the mountain and reported three unidentifiable 'friendlies' departing the site during the attack, the statement of Lao Major General Singkapo to a US military officer ... three Americans were captured ... and moved to Muang Son, the ... (JCRC) report of a wartime signal intercept indicating that three American prisoners had been taken to Muang Son three days after the attack ..."

In 1994, The Last Firebase Archives Project wrote that Ann Holland found in her husband's files a report that described a POW from Phou Pha Thi that fit her husband. A Russian document depicted the sentencing of a "Arnold Mikhailevich Holland" for "counter-revolutionary activities" in the Soviet Union. Mel Holland's full name is Melvin Arnold Holland. The obvious reason for Holland's transfer to the Soviet Union would be his knowledge of the radar designed to guide US warplanes onto Moscow in the event of war. That plus the failure of the Soviets to get pictures of the phase array of the radar prior to the fall of Phou Pha Thi, Site 85, Channel 97. (**USV, Aug. 19, 1994**)

Minarcin told me that an even more classified story of Site 85 would answer my questions. A Pentagon report claimed that Patrick Fallon, was interrogated by 12 Russian officers in 1983 in Laos (Minneapolis Star-Tribune August 23, 1992). Was it the possibility of three POWs, the "dope" angle, or the Soviet angle that reclassified the CHECO report? Did the "dope" keep Site 85, a strategic asset, from being protected by American forces? Did the CIA believe too many eyes would compromise too many secrets?

The dope angle

In 1978, LTC Albert Shinkle was asked, "Did you read Al McCoy's book ... on Laos and Vietnam?" (Question is about a classic book on dope trading in the area.) Shinkle replied, No. Congressman Lester Wolff then asked Shinkle, "Do you know anything about any drug traffic that took place there?" Shinkle replied, "Let me give you a background ... you can draw your own conclusions."

Shinkle continued, "I have only hearsay... that the C-47's ... were running opium and probably opium base... in South Vietnam into Thailand. I have never personally seen any opium on an airplane in Laos ... flown by the Laotians or by Air America..." Wolff asked, "You note that there was heavy traffic in opium in Laos?" Shinkle replied, "There were two kinds of traffic ... some of the Meo raised opium, incarcerated it ...the Burmese opium was transported into Thailand by dissidents."

Wolff asked, "In your intelligence gathering you never heard of any —" Shinkle replied, "We heard of it, but we made a decision in Air Force Intelligence to stay out of the opium business. If we got any information, accidentally... we immediately turned it over to DEA in Bangkok." One of his questioners asked, "Was information turned over to him?" Shinkle replied, "Yes, Sir." Shinkle was asked, "Relative to opium?" Shinkle replied, "Yes, Sir. As a matter of fact one of our agents ... was approached by a person willing to transport heroin to Hong Kong and we cooperated with Bill Wongsak in DNDD ... We let them use our agent, ... a Frenchman, to transport two suitcases of heroin to Hong Kong, so that the Hong Kong police could pickup the receivers. That almost got our agent blown away."

Shinkle was asked, "... in order to gather intelligence, we're permitting the Lao to traffic; that was their payoff." Shinkle replied, " ... we were not letting them do that so we could gather intelligence, ... we were looking the other way to let them make money so that they would let us fight a war in Laos."

Wolff contended, "... the amount of narcotics traffic... within our military... was one of the turning points of the war ... the help that we were giving these people, they were actually destroying some of our troops in the area." Shinkle replied, "I would accept that logic, and ... while having no personal knowledge of it, it was common gossip in Laos that this was being done, ... CIA aircraft or Air America aircraft transporting ... narcotics. I never saw a Royal Lao Air Force aircraft transport any either, but I didn't always go out and look..."

The defense of Khe Sanh

A contrast from another battle fought in the same TET offensive period will show how a strategic site should have been defended vice the way Site 85 was not. Khe Sanh was located astride the strategic route 9 coming out of Laos. Situated on a strategic plateau, with a sheer drop off on one side, it was valued for intelligence gathering in Laos. It was targeted by the North Vietnamese for capture prior to the

TET offensive (1968). The White House, concerned about the defense of Khe Sanh, wanted no repetition of Dien Bien Phu.

The base was surrounded. TSQ bombing played a deciding factor in its successful defense. Enough air power and ground forces was applied to the defense of Khe Sanh that it held.

The Marine and ARVN defenders were outnumbered by fifteen to twenty thousand enemy troops to their six thousand. The enemy had every advantage from cover, concealment, and artillery. They did not, however, have air power. Twenty-two thousand sorties and eighty-two thousand tons of bombs were dropped to hold this base. There was no political sensitivities except "No Dien Bien Phu." Unlike Site 85, Khe Sanh was fought for like the strategic outpost that it was. (A **SOG** base was also at Khe Sanh - see later chapters on SOG)

The families of the EC-47 and site 85 case have seen what cover-up and deceit are all about. In 1978, soon after Ngo Phi Hung testified and the Pentagon admitted its part in the EC-47 case, a congressional delegation left for Indochina. The CIA told the congressmen that Hung was not a credible witness. Representative Henson Moore was told that there was no evidence to substantiate the assumption that men from the EC-47 survived the crash. The CIA briefing on Hung was remarkable since CIA had not questioned Hung. Moore, to his credit, found the EC-47 explanation less than credible. (**Personal interview with Moore's staff in 1978**)

This delegation received the eleven remains from Vietnam and four from Laos. Most of the congressmen praised the Communist regimes for the "progress" on the MIA question. News stories told of the difficulty in resolving these cases. Previously, Frank Sieverts testified the Vietnamese told him the "easy" cases were resolved. Congressman Sonny Montgomery already expressed his view that only one hundred or so cases could ever be resolved.

Remains returned tell their own story

The remains returned in this 1978 trip, give this line of reasoning the kick in the solar plexus that it deserves. One set belonged to Navy LCDR Vincent Monroe. He was shot down in 1968. Right away, the Communists announced the capture of two men where Monroe went down. His back-seater was returned in Operation Homecoming. Intelligence information showed Monroe was a POW.

Another set of remains was that of CPT Glendon Lee Ammon. For over eleven years, our government kept from Ammon's family intelligence showing his probable capture. It is not known when he died. The Communists remained silent.

A third case, that of Air Force CPT Jack W. Weatherby, illustrates the type of difficult cases that Hanoi can resolve. Weatherby was an RF 101 reconnaissance pilot. Orders came to pinpoint a SAM site near Yen Bai, an important railroad marshaling yard. Since the SAM locations at Yen Bai were mobile, aerial reconnaissance was needed prior to further bombing. This was his second mission against a SAM site in three days. (**Unarmed and Unafraid by Glen B. Infield and AP, Yen Bai references**)

Weatherby and his wing-man, MAJ Jerry Lents, headed north from Tan Son Nhut. Forty miles from the target area, the two men leveled off at 200 feet. Weatherby was hit by ground fire. Lents saw flames streaming out of Weatherby's plane. He started to radio Weatherby to get out when the plane exploded. The tail section came off in one piece. The plane dissolved in a huge orange fireball. The entire incident took only fifteen seconds. Jack Weatherby was posthumously awarded the Distinguished Flying Cross.

Here, Hanoi returned remains, seemingly in a remote area and cooperated for a change. Incorrect, as Yen Bai was historically an important military base, containing a railroad and a marshaling yard. Large contingent of Vietnamese, Chinese Communists, and Russians were in the immediate vicinity. In all, it was an easy case to resolve. (A footnote — Yen Bai will become more familiar to the reader as you progress in this book.)

The Monroe, Ammon, and Weatherby cases are illustrative of the MIA accounting problem. Even more graphic is the case of Dominic Sansone. Through a mix-up, Sansone was buried at Tan Son Nhut Airport. Hanoi knew he was there. Washington knew he was there. It was not until 1985 that Sansone's remains were returned to the United States. Until that time, though, Hanoi used the case of Sansone to accuse us of expecting "miracles" out of them when we could not even keep track of our own dead.

Let's be blunt. Hanoi lies about the information that it possesses. It has piles of military ID cards in "military museums;" custody of men they deny holding; and warehoused hundreds of remains. Hanoi has returned few remains. Little accounting occurred in Laos. Each time Hanoi returns a set of remains or two, our government hails the progress being made. Few solid cases have been resolved. One notable exception is Navy Pilot Ron Dodge, whose captivity was captured forever on film and the cover of **Life** magazine. Otherwise, men photographed in captivity mean little to Hanoi. There can be no letting up on the pressure on both Washington and Hanoi. Prisoners need to be repatriated and remains returned.

Our men administratively resolved

All MIAs have been "administratively resolved." Of the more than 2500 (or 4400) cases, about 200 cases have been resolved by the return of remains. Some of these "bodies" are no more than a handful of bone fragments. On October 5, 1990, four servicemen, buried at Arlington National Cemetery, were "unaccounted for." DOD admitted, "two of the caskets of 'remains' contained no bones at all ... *The two coffins were empty."* In February 1994, the government attempted to resolve the case of the entire EC-47 crew on the basis of one molar tooth.

Many cases will never be resolved. Some MIAs went down over the sea or in unknown remote locations. However, Hanoi can resolve a great proportion of the cases. MIAs have been "accounted for" on the flimsiest proof. A lapse of time and Communist silence was sufficient.

The foregoing is a brief outline of the problem facing the MIA / POW families. A former enemy does not release information. Their government consistently turns its back on them. The 1205 document says Americans are prisoners. Evidence mounts that many were transferred to Russia or China. There is also solid evidence that Americans are detainees closer to Washington, D.C. than to Hanoi.

None of this information was easy to obtain. The government argues in court that all efforts to obtain MIA information is undertaken while trying to defeat Congressional efforts to have "truth bills" passed. DIA argues against further declassification of reports. Poppycock! When some "newly declassified reports" were released in January 1994, the information contained in those reports (**Washington Post, January 1994**) was older and less reliable than that released in 1979.

In two cases, information concerning the fate of MIAs never made it to the families until 1990 and 1991. In both cases, I released that information. Even today, the reason for both of these men being listed as POWs is unknown to the families despite many requests for that information.

The executive branch has been untruthful to the courts; the legislative branch; destroyed evidence; behaved in an illegal manner; and deceived the American people. This is a shocking story. Some people will not believe it. Some will recognize a massive cover-up. Men died in captivity while this story was being written. President Carter wanted to establish diplomatic relations with Hanoi. President Clinton, to "heal the wounds of war," in February 1994, lifted the Vietnamese trade embargo. There were no unreturned POWs and unaccounted for MIAs. Diplomatic relations were later restored and still no unreturned POWs and MIAs.

The numbers the government uses concerning the MIAs are misleading. In World War II, the bodies of twenty-two (22) percent of the men killed or MIA were never recovered. In Vietnam, the figure is about four (4) percent. A quick comparison gives the impression that the Vietnamese have done an admirable job. A closer look provides a totally different perspective. For example, the 22 percent figure includes Navy men lost at sea. We had no such experience in Vietnam. Of the 78,794 men not recovered, about 9000 to 17,000 were declared dead on the basis of presumptive findings of death. That works out to about two to five percent. (**Final Report Montgomery Committee**)

Some of these nine to seventeen thousand men were actually POWs (as explained later in the book). The two to five percent becomes smaller.

For clarity, consider that in World War II, we were considered the victors. We had the time and resources necessary to find stragglers or persons in remote prison camps. The situation was not the same in Vietnam. We were the losers. There was no opportunity to comb Vietnam for hidden prison camps (not officially anyway). Early in 1985, the Laotians allowed the United States to excavate a site in their country. We paid a monetary price for that privilege, however. The Laotians plainly stated it would be the future price for any "cooperation." Our recent access to Vietnam produced "contrived results."

In World War II, three percent of those classified as bodies not recovered were men who could not be identified. No soldier from Vietnam qualifies as an unknown soldier. The four percent figure for Vietnam is highly suspect. Unrefuted testimony given by Dermot Foley and documented by the minority staff of the Senate Foreign Relations Committee, shows the true figure is very likely to be closer to eight percent. The difference is approximately twenty-four hundred findings of death, with no proof, made before the end of the war.

Eight percent in Vietnam versus two to five percent in World War II. Keep those figures in mind as you read the government's declarations of satisfaction with Vietnamese performance in accounting for our missing.

What's the big deal — the harm done?

What harm is done if a man, declared dead, later returns. First, if his wife remarries and he should return, it is doubtful that the new marriage would be valid. Marriage is governed by state rather than federal law. Second, money distributed at the time of "death" probably cannot be recovered. The same uncertainty applies to any other property. The government has no provision except for back pay.

A wife is perfectly free to remarry and still leave her husband in a missing category. State law has remedies. Any next of kin has the right to be represented by a lawyer in any given situation because of a man's MIA status. It is only the MIA who has been denied his rights.

In civilian life, if a person disappears for a period of time, a surviving spouse or other party with a vested interest can seek a determination of death. It has to be proved that all reasonable means of finding the missing person has been exhausted. Then, a determination of death may be made. The burden of proof is upon the person seeking such a change in status.

For the MIA, there is no such requirement. Some POWs are alive today. The government has not exhausted every reasonable effort to account for them, ignoring Vietnamese statements that they hold POWs. It adopted the attitude that if the men are alive, not much can be done to recover them. An exhaustive study of this balance between the rights of the MIAs and the families is in the testimony Dermot Foley gave before the House Select Committee on Missing Persons in Southeast Asia (94th Congress 2d Session).

Government embarrassed, Garwood returns

In 1979, an "embarrassment" came home. Marine PFC Robert Garwood emerged from captivity in Vietnam after fourteen years. The government portrayed him as a collaborator. Later, we'll examine his case. I talked with him and did research for his original lawyer, Dermot Foley. I first believed he was a traitor. I no longer hold that viewpoint.

The government made no special effort to find him, writing him off as dead just before he came home, through his own ingenuity. Our government believed the Vietnamese claim of his "demise."

During the Senate POW Hearings in 1992, both former Secretaries of Defense Melvin Laird and James Schlesinger said they believed "the US government knowingly left American servicemen behind..." (Washington Times, 9/22/92) Laird said he cannot explain why Nixon never challenged the assertion all POWs were returned. (Washington Post 9/22/92) No Deceit?

One final point on the belief in the Vietnamese. In 1993, a Soviet translation of a Vietnamese report from General Tran Van Quang, dated September 15, 1972, was found. A short synopsis of this explosive document is that Quang told his superiors the Vietnamese held 1205 American prisoners of war at that time (only 591 came home). 1205 American prisoners! What happened to them?

Why the secrecy? "The Government of the USA knows well about this, but does not know the exact number of prisoners of war, and is able only to surmise approximately about them on the basis of its losses. That is why, in accordance with the instructions of the Politburo, we are keeping secret the numbers of prisoners of war." (*From the document — English Translation*)

The government was wrong about Garwood — it is wrong about men being left behind — it is wrong *about the men who have returned clandestinely.*

Trail to Captivity

Two hundred miles Southwest of Saigon lays the legendary "Forest of Darkness," the U-Minh. A traditional stronghold of communist forces, it served as a detention area for American POWs. According to DIA, all known POWs captured prior to 1969 were executed, died from illness, released, or escaped. They lied.

The late COL James N. "Nick" Rowe, a prisoner in the U-Minh and Nam Can Forest, recalled, in his book **Five Years to Freedom**, that "constant reference by the guards to a *new POW* gave me hope that I'd have someone soon with whom I could communicate." (*Emphasis added*) On January 13, 1968, he was taken to a series of propaganda movies. During intermission, **he saw not one but three** American POWs in attendance. Who were these men?

Charles A. Dale and David S. Demmon became MIAs on June 9, 1965, lost to the East of the U-Minh Forest. According to known VC procedure, these men were taken there if captured. Several candidates exist for the "third man." In 1974, the Pentagon listed their cases as being unlikely to be resolved. I wrote in 1979 that sometime later, probably in the 1976-77 time frame, our intelligence agencies accumulated information causing the Pentagon to state positively that the Communists could resolve the cases of Dale and Demmon.

I did not yet know that in 1977 intelligence was being reviewed showing Dale and Demmon survived. Reports from 1966 had Dale and Demmon in a specific prison camp. Eleven years after the fact, despite clear written records, DIA decided that the intelligence was wrong.

The reason given was that no one else had seen them. Were Dale and Demmon two of the three men seen by Rowe? The government, at the time of reclassifying them to presumed dead, wrote "all ... information ... has been given careful consideration. The circumstances attendant to ... disappearance, plus the lapse of time without ... information ... can lead only to the conclusion ... no longer alive. Further, the debriefing of returned prisoners ... revealed no information of ... fate."

Unknown to the families was that buried deep in classified archives, was a series of reports from the U-Minh and Nam Can Forests showing Americans prisoners including early 1973. (I have seen reports of Americans reported alive as late as 1988) No one emerged from the U-Minh to report any POWs left behind. No one referred to the three POWs seen by Rowe. The government did not tell about refugees seeing Americans in the U-Minh. The families were not told of the multiple rescue missions in the U-Minh. Possibly, Dale and Demmon were two of the men that Rowe saw. Dale was reported, in 1986, alive, as will be seen later.

In 1994, I talked with Daniel Pitzer, a person captured with Rowe. He told me Rowe did not know the identities of those he saw. Since Rowe could not identify them, they are "uncorrelated cases," and "do not exist."

Discrepancies existed between the number of POWs Hanoi said it held and the number of men that we knew were prisoner. The 1205 document confirms Hanoi held hundreds of captives back. Henry Kissinger finally wrote, "Equally frustrating were our discussions of the American soldiers and airmen who were prisoners of war or missing in action. We knew of at least eighty instances in which an

American serviceman had been captured alive and ... disappeared. ....." (**Years of Upheaval** - Boston: Little, Brown, and Company pp. 33-34)

Discrepancies and the trail to captivity

On June 7, 1964, SGT Robert L. Greer and SGT Fred Scheckengost took a motorcycle ride near Da Nang. Villagers reported seeing them, clad in black pajamas, being led away by VC forces. They were listed as POWs. Greer and Scheckengost were "accounted for" on 11/20/90. (Official accountings may not be what they appear to be.)

CPT George Clarke Jr. was an RF-4 pilot lost over Laos October 16, 1967. In April 1968, his parents were informed by Pentagon spokesmen that a released POW reported him being held in an NVN prison. A short time before Christmas 1971, they were told, "It has come to the attention of the Air Force" that Clarke needed eyeglasses. Again, it was not mentioned how that information was gathered. Packages sent to Clarke were returned by Hanoi. Clarke is unaccounted for.

Ironically, I found out in 1991 that the person in the plane with Clarke was the son of a neighbor of mine, Richard Appelhans. In 1987, Congressman John Rowland (R- CN) discovered that Appelhans was listed as a POW and not negotiated for in 1973. The family of Appelhans did not know this. In 1999, they still do not know the circumstances of his capture. Appelhans is unaccounted for.

A classic case of gall involves the capture of Navy LT Ronald Dodge. He was shot down over Nghe An Province May 17, 1967, safely ejecting from his plane and observed on the ground. He radioed his wing-man: "Here they come. I'm destroying my radio" and Vietnam boasted of capturing a "U.S. bandit pilot."

A few months later, the French magazine, *Paris Match*, ran a photo of Dodge, led by his captors. The East German propaganda movie, **"Pilots in Pyjamas,"** featured his captivity. The Vietnamese refused to acknowledge him until 1981, when, fourteen years after capture, they returned his remains.

On February 18, 1969, CPT John M. Brucher ejected from his F-105D aircraft over Quang Binh Province, near the Laotian border. He immediately established radio contact with rescue forces and reported landing in a tree, suspended in midair with a dislocated shoulder. Rescue helicopters departed before Brucher could be found. He reported being unable to disengage from his parachute. On the second effort, the next day, searchers found the parachute, in the tree, empty. In 1973, negotiators failed to ask about him. He ceased to exist, unaccounted for.

Another classic example of Communists denying the obvious is CPT David Hrdlicka. Captured on May 18, 1965, the Laotians broadcast a letter attributed to Hrdlicka. The letter was lengthy, similar to those POWs were tortured into signing. *Pravda* ran a picture of Hrdlicka in captivity. Radio Peking quoted Laotian sources saying Hrdlicka was a prisoner. Congressman Robert K. Dornan provides this look at Hrdlicka's case: "My best friend ... in the Air Force ... David Hrdlicka, ... I am the godfather of his oldest child .... He was photographed in captivity as late as 1968 or 1969. He was almost the object of an international prisoner transfer ... There were tape recordings ... and photographs of him ... His wife found out about his missing ... status through a newspaper photograph in Moscow ..."

The Communists tried several subterfuges with Hrdlicka. First, the Vietnamese released a separate list of men captured in Laos as being the only POWs captured and held. All were captured by the North Vietnamese forces and held prisoner in North Vietnam. Next, they said the Pathet Lao did not have facilities for holding prisoners. All men captured were executed within a few days of capture. Hrdlicka was declared dead with no proof of death.

Dr. Roger Shields, POW expert, said, under oath: "I have very serious questions about his status having been changed without ... getting a statement ... they knew nothing ... because he certainly was alive, ...they knew ... enough to tape and photograph him, and that kind of status change I would object to." (*Hopper V. Carter* **77C1793, US District Court for Eastern District of New York**) Hrdlicka remains unaccounted for and was on Rowland's list.

COL Robert D. Anderson, USAF, and his navigator, George Latella, were flying an F-4E aircraft when forced down on October 6, 1972. Both Anderson and Latella parachuted with Anderson establishing radio contact stating: "I have a good parachute, am in good shape and can see no enemy forces on the ground." They landed several hundred yards apart. Latella was immediately captured. Anderson was not heard again on the radio; his automatic beeper did not transmit. Radio Hanoi, however, announced the capture of **pilots**. Anderson and Latella were the only men lost on October 6, 1972. Latella returned in 1973.

In July 1983, COL Anderson was described in the DOD POW-MIA Fact Book as one on "whom there is 'hard evidence' (e.g., post-capture photography, U.S. or indigenous eye-witnesses to capture or detention, intelligence reports) that they were captured or detained by communist forces." He remains unaccounted for.

Closely associated with David Hrdlicka is COL Charles Shelton. Lost on April 29, 1965 over Sam Neua, Laos, his 33d birthday, his wing-man saw him parachute safely. Shelton radioed he was all right. Intense gunfire kept rescue aircraft from executing a pickup. For two days, search parties followed Shelton's emergency beeper without finding him. Shelton was declared a POW, based on intelligence reports of his capture and other "sufficient evidence." Subsequent intelligence reports showed him with Hrdlicka. Two abortive attempts were made to rescue him. This author reviewed formerly classified documents clearly showing Hrdlicka with Shelton and seven or more other POWs. As for the abortive rescue attempts, referred to in the original version of the book, it was determined that in 1970, he escaped from captivity; was in the hands of the Free Lao forces; and forced back into the hands of the communists. The operation was called "Duck Soup."

Symbolically, Shelton was known as the "Last POW." The government chose not to declare him dead as an indication of our "firm resolve" to end the POW/MIA dilemma. Tragically, however, Shelton's wife, Marian, in 1990, after years of rearing children into adulthood; being the wife of the "Last POW;" and being vilified by government representatives as a hysterical wife, took her own life.

I knew Mrs. Shelton. I gave reports I found in declassified documents to her lawyer. I met her many times at POW family functions. I last saw her in mid - 1989 where I had dinner with her, the Cressmans, Congressman Bill Hendon, and others. We had our own "intelligence briefing" session. We also discussed, in more private settings, reports that I had come in possession of. The Communists have said nothing concerning Shelton's fate.

SGT Donald Sparks was his company's point man. He was wounded and cut off from the rest of his outfit in an ambush on June 17, 1969, near Chu Lai. No one was able to reach his area for almost twelve hours. When help arrived, Sparks was gone. Originally, Sparks was listed as MIA.

On April 11, 1970, on a Viet Cong body, our soldiers found a letter from Sparks addressed to his parents. He assured them of his good health, although in solitary confinement for ten months. Experts confirmed his handwriting. His status changed to POW. Subsequent intelligence reports showed his continued survival.

SGT Russell P. Bott was lost in ground action on December 1, 1966. He was part of a combined Special Forces/Vietnamese reconnaissance team (probable SOG) inserted into Laos just below the DMZ. His team got into some heavy action. They engaged in at least two fire-fights before being surrounded by a superior enemy force. Air rescue was impossible. The team was ordered to evade. Bott ordered the Vietnamese to evade while he guarded his wounded team leader, Willie Stark, also an MIA. His radio broadcasted the fight on the ground with Bott expending his remaining ammunition, providing a cover for his friends. The South Vietnamese reported Bott's capture, hearing the orders to tie his hands. Bott was later seen in a village as a POW. Bott was on the Rowland list; possibly was seen in captivity by Ngo Phi Hung; yet, he was declared "dead." The communists choose not to contradict what our government believes.

CPT Richard Bowers, a member of a three man Mobile Advisory Training Team (MATT), assigned to Tam Soc operations base, awoke on the morning of March 24, 1969, to find his team and Vietnamese allies under attack. He was calling for help on the radio when it went dead. When a relief element arrived, all the Vietnamese defenders of Tam Soc were dead. One of the three American was also dead. A Vietnamese civilian captured and later released saw Bowers and the other advisor, SGT Gerasimo Arroyo-Baez in captivity, dressed in black pajamas, being led into the jungles. Intelligence reports showed Arroyo-Baez alive and well in a Viet Cong prison camp. Hanoi said Arroyo-Baez died in captivity.

DIA documents show that Arroyo-Baez survived his capture. Captured documents show that the U-Minh prison system, where Arroyo-Baez was held, had difficulty reporting the number of men in captivity. One report, correlated years after the fact to Arroyo-Baez by DIA, showed the VC had trouble moving captured Americans into the U-Minh, stating captured Americans were held in place until the security situation improved. This "uncorrelated" document, showed Arroyo-Baez alive in the early 1970's. On October 8, 1971, a SOG mission just missed getting Arroyo-Baez out of a VC prison by hours. (**SOG**, pg. 279-80)

In 1985, the remains of Arroyo-Baez were returned to the United States. There are conflicting reports on the survival of Bowers, who was on Rowland's list.

When it fits Hanoi's purpose, information will be found that has been denied for years. It took nine years to return Monroe's remains - Dodge - fourteen years - Arroyo-Baez - sixteen years. How long did they survive after capture? Such a determination can be made if the government really wants to know.

LT Arthur Ecklund and CPT Perry Jefferson were lost on April 3, 1969. They were on an early morning air reconnaissance mission northeast of Phan Rang Air Base, SVN. It was Jefferson's last mission before rotating home. Ecklund was in the Army and Jefferson in the Air Force. A two day air search failed to locate either man. A short emergency beeper signal, however, was heard on the second day. Subsequent intelligence showed two Americans being captured, wounded, and moved to Secret Base 22. The report was specific as to time, place, and aircraft.

A ground force was inserted to find them. They found evidence of recent enemy activity. An evaluation stated, "Field reports received ... indicated the two air

crew members were captured and held in the general area of the source's sighting."
Neither men was acknowledged by either side.

In August 1972, Mrs. Michael Estocin received back from Hanoi a package she sent to LCDR Michael Estocin. Hanoi declared in 1970 that Estocin had "never been detained." Intelligence sources saw him in NVN. The return of the package was heartbreaking. Yet, there was something odd this time. There was a slit in the top. Inside, Mrs. Estocin found items added to the package. One was a crudely cut, hand sewn bootie with two *M*s cut out of felt on it. (**Michael's** wife's name is **Maria**) Inside the bootie were three hearts. (The Estocins have **three** children). Mrs. Estocin brought this to the attention of the Navy. The Navy denied knowledge of how this might have happened. Estocin was on Rowland's list.

What we have said happened

Navy LT Barton Creed was shot down over Laos on March 13, 1971. For over two hours, Creed communicated with other pilots. Suffering from a broken leg and arm, Creed evaded while rescue craft hovered sometimes only thirty feet away. Intense gunfire caused four rescue attempts to be aborted. Pilots saw Creed, surrounded, when he radioed, "Pick me up now. Pick me up now. They are here." One returned POW reported seeing the Creed's ID card. He remains unaccounted for.

LCDR Donald Lindland was flying over Haiphong in late 1972 when shot down. Lindland and his navigator ejected and were separated by some two to three miles. The navigator was captured and returned in Operation Homecoming. Lindland avoided capture for twenty-four hours. Radio Hanoi broadcasted an A-6 Navy plane was shot down and its "aggressor **pilots**" captured. CDR Lindland was seen alive by pilots on his strike going through a rice paddy towards the river separating him from his navigator. Hanoi returned his remains on 6/3/83.

B-52s played an important part in ending the fighting in Vietnam. The Vietnamese, having shot all their SAMs, had no defense against them. A B-52 attack was a very demoralizing experience. Aboard one B-52 shot down on December 21, 1972, were CPT Donovan Walters and MAJ Edward Johnson. There were seven men aboard their aircraft, and Hanoi gave information on only three. The aircraft commander, after repatriation, told debriefers he saw Johnson's name on a North Vietnamese list. During interrogation, he heard Walters name mentioned in the next room. Another member of the crew saw Walters' ID on the table in his interrogation room. Walters, Johnson, and two others from the crew had their remains returned on December 15, 1988.

Journalists also suffered the loss of verified deaths and the torment of MIA friends. Sean Flynn, son of actor Errol Flynn, and free-lance cameraman Dana Stone were on assignment for *CBS News* covering Cambodia. They left Phnom Penh on a rented motorcycle. Near a eucalyptus plantation in Eastern Cambodia, the two men were captured by combined North Vietnamese and Viet Cong forces.

An intercepted radio message from COSVN showed Flynn and Stone as captives. Several defectors reported that a few weeks prior, orders were circulated saying captured foreigners were not to be harmed. They were to be passed up the chain of command as rapidly as possible. Reports from mid-1971, have Flynn and Stone shot to death. The Cambodians and Vietnamese have been "stubborn" and "indifferent" in providing information on their fate. Both were on Rowland's list.

Welles Hangen was an *NBC News* correspondent in a combined group of *CBS* and *NBC* personnel when they were attacked in Cambodia. Hangen was captured with two other personnel. Intelligence reports showed Hangen and his fellow prisoners surviving for three days before being executed. In 1992, Welles Hangen's remains were recovered. He was on Rowland's list.

In 1974, Charles Dean and Australian Neil Sharman were captured at a checkpoint in Laos by the Pathet Lao and detained at Ban Photan. Seen alive by several sources, two contacts were given their photographs in February, 1975. The Lao government denied knowledge about them. Dean's family traveled to Laos and at the family's request, our embassy in Laos issued a presumptive finding of death. The family announced being reconciled to the "death" of their son. The Australian government kept the case open because they considered Sharman alive. There is no proof of their death. Both were on Rowland's list. Both have reports unofficially related to them as being alive well into the 1980's.

On January 27, 1973, Navy CPT Harley Hall was shot down near Quang Tri. Hall, a former commander of the Blue Angels, was seen discarding his parachute. Other intelligence showed his captivity. A 1980 DIA list said that Hall was killed. Despite clear evidence of his survival, Hall was not on the 1973 negotiating list. Abandoned by his government, his remains were returned on 1/25/93.

One fascinating story from this morass is that of Air Force LT Earl P. Hopper Jr. Young Hopper was shot down on January 10, 1968, over Hanoi by a SAM. Neither Hopper nor his pilot, CPT Keith Hall, were hurt by the blast. Hall was able to bail out while Hopper continued towards Laos. Other pilots marked Hall's position and followed Hopper's plane. Later, the accompanying pilots reported seeing two objects from the jet, the canopy and the ejection seat.

They reported picking up two emergency radio signals, one strong and one weak. Hall was captured approximately forty minutes after bailing out. Hopper was tracked for three days via the beeper. About the third day, a pilot reported hearing Hopper's recognition code and saying, "LT Hopper, if that's you, give me 15 second intervals (in his radio signals)." The pilot received six fifteen second intervals. This information was released to the family in February 1968.

Hall was returned. During his debriefing, and later in conversations with Hopper's family, he recounted an incident that occurred two and a half years into his captivity. He was pulled out of his cell and interrogated at length about Hopper, including his marital status, hometown, hobbies, etc. Being the first time flying together, Hall had none of this information. When one guard left, Hall asked if Hopper was incarcerated. He received a non committal shrug of the shoulders.

In April 1980, the Air Force held a status hearing. After several days of testimony, the case was put on hold for another two and a half years. On July 14, 1982, Earl Hopper Jr., the last POW/MIA in North Vietnam, ceased to "live." Hopper's parents filed for POW compensation pay at the urging of their casualty officer. A Department of Justice committee determined, "... Earl P. Hopper Jr. survived ... and was captured on January 10, 1968. ... remained a prisoner of war from that date until April 1, 1973, the date ... the last known prisoner of war was returned..."

In 1984, additional information concerning Hopper surfaced through friendly and reliable sources. His CIA file revealed they always listed him as a POW. His file showed that the agency tracked him as he climbed the most rugged and highest mountain in the region (possibly Phou Pha Thi) heading for a "safe" area in Laos. Heavy concentrations of NVA and Pathet Lao troops searched for him. The CIA sent a Free Lao team to extract him. When Hopper knew he was in imminent danger of being captured, he locked the transmission key on his radio into the "on" position marking the location of capture. The time, place, description of the area, and other details suggests that Hopper was climbing towards a CIA Lima Site.

LT Hopper's father received data, unofficially, from a sensitive private source, that a computer profile of Hopper, his personality traits, all known incident data, and the known treatment of POWs, states there is a 55% probability that he is alive today. He was on Rowland's list.

LT Arthur H. Hardy, USAF, was lost over Laos on March 14, 1972. One report correlated to him by date, location, and aircraft showed him unconscious, held by four NVA soldiers, with a head wound, impaled upon a sharpened bamboo stump as "punishment." All of Hardy's equipment, outer clothing, and identification had been stripped from him. Higher headquarters used it as proof of his capture. Soldiers told the source Hardy died before reaching the local NVA field hospital. The source was provided with a general description of the burial location. His remains were finally returned on 9/20/83.

James Henry McLean was lost on 2/9/65. He was a medical advisor with a SVN RF unit in Phuoc Long Province. According to released and escaped SVN POWs, McLean was captured, unhurt. Others saw him in a prison. He was last seen in captivity in late 1966. Besides the first hand reports, US intelligence captured VC documents substantiating McLean's capture, although officially they are "uncorrelated." McLean is on Rowland's list.

Hanoi is not ignorant of the fate of these men. Our government is grossly negligent, making one excuse after another for Hanoi's refusal to supply information. In 1987, General John Vessey, Presidential Emissary on POW/MIAs testified, "The Vietnamese side asserted that they also had 'Humanitarian Concerns' ... 1.4 million war disabled, 500,000 orphans and many destroyed schools and damaged hospitals... these too would have to be addressed if there is to be progress on the humanitarian concerns of the United States" (POW/MIAs). (**Vessey Mission Sept. 30, 1987 House Committee on Foreign Affairs pg. 5**) (As a side note, if a child was 8 years old in 1972, the last year of the bombing, that "child" would be 23 years old in 1987. Orphans from our involvement?)

An unenviable track record

A fascinating story is that of CWO Michael B. Varnado. It is both intriguing and frustrating. Varnado was shot down over Cambodia on May 2, 1970. Aboard the helicopter with him were seven Americans. (This story is developed from: the testimony of his mother, a DOD summary, a DIA summary, the prepared statement of a POW, congressional sources, and an affidavit.) As all men exited with no injuries, they came under intense enemy fire. One man, Private Tony F. Karreci, evaded. He saw one man taken prisoner and one man killed at the scene. A rescue attempt was mounted. A five day search turned up no bodies or evidence of graves.

Subsequent intelligence reports were received about four of the remaining seven men, excluding Varnado. In 1973, the Communists listed Varnado as dying in captivity. Varnado's family held a memorial service on Easter Sunday, 1973. For the family, the war was over until the Army showed them a new intelligence report.

An indigenous agent in China said Prince Sihanouk received a telegram stating that two Americans, Glenn Harris and Michael Varnado, were being held prisoner in Kratie Province, Cambodia in July 1974. The Prince read the telegram and returned it to the messenger.

The Army promptly refuted that intelligence report. Two returning POWs stated they had seen Varnado while a prisoner, wounded, but being transferred to a hospital. Another intelligence report reported the death of a serviceman, correlated to Varnado. According to Colonel Chester Bobinski, these reports were conclusive evidence that Varnado died. The Varnados asked why did the Army give them this information if they considered it invalid? The Army's answer was correct in stating the family should be in full possession of all information pertaining to the men even if it is of little value. The Army's information, however, needs scrutiny.

Returning POWs did not agree that Varnado could have died from his wounds. LTC Raymond Schrump saw Varnado prior to his arrival at the hospital, with a serious wound. If treated within a week or two after he saw him, however, his chances for survival were excellent. POW John Sexton said, "he had a slight leg wound and was otherwise in good condition."

This brings us to the intelligence report. The Army stated that their indigenous intelligence source in China was untested, producing both good and bad intelligence in the past. The Army tried to recontact him with new questions. They included: "Did the source actually ... read the telegram ... read or speak English? If he did not read the telegram, how did he come by the information? Could he have obtained the names of Varnado and Harris by other means?" The recontacting was not accomplished. In October 1975, another opportunity presented itself when members of Prince Sihanouk's entourage defected to France. The Army tried to reach these persons also, but without luck. On this basis, the Army ruled the information to be invalid. They also had a "credible" eyewitness to Varnado's death.

This eyewitness reported the officer who died was a Major. Varnado was a Warrant Officer. The date of the helicopter shoot-down is incorrect, as is the supposed date of death. This source, a Cambodian security guard at a VC hospital in Cambodia, said four persons were killed in the helicopter crash and buried at the crash site. Two who died were Vietnamese. There were no Vietnamese on Varnado's helicopter. Furthermore, the Army searched the crash area for five days and found no one buried. Finally, the medical chart on the "patient" listed him as being in the Air Force. Varnado was in the Army. This was the "credible" evidence.

Congressman Lester Wolff (D-NY), traveled to China with an Army prepared list of men lost in Cambodia. He presented the list to the Cambodian Embassy in Peking. Michael Varnado and Rodney Griffin were not on that list. Both had previously been declared dead. The name of Glenn Harris, however, was on the list.

There is one curious footnote to this case. The Army, in preparing some reports on this case, did spell **Glenn** Harris as **Glen**, as did my publisher in the original version of this book. The indigenous source in China, suspected of not knowing English, spelled **Glenn** correctly.

All the information available shows that the U.S. Government attempted to deal with Cambodia in getting back Griffin, Harris, and Varnado. However, it is quite probable that they were almost always in the hands of the Vietnamese. In 1970, the area they were lost in was the home base for COSVN. When ARVN pushed into Cambodia in 1971, COSVN moved to Kratie, Cambodia. The PRG stayed in that country until they won in 1975. (**Viet Cong Memoir pgs. 184, 196**) Varnado's remains were returned on 4/27/89 by Vietnam. Nothing has happened in the Harris or Griffin case. The 1205 document says POWs existed in 1972, captured in Cambodia.

The government creates the impression that all POWs have been accounted for. Returned POWs "indicated that many others listed in an MIA status did not enter the captivity environment." The implication was if a man was not identified by the "intricate communication and personnel accounting system" maintained by the POWs, he was probably dead. LTG Walters of the CIA, said: "Careful analysis of all debriefing of returnees from North Vietnam ... established that all men **known to the returnees to have been in the prison system** had been accounted for. The returnees knew of men who **had been seen in captivity ... but not in the prison system**; many of these were not accounted for .... (Emphasis added)

Let's look at the system

The implication that returning POWs accounted for all of their cell mates does not stand up to scrutiny. Former POW CPT Eugene "Red" McDaniel, stated he once sincerely believed that all POWs had been accounted for. However, while working in a liaison capacity on Capitol Hill, he got to know RADM Jerry Tuttle and LTG Eugene Tighe, both of DIA. Based upon the sheer weight of evidence available to DIA, CPT McDaniel changed his mind. He is convinced American POWs were left behind. His fellow crew member, LT James Kelly Patterson, survived his loss incident. Patterson broke his leg upon landing and maintained radio contact with rescue forces for two days. He further reported that enemy forces had taken a recovery kit which had been dropped on him and that he had moved up a hill for safety. McDaniel had been urged by DIA to tell Patterson's family that he had died. He was on Rowland's list.

The POW system of accounting for fellow POWs was good, but not perfect. Returned POWs included men not entered into the "system." Of our MIAs, some entered into the system only because their ID cards had been seen. One would think that seeing an ID card would not be a strong case for presuming a man to have survived.

Air Force COL Norman Gaddis was shot down on May 12, 1967. (This story is a composite from **The Raid** and **POW A Definitive History.**) He was held in solitary confinement for over two and a half years, out of communication with the rest of the POWs. Not one American saw him. His name entered the system because one prisoner saw a picture of his ID card in a North Vietnamese magazine. He was still another unaccounted for POW. After the attempted prisoner rescue at Son Tay in 1970, the Vietnamese consolidated the **known** POWs. Then, Norman Gaddis first was seen! Ironically, he was known to intelligence outside of Vietnam before the POWs knew about him. His ID card also appeared in "**Pilots in Pyjamas.**" (I first learned this in December 1996 by viewing my copy of the film)

Where had he been held captive before the consolidation? For almost four and a half years, Gaddis was in a section of the main prison compound in the center of Hanoi, "Heartbreak Hotel," a receiving station for prisoners incarcerated in Hoa Lo Prison (the Hanoi Hilton). He was inside the main North Vietnamese prison and no other POW had seen him! Yet, now the government wants us believe that no prisoner was unknown to returned POWs.

Our intelligence identified only nine of the thirteen identified prison camps the Vietnamese kept returned prisoners in. By November 21, 1972, DIA had confirmed only eight of the nine. Returned POWs, like MAJ. Mark Smith, made numerous references to a "bad boy's camp" they were threatened to be sent if they did not cooperate with their captors. Sexton said they were threatened with being sent to "a punishment camp." The Vietnamese told them that their chance of returning this camp was almost nil. Declassified documents named one location as a "bad boy's camp;" Yen Bai. One inhabitant of Yen Bai was **Robert Garwood**. I asked a former POW how accurate the "system" was. My source spent five years in the Hanoi Hilton. He spent time in solitary confinement as "uncooperative." He knew of persons in the prison system not accounted for. He flatly stated that it was impossible for the POWs to account for all the persons in prison because the prisoners generally knew only about their own compound. The data base for the identification system did not grow until after the Son Tay raid. The prisoners were brought together to provide the maximum security against another raid. My source said it was reasonable to assume that some maximum security prisoners had not been brought into the Hanoi Hilton.

After President Nixon ordered the mining of the Haiphong Harbor, some 220 prisoners were moved from Hanoi to a prison camp known to POWs as "Dogpatch." The official U.S. explanation was that the Vietnamese moved the men to break up the POW organization operating at the Hilton. My source said the move was made because the Vietnamese feared an invasion. This move precluded the rescue of all POWs because of the distance from the other POW camps. The Vietnamese feared another Son Tay. Such an invasion was planned if peace negotiations continued for an extended period without any visible results. (Discussed at length in **The Raid**)

DIA reports revealed that **eighteen further prison locations** were suspected of containing American POWs. The 1205 document said other POW camps were opened after Son Tay, holding unacknowledged prisoners. DIA's documents show "possible prisons" reacting to the Son Tay raid.

Further, prisoners returned in 1973, contained no severe mental cases, no severe burn cases, and no amputees; contrary to all expectations of medical authorities. Declassified documents assert POWs still captive include severe mental cases, severe burn cases, and amputees. Some captured men probably did not survive the initial brutal interrogation and sadistic torture sessions. Some, like Norman Gaddis, were put into isolation, their presence never revealed. The Vietnamese revived some former French prisons. When China began some of its well-publicized border incursions in 1979, Vietnam exfiltrated groups of men out of Vietnam into Laos for "procedural safeguard." Such reports started to occur again in March and April 1992, before Smith reported them in Laos, in Vietnamese "care." Some spent time along "Prisoner Highway." Others were part of a brutal, heinous, experimental system implemented by the Vietnamese, Russians, and Chinese conducted in several countries.

In September 1987, Congressman Rowland asked a question of Ann Mills Griffiths, of the League; David Lambertson, the State Department; and General Vessey, Presidential Emissary concerning discrepancy cases.

Mr. Rowland: Do you believe we left men behind ... in 1973?

Mrs. Griffiths: Yes, I said I certainly do.

The answer for Vessey and Lambertson was provided by DOD. It said: "We have no information to indicate that any of the sixty three individuals were alive at the time of Operation Homecoming in 1973." On that list were the crew members of the EC-47 and men on Rowland's list. The same question was asked in 1992 and 1996. In 1992, several former officials finally conceded that men were left behind. In 1996, several former officials in the accounting process, fired because of their beliefs, said yes, they felt men were still alive.

The doubt lingers on because of the admission of the Vietnamese that they held 1205 prisoners in late 1972. The government will attempt to explain the whole document away with tortured language that almost duplicates the hairsplitting ability of President Bill Clinton attempting to explain something with the outcome hinging on what the definition of "is" is. Their hair splitting, however, has much more damaging effect upon the psyche of the security of the United States than the philandering of a wimp President who in early 1999 promised to have records examined to see if American POWs existed in the former Soviet Union.

Are there still Americans captive in Vietnam and elsewhere? We are dealing with multiple trails of deceit. The answer to both would seem to be yes.

Are They Still Alive?

The tall stern Mississippi Congressman asked Ngo Phi Hung how he was the only refugee reporting Americans in the building he testified about? This Congressman, G. V. (Sonny) Montgomery, knew the question was based upon a false premise. Hung replied that the walls surrounding the building were high and he had access to the building because of his papers. Further, the "Final Report" of Montgomery's own Select Committee stated on page 69 that there were hundreds of thousands of documents dealing with sightings of Americans in Vietnam and elsewhere. These documents contain over four thousand sighting reports and accompanying evaluations. Parts were released to the families in early 1979. Some of those reports corroborated what Hung testified to. On September 30, 1987, in the Vessey hearings, more declassification of materials pertaining to the POWs/MIAs was asked for, especially material given to the Vietnamese.

Mr. Rowland (CN): ... let me ask this very simple question. You would have no problem... giving this same information ... given to the Vietnamese ... to the Congress and to this committee, but certainly to the American people.

General Vessey: ... that ... needs to be wrestled out technically —

Mr. Rowland: General, ... we have given it to the Vietnamese; ... should we be afraid to give this to the American people?

General Vessey: ...I think it is important that the intelligence and technical people look it over and decide what —

Mr. Rowland: Why should we be concerned about intelligence when we have already given it to the Vietnamese? ... who are we hiding it from? ... the American people... members of Congress, the families. ...

General Vessey: You have it so it is obviously not being hidden from the members of Congress .

Mr. Rowland: Oh, I have it. You don't know what I went through to get this. ... I don't even want to get into that... And I only have 70 of the cases.

General Vessey: I think this is an argument that I don't really want to be in ... but ... you ought to ask yourself, is the issue of resolving the POW/MIA business served by disclosing the information?... If it is served ... I am in favor... If it is not served ... then I am opposed ... I recognize that men of good will may disagree on whether or not it does, but you people ought to -

Mr. Rowland: General, ... the answer is very simple. The American people would be outraged if they knew this information ...the live-sighting information ... that we left guys behind in 1973. The follow-up question ... for Mr. Lambertson is what has the ... State Department done to bring the men home after 14 years?

General Vessey: ... I think the American people are already outraged ... I don't think there is any question .. .

Mr. Rowland: If you give them the rest of that information; you haven't seen anything yet, General.

Congressman Solarz (D-NY) asked finally "Can you undertake, Mr. Lambertson, ... to get us an answer? This appears to be a very reasonable request. I must say there would have to be a pretty compelling justification for not making public what we have provided to the Vietnamese."

The official response (**pg. 107** of the hearing) was: "The information provided to the Socialist Republic of Vietnam (SRV) ... consisted of selected incident and personal data extracted from the case files ... presented in a narrative format. Copies of the negotiation narratives ... are being conveyed to the Subcommittee ... The administration asks that the Subcommittee restrict access to this information ... Such protection reduces the potential for ... gross misinterpretation ... by unqualified individuals....The next of kin...have latitude to release or reveal it.... this precaution preserve the family's privacy, ... serves as a barrier to misuse of the information for ... possible emotional or financial exploitation of affected families."

Some Early Sightings

Early on May 2, 1975, near Rach Gia City, two Vietnamese men sat engaging in small talk. Suddenly, there was a commotion behind them. Everyone ran to the riverside to catch a glimpse of a docking sampan containing five VC and two American POWs, one white and one black. The white man appears about thirty years old and is quite thin. The black man appears to be about the same age, but a little heavier and more solidly built. The men have traces of tears on their faces.

The Communists spend twenty minutes in Xeo Ro before departing towards the U-Minh Forest. Perhaps they went to the Can Gao Canal. The POWs would learn it's new name, the "Hate Americans Canal." Possibly, they joined other Americans being held in the same area.

Trinh Hung is a friend of these two Vietnamese. He was living in the same area when another sampan arrived in October 1975. Again, there are two Americans. This time, both are white and thin. They are lying on the bottom of the sampan, hands tied behind them. Their heads are shaven, like those of Buddhist monks. Their captors encourage the onlookers to taunt the helpless Americans, even to beat at them with small sticks until they leave towards the U-Minh Forest. Hung explains the Americans were detained in a forced labor camp, sealed off and forbidden for the local people to come near. Numerous persons see the Americans however, and unveil what they have seen.

A refugee named Hong saw Americans in the U-Minh Forest. On June 6, 1975, he is arrested by Communist cadre. He ends up in a concentration camp, Canal Number 7 Camp in the U-Minh Forest. A week later, he arrives at an auxiliary detention center. Life is severe. Inmates are detailed to cut wood three kilometers south, near a prohibited zone.

In early August 1975, Hong joins Mr. Long, a communist cadre doing time for a crime against the revolution. Long, familiar with the area, makes sure other prisoners do not attempt escape or enter the prohibited zone. The two men look for beehives and honey. Climbing a tree containing one hive, they look across a small canal to the South. They see five men. Three are tall with shoulder length hair. Two are Vietnamese guards. Long tells Hong "they are Americans." He becomes very excited. They are on the edge of the prohibited zone, called "Camp T." He tells Hong "don't repeat a word of what we saw or we will be severely punished." Only in a Thai refugee camp does Hong tell his story. (**From DIA files**)

After reading an advertisement in <u>**Trang Den,**</u> a Vietnamese Language newspaper, a woman writes to say that she knows of a large number of Americans being held in Vietnam. A friend visits her after being released from a Communist concentration camp in North Vietnam. He was held with a cousin. He says many Americans are held prisoner with Vietnamese POWs. They are being used as bargaining chips to extract war damages from the United States.

A Wartime Sighting

In August 1974, a rallier reports seeing six POWs in the U-Minh Forest in 1970. He adds that he has kept track of them until just before he rallied. The Air Force flies reconnaissance missions over the U-Minh that December. The report "confirmed the existence of a factory-like building as well as man-made structures in the reported PW camp location. Aerial reconnaissance further confirms source's diagramming of the various canals to include the camouflaged canal entrance and the security check points." We'll visit this site later.

Camp T

Two reports confirm the existence of Camp T in the U-Minh Forest. One is a captured Viet Cong document describing Camp T as the main prison headquarters for VC Military Region Three, including the U-Minh Forest. At least two Americans were being held there in early 1970. Another report says released South Vietnamese army personnel were held in Camp T in early 1970. They did not see American POWs, but added that "foreigners" were in the regional prison camp. The captured VC document named Camp T as the regional prison camp. Other documents affirm the responsibility for holding, securing, and interrogating American POWs rests with the VC regional level.

Camp T is described as being divided into two sections, one for Americans and one for Vietnamese. It would not be unprecedented for the Vietnamese to be unaware of the contents of the other section of the prison. Colonel Rowe wrote that some of his prison locations were divided into various sections to keep the Americans from knowing who else was incarcerated. Intelligence documents show that prison camps throughout Vietnam used "T" as the designator for regional activities. Bobby Garwood was held in various camps using a "T" designator in front of the number of the camp. Other military units also used "T" for the regional designation. COSVN, the overall VC headquarters, had the designation "R."

The debunking begins

I asked in 1978 how DIA would explain away the above reports and the following ones. In February 1972, agents see three Americans in the U-Minh. It gets reported in November 1972 to the CIA. JPRC evaluates, saying, "the above information ... is **extremely probable**. Numerous reports of U.S. POWs have been received ... The camp description provided by source is typical of POW camps built in swamp areas." (JPRC is a cover name for SOG)

In early 1973, similar reports are received and passed on to the JCRC. They say it is "extremely possible" for American POWs to be in the U-Minh. In 1978 I asked why it was probable Americans existed in November 1972 and early 1973 but not in mid 1973. (JCRC is a successor to JPRC)

I hadn't yet read all the "uncorrelated" reports. They answered both questions. They contained the cable concerning Nguyen Thahn Son. In earlier pages, I stated that 1974 was the year of "declare them dead." The State Department, through Sieverts, however, holds the record for debunking. He stated that if POWs were not on the Vietnamese list and did not come home, they must be dead. (**January 28, 1973** *New York Times*)

Let's examine some newer reports. The following reports are from the American Defense Institute (ADI) and their POW Policy Center. A woman refugee saw two Americans while delivering food to her husband. They are in the Rach Gia prison, their hands bound behind them, sticks under their arms. She saw them delivered to the prison. American investigators find a refugee who worked at that prison. He tells American intelligence that American prisoners are there. A Chinese businessman, also a prisoner in Rach Gia prison, said his cell mate was American. His story is verified by polygraph.

A former ARVN soldier has an American POW cell mate while in Rach Gia. This POW, chained to a ring in the floor, a Marine Corps pilot says his name is "Bolick." Another refugee, later in the same cell, remembers the name "Bolick" also. (On the MIA list is James Richard Bohlig, a Marine aviator lost in South Vietnam) In 1988, my home state paper, *The Arizona Republic*, ran the picture of a man identified as an American held in the U-Minh Forest.

Now, let's take a look at some similarities in these reports. The lady letter writer remembers Communists talking about holding the Americans hostage for "war reparations." Ngo Phi Hung said the guards holding the Americans affirmed the Americans were being held for the money promised as war damages. Nguyen Cong Hoan, a former communist assemblyman, told congressional sources Americans were being held in North Vietnam as bargaining chips for war reparations.

Declassified documents support the refugee reports. There have been reports of both South and North Vietnamese officials stating that American POWs were bargaining chips for future negotiations. A leader in a VC re-education camp in the VC Ca Mau area said Ca Mau was to be one holding area. Ca Mau contains the U-Minh Forest. The 1205 document affirms the communist plan of holding POWs for reparations. The Peace Accords themselves affirm the American duty to pay reparations (when examined in Vietnamese).

How many times does the name "Rach Gia" have to come up before analysts notice the agreement? Rach Gia and Xeo Ro are near the northern end of the U-Minh Forest area. I located a Vietnamese source who came down the "Hate American" canal towards Ca Mau City (province capital of An Xuyen). He put various landmarks in their correct perspective. In addition, he added a connecting river not shown on the map he was working with. He placed a holding camp, "Canal # 7" at about the same spot as Hong did.

Another major similarity was the stated number of Americans held prisoner in North Vietnam. Nguyen Cong Hoan put the number at about two hundred fifty. This is the number heard by Ngo Phi Hung. Several reports, received by DIA, show refugees seeing two hundred thirty American POWs near Bat Bat prison in North Vietnam in 1976. A Vietnamese doctor treated these 230 Americans in October, 1977. Eleven Americans die from illness and malnutrition.

This type of report of large numbers of American POWs in North Vietnam also circulated in North Vietnamese military circles. The lady from Japan reported that her friend, a former prisoner in North Vietnam, heard of "many" Americans being held there. In early March 1977, a military defector living in Thailand tells reporters it is "common knowledge" among his military comrades that there are Americans held prisoner in North Vietnam. These prisoners are "moved around fairly frequently." John LeBoutillier, a former member of the House POW Task Force, wrote in the *New York Times,* on August 20, 1984, that DIA analysts privately conceded that in Laos about 200 - 250 Americans were being held.

Mike Mielke, a retired army man living in Saigon, with his family, after the Communist conquest, served as a volunteer coordinator for VIVA. He had freedom of movement as long as he obeyed the rules. He would shop with his Vietnamese wife and they would run into groups of ladies from North Vietnam. They talked about Mielke. Commenting on his freedom, they said, "That's an American. We thought all Americans were up North." Critical that he had no guard on him, the shoppers from the North talked to each other about an American community numbering about 200 persons located near the Vietnam-China border.

DOD goofs

In May 1991, the Republican Staff of the Senate Foreign Relations Committee relates a 1987 refugee account of a capture of an American pilot in 1968, around Do Son, near Haiphong. The refugee described seeing a tri-colored parachute. The American swam out towards the ocean to escape capture, firing his pistol at the pursuing Vietnamese. Once captured, he is stripped of his one-piece flight suit, placed in the side car of a motorcycle, driven across Do Son airfield, and taken to an awaiting Chinese automobile.

An early DOD evaluation concluded this fisherman saw the capture of James M. Hickerson, captured near Do Son, repatriated in March 1973. The Republican staff received a letter from Hickerson in April 1989 detailing his capture. He is disturbed by the analysis attributing this capture to him. Hickerson was shot down near Do Son, on the inside of the peninsula, and could not swim out towards the ocean. He denies firing a pistol before his capture. His parachute was white, not tri-colored. His Marine utility uniform consisted of pants and a shirt, not a one-piece uniform. He was taken to prison on the back of a bicycle; not in a jeep.

If the fisherman did not see Hickerson, then who did he see? The Republican Staff reported CDR James E. Dooley was shot down on October 22, 1967, while conducting a bombing raid near Hanoi. He crashed to the South of Do Son island. Fellow pilots see his aircraft after being hit crashing about one mile offshore near Do Son. They do not see a parachute. Dooley is officially listed as KIA-BNR (killed in action — body not returned). In 1973, however, a repatriated POW reported seeing Dooley's name written on a prison cell wall in Hanoi. Two released Thai Special Forces soldiers identified Dooley as a fellow inmate. A Communist propaganda photograph of captured US pilots in Hanoi, dated after Dooley's shootdown, bears a "partial profile of a person that strongly resembles Dooley."

A second look at this shoot-down by DOD refuses "despite these sharply contrasting differences between the actual events of Hickerson's capture and the fisherman's description ... to change its original conclusion that the captive witnessed by the fisherman was Hickerson." (SFR pg. 6-3,4)

The Republican staff evaluates. "The fisherman may indeed have witnessed a capture, but the description of events more closely resembles the capture of Dooley, not Hickerson.... a significant question remains: was Hickerson's shoot-down correlated to the fisherman's live sighting report ... because Hickerson was repatriated, and ... sighting could be 'resolved?' ...In ... April 10. 1987, the JCRC ... sent an evaluation of the Dooley file to the National Security Council ... The message says that Dooley's case was presented to North Vietnamese officials in August 1984 ... during a POW/MIA technical meeting ... Were they looking for remains, or were they trying to ascertain the fate of a person believed to have been a POW ... ?"

In April, 1992, BG Edwin Lacy deposes, under oath, about the difficulty in on the spot evaluations. "I did have one occasion that I was flying with a new pilot ... He took ground fire, on fire, and ejected. He had a chute that streamed. The chute did not open. He hit the ground. I came back and reported that there was no way for him to survive. Five hours later, ... he hit in the mud, he had compound fractures of the legs, and crushed discs, but he survived." Lacy is asked, "So, he was rescued?" He replied, "Yes, but again, my initial report was that he was a fatality. ... things happened so rapidly that you see something ... based upon experience .... you say there's no way that anyone could survive. But ... he survived."

Laos — the "black hole of MIAs"

The focus shifts to Laos. LTC Albert Shinkle testifies on July 1, 1978 about first hand knowledge of American POWs in Laos collected while with the Defense Attaché Office (read DIA). He knows of eight or nine American POWs located in an unnamed cave in a specific valley about ninety miles to the North Northeast of Nha Kha Phanom Air Force Base in Thailand. These confirmed sightings have men captive until some month in 1972. Shinkle cannot remember the exact month.

Shinkle's testimony is corroborated by a declassified Air Force Report dated November 12, 1973. I found this report that says as part of a list of **known POW camps in Laos**, located in an area **approximately 90 miles** to the North Northeast of Nha Kha Phanom Air Force Base, is an "**undesignated cave prison camp**" that is "known to have existed, and maybe still does" **in September 1972**, held Americans. A comparison of the name of the valley given by Shinkle in his testimony with the information in the Air Force report together with a map survey shows a village at the grid coordinates in the Air Force Report whose phonetic name is remarkably similar to the name of the valley given in Shinkle's testimony. The two items substantiate each other. You'll see more of this valley later in the book.

Shinkle testifies about his knowledge. "The most telling piece of evidence ... as to there being Americans alive in ... 1973 in Laos, while I was on active duty, comes from the only mission that the Air Force clandestine intelligence units were allowed to put into Laos ... The CIA, ... hired many Thai mercenaries to cross the border into Laos ... One of these trail watch team members was captured... put into a prison camp in Laos; he eventually escaped, ... reported to his CIA supervisor, was not debriefed, and went on his way. We were curious. ... an Air Force ... Captain, ... Jack Corpsman, ..., got him, sat him down, ... there were between six and eight Americans alive in that same prison camp that the Thai had been in..."

Shinkle explained that part of the Thai culture, not volunteering information unless asked for, explained why the CIA supervisor was not told of the American presence. He continued, "... this Thai man ...was held in a cage above ground... could see the flying helmets ... the flying uniforms ... periodically, ... the Pathet Lao, would bring out of an underground cave, some white men, who were wearing shorts, and they had a large hardwood hobble on one leg. ... the right leg."

After telling Congressman Tennyson Guyer the location of this cave, Shinkle continued, "... They were running around in a circle, apparently, to exercise. And, he knew one word of English, and he'd shout it ... Some times, they'd shout back. .... tried to talk to him. ... when he got back to Thailand, and we debriefed him, we organized the only helicopter insert mission that we ever were allowed to put into Laos. .... We were late when we got our team in there. The American prisoners had been moved northward some two months prior ... I have footnoted with independent sources that can verify those things which I say ...."

Another part of Shinkle's testimony centers upon his developing sources within the Lao government. He is told about "several tens" of Americans held prisoner, at least until early 1975. They are held as bargaining chips in further negotiations with the United States. He elaborates on one source. "The source of information ... one of the Lao pilots that I worked with... carried in his wallet... a letter from a very high ranking Pathet Lao government officer, who, indirectly, was a member of his family.... We eventually asked this man to cooperate with us ... "

Shinkle continued, "This man (the Laotian official) ... said ... I've got between 30 and 60 American POWs that aren't in the system. I'm holding them back for insurance.'... This is 1974, 1975." Wolff asked, "1974 and 1975, and alive..." Shinkle answered, "Yes, Sir. His exact words were in Lao, ... 'I have several tens...'" Wolff asked, "the man who said that he had several tens of prisoners is now a Laotian official?" Shinkle answered, "... at the time, I do not know his current position."

There is a large volume of intelligence showing Americans alive in Laos. The CIA listed live POWs in Laos during the 1960's held in Sam Neua. Laos is called the "black hole of Southeast Asia" with many men disappearing off the face of the earth. The Air Force intelligence study cited in the Shinkle testimony is significant for another reason.

Thirty percent survived in Laos

This study showed that of the four hundred forty-seven cases, **over thirty percent survived** their loss incident (138 actual). Of these 138 known survivors, only 10 returned to the United States. Of these ten, not one had been captured and held by Laotian forces except for a few days. Of the remaining 128, thirty-three possibly died in captivity. This total is uncertain because only a couple of cases have been "confirmed" by the return of remains or the first hand sighting of an actual death. The newly "discovered" one hundred men possibly had a survival rate of thirty percent also. This report stated however that these American POW losses were "of historical interest only."

A 1970 CIA document showed that in late 1968, twenty-seven American prisoners were moved from Laos to North Vietnam for a prisoner exchange. Another acknowledges that our negotiating team in Paris was aware of this move and believed it to be accurate. CIA "confirmation" dictates their agents had seen these twenty-seven Americans on more than one occasion and by more than one agent.

It would be pure speculation to ask whether this contemplated exchange involved Charles Shelton or David Hrdlicka or was the exchange described by former CIA analyst Frank Snepp in his book **Decent Interval**. We could further speculate if this move involved an exchange engineered in South Vietnam by the CIA near Tet 1968. Official reports, however, are still classified as part of the unreleased "**Pentagon Papers**." The "1205" document shows 43 POWs from Laos as prisoners in Vietnam in September, 1972. Very similar to numbers just shown.

Recent POW reports

A Pathet Lao prison guard defected from the "Muon Aet" prison where he guarded Americans. One was named "Armstrong." The U.S. reports two pilots named Armstrong missing in Laos. (**These reports are from ADI files**) A prison camp near "Muong Ka" in Northern Laos contained 50 Americans. This report is confirmed by polygraph. Five very thin American POWs were seen handcuffed, wearing ankle chains, and each tied to the other with rope. A Laotian who passed a double polygraph test saw five American pilots in a prison camp in "San Nuea." "Ban Na" was the location of a prison camp with twenty-five American POWs.

The Mugia Pass was a nightmare for American pilots with many planes lost there. Refugees report eighteen American POWs are held in a cave on the southeast slope of "Hill 1492," three miles south of the "Mugia Pass" near route 12. In 1992, Gen. Lacy testified , "We put US Marines into Mu Gia Pass in North Vietnam... US ground forces were not supposed to be ... in North Vietnam." The 1205 document says among the held back prisoners are infiltrators into the area between Laos and North Vietnam.

In 1982, radio intercepts show U.S. POWs being moved to mines in the Attopeu Province area. An escaped Laotian Air Force Officer saw American POWs "working like burros" on a road construction crew near Attopeu Province. American POWs were seen in a prison camp near "Phu Him Lek Fai" village at map coordinates YB 3349. This is near the "Xe Kaman" River.

A defecting Laotian Major saw fifteen American POWs in a cave prison thirty-one kilometers southeast of "Mahaxy" Laos. Three or four were dark skinned. One POW had a tattoo of a flower on his shoulder.

From the mouth of the enemy

In September 1968, Soth Petrasy, the permanent Pathet Lao representative in Vientiane, told a U.S. official that American pilots were generally kept near the locations of their loss and were "throughout Laos from the South to the North." On May 1, 1971, Petrasy confirmed that prisoners were held in various regions of Laos. In February 1972, (**From DIA documents**) Petrasy gave his estimate of prisoners held, "Several tens of prisoners are presently being held by the Pathet Lao." Twice more during 1972, he said that "There are many American PWs held in the liberated areas of Laos." In April 1972, Prince Soupanouvong of the Pathet Lao said the American POW issue would be settled once the Americans stopped their "aggression" in Laos.

Many government officials diminish Petrasy's wartime statements. This exchange between Congressman Robert K. Dornan (R-CA) and General Tighe on June 5, 1979, in Executive Session, rebuts that downgrading.

> **Mr. Dornan**: ... is there any way of us getting the information out of Laos on Americans there, ... any way we will ever be able to confirm ... there were Americans alive in January 1973, in Laos, and ... truthfulness to Soth Petrasy's statement ... up to 180 Americans alive?
>
> (*Deleted*)
>
> **General Tighe**: ... My belief in our ability to find out specifically what happened in that country is very high, **if you want to get it.** (**Emphasis added**)
>
> {*Deleted*}

POWs alive in Laos when "last POWs" came home

Is it possible that these informants, former enemy personnel, and just plain "folks" were having illusions? The American government thought so. Today, these reports are written off as "contrary to known communist precedents," "unconfirmed," "uncorroborated," or "uncorrelated."

In the "uncorrelated" documents, when a person passed on verified information he was called reliable. The same person, however, reporting live POWs, was not believed because "the Communists say they aren't holding American prisoners."

Yet, the government did not hesitate, in April 1992, to believe 552 Americans were killed by peasants during the war. (*AP* wire story)

Some confirmations

A confidential memorandum, dated August 13, 1976, from Congressman Paul McCloskey (R-CA) confirms reports of prisoners. McCloskey recites conversations held between General Vang Pao and Congressman Benjamin Gilman on January 16, 1974. Vang Pao informed Gilman of "8 to 10" American pilots being held by the North Vietnamese to extract "technical information from them." Vang Pao expanded, saying that these men "broke" under Vietnamese pressures and were "cooperating," in exchange for survival and increased "comforts" such as food, medicine, and relative freedom. Part of this cooperation involved defusing unexploded ordnance along the Ho Chi Minh Trail, the Plain of Jars, and Sam Neua.

Vang Pao said the reports began in 1968 ending in 1975. The later reports specified the number of prisoners being 8 - 10. One source saw the prisoners working and were identified by Vietnamese captors as Americans. He extended a hypothesis making the Vietnamese and the Pathet Lao technically correct about POWs. If North Vietnamese held American POWs in Laos, the Vietnamese could state no POWs were in Vietnam and Laotians could claim they held no prisoners.

McCloskey said the CIA analyzed these reports and only expressed doubt about Vang Pao's hypothesis while confirming the capture reports with sources unrelated to him. Their reports of one to nine Americans being held in the Laotian panhandle region were from late 1973 to early 1975. Polygraph tests showed some reports were true. McCloskey concluded "... we cannot write off the possibility of 8 to 11 Americans still being held in Laos, presumably by NVA authorities."

While McCloskey thought the CIA was doing the evaluation of this report, DIA did the actual work and passed it verbatim to CIA. Portions of the actual evaluation appeared in the "uncorrelated documents." These reports also show State Department officials attempted to keep Congressman Gilman from releasing Vang Pao's information. Monitoring his activities, some government officials were not happy at Gilman's publicizing the existence of American POWs.

During the Montgomery hearings, the CIA was asked if Americans were still alive in Indochina. GEN Walters answered they had "no confirmed" evidence; no "hard evidence"; and finally, "Now, I can't tell you there isn't any. All I can tell you is there is not evidence available to us at this time."

The late ADM John McCain, former CINCPAC, said if he had access to reports he had seen, he would be able to prove Americans being held prisoner in Indochina. Admiral McCain's son is Senator John McCain (R-AZ). He saw numerous intelligence reports of American prisoners. Unfortunately, then being classified, the Admiral could not access them at the hearings.

Walter Cronkite testified his Journalist committee spent months seeking information on their missing colleagues. They uncovered a large volume of evidence showing journalists alive in September 1973 with Kratie City, Cambodia as a central detention center for prisoners. This is the same area that Michael Varnado reportedly was held in mid-1974. It was also COSVN headquarters. The journalists interrogated former enemy ralliers, returned ARVN POWs, and civilian sources.

Reports on Missing Journalists

One military rallier talked with two of six journalists held by the North Vietnamese on May 30, 1970 in a house four kilometers from Kratie City. This man passed a lie detector test given by Army Intelligence specialists.

A second eyewitness, a former ARVN POW, saw six Caucasians being moved by North Vietnamese just outside Kratie City on May 1, 1972. He asked his guard if they were American military advisers. The guard replied "No, they were correspondents of the imperialist side." Another POW saw six Caucasians marched under armed guard in the immediate vicinity of Kratie City in mid-1972. His guard also said that they were imperialist journalists.

The committee dispatched investigator Zalin Grant to South Vietnam after the cease fire in 1973. He interviewed 3000 of the 4300 returning SVN POWs. Reports, from 25 unrelated sources, showed the journalists held in a fifty kilometer radius of Kratie City as late as March 1973.

Gavin Scott, a correspondent for **Time-Life**, at Tan Son Nhut in the summer of 1973, had a Viet Cong General tell him, in a private conversation, that American journalists were prisoners along the Vietnamese-Cambodian border. Scott later accompanied VC guides eventually to Kratie City. The Khmer Rouge manager of the area stated that he was aware of foreign journalists captured by the Viet Cong and detained by the Cambodians. Among this group of journalists was an "actor who was working for **Time Magazine** and *CBS*."

Scott noted the obvious hope was confusion of the nature of the persons being held. Possibly Sean Flynn and Dana Stone were held together. Flynn was working for *CBS* and was the son of an actor. Dana Stone was working for *CBS* but also for **Time**. Obviously, American journalists were still alive in late 1973.

The Vietnamese are not cooperative

Donald Dugan, a man with thirteen years of experience in Laos, provided Mike Mielke with this information. He said Americans were seen at a road junction outside the Sam Neua complex in 1973 and 1974. These prisoners were exercising, gathering wood, and tilling the ground. No specific numbers were given, but the translation equaled "a group of them."

Mielke last heard of the American community in North Vietnam in July 1976. The information was passed to Mr. Anthony Suarez, CIA. Mr. Suarez passed it to DIA. (**Uncorrelated documents**) According to Mielke, DIA felt, "I was considered to be a very reliable accurate source... " *Apparently Mielke's information coincided with DIA's information.*

The Communists insist they hold no live Americans prisoner. They specifically denied Ngo Phi Hung's report, ascribing it to a Chinese plot. When these denials were given, Arlo Gay was in a prison camp just outside Hanoi. Tucker Gouggelman, a retired CIA officer, was a prisoner in Chi Hoa prison in Saigon. Gay was a commercial fisherman seized in Rach Gia in April 1975, and moved to Hanoi in October. Gay was suspected of being CIA because of numerous requests about him. When convinced that Gay was a fisherman, Vietnam released him.

Official reports say Gay had no information concerning American MIAs. Declassified reports, however, show a cell where Gay was a prisoner, had scribbling on the wall, "LTC Comb" followed by other writings "GI or G1 / I / Corps / **PINE** G4 FWD / CP Arr from Danang Apr 23 1975 Depart". Gay learned a man with European features had been incarcerated in that cell shortly before he arrived. Who? Operation **PINE** is covered in Chapter 11.

Tucker Gouggelman returned to Saigon in April 1975 to find family members.

He missed the final airlift and was trapped with other Americans. He was seen by Mike Mielke. Another source saw him arrested in front of the Ambassador Hotel. A third source saw him in Chi Hoa prison.

A retired CIA official from the Phoenix program, Gouggelman did not receive good treatment. The KGB and other Communist intelligence organizations interrogated him. Gouggelman was well informed on U.S. intelligence operations in Vietnam and elsewhere in Asia. All questions concerning his welfare were rebuffed. Gouggelman died while in prison, apparently in June 1976. Officially, he died due to natural causes. He was fifty-five when captured. It took over a year for the Vietnamese to repatriate his body. Unverified reports said that this natural death entailed broken bones in many parts of the body, similar to a torture session.

In 1992, while traveling in Vietnam, Senator John Kerry (D-MA), head of the Senate POW Committee, was deceived by the Vietnamese. He was told by officials that "no Americans were ever held" at the prison he was at. Eight months later, an American civilian, held at that prison for years, told investigators that he "was moved from the prison only one day before the arrival of Senator Kerry and moved back into the prison two days after the Senator departed. (Letter Garnett Bell to Senator Frank Murkowski, 12/28/94)

Congressional delegations "seek information"

This section is difficult to write. I will not cover all congressional delegations seeking information on MIAs. Except for a few Congressmen, the results have been the same. The U.S. Government professes all men are dead.

One delegation, in March 1977, asked if prisoners were in Vietnam. The answer was no. Ngo Phi Hung was tracking POWs. The official Vietnamese greeting party read the **Final Report** of the Montgomery Committee "concluding" that there were no live POWs. Bobby Garwood was captive. Congressman Montgomery, was a member of this delegation. It would have been a major diplomatic blunder for Vietnamese to "discover" anyone while he was in the country.

In August 1978, another delegation went to Vietnam and Laos. Questions are asked about live POWs. The answer was there are none. This trip took place after Ngo Phi Hung testified. A few months later, Bobby Garwood appeared. In Laos, POWs are seen in a location that leads to a **rescue mission**, in 1981. The leader of this delegation Montgomery. He received a request that a League member accompany the delegation. That request was denied. Also denied was a request from Congressmen Gilman, Guyer, and Dornan that they be permitted to go.

In December 1984, another delegation went to Vietnam and elsewhere in Southeast Asia. The leader of this delegation was Congressman Montgomery. There are a few changes. Official government statements inched towards concluding some men were alive and prisoner. The rescue mission had been mounted in 1981. Some things do not change, however. The report of this delegation made no mention of these activities. This report recounted the times Communist leaders said "no Americans were held captive in Southeast Asia."

My congressman, Bob Stump, was with that delegation. I told him that men were probably captive. Yet, I was not surprised no one deviated from the report because Stump told me that he had been told as a member of the House Permanent Select Committee on Intelligence that no American was held captive. If anyone was alive, he was either a defector or a drug addict. "All reports on live MIAs were proved false." I believe Congressman Stump was told this in his official capacity.

The Chairman of that committee told me on July 19, 1985 he was unaware General Tighe had testified that Americans were prisoners in Southeast Asia. (**Interview with Congressman Matt McHugh**)

Some people deny the government holds that view. Ann Mills Griffiths testified on September 30, 1987, at the Vessey Committee hearings: " ... the U.S. government ... does not prejudge the circumstances of any American who would return. They don't categorize them ... it is not a prejudicial situation. They want any and all Americans under any circumstances to be returned to this country."

In direct contradiction to this statement, Issue Brief IB88061 "MIAs in Indochina and Korea," August 5, 1988, (used for briefing members of Congress) tackles the issue "Are Americans remaining in Indochina Voluntarily" (**pg. CRS-10**). The statement starts "Some have suggested ... if the reports ... are accurate, these Americans may not be held against their will. They cite the case of PFC. Garwood as an example." It continues, "The U.S. Government ... **does not** seek the forced repatriation of Americans living in Indochina voluntarily, but that it would like to notify their families of their status. The Vietnamese have denied ... Americans are living in areas 'under their control,' ... not explicitly rule out Americans living ... not 'under their control.' In addition, the U.S. Government policy statement cited above ... is careful to refer to 'Americans ... still being held against their will.' It is possible, therefore, ... *at least a few Americans remaining in Indochina voluntarily is considered greater by U.S. Government authorities ... than that of Americans being held against their will*, but they ... would not classify any American as being present ... voluntarily until all facts were known." (**Emphasis added**)

The fact that this Congressional Briefing Paper even suggests what it did is explicit evidence that the views of Congressman Stump and others is not coincidental. The fact that Americans are held against their will is systematically downgraded. I heard ADM Paulson say that he was not interested in bringing back defectors. Actions and attitudes speak volumes about commitment.

Time has not changed the results of Congressional visits. In 1991 and 1992, Senators on the POW Task Force made numerous trips to Vietnam and almost all concluded that there was no evidence of live POWs. One notable exception came in 1993 when Senator Bob Smith (R - NH) went to Vietnam with Bobby Garwood and found evidence supporting Garwood's assertion of being a POW and other Americans also being held as POWs. (More on this in my discussion of Garwood.)

Alive or not alive - factors to consider

We've examined governmental factors of why the POWs were probably still not alive earlier. In 1988, the Congressional Brief (cited above) added a couple of new twists. It stated "Despite thousands of reports, exhaustive interrogations, and formidable technical means at the disposal of U.S. intelligence agencies, not one report of a live American has been validated as to where the individual is being held, **who he is**, and when he was or is being held. Much of the 'evidence' cited has proved to be relevant to already accounted for Americans, wishful thinking, or fabrication." The second one said "It makes no sense for the Vietnamese to keep live Americans as negotiating assets. American outrage over the sudden revelation of live Americans being held would preclude the softening of U.S. attitudes toward Vietnam that the 'bargaining chips' had ostensibly been held for. Furthermore, live Americans would be perishable assets which diminish in value as time passes — if they exist, they have been kept under wraps for 15 - 27 years and have as yet served no useful purpose to the Vietnamese and Laotians."

There is no question that prisoners would face many difficulties in staying alive. All the elements listed by the government against survival (i.e., sickness, hostile populace, disease, etc.) are valid. Nevertheless, 591 known returnees survived exactly the same conditions for periods of time up to nine years. The Congressional Issue Brief continued, "Even though many people held in Communist prisons die, some do survive until eventual release (such as Germans and Japanese taken prisoner by the Soviets in World War II and not released until the mid 1950's; American intelligence agents held by China from 1952-72; and Communist countries own political prisoners who served full terms of 10-25 years.)" I was told by one man of a German acquaintance of his, captured by the Soviets and released in 1954. He had been captured in 1918, thirty-six years earlier.

There is no evidence validating these 591 men were the only men surviving such circumstances. The 1205 document says 671 more survived. The government relies upon the word of the Communists. The 1205 shows prisoners who have not been returned. Completely ignored are the instances of these prisoners being subjects of secret high-level negotiations concerning possible prisoner swaps. Hidden until 1993 was GEN Quang telling his Politburo, " ... The number of American POWs has not been public ... We have kept this figure secret. **... I will report to you, Comrades, the exact number of American POWs. The total number ... comprises 1205 people....**" (**1205 document Emphasis added**)

As seen, available evidence weighs against the government's reliance upon the Communists word. The cases of Neil Sharman, Charles Dean, Arlo Gay, and Tucker Gouggelman show that the Communists will lie about holding American prisoners. Until 1979, the Communists denied holding Robert Garwood; until 1985 they denied holding William Mathers (a yachtsman whose boat strayed into Vietnamese waters); and until his release in 1986, held incommunicado Robert Schwab (who went to Vietnam looking for his Vietnamese girlfriend).

Further, in 1962, eight years after the end of the French Indo-China War, Vietnam made a plain statement wiping out denials of holding French prisoners captive. They said: "After a long period of negotiations ... on the repatriation of French solders who had surrendered, on October 25 ... Republic of France ... (stated) that it had been authorized to work out a plan for transporting, ... French soldiers who had surrendered and who had applied for repatriation."

Of greater importance, however, are the unrefuted sightings of live Americans in captivity. In rebuttal, the government argues that these sightings are "unconfirmed" or "uncorroborated." The **<u>Final Report</u>** relies upon the testimony of General Walters and Dr. Shields as "proof" of the unconfirmed nature of the sightings. For example, General Walters did say: "There are cases where we are certain that the communist governments of Indochina could account for the fate of persons known to have been alive in captivity since 1973 ... But, we have no firm evidence that American PWs from the period before 1973 are still being held."

Dr. Shields added in other testimony: "As for how many men are still alive, it's certainly possible that some men are, but .. **we have not been able to put our hands on a missing man who is alive and say he is alive.**"

This emphasis upon the lack of **confirmed** sightings and the **lack of names** points up the very weak foundation of the government case. What constitutes a confirmed sighting? Some sightings of POWs have been "uncorrelated" because "the information cannot be directly correlated to any known POW in the area at that time." Translated, that means that the intelligence community did not know in advance that a particular man had been transferred to the sighting area and therefore the reports were "unconfirmed."

I was told by Navy CPT Raymond Vohden, then the principal military advisor for PW/MIA matters, that he considered it significant that all the sightings failed to come up with a name associated with the alleged POW. The government expects refugees to go up to a captive POW, ask him for his name, or grab an ID card or dog-tag off him to validate the sighting. The lack of names does not invalidate the sighting. It does give the "investigator" an excuse to call it "unconfirmed."

The declassified "uncorrelated" documents confirm our worst fears. Even if names come out accompanying the reports; even if fingerprints came out with reports; or even if pictures came out with the reports; none of this matters. There is still a way to make the report "unconfirmed."

Let's see what it takes to "confirm" a report. The CIA in 1973, through document 317-09086-73, detailed criteria to confirm a POW report. What was needed was a detailed description of the POWs, specific data on where the POWs were lost or captured, and information concerning the loss incident. They used these criteria to confirm this POW report to a specific POW. Another CIA document, 317-09129-74, dated in 1974, added that specific names of individuals involved in a loss incident would be helpful if dates were fuzzy due to a faulty memory.

The March 22, 1983 testimony of RADM A.G. Paulson from DIA before the House Subcommittee on Asian and Pacific Affairs, discussed confirmed or correlated refugee reports. "These reports that have been correlated to accounted for Americans who came back in 1976 and Private Garwood in 1978 (sic) were truthful. One cannot conclude that the remaining 216 sightings were purposeful attempts at deception simply because no one has returned to confirm them." Later, he stated "we have live sightings in areas that we know Americans were being held in during that time frame. We have live sighting reports of nonspecific locations and times and in geographic areas that are not defined except the Mekong Delta."

Here, Paulson says DIA does not doubt the truthfulness of reports that Americans were left behind. The problem was that they lacked specific locations of sightings and the specific identification to correlate the report to a specific person. In other words, the report cannot be confirmed. The people do not officially exist.

In his testimony on June 27, 1985, LTG Tighe was asked what it would take to prove a live sighting. He stated that it would take a person on the ground that we had confidence in to confirm what some other person reported. That person could either be American or Vietnamese or some other nationality that we had complete confidence in. Even then, people following the government's official line will find a way to discredit a "confirmed report."

Unconvinced? In 1981, fingerprints were brought from Laos that had about six potential names attached to them. In 1987, a photo came out of Laos with a name attached (it appeared in **Life** Magazine). In 1988 a photo came out of the U-Minh Forest with a name attached. In July 1991, a photograph with an apparent date of May 1990 of 3 men came out with three names attached to the photo.

The result? In 1981, the fingerprints were "too fuzzy." In 1987, the DIA said it wasn't the man named. It could have been anyone at anytime in any location. In 1988, the photograph was unconfirmed. In 1991, all the family members said yes, the photos matched our missing man. Comparison photos appeared to match the men. Hanoi said no. One man was returned to you dead last year. DIA said no. The bones sent back as this man were nonhuman. General Vessey, presidential envoy on POWs MIAs said that he was "unimpressed" with the photo.

One component in the government's argument is the information contained in the MIA files weighs against the chances for their survival. The **Final Report** stated, "The most important single document pertaining to a missing serviceman is the case file maintained by the parent service." Many families expressed suspicion these files were incomplete with classified information omitted. The Commanding Officer of the JCRC was asked if the files had been purged of information. He answered no. General Walters was asked "No intelligence information is being held back ... ?" He answered, "Absolutely none, Mr. Chairman. It would be inhuman to do such a thing to the families."

The RC-47D Case

Perhaps the two men speaking those words did not know information was being kept back from the families. Files did not contain some information because it had been destroyed. The families, Congress, the courts, and even members of DOD have been misled on the issue of "complete files." Taking first the question of purging files, the case of Vincent Chiarello shows what happened in the past.

Chiarello was aboard an unarmed RC-47D Command and Control aircraft originally thought to be shot down over Laos on July 28, 1966. With him were MAJ Galileo F. Bossio, CPT Bernard Conklin, LT Robert J. Di Tommaso, SGT James S. Hall, CPT Robert E. Hoskinson, SGT John M. Mamiya, and SGT Herbert E. Smith. This particular case is one of "covert war," destroyed documents, "national security," and cover-up.

Originally, the plane was officially thought to have been shot down over Sam Neua, Laos. The **Top Secret** report discussing the initial downing said that the plane had been forced down by Migs. The mention of Migs seems to be at least one of the triggers causing an otherwise **Secret** report to be upgraded to **Top Secret**. What I did not know until February 1997, was my original supposition was correct. On September 3, 1964, Under Secretary of John McNaughton wrote a Top Secret Memorandum outlining situations under which the United States might escalate military operations, if it could be justified. Among those justifications were "Down of U.S. recce (recon plane) or U.S. rescue aircraft in Laos (likely by AA, unlikely by MIG) ... MIG action in Laos or South Vietnam (unlikely) ... (**Pentagon Papers** pg. 357) This paper was drawn up for electioneering consumption by President Johnson. It said, "The relevant 'audiences' of U.S. actions are the Communists (who must feel strong pressures), the South Vietnamese (whose morale must be buoyed) ... and the U.S. public (which must support our risk - taking with U.S. lives and prestige). During the next two months, because of the lack of 'rebuttal time' before elections to justify particular actions which may be distorted to the U.S. public, we must act with special care — signaling to ... the U.S. public are behaving with good purpose and restraint." (***Ibid.***)

Ambassador Sullivan thought it necessary to protect the information that Migs were involved in the shoot-down. One message read "Assume that we will adhere to the policy of confirming that aircraft was on reconnaissance mission." The Embassy wanted to know the "precise language" Washington would use in discussing the case. The entry of Migs into combat obviously was worrisome because no Migs were supposed to be in Laotian airspace. It was undesirable to publicly confirm an attack by Migs took place because the attack may have been an "isolated instance" and not a "real" entrance of Migs into the Laotian campaign.

On the same day as the shoot-down, a person on duty in the casualty section of Headquarters, 7th Air Force received word of the initial shoot-down. The message he received plainly stated that the C-47 was under attack by Migs and being forced down by Migs. Radar indicated that the force-down took place over NVN. On July 30, 1966, the duty officer at the command post asked for the information on the C-47 incident, destroyed it, and told the person who had the report to "forget the information on this piece of paper as if it had never happened." (*Hopper v. Carter*)

In August 1970, the Air Force held a status hearing. A dispatch from the State Department to the Laotian Embassy requested "all information" on the mission. The request asked for specific guidance as to which parts needed special protection because of their sensitivity. In 1970, other agencies did not know about the Migs. Something else was on the minds of the planners at both the State Department and the Embassy in Laos.

First the matter of the Migs. The reply stated that "we have researched all files concerning downed aircraft and neither CAS (the CIA), AIRA (the Air Attaché's office or DIA), or EMB (embassy), has any information concerning flight ...." This reply is incredible. The Embassy was responsible for classifying the initial shoot-down report. Can't find anything just four years later?

The message continued, "We speculate rpt speculate that aircraft was probably involved with initial survey activity for MSQ on Phou Pha Thi (site 85 UH 6860) which was bombed by NVA in January 1968 and was destroyed on 11 March 1968." We know the mission of Site 85. The Commanding General of 7th Air Force said that Ambassador Sullivan was politically opposed to site 85 because it might "appear" that Laos was being used for military purposes in the war.

That the CIA, DIA, and Embassy could not lend a hand in 1970 for information on this case is ludicrous on its face. CIA set up and ran Phou Pha Thi as a guerrilla base of operations. DIA kept track of and operated the TACAN site and MSQ site. The Embassy was in charge of it all.

What is absolutely ridiculous is the sensitivity about this site location. In 1978, the families in this case learned about site 85 but not its mission. General Momyer of 7th Air Force was writing his book and openly talking about the site and its mission. In July 1985, a 1974 message giving the location of Site 85 or channel 97 was still classified in another case. The Air Force Casualty Officer was absolutely horrified to learn that persons knew about site 85 and the MSQ radar on it. I saw the look of terror on the face of the casualty officer when site 85 was being discussed. The head of DIA, however, on the spot, declassified the message pertaining to site 85 so that the family involved in this particular case could keep it. Over the years, the Casualty Office, Air Force, CIA, DIA, and others caused unknown harm to themselves, countless families, and the issue by playing around with this one piece of information. Phou Pha Thi's location was not a national secret.

On June 22, 1973, a confidential review of the C-47 downing noted that on May 16, 1972, all next of kin had been notified that they had received all information pertinent to the case. Paragraph 2, however, read the next of kin "have not, repeat have not, been advised of the presence or contents of confidential IR 1516-

Are They Still Alive?

0086-71 (5800-05-6) or the **Quan Noi Nhan Dan** 6 Jan. 68 newspaper article or any message traffic pertaining to any data about the above two sources ... on their visits to this office. NOK have never been shown any classified documents surrounding loss ... be advised that this case is one of the most sensitive that has been handled by casualty division."

What was withheld? The referenced IR stated that Lieutenants Chiarello and Di Tommaso survived the crash and were prisoners. An eyewitness gave an extremely detailed and verifiable account of the loss in a credible manner.

What was sensitive about the case? If the plane went down over Laos, as originally suspected, the entrance of Migs into the battle might have meant the entrance of Soviet pilots into the fighting. Sullivan testified to Congress in 1970 that Soviets flew support missions in Laos in the 60's and over 500 Soviet personnel were involved as early as 1961. CIA logged information that the Soviets were involved in flying missions over North Vietnam as early as 1967. The Commanding General of 7th Air Force suspected that Soviets flew numerous missions in South Vietnam. Soviet helicopters were found and destroyed by SOG units in Laos.

One item in the June 22 document shows dramatically the hostility shown to families. It read, "Mrs. ——— (I delete to protect the family names involved) has visited Casualty Division on several occasions.... Expect her to be somewhat hostile in her attempt to gain additional information on her husband's loss. Col.———, Air Force Retired, (NOK) is relatively unstable emotionally." The Colonel is well respected. His many trips to Laos probably earned him the enmity of the Air Force. After years of stonewalling, who could blame the wife if frustration drove her to being "somewhat hostile?" What NSA material has been withheld?

The case still holds doubts. The "remains" of Chiarello, Conklin, Hall, Mamiya, and Smith, were all "returned" on March 2, 1988. An interesting phenomena is Hanoi returns groups of "remains" from the same incident on the same day while others from the same incident are not returned. MIA or Alive?

Information suppression continues today

Some argue all of this took place in the past. Ann Griffiths of the League testifies often: "There are other real dangers to priority efforts now being made which... poorly serve the objective. Legislation ... to publicly release sensitive intelligence data on the live prisoner issue defies logic and is strongly opposed by the League. *As a matter of U.S. government policy, the family members receive, after initial evaluation, all information which does or may pertain to their own individual case.* Public release... appears aimed at generating domestic pressure against our own government, rather than gaining the release of Americans alive or dead." (**Emphasis added. Vessey, Sept. 30, 1987 pg. 27**)

Let's examine reactions of former government officials who had been assured about document releases. In *Hopper v. Carter,* the government furnished the trial judge for his inspection *in camera,* files purporting to be the only information withheld from the family of CPT Michael Bosiljevac. The judge inspected the files and reported that in his opinion, there was nothing withheld which was not substantially the same as the materials revealed in the file available to the family.

Since then, Mrs. Bosiljevac received FOIA information pertaining to her husband, who was lost in September 1972. A sworn affidavit in the *Hopper* case showed an examination of the materials received by Mrs. Bosiljevac was substantially and significantly more than had been released to her in the past. The affidavit alleged significant information was withheld from the judge and the court.

In 1978, Dr. Shields was deposed and shown several cases, all presented to the court, in which information suppression took place. Shields examined the cases and stated that he was "frankly appalled" that these cases represented breaches of directives issued to insure that information was going to the families. He had been assured such suppression was not occurring.

From personal experience, I have worked on many cases since I first started research on this book. Despite assurances from all sources, I can state that today, December, 1999, the government still plays games on releasing information.

In July 1985, it took the personal intervention of the head of DIA to release two innocuous pieces of information to family members. One concerned Phou Pha Thi's location. Another piece of information, used to help determine that two MIAs "died," was found not have pertained to the case at all. This was determined seven and eleven years after the men had been declared dead. Why this information was in the men's files in the first place has not yet been furnished to the families.

In 1987, Congressman Rowland released information he gathered. I received that information through the Forget Me Not organization. I set the information aside to "look at it later." In 1989, I received information about my neighbor's son being a POW. I knew the family had never mentioned him being prisoner. Rowland's material was the same I received in 1989. Their son was listed as captured and not negotiated for in 1973. They were unaware of this information in 1989.

In 1990, I read where MIA Tom Beyer's family had "celebrated" his 50th birthday. I cut the article out for reference. Months later, in 1991, I was researching for this edition of the book. I came across a document showing the **government thought** Beyer had been seen in captivity. I contacted the family. The family never knew of this documents existence. Through the intervention of the office of Senator John McCain, they obtained a copy of the report. I sent a copy of what I had so they could compare their copy with mine. It took only twenty-one years and a chance reading for the family to first learn that perhaps their son survived. By December, 1999, they have not received any reason why the government believed, in 1968, that their son was held in captivity.

What we have then is nothing less than a cover-up of massive proportions. Sometimes the victims of this cover-up have been willingly "duped" by executive branch members. This was true of the staff of the Montgomery Committee. They were so eager to prove that live Americans did not exist that they took from MIA files some of the most bizarre cases to prove that the MIAs could not have survived their loss incident. The staff failed to consider the **survival** of some returned POWs under unusual and bizarre situations. The following cases are presented to show mistakes can be made.

Outside of Bobby Garwood, the person held captive longest in Vietnam was Army Captain Floyd Thompson. (**Grateful appreciation is given to John Hubbell for his permission to use material from his book <u>POW: A Definitive History</u> to develop these incident recitals.**) Captured in early 1964, Thompson was mostly held in southern Vietnam. He was often seen suffering from ill health, and described as a walking skeleton. The United States government had no knowledge of his status. His survival was a shock to most who had seen him. Despite the "best estimates" of the intelligence community, Floyd Thompson survived.

Edward Alvarez was a prisoner for the longest in North Vietnam (again outside of Robert Garwood). When shot down in 1964, no one saw his parachute display. It was natural to assume he had not survived. He realized that unless he made a public statement no one would know that he was a prisoner. Not until he made that statement was his official status was changed to POW.

Robert Purcell was flying at two hundred feet when both his wing-man and the flight leader reported seeing him shot down. There was no parachute deployed and the plane was completely engulfed in flames. Everyone assumed Purcell died in that crash. Purcell survived, despite the government's best estimates.

Bill Franke's loss dictated that he "could not" have survived. He was declared KIA. The family had a memorial service for him. One and a half years passed before it was discovered he was alive because his name had been memorized by LTC Robinson Risner, passed on to RADM James Stockdale, and by some way Stockdale got his name to intelligence personnel. (**In Love and War pg. 159, 249**)

Stockdale also wrote of the loss of Navy LT Ed Davis. Stockdale declared him dead because of the angle of descent on a night bombing mission; his "Mayday" at 1000 feet; and not seen exiting the plane. A flight member saw the fireball as the plane hit the ground. He later told Stockdale he had exited just before the crash. Risner also memorized his name. (**In Love and War, pg. 92, 159**)

The circumstances of the loss of Seaman Douglas Hegdahl were so bizarre that even the North Vietnamese, who rescued him, were skeptical of his story. Aboard a ship several miles off the North Vietnamese Coast, he came top side to watch the action. During a salvo, he fell overboard. After a search, the decision was made that he had drowned. Later Hegdahl was ordered by his POW superiors to accept early release to bring out vital POW information for our intelligence agencies.

LTC Albert Shinkle testified: "Numerous times ... there was a shoot down in which there was a good chute. The pilot got out ... alive... other men were in radio contact with him .... He did not get returned ... He's still ... in Laos, in my opinion. ...this happened numerous times." (**Testimony 1 July, 1978**) The point is odd loss circumstances do not equate to a dead MIA.

No one believes all the MIAs are alive. However, the Communists can account for hundreds of those men who are still missing. The balance of this book will continue the evidence of Americans still alive. It will also give equal recognition to the fact that MIA families want to know the fate of their men, even if that means learning that they are dead. The argument continues that to maintain a cover-up would require a massive effort, especially in the era of press leaks. This question of cover-up, deceit, or mind-set to debunk will be openly and frankly looked at.

The contention is that it makes no sense to hold back negotiating chips all these years and not attempt to bargain them for concessions. To gain a proper perspective, we will look at past wars. By looking at the Communists past performance, we can gain an understanding of their actions. Also, by examining the past performance of the U.S. government, we'll see that its shocking performance for the Vietnam War is no different than actions in past conflicts.

What some experts say

This examination will focus upon three conflicts. The French Indochina War, the Korean War, and World War II. Actions taken in these wars and in the first critical year after the end of each conflict laid the foundation for actions taken by our government after the "pull-out" in Vietnam. Each era will be given a thorough examination although a whole book could be written on each war. The research will focus on answering the question — are POWs alive today? I believe so and many experts say the same or similar thoughts:

* LTG James A. Williams, former DIA Director and chief of Army Counterintelligence: "The conviction that the many reports, the known perfidiousness of the Communist governments ... implies that some of the many missing must have survived... Americans may be alive in communist ... Southeast Asia." **(Letter to Congressman Henson Moore, 24 December 1981)**

* LTG Eugene Tighe, former DIA Director: "It was inevitable ... to draw the conclusion that ... Americans still in Vietnam ... weren't there because they wanted to be .... some fifty American military personnel still alive in Vietnam." **(ABC interview and a prepared statement to POW Task Force June 27, 1985.)**

* LTG Daniel O. Graham, former DIA Director: " ... I have kept a close eye on the evidence ... and believe that some of our men are still alive and imprisoned..." **(Letter to former Congressman John LeBoutillier, November 19, 1984)**

* Former Congressman Bill Hendon - POW Task Force member and DIA consultant supports Tighe but "feels that his number of estimated POWs being held is too low. I have seen much of the intelligence that General Tighe has seen. There is no question that the men are there." **(ABC News Broadcast May 7, 1985)**

* Colonel Millard A. Peck - Chief of the Special Office for ... (POW-MIA) — DIA: "I had heard the persistent rumors of American servicemen having been abandoned ... the government was conducting a 'cover-up' so as not to be embarrassed.... I observed that the principal government players ... conducting a 'damage limitation exercise'... The mind-set to 'debunk' is alive and well ... It appears that any soldier left in Vietnam, ... was, in fact, abandoned years ago ... I think there's a strong possibility ... of live POWs. If I were to hold hostages ... it would be a very tightly compartmented program, and very, very few people would be in on it.... I don't think these people are working in fields per se, I think they're in closely guarded facilities." **(Letter of resignation 12 February 1991, Testimony May 30, 1991, House Subcommittee Asian and Pacific Affairs)**

* GEN MAJ Jan Sejna, former Communist official in Czechoslovakia until his 1968 defection and former DIA official: "I believe they are in Korea, Vietnam, China, and Russia" (September 17, 1996)

* North Vietnamese General Lieutenant Tran Van Quang at the Politburo Meeting 12 September, 1972: **"I will also report to you today on American POWs captured** on the various fronts of Indochina ... The peoples of the world ... want to know the exact number of POWs located in North Vietnam. Allow me to inform you specifically on this matter.... that **the 1205 American POWs presently in prisons of North Vietnam** include: 624 aviators captured in North Vietnam; 143 aviators captured in South Vietnam; 47 diversionists and other American servicemen captured in North Vietnam; 391 American servicemen of other categories, which includes 283 captured in South Vietnam, 65 in Cambodia, and 43 in Laos.

All of them are presently in prisons in North Vietnam..." **(1205 document Emphasis supplied)** Who would know better than the Vietnamese if American POWs were held back for ransom?

Background to Deceit

A quick introduction

It was spring, 1951. PFC. Robert E. Meyers, Greencastle, Pennsylvania, was a head equipment operator in Korea. He was captured. His parents learned of his missing status from his buddy. The government did not notify them for another week. (**September 1973 edition of The Voice**)

Shortly afterwards, the China Photo Service in Peking, released a photo of eleven men in a North Korean prison camp. In the middle of the back row was Meyers. The caption identified the men as Pennsylvania POWs. The Communists listed Meyers as being in the picture. His parents positively identified him.

The father, Raymond Meyers, contacted congressmen, returning POWs, and other sources to obtain information concerning his son. No one, including one of the men in the picture, had any further information. One year after his capture, he was reclassified as "presumed dead." The war had not even ended.

MAJ Wirt Thompson, U.S. Army, was lost in 1944. His family was told he was KIA. (**SFR-3-27**) In 1955, a German repatriate emerging from the Soviet gulags saw Thompson who had been held at Budenskaya prison near Moscow and at Tayshet labor camp. Not until early 1991 was Thompson's daughter told. Thompson was one of *more than fifteen thousand* American POWs, captured by the Germans, "liberated" by the Soviets, who disappeared behind the Iron Curtain.

Georges Boudarel was a Frenchman "who acted as a deputy political commissar in Vietnamese prison camps during the First Indochina War." (**SFR 9-1**) A member of the Communist International underground in Southeast Asia, he taught in the French school system. He was accused by Claude Bayel, a former POW, in a book (**Prisonnier au Camp 113**) of being the one who tortured him. Boudarel dropped out of sight until 1991. On May 6, 1991, the *Figaro* newspaper showed that of the 39,888 VIet Minh *prisoners*, 29,954 were **not returned** including **2,350 French Nationals and 2,867 Legionnaires**.

The problem faced by U.S. authorities and family members is that Communists believe in to the victor goes the spoils.

The Korean experience

The Korean War ended in 1953. The State Department told MIA families to be patient. Let the "experts" take care of the problem. Raymond Meyers waited. In June 1973, twenty-two years later, Raymond Meyers first learned that his son was one of 389 men *officially* listed as a prisoner in Korea, but unaccounted for.

Three hundred eighty-nine men captured and abandoned. There was no outcry of indignation from anyone. Why? Because of "National Security" interests.

The United States was not prepared for war in Korea. During World War II, the Germans had a formal POW system with good records. The U.S. intelligence had almost the same information gathered from radio intercepts. Korean War families assumed prisoner repatriation after the fighting. The nation won a "total victory" in World War II. They could not conceive of a United States so paralyzed politically that it would accept anything less in Korea. Ironically, they got just what was expected. The package was just wrapped differently.

The Koreans and Chinese were brutal captors, perpetrating heinous acts upon captured personnel. In February 1951, a Korean guerrilla commander secretly ordered his American POWs executed by making them bayonet "dummies". Prisoners resisting or dying too slowly were bludgeoned to death. Other prisoners died in "medical experiments," including practice amputations. The operation was KGB run and continued into the Vietnam war. (**House National Security Subcommittee on Military Personnel**)

The Chinese established a formal POW system. Men were processed soon after capture. Of the known POWs, only GEN William L. Dean was held exclusively by the North Koreans. At the prisoner exchange in 1953, the Communists released the POWs in two groups. 5133 men were returned. During negotiations, a Chinese diplomat got drunk and told Dag Hammarskjold, then head of the UN, that the Chinese government held fifteen American flyers hostage as "political prisoners." It took two years of negotiations to obtain their release. Two CIA types were released in 1971 and 1973, almost twenty years after the hostilities ceased.

In 1954, GEN Mark Clark wrote in his biography **From the Danube to the Yalu** the United States had "solid evidence" that the Communists held onto hundreds of US POWs. GEN Eugene Tighe told Bill Paul of the *Wall Street Journal* the United States had evidence of American POWs left behind in Korea. He added we had no leverage to get them back. In September 1996, COL Phillip Corso, a former military aide to President Eisenhower testified, "In the past, I have tried to tell Congress... that in 1953, **500 sick and wounded American prisoners** were within 10 miles of the prisoner exchange point at Panmunjon, but **were never exchanged.**" Congressional investigators for Dornan's Committee found declassified documents showing the Pentagon knew that over 900 POWs were unreleased by enemy forces. In April 1997, US military officials, in Phoenix, told an audience that Corso "was mistaken" in his information.

What became of Robert Meyers and others? The official answer was provided in 1976 by GEN Walter Druen, head of the Air Force Military Personnel Center as he told the Montgomery Committee that at the end of the Korean War, the Air Force carried 888 personnel in a missing status. 217 were repatriated leaving 671 still missing. The Chinese acknowledged holding 15 prisoner who were returned to American control in 1955. Prisoner debriefings provided conclusive evidence that 209 died while in captivity. That left 447 men still missing.

Status judiciously resolved

Druen said that by August 1954, these 447 cases were "judiciously resolved" by findings of death. He added, "It is especially noteworthy that none of these men declared dead, ever showed up alive." The judicious resolutions provided the families with a "measure of relief." Other services acted in a like manner.

What hypocrisy! Was Raymond Meyers filled with relief to find out that his son was one of "389" abandoned in Korea? How about the little old lady that I will call "Mary" who called Dermot Foley once a year to say, "'Joe' is X number of years old today, if he is still living. You know," she continued, "all I want to know is what happened to him. Is that too much to ask?" "Joe's" status was "judiciously resolved" at the end of the Korean War. Was he one of the 900 abandoned? "Mary" may never know, if she's even still alive.

How any person, in or out of uniform, can sit before a committee of the people's congress and tell the people's representatives that their constituent's sons, husbands, and neighbors had "been judiciously resolved" with the knowledge provided earlier by Tighe, Corso, and Clark is beyond my comprehension. I have been in uniform and I have been involved in elected politics. I would resign before I would go before these men and tell such tripe.

Hard evidence on Korea

The majority of the evidence on abandoned POWs comes from the Republican Staff Report. They were also exposed to material from writers like James Sanders, Bill Paul, and others. I will use their official documentation and present my interpretation. Their evidence is examples of neglect, abandonment, and cover-up.

In 1953, the switching of prisoners took place. It was agreed that no one would be forced to go to either side. Twenty-one Americans stayed in Korea. An intelligence estimate showed 8,000 unaccounted for. (**SFR page 4-2**) After debriefings, in 1954, the Assistant Secretary of the Army estimated that 954 Americans were "believed to be still held illegally..." Clandestine operations forces were attempting to recover at least one to prove men were being held. One complicating factor was the "money" bugaboo. It cost the government over a "million dollars annually" to keep the men in a missing status. Thus came the decision to presume them dead.

In May, 1996, Corso testified that in early 1955, Yuri Rastvorov, a Russian defector told him, "US and other U.N. POWs were being held in Siberia." Thus, while intelligence showed people in captivity, in 3 months, three hundred men were administratively "killed off." Another 313 were on the "hit list." 275 were listed as probably killed in prisoner status based upon reports by returning prisoners. Twenty-one were given dishonorable discharges. Two returned to military control and four were left to be investigated (their fate was like the others — presumptive findings of death). (**SFR page 4-3 from a declassified report**)

In June 1955, a classified report sheds a little different light on the "political prisoners" held by the Communists. Prompter action was taken on the fliers held because in November 1954, the Chinese announced that 13 of the 15 had been sentenced for "spying." This caused a political uproar among US citizens and a demand for political action to effectuate their release. (**SFR 4-4**) Wing Commander, Donald Skene, brother-in-law of repatriated British flyer Andrew R. McKenzie, said that McKenzie had been held prisoner with other American airmen not on the list of political prisoners referred to above. (*New York Times*, **December 6, 1954**)

Our ineffectual attitude towards recovering captured soldiers developed in a 1955 classified study which said in future "peripheral 'fire-fights'..." our alternatives would be limited to political initiatives and some special type recovery operations. Acknowledging there were personnel "now in custody of foreign powers," with alternatives "limited," the problem becomes a "philosophical one." After all, wars mean casualties and we must "learn to live with this type of thing." We may have to adopt a "rather cynical attitude" and instill in the soldier a much more effective "don't get captured attitude." (**SFR 4-5**) This is quite a change from Roosevelt's attitude of your kingdom gone if you don't release American hostages.

While this wimpish study was being prepared, a Greek immigrant reported to our intelligence officials that he had seen American POWs being sent north from

China to the Soviet Union. The Air Attache who interviewed the immigrant reported that he saw hundreds of prisoners, in American uniforms, being sent to Siberia in late 1951 and 1952. They were observed at the Russian -Chinese border at Manchouli. Sleeve insignia indicated that some were NCO's in the US Air Force. All were conversing in English.

The informant was interrogated on two occasions by the Assistant Air Liaison Officer and the *Consulate General agreed the information as probably true. The* train station was divided into two sections, one on the Chinese side and one on the Soviet side. The stop was made to change the undercarriages of the trains to accommodate the different gauge of tracks used by both sides. Multiple sightings took place with a very close Russian friend informing him of subsequent POW shipments, which happened "often." (Declassified DOD Documents)

On April 19, 1954, Secretary of State Dulles informed our embassy in the Soviet Union that the report *corroborated* previous reports UNC POWs might have been shipped to Siberia. He requested they approach the highest level of the Foreign Ministry showing American Prisoners had been transported into the Soviet Union and were in Soviet custody and request their repatriation at the earliest possible time. Dulles reemphasized that this information was reliable. (*Ibid*)

The cover-up continues on Korea

In an August 1990 interview, LTC O'Wighton Delk Simpson, the Air Attaché who interviewed the **Greek** emigre, recounted his report with Dak Rhee, writer for *US Veteran News and Report*. Simpson never saw the report after he mailed it. In 1985, his report was evaluated by DIA. The DIA evaluation said, 33 years after the fact, that the (**Polish**) émigré saw French POWs from Indochina being sent to France. Black POWs, noted many times by the émigré, were supposed to be Senegalese troops who fought for the French. Ignored was that these "French" and "Senegalese" troops conversed in English. Not explained is why these "French" troops were wearing U.S Air Force NCO uniforms and were being sent home in 1951 and 1952, not in 1955 (as stated in a fact sheet by DOD).

A better explanation

The CIA had a better report (**SFR pg. 4-7**) explaining the black POWs. CIA document **SO 6582** stated that "One Republic of Korea soldier who was captured by the Communists ... was sent to a war prison camp at Pyoktong.... This camp ... had about 1000 American war prisoners, ... about 700 were negroes (sic), approximately 1,500 ROK prisoners and about 300 civilian employees ..."

On April 29, 1954, the Assistant Secretary of the Army was told by General Young that the report from the Greek Émigré "corroborates previous indications UNC POWs ... shipped to Siberia during Korean hostilities... and are now in Soviet custody. ..." (**SFR pg. 4-7**). A July 1952 CIA report showed Negro POWs in custody in large numbers. One specific camp numbered three quarters of the POWs as blacks. The same report showed that there were camps in which the prisoners would not be repatriated. (**Ibid. pg. 4-8**).

The Soviets replied the assertion that American Prisoners of War from Korea had been transferred to the Soviet Union is "clearly farfetched" and there are not *any such persons* in the Soviet Union. (DOD declassified documents)

The Minority Staff pointed out a fact with implications for Vietnam since the Soviet Union supplied much of their political doctrine. The Soviet response predicates denial of access to the men on its refusal to characterize the US personnel as "prisoners of war." The Soviets made it a practice to refuse to acknowledge the US citizenship of the US soldiers; as a result — from the Soviet's standpoint — the Soviet denial is accurate. We now know that some of the POWs were prisoners who were experimented on and sent to the USSR for long term observation.

Denial of information to Congress began well before Vietnam. In 1953, Senate Majority Leader Lyndon Johnson, inquired about 944 unreturned POWs from Korea for a constituent. The State Department attempted to respond by phone. Johnson wisely asked for a written response. After four drafts, the water-downed answer indicated only that some Americans might be in communist custody. Earlier versions contained information on why 944 Americans were considered in custody in communist hands. (**Staff Report (SFR) contains all versions in the original**).

In 1960, the State Department received a dispatch from Brussels stating that two American POWs were seen working in a Soviet phosphorus mine. The two POWs were named. However, when the government released the "sanitized" version of the dispatch to the *Washington Times* in March 1991, the names were excised to protect their privacy. The **Staff Report** appropriately said "It is absurd that the US government, having abandoned soldiers to a life of slave labor and forced captivity, is attempting to protect the same abandoned soldiers' 'privacy'."

In January 1991, *The Free Press Enterprise*, interviewed Phillip Smith, a Vietnam War POW shot down over the Gulf of Tonkin. He was in solitary confinement for seven years in China. He was shown two American POWs during his captivity who were held from the Korean War. They were released in 1973. Smith reported the Chinese told him that they would hold him like the others until he recanted.

In June 1986, Robert Dumas, brother of a Korean MIA, taped a conversation with COL Henry Land, number two man in DOD on MIAs. In that conversation Land said (from the *Wall Street Journal*) "The bottom line is that until the North Koreans get to a position and they want to release prisoners and the remains that are up there (pause) They will do it when they feel it is to their advantage." Bill Paul, writer for the *Wall Street Journal* (who has a copy of the tape) said "a careful listening to the 10 minute tape leaves no doubt that Colonel Land is knowingly differentiating between live prisoners and remains, and ... both are still in Korea."

A finale to Korea

On May 28, 1990, five remains were returned and on June 23, 1991, eleven more were returned. Senator Bob Smith (R-NH) met with Korean officials and asked about the recovery of remains; accounting for POWs, and an accounting for those shipped out of country or who chose to remain. (*UPI dispatch*)

The State Department, in an April 15, 1991 press advisory, said "in the interest of following every credible lead ..." they would ask the Soviet Union about "any additional information on any other US citizens who may have been detained as a result of World War II, the Korean conflict or the Vietnam War." They asked specifically about — "two U.S. planes shot down in the early 1950's." I know from my position in the US Army EW School, that these planes were **vectored** into Soviet Air Space before being shot down (meaning they were electronically lured).

The Staff Report (**pg. 4-9**) noted that they did not ask the Soviets any specific questions about any non-repatriated POWs from World War II, the Korean War, and the Vietnam War. It also noted that the request "repeated the mistake of asking for information only about US citizens that the State Department made 37 years earlier." Further, the report said "It seems apparent that if the Department of State had expected to get solid information from the Soviet government, then ... (they) would have sent a much more comprehensive and appropriately phrased request."

I want to address a statement that it is noteworthy that no one after the Korean War came home who had been missing and later presumed dead. However, in September, 1996 testimony was taken that in 1979, Romanians touring North Korea took a wrong turn at a collective. 10 men, one with blue eyes, were seen. These "farmers," in their 50's, were American POWs. Investigators, in 1995, found a second eye witness, in Romania, to the sighting. DIA acknowledged, in 1996, that "10 - 15 possible American POWs" could be in Korea, 43 years after the war.

This same government wrote three years before this sighting, "The implied lesson for future American involvement in armed conflict with Communist Forces was that US expectations for POW/MIA accounting far exceed actual performance." (**Final Report pg. 77**) The writers of the report ask that we imitate this cowardice and follow the legacy from Korea.

A postscript

The National Alliance of Families for the Return of America's Missing Servicemen from World War II, Korea, and Vietnam ask us to remember the following men mentioned by name in State Department dispatches and the prisons they were left in: * William G. Robertson - Kiev; * William Baumeister - Kubischev; * Jimmy Fabian (seen by four different sources); * William Bizet; * Harry Hopkins - Rasaifka & Verch Uralsk; * James Biber - Torgau; * The censored American LT. and SGT. seen in Camp 37 near Bulun (those men mentioned earlier censored to protect their privacy); * Joe Miller - Karabas prison & Koragunda Coal Mine.

Most of the documents were dated in 1955. Now, 1955 seems like a long time ago and no one is probably surviving today? On 9 March 1988, The CIA sent a memorandum to COL Joseph Schlatter, DIA, concerning "Alleged sighting of American POWs in North Korean from 1975 — 1982 (censored):

* April 1980 - " (censored) sighted two Americans in August 1986 (sic) on the outskirts of Pyongyang (censored) about 10 military pilots captured in North Vietnam were brought to North Korea."

* April 1980 brought a second report "apparently describes the same incident" (censored for the rest of this report)

* The son of a bodyguard to the late Kim Il Sung defected in 1996. He reported seeing American POWs in North Korea numerous times between 1982 and 1993. (*Asia Times*, Bangkok, Thailand)

From 1953 to 1993 is 40 years. Forty years from 1975 (end of the Vietnam War) is the year 2015. Think about it!

First Indochina Conflict

We can learn about the present policies of Vietnam by examining their conduct at the end of the French Indochina War. The agreement ending the fighting was signed on July 20, 1954. (**Testimony of Anita Lauve, DIA expert, before the House Select Committee in 1976; SFR Chapter 9**) This agreement provided for the return of prisoners, an accounting for MIAs, and the repatriation of remains. The deadline for fulfillment of the agreements was September 9, 1954. The Vietnamese initially refused to allow C-47 transports into the airstrip at Dien Bien Phu to evacuate the seriously sick and wounded. The French were not allowed to evacuate Vietnamese POWs serving with the French. The Vietnamese forced survivors of Dien Bien Phu to march over 600 kilometers to freedom.

The "Freedom March" rivaled the detested Bataan Death March. Up to fifteen men died each day. Others were ravaged by disease. Conditions were so abominable, the French censored news reports about the march, not wanting to give the Vietnamese an excuse for not releasing men still in captivity. Despite this, by the deadline, Vietnam had released only one-third of the POWs that France claimed it was holding. After debriefings and a recognition that many Vietnamese POWs were either defectors or refugees to South Vietnam, the French still claimed that Vietnam was holding some ninety-five hundred prisoners.

Despite denials, over the next two years, Vietnam returned to the French Command three groups of alleged "ralliers" totaling 380 men. During the same two years, the Vietnamese "escorted" three groups of men, totaling 450, across the Chinese border, through the Soviet Union, into Communist controlled Eastern European countries. These men were described as "ralliers." Reliable reports had several hundred French Legionnaires returning the same way. Not all were "ralliers." In the late 1960's and 1970's the Vietnamese released several hundred North African Legionnaires and well over one hundred European Legionnaires to their home countries. Not all these men remained in Vietnam voluntarily either.

LTC Al Shinkle reported what Air Force intelligence knew. "In 1969, the North Vietnamese, ... released 12 Spanish Nationalists ... of the French Foreign Legion ... held prisoners for 15 years..." Congressman Wolff asked if information prior to their release showed they had been held involuntarily. Shinkle replied, yes. He further said that Colonel Iles, 1137th Field Activities Group, asked permission to see the Spanish repatriates. CIA denied him permission. Shinkle said the Air Force wanted to know if they had seen Americans in captivity. Iles specialized in POW information for the Air Force Intelligence Group.

The Minority Staff Report, using a larger data base, provides information about these POWs. The Soviet Union went to Vietnam to take home "their people." French Legionnaires with backgrounds from Soviet occupied countries were forcibly repatriated to the Soviet Union. This explains some of the previously mentioned movements. This took place in 1954, and not in 1952 as the DIA tried to portray in the movements around Manchouli. The number moved appears to be substantial.

Now, a technical point emerges. No, the Vietnamese did not hold these men back, the Soviets did. They were not held in Vietnam, but in other countries. That is why you will see me refer to men held in Southeast Asia or elsewhere. It makes not a whit of difference where they are held as long as they are not free to come home. **Don't think for a minute that our United States intelligence is so incompetent or blundering that they don't know where these men, as well as our POWs, are being held. Political they are. Incompetent they are not.**

Some of the French releases were done to make room for new American POWs in former French Legionnaire prisons. The Minority Staff said, "Robert Garwood, a former US POW who returned from Vietnam in 1979, stated that during the mid-1970's, he saw French prisoners being used as forced laborers in a North Vietnamese dairy farm not far from Hanoi... former Legionnaires ... they had no home country to accept them after the war." The footnote said "Garwood's information on French POWs still being used as forced labor by the Vietnamese was not verifiable without access to classified files." Soon, we'll look at this dairy farm.

With regard to MIAs and those killed in action and whose bodies were not returned (KIA-BNR), the French faced an equally tough time. They received no information concerning the MIAs. The Vietnamese insisted that all POWs had been returned. If the men were missing, they were dead.

The French repatriated remains of known dead soldiers at a huge secret cost. Vietnam considers repatriation of remains a means of securing long-term monetary support. They charged for disinterring remains and maintaining cemeteries in Hanoi. The costs escalated to totally unreasonable levels. The French paid to receive remains. Actual cemetery maintenance was almost nonexistent.

Only those remains of known KIA / BNRs buried by the French in French cemeteries have been returned. No prisoners who died in captivity have returned. The Vietnamese regarded the return of remains as a business deal; not "humanitarian concerns." Diplomatic relations did not speed up the return of the remains.

Until 1991, the Vietnamese did not allow inspection teams into their country to locate remains or graves. Anita Lauve testified they could be afraid that we would abuse the opportunity similar to how they abused it in South Vietnam after the 1954 armistice. They used their "inspection teams" to contact the local Communists cell groups. One high-ranking inspector caught in contact with local subversive groups later showed up during the war as a ranking member of COSVN.

They are afraid that we might locate prisons in Vietnam. Bobby Garwood and US Senator Robert Smith, (R - NH), in 1993, located Garwood's former prison area. An *ABC* camera crew, with Congressman Bill Hendon, proved the veracity of a person who said he had seen Americans in prison at a specific location in Hanoi. The communists restrict travel to suspected locations unless there is a long period of "pre-warning" that a visit is requested. A congressional committee was denied access to an area where hundreds of remains were warehoused.

The fighting in Vietnam is not over and the Vietnamese do not want confirmation of this. Who wants persons contacting the "Enemies of the State" as the North Vietnamese did many years ago?

The League of Families is formed in the US

Indifference by our government, and deceit by the Communists, lead the families of POWs and MIAs to band together. In 1969, Mrs. James B. Stockdale, wife of POW and Medal of Honor winner Vice ADM James Bond Stockdale, received permission to insert a paragraph in the family letters giving her San Diego address if they wanted to receive her newsletter. In 1970, a bipartisan group called An Appeal for International Justice was formed in Congress under the leadership of Senator Robert Dole. A mass meeting in Washington, D.C. on May 1, 1970 lead to a group for the families.

On May 28, 1970, the National League of Families of American Prisoners and Missing in Southeast Asia (The League) was incorporated. As conceived, it was a non-profit, non-political, tax-exempt organization financed by the families and contributions of concerned citizens. Voting membership is denied to concerned citizens. I say deliberately, "as conceived," because the League became an extension of the government. The League's Executive Director sits on government councils and helps conduct foreign policy negotiations on the MIAs and "related problems." She held a secrecy clearance and possibly signed a secrecy agreement. The League newsletters are embarrassingly a cheering section for the government and a jeering section for those the Executive Director chooses to chastise. Many family members choose to join or form other POW/MIA organizations, continuing the original purposes of the League. Many still retain League membership.

Bringing the problem to the attention of the public

The POWs were kept in the forefront of the nation's conscience by the distributing of POW and MIA bracelets. Originally, the League and Voices in Vital America (VIVA) sponsored the sale of the bracelets. Several million bracelets were sold. I bought mine in October 1972, shortly before leaving active duty. I specified an MIA. Twenty-seven years later, I still wear it, dated Jan. 16, 1967. I wonder "What happened to Fredrick Wozniak?" Until I find out his fate, I will wear his bracelet.

Increased publicity about POW treatment lead to the prisoners being tortured less often. Hanoi found America cared about its prisoners. The Vietnamese re-molded themselves as guardians of virtue and kindness towards our prisoners. They brought celebrities to prove the prisoners were treated humanely. Jane Fonda reciprocated by calling our men "liars and hypocrites" when they revealed the torture suffered by Vietnamese captors. For 591 families, the ordeal ended in early 1973. Prisoners came home. MIA families made a decision to keep quiet during the POW return. It was difficult. The assurance was the Peace Accords would provide an accounting for their men within sixty days. In Hanoi, the 1205 document shows the POWs had another purpose.

The phony Peace Accords

The Peace Accords were not designed to provide an accounting. There were no provisions for a timetable for an accounting because Secretary Kissinger said there was no telling how long an accounting would take. He wanted to give the North Vietnamese no excuse to quit looking for remains and information. Off the record, he told a family meeting in San Clemente that he did not think that the North Vietnamese would live up to the accords because there was no way to enforce them. (**House Select Committee Vol. 5 pg. 133**) Later he said Americans were probably being held prisoner in South Vietnam, Laos, and Cambodia. (**House Select Committee Vol. 3 pgs. 82-83**)

We left Vietnam in exchange for our POWs. There was no timetable because the government expected to declare all the men dead within one year. Why? All the phony rhetoric about "Peace With Honor" was just that. Kissinger met with the Chinese on June 16, 1972. The then secret records of his conversation with Zhou En Lai recorded him saying "The trouble with the North Vietnamese... was that they were too greedy and wanted everything at once. They were afraid of the process of history.... couldn't it see the whole process as two separate stages. The first step... would be the American disengagement. *History would then run it's course in Vietnam...*" (<u>The Palace File</u> **pg. 63 - Emphasis provided**).

After the "last" POW returned, DOD announced where the United States was unable to find any information concerning a man; where there was no information that he was alive; and where there was no indication that information was forthcoming; then presumptive findings of death would be issued. "It is not our intention to continue a man in a missing status and to continue carrying the family in that state of anxiety and uncertainty." (**House Select Committee vol. 4 pg. 58**)

DOD estimated an accounting would take three to five years and fully intended to have a rash of status reviews; declaring everyone dead within one year. The

Pentagon did not expect Vietnam to provide an accounting anymore that Korea did. A DOD spokesman stated, "... within the next year, everyone will have had a status review and a change to KIA who has not shown up ... " (**House Select Committee vol. 4 pg. 241**).

Frank Sieverts told the *New York Times*, (January 28, 1973), if a man did not appear on the Vietnamese list of prisoners, the assumption was he was dead. In Hanoi, General Quang had told the Politburo, "Currently, we have 11 prisons where American POWs are held... Each prison holds approximately 100 POWs... through them, we are attempting to gain an understanding of the current situation which has developed in the American Army, extract the material and information we need, and determine our position toward them." These prisoners never came home. On September 17, 1996, Robert DeStatte testified, "My belief ... (is) we did not leave anybody behind in Vietnam at the end of the War..."

The Moose Memorandum

One year and a day after the signing of the Peace Accords, the Senate Foreign Relations Committee held public hearings to assess the MIA situation. Under "normal circumstances," a year and a day would end the MIA issue. Status reviews are usually over. The government sensed that the families would not let Korea happen again. In a private Committee memorandum, Dick Moose provided members with guidance on how the MIA issue was perceived. The families were at an important crossroads. Hanoi gave no information on the MIAs. According to Moose, the families know there was little chance of POWs being held and little chance Hanoi would provide further information. The families "are understandably reluctant to acknowledge this reality — even to themselves."

He added," Officials ... are equally reluctant to speak frankly ... the families are ... reassured — out of compassion ... political caution ...— that every effort will continue to be made to obtain an accounting ... Such assurances serve to keep the families' hopes alive and fuel their efforts at obtaining additional action ..."

Moose stated many League leaders recognize the government did all it could to achieve an accounting. Some preferred to see the League "quietly fold." This "reasonable attitude" was opposed by what Moose called a "minority element in the League," "militants" who wanted to continue an increasingly futile campaign to obtain an accounting. Board members agreeing with Moose were "moderates."

Moose revealed his deceptive thinking. Official figures differed from MIA group figures as nearly two hundred men were reclassified because of presumptive findings of death (PFOD). Moose understated, "Despite these presumptive findings, the individuals involved are still, **in a sense**, unaccounted for." (**Emphasis added**)

The families questioned the sincerity of the Nixon administration and Congressional leaders. Moose answered: "There appears little likelihood that the North Vietnamese will do anything substantial ... to facilitate an accounting ... they probably have little to offer beyond ... additional deaths ... and ... repatriation of remains. There **may** be some prisoners in Laos, ... the Administration must ask itself **what price it should be willing to pay for such limited returns**." (**Emphasis added**)

In Hanoi, the Vietnamese were preparing for victory. The 1205 document carefully laid out the political steps they would take to undermine the RVN government. On the issue of POWs, Quang told the Politburo, "We still have among us Comrades who think: why do we keep these POWs and not take advantage of the Nixon proposals? ... This is not political horse trading, but rather an important condition and serious argument for successful resolution of the Vietnam problem. That is why the matter of the American POWs has great significance in exposing Nixon's designs ... when the American government resolves the political and military issues on all three fronts of Indochina, we will set free all American POWs. We consider this a very correct course..." One year away from release, and the US Government, under the guise of the Phony Peace Accords, sold the men out.

Deception continued in the Carter Administration. On January 21, 1980, Michael Oksenberg wrote to Zbigniew Brzezinski, National Security Advisor that: "A letter from you is important to indicate that you take recent refugee reports of sighting of live Americans 'seriously.' This is simply good politics; *DIA and State are playing this game,* and you should not be the whistle blower.... say that the President is determined to pursue any lead concerning .. live MIAs." (**Emphasis added**)

On May 23, 1990, Harriet Isom, Chargé d'affaires to Laos said, "America's... future in Indochina involves complex negotiations with Russia... China... Vietnam, Laos, Thailand... Kampuchea... there is a greater destiny for our foreign policy ... **the POWs are expendable** ..." (**Task Force Omega, Emphasis added**)

The beginning of the battle of the families

Moose was correct about 1974 being a crossroads for the League. A schism existed within the League. His numbers were wrong, though. The "minority element" whipped the "moderates" in 1974 and held sway until the mid-1980s.

Why did this battle occur in 1974? The statements concerning status changes were plain enough. The families discovered the intelligence agencies identified only nine of the thirteen identified POW prisons; nine men originally classified as KIA were actually POWs; and men came home not on the POW lists. In 1996, it was discovered that one man, originally listed as MIA, and whose "remains" were returned from Vietnam, actually lived in the United States since 1970.

One man spent five years in Hanoi. His mother was told that he was an MIA. Early returnees informed the State and Defense Departments of his prisoner status. These departments told the returnees it was their prerogative not to inform the mother her son was alive. (**House Select Committee Vol. 3 pg. 86**). This family went through two more years of anguish because the government wantonly chose to deceive the family. Thus, the families chose to keep the pressure on the government. Also, during this time period, friendly secret elements in the government began the leaks to the families telling them of the survival of the POWs.

Unfortunately, the "discovery" of more POWs than were acknowledged and the "discovery" of more camps than we "knew" about, worked to the advantage of the communist cover story that all men were released. Politics on our side played well to the military deception practiced on their side.

World War II sets the stage for government deceit

POW cover-up and deceit began with World Wars I and II. I will cover World War II only as it's history sets a precedent for Vietnam. The Senate Minority Report adequately covered WWI

A young army captain in military intelligence was killed **after** the end of World War II. I first thought his case was about political deception rather than POW matters. The Senate Minority Staff changed my mind. This man served illustriously as an intelligence officer for the legendary Claire Chennault of the Flying Tigers. He was directly responsible for setting up a network of agents in China behind the Japanese lines because of his skills in the Chinese language. His network was primarily responsible for the sinking of tons of enemy shipping and the saving of many lives. He was directly responsible for the saving of the lives of Dolittle's Raiders after the attack on Tokyo. As a committed Christian missionary, he could have escaped service. Instead he chose to serve with the rather unusual proviso that he be allowed to preach on Sundays. This request was readily granted.

He was appointed head of a Mercy Team who provided for the safe release of Allied and American prisoners in Japanese prison camps under the control of either Soviet or Chinese Communists. He was on such a secret mission when he was killed. The family was first told he had been killed by a "stray bullet." Thirteen years later, they found out the stray bullet came from our "allies," the Chinese Communists. Not until the 1970's was it discovered that Captain John Birch had been brutally murdered. In 1991, it was learned that Birch had been denied access to a Communist POW camp. Additionally, DOD chose to wait until after Nixon traveled to China to release more Birch documents. Pure diplomatic droppings.

Precedence for Vietnam

In World War II, up to 20,000 American POWs disappeared into Soviet Gulags. Our government made perfunctory inquiries about the men and then classified the whole matter. It was reported in the April 19, 1945 edition of the *New York Times* that the **United States captured "Germany's complete roster of prisoners of war** ... an itemization of all captives ... since the outbreak of the war... the **latest whereabouts of Allied prisoners of war**... prisoners who have died since their capture..." (**emphasis added**). Perhaps, this story was a cover story for another way that we knew about the status of our POWs. During the war, we intercepted nearly every radio transmission from Germany, often before the German receivers did. What went over the German airwaves about POWs, we probably knew.

Our military leaders worried about the numbers of POWs returned from German POW camps "liberated" by the Soviets. The numbers returning to US control were not tallying with the records. On 10 May 1945, General Golubev of the Soviet Command, responsible for repatriation of American prisoners wrote, "... the **last** group of liberated Americans in the general amount of up to 5,000 will be transferred ..." (**Emphasis added**)

This was unsettling to the Americans. An Urgent Top Secret dispatch from US Ambassador W. Averell Harriman earlier informed the President on March 8, 1945, he "was outraged" that "the Soviet government has declined to carry out the agreement (on POW repatriation) signed at Yalta... there appears to be hundreds of our prisoners wandering about Poland trying to locate American contact officers... In addition ... there are a number of sick or wounded who are too ill to move. These, Stalin does not mention in his cable. Only a small percentage of those reported sick or wounded arrive at Odessa."

Odessa, a Black Sea port in the Ukraine, was the area in the Soviet zone where American contact officers were allowed to repatriate American POWs.

On May 12, 1945, the *Associated Press* reported from the Allied Headquarters in France that nearly 38,000 American prisoners were still in the Russian zone of occupation. "Supreme Headquarters has twice requested a meeting or an agreement to arrange their return." There is quite a discrepancy between 38,000 and the 5000 reported by the Soviets.

Message S88613, dated 19 May, 1945, from General Eisenhower to General

Marshall estimated that 25,000 Americans were held by the Soviets. Marshall replied, "concerned over report that 25,000 U.S. prisoners still in Russian hands." By May 28, 5,241 Americans had been returned to US control. That coincides with the amount that Golubev said to expect. On May 30, General Marshall wrote to General Eisenhower "15,597 US POWs now in Marshal Tolbukhins hands."

The British were also involved. A TOP SECRET message from the British Air Ministry Special Signals Office to the Joint Staff Mission in Washington, D.C. said "There are still a number of British and American PWs in Soviet hands including 15,597 Americans and 8,462 British released by Marshal Tolbukhin."

The message continued, "We consider that Soviet government should be informed of Marshal Tolbukhins action in paragraph 1 above and pressed to issue immediate instructions to him for exchange of British and American PWs overland. We suggest that directions of combined Chiefs of Staff should be repeated Moscow and that Heads of respective Military Missions should be instructed to approach Soviet authorities in conjunction with embassies. As no further shipping is scheduled after end of May for evacuation from Odessa, issue of necessary instructions to Marshal Tolbukhin is of **extreme urgency**." (**Emphasis added**)

On 31 May 1945, a TOP SECRET message, 1009, was sent from MG John R. Deane, of the US Military Mission to Lt. General N.V. Slavin, Assistant Chief of Staff of the Red Army saying: "I have had a cable from General Marshall ... he has received information which **indicates** that 15,597 United States liberated prisoners of war **are now** under control of Marshal Tolbukhin. ... his information is that Marshal Tolbukhin proposes to continue the evacuation of these prisoners of war through Odessa, rather than repatriate them westward... He has asked me to obtain information on this subject and reply to him urgently." (**Emphasis added**)

The message continued, "I have been informed by General Golubev that **no more American** prisoners of war would be repatriated through the port of Odessa and that all would be repatriated westward and overland." (**Emphasis supplied**)

The implication in this series of messages, uncovered by Bill Paul of the *Wall Street Journal*, James L. Sanders of the Legal Affairs Council, and one provided to me by the Pentagon, is obvious. As of 31 May 1945, 15,597 American and 8462 British POWs were in Soviet hands. This got publicized widely.

The Pentagon responds to charges of abandonment

In early 1989, DOD responded. While attending the 1989 League meeting, I went to the Pentagon to get a copy of their response. The Pentagon said, "The Department of Defense found these charges very surprising... the seriousness of the allegations mandated an in-depth review to determine the extent of their validity...." DOD said that in September 1988, both British and American officials found "a series of World War II communications with a direct bearing on this matter."

Their documents begins with the May 29, 1945, message from the British Air Ministry, quoted earlier. The second message from the Joint Staff Mission, dated 31 May 1945, expressed "incredulity at the statements... that 15,597 Americans and 8462 British POWs released by Marshal Tolbukhin were still in Soviet hands and that Marshal Tolbukhin intended to continue to evacuate British and Americans to Odessa" (eastward).

The 31 May "Top Secret" message continued, "War Department enquired position from A.F.H.Q. who have today replied that the figures quoted by you refer to Russian Nationals held by US and British forces in Italy and not to American and

British liberated PWs in Russian hands. They also showed our representatives a message from General Deane to General Marshall of which the following are extracts: 'Deputy Head, Soviet Repatriation Committee informed me on 12 May that henceforth all repatriation of American POWs would be westward and overland. Admiral Archer was informed by Soviet repatriation committee on 27 May that instructions would be issued to stop sending British Officers, soldiers, and civilians to Odessa also that henceforth those allied PWs liberated in Southern Regions would be despatched to Gray to be handed over to Eight Army.'"

On June 2, 1945, a Secret Message, cited as 98091 31 May 1945, went from the British War Office to A.F.H.Q. that asked "Do figures 15,597 USA accounts and 8462 British accounts refer to numbers American and British PWs in Soviet hands or Soviet nationals held by US and British forces in Italy awaiting repatriation." A June 3, 1945 reply, cited as FX 87043, went back to the War Office from A.F.H.Q. stating, "Figures did refer Soviet citizens then held by US and British."

The Pentagon noted that "further confirmation of the status of American POWs was discovered... in April 1989." That message, dated June 1, 1945, said "The 25,000 prisoners of war reported in S-88613 as being in Russian hands was an estimate of 19 May. It has been subsequently determined that of this number, several thousands were in transit or already under US control and not yet reported on nominal rolls on 19 May."

This "secret" document, signed by General Eisenhower, went on to say "The numbers reported as returned to US control are as follows: A. From 1 to 23 May, 23,421...B. From 23 to 28 May, 5,241...C. It is now estimated that only small numbers of US prisoners of war still remain in Russian hands. ... scattered singly and in small groups as no information is available of any large numbers in specific camps... Everything possible is being done to recover US personnel and to render accurate... reports to the War Department."

The Pentagon states that these documents uncovered should clear up the "misunderstanding" about the "appearance" of 15,597 Americans and 8462 British being held by Soviet Forces. They ended by saying, "We hope this information provides a clearer understanding of these important issues."

Let's look at this "misunderstanding"

Well, it sure does! The original documents cited present a precise picture, move along in a clear logical pattern, with no internal contradictions. They freely refer to each another. It is exactly what one would expect to find in a series of *original undisturbed* set of documents.

The documents "found" by the government are full of what can generously be called errors and contradictions. For example, the message cited by the Pentagon as originating on 31 May stated plainly that the War Department inquired from A.F.H.Q. as to the discrepancy between PWs and foreign nationals. It continued that "today" they replied the 15,597 and 8462 figures applied to Russian nationals held by the Allies. The problem is that the inquiry was dated 31 May (98091 — PW2 — 31 May 1945) and was dispatched 2 June 1945. The reply (signed by General Alexander) was to "98091-PW2- of 1 June 1945" and was labeled "FX 87043 cipher 3 June." The Pentagon concurs: "The misunderstanding was finally corrected by a message ... **dated June 3, 1945**, which affirmed that the figures ... referred to Soviet citizens held by US and British forces." (**Emphasis supplied**)

Other contradictions in the Pentagon version include the message that on 31

May, Washington was quoting General Deane, referring to a conversation he held with General Golubev, on May 12, when on May 10 Golubev had already told the Americans that by the end of May "up to 5000" PWs would be the end of the flow. It further ignored that on 31 May, General Deane was still inquiring about 15,597 US and 8462 British PWs to the Russians. (cited in the Pentagon review).

The Pentagon would have us believe that General Alexander was confused. On 31 May he was supposed to have told the War Office that the figures referred to Russian Nationals. However, General Deane wrote on 31 May that "Field Marshal Alexander has also cabled to me stating that the **repatriation of prisoners of war** in Marshal Tolbukhins area **continues...** through Odessa." (**Emphasis supplied**)

There are numerous other problems with the "discovered" messages. One serious internal contradiction is that all the messages in this series should be Top Secret. The reason for this is a cardinal rule, if you refer to the specific contents of a classified document, your message or document carries the highest classification marking of the document referred to. There are exceptions where separate paragraph markings may designate a lower classification. Thus, when messages being referred to carried a Top Secret designation, then Top Secret would be the markings on the new messages. Such was not the case with the "found" 1945 documents. Documents 98091, FX87043, and FWD-23059 (the Eisenhower 4 June message) were all labeled Secret. This is a much lower classification and this breach of security would not have been allowed, considering the sensitivity of the subject discussed and the high headquarters doing the communicating. Further, cryptographers told me the "found" messages were not in the proper W.W.II format.

The Minority Staff Report reported that on May 30, 1945, General Kenner, Surgeon General for General Eisenhower, received a memorandum saying about 20,000 U.S. POWs were being held by the Soviets. This is two days before the supposed Eisenhower memorandum.

On June 5, four days after Eisenhower's supposed statement, the Army's figures showed that over 12,500 persons never made it from Soviet hands. (**SFR pgs. 3-21 & 3-22**) On February 25, 1946, a chart showing POWs and MIAs from the German theaters ending December 31, 1945, showed significantly high figures for "current status POWs," "MIA current status" and declared dead MIAs. The totals were close to the 20,000 figures mentioned and nowhere near the "small numbers" reported in the supposed Eisenhower memorandum. (**Ibid. pgs. 3-22, 23**)

Finally, an April 13, 1945, a TOP SECRET cable from the Department of State noted that the Soviets were already in Bari, Italy where "after a minimum of processing they (Russian nationals) are flown to Bari (from Florence) to await shipment to Russia." This contradicts the confusion over the identities of Russian nationals versus American POWs and British POWs among the highest ranking American and British generals. This cable plainly shows that processing of Soviet nationals had been taking place for almost a month and a half smoothly.

I believe that 15,000+ American PWs were kidnapped by Soviet troops and were part of the nine to seventeen thousand men presumptively ruled dead by our government (**Final Report**).

A cover story was needed to deflect public opinion and those supplying it did a sloppy job. What I mean is this. If you are trying to hide something, you need to develop a cover story. While on active duty, I was trained in Tactical Cover and Deception. Later, I served as a researcher for the Tactical Cover and Deception team at the Electronic Warfare School. We learned, as part of our training, and taught as part of our curriculum, how to develop such stories. As learned, cover stories must be close to the truth. My research showed how other countries and other services developed their cover stories. This was a sloppy job. Their problem was that they didn't have sufficient time, as the State Department did, after Pearl Harbor, to cover up their mistakes. Friendly leaks helped too.

The 31 May 1945 cable from General Deane said, "I have had a cable from General Marshall in which he stated he **has received information which indicates** that 15,597 United States liberated prisoners of war **are now** under control of Marshal Tolbukhin." The wording, to me, because of the exactness of the numbers of American prisoners given implying an exactness of knowledge — which could not be revealed — like an allied intercept of Soviet communications or an allied agent net with precise information. That would explain the reluctance to disclose information — although precious little, if anything, should remain classified now about World War II.

Yeltsin has his say

Russian President Boris Yeltsin shed some light on the situation from all wars. On June 14, 1992, he wrote to U.S. Senators, "... As the ancient used to say, the war is not over while the last killed soldier remains unburied... By my decree, a State Commission ..." was appointed to examine the claims of US POWs being transferred to the Soviet Union during all wars. Preliminary findings at that time showed that over 23,000 American POWs in World War II were interred at one time. He added that the majority of them (22,554) were released through the established lines, like Odessa. He added, and his advisor agreed, that not all were returned. At least 39 were identified as being held, as possibly as late as 1992.

In Korea, 510 of the "MIAs" were identified as being captured by the Koreans and Chinese. An additional 262 airmen were identified as being taken prisoner. He found no documents showing any transfer of POWs to Korea. The only Vietnam soldiers were those who were AWOL and never made it to Vietnam. Yeltsin said, "no data is as yet available."

Since his letter, much has been learned. The former KGB and GRU are not always cooperative. Finding the 1205 document caused the Russians, in whose files the information was found, to ban further access to the Australian researcher. In December, 1992, the U.S. Government wrote to the American members of the US - Russian Commission to find US soldiers that "We have compelling evidence that this (transfer of Soldiers) happened (in Korea) and we need to identify and account for these men."

The **Washington Times** quoted a State Department Cable on December 30, 1992 saying that Russians were using "intentional tactics of delay and obfuscation" to help protect former and current government officials knowledgeable of American POW internment in Russia. The confidential cable also said the top priority of the US investigators was not to search for living American prisoners. When the commission went to remote cities like Pechora, Vorkuta, and Khabarovsk, they found that unexplained fires destroyed the relevant documents only hours before their arrival. (**Tacoma Morning - News Tribune, Nov. 7, 1992**)

FBIS reported on 23 April, 1993 from the former Soviet Union a broadcast stating, "Over the year we were able to clear up the fate of 22,000 Americans who found themselves on the territory of the former Soviet Union. Among them is a large group of former Americans mainly of Slavic descent who while in the Soviet Union were taken repressive actions against (sic) by the Stalinist regime and spent many years in concentration camps.... those who remained alive feel themselves like native Russians, ... do not want to return to the United States." The schizophrenic American investigators pressed the Russians not to reveal many documents found as it would hurt the relations between Russia and the United States. (*N.Y. Times*, **Feb. 18, 1994**)

Finally, US CDR Chip Beck, a former CIA Station Chief and Naval Foreign Counterintelligence Agent (Ret. 1996) wrote to the **US Veteran Dispatch** (USV) in their January 1997 edition "... the current 'mad dash' to admit former Warsaw Pact countries (into NATO) is being done at the expense of America's unrepatriated ... POWs from World War II, Korea, the Cold War, and Indochina ... Aggressive pursuit for the knowledge of what happened to 6000 - 9000 POWs, who were transferred to the Soviet Gulag between April 1945 and the early 1970's, is too difficult and might retard more important policies..." (according to US officials and not Beck) "... According to official declassified American documents from 1945, an estimated 6000 - 7000 US POWs mysteriously failed to be accounted for ... Stalin learned an important lesson from this experience. He knew he could exploit foreign prisoners of war, even Americans, with impunity -- and get away with it .... Some of the more interesting admissions that the transfers took place come ... from Eastern European personalities in the former Warsaw Pact countries ... representatives from more than one former Warsaw Pact country make it known to me and a couple of colleagues that Sejna's stories were substantially true ... they believed their governments would be willing to provide the United States with documents, witnesses and other information they still have on the transfer and POW exploitation programs if it would assist their entries into NATO..."

The United States internal documentation says thousands of Americans did not return from Soviet internment. We need the men back. Perhaps President Clinton would help for a donation to the Democratic National Committee. A clear formal resolution from Congress tying aid and other help to their return is needed. Anything short would be a sham. More proof of Americans being transferred to the former Soviet Union will follow in a later chapter.

The families' feelings

How do the families feel about their "abandonment?" COL Vincent Donahue summed up the feelings of a large group of families when he testified before the House Select Committee in 1976:

"What I am trying to tell you here is, whether by misguided conviction, by order, or by design, the DOD personnel involved ... do not believe, will not believe, that any MIAs or POWs are alive 'unless they are deserters.' And that the Center and DOD seek a declaration of findings of death in all cases." This prophetic statement in 1976 goes uncontradicted through all these years.

Deceit and deception are ugly words when used in the context of governmental action. Yet, as this chapter clearly shows, the precedents are there. No sweet words, no whitewash, no amount of "massaging" has been able to change the written records. World War II, Korea, Vietnam. Deception, cover-up, deceit, over abandoned men.

Deceit Through Public Investigation

This chapter shows some early responses to the cry of the families for this display of official concern.

The House Select Committee "Investigation"

Family pressure and genuine concern by influential congressmen caused the House to appoint a Select Committee to conduct "a full and complete investigation" of the MIA problem. They also examined the problem of returning known KIA remains. A third charge was determining the need for international inspection teams to find if men were held prisoner. The mandate was plain enough. Start with a neutral position and let the evidence point to the men being alive or dead.

Appointed were Representative G. V. "Sonny" Montgomery (D-MS), Chairman, Democrats Henry Gonzalez (TX), John Moakley (MA), Patricia Schroeder (CO), Richard Ottinger (NY), Tom Harkin (IA), Jim Lloyd (CA), and Republicans Paul McCloskey (CA), Benjamin Gilman (NY), and Tennyson Guyer (OH).

One committee member, McCloskey, stated before the hearings began, no POWs or MIAs were alive. He speculated that only a small number of MIAs could ever be accounted for. He gave no supporting evidence for his claims. (**National League of Families,** *"Analysis of the Final Report of the House Select Committee,"* **April, 1977, page 3.**) Later, he took an opposing view.

The "Montgomery Committee" was allocated $350,000, roughly half of the Presidential Commission on the Olympics, to conduct a fifteen month investigation. Thus crippled, the committee could not conduct any independent investigation. The committee staff took at face value studies prepared by the agencies investigated and then presented them as done independently by the committee.

An illustration of this cozy arrangement is a DOD study on POW camps in Vietnam. On April 26, 1976, Dr. Shields replied to J. Angus McDonald, the Committee Staff Director: "This letter is in response to a request ... for **unclassified information** pertaining to U.S. PW camps in North and South Vietnam" (**Emphasis added**). **The** DIA annex to this study asserted: "A total of 13 facilities in North Vietnam were used as permanent detention camps for U.S. prisoners of war."

Nine of these thirteen camps were identified by our intelligence. Taking only this DIA information, the reasonable assumption is 13 camps was the total number of POW camps in North Vietnam. In 1979, I failed to find the discrepancies.

Camp, camp, who lost the camps?

The December 1978, DOD release of previously classified files contained study number DI-367-18-72, "Prisoner of War Camps in North Vietnam (U)," prepared in November 1972. It served "as an intelligence aid for the debriefing of released U.S. personnel ..." (The (U) means the title is unclassified) "...There are **eight confirmed** prisoner of war camps in North Vietnam ..." Eight camps were identified only months before the war ended! The shocker came: "There are 18 **possible** prisoner of war camps in North Vietnam... used for the detention of American prisoners on a permanent basis."

Suspect camps? The DOD study for the Committee never mentioned suspect camps. I scrutinized both DOD reports to resolve discrepancies on locations.

A POW camp, "Briarpatch," located 105 miles to the North, Northeast of Hanoi, was missing on both lists. In May 1972, 220 prisoners were moved there with none of our intelligence assets picking up this movement. The four remaining camps were not on the suspect list either. We did not have a clue they existed. What a different picture from that painted for the Select Committee and the public.

Families painted as "professional MIA celebrities"

Problems which occurred included one half of the committee's budget was unspent at the end of the fifteen months. The staff and some committee members were predisposed to find nothing showing Americans were alive. McDonald, the Staff Director, developed a deep animosity towards the families. League board members learned he publicly said; he detested the families; was on a collision course with them; and some were "professional MIA celebrities." (**Affidavit of Dermot Foley, *Hopper v. Carter*, pg. 15**) In a confrontation on July 6 1976, McDonald admitted statements attributed to him. He was sorry the League found out, but would not retract them.

The League asked Montgomery to either discipline or replace McDonald. He did neither. (***Ibid.***) The League later charged Montgomery solicited support terminating the committee with the conclusion all MIAs were dead. Montgomery told news reporters that he had a commitment from a "majority" of the committee supporting this view before the hearings were completed!

The Select Committee conducts an "investigation"

Let's examine the investigation and the findings. These findings, illegally filed, are the cornerstone of the government's cover story all the MIAs are dead.

The coverage of Walter Cronkite in the **Final Report** gave no details of the massive interrogation undertaken by the journalists. The Staff said that the journalists' committee produced no reliable information of survival since 1973 and the Cambodians said they had "absolutely no knowledge of missing Americans." With this, Cronkite's testimony was dismissed.

General Vang Pao was not as fortunate. With no public record of his statements, the staff distorted his views. They noted his report of eight to ten Americans held prisoner in Laos only because Gilman put it in the **Congressional Record**. The staff dismissed it with faint praise: "Never doubting that the General had received such a report... the Select Committee conducted ... close scrutiny of the records of the intelligence community and two interviews with General Vang Pao for additional information, details, or evidence." (**Final Report pg. 94**)

That was the McCloskey letter discussed earlier. The close scrutiny of intelligence consisted of asking the CIA to evaluate Vang Pao's evidence. The result printed in the **Final Report** was a travesty. The CIA told McCloskey it confirmed the information Vang Pao presented. The staff reported however, "no evidence was ever turned up by the American intelligence ... to substantiate these reports."

Vang Pao said his reports probably related to the same group of men. The staff said that it was not clear that all reports related to the same men. McCloskey said he wanted the report to show the possible presence of eight to ten men in Laos. The staff determined the report had no importance.

This "close scrutiny of intelligence community" records failed find the 1974 State Department shadowing of Congressman Gilman. Secretary Kissinger tried to dissuade Gilman from publicly commenting on the Vang Pao interview.

(**Uncorrelated documents**) One staff member, Job Dittberner, called Vang Pao a "flaky, senile old man." (**League analysis pg. 9**)

People testifying no Americans were alive were quoted extensively. The staff quoted, out of context, one MIA wife making it appear she agreed with status reviews being continued. She was adamantly opposed. (**League Analysis pg. 17**) **Then came the "conclusions."**

The Select Committee's "conclusions"

The most dramatic conclusion was the committee's decision no Americans were prisoner in Vietnam or elsewhere. The Vietnamese could only return about one hundred fifty remains in an accounting. If captive, it was unlikely that the United States could secure their release. The committee took faint notice of unreturned Americans surviving their loss incidents. The passage of time with no information constituted strong evidence the men were dead. After all, no one from World War II or Korea ever returned after being declared "presumptively dead." There might be one or two defectors or deserters. This conclusion was called the result of a "careful, studied assessment" of all intelligence acquisitions over the previous fifteen years. Unknown to the Committee, these same agencies squelched the reports of transfers of prisoners to the Soviet Union and the supporting evidence.

An important recommendation was that status review hearings be resumed. The report claimed that the Missing Persons Act adequately protected the rights of missing servicemen and their dependents. Noting the imprecise and incomplete information furnished the families, the staff claimed these errors were "faulty interpretation of regulations" rather than an official policy.

The committee urged that the vast volume of information not studied be declassified. It recommended the reversion to the Korea example and declare dead, within one year of the end of the hostilities, all persons not released. The claims of Americans left alive in Indochina were "gut feelings" of well-intentioned persons. In contrast, their conclusions represented the "careful studied assessment" of the intelligence community. However, the intelligence community never said what was claimed and never corrected faulty interpretations of deliberately vague statements.

"Evaluation... is a subjective procedure"

General Walters said the DIA held approximately three hundred reports of sightings of U.S. personnel in Laos alone. Most, *but not all*, of the information could not be correlated to MIAs. **DIA held information on live POWs in Laos, but was not certain who had been seen.** Further, he stated that the "careful, studied assessment" was only a series of siftings by analysts. Walters admitted the evaluation process was not void of subjective judgments. As General Williams confirmed in 1981, "thus, regardless of the methodology ... used to verify a source's report, **in the end it is the analyst who weighs the information ... provides the human equation. ... the evaluation ... is a subjective procedure based upon the experiences and judgment of the analyst ....**" (**Emphasis supplied**) General Tighe testified in June 1985 that you can either try to prove or disprove a report; help your case, hinder your case, or to find out the truth depending on your goal.

The report endorsed the Korean War policy, leaving the fate of an MIA in the hands of our enemies. This happened in the past and the report recommends it for the future. I wrote, in 1979, the lesson for future wars is clear: **"Fight well but don't get caught; we may be too busy to worry about your fate."**

A Senate researcher validated my words. A classified report, from June 8, 1955, said: "The problem becomes a philosophical one. If we are 'at war,' ... losses must be expected... we may be forced to adopt a rather cynical attitude ...which would (1) instill in the soldier a much more effective 'don't get captured' attitude..."

This the legacy we want to bequeath future generations? In high school ROTC, I first learned the Code of Conduct. Part dealt with being a prisoner of war. I looked at those pictures of prisoners and wondered if I could live up the expectations. I remember well the explanation — If captured, **I would** do my best to **resist** because **my country would** attempt to **get me out and would never forget me.** That explanation was a hoax. Our country forgets POWs for political expediency.

How to create a majority where none exists

The public was told that a committee majority endorsed these conclusions. Only the separate views of Congressman Moakley and dissenting views of Congressmen Gilman and Guyer were printed. However, the committee was evenly split over two major points. These were that all the men were dead and that status reviews ought to be continued. Kept off the report were two other dissenters, Congressmen Lloyd and Ottinger. (**Affidavit of Gilman, his** *Amicus Curiae***, Feb. 4, 1978; affidavit of Foley,** *Hopper et.al***, May 30, 1978; League Analysis**)

When the committee met to discuss the **draft report**, committee members were in and out; two known dissenters could not attend; and the discussions were not completed. No vote was taken on the conclusions and recommendations. Congressman Ottinger wrote: "...the select committee held its first meeting to discuss the draft report .... There was considerable disagreement ... the issue is ... unresolved." (**League analysis pg. 4**) However, Montgomery ordered the incomplete report to the printers. Ottinger's name was "inadvertently" left off as concurring with Congressman Moakley. Congressman Lloyd's attempt to have his name attached to the views of Moakley was also ignored. (**Appendices D & E**)

The report was fraudulently presented to the public. The Staff Director stated in a sworn affidavit the report represented the views of eight members. Further, he said three of the five members seeking to dissent had no serious disagreement with the Final Report. (**Foley affidavit May 30, 1978, pg. 15**) The Gilman affidavit, contains, however, letters, memoranda, and dissenting opinions from five Congressmen proving the committee was evenly split. (**Appendices D through G**) Further, the Report was adopted contrary to House and Committee rules. Gilman argued no vote on the report was taken. The court was similarly deceived.

On January 31, 1977, Montgomery presented the "authoritative report" to President Carter. He refused to allow known dissenters to participate. Moakley, however, wrote to Carter, and showed that outright dissent was voiced by two members on status reviews. He added three others concluded no evidence had been presented that Americans were all dead in Indochina. On the status review problem, he said 3 members urged the President to be careful before resuming them. **"This even split must be seen as representing the true views of the committee."** Moakley urged the President to meet with the "real experts," the families.

That meeting took place on February 11, 1977. President Carter assured League members he understood their concern about status changes. He would not allow Vietnam into the United Nations until personally assured of an adequate accounting of MIAs. He would not conduct unsolicited status reviews without exhausting all avenues of MIA information including appointing a Presidential Commission to go to Hanoi. (**League Analysis and interviews with participants**)

The Woodcock Commission goes to Hanoi

The Presidential Commission consisted of Leonard Woodcock, UAW President; Senate Majority Leader Mike Mansfield; Marian Wright Edelman of the Children's Defense Fund; former Ambassador Charles Yost; and Representative Montgomery. This commission was charged with seeking "information about our missing men and the return of any recoverable remains." They were to "receive the views of the governments in Indochina on matters affecting our mutual relations." These members were first cleared with Hanoi and found "acceptable."

In a DOD briefing (**Appendix A**), the Commission was given evidence of men, like Ron Dodge, who were alive at one time. The Defense Department gave photographic evidence of men known to be dead but whose remains had not been returned. A radio photograph, originating in Hanoi showed ID cards of four naval officers shot down in 1967. Two returned in Operation Homecoming. The other two, Walter Estes and James Teague, were identified as being captured. The Communists refusal to comment on them made "questionable the Vietnamese's claim of no additional information." Finally, in October 1977, ten years after their capture, the Vietnamese returned the remains of Estes and Teague.

Explicit pictures were exhibited to show conclusively the Communists vast reservoir of information. The briefer, COL C. M. Matthews, added, "We cannot really accept the other side's denial of knowledge..." Matthews anticipated a question saying, "... we would say that it would be reasonable to expect an accounting ... a total of 1339 men."

The Commission report emphasized being furnished copies of the **Final Report** and reading it thoroughly. The Commission noted the Defense Department briefing, yet missing was the realistic expectation the Communists could account for 1339 men. Instead, the Commission reiterated data showing that our MIAs only accounted for 4 percent of the men killed in Vietnam versus the 22 percent figure from World War II. This impressed upon the Commission the need to be realistic in its expectations for a future Indochina accounting."

The need to be realistic in expectations

What was their realism? The "Perspective" section of the **Final Report** stated "The purpose ... is to ... contrast statistics of previous military experiences with ... the recent Indochina War... World War II spanned continents, ...Casualties were enormous... measured in thousands ... tens of thousands, and ... millions."

However, the American part of those "millions" was 78,794. We controlled the real estate where most of the deaths took place. In Vietnam, we accessed virtually none of the land where prisoners were held. Without these qualifications, any comparison of World War II and Vietnam statistics are meaningless.

World War II produced between nine and seventeen thousand presumptive findings of death, nearly the number of believed abandoned POWs. The Final Report never even hinted at this problem. Commission members were told that the DRV Deputy Foreign Minister, Phan Hien, also read the **Final Report.** Thus, the Vietnamese knew what the Americans expected and did nothing to disappoint them.

Commission members were "wined, dined, and shined." They knew Hanoi could produce remains, POW information, and personal effects. The Commission received the remains of twelve men and the promise more later in the year. They reported lamely the Vietnamese were probably capable of providing more information but chose not to do so at the time.

The Commission stated it was usually not restricted where it could go. Not reported, however, was the Vietnamese denial to visit the "War Crimes Museum." Some POWs were forced to go to the War Crimes Museum and found ID cards, pieces of planes, and articles to help resolve MIA cases. The Vietnamese stopped showing POWs the Museum when they noticed them taking notes of names on the ID cards. (**POW, pg. 586**).

The Commission findings were an instant replay of the **Final Report**. Montgomery, the onetime hawk considered Hanoi to be the liberator of South Vietnam. (***Human Events*, Sept. 23, 1978**) President Carter referred to him as the leader to open normal relations with Vietnam, (since relinquished to Sen. John McCain)

The significant difference between the two reports is the Commission declared no Americans were alive in Vietnam. Later, Robert Garwood returned alive.

Woodcock reported the Commission impressed upon the Vietnamese and Laotians the desire for an accounting. "We had a 'realistic attitude' towards the MIA problem." The administration wanted the problem resolved in a "reasonable way" **removing it** "as an obstacle to normalization." (**Wolff Committee pg. 7**)

Woodcock believed the Vietnamese information was the best they could under the circumstances. He explained the terrain, the climate, the circumstances of loss, the passage of time, as reasons the Vietnamese could not provide us with a total accounting. (Missing is the *ad nauseam* explanation of baby tigers dragging bodies down the jungle trail) Asked what they could do, Montgomery answered: "... I would say 100-150 would be the maximum I think the North Vietnamese could give us information about." (**Wolff Committee pg. 10**)

Woodcock noted the Vietnamese "clear, formal assurance" of looking for MIA information. "...take steps towards normalization, ...would significantly move up the process ... to the MIA problem." Montgomery pushed for PFODs: "(to) ...close ... the final sad chapter in Vietnam." (**Wolff Committee pg. 14**)

Carter breaks faith with the families

After approving the report saying, "We are satisfied with what's been done," (**Wolff pg. 74**) Carter instructed Secretary of State Cyrus Vance to drop opposition to Vietnam's entry into the United Nations. Publicly, the administration dropped opposition because of support of "universality of membership." Undersecretary of State Richard Holbrooke denied admitting Vietnam into the United Nations was giving " up a bargaining chip for MIAs ..." (**Wolff Committee pg. 37**)

President Carter knew Ambassador Andrew Young testified two weeks prior to the family meeting the United States was going to approve Vietnam's application for UN membership. He suggested the United States and Vietnam would open talks to normalize relations. (**Vietnam: Problem of Normalizing U.S.-Vietnamese Relations, issue brief IB77018, Library of Congress, April 3, 1978, pg. 16**)

The next day, the State Department confirmed Carter would seek normalization of relations, adding there was still expected an accounting for the MIAs. Mr. Holbrooke claimed "... the decision was based ... not on approval ... of the individual country's behavior in regard to ... MIAs ..." (**Wolff Committee pg. 38**)

The President, in August 1977, recommended that status hearings resume. We received only twelve remains and a promise of more in the future. Those twelve remains were announced in September 1976. The Ford administration said this return was inadequate. Carter felt that it adequate to "fulfill" a campaign promise.

I wrote to Jody Powell, Carter's Press Secretary, asking how the President could allow the Vietnamese into the United Nations and resume the status reviews considering his promises to the families. His reply, via DOD, said, "President Carter has not changed his attitude about obtaining the best possible accounting ...." The Vietnamese "formally agreed" to furnish **all available information on MIA remains** as they were recovered. President Carter wanted to: " ... start the process ... to be ... our friends ... a more ... free society..." On the efforts of the Select Committee and the Woodcock Commission he said, "They've done a great deal to ... return those bodies since that time." (Note no live POWs)

The reply to my question about status changes was, "Status Reviews and accounting are two distinct issues." Status changes could not prejudice an accounting. The President remained firmly committed to an accounting. The passage of time required the continuing of status review hearings.

At this time, Ngo Phi Hung was remembering the POWs he personally saw. The Soviets were looking over the 1205 POWs for those they could further exploit. Garwood was still in captivity and a draft evader was beginning his ascent to higher office in Arkansas. President Carter broke his promises, choosing instead to deceive the families. He knew the suffering of the families since his own uncle had been an MIA, declared dead, and later found alive in a remote prison camp.

Public investigations a sham exercise

This public investigation was a sham. COL Vincent Donahue testified on February 25, 1976, "From the first, ... the MIA issue has been mishandled by State and by DOD." (House **Select Committee vol. 3 pgs. 83-84**) He reminded the Committee that LTC Kain, assistant to GEN "Chappie" James, leaked to the press the theory families did not want their next of kin declared dead to continue receiving their pay and allowances.

Frank Sieverts told Donahue: "If I had my way, I would have all of the MIAs presumptively declared dead immediately, and ... bring an end to the anguish and pain ... these nice families have." Donahue responded: "Is he so naive or stupid that he thinks that by the stroke of a pen ... of a PFOD panel... he is going to answer the ultimate question in the hearts and minds of the loved ones of the MIAs?"

The families noticed the many holdovers from Henry Kissinger's tenure at the State Department. Nearly everyone involved in the accounting process was a Kissinger protégé. One National Security Adviser who privately admitted MIAs were alive (Bud McFarlane) was with Kissinger in Paris. Another, Brent Scowcroft, was Kissinger's assistant in 1973.

In the April 24, 1985 ***Wall Street Journal,*** GEN Tighe, voiced his apprehensions: "Some people have been disclaiming good reports for so long that it's become habit forming;" some had a "mind-set to debunk." His testimony on June 27 asserted, "The attitude of a few could have had a significant impact ...(on) the ... accuracy of the evaluations ... ***Judge a report - phony for any reason - it's not likely that report would be used to cross-check others*** nor is its author likely to be interrogated.... whether or not it ... had an impact on a willingness by my superiors to believe (Americans were alive) — I have no way of knowing. From there to a U.S. effort to recover, ... is a great and unknown distance." (**Emphasis added**)

Suspicions continue between families and the government. This public inquiry was a phony attempt to answer the "ultimate question," POWs, alive? The hearings provided publicity about the MIAs. The **Final Report** was fraudulent. The words of Donahue, spoken years ago, are on target: "Had our government acted promptly ... and ...not engaged in years of rhetoric ... these men who were alive at the time might still be alive today — if indeed they are no longer alive."

And the deceit goes on

New evidence of "deceit through public investigation" has arisen. The Wolff Committee gave way to the House POW Task Force. The POW Task Force has always been headed up by a Republican in the Democratic House. (Since the Republicans took over in 1994, other committees have looked at POW matters.) Among the chairmen of the Task Force have been: * The late Tennyson Guyer - A real gentleman and a force for POW/MIAs * Robert Dornan - A scrapper for POWs and knowledgeable * Ben Gilman - Fought the lonely fight in the Montgomery Committee * Gerald Solomon - Stated his personal view that POWs are alive and held against their will (June 17, 1985 and reaffirmed to me Jan. 21. 2000)

Despite the Republican chairmen, the power was wielded by Congressman Stephen Solarz (D-NY). His priorities were more concerned with the ethnic makeup of the South African government than with the question of live POWs.

Here are some criticisms of the way the US has looked for POWs / MIAs by some members of the POW Task Force: "Beyond a shadow of a doubt, U.S. military personnel are being held alive against their will in Southeast Asia.... President Reagan and President Carter have both been kept in the dark on the true nature of the intelligence." (**Congressman Bill Hendon, November 11, 1983**)

"As a member of ... Congress and ... the Task Force ... I will state categorically that there are American POWs being held against their will ...." (**Congressman John LeBoutillier, December 8, 1982, interview with author Diane Taylor.**)

Congressman Dornan had private assurances from DIA officials that American POWs are being held prisoner. Congressman Douglas Applegate of Ohio charged a cover-up was in progress in August 1984. Congressmen Hendon and LeBoutillier told me a cover-up, at mid-level DOD and DIA, has been underway for years.

These men had oversight responsibility on the issue, saw the reports, read the report analysis, and asked the tough questions. They paid a price for their views. They were criticized, ridiculed, and lambasted for being outspoken.

The U.S. stance was : "... we have ... been unable to prove that Americans are still detained ... the information ... precludes ruling out that possibility. Actions to investigate live-sighting reports ... continue to receive necessary priority ... based on the assumption ... some Americans are still held captive. Should any report prove to be true, we will take ... action to ensure their return."

Since 1991, resources doubled to a reported 222 persons working on the issue. With spokesman saying that there was no evidence that Americans were being held in Vietnam, what are 222 persons doing? In September, 1996, Dornan asked that question in his usual tactful manner: "If the Communist liars in Hanoi are telling the truth... gospel truth and they are really cooperating fully, effectively, totally, passionately, all the crap words we heard out of the Senate Committee, if... there is nothing left but dust and the bones of a few heroes, then why do you exist?... That is the problem DPMO has boxed itself into. If everything you say... is true, then there is no reason for you to exist... you can either retire or look for analyst jobs somewhere else..."

The position is structured so that you can look forever and not be responsible to do anything. The statement says, "We will take appropriate action to ensure their return," Only if a report proves "to be true." And who decides? General Tighe said "From there (a willingness to believe) to a U.S. effort to recover, as you are well aware, is a great and unknown distance."

Walking that great and unknown distance

Let's examine the difficult task of insuring that persons with responsibility to recover have the proper information on which to formulate policy. On June 5, 1979, in Executive Session: **Mr. Dornan**: Do you personally believe that Americans were probably still alive in January of 1973?

General Tighe: ... **a personal belief, yes, there were some live Americans**. However, we have no hard evidence that any ... are alive and being held prisoner ...

Mr. Dornan: (Deleted)

General Tighe: (Deleted)

Mr. Dornan: (Deleted)

General Tighe: (Deleted)

Mr. Dornan: (Deleted)

General Tighe: That decision would have to be made by the State Department

Mr. Dornan: But eventually, it should come out?

General Tighe: Yes, sir.

Stated assurance - POWs held against their will

On June 25, 1981, I knew GEN Tighe was testifying but was unable to be at the hearing. A newspaper reporter I knew was there with some potentially "explosive" questions we wanted asked. Ron Miller of *ABC National News* called me and asked what was going on. I told him that Tighe was going to testify and there were some questions going to be asked of him by this reporter and there might be the opportunity to get some good answers on tape. *ABC* was at that hearing. What happened made headline news for years to come.

The questioning began routinely. Quickly, however, Congressman Solarz became intrigued by General Tighe's point of DIA's working assumption. He asked, "Is it the conviction of DIA that there is ... at least one American serviceman ... held against his will in Indochina?"

General Tighe replied, "My personal conviction and stated assurance is that there is at least one American being held against his will in Indochina."

Congressman Solarz: "... there are at least **two hundred eight sightings of live Americans** ... you have not been able to track down ... does the weight of the evidence suggest ... American servicemen are ... in Indochina?" (**Emphasis added**)

General Tighe: Yes, sir.

Mr. Solarz: And ... American servicemen being held against their will...?

General Tighe: ... yes in answer to both questions, sir.

Mr. Solarz: Now, have you testified to that effect, previously, General?

General Tighe: I have not been asked the question in exactly that way, ... as far as personal convictions .... (Remember the testimony of June 5, 1979 and you will see that something has caused the General to change his mind.)

Mr. Solarz: ... *this is a conclusion that ought to be given great weight, ... by every member of ... Congress. ...* (**Emphasis added**.) ...with all due respect to ... your agency, that was not an impression I had previously received.... there are a lot of reports, ... unfounded ... chances were nobody was ... alive. But you feel otherwise... what leads you to that conclusion?

General Tighe: I would like to defer that to the closed session.... this is a very fast-moving train of evidence. I would like also to clarify the means ... to verify ... these reports that... have checked out .... our ability to check is ... circumscribed.

Mr. Solarz: ... your testimony is that in your judgment, the weight of the evidence indicates ... Americans still ... being held against their will in Indochina.

General Tighe: Yes, sir.... That is my own personal judgment...

Mr. Solarz : And do you have any sense as to how many are being held ...

General Tighe: I have none.... those reports that we take most seriously, ... involve more than one. That is about as far as I can take that.

Not only did General Tighe change his mind publicly, he was more forthcoming in December 1982, telling author Diane Taylor that he had seen more POW/MIA information that any other man in the world, "The evidence is clear to me that ... Americans are being held, ... in Southeast Asia."

Not toeing the "party line" costs

Think of the significance of this charge. The head of the military intelligence agency obligated with finding if servicemen are prisoners tells an author and a congressional committee he believes servicemen are held prisoner. He is going against what I called in 1979 the "party line."

Retribution came. In his December 24, 1981 letter to Congressman Moore, LTG James Williams, wrote that although Tighe testified as to his personal opinion, the official opinion at DIA was they "could not prove that Americans are indeed still detained in Indochina." That response was mild. Tighe was the victim of "revisionism." DIA officials testifying in other settings said that what Tighe "really meant" was that we had to operate with the mind-set that Americans were left behind. He really "did not" mean to imply there were POWs.

Tighe also was lambasted by League officials. They stuck to the strict government position of no proof of prisoners. Some insinuated Tighe mismanaged DIA to the disadvantage of the MIAs. I heard that charge made at the 1985 League Meeting in the Inter-Agency Forum. George Brooks, League Chairman took the lead on Tighe. No one from DIA, State Department, nor National Security Council came to Tighe's defense. Although charges emerged that a cover-up concerning the existence of live MIAs was underway, GEN Tighe specifically denied a cover-up existed. The persons attacking Tighe's veracity did not care. The charges of cover-up became loud enough that some in the media decided to investigate.

The General doesn't budge

Bill Paul of the *Wall Street Journal,* on April 24, 1985, Tighe as saying that there existed a mind-set in certain persons to disbelieve Americans are prisoners. *ABC News*, in May 1985, elicited the opinion that at least fifty to sixty live POWs were prisoner. This was based, Tighe said, on reports he remembered seeing as DIA Director. He added unless something extraordinary happened to disprove the reports, that estimate still stood. In the Paul article, Tighe admitted he was ashamed of some poor analysis work done at levels below him while he was Director.

The House POW Task Force invited Tighe to testify on July 27, 1985. I watched the hearing. The General was under attack. In his prepared statement he said: "I have ... received some harsh criticism for my activities ... and some generous praise."

Two questions to him were, "Previously, when you testified as Director ... you indicated ... no evidence of Americans in Indochina. Does your recent statement indicate that you have received information subsequent to your testimony ... in 1979 ... to alter your view? Did you ... as Director of DIA, state that you wouldn't ... be surprised if Americans were being held?"

Talk about short memories! You have already read the 1979 and 1981 statements. The questions came from Mr. Solarz. Tighe answered in part: "You will recall, ... when I testified ... on 25 June 1981, ... I said ... there was no way I could prove that Americans were held against their will ... it was my view that they were. The evidence was very convincing to me... I wish we had as good human intelligence available on Americans we believe ... held captive in other parts of the world... The '50-60' was based on my memory of **three areas of particularly convincing sightings**.... large numbers of unclassified reports... pointed to the existence of live Americans held... I have not altered my views... I've seen no evidence to counter ... these reports. ... a great many were very believable. *I testified officially that I always held there were live American POWs still held against their will but could not prove it."* (**Emphasis supplied**)

Trying to undermine the General

The questions seemed designed to diminish the value of the General's public statements of live Americans held prisoner. Commodore Thomas Brooks of DIA testified, "To date, we have not yet been able to prove that Americans are still being held captive .... our basic ... operating assumption is that ... some Americans *may still be* held captive .... (**Emphasis supplied.** Note the subtle difference between this and what Tighe testified, "My personal conviction and stated assurance is that *there is* at least one American being held against his will in Indochina.") Brooks also asked, "I would only hope that those individuals who levy conspiracy charges against DIA either refrain ... or else produce the 'proof' that ... when challenged, they are unwilling to provide." (**You'll get your wish in this book!**)

Examining that "great and unknown distance" GEN Tighe referred to; Richard Armitage was asked: "Assuming that the DIA found conclusive evidence that an American was being held in Vietnam. What would the next step be to guarantee his immediate and safe return... ?" He answered, "Given the expressed pledge of the President and the priority throughout the government backing that pledge, should we find conclusive evidence, it would be a subject of immediate consideration at the highest levels ... to determine the necessary action to secure release of anyone still held." (Someone please decipher this for me!)

Vessey - a new start - the same result

In "February" 1987, President Reagan appointed GEN John W. Vessey Jr. as his Special Emissary on POW/MIA affairs. He and a delegation left for Vietnam on August 1, 1987. Vessey described the trip as "positive, correct, and business-like. Protocol and administrative arrangements were appropriate for a delegation headed by a Presidential Emissary." (At first, I honestly believed that February was the time Vessey was appointed. In Chapter 11, you'll see that even in small details, the government lies to keep their deceit rolling.)

Vessey said, "Concerning the question of live American prisoners, the Vietnamese insisted ... they held no American prisoners. We made it very clear ... many questions ... must be answered before the American people ... could accept that assurance... most Americans ...believed Vietnam held live prisoners."

His trip was discussed until Ann Griffiths testified. In a short space of time, she attacked two Congressional bills seeking to declassify POW information; a reward offer of two million dollars sponsored by several Congressmen; ... POW/MIA families generating publicity for the reward offer; a former Congressman as a "conspiracy and cover-up theorist"; several respected POW organizations; and said "...The Congress... should devote attention to such situations which constitute a grave danger to the issue and efforts to resolve it."

By 1987, the Families' watchdog had become the government lap-dog.

Congressman McCloskey (D-IN) asked, "Mr. Chairman... we just heard a publicly concerned organization and a former Congressman slandered through ... Mrs. Griffiths testimony ... Would it be possible to have Mr. Hendon and Mr. McDaniel and the American Defense Institute come here to answer these charges ...?"

Mr. Solarz replied, "The subcommittee will ... take your request under consideration... I have... invariably found Mrs. Griffiths' observations to be accurate .."

Mr. McCloskey countered, "In all due respect, there is not monolithic opinion out there in the POW/MIA community..." Solarz retorted, "... this wasn't the first time, nor will it be the last that controversial statements are made ... if Mrs. Griffiths feels as strongly ... she has an obligation to share her concerns...."

McCloskey again asked that those maligned be given a chance to defend themselves. Mr. Solarz replied, "We might just do that. We might also want to have ... the Justice Department testify as to whether there is a potential case of mail fraud here. If, ... these allegations are ... true, ... a scam is being run ... people are being asked to contribute on a false basis."

At this point, Mr. Rowland of Connecticut interjected, "I would like to continue ...(what) Mr. McCloskey brought up, and I think that the comments that you are throwing out ... heighten some of the rhetoric . ... " (**Vessey pgs. 29-30**)

Where did the official policy go?

Mr. Solarz: Let me begin with you, General Vessey ... in your personal judgment, do you believe ... Americans being held captive ... in Indochina...?

General Vessey: ... I do not know ...We have evidence ... we had people alive... you have the repeated assurances ... they hold no live prisoners... There is evidence on both sides ..."

Solarz asked Griffiths how many men she thought the Vietnamese could account for. She replied "I would say surely on 200 plus that General Vessey took plus a substantial more... It is an impossible number to put a finger on." He asked about POWs that we had evidence were alive at one time but who did not return. Griffiths replied that DOD or DIA would have to provide an answer. One statement stands out in that answer: *"We have no information to indicate that any of the 63 individuals were alive at the time of Operation Homecoming in 1973."*

I thought deceit may have ended in 1990 and 1991. A report from the minority staff of the Senate Foreign Relations Committee made the first in-depth investigation of the POW/MIA issue from looking at classified and formerly classified reports. You have read some of their findings. You will read more. One part from the May 1991 report is significant: "After examining hundreds of documents relating to the raw intelligence, and interviewing many families and friends of POW/MIAs, the Minority Staff concluded that, **despite public assurances to the contrary, the real, internal policy of the U.S. government was to act upon the presumption that all MIAs were dead.**" (**Emphasis added**)

Because of the diligence of the members of the Minority Staff, a Senate Permanent Committee on POWs/MIAs was formed. We'll look at their results in chapter 13 devoted to the Committee.

The statements of General Tighe became the rallying cry for a new and renewed effort to break the POW logjam. On August 2, 1991, *ABC's 20/20* revealed that an overwhelming majority of American citizens feel that POWs are alive and that the government is not doing enough to get them home.

A small preview and challenge

In the next chapter, we will examine the "fast moving train of evidence" referred to by General Tighe. I do not have all that General Tighe saw. I have read, however, a great deal of background material, refugee reports in the hundreds, declassified reports in the thousands of pages, plus my own investigation. However, the best is still under lock and key.

The end to this chapter is necessary to introduce the next chapter, "Intelligence Cover-up." Until President Clinton, the rhetoric on POWs became better. The action, however remained the same. Those who charged cover-up and deceit became reviled. General Tighe was described as "senile." POW relatives were characterized as "distraught." Garwood, the one POW who made it home was vilified. Honest, patriotic, people differing with the government had their integrity, motives, and character attacked by a government sanctioned organization or their government allies..

As the author of the book first using the words "cover-up" and "deceit," I take as a personal affront any challenge to my integrity or of those with whom I work. To all apologists I say: "I do not back down from what I write now, have written in the past, or present in other forums. A cover-up has occurred in the past. Either incompetence, cover-up, or 'mind-set to debunk' is in operation today. You've never called me to testify, despite my attempting to do so. There is no halfway 'happy medium.' That belongs to politicians. Statesmen act — politicians whine."

What I did not know for a long time was that another force was at work against the POWs. It emerged with President Clinton. A policy, meager as it was, insisted that Vietnam would not be recognized, a trade embargo would not be lifted, government rhetoric on the issue would not be changed until a satisfactory accounting on the MIAs was accomplished. With President Clinton, that all changed. As will be shown, the change came about, not because any proof emerged that they were dead - not that any proof emerged that remains could not be recovered - not that any proof emerged that Hanoi had exhausted all means of cooperating. No, the policy changed because of money. Not just any money. But campaign money - to seize power - to keep in power - turned the head of a man who shirked his duty, denounced his country in wartime, and then when presented with proof of live men, turned his head, as he had done so many times before and went on to enjoy life while the heroes suffered in captivity.

Intelligence Cover-up

This chapter is called Intelligence Cover-up. Before getting specific, some definitions are in order. I will lay out qualifications for what I will maintain. I have been a student of Vietnam, its history, culture, politics, and military situation since 1963, a senior in high school. During the war, I served as an intelligence advisor in the Vietnamese Phuong Hoang or Phoenix program. I developed sources within government, Vietnamese, and POW/MIA communities. One contact, the late Father Raymond de Jaegher, was a confidant to President Ngo Dinh Diem. I trained in intelligence, infantry, Electronic Warfare, Deception, and Counterinsurgency.

My initial interest in Vietnam grew from discovering the first Military Advisory Chief was LTG John Wilson "Iron Mike" O'Daniel. Was he a relative? It's not important. It was enough to get me interested. My POW interest develops from 1969 when assigned the task of finding POWs. I have lived in an intimate knowledge of Oriental habits and culture since being an advisor in Vietnam. I became a student of communist tactics in 1960.

Intelligence, either military or political, is usually a guesstimate. A good intelligence officer must first be a good enemy operations officer. Indispensable is knowing their strategy, ideology, and tactics. Possibly, you can anticipate their moves. You seldom have a "smoking gun" telling you what an enemy knows or plans. Here, we are fortunate to have two such "smoking guns," the 1205 document, and an eyewitness to the transfer of our POWs to Moscow and elsewhere.

There are various ways to gather intelligence. Some are sophisticated and some are old fashioned. A good intelligence program relies upon a mixture of input. Although trained in a variety of information gathering methods, I confess a weakness for old fashioned methods. I prefer eye witness reports and documentary evidence. I see their reliability in situations where newer methods are limited. Our KH-11 satellite is remarkable. It can read plates off a car from a high distance in the air. It cannot see a car in a garage, however. An agent can enter that garage. You can read the 1205 document. You can debrief former General Major Jan Sejna.

I like radio intercepts which give you an unvarnished look into the enemy camps. It is like running a wiretap. We received radio intercepts on POW movements and some lead to a rescue mission in Laos.

Now, for a secret. What differentiates between what you have been doing since beginning the book and what an intelligence analyst does? Very little. In reading the POW reports, you begin forming an opinion based upon factors you consider relevant to come to a conclusion. The same is true in the intelligence field. The difference being a command emphasis on what is needed to be known "at the top." The need to protect from enemies our interests and where we obtain our information is what "classification" is all about.

Intelligence then is the by-product of gathering material, reading it, analyzing it, and reaching a conclusion, in theory anyway. As James Srodes, biographer of Allen Dulles, "**Master of Spies**" put it, the real secret of intelligence is that it is politicized. Analytical conclusions are freighted with political bias, opinions, and agendas. (Pg. 325) With this very rudimentary understanding of intelligence, let's concentrate on defining cover-up. In intelligence, there is a gray area between knowledge and presumptive "proof." For example, LTG Williams wrote, "Thus regardless of the methodology ... in the end, it is the analyst who weighs the information ... provides the human equation... the evaluation ... is a **subjective** procedure based on the experiences and judgment of the analyst weighing all the evidence available." (**Emphasis added**)

You can use the available facts to either prove or disprove a point, as Tighe testified to. The proof or lack thereof depends upon your individual bias or upon "command emphasis." Officially, the United States policy is one or more Americans are held captive. The command emphasis should be to "prove" this fact.

Quite the opposite happened. The Senate Minority Staff Report says, "For Vietnam, the U.S. government has at least 1,400 such reports (first hand sightings) including reports ... received in 1991; ... In addition ... thousands and thousands of secondhand reports ... full of detail such as 'my brother ... saw 11 American POWs being transported in a truck to such and such a place.' Yet, amazingly, the U.S. government has not judged a single one of these ... credible." (**SFR pg. 6-1**)

If the command emphasis is to prove live POWs; if the evidence supports the thesis; if deception is absent; if the evidence is clear and consistent; and if the product is "No live Americans;" this is cover-up pure and simple. Additionally, the standards used to "prove" a point are such that no report or combination of reports ever meets the definition of "proof." With these parameters guiding us, we can have a basis of understanding to determine if a cover-up exists, as defined.

The government says releasing "uncorrelated" reports will enable "amateur" intelligence analysts to detect live POWs where none exist. Classification of reports "serves as a barrier to misuse of the information for the possible emotional or financial exploitation of affected families." (Not a legitimate use of security classification) Releasing the 1978 reports made clear the presence of live POWs. All POW MIA families want is the truth. If that means that their man is dead, they can handle that. What they cannot stand is patronization and lies.

Doing the analysis

In chapter three, a sighting by refugee Trinh Hung was presented. Hung lived in the United States and lacked the insinuated incentive to fabricate a story, coming here. The DIA requested Hung be debriefed. When the U-Minh Forest was mentioned, someone decided that Hung would not be interrogated, being ordered "from the top." (**George Brooks testimony Aug. 9, 1978 Wolff Committee**)

Others questioned Hung including a former POW; interpreting was a professor from the University of Pittsburgh; and a licensed polygraph operator. The consensus of those involved was that Trinh Hung was telling the truth. His story was sent to DIA for comments. DIA said that it "contained certain elements ... contrary to precedent, and which, therefore, tend to cast suspicion on his story." (**November 28, 1977, letter from CDR Bruce Heller to Navy CPT Ray Vohden**)

I became involved in **December** 1977. My reaction was "DIA is lying on this story." Dermot Foley used parts of the following analysis in *Hopper v. Carter*. Let's look at Hung's story the way an analyst should. The overall analysis casts suspicion upon DIA's ability to tell the truth. His story is full of details with the ring of truth. Point one made by DIA was that although the Vietnamese were known to have a record of POW abuse by an angry populace, they did not normally condone such action. They had directives assuring the safety of Americans because of their value as political bargaining chips. This answered Hung's contention that guards encouraged the populace to hurl insults and accusations at the POWs, beating at them with small sticks.

In the Hanoi March, officials so inflamed the populace our men barely completed it alive. (**Hubbell, POW, pgs. 182-199**) By contrast, the East German propaganda film "**Pilots in Pyjamas**," has one certain "grandma" being particularly "vicious" and "always present," regardless of the POW being talked about, that the staging is very evident, thus justifying Hung's contention.

Looking at both sides of the story

One could make the outwardly plausible case that the NVA and VC were "independent" of each other. POW treatment in the North did not equate to the South. Arguing from that perspective, in December 1968, our forces captured a document on the Viet Cong "rational use" of POWs in captivity. (**Select Committee, vol. 5, pg. 124**) This political "after action report" outlined actual POW presentations to the populace. The VCI then analyzed the presentations to formulate guidelines.

One stuck out. It was the presentation of returned POWs Daniel Pitzer and Edward Johnson, who were held with COL Nick Rowe. In 1967, they were taken to "liberated areas" as examples of "American aggression." The VC wanted to install in the populace a hatred of the United States. They also wanted to establish a policy of how to handle US and ARVN POWs in order to free the POWs' minds from "enemy" indoctrination by destroying their "haughty and self-conceited feeling ... Americans are second to none." This was the first American POW exposure in the U-Minh Forest.

Pitzer and Johnson were brought to a village by boat. At the outskirts, the words are shouted, "We have got two Americans." Seven persons are allowed to wade into the water armed with knives and axes. They approach the boat while others on shore are encouraged to display a "very angered attitude" by unceasingly shouting anti-US slogans. When Pitzer and Johnson returned to Rowe, they tell him this show was one of mere braggadocio. This policy contains no contradictions to the Trinh Hung story and was known to American intelligence as authentic.

A second "discrepancy" DIA found was his description of the POWs. They had their heads shaved like Buddhist monks. DIA countered that no U.S. POWs returned saying their heads were shaved. Further, this description did not match one given by a refugee who saw American POWs with long hair in the U-Minh Forest. (**Letter Heller to Vohden op. cit.**) Two POWs from North Vietnam, George McKnight and Douglas Hegdahl, reported their heads shaved. Hegdahl's head was shaved twice. (**Hubbell, POW, ppg. 356, 378, 454**) Le Thi Anh, in a sworn affidavit, asserted shaving the head was a traditional form of showing disgrace.

What is the discrepancy? The Vietnamese not showing a POW in disgrace? A definition of a shaved head? Hung's wording said the heads were shaved like monks. Vietnamese monks have a variety of shavings from close hair cuts to complete shavings. Wartime and post 1973 declassified reports contain numerous eyewitness accounts of US POWs with their heads shaved. DIA, however, called them "uncorrelated." By DIA standards, they do not constitute a precedent. A carefully worded analysis allows the analyst to not lie directly while supporting a predetermined goal. Looking at the other aspect of DIA's objection, another refugee saw Americans with long hair. DIA didn't like that report either. Did they consider the possibility two refugees described two different sets of POWs?

A third discrepancy examined

DIA made a third point. Historically, the U-Minh was a place of detention for American POWs captured in South Vietnam. Most, however, were captured before 1969. A single confirmed American prisoner detained there after that date died in the latter part of 1972. DIA asserted the statement of a friend of Hungs that prisoners were taken from their former hiding places in North Vietnam south into the U-Minh to keep their existence a secret was contrary to the experience of every confirmed US POW. After the Communist takeover, DIA argued, captives were taken north into the Hanoi region for detention. During the war, this policy was restricted to POWs captured in northern South Vietnam. After the Communist takeover, DIA claimed persons captured as far south as Rach Gia were taken to Hanoi prisons. They offered Arlo Gay as an example of that policy.

Before tackling DIA's multifaceted objection, I will add that I served my last six months in Vietnam in the areas just to the East and just to the South of the U-Minh Forest; the District compounds at Thoi Binh and Song Ong Doc respectively. I had operational intelligence responsibility for parts of the U-Minh Forest. Thoi Binh is located just down the canal from the compound COL Rowe was operating out of when captured.

The DIA correctly states the majority of POWs were captured before 1969 because most of our forces in the Delta were gone by mid-1969. Another DIA analysis added about the U-Minh: "...by the end of 1968 ... known US POWs had either been released... died... executed... or escaped." **(Select Committee, vol. 3, pg. 307)** The key words are "confirmed prisoners" and "known US POWs." Nick Rowe saw three prisoners in early 1968, although he did not know their identities. They existed, however. Dale and Demmon were detained in the U-Minh. Two prisoners Rowe described as almost dead when the VC took them away to a hospital were in the U-Minh. This gives five possibilities for the men Trinh Hung saw. Unfortunately, two known POWs in the U-Minh, Rocky Versace and Kenneth Roraback were executed and decapitated, eliminating them as persons seen.

Declassified documents show two 1968 rescue missions in the U-Minh. They were looking for **eight** American POWs. The attempts failed to find the Americans, but those rescued said the Americans had been evacuated just prior to the rescue forces arriving. This brings us up to possibly thirteen men. Also included is the 1974 sighting of Americans in the U-Minh. By coincidence, one name given then was one of the confirmed POWs that DIA said died prior to 1969.

Contrary to DIA's "precedents," the 1205 document says Vietnam expanded the number of POW prisons at the same time DIA said the number contracted.

My three reports

While serving in Thoi Binh and Song Ong Doc, I received at least three reports concerning POWs in the U-Minh Forest. One report was developed by another intelligence agency. One was developed by my intelligence agents. The third came from "reliable higher US intelligence sources."

Air Force intelligence interviewed a Hoi Chanh who saw US POWs in the Nam Can Forest, which DIA refers to as the "southern U-Minh" area. My agents, in 1969, saw US POWs in an area of canals up the Song Trem Trem from Thoi Binh. Nick Rowe's areas of captivity corresponded with these two reports. This is also the same area where rescue attempts were made in 1968.

The higher U.S. intelligence sources reported that American POWs were located in the middle of the U- Minh. I presumed then and do now that these "higher intelligence agencies" involved more sophisticated means of locating POWs than agents, like SOG. We were explicitly warned not to fly over this particular location as it might cause the VC to move or dispose of the POWs being detained.

For DIA to be correct, then our agents, ralliers, and "higher intelligence sources" (not to mention COL Rowe) all saw non-existent persons after 1968. We also attempted to rescue nonexistent persons seen by real POWs.

Regarding the objections DIA posed to the reported prisoner moves, DIA contradicts itself. Arlo Gay was captured in Rach Gia; then taken South to the U-Minh; moved to Can Tho, still in the Delta; then six months later he reaches Hanoi.

If Gay is offered as a precedent of Communist movement of prisoners, how do they explain the fate of Tucker Gouggelman? He was captured and held prisoner (as far as anyone knows) in Saigon's Chi Hoa prison until his death. The comparison is valid because Gouggelman was a CIA agent and Gay was suspected of being one. (Some early "discredited" "uncorrelated" reports were of Gouggelman and Korean diplomats held in Chi Hoa prison.)

DIA also forgets it's document, "US PW Movement to North Vietnam," which paints the following picture of US POWs captured in the Delta after 1968: "... the Communists did not feel it was to their advantage to consolidate these PWs as ... the earlier captured group. Instead, Americans captured ... after 1968 remained in the general vicinity of their capture ..." I know the Communists did not move prisoners because the tactical situation changed in 1969. The movement of POWs would have been difficult. Further, the U-Minh would have to be considered a "big cell" if it is offered as proof of consolidation. Read the book **Five Years to Freedom** to see how "consolidated" COL Rowe felt. 220 men were moved from Hanoi to the Chinese border in 1972, contrary to known precedents. It was done to meet a potential strategic emergency, a possible invasion of Vietnam. The 1205 document and DIA photos show the moving of POWs after the Son Tay raid. DIA said this movement was to "consolidate" the prisoners. LTG Quang said the prisoners were moved to "expanded" secure prisons to prevent future rescue attempts. Whose interpretations do we believe, DIA or the man in charge?

The Communists moved POWs as it suited their needs. The uncorrelated reports prove that POWs were moved during the war years as needed. DIA fails to accurately portray the Vietnamese as disciples of the Chinese and Russians in tactics, masters of the art of tactical and strategic deception.

I don't know that Trinh Hung correctly related what he saw. I know DIA refused to question him. His story, not the first to come from the U-Minh, cannot be shunted aside. Are our intelligence agencies so weak we cannot penetrate the porous borders of Vietnam to conduct investigations? When General Tighe said POW information is available "if we really want to get it," what did he mean? Are some of our methods so sophisticated and "secret" that we cannot use the intelligence gathered for fear of compromising how we got it?

Finally, two refugees reported that while members of a resistance group active after the 1975 defeat of Saigon, their commanding officer (who they named), ordered them to "find out the whereabouts of ... American POWs ... being moved to the Vinh Chau region." These two men penetrated the "Palm Forest of Darkness" in Vinh Chau District, Ca Mau Province. This is the U-Minh Forest. Once there, they saw first one and then two, US POWs located where there was a camp "reported to be holding 32 US POWs."

Now the candidates for Trinh Hung's story being correct is at least 32.

Why look at history?

Why look at history? This is 1999 (or what ever year you read this book). You want to know about recent reports. Hang on, we'll get there. I work from a very logical position. The only way that Americans can be there (wherever there is) is for them to have been alive from the beginning (after 1973). I am deliberately spending time laying the foundation for some of the later reports.

The story from Hong, from chapter three, also about the U-Minh, likewise received shabby treatment. First, the analyst ruled out the possibility of the sighting by Hong being related to the holding of Arlo Gay in the U-Minh because of the time differences. If Hong had seen only one American, they would have correlated this report to Arlo Gay regardless of the time difference. Arlo Gay has been "correlated" to being black, white, tall, small, skinny, husky, or any description.

As LTG Williams testified on August 8, 1984 about a measles map type of reporting; "I alluded ... that our live sighting reportings ... look like a measles sheet when ... plotted on a map. We ... received many reports on an American ... in the same geographic area. **We could say ... an American in the area, but we didn't know who he was**. ... it was ... PFC Garwood." **(Emphasis added)**

Thus, with one swift kick, Williams knocked out many reports as being "correlated" to Garwood. What Williams did not say, however, is just as instructive. Those reports verified Garwood being a prisoner. Those reports Williams alluded to did not include the ones which told of many Americans being held in the exact same geographic area as Garwood. Then, Garwood had not been debriefed, making it difficult to say how the reports pertained to him. **Officially**, DIA did not know where he was a prisoner. So, the "confirmed" reports were "correlated" to Garwood while others, from the same area, were "uncorrelated" and thus invalid.

DIA claimed Hong surfaced the report to call attention to himself in the refugee camp. At this time, in 1975, most refugees were unaware the United States was interested in POW reports. That policy did not change until 1978 when the State Department put up signs asking for the information. Hong's interviewer said the two men indicated a desire to emigrate to the United States. A story of American POWs could be a useful tool in accomplishing their goal. DIA found a couple of other faults with the source. The first was his friend issued a warning that one of the Americans was fluent in Vietnamese. The second was the JCRC investigator could not believe the local Viet Cong leader who acted as a guide having so much freedom since he was sentenced to an eight year term for an unspecified crime.

DIA further created doubt saying there was no chance for follow-up on the sighting because of the lack of description of the men and the lack of corroboration to the story. Unsaid is if a POW was found, Hong could verify who he saw. If not, we would then have one "confirmed" POW and two "uncorrelated." The analyst said, "In conclusion, the source's allegation of ... Prisoners in the Rach Gia area cannot be confirmed or refuted, but both refugees' motivation in surfacing the story possibly could be self-serving."

It's possible that their motive was spelled out in a letter to the League: "We let you know ... because we were so surprised when listening to ... (VOA) they said that the American Missing ... are considered to be death (sic). We hope ... this letter ... and our news will bring ... a new hope in this Xmas and New Year."

DIA failed to report at least one of these refugees lacked the motive of calling attention to himself to come stateside. His brother had been a resident since 1967. Officially, the policy was supposedly to allow refugees the opportunity to surface MIA information. Frank Sieverts, said, in a sworn declaration and personally to me, "every refugee has opportunities while in ... transit areas to provide information on American POW/MIAs, ... for such information to reach responsible United States officials for follow-up and reporting." This "opportunity", however, also gave investigators a reason for rejecting the report by calling it "self-serving."

Hong and authenticity

Hong's story has a solid ring of authenticity. I have, from another refugee source, verified an interment camp existing on Canal Number 7 at the same time that Hong reported his. My source placed Canal Number 7 in the same location as Hong. He and Hong did not know each other. He told me of numerous other "re-education" camps for Vietnamese in the U-Minh Forest.

Second, Communists keep areas containing American POWs off limits. They surface POWs only to achieve specific propaganda purposes. The warnings of severe punishment to those violating the "prohibited zones" is believable. I am not concerned about the freedom allowed the VC imprisoned with Hong. I remember some wartime VCI standing accused by their brethren of crimes, coming to us through Chieu Hoi centers. From the context of the story, it was evident this VC was terrified enough of punishment, he would never contemplate escape. Also unsaid by DIA was that in the U-Minh Forest, Nick Rowe and other POWs also at times were untended, Rowe to the point where he escaped a couple of times.

What intrigued me about the DIA analysis was the sentence "Any possible relationship between these claimed Americans and the alleged four Americans paraded through the streets of Chau Phu is open to speculation." Since Chau Phu is close to the U-Minh, I asked Commander Bruce Heller of DIA, for a copy of DOD document "Recent Reports of US PWs and Collaborators in Southeast Asia" dated May 1977, report number (DDI-2430-9-77).

The report, now you see it, now you don't

I was shocked with the reply from Navy CPT Raymond Vohden, the principal advisor, Office of POW/MIA Affairs, DOD. He said the report did not exist. He assumed I was referring to a compilation of sighting reports being prepared for release in the near future. Vohden was not ignorant of the report. A letter from Heller to him dated November 28, 1977, said: "Tran Van Hanh's statement was noted and evaluated in a compilation of US PW sighting reports DIA ... published in May 1977, titled "Recent Reports of US PWs and Collaborators in Southeast Asia" (... DDI-2430-9-77). A copy of that write-up is provided as enclosure 4. "

I brought this to Vohden's attention at Ngo Phi Hung's hearing. I inquired why I could not have a copy of it. He expressed shock about my having this partial report. He said "it was classified." When I told him that my copy did not have classification markings, he quickly dropped the whole subject.

Lack of detailed analysis

In the DIA studies I've seen, I've been aghast by the lack of comparison in the refugee sightings. Common denominators abound in the reports. At least four reports told of Americans held prisoner in the Rach Gia/U-Minh area in 1975. Two revealed Americans being held in a "prohibited zone." Two reports described the same mode of transportation. The destination was the U-Minh Forest. A third source saw Americans in the U-Minh.

Judge a report to be phony ....

Before 1979, the only known comparison by DIA was the analysis noting the dissimilarity in hair length in two refugee narratives. Tighe testified that if a report were judged phony, it was unlikely to be used to cross-check future reports. All reports officially have failed. The Senate Foreign Relations Minority report stated: "The DOD ... has received in excess of 1,400 firsthand live-sighting reports ... With the exception of a very small percentage ... 'unresolved,' DOD has concluded ... do not pertain to any American POWs ... there is little reason to assume that the few ... still 'unresolved' will ever be determined ... valid ... many ... 'resolved' live-sighting reports should be reexamined.... the ... DIA explains away (their) validity ... with a flawed or... questionable analysis.... used in a rigid, bureaucratic manner ... to ... close the files... DIA's analysis ... reflects an approach ... geared toward disproving each live-sighting report, rather (than) receiving ... the 'necessary priority ... based on the assumption ... Americans are still held captive.' Thus, DOD has been able to construct a rationale to discredit 'officially' nearly ... every live-sighting report.... Once an analyst makes a conclusion, it seems to be cut in stone." (**Sounds like what I wrote in 1979.**)

Let's look at the record

In June 1973, Nguyen Thanh Son emerges. He's the rallier who saw live Americans the State Department asked the media to ignore. The EC-47 case is being covered up. In North Vietnam, 670 POWs have not been released. KGB agents are ready to interview more POWs for their purposes.

On November 2, 1972, February 15, 1973, and March 3, 1973, JPRC received reports of POWs in An Xuyen and Kien Giang Provinces. This corresponds to large portions of the U-Minh Forest. JPRC said that for many years, it received reports of prisoners in the U-Minh. These new reports are called "extremely probable" and "highly plausible." These wartime evaluations starkly contrast to current DIA evaluations of U-Minh sightings.

A "friendly foreign intelligence agency," reported on May 4, 1973, that the VC Military Region III Headquarters held an April meeting for certain District Committees in a three Province area. They discussed post cease-fire activities. American and South Vietnamese POWs were to be used as a "bargaining chips at future peace talks." Viet Cong Camau and Chuong Thien Provinces were designated as the holding areas, including the U-Minh Forest. The report is called "probably true" from a "usually reliable" source. Sounds like Trinh Hung's story.

In the Soviet Union, the Soviet Politburo is told that 1205 POWs are in captivity. Only 591 return in Operation Homecoming. The others are bargaining chips. Some POWs are arriving in the Soviet Union, through Czechoslovakia, for examination of the war from the American side, others for medical experimentation, including practice amputations and examination through chemical interrogation.

In Laos, on July 24, 1974, three Caucasians, described by local villagers as Americans, are seen in captivity. The source was polygraphed and the "results substantiate source's claims that he ... observed three Caucasians ... "

A report that meets DIA's own criteria

In August 1974, in the U-Minh Forest, a Viet Cong rallies. He saw six American POWs in 1970 and kept track of them until just before he rallied. Air Force reconnaissance missions over the POW camp in December "confirmed the existence of a factory-like building as well as man - made structures... further confirmed source's diagramming of the various canals ... the camouflaged canal entrance and the security check points. Area in which both factory and PW camps are located is considered hostile." His polygraph examiner said, "no deception had been indicated." Unfortunately, the recon photographs cannot show the actual contents of the buildings. The polygraph summary says, "source's polygraph examination, however, basically supports his reports."

To confirm a report, DIA looks for ways in which the original sighting can be "strengthened and supported by technical means." If there are a series of reports concerning a certain area, it is hoped that "at least one source's credibility will be enhanced by a polygraph examination." GEN Tighe affirmed if a report was specific as to time, location, and the source showed an intimate familiarity with the given terrain and the source passed a polygraph, his reaction would be he probably would tend to believe that source.

In this particular case, we have a rallier who saw six American POWs in an area where JPRC already believed earlier reports of prisoners. In April 1972, American intelligence reported a PW camp with 3 Americans, about 17 miles from this location, in Thoi Binh District, An Xuyen Province. The 3 Americans were two white and one black. In 1968, another report had 3 Americans held prisoner near here; two white and one black. US intelligence reported, "A later RVN raid... repatriated ARVN POWs, but no US personnel." The reported camp is "near canal 17, on the NE side of the Trem Trem River, ... Kien Giang Province." **The source believes the camp to have been in existence since 1969**.

Further, this source claimed to have been a prisoner in the camp. He saw between 500 - 600 prisoners consisting of Vietnamese, Cambodian, Montagnard military and political prisoners, "as well as six Americans." He described three of them. They were two white and one black. In addition, he gave two names. Known to me through computer records, **one** of the **names matches a confirmed POW in the U-Minh Forest**. He was previously listed as died in captivity. The rank assigned to this POW is correct. The name of the second white POW does not match names on my computer records. The black POW "had a heart tattooed on his chest and both arms."

The rallier continues. The black soldier was wounded in a mid-1973 escape attempt. The wound has now mended. It is believed the POWs were special forces "who may have been captured as early as 1964." The confirmed POW was captured in 1965. DIA admits all known POWs in this area were captured prior to 1969. In describing the camp, he says there is a canal network being the primary means of overland transportation. "This area is part of the U-Minh secret zone, a traditional communist stronghold..." He gives a map location using his memory, assisted by two US interpreters. He also reveals another source of information, a female merchant, "who ... sold supplies to the wife of one of the PW camp cadre... the female merchant last returned from the communist area on 18 August, 1974." Aerial reconnaissance "confirms the existence of a factory - like building as well as man made structures ... further confirms source's diagramming of the various canals, to include the camouflaged canal entrance and the security check point."

The rallier's story passed all tests except for the crucial one — it went contrary to the expressed Vietnamese profession that American POWs had been returned.

However, there is more to this account. The 1968 raid occurred differently than DIA described it. They reported "no Americans were found." I located the original report. On August 27, 1968, two ARVN PWs escaped from the PW camp with JPRC receiving the escape report on August 28. The camp contained 35 Vietnamese PWs and 8 US POWs. On August 30, a raid was conducted including a US Navy SEAL PRU advisor, 9 PRUs, and the two escapees. JPRC furnished specialized equipment to help in the operation.

The raiding party advanced from an ARVN outpost, only 3000 yards from the POW camp. At daybreak, a reaction team of 60 PRUs and four gunships arrived and "attacked the guards... killed two VC while the others ran. The reaction force landed and cordoned off the area....A total of 49 VN prisoners ... were ... shackled ... in trenches filled with water chest deep. They were ... interrogated immediately regarding the US PW... the US PW had been removed ... on 28 August by an estimated enemy BN (battalion) ... A search of the area revealed no clue as to the fate of the 8 US. .. **The sources were rewarded by CORDS for their services.**"

In the case of our rallier, it was determined that "it is believed unlikely that any US personnel are still there..." This despite the report of the polygraph exam which "basically supports his report" of US POWs.

I also found more reports to evaluate the ralliers report. In March 1973, the JCRC reported"... the presence of four to six US POWs in the delta region for several years..." including "three caucasian and one negro POW..." Continuing, "infrequent sightings of small groups of US personnel have come from the U Minh Forest area..." **In September, 1971, the CIA reported** the existence of a VC prison camp in the Nam Can Forest for both US and ARVN prisoners. Nick Rowe was held in both the Nam Can and U Minh Forests.

Only **three months later**, the CIA reports "... six ... (POW) were held... located within ... (VC) Military Region 3 (MR-3) ... headquarters ... Two of the POWs are majors; three are captains (two of whom are Negroes); and one is a first sergeant. The six were captured in the U Minh Forest ... dates ... unknown; **all are believed to have been detained for several years**... A 100 man company of the VC U Minh local force battalion is located nearby..."

In 1969, I received reports of US POWs held in the area up the Trem Trem river, near some numbered canals. It is in the same area where Nick Rowe reported seeing his three American POWs in January, 1968.

This rallier reported POWs in a specific location, at a specific time, and showed an intimate knowledge of the terrain to include hidden check points and descriptions of buildings. He passed a polygraph test. His story was strengthened and supported by technical means (aerial reconnaissance). Further, the government's own holdings included reports of POWs in the same specific areas mentioned by the rallier. He gave the names and ranks of two POWs. One name was of a confirmed POW seen in captivity by Nick Rowe. The descriptions of the POWs fit other reports. The ranks fit other reports. The named river was the same as several other reports. The U-Minh local force battalion mentioned in a confirming report is known to me. It is the U Minh 2 Battalion. It operated in both Thoi Binh and Song Ong Doc Districts. There is no contradictory information in this first hand sighting of US POWs in a camp in 1974 where the rallier had been held himself.

The conclusion? We knowingly left US POWs in the U-Minh Forest.

1205 confirmations?

In April 1975, Saigon falls and refugees flee Vietnam by the thousands. POW reports grow in numbers and quality. In September 1975, Aleksander Solzhennitsyn addresses the AFL-CIO. He touches on the POW/MIA problem. He says Communist governments brag to their allies about holding American prisoners.

CIA confidential agents report (1976-77) that Vietnamese military cadre reveal the SRV withheld American prisoners from the exchange to use them as future bargaining counters. CIA agents report (Feb. 1977) American POWs from "wealthy American families" being held as a trump card for financial aid to the SRV. Another CIA agent reports that the SRV categorizes MIAs from dead to "good" Americans living in the SRV. GEN Quang tells the Politburo about reactionary POWs (one of three categories), "we understand ... these officers come from rich families." He categorizes the captives as, "progressive, neutral, and reactionary."

First hand reports from a former ARVN officer POW in North Vietnam and a doctor doing North Vietnamese government work say they have either seen official SRV documents pertaining to POWs or have heard SRV army officers talking about the American POWs still being held.

In early March 1977, a "generally reliable" CIA agent with "extensive contacts in international political circles" quotes an SRV "Ministry of Foreign Affairs Official" as saying Americans remaining in the SRV were either married to Vietnamese women or had been judged guilty of "crimes against the Vietnamese people." Both were attending a conference of government press representatives from nonaligned nations in Tunis, Tunisia. Nick Rowe reported that while held prisoner, he was adjudged guilty of crimes against the Vietnamese people. Until he confessed, he could never be released.

The Vietnamese believed that 1977 would bring "normalizing" of relations. Carter's election portended that decision. However, in January 1977, a CIA agent reports that American POWs and some defectors remain in Vietnam. He says their presence poses problems to the expected new diplomatic relations.

Another agent reports in February an overheard private conversation where Hanoi acknowledges where U.S. pilots shot down are buried. Next, this SRV official states "we have American POWs" who won't be released until financial aid from the US was forthcoming. He continued Hanoi was in contact with MIA families and the prisoners are the one trump card that the SRV possesses. "We will take advantage of this situation in negotiating with the US for aid in economic reconstruction." Quang revealed his strategy: "**We intend to resolve the American POW issue in the following manner**: ... 3. Nixon must compensate North Vietnam ... If we take a path of concession ... and release POWs... we would lose much ... this issue must be resolved on the basis of military and political aspects.... we are convinced that our position concerning POWs ... continues to be correct..."

In 1993, it was revealed this overheard conversation was between an Indonesian Diplomat and Vietnamese Vice Foreign Minister Phan Hien. Bill Hendon said he believed the Indonesian diplomat's account of the conversation as the "agent" was a listening device. In April, 1993, years after release, the CIA now views the report as a "fabrication." (*NY Times*, **April 18, 1993**)

Ngo Thanh Giang in the SRV Ministry of Foreign Trade said, a CIA agent reports, in March 1978, that Americans are in the SRV, with some confined and others are "happy to be in Vietnam." Among those "happy" to be there are those married to Vietnamese women.

The refugees come with their stories

Refugees fleeing the communist tyranny arrive in camps scattered throughout the world carrying accounts of live POWs, burial locations, and descriptions of current prison locations. This flood of humanity includes former VC, defectors from communist governments, Vietnamese of Chinese extraction, former Thieu supporters, and former non-Communist Thieu opponents. All say **American POWs have been left behind.** Some of the following League acquisitions I read doing work for Dermot Foley. Others are extracts provided by DIA to a Congressional Subcommittee before their travel to Hanoi in 1979.

In February 1979, JCRC interviews a refugee in Malaysia. He tells of POWs he saw in mid-1971 and an American he saw in Yen Bai in mid-1975. This American lived with camp cadre and lectured American POWs. (This report referred to Bobby Garwood. This person was expected to testify at Garwood's trial. He did not, however. Garwood was a prisoner here. Had Garwood been a defector, this source would have been used by the government in the trial.)

A Vietnamese pastor is interviewed in March 1979. His cousin was held in Chi Hoa prison from 1975 to fall, 1978. He saw a white American and three Koreans imprisoned. (**Tucker Gouggelman and two Korean diplomats were prisoners in Chi Hoa.**) These sightings of Koreans are also the topic of conversation between Dornan and Tighe in the redacted 1979 Executive session covered earlier. Further, in mid- 1979, the United States verified the Vietnamese held two Korean diplomats hostage since 1975. In May 1991. The Minority Staff Report said: "During their imprisonment, the South Korean government negotiated continually ... The Vietnamese never admitted ... the South Korean POWs were ... in prison. Even after ... presented ... incontrovertible photographic evidence ... the Vietnamese government continued to deny holding the men ... in 1980 — the Vietnamese government repatriated the two prisoners ... after their release, the Vietnamese government denied that it ever held the men." (**SFR pg. 9-4**)

A former judge and congressman from Vietnam claims high officials in the Communist government told him they hold American prisoners.

A reporter/photographer in Kowloon, Hong Kong, in 1978, says Americans helping Vietnamese resistance soldiers were captured in 1977. (Several refugees have similar stories of Americans helping the resistance movement. **Kiss the Boys Goodbye**, deals with this subject in detail.)

A refugee in Malaysia in February 1979 says his lecturers in a reeducation camp claim Vietnam is holding American POWs who will not be released until the United States recognizes Vietnam. (There are several reports of a similar nature from other refugees. One specific camp, Ba Vi, will be examined later in the book)

From Paris France, in June 1978, a refugee says he knows the location in the U-Minh Forest where fifteen American officers were being held in spring, 1975. This refugee is different from all the previous ones examined.

Nguyen Cong Hoan, a congressional member of both the non-Communist and the Communist governments, says a North Vietnamese official stated, in June 1976, that "among the Americans listed as missing, there are some still alive in Vietnam." The DIA says (pre 1205 document) there was no information to substantiate this as unreturned POWs would contravene the 1973 Peace Accords.

A Laotian, in a sworn statement in 1978, says he has information concerning the capture of Captain Morgan Donahue in 1968. DIA dismisses out of hand Donahue's survival. (Reports about Donahue's survival continues through at least 1987. One account is in the "uncorrelated reports.")

Government officials reiterate, "Refugees ... from Vietnam are virtually the only ... source of information on possible alive Americans ... it is essential that all stations be alert for ... information Vietnamese refugees ... have."

A September 1978 refugee report from Malaysia is a Hanoi official told him American POWs are held in a "special" forbidden area outside Hanoi. The number of POWs estimated is more than one hundred. (For all the language skills in DIA and JCRC, it is interesting both passed on this refugee, Tran Ai Quoc or Tran the Patriot. It's an obvious play on Ho Chi Minh's revolutionary name, Nguyen Ai Quoc.) (This report coincides with the number of POWs in each 1205 POW camp.)

In October 1978, a source reports knowing about American prisoners in North Vietnam by reading a document issued by the Political Bureau of the 5th Military Region. All cadre and high ranking officials are asked not reveal information concerning Americans held in North Vietnam; it's a State secret. He has a copy of that memorandum. (JCRC did not follow-up for at least six months. The source writes he stills wants to help the families but is "not happy" with the US government.) Quang is a cadre in the 5th Military Region.

230 American POWs are reported by several individuals as imprisoned in Bat Bat, Son Tay Province in 1976. In October 1977, a Vietnamese doctor reports he treated these 230 prisoners; but eleven die. The remaining prisoners suffer from malnutrition. Bobby Garwood reports POWs in Bat Bat in this time frame.

One refugee reports from November 1977 to July 1978, he was incarcerated with forty-nine (49) POWs at Tan Lap prison, Vinh Phu Province. While there, two died, one in November 1977 and the other in May 1978.

Two refugees report seeing POWs in Haiphong prison. One recounts seeing two Americans in April 1977 and the other saw four in September. The two prisoners were sent to the prison hospital for treatment. Security guards reported they were being held to obtain aid from the United States.

Le Dinh, a defector in 1975, served in North Vietnamese intelligence. He reported considerable information on US POWs still detained in North Vietnam. Specifically, a synopsis available to me, says Dinh has information on 33 American pilots being held in Hanoi. Dinh also has intelligence information on the categorizing of US POWs during and after the war which apparently has a determining affect on who was returned and who was not.

One Laotian prisoner, who worked for the USAID in Laos, in late 1975 was stopped by Communist forces who found his USAID card. He was imprisoned in a camp "about 3 1/2 hours east of Aieng Xay." At this camp, were 5 Caucasians identified as Americans by guards. The Americans were still there when the source left the camp in 1976. (As we will see later, they were still prisoners in 1981)

1979: A turning point for some

1979 was a turning point for some officials. One reason are the refugee reports. I read most of the 1979 and earlier refugee reports. Officially, these reports are "uncorrelated," but two were used to help launch a rescue mission.

One refugee report proved to be significant. Giang answered an ad in a Vietnamese Magazine on October 23, 1978. Conversations took place between Giang and the League by "telephone, cables, and letter." The League "worked hard to have this refugee released to US. He is ... category 1, top eligibility, ... agrees to testify. DIA ... asked to stay clear until his arrival in US."

Giang was held with 49 Americans at Tan Lap Prison. His report was turned over to a House Subcommittee prior to their leaving for Vietnam in 1979. By August 1979, Giang was still not in the United States. General Tighe got involved on August 10 when he wrote to Secretary of Defense Harold Brown, "if the substance of Giang's information is true, then its importance goes without saying." The memorandum continued, at present Giang was ineligible to entry into the United States. Tighe appealed, "As reported, Giang's story of capture and confinement with Americans is plausible. His report agrees in some instances with confirmed information and yet there are some important discrepancies." To clear up those discrepancies, Tighe needs Giang.

Brown wrote to Secretary of State Cyrus Vance on August 17, saying that despite attempts by DIA to intercede with the State Department, Giang was still being denied entry. Vance was asked to help. He wrote back on September 17, "I share fully your desire to check the veracity of Mr. Giang's story ... the decision of the (INS) not to admit Mr. Giang ... consider approaching the Commissioner of Immigration to have the decision changed..." Turf battles aside, someone made the decision not to allow Giang in. He also had information confirming portions of the 1205 document.

Remember, Giang passed on previously "confirmed" information. DIA was never able to resolve the discrepancies. The discrepancies were not necessarily with Giang. If you know a fact and someone comes along and agrees with you on the fact you know and then brings up something you don't know, there is a discrepancy. It can be a discrepancy and still be true until the data base is updated reflecting the new situation, eliminating the discrepancy.

I learned more about Giang from files I obtained earlier. Tan Lap is a remote camp 100 kilometers west of Hanoi. Giang was captured in Laos in the early 1970's. He was in Tan Lap from 1973 - 1978. Tan Lap is also the location of my "dog-tag report." Bo Gritz interviewed Giang in a refugee camp. Tan Lap also generally corresponded where Bobby Garwood was held through 1979. Bobby told Tighe in 1987 about a prison camp where Americans captured in Laos were held. Quang told the Politburo some Americans captured in Laos were held in North Vietnam.

On May 17, 1979, Dornan asked a prophetic question of Robert B. Oakley, the State Department. Dornan said eighteen months prior, he met with Dr. Kissinger, and asked about the MIAs. In particular, he asked about Vietnam's knowledge of deceased MIAs. Kissinger said , "I resist using the word warehousing, but ... they have this information, if not in boxes of bones, warehoused, to be used for political purposes." Dornan asked Oakley if he had further information. Oakley said he did not know. Dornan pointed out Dr. Kissinger added, "Of course the Vietnamese have several hundred cases they could account for immediately."

Can't hide a good sighting forever

In August 1979, while in Hanoi, Bob Dornan received a significant story from a *CBS* journalist. Swedes working in the country knew about American POWs in a prison camp yelling at them as they passed by. The story is similar to one heard by millions in December 1980 concerning Swedes seeing POWS doing forced labor and yelling, "Tell the world about us." Remarkably similar in detail, they differ only in the nationality of one participant and the slogan yelled. DIA devoted much effort to debunk this particular story. They said the story, near the Swedish (**Bai Bang**) paper mill, was a fabrication.

I am not convinced it is bogus. When I contacted DOD in 1981, I was told an interview with the Swede produced nothing. Besides, the encounter actually occurred in *early 1978*. Trusted sources tell me DIA interviewed the wrong man.

On *March 10, 1978*, our embassy in Stockholm received a letter from someone in Sweden (the name was censored) concerning a relative of theirs working on a construction site (this name too was censored). The location was near **Bai Bang** . While on a trip near there, the relative came across a prison camp housing Americans. Fearing reprisals while the relative was still in the SRV, there could be no more specific information concerning the number of Americans or their location. Our State Department averred, "SRF had received similar information and is pursuing the matter." SRF is an intelligence arm in our State Department.

In one declassified report, a foreign diplomat traveling to a (censored) project near **Bai Bang**, saw, in 1977, a black person on a work detail. Keeping count on this one story, it was received by a Congressman, a Swede, our Embassy in Stockholm, the POW coordinator, and State Department intelligence several times. All the stories are similar, specific as to location and time. Sources say it is "common knowledge" that Swedes know about live Americans in the SRV.

Dornan took his report to DIA and went one step further. As he related to me in 1981, on October 29, 1979, he was in a one-on-one situation with President Carter at a reception. For a brief moment, standing eyeball to eyeball, Dornan asked Carter if he had knowledge about Americans being left behind in Southeast Asia. The President replied, no, he knew only about remains. President Carter, like General Tighe before him, will have a change of mind.

Dermot Foley wrote me **on April 23 1980**: "Dear Larry: Enclosed ... is a copy of a letter dated 6 August 1979 from Charles F. Trowbridge Jr., from DIA to the ...League... I also attach the various enclosures ... consisting of "Six case files providing information from Southeast Asian refugees regarding U.S. prisoners in SEA" ... regarded as very creditable ... this is the material which was given to Congressman Wolff ... prior to their trip to Hanoi last year ... quite obviously, if it was weak, it would ... detract from rather than enhance any arguments ... to the Vietnamese urging them to provide an accounting. These six cases, as you know, are the mere tip of the iceberg. **We ... have ... hundreds of DIA reports and DIA candidly admits that they are withholding many hundreds more**. I trust you will find this information useful ... Dermot Foley" (**Emphasis supplied**)

The important refugee with a big story

In November 1979, I became aware of an important refugee with vital information. I earlier wrote about Dornan's quotation from Dr. Kissinger concerning "warehousing" POW remains. Dornan included that in the original forward. Two days after a press conference, in January 1980, announcing the publication of my original book, a Congressional Subcommittee charged a "mortician" had proof of the warehousing of 452 remains in Hanoi. Loc is the "mortician" and I believe him to be a former "cadre" of importance.

Loc had information on both POWs and remains. He first testified on June 27, 1980, under oath. Before Loc's testimony, General Tighe testified that Loc had been polygraphed, thoroughly investigated, and DIA believed him totally. Loc testified that the SRV had warehoused over 400 remains the SRV could release immediately. He claimed all remains released to that time had come from this carefully preserved storehouse of American heroes.

Wolff's Congressional Delegation confronted the Vietnamese with evidence Loc furnished during his debriefings. The Vietnamese denied knowledge of the remains and refused the delegation permission to visit the building where the remains were stored because the building "was too far away." In reality, the delegation passed it on the way back to the airport. Months later, with great fanfare, the SRV allowed inspection. To no one's great surprise, the building was empty.

Controversy surrounds Loc's claim concerning the "452" remains. The Vietnam Veterans of America national leadership told me that they did not believe him. DIA would not tell them how the information was cross-checked. Greg Kane told me that it was part of a Chinese conspiracy to embarrass the Hanoi government.

The testimony directly contradicted Montgomery's estimate that Hanoi could account for only 100-150 remains. He told news sources he could end up with egg on his face. He asked DIA how valid was Loc's polygraph examination.

In April 1997, DOD publicly degraded Loc's sworn testimony when questioned about it by me in a public forum.

On September 30, 1987, Ann Griffiths was asked by Congressman Solarz in how many of the 2413 cases could the Vietnamese provide "meaningful information." Griffiths replied, "I would say surely on 200 plus that General Vessey took, plus a substantial number more... it is an impossible number to put a finger on." Mary McGrory, on the other hand, asked in August 1991 how the Vietnamese could account for MIAs if they knew nothing.

In 1994, a book was written by a former writer for the *Washington Times* debunking the idea MIAs are alive today. In 1992, DIA sponsored writers wrote about the "big dark secret" of Hanoi (all the men are dead).

Loc and MIAs - alive and dead

Loc's electric story was he processed and observed the remains of 452 MIAs. In addition, he saw POWs in captivity. Not everyone believed his story since it proved some POWs were alive. It also proved that the communists lied about the pace they could accomplish an accounting on MIAs.

On June 6, 1983, DIA replied to Montgomery. Loc was polygraphed twice. The first time was in Hong Kong, by non-DIA personnel. The results indicated skepticism about his processing American remains. Loc was brought to the United States and reexamined by DIA's PW/MIA experts and by a senior US mortuary specialist. He underwent a series of polygraph examinations. "The mortician responded to all questions with no indication of deception." DIA's letter continued, "Our assessment ... is not based solely on the polygraph results. Our investigation obtained other evidence that supports the validity of his claim to have observed the remains of American servicemen."

DIA located a former French military representative who verified that Loc helped regroup French remains. Loc brought with him several documents, believed genuine, pilfered from the communist files supporting his claim. In addition, an American delegation photographed Loc in Hanoi on March 6, 1974, performing technician duties during the ceremony turning over the remains of twelve American MIAs.

Loc last observed the remains at 17 Ly Nam De Street, a former POW camp, in mid-1977. DIA's letter concludes, "... our polygraph examination and the other evidence gives us complete confidence ... the mortician was truthful ... he ... personally observed the skeletal remains of ... 400 American servicemen in Hanoi... "

The story of Loc continues. Here, DIA does not agree with DIA and the League does not agree with the League. Loc's testimony, under oath, is significant because DIA believed him concerning the remains. Loc also testified seeing three or four American captives in Hanoi after 1973. This part of the testimony was not supposed to be made public. It took four years to emerge. I'll discuss these points from a personal perspective to keep confidential some people with whom I work.

My initial source, Jon Holstine, said Loc knew about live Americans. He did not elaborate. Eventually, through sources, I discovered that Loc presented detailed descriptions of the captives, so detailed that identification busts were made of them. Either Loc or DIA, a point in contention, had a 75% confidence factor in the identity of two men and a 50% confidence factor in the identity of the third.

The Loc controversy

Page 9 of a League booklet says "The mortician never spoke to the three, nor was he able to provide the US government with their names or other identifying data." This is an "Official, unclassified evaluation" of Loc.

A July 6, 1984 "Question and Answers Guideline", prepared by DOD for the League, said on page 2, "The mortician did provide us with information about ... Caucasians who he was told were Americans. However, we have been unable to independently verify this portion of his testimony."

On July 17, 1980, just after Loc testified, there was an Intergovernmental Agency forum conducted at the League Meeting. I was present when Loc was discussed. Government officials conceded Loc knew about live Americans. Yes, he gave detailed descriptions of the men. A State Department spokesman said the families "did not want to know what was known" about these men. The clear implication was they were "defectors." Besides, "It was classified."

The 6 July 1984 "Guidelines," added, "The mortician indicated that these Americans were not POWs in the classic sense. However, I should point out that the USG (government) does not characterize anyone who may be in Vietnam as being there of his own free (will) until all the facts are known."

The June 25, 1981 testimony of Tighe verified Loc identified these Americans.

Let's examine each phase of testimony by and about Loc. He testified on July 17, 1980. Three days earlier, I was told he was scheduled only to testify about remains. Trusted friends and I planted detailed questions with the Congressmen scheduled to question Loc. An exchange between Congressman Gilman and Loc made the following points. Loc observed three Americans under the Military Law jurisdictional area. This division took very special care of them. Loc first saw them in 1969, many times in 1970, and until 1974.

Digressing, the reader needs an appreciation of what I observed as the printed record does not reflect the red faces abounding then. Loc is questioned about items not on the official agenda. General Pickney, DOD, sitting on a raised podium waiting to testify, appears ready to break the pencil in his hand. His face looks livid. Admiral Jerry Tuttle of DIA is in the audience attempting to fade into his chair. Ed Palmer, Counsel for Democrats, is frantically shuffling between witnesses and Jon Holstine, Counsel for Republicans, pointing his finger saying, "Where are these questions coming from, Jon?" Jon throws his hands up in an "I don't know" signal. Prepared people sitting behind the Congressmen are half shouting questions. The audience realizes this hearing has become an unrehearsed give and take session.

Soon, Loc is excused as a witness "due to lack of time remaining." Congressmen follow him out of the hearing room. Inside, the "show testimony" continues. The families are now ready to confront some of the Executive Department witnesses in the forum discussed earlier. This ends round one of the Loc story.

Loc and live Americans

Round two came on June 25, 1981, when General Tighe testified the *persona vita* of Loc had been cross-checked and verified. His polygraph indicated that he was practicing no deception. **Tighe added that the allegation that the SRV was holding and maintaining over 400 sets of remains was judged to be valid.**

He added imperceptibly: "In addition ... I have a great deal of faith in the means ... we interrogated and cross-checked the testimony of the Undertaker who passed his tests for veracity on the remains issue, and **who also identified live Americans.**" (**Emphasis added**) This part got lost because only moments later he dropped his bombshell testimony that Americans were held captive in Southeast Asia.

Phase three of the Loc story came on March 22, 1983. I was told Loc saw these Americans much later than 1974. My sources insisted they were last seen in 1979. VADM Paulson, DIA, testified that Loc saw three "Americans" (accurately, DIA, except for Tighe, always calls them Caucasians) under circumstances indicating they were "not prisoners of war in the classic sense." He conceded they were "closely supervised." He acknowledged he could not eliminate the contention they were prisoners. He conceded "The last date of sighting was 1979." It took four years, and "friendly leaks," to get DIA to admit the truth.

Now for the cover-up or confusion of the highest order. The League publicized "facts" from "official" and "unclassified" sources. "... The mortician also reported sighting three Caucasians ... he was told were Americans ... on several occasions ... in Hanoi. Although ... in the company of Vietnamese personnel, there was no indication they were under guard or otherwise captives." (**pgs. 8-9 of League book**)

The July 6, 1984 "Guidelines" said, "the mortician indicated that these Americans were not POWs in the classic sense." The July 1983 "POW/MIA Fact Book" said, "In 1980, a Vietnamese mortician of Chinese ancestry told US officials ... remains of ... 400 Americans were warehoused in Hanoi.... the US Government believes the information ... is very credible." (**pg. 13**) There is no mention of POWs.

On January 25, 1980, Ann Griffiths received a DIA extract about Loc, "Source also reported seeing 3 Caucasians in ... **1979** at the facility where he was processing the American remains. He was told by the **guards** the three were **American prisoners** ... The 3 ... **were loosely guarded** while ... in the compound ... the source as credible." (**Emphasis added**)   (17 Ly Nam De St.)

I talked with Ron Paul, in the mid 1980's, who told me the Americans Loc saw were not defectors but Americans of a "special category." He added that there is reason to believe that the identities are known, but not verified.

In early 1980, approximately three weeks before Loc testified, I called General Tighe's office and asked about the three Americans and the identification busts mentioned earlier. I was told that DIA was aware of the information and immediately put on hold until another voice came asked my interest in the subject. He referred me to a PR Department. Here, I was told he would have to check out what he could tell me. He then said that he didn't want to probe, but that he thought that all this information was on a "close hold" basis with Congress. Two days later, he called back saying the material was classified and could not be released.

Solving the Mystery

In November, 1991, Garnett "Bill" Bell testified before a closed session of the Senate Select Committee on POWs saying based upon the detailed descriptions provided by Loc, he thought he could identify these POWs. In July, 1994, the National Vietnam Veteran's Coalition released four names, plus six others Bell believed survived. The four at the mortuary were: Kit Mark, Charles Duke Jr., Jimmy Malone, and Robert Garwood. Garwood also testified seeing POWs at the Mortuary. DIA disputed him. The other three were captured under circumstances dictating them being prisoners. DIA disputes their being captive at any time.

Also believed to be alive are: McKinley Nolan in 1974 in Cambodia (by 1978, Nolan a probable deserter, was written off as dead); Dallas Pridemore in Cambodia in 1974; Bennie Lee Dexter, 2 Caucasians and two blacks (names unknown) in Western Tayninh Province in 1974; and two (Edward Reilly and Clemie McKinney) whose remains have been returned. Pridemore, Dexter, and Reilly were three men on the 1987 list released by Congressman John Rowland, all as POWs.

In addition, Dexter was originally listed by DIA as being killed in 1966 and listed as a category 1 MIA; Pridemore was also listed as a category 1 MIA; Mark and Duke were listed as category 3 MIAs lost in 1970; Malone was listed as a category 4 MIA; Reilly was listed as a category 1 KIA (his remains were returned 4/27/89); and McKinney was listed as a category 4 USN pilot shot down and lost over the water in South Vietnam (his remains were returned on 8/14/85).

Finally, Dexter and Reilly were on a list in 1988 for whom negotiations were being made in Sweden. (See Chapter 11)

The saddest part is that in 1994, Mrs. Jane Duke Gaylor, 73, was arrested for demonstrating at the White House seeking information on her son, Charles Duke, Jr. She told reporters she was 73 and probably did not have another 23 years to wait for information on her son. All she wanted to do was to be able to hug and kiss him one more time. She lamented being "naive" in the early days and believing the government about her son.

Do any of the remains returned show tangible signs of verifying Loc's story? On July 14, 1994, in the *Wall Street Journal,* Barry Wain, editor at large of the *Asian Wall Street Journal*, wrote about Loc. In the 1990's, Wain reported, Vietnamese confirmed to our investigators that Vietnamese officials continued to warehouse remains well into the 1980's. Even though DIA said that Loc processed 452 remains and hundreds have been returned, many of those remains were non Caucasian and showed no signs of long-term care. The logical inference is that "Loc's" remains are still in Vietnam, awaiting the appropriate time to "surface."

Wain was skeptical of the assertion that Vietnam can rapidly account for hundreds of missing Americans. But after seeing official US documents he now believes it. According to Wain, over 180 identified remains returned by Vietnam have shown evidence of long-term storage including disinfectants and preservatives. This provides "hard evidence, confirmed by forensic scientists." DIA, according to Wain, estimates that between 435 and 560 remains could be returned immediately. The high number is consistent with an estimate that in Haiphong, several hundred other remains were known about by Loc.

In April 1997, attempting to discredit Loc, officials from DPMO told me a new evaluation of his information concludes that only a couple hundred remains are still part of what he saw. DIA asserted Loc "processed the skeletal remains of about 300 ... he observed an additional 100 remains ... processed by other technicians ... the ... polygraph examination and the other evidence gives us complete confidence ... (Loc) was truthful" about the 400+ remains in Hanoi.

If Loc's case doesn't constitute cover-up, incompetence, or debunking, then these words have lost all meaning. The **Final Report** conclusions on the return of remains have been proven to be erroneous. The one question remaining is do any of the remains show signs of torture, execution, or other maltreatment?

This chapter is called "Intelligence Cover-up" because refugee reports, communication intercepts, and POW debriefings were kept from MIA families.

The government becomes repugnant

Charles Darr was aboard a B-52 shot down near Thud Ridge, near Hanoi, on December 20, 1972. (**Hopper v. Carter**) The Air Force denied any knowledge of his fate. Using FOIA, however, Darr's wife obtained documents showing Darr was captured. She was an original plaintiff in *McDonald v. McLucas*.

The government possessed and classified part of their data base, known as the summary sheet, which contains MIA information derived from various sources. In Darr's case, one entry read a returnee, Ernest Moore, said the last known location and status of Darr was that he was a prisoner at the "Zoo." This prison was located in the Hanoi suburbs and was used primarily as a holding area for POWs captured after December 1971. A report dated December 14, 1977, stated that there had been an enemy statement regarding Darr. Witnesses reported hearing multiple beepers from the plane. One witness said the plane "was under control ... I'm convinced that all crew-members bailed out successfully..." He estimated the men should have landed on Thud Ridge, meaning almost instant capture. The same man reported hearing four to six beepers lasting at least five minutes.

Such information suppression leads to the issuance of a PFOD. In this case, DOD was unfriendly. Mrs. Darr was approached by Major Ed Silverbush, Air Force Casualty while a plaintiff in *McDonald*, a serious breach of judicial conduct. The offensive nature of this contact was repugnant. (*Hopper v. Carter*)

On August 27, 1974, Mrs. Darr and members of her husband's family met with Silverbush. They were told he was touring casualty offices and wanted to meet family members. The Darrs were the only family present. With Silverbush hostile and aggressive, the meeting became disturbing. Silverbush expressed disappointment Mrs. Darr came with members of her husband's family. He frankly stated he preferred to talk with wives alone since it was time for the wives to get on with their lives because there were no MIAs alive. He charged that the relatives of the men were obstructing the wives by delaying the status reviews. Mrs. Darr informed Silverbush there was no conflict in this family.

Silverbush then accused wives refusing to change the status of their husband, and supporting litigation like *McDonald,* with betraying their husband's organization. Silverbush was informed Mrs. Darr was a plaintiff in *McDonald*. Not slowing down, he discussed the trial with open hostility, claiming knowledge about Foley's trial strategy bordering on pure fantasy. Silverbush planned to do the same thing at other Air Force Bases, especially Blythesville AFB and Barksdale AFB. Only through the persistence of the families in pursuing an accounting have these instances of governmental misconduct been revealed.

Sixteen years after shoot down the remains of Charles Darr, Randall Craddock, Bobby Kirby, and George Lockhart were returned (12/15/88). One earlier set of remains, Ronald Perry were returned in 1975. One, James Lollar, returned in 1973. **(From various sources including Dermot Foley, litigator for *McDonald*)**

The best laid plans of mice and men

Sometimes attempts to squash speculation on reported sightings opens more questions than it answers. For example, in the Vang Pao case, the CIA said, "It is unlikely that his sources could have reported enough information to establish ... that they had actually seen Americans and not other nationalities ... dubbed 'Americans' for camouflage purposes." Who goes around Laos in the company of Vietnamese and Laotian troops disguised as American POWs? Russian advisers? Cubans? The CIA knows all the above as true.

The CIA claims Americans held by Laotians would not have the skills to defuse ordnance. Most would not. However, they might learn in exchange for better treatment, like not being beaten as often. POWs can hope their government didn't abandon them only so long before cutting the best deal available.

The Vietnamese had extraordinary skills in defusing ordnance and making it into booby traps. High-ranking former South Vietnamese military officers were used in the same areas to defuse ordnance. They were no more qualified than our men. One source of mine saw Vietnamese captives so being used in a location in South Vietnam. Perhaps the CIA confused the issue to hide some sleazy activities, like running drugs, for example.

Smith v. Reagan - New men step forward

On September 4, 1985, a class action suit was filed in the US District Court for the Eastern District of North Carolina. Called ***Smith v. Reagan***, it was filed by three Green Berets to force the government to seek a full accounting of MIAs, and release of POWs by means, short of war. The plaintiffs were members of a Special Forces outfit stationed in Korea who gathered POW information and cultivated foreign intelligence sources in Thailand and elsewhere.

This case attracted many persons with narratives of live POWs and the efforts to frustrate the POW/MIA movement. I filed an affidavit in this case. My particular information will be examined later.

LTC Robert L. Howard, a former SOG operative, was one plaintiff. The recipient of the Congressional Medal of Honor and recommended for it twice more, Howard had thirty years of active duty experience. From September 1983 to May 1984, he was in charge of a Special Forces team with responsibility for developing intelligence on sightings of POWs, remains, crash sites, material from crash sites, agent network reports, and personal contacts with foreign intelligence officers.

By May 1984, Howard was convinced Americans were prisoner in Laos, and possibly in Vietnam. He cultivated senior foreign officers. In furtherance of this aim, he went to a luncheon in his honor at Lop Buri, Thailand. With Howard was MAJ Mark Smith, SFC Melvin McIntire (both from Howard's unit), LTC Paul Mather (JCRC), COL Alpern (Military attaché in Thailand), the Commanding General of the Thai Special Forces Command, and four Special Colonels of the Thai Special Warfare Command.

Howard charges several things occurred then. His first allegation is Mather and Alpern compromised an intelligence source by openly revealing the relationship between his unit (SFD-K) and these Senior Thai officers. He asserted they openly revealed the Thai General provided information concerning live Americans. Howard affirmed the security breach was designed to undermine the suc-

gence gathering mission of the SFD-K concerning live POWs.

Howard confirmed one Senior Thai official told him about American POWs. Despite that security breach, Thai officials were still ready to help. Howard stayed an additional eight days. He participated in a training exercise believed designed to discredit his detachment. Specifically, he, Smith, and McIntire were in jeopardy of being killed or captured by a hostile force if the exercise went off as planned.

Fortunately, McIntire became suspicious about the mission. He concluded they were about to become engaged in an illegal border crossing into Laos. Howard declares that, subsequent to this exercise, he was officially accused of participating in an unauthorized cross-border activity. He believes the accusation was made to make the intelligence gathering of his forces more arduous. He affirms that POWs exist and that DIA deliberately ignored reports establishing that fact. He believes the number of POWs in captivity to be more than one hundred.

SFC Melvin McIntire spent from February 1982 through August 1984 with SFD-K. His mission was locating, identifying, and possibly rescuing POWs from Laos, Cambodia, and Vietnam and recruiting agents. His direct orders were to renew contacts; establish new contacts; and verify or deny live POWs existing in Southeast Asia. To establish this agent net, he traveled every sixty to ninety days on ten day trips. In ninety days, he gathered intelligence reports showing live POWs.

His next step was to cross-check the information for corroboration while eliminating receiving the same information more than once from the same source. His superiors ordered him back for more information. His sources were distrustful of both DIA and CIA and felt there was corruption in the refugee program and in JCRC. McIntire developed ten sources he considered to be credible and reliable ranging from drug smugglers to the highest level of a foreign military power.

McIntire verified live POWs from these sources while charging that DIA, CIA, and others discredited his agent reports though developing through their own sources the same information. McIntire estimated about two hundred POWs in captivity.

We could have extracted live POWs

McIntire reported in 1983 that it was possible to extract live POWs from Laos. It took time to coordinate movements. By January 1984, his sources believed two prisoners could be extracted by May. McIntire relayed this information to his superiors. His reward was being personally debriefed by the 501st MI Group, told to remain in country, and cease activities in Thailand. Additionally, in August 1984, he was sent back to the United States six months before his normal rotation time. Through a prearranged set of communications, McIntire received additional information concerning live POWs. This information he forwarded to MAJ Smith.

McIntire took intelligence reports, memorandums for record, and source information relating to live POWs and showed them to three different organizations in the United States. He later received direct orders to destroy vital POW intelligence. After attempting to work within channels, McIntire returned with Smith to Southeast Asia to keep the project alive. In mid-1985, McIntire received information about sixteen POWs, two of whom were in a position to be repatriated.

This information was relayed to DIA. By September, DIA had not yet debriefed him. McIntire believes no one in government cares about the POWs.

A POW helping other POWs

MAJ Mark Smith received a battlefield commission from General William Westmoreland in 1968. In 1972, he was captured and held prisoner until repatriated in 1973. His medals include the Distinguished Service Cross, the Silver Star, nine awards of the Bronze Star, four awards of the Purple Heart.

Smith, detachment commander of SFD-K since 1981, had the intelligence mission of gathering information on Korean, Thai, and Asian special operations groups of interest to the United States. The subject of POWs came up in July, 1981. Smith was approached by a Thai General Officer about LTC James "Bo" Gritz. The General said Gritz's information about POWs supported information from his forces. This was at the time "Fort Apache" was being reconned for a rescue mission.

Smith's personal opinion then was there were no live prisoners and so told the General. Smith then received a complete briefing of known and suspected locations of POWs. All were in Laos. The General avowed this intelligence was gathered mainly through efforts of Thai reconnaissance teams. The General inquired if Smith had a secure channel for intelligence to the United States bypassing the Embassy, CINCPAC, and JCRC. Smith was assured POW facts would continue as long as sources were protected. Smith communicated with DIA and was assured that no one in the Embassy in Bangkok would be informed of the identities of his sources. From then until April 1984, Smith traveled every sixty to ninety days to his agent network consisting of Lao, Free Vietnamese, and Thai personnel. Although "chartered," Smith was plagued by compromises of sources including a Lao agent being shot by Vietnamese. After this, Smith attempted to bypass normal American military intelligence channels.

In less than a year, Smith was convinced POWs existed. He came to this conclusion by checking reports from fifty agents, cross matching corroborating information, and weeding out possible double reports from the same sources.

Forget the POWs

In April 1984, Smith received word three American POWs were available for repatriation. When this information was made available to a certain US Major General, the 501st MI Group, and to the CIA in Seoul, Smith was told that all SFD-K operations to Thailand or to Southeast Asia were terminated and unauthorized. SFD-K was to have no further role in developing POW information. He was told if he had any desire to make his next promotion, he would forget the POW/MIA information developed.

Smith was further told it would be smart of him to put through a paper shredder a folder entitled "Possible American/Allied POWs in Southeast Asia, dated 10 April 1984." He was ordered that under no circumstances would he be permitted to see a certain General Officer in Washington, D.C. about this matter. (**See chapter 11 for further information**) Smith corroborated the story of Howard and McIntire about the training mission in December 1983. He joined a training mission with Thai troops to "infiltrate," by parachute, "aggressor" territory.

Smith and his group were leery of this mission. The USAF crew had received orders from the Command Center at Clark Air Force Base to change the original flight plan. This caused McIntire to recalculate where they were going. If the mission had come off as planned, the participants would have landed approximately twenty miles inside Laos. This training exercise of "infiltration of an aggressor nation" had Thai troops fully combat loaded. MAJ Smith said, "The significance of this operation ... was ... all factors clearly indicated that someone, ... given a green light for ... Laos, ... the Thai military ... were prepared ... the US Air Force ... received ... instructions ... to fly ... and the aircraft ... a stealth type aircraft clearly intended to facilitate the infiltration in Laos in a clandestine manner without informing either myself, SFC McIntire, or LTC Howard."

I saw POWs

To bolster their claims of live POWs, Smith surfaced an informant. The man's name (fictitious) is John Obassy, a resident of Southeast Asia since 1967, who saw live POWs. He was an "entrepreneur and government contractor" with experience in Vietnam, Laos, Cambodia, China, and other Asian countries. He financed, distributed, and personally administered medical relief to the hungry, sick, and wounded in Communist controlled areas. He became a target of opportunity for our intelligence. He spurned their advances because of not being in accord with the "CIA and American foreign policy in that region then." In addition, DIA and DEA attempted to recruit him. He added, as a businessman engaged in imports and exports, "I did not want to get involved with ... CIA. I had my own business ..."

To finance his humanitarian efforts, he bought precious metals and stones from the free-Lao and sold them on the international market. During this activity, he saw the POWs, first in 1976-78. He described "Americans who I presumed were doing similar activities as mine ... I now know that these Americans were former prisoners of war because ... members of the American intelligence community confronted me with photographic evidence of my presence ... with these Americans in Laos. I was informed ... these people were in fact prisoners of war.... I personally spoke to these people (prisoners) who confirmed to me that they had been left behind. There were approximately twenty to thirty ... in different areas that I talked to. They were afraid to leave their sanctuary areas in Laos. I was ... shown by the free-Lao, sites or camps which had male Caucasian ... prisoners — some were in chains ... heavily guarded by Vietnamese... also guarded by other nationalities. I estimate ... nine of the prisoners were Caucasians and that forty to fifty ... were North Americans. I did not ... speak ... because of the extreme security measures involved.... these prisoner details were all mining for gold."

Obassy said the last time he saw these men was in October 1985. The number of men in the work detail was thirty-nine.

Obassy decided to get involved and went to a US embassy official "personally known" to him and gave the person a seven page report, a three page attachment, twenty-two photos, and told him that these men could be extracted if an "immediate extraction operation were mounted." Obassy said "I personally took these photos in Southern Laos, and I provided specific grid locations where these people were located... I gave this information thinking that immediate action would be taken, but instead I was offered immediate employment by the CIA."

Obassy said that this employment was not related to prisoners and would have removed him from his contacts and opportunities to travel freely throughout Laos. When he declined, his reputation suffered "... my personal life and my economic well being. Since 1980, I did not report ... information to the US Embassy because of the lack of interest in the information ... I had reported earlier."

Obassy meets Smith - extraction told possible

John Obassy first met Mark Smith in December, 1980. Smith was given Obassy's name at CINCPAC. Obassy said that Smith was given his name because "I was considered to be the only positive source with current knowledge on the subject of live prisoners of war." Obassy was Smith's source from then to 1984 providing "current information ... about ... my trips into Laos and ... prisoners ... I ... told Major Smith that I was to remain anonymous ... if ... approached by any other person... on this subject that I would immediately end our relationship."

Obassy responded to Smith because "he was a former American prisoner of war and hopefully would respond." Since Smith was skeptical about live POWs, Obassy introduced him to a senior Thai General, a personal friend. Obassy avowed "... I was present with Major Smith and this Senior Thai Officer when ... American POWs was being discussed " and intelligence confirmed their existence.

In May 1984, Smith was told three POWs could be released if the communist criteria could be met; "... a set of conditions ... agreed ... by the American government... endorsed by a third government ... an exchange would be made ... if political asylum was given to certain members of the Laotian communist government... Major Smith would ... receive these prisoners. I ... made the actual contacts with the Free-Lao" Obassy said. Smith said this extraction was known by a "code word" given to him by the Senior Thai General. This extraction, when known to the US government, caused SFD-K activities to be closed down. In **Kiss the Boys Goodbye**, it was related that when the three were brought to the border, no U.S. officials were there. The prisoners were returned and one died. (**pg. 96**)

Smith, McIntire, and Howard were charged with an illegal border crossing in the December training exercise. All were found innocent. Pressure was put upon investigators to find them guilty and ruin their credibility. Tracy Usury served in the Army Criminal Investigation Command (CID) before Senators Jesse Helms and Charles Grassley appropriated him for their POW/MIA investigation. He testified before the Senate Veteran's Affairs Committee in Minnesota on February 7, 1991. He was asked if the government "acted improperly to intimidate, coerce, or discredit sources which have valid information concerning living POWs..."

In his prepared statement, Usury said "It is the staff's position that the answer is YES." He cited an example. "During the period 1984 through 1986, while ... in the ... Criminal Investigation Command, I was the Investigating Officer in which MAJ. (Ret.) Mark Smith levied allegations against certain military officers who ... failed to take appropriate action concerning information provided ... on possible live American POWs being held in Laos. ... there was pressure placed on me, by superiors, to gather evidence discrediting MAJ. Smith, rather than to pursue the allegations made by Smith...During the ... investigation, ... I found ... one instance, Smith's source ... was deliberately compromised by ... the Defense Attaché's Office ... The normal investigative process was not allowed ... to prevent potential embarrassment to an Army general; statements ... concerning Smith's mission ... omitted ... information... giving the impression ... Smith was acting without authority ... his chances for promotion violated through ... manipulation...."

Usury ended, "... after the fact, Smith's superiors did take steps to determine if Smith's information was valid; however, ... Smith was so disgusted ... he ceased cooperating with the Army." Smith eventually went back to Asia to continue his quest on POW information. In July 1994, he appeared on the AIM television program, "The Other Side of the Story." There he claimed the Vietnamese military was prepared to release 572 Americans held in Laotian prison camps. These men were dumped there by Hanoi after President Clinton abandoned the economic embargo. Their orders were to dispose of them. Rightly fearing retribution for war crimes, the army commanders sought other ways of getting rid of them, including giving them to the United States. **(AIM Report, August, 1994)**

Finally, John Richard Taylor, a former Assistant G-3 (Air) in Headquarters, 7th Air Force, affirmed that in early 1972, while assigned to "Blue Chip" at Tan Son Nhut, his unit had intelligence confirming 30 - 34 POWs near Cambodia. Some of these POWs were American. "A mission was planned to make an extraction of American POWs at this particular camp. We had ... confirmed this as well as the exact location of this camp... the mission to extract and rescue American POWs was called off. A senior USAF General Officer ... specifically told me the mission ... had been called off by 'Washington' because 'Henry was negotiating.'"

Deceit by government officials?

The implications of a cover-up are there for all to see. There are other examples we'll examine as we come to the end of this section of "Intelligence Cover-up," a prelude to the next chapter, "Deceit and Cover-up." On October 9, 1985, Robert McFarlane, then National Security Advisor, addressed an industrial group in Washington, D.C. in an "off the record" session. In the audience were former Congressman John LeBoutillier and John L. Thorton, an investment banker. These two made a tape of McFarlane's POW / MIA comments. I saw a transcript of the recording. McFarlane was asked how he felt personally about the POWs: "How I really feel ... there have to be live Americans ... a lot of evidence given by people who have no ulterior motives ... they're telling things they have seen."

I have been at many "off the record" briefings by senior officials. Their reflections are closer to the truth than in other forums. At a similar gathering, I learned from a former Air Force Chief of Intelligence that the combat ready Soviet training division in Cuba was known to every President from Kennedy on. This was contrary to the public position then being presented.

In early summer 1985, USN CPT (Ret.) Eugene "Red" McDaniel, a former POW and Chairman of the American Defense Foundation swore in an affidavit to a 1985 conversation he had with Richard Childress: "I specifically recall ... receiving a telephone call from Mr. Childress ... which lasted approximately one hour, Mr. Childress and I discussed the POW/MIA problem... I specifically asked ... if he thought we had Americans still ... in captivity ... He responded ... 'you're damn right I do.' I recall also discussing what was being done ... Mr. Childress told me that he specifically briefed the President on the POW/MIA issue." and "we would expect to get some ... back... in two or three years." McDaniel answered "... in my opinion, that was too long, that we were running out of time."

If these two statements, made by responsible officials with access to POW/ MIA intelligence, do not verify a cover-up, then the word does not exist. I am reminded, in Arizona in 1974, I was in the campaign of Robert Corbin, the former Attorney General. He had just finished addressing a group of supporters. A small group of us went back to Corbin's hotel room. Corbin told each of us that if he ever took a position different out of the public eye, than he advocated publicly, then his advice was to support someone else. I reminded him of this conversation in 1990. He still felt the same way. This is public trust of the highest order.

One more honest man steps forward

In deciding the format of the rest of the book, I feel the don't hold anything back approach is best. Courts have been tried. Investigations have been tried. I've personally picketed the White House. I've worked in the system. Now is the time for the best shot approach. Why?

The late COL Nick Rowe wrote his greatest fear was dying forgotten in a POW camp. The well known cartoon character, "Sgt. Mike," made post fighting appearances in POW/MIA publications. In one, he is marking days, and years, upon his cell's rock wall, saying if someone did not care soon, even he would forget he was a POW. This cartoon appeared in 1973!!

Why is the government hiding information? One reason could be that the government did things it wishes to keep secret. Possibly the government wants to protect "code-word" operations currently in progress. Some have "more important things" to worry about, cushy jobs, pensions, kids to educate, than routine things like how many bugs are in the rice and "why has my government forgotten me." In trying to establish things like relationships with Hanoi, China, and campaign contributions, they have forgotten mundane subjects like the POWs.

Probably, all of this is true. In the last version, I wrote, "Government bureaucrat, and retired officers, think about what you know and contemplate this paragraph." One officer decided honor came first. COL Millard Peck resigned as Chief of the Special Office for Prisoners of War and Missing in Action on 12 February 1991. He explained, "... the job was highly contentious and extremely frustrating... no one would volunteer ... because of its complex political nature.... I had heard the persistent rumors of American servicemen ... abandoned in Indochina ... a 'cover-up' ... I was curious ... and thought ...serving as the Chief ... would be an opportunity to ... help clear the Government's name."

Peck heard this office described as the "black hole" where reports disappeared. He was intrigued by the fact that eighty-three percent (83%) of active duty military personnel felt that live prisoners existed. He added, "worse yet was the implication that DIA's Special Office for POWs ... was an integral part of this effort ... to not embarrass the Government...." He volunteered to prove the critics wrong.

"My plan was to be totally honest and forthcoming ... aggressively pursue innovative actions ... to clear up the live sighting business, ... refurbishing the ... honor of DIA. ... I was not really in charge of my own office, but ... whipping boy for a ... Machiavellian group ... outside of DIA. What I witnessed, ... could be euphemistically labeled as disillusioning." The promise to address the POW/MIA issue as the "highest national priority" was a "travesty." People created "manufactured crises" of "little substance and no real results... the mind-set to 'debunk' is alive ... and continues to pervade the POW-MIA office, which is not necessarily the fault of DIA."

He found that analysis was done to find fault with the source; leads were not pursued; and efforts to pursue leads were cut off by "busy work" tasks from other areas. He said that "a number of these grandiose endeavors bordered on the ridiculous, and — quite significantly — there was never an audit trail." "There was, and still is, a refusal by any of the players to follow normal intelligence channels in dealing with the POW-MIA office."

DUTY - HONOR - INTEGRITY - Gone?

Peck said "... the entire issue is being manipulated by unscrupulous people in ... or associated with the government. Some ... for personal or political advantage and others ... as a forum to ... feel important, ... this issue is being controlled and a cover-up may be in progress. The entire charade does not appear to be an honest effort, and may never have been."

He called it strange that an intelligence office became a "lightning rod" for people to strike out at, a "toxic waste dump" to bury the whole "mess" out of sight and mind. He charged that persons outside of DIA really ran the whole show. He then accused what others had mouthed — the League was a government shill, especially the Executive Director.

On the subject of Griffiths, he said "One wonders who she really is and where she came from;" a supposedly uncleared person seeing "top secret, code-word message traffic... ahead of the DIA intelligence analysts.... she is adamantly opposed to any initiative to actually get to the heart of the problem, ... interferes in or actively sabotages POW-MIA analyses or investigations... Her influence in 'jerking around' everyone and everything ... goes far beyond the 'war and MIA protester gone straight' scenario."

He stated, "In some respects,... I have managed to satisfy my curiosity... From what I have witnessed, ... any soldier left in Vietnam, even inadvertently, was, ... abandoned years ago, and that the farce ... being played is ... political legerdemain done with 'smoke and mirrors', to stall the issue until it dies a natural death."

Not so cryptically, he told his superiors "So as to avoid the annoyance of being shipped off to some remote corner, ... in my own 'bamboo cage' of silence somewhere, I further request that the Defense Intelligence Agency, ... assist me in being retired immediately from active military service."

On May 30, 1991, he told Congress: "In closing, let me reiterate three points: a. Accountability - Accountability of remains will not necessarily solve the live-sighting question... accounting for the remains... we will never know exactly what happened to them... b. Normalization - Normalization will cost us all of our leverage... the game is over, and short of a new war, we will never have the opportunity to learn the truth. This is a fleeting window of opportunity and we don't want to be the ones to close it... c. Golden Opportunity - ...We have an historical opportunity to ...clear up doubt about a lingering question... a great opportunity... to close ranks and work together... to secure not only the truth... but bring a lasting and viable Pax Americana - on our own terms - throughout this troubled region..."

Even though I have never met the man, I can only add that this is a fitting ending to this chapter of "Intelligence Cover-up" and a great way to preview the next chapter, "Deceit and Cover-up."

Deceit and Cover-up

During the Vietnam War, U.S. Studies and Observation Group personnel (known as SOG or Special Operations Group), operated in Laos, North Vietnam and Cambodia. Their missions would include planting sensors along the Ho Chi Minh Trail; verify enemy positions in Laos, Cambodia, or North Vietnam; locate and cut enemy POL (petroleum, oil, and lubrication) lines; or rescue POWs. Many times, these patrols were able to return with few people knowing what they had done.

On at least four occasions, however, the personnel were not lucky. These units, a combination of indigenous and American personnel, were discovered by North Vietnamese forces. In the ensuing fire-fights, these patrols became surrounded. They radioed for help. Ordinarily, this would bring a rescue attempt. On these four occasions, however, the response from headquarters was quite different.

We were not officially operating in Laos, Cambodia, or North Vietnam. In 1970, President Nixon said publicly we lost no men in ground combat in Laos. Now, the command was faced with the possibility of covert operations exposed to public scrutiny. Congress might specifically prohibit these "covert operations."

A decision was made to napalm our own forces. The men were subsequently listed as missing in action. Their losses were never acknowledged. In 1979, when I first wrote this, I had few clues to work with. I knew these operations occurred. My contacts had access to details. The more I probed, the more I learned about covert activities outside my own program (the Phoenix program).

Successful covert operations require compartmentalization, called the "need to know." Having a Top Secret clearance, does not allow you to see all the documents at that classification level. You see and learn details because your job performance requires that you "need to know" certain facts to get your task done.

In 1979, when I first wrote just about the cross-border activities and the napalming, I was attacked by government agents probing where I obtained my information. When I refused to tell, they said I was indulging in the "myths" of Vietnam. By 1986, I had learned about SOG and it's various names of CCN, CCS and CCC - Command and Control - North, South, and Central.

Now, I have learned of other intelligence collection programs known as Oak, Pine, Black-Beard, Gunboat, Rapid Shave, Bent Axle, Nantucket, Corral, Sunshine Park, Vesuvius I, Big Mack, and others. In addition, I have learned of agencies such as SACSA, TRU, C.E.E.A., SRF, OSA, and others. Some of their functions involved intelligence on POWs/MIAs. I know we planned rescue missions and offered rewards for information on our POWs. These rewards led to the successful extraction of allied POWs and just missed getting our own men.

My own program, Phoenix, had as one of its top missions, the location of prisoners, both Americans and allied. This was collateral to our function of identifying the VC party functionaries whose job it was to hold the men prisoner. Among our essential elements of information or EEI, was finding the location of any American, Vietnamese, or Allied POWs. Special intelligence collection requirements or SICRs were used with the EEI to direct operatives in collecting information. They provided the guidance on where to employ assets to gather that information.

On the cross-border operations, the decision to napalm our own men was possibly wrong. Some say it never happened or it was called in by the SOG personnel in trouble. In the case of Lima Site 85 or channel 97, we napalmed it. Why? To have "plausible deniability" of operations in Laos. The decision for us "not to be there" when Vietnam built major highways for transporting troops and supplies lead to major US casualties and was a huge political and diplomatic blunder.

When Phou Pha Thi fell, the other side made not a peep. The news media heard about the fall of the site, but few persons would comment on it. We had numerous documents concerning the subject. For example in January 1969, the CIA learned that prisoners of one Pathet Lao prison were harangued about "Pathet Lao Forces were defeating the Royal Lao government ... and at Phou Pha Thi, 500 Royal Lao Government soldiers and 20 Americans were killed ... radar equipment was captured (sic)." The guards likewise probed their prisoners about: * The presence of Thai soldiers in Laos and the possibility of training of Lao soldiers in Thailand; * The presence of American soldiers in Laos; and * The possibility of a military entry into Laos by President Johnson or Vice President Humphrey

Each side had secrets. The decision to bomb our troops was not unique to this war. People were expendable if the mission so required. Most times, the decision was necessary. Sacrificing men, however, to uphold some "gentlemen's agreement" is ludicrous. A government capable of ordering men napalmed in wartime is capable of deceiving our nation about MIAs being held prisoner.

Let's look at the secrets

This chapter will delve into official deceit and subsequent cover-up. Dermot Foley caught on quick to certain types of deceit since he had excellent sources. His probing in **Hopper v. Carter** was not random. Helping in some of his research enabled me to understand his leading. In the following exchange, Shields was asked about what provisions were made to ensure the sensitive and secret material carried aboard aircraft did not fall into enemy hands. The enemy copied circuits, circuitry, and anything else they could not manufacture on their own.

Mr. Foley: Were any EA-6Bs in use?

Dr. Shields: I think that the AWACs has not been used anywhere (1978)... (Note: E-3A AWACs had flown though)

Mr. Foley: ... were provisions ... made that the sensitive equipment on those planes would not fall into the hands of the other side, even if there was a casualty?

Dr. Shields: I think extreme measures would ... (be) taken.

Mr. Foley: Were they not, in fact, taken?

Dr. Shields: ... I am sure that extreme measures were taken ... The C-47 is a very old aircraft. You could put a lot of sophisticated equipment —

Elaine Buck: ... What is the purpose of this ... testimony?

Mr. Foley answered, "He knows where I am going." The immediate purpose was to expose the expected reaction from the command structure if a sophisticated plane went down carrying highly secret electronic warfare and surveillance equipment. Several were shot down and MIA casualties occurred.

Mr. Foley: What measures were taken to see to it that the equipment didn't fall in enemy hands?

Dr. Shields: ... There are several things you could do.

Elaine Buck: I object... If he has no knowledge ... I see no relevance.

Mr. Foley: ... he knows what I am talking about.

Closing in on another "Secret"

Dr. Shields: ... one way ... You could simply put it in air strikes... if you thought there was some equipment that might be compromised, you could put in individuals to blow that equipment up. (In the EC-47 case, eye witnesses said that after the American para-rescue personnel left the site in 1973, they watched the plane burn even more intensely than before the Americans arrived.) .... if there were sensitive equipment concerned which could be duplicated... the precautions would be taken....

Mr. Foley: You are aware of ... the AC-130? ...

Dr. Shields: ... it was a gunship... it flew ... night missions to intercept materiel coming down the Ho Chi Minh Trail. That is all I know ...

Mr. Foley: Are you aware of any policy with respect to the destruction of that aircraft, if it went down?

Dr. Shields: All I think is what you told me about an article that was written...

Mr. Foley: Where would one go to get information ...

Dr. Shields: The Chairman of the Joint Chiefs of Staff ....

Mr. Foley: ... you testified ... some kind of definite steps would be taken, ... you did not know what they were.

Dr. Shields: Well, when you said sensitive or sophisticated or secret, and ... on occasion we would bomb our personnel carriers ... or trucks, ...when they were overrun. ... keep the materiel from falling into the hands of the enemy.

Mr. Foley: ... there is no higher priority than just the destruction of stuff that —

Dr. Shields: ... a lot of the equipment was destroyed to prevent it from falling into the hands of the enemy, ... I would assume it to be more sensitive or sophisticated equipment. (Dr. Shields referred to an article in a service newspaper (Fred Reed "Spectre", **Times Magazine**, April 3, 1978) about the AC-130 or Spectre. Reed said it was one of the great untold stories of the Vietnam War: "Spectre is the legendary night-fire gunship ... a lumbering cargo plane turned into a dark killer. The military has only recently loosened the security wraps. Gunships were so secret that if one was shot down — only a half dozen were — command sent a fighter to bomb the wreckage.")

I confirmed, through my sources, the command policy to bomb downed AC-130s so that the aircraft was destroyed and the equipment decimated. The official list of MIAs confirms a half-dozen downed AC-130s with a loss of over fifty MIAs. The emphasis seemed to be more on equipment destruction and less on the fate of those who manned the planes.

The AC-130 first emerged in 1967. Former Air Force Commander GEN William Momeyer said, "At first, I was quite skeptical about the advertised capability of the aircraft to kill trucks... however, the results more than confirmed the advertised potential. (**AP pg. 211**) Initial ships were armed with two 7.62 mm and four 20 mm guns ...used in operation **TIGER HOUND**... The Pave Aegis carried a 105 mm gun. Onboard sensors included Low Level TV (LLTV), infrared (IR), and radar. Later sensors included laser designators to pinpoint targets and direct bombs towards them. By **COMMANDO HUNT V**, late 1970, AC-130s were knocking out 4 times as many trucks ... as the B-57." (**CORONA HARVEST**) This state of the art electronics dictated the command policy of bombing crash sites.

The Thomas Hart affair

In February 1985, our government was allowed to excavate an AC-130 crash site in Laos. Fourteen men were aboard the plane. One returned to American control, leaving thirteen MIAs. The excavation "determined" all thirteen MIAs were positively identified. Officially their cases were closed 2/21/85.

On August 9, 1985, Anne M. Hart, wife of LTC Thomas T. Hart III, MIA, filed an affidavit in *Smith v. Reagan* concerning the downing of this AC-130. She previously refused to accept the remains of her husband from the excavation because of certain case irregularities. LTC Hart served in the Air Force from 1960 to 1978 when he was officially declared dead from his December 21, 1972 crash. Shortly after the crash, Mrs. Hart was notified that her husband was MIA and received several contradictory reports about the crash. Later, she served the League as Vice-Chairman. She made a trip to the Pakse crash site (her husband's) in 1982.

The "biographic report" contained in government computers contains "all" correlated material connected to the MIA in extract form. This extract was supposedly made available to the families. Mrs. Hart said the following evidence given to her in July 1983 shows her husband survived the crash.

On the night of the crash, a Pathet Lao Officer heard a low-flying aircraft explode in the air and later heard the ground impact explosion. A squad from his battalion found five parachutes with their canopies deployed. Of the five parachutes, two were charred. The next morning, another search was made. Partial remains of several individuals were found along with two small piles of bloody bandages. No remains of entire bodies were found. The partial remains were buried near the nose section and were estimated to represent at least five or six men.

A July 1973 report stated an "evader symbol," with the numbers 1973 or 1573 and the letters "TH," was found near the crash site. It was believed that the numbers were the year or an authentication number, while the letters indicated a person's initials. **"This was thought to be Captain Hart**;" declared the biographic report of **James Ray Fuller**. Mrs. Hart first saw it in 1983! After the excavation at Pakse, the government declared all thirteen MIAs "identified;" their remains recovered and returned to families. (Photo at www.angelfire.com/ma2/georgemacdonald/)

A companion exhibit to Mrs. Hart's affidavit was a declaration of Michael Charney, a Ph.D. in Anthropology and a forensic anthropologist. His credentials include being an Emeritus Professor of Anthropology and Affiliate Professor of Zoology at Colorado State University. In addition, he is the Director of the Center of Human Identification and the Director of Forensic Science Laboratory at Colorado State University. Outside the University setting, he is a qualified expert in forensic anthropology in murder, abortion, and paternity cases and a recognized expert in the field of human identification.

Charney examined the documentation provided by CIL on the alleged remains of LTC Hart. He also examined the bone fragments identified as the "remains" of Thomas Hart. He declared, "based upon said examinations and upon my experience, ... it is scientifically impossible to identify said bone fragments as the mortal remains of any individual. ... are from the same individual or from several individuals, or to tell the sex, age, height, weight, race, or right or left-handedness of the individual ... from which any or all of the fragments may have come."

He concluded, "... the findings of the United States Army Central Identification Laboratory, Hawaii, ... are highly speculative and unreliable. It is impossible to determine whether these fragments are from LTC Hart or ...whether they are even from any of the crew members of the AC-130A aircraft in question."

Mrs. Hart provides an anecdote to the Pakse affair giving an insight into governmental absurdity in MIA cases. While Anne was at the Pakse crash site, she was given small bone fragments. CIL later identified them as human remains. In 1985, Mrs. Hart received the purported remains of her husband and the associated documentation. CIL identified those same two bone fragments as belonging to LTC Hart. A coincidence or attempted shock effect?

The inanity does not end here. This Spectre 17 case was evidence in the Montgomery Hearings, including the previously mentioned report on open canopies. The summary ended: "In addition ... there have been several others that relate to the Spectre 17 downing ...." A letter from Dr. Roger Shields, dated June 3, 1976, contained another comment concerning the cited bandages. The Pathet Lao political cadre stated, "**Those who were alive** must have bailed out prior to the impact." The report continued, "Although the source stated that the items located were bloody bandages, ... this was merely the opinion of this man. The possibility exists that the items were parts of the parachutes or clothing of some of the crew-members who were involved in the incident." (**Emphasis added**)

Rush to judgment - Hart Case

The government presented a story of death with credibility given to the story except for the part about possible survivors. They did **not** present to the Committee the classified report showing an evader symbol was found. Other important material apparently escaped their notice. A person present at the Pakse crash site told me that coming in by air towards the site, there is a noticeable swath in the trees extending for some 3 - 4 kilometers, ending at the impact area. At the impact area is the nose section with no evidence of bomb craters. A scenario emerges.

An explosion in midair immediately leads to two men exiting the plane, one voluntarily and one blown out by the blast. As the plane goes down, more men are able to evacuate. The plane disintegrates while cutting through the trees. The parts left at the impact site are not large enough to engage command policy of bombing AC-130 crash sites. Equipment is littered all over the countryside.

The next day, an indigenous friendly force goes to the crash site and recovers the arm of one man. He is identified by fingerprints. Hostile fire causes this team to retire early. The report of charred parachutes is consistent with men exiting a plane with encroaching flames. The bloody bandages is also consistent. Finding only a few bones at the crash site indicates either only a few remains were at this site or it was "**salted**." LTC Hart probably survived, leaving an "evader symbol."

Those who wonder how we find out

Some readers wonder how Dermot Foley questioned a former government official about incidents not yet made public. The government often asks that question. Someone wondered how he received his information. Someone made surreptitious attempts to obtain information from his MIA files. Foley anticipated such attempts and took steps to protect the information. The government's night operations, including kicked in office doors, proved fruitless.

The same is wondered about this book. Some material is "classified" or "privileged." Few have read the CHECO report on Phou Pha Thi. Few have read as many details as you have in this book. A CIA Director, testifying in a closed session, had a book called **Missing in Action: Trail of Deceit** placed upon the table in front of him and was told, "read this, you might learn something." A DIA

Director received a phone call three weeks before a key witness testifies and is told what he is going to testify about. The DIA tells a researcher for *60 Minutes* they have debriefed Bobby Garwood. A DIA Deputy Director asks this author, in late 1986, please tell us what he tells you, we have not debriefed him yet!

Because of reports in this book, certain people take an extraordinarily acute interest in the traveling habits of myself but others I know. For example, in 1985, I took a quick trip to North Carolina to file my affidavit in *Smith v. Reagan*. Caution was taken to make sure I met the right people. Photo IDs were required both of myself and the awaiting investigator for Mark Waple. Within twenty-four hours of my return, I was told not only where I had been but why I was there. Only a limited number of people knew the details of the trip, all family members. Of course, trip details were worked out over an unsecured telephone line.

In 1989, I traveled to Washington, D.C.. I kept where I was staying known only to one other person and myself. On arrival, my "confirmed" reservations were lost. I was given new reservations. I traveled to meetings by cab part way and the subway the rest of the way. Leaving town, I was picked up by a cab to be taken to the airport. I wore or carried nothing indicating interest in the POW/MIA issue. The cabby and I engaged in small talk. Entering the airport, the cabby asked me questions about the meetings I had been to and what I thought of the POW issue. Not once did I tell him where I had been or what I was doing. (I did make a phone call, in D.C., from the hotel, to a contact over an open line saying where I was.)

Once, I talked to a source over the phone. Previously, I invented details and pre-mailed them to this source. We tested the theory we had propounded to Ross Perot that phone lines of some activists were bugged. The invented details were discussed. Within two days, government officials asked my source about those details. No other mention had been made in any other setting about those details.

During the Senate hearings on Smith - McIntire, I received a phone call from Scott Barnes. He told me the substance of what he was going to testify about. Shortly thereafter, I received a phone call from a person "extraordinarily involved" in the POW issue. He was in the forefront of an attempted discrediting of Bobby Garwood. He invited me to his home when my book first came out and asked about my sources on the napalming incidents. I refused. He agreed with the substance of my book. In a book review, however, this active duty person derided the incidents as part of the "myths" of Vietnam.

He turns up in many places involving investigation into this issue. He told me in early 1980 that he watched family members, gauging their reactions, as they viewed film clips, released by the government a couple years earlier. He is suspected of being a DIA operative. Once, while reading a publication advertising for information concerning a resistance movement in Southeast Asia, I noticed a pen name of this man in the advertisement. He was still on active duty.

He denies the allegations. On November 12, 1986, he wrote, "Wrote to you some months back asking for information ... Received no reply and thought perhaps my letter had gone astray. Recent information, however, indicates you did in fact receive my letter, but did not plan to reply, in that you believed I was working for DIA, etc." The only time I questioned where he worked was with one of my contacts over an open and unsecured line. He continued, "On one hand, you disseminate information that I'm a government 'spook,' yet you also refer to me in the book as a '... writer friend of mine ...' when referring to specific instances of

Soviet involvement in Vietnam..." He asked why, adding, "For your edification, I'm not nor have I ever been a 'spook,' and have no affiliation with DIA. That story made the rounds ... and I've been told it originated with David Taylor. ... it ... climaxed with Mark Smith's absurd testimony ... alleging that I had disclosed 'Obassys' identity to the press, worked with Murkowski, and am now masquerading as a dentist in Subic Bay. Interesting, but untrue." He said that many persons claimed to see proof that "I work for DIA... etc." but they never seem to "be able to produce the proof..." (He knew what Barnes told me however)

A coincidence, you might be thinking. I used to think so. I was taught from fourteen years old in high school ROTC these things did not happen, my government did things honestly. I did not want to believe differently. I found that others had this happening to them too. Not just activists, but researchers like Monika Stevenson who wrote **Kiss the Boys Goodbye**. Minor annoyances, yes. I wonder if COINTELPRO really disappeared? I read their reports on active duty. Is it now known by another name, reactivated in 1981, as reported to me by Mark Smith. One further coincidence. The only time I every hear from him is when another book is reported ready for publication. Got a Christmas card from him in December, 1996, with no return address this time. Publication was expected in early 1997. Would have missed some good material if that date had held true.

Another case of mysterious remains

Kathryn Fanning also filed an affidavit in *Smith v Reagan*. Her husband, MAJ Hugh Michael Fanning, a Marine aviator, was shot down over North Vietnam on October 31, 1967. On September 24, 1976 he received a PFOD. On July 17, 1984, the presumed remains of MAJ Fanning were returned with services held in Oklahoma City. In July 1985, Mrs. Fanning examined her husband's files and found reports indicating MAJ Fanning was a prisoner. She previously believed the government had given her everything. As she said, "this obviously did not happen."

On August 23, 1985, Kathryn Fanning had the "remains of her husband" exhumed. The remains were first examined by Dr. Clyde Collins Snow, a Forensic Anthropology Consultant to the Oklahoma State Medical Examiner. Dr. Snow stated the examined remains could not be identified positively as Fanning. Next, she went to Dr. Charney. He examined the paperwork submitted by CIL. Dr. Charney announced, "It is not possible to positively ... make an identification of the skeletal remains as ... Major Fanning. In none of the submitted papers ... any statements as to how such an identification was made. Further, claims ... as to the sex, race, age, height, dexterity, musculature cannot be scientifically supported ... With race undetermined, this leaves the estimate of height in question."

Mrs. Fanning recalled, "I was led to believe ... that skull and dental material were used ... in the identification process." Dr. Charney wrote: " ... "The skull or pertinent portions ... was not on hand." Mrs. Fanning proclaimed, "I have been intentionally misinformed not only about the circumstances surrounding my husband's disappearance but also about the identification of my husband's alleged remains.... I believe ... a possibility that my husband is alive ..."

The CIL-HI fraud part of cover-up and deceit

As a result of numerous reports like that of Mrs. Fanning and Mrs. Hart, Congress investigated the CIL facility in Hawaii. (**House Armed Services Committee, Investigations Subcommittee, 99th Congress, 2d Session, 1986 "Activities** of the Central Identification Laboratory") In 1991, the Senate Foreign Relations Minority Staff released their findings about CIL-HI. Official records show, by 1990, some 255 sets of remains were repatriated. The Executive Department refused to tell the staff how many remains came from excavations. This is important because up to 520 remains were in Vietnamese custody when Loc left in 1979. Loc testified most remains repatriated before then were from that "stockpile."

How many of those 255 belong to MIAs? The Senate Minority Staff charged that "many ...technicians ...lacked advanced training in ... forensic anthropology. Prior to 1986, CIL-HI's technicians referred to themselves as 'doctors,' when ... they have never been awarded doctorates in medicine or any other recognized ... discipline." Dr. Charney said, "This facility... entrusted with the analysis of ... remains of our servicemen ... is guilty of unscientific, unprofessional work. The **administrative and technical personnel have engaged knowingly in deliberate distortion** of details... to give credibility to otherwise impossible identification."

The Staff continued, "**The senior anthropologist** ... did not hold a doctorate in the field of anthropology but, had worked in the field of forensic anthropology since the end of World War II.... he **insisted on using** a theory he developed ... **that was rejected** by the anthropological scientific community."

Dr. Charney was joined by Dr. George W. Gill, a former secretary of the physical anthropology section, American Academy of Forensic Sciences, and a member of the Board of Directors of the American Board of Forensic Anthropology. Dr. Gill stated, "It is clear ... that the problem in **the CIL-HI reports** results from either **extreme carelessness, incompetence, fabrication of data**, or some combination..." It has been estimated that **80 sets of remains may have been falsely identified**. (SFR, pgs. 8-3 to 8-5 Emphasis added.)

The "official government line" theory

Why didn't information on CIL-HI, the EC-47, the Hart case, and other cases of suspected live POWs come out years before they did? Dr. Roger Shields provided one answer when he testified about the EC-47 case. (This, does not imply that I believe Dr. Shields has been a part of this. On the contrary, he helped the cause along.) Dr. Shields said simply, "I do not want to go to jail."

This simple reply deters many persons from offering POW information. Revealing information contrary to the government "official line" is not conducive to promotions. GEN John Singlaub publicly questioned President Carter's position on Korea and was "retired." COL Laird Guttersen, a returned POW, went public with his doubts about the official government line on POWs and was "retired." GEN Tighe was treated shabbily by his "peers" when he told the truth. Mark Smith, Melvin McIntire, and Robert Howard had their reputations besmirched. Colonel Peck was vilified. LTC Shinkle was treated with disdain.

There is the ever present fear of fine, imprisonment, or civil suit for persons once having access to POW information. Frank Snepp can tell you how much of his royalty payments on **Decent Interval** he could keep because he did not clear it with CIA censors. (One might ask now how can I write and not worry. Simple, I am writing about classified materials I did not have direct access to. As a member of the working press, I am further protected by shield laws. Besides, those who want information out have managed to find me over the years.)

I maintain there exists an "official government line" concerning MIAs from which agencies cannot deviate. A document found by Karen Martin supports this theory. Martin, the wife of an MIA lost in Cambodia in April 1973, found an inter-office memo, dated April 2, 1974 from COL Archie Gratch, chief of the Air Force Casualty Service referring to a conversation he held with GEN Kingston, a former head of JCRC. Mrs. Martin wanted to see him concerning her husband. The General did not want to see her, but he could not do anything "to get her turned off." Kingston requested guidance from Gratch to "what the party line would be" in the meeting with Mrs. Martin. (**Select Committee, Vol. 4, pgs. 92-107**) The memo continued this case was rather unique in that now the services had to notify the next of kin on a pending change of status. Family members were also allowed to attend the hearing.

Gratch wrote Kingston, "Hopefully by the 27th (the day of the proposed meeting), this will have been taken over by events. There is a good possibility the status could be changed by that time." He added if Mrs. Martin insisted upon the meeting, Kingston would be informed of "what the general party line is regarding status changes and search for remains." He would also be provided with background material on Mrs. Martin.

It can be argued the phrase "general party line" is just "shorthand." I have material suggesting the "party line" continues. The **official policy** on POW/MIAs is: **"Although we have thus far been unable to prove that Americans are still detained against their will, the information available to us precludes ruling out that possibility. Actions to investigate live-sighting reports receive ... necessary priority and resources based on the assumption that at least some Americans are still held captive. Should any report prove true, we will take appropriate action to ensure their return."**

Since 1979, the official government line moved towards acknowledging live POWs. On July 6, 1984, DOD prepared a "Question and Answer Guideline" for the League. In 1985, I questioned POW Coordinator LTC Gerald Venanzi about this guideline. He said, "Yes, I know about it. I wrote it." One question asked if the government was inching towards recognition of live POWs. The **answer given was the government official position** seen above. Curious, I used that phraseology with certain League officials when I was on friendly terms with them. The next question was, "What is your **personal view** of the possibility that Americans are being held captive in Indochina." The official answer is "**My personal view** is the same as my professional view which **is reiterated in the official USG position** on this subject." **This is a party line**, and for a "private" organization.

LTG Williams, DIA was asked in 1984 by Congressman Solarz;"... you said it was the operating assumption of the DIA that Americans were being held against their will ... You also said you had no firm evidence that would conclusively prove that. But... let me ask you for a purely personal judgment...do you think that Americans are being held... in Indochina today? What is your personal judgment?"

Williams answered, "I don't know. It's that simple." No personal view? In the same hearing, Williams said that 56 people had taken polygraph tests; 39 involved purported first hand live sightings; 13 indicated no deception involved; 5 involved reports of individuals "... seen in a prisoner - of - war environment;" and only one was a fabrication. How far does this "party line" extend?

The League a family spokesman or government?

On November 11, 1985, Ann Mills Griffiths and Congressman John LeBoutillier squared off on *CNN*'s "**Cross-fire**" program. The topic discussed was POWs and the taping of Bud McFarlane, including his professional views versus his personal views on live POWs. Griffiths defended the government's position on POWs and gave her personal view men were alive. She did not, however, present the position of her "employers," the League. Their stance, adopted on October 27, 1979, by an unanimous board vote is: "The Board of Directors of the National League of Families of American Prisoners and Missing in Southeast Asia has obtained sufficient evidence to prove that American Prisoners are being held in Southeast Asia."

The League Newsletter carrying this declaration (November 27, 1979) continued, "The preponderance of evidence clearly indicates that Americans are being held against their will in Southeast Asia, contrary to statements made by spokesmen from the Departments of State and Defense." As late as June 25, 1981, Griffiths testified, "The people ... will not be tolerant of knowledge that our own servicemen are still held captive ... 8 years after being assured ... that all the prisoners had been returned. ... intelligence ... indicates that U.S. prisoners are currently held captive. The public is becoming more aware of a lack of effective effort..."

In the Vessey hearings, she said, "I have repeatedly testified ...my view ... the League's view, that Americans are alive in Southeast Asia. However, we base it on the facts ... the discrepancy cases... currently under investigation ..." There is a qualitative difference between what Griffiths said and what the League adopted. The League stance was based on less evidence than was available in 1981, 1985, or 1987. In those days, they were "Rambos" and "extremists." Political acceptance, however, breeds familiarity and a watering down of views. Much like the Pentecostals, who used to be "those people across the tracks," today, they're the church to attend. In many cases, the dynamic Spirit filled doctrine that brought them to where they're at is watered down to gain public approval.

The emphasis on "personal opinion" comes from Tighe's testimony in 1981. It played a role with McFarlane and Childress. General Tighe giving his personal view, which reflected his professional view, set the standard. He also helped in many ways which cannot be publicly acknowledged.

While League Chairman of the "Refugee Data Committee," George Brooks in 1979 developed an "informed opinion" as to the veracity the government position. After reviewing 231 refugee reports, Brooks said, "The claim is ... not made that each refugee report is absolutely true, but when no credence is applied to any ... refugee reports, the motives of the investigators are more suspect than ... the sources." The Senate Minority report said over 1400 reports have been studied with the government not finding one valid. It was the refugee reports, not discrepancy cases, that caused the League to adopt their 1979 position.

What "independence" can the so-called watch dog of the government have when the League Executive Director sits on a committee developing government policy on the POW/MIAs and "related" issues? Colonel Peck wondered, "who she really is and where she came from." Senator Robert Smith (NH) asked during the Vessey hearings: "I did read that some representative of the League had made some requests. Has the United States Government — I think sometimes there is some confusion here — the League is not the United States Government — ... ?"

The confusion arises sometimes from the government. Richard Armitage testified on August 8, 1984, "In February ..., I led a US delegation to Hanoi.... the highest level Executive Branch visit to Vietnam ... Much of the planning and coordination ... was conducted by Mrs. Griffiths..." Paul Wolfowitz, State Department, also testified, "The Department of State is the Chairman of the Interagency POW / MIA group (IAG) and participates fully in the planning of United States actions ... on the POW / MIA issue... participating IAG members ... and the Executive Director of the League of Families ... the government to government efforts ... "

In September 1996, Bill Bell, a former government official gave a first hand account of the cost of transgressing the "official line." Congressman Dornan asked, "were you coached by the Department of Defense as to how to answer congressional questions?" Bell replied, "Back at the time (November 1991) they had what was called 'murder boards' where people would go and discuss the questions... In this case, I think they went a little too far, because myself and others were taken into a room and given a list of the questions... what we really were dismayed about in this instance is that we were given answers to each question. No one came right out and said 'you must use these answers,' but when you have a superior and your chain of command, the day prior to a hearing, ...it's a safe assumption that individual desires you use those answers..."

Bell testified in that closed 1991 hearing that he believed Americans had been left behind in 1973. Dornan picks up later in the 1996 hearing "The last question I asked you, Mr. Bell, was did you testify that, in your opinion, American prisoners remain and your answer was, 'Yes, sir, I did.'... That cost you your job, testifying frankly to a closed Senate Committee hearing?" Bell replied, "... the Vietnamese went to my superiors just before I testified, in my presence, and what they said to my superiors was that we are very concerned about what Mr. Bell will say--"

Dornan asked, "This is in Hanoi?" Bell replied, "Yes, sir... during one of the technical meetings..." Dornan exploded, "That's outrageous." Bell continued, "...This was one way that I felt they were trying to intimidate me... They did this quite often... After I testified, they... denied me a visa to reenter Vietnam and assume my duties... Finally they did, but by that time I think they had reached an agreement with my employer, that I would not be there long..."

There is a "party line" on POWs/MIAs. Deviate from the "party line" and consequences follow, even for the press. I was excluded from a policy speech given by the Secretary of Defense covered by other media. I wore my photo ID, issued by the Arizona Department of Public Safety, and carried my press card issued by the legislative leadership giving access to the floor of the Arizona Legislature. League officials said I was not a legitimate press person. My transgression? I criticized the League and Ms. Griffiths.

Backtracking, were the decisions in the Martin case decided upon the facts or the "official party line?" Karen Martin received word of the status hearing on April 12, 1974. The hearing, on April 16, was scheduled fifteen hundred miles from her home. That gave her four days to hire an attorney, travel the fifteen hundred miles, review her husband's files, and prepare a defense. This is what the services deemed adequate notice to protect MIA rights. Fortunately, she was able to postpone the hearing until June. During that time, the navigator's father traveled to Thailand and found an intelligence report in the JCRC field office not appearing in Mrs. Martin's files. It suggested both men survived the crash.

The Casualty Office told Mrs. Martin there was no existing intelligence indicating anyone survived. They also stated only deserters and deviants were alive in Indochina. Senator John Kerry, (D-MA) used **this** party line in August 1991 prior to chairing a new Senate "investigation." Mrs. Martin was further told her challenging the status change was an unfair, unnecessary, burden on the navigator's wife who wanted her husband's status changed. Shades of the Darr case.

Asking the fox to watch the hen house

The panel picked to review the evidence consisted of three officers from the casualty branch. That is equivalent to a junior officer investigating the general's wrong doing and having the general sitting in judgment of the junior officer's work. Upon objection, the military appointed an independent board.

As evidence, the government presented Communist broadcasts indicating the men were dead. Earlier, the government urged Mrs. Martin to discount these same statements as being propaganda. The statements contained the wrong day, the wrong place, and did not mention any names of who was killed.

For Mrs. Martin, there was the JCRC intelligence report from Thailand. The report showed her husband and the navigator in captivity. There were affidavits concerning the examination of the airplane showing that Captain Martin could have ejected before the crash. (A 1980 list on Martin and his navigator, Samuel James, show that an undated **FBIS** report lists both men killed and their bodies charred. There have been no remains returned. **FBIS** stands for Foreign Broadcast Information Service) These affidavits were difficult to come by. The casualty office "forgot" to notify Mrs. Martin that officers were attempting to contact her. Only by her lawyer going through the casualty file did they find these attempts.

Mrs. Martin prevailed. Her husband was kept as MIA for a while longer. Whether or not the father of Captain Martin being an Air Force Major General and in attendance at the hearing had any bearing on that outcome is open to conjecture. The pattern of information suppression is no coincidence. There is a "party line" on MIAs. No deviation is tolerated.

The 1984 "Question and Answer Guideline" describes " the relationship between the USG and the League ...." "The USG works very closely with the League on the POW/MIA issue. The ... Executive Director is a fully participating member of the POW/MIA Inter-agency Group ... develops policy and recommendations ... plays a vital and integral role in this function." How independent can the League Executive Director be having this official relationship? I believe that the answer is found in League publications. Her position often changes with the government.

The Communists have their "party line" too

Some MIAs are dead, perhaps the majority. The Communists cannot account for all of the men. According to DOD, of 2546 men listed as MIA or KIA / BNR, 436 men were "nonrecoverable." These men were known to be dead including "a pilot who crashes into the sea" or an "**incinerated soldier**." However, the Communists have accounted for some men in this category. I know they can account for those they tortured and transferred to Russia and China.

The Communists have their own party line and agenda. During the week of July 20, 1984, the Vietnamese announced the return of eight remains (POW/MIA Recognition Day). This continued the pattern of responding to increased awareness of live POWs begun in 1981. During the same "recognition week" the remains of POWs, including Ron Dodge, were identified. In 1985, the Communists announced the return of twenty-six remains on July 7. This "body charade" has a subtle message. To then, virtually every return contained one or more "easy" or "famous" case. For example, Ron Dodge, Donald Lindland, Erasimo Arroyo-

Baez, Robert Sherman, and Milton Vescelius were all known POWs. Stephen Musselman, Lyn Powell, Farrell Sullivan Jr., Michael Doyle, Monty Mooreberg, and Dominic Sansone were all highlighted in either the Woodcock briefing or in negotiation folders given to the Wolff Committee.

The subtle message is "we know a lot more and what are you willing to pay for it?" In many cases, the remains returned were from the same plane returned together or were in chronological order on our MIA list. The Vietnamese for years played this game. The unanswered question is the US government cognizant of this subtle message? The message of the 1205 document, "why do we keep these POWs ... This is not political horse trading, but rather an important condition and serious argument for successful resolution of the Vietnam problem" is a party line.

Rescue mission - answers and some questions

Earlier, we saw where General Tighe subtly changed his public stance on live POWs. President Carter also changed his views, although not publicly. His October 1979 answer of no to Congressman Dornan changed in September 1980, during a campaign swing in Philadelphia. As he waded into the crowd, he was asked if he was keeping on top of the POW issue. He said, yes, walked on a couple steps, returned to the questioner, leaned over, and asked, "Do you know there may still be live Americans over there?" (**The man to whom Carter spoke**)

A third person changing his mind is President Reagan. While addressing a breakfast meeting of the American Legion in February 1981, he was asked about POWs. He quoted Congressman Montgomery that no POWs were alive. However, by March 21, he was considering a rescue mission.

A rescue mission? The official position was there was no credible evidence POWs were captive. Yet, a rescue mission was planned. The following is based upon personal knowledge and from identified sources.

In March 1981, I was in Washington, D.C. celebrating the conservative Presidential victory at the Conservative Political Action Conference (CPAC). I knew some victors. By invitation, I was also to brief the staffs of Congressman Jack Kemp and Senator Roger Jepsen on POW matters. They were considering a bill making the POW problem one of a "human rights" violation.

At this time, *ABC Network News* was running a multipart series about live POWs in Laos. Several Laotian guerrilla leaders claimed holding "tens" of POWs. In addition, they mentioned private operations in Laos either planned or scrapped. (I had some input on private operations that had been scrapped) Behind some closed doors, government officials were not so silently cursing the series and the effects the series might have upon a rescue mission.

I also met with my contacts. The first stop was Ann Griffiths who previously showed me negotiating strategies presented to the POW Inter-Agency Group. She also showed me the new JCS POW statement adopted the day after the presidential election, prior to it's adoption. In 1981, we still were able to talk. We discussed alternative measures the new administration might take to resolve this problem. One item she mentioned caught me off-guard, a rescue mission. Previously, no one discussed a rescue. The primary reason given was we had no idea where the men were incarcerated. I also presumed the U.S. lacked the intestinal fortitude to pull off a rescue mission. This attitude was expressed to me by former DIA Director, LTG Daniel Graham in 1977. Then, we contrasted the long Son Tay Raid planning period versus the short planning period by Israel at Entebbe. Likewise, with the botched Iran rescue mission fresh in mind, some thought we lacked the technical means of handling a POW rescue. This feeling was expressed by Senator Barry Goldwater, in his book **Goldwater**, when he talked with a leader of both Son Tay and Iran, LTC Myron Beckwith. (**pgs. 344-48**)

I presumed Ann was discussing a governmentally sanctioned rescue. I did not know then she was also involved in a "private" rescue headed by a retired Special Forces Officer, James "Bo" Gritz.

I next checked with Jon Holstine. Holstine and I talked many times on the POW issue, professionally. I would bounce ideas and theories off him. He would steer me in the correct direction. I never asked for any classified information. You can develop things merely by listening. I asked Jon how a rescue mission might fly. Having just come from Griffith's office, I was curious about this new tack. Iran came up. We both concurred lack of training botched the mission. Jon was non-committal about a rescue mission, but would not rule it out. I still felt, however, that Ann was undergoing wishful thinking.

In CPACs, well-placed persons come to you as speakers. The next person I sought out was National Security Advisor Richard Allen. I knew him by reputation, as an intellectual force in conservatism. By coincidence, Allen lived in New Jersey less than fifty miles from me. He spoke to the delegates on a variety of topics and opened the floor to questions. I persuaded a former Vietnamese Army Officer to ask about POWs. Allen answered the administration was then studying several open options; adding these discussions were in a delicate state. There was a tone to the answer suggesting more than was overtly said.

The next speaker was Graham. On a professional level, he and I were both authors, published by the same publishing firm, Arlington House. His book **Shall America be Defended? Salt II and Beyond** and mine, **Missing in Action: Trail of Deceit** both came out in 1979. I knew he served on Reagan's intelligence transition team. I knew if I asked him a question, I would get an answer. So I asked, "Do you feel that American POWs are still alive in Southeast Asia." His answer was, "*Sure, we know where six or seven POWs are and we intend to do something about them.*" (Later I knew I misunderstood the number mentioned)

Can you keep a secret?

I came across a state secret. The Reagan administration was ready to launch a rescue mission into Laos. (It being mentioned where the men were held) Almost immediately, a problem arose. I still had not briefed the Congressional staffs on the issue. At Jepsen's office, I discussed the current situation. This briefing did not go well as I was burdened by secrecy considerations. I needed to know more to keep compartmented what could disrupt a rescue by something I might say or do.

I sought out Congressman Dornan. I knew that he was cleared to know about a rescue. We talked. Besides writing the original forward to this book, politically, we worked together on a tough reelection campaign of his. One challenger was a Libertarian friend of mine. Another friend, Dr. Bob Moffett, served on Dornan's staff. I first met Dornan at CPAC 1977.

Now, I laid out for him what I had been told and by whom. He began weighing out the options. He toyed briefly with bringing the whole thing into the open. I earlier told him of my encounter with the man who told me about Carter's conversion on POWs held captive. Dornan heard for himself what was told. On the rescue mission, he told me to be prepared to add a new chapter to my book concerning a rescue. "Be ready by Christmas — no, on second thought, make that by the 4th of July, Independence Day." I was told the approval for the rescue operation was "on the President's desk." Now, I was hooked, secrecy wise.

Why no rescue? Publicity or conspiracy?

What happened? A lot of things. There was satellite and SR-71 imagery of a Laotian camp having all the characteristics of a prison camp, including a distinctive picket fence. Photos showed people on the ground, too tall to be Vietnamese, working a piece of ground, using tools with handles too long for average Asian use. The crops grown were not conducive to an Oriental diet. On the ground were the letters "B-52," or "52." This camp was active. (This is the same camp discussed in the EC-47Q chapter.) In October 1990, I met Colonel Gritz. I had a purported sketch of the prison. In two seconds he told me that the sketch was true, who did it, and the actual photos were still Top Secret, SI, (Special Intelligence).

Tighe's fast moving chain of events

A reconnaissance mission was ultimately tried. Press reports said nothing was found. However, I learned more. The target was a detention facility near Moung Nhom Marrot, near Thakket. The prisoners were later moved to an area along Se Thamouk (or Thamouk river). Both regions were well known as being prison locations. There have been indications that photographs were taken at this second location with Caucasians visible. On June 25, 1981, after Tighe's explosive statements, a closed session of the Solarz subcommittee examined Tighe's fast moving chain of events leading to his public statement. The following is (at the **Confidential** level only) what happened from committee records.

Attending were LTG Tighe; RADM Jerry Paulson, DIA: LTC Jack Kennedy, DIA; Fred Brown, Deputy Secretary of State; Dornan; who discussed:

Subject Nhom Marrot:

Sources: 1. Redacted (my choice) - As an employee of USAID, source reported sighting 5 Caucasian prisoners in January, 1976 in Laos. A first hand sighting. Passed polygraph. USAID employment verified. (This is the USAID employee, discussed earlier, imprisoned with the Americans)

2. (Redacted) wrote letter to Vang Pao on April 19, 1979, saying 18 US POWs and 25 Lao Prisoners were being held in a cave near Nhom Marrot. The information was relayed to (redacted) by a resistance leader named (redacted). The prisoners were moved into the Nhom Marrot area on 10 March, 1975. The letter said they were being held in a cave near Kham Keut. (**DIA Note**: not clear if it was referring to a previous detention site or the same one) It also said 2 US POWs, 1 Australian and 1 Japanese prisoner were held in an adjacent cave. (**DIA Note**: briefer noted that it took some time before this letter reached US government ...)

3. **Photography** — Cave area apparently identified. Imagery of October 1979 through 1980 "generally correlates with description of detention area." One cave located. Foliage heavy — other cave entrances possibly concealed.

4. Same **source** as in 2: In November, 1979, reported the detention of a Lt. Col. Paul W. Mercland, near Moung Nhom Marrot. DIA found no correlation "Mercland." However, a Major Paul W. Bannon was lost in Laos in 1969. (**My note**: Major Paul W. Bannon, USAF, was lost on 4/12/69) Briefer noted it was not uncommon for POWs to assume they had been promoted while in captivity and would use new rank designations — hence the LTC. Tighe commented that

Mercland sounds like 'American' and made the supposition that source may have dropped or mistakenly supplanted 'American' for last name. One source passed polygraph test(s) in 'September /Oct 1980.' Other not given polygraph.

5. 'Sensitive Source' (**DIA designation**) — In November, 1980, a 'sensitive source' reported that 30 US POWs were being held near Muong Nhom Marrot. The information reportedly provided to source by LPDR officials, reliability unknown. However, **source** who passed information from original source **evaluated as 'very high in reliability.'**

6. **Photography** - Imagery from 4 December, 1980 indicated secure detention facility near Nhom Marrot ... not constructed in Imagery of April, 1978. The number '52' was ... stomped in the row crop area of the camp on 30 December, 1980 imagery. Group of people continuously observed.

Admiral Paulson comment, 'It was based on that evidence, Mr. Chairman, that the recommendation was made that we had enough significant evidence to attempt verification ... by this time (Dec. 1980) Dick Allen, Jim Buckley and Secretary Haig ... briefed on this information.'

Dornan interjected at this point that he was briefed by Tuttle, while still at DIA, that 'prior to November 1980, but about the same time area, a broadcast ... referring to 27 American POWs moving from a camp up north to this camp ... prepared for occupancy, some time around this period.'

Dornan - 'Remember Admiral, you (**Note** - referring to a previous briefing presumably in May or June 1981 after Paulson replaced Tuttle - **DIA note**) had not heard of this and one of the other Colonels ... said that is right.'

Paulson did not respond. Tighe said he was not aware of the message.

(**Committee note** - ... in the file folder in which this transcript ... kept, ... the conversation regarding the **radio intercept** ... It was noted ... that every mention of '**radio broadcast**' or '**intercept**' was lined through and **replaced** with the word '**information**' or '**intelligence**.' It is probable... the final transcript has no reference to a 'radio broadcast.' ... not clear why ... may have been to allow storage at a lower level of classification.) (**Emphasis supplied**)

I'll add a note. Kham Keut is probably the same Kham Khut LTC Shinkle testified about in his operation to rescue live Americans and the same area in the 1973 Air Force Intelligence study with a confirmed cave prison, holding Americans. This 1980 time frame is when Carter changed his mind.

Back to the mission

A reconnaissance mission took place in Laos prior to May 20, 1981. Word of the mission leaked to the press. To their credit, the media kept the information quiet until DOD quit telling them to hold onto their stories. On that day, I received a call from Ron Miller. He and I cooperated many times on POW/MIA stories. He asked me what I knew about a Laotian mission. I told him some of what I relayed here. He told me that DOD had just told the media that all men associated with the reconnaissance mission were out of country.

I undertook to find out more. The media was being told by DOD personnel, "The mission revealed no live POWs." How, I wondered, could a rescue mission make its way to Reagan's desk with no one there? I smelled a rat.

I called the Senate Intelligence Committee and reached Earl Eisenhower. I asked about the Laos mission and was told Thai Intelligence Forces, combined with Lao personnel, pulled it off. I asked about photographs that Senator Goldwater had been quoted as saying men in the photos looked like Americans to him. Mr. Eisenhower refused any comments about any photographs.

At the Pentagon, COL Jerry Grahowski told me there was no corroboration any operation took place. He did confirm, however, the existence of the camp satellite photos. In talking about the particulars of the photos, he degraded their significance. In discussing the size of the men, he pointed out that Koreans and Chinese were also larger than the average Vietnamese. (**Note: The May 21, 1981** *Washington Post*'s **Pentagon sources suggested the Caucasians might be Russians, not prisoners.**) When asked how satellite photos got to Gritz, I was told he had many friends in the Pentagon or he could have received them from the League. SI, the photo's classification requires special compartmentalization and handling.

Grahowski did not explain what Koreans or Chinese were doing in a Laotian prison, using tools better designed for Occidentals. He did not explain why Asians were growing food better designed for Occidental diets. He never tackled the question of what a "52" or "B-52" meant, scratched in the ground. He gave up attempting to explain away the obvious.

A July 15, 1981 letter to Betty Foley, says it all. The letter I saw says: "I ... signed a proclamation naming July 17 as POW/MIA day... that... means little unless we keep on trying to learn the whereabouts of our men missing... alive or dead... we've been unable to substantiate ... reports concerning Americans in Vietnam, Laos, or Cambodia. But ... we shall continue trying. **... our effort must be ... without publicity. We weren't helped ... by the news story about our mission in Laos...** we will continue.... (**Emphasis added**)   (s) **Ronald Reagan**

What happened to the rescue? The one word reply of COL Rowe, leader of the mission, in **Kiss the Boys Goodbye**, was conspiracy. President Reagan said it was publicity. The two might not be mutually exclusive. Let's examine publicity.

In March 1981, **ABC News** ran a legitimate news story with no one knowing a government operation was planned. Also, the Florida paper, the *Sentinel Star*, ran a story about a "private rescue mission" headed by Bo Gritz. I did not see this March 26 story, until July. The article quoted "self-proclaimed mission organizer Ann Griffiths" that despite contrary reports the Gritz mission " is definitely on."

In the article, Gritz alluded to satellite photos showing the existence of POWs in January, 1981. Grahowski said that if it were true, then Gritz had assets beyond the capability of the US intelligence community. This misleading statement is typical of what DIA has done over the years. Literally, the last known photo was taken in late December 1980, as noted above.

In early April, columnist Jack Anderson ran a small piece in his column saying American intelligence officials knew about the existence of a Laotian POW camp because of an informant, close to the camp. I remember reading the article with an unprintable reaction. I was positive the rescue mission was being compromised. At this time, I was receiving, from several sources, information indicating there were two separate rescue missions planned. The reason was that two different sets of numbers of POWs were being discussed and possibly two separate locations. I had not read or heard yet about Gritz. I had, in fact, discussed more than one private mission with Miller.

Apprehensiveness turned to fear additional POWs might be taken when I received a call from a Washington, D.C. based reporter highly cognizant of the POW issue. This person asked me what I knew about a rescue mission being planned for

Laos. I told this person to sit on whatever he thought he knew and not to print anything until I could get back to him.

Next, I received a call from a California-based private POW organization. The leader was related to a well-known POW and reportedly had ties to Gritz. At this moment, the woman was telling me about a reported raid into Laos, the photos, and the "B-52" imagery. Again, I told this individual to sit on what she thought she knew and not to spread that word around. I never told either why.

Compromised? You bet!

I had this sickening feeling the government planned rescue mission was compromised and would end with more prisoners. I called Foley. We arranged to meet immediately! Over a period of two meetings, we discussed what we knew. (We met at the Vince Lombardi exit on the New Jersey Turnpike. This exit was picked because it was convenient to Foley's New York Office, coming from the North and my house, coming from the South. It was the only exit where both of us could turn around without leaving the Turnpike and return to our respective originating locations. Most importantly, it provided a private location to talk without being overheard by outsiders.) I soon found that Dermot also knew about a rescue mission, plus more. He knew about a place where twenty-six or twenty-seven POWs were being held. I told him about my six or seven and who it was that I had talked to.

The conclusion we came to was either we were talking about two separate operations, or one of us misunderstood what he had been told. With more independent checking, I know we were talking about the same mission. Independently, we discovered COL Nick Rowe's operation. Foley's numbers matched. I misunderstood mine. Besides, Foley's source was Rowe.

This mission had been compromised. Through appropriate means, Foley got word to the Pentagon something was amiss. That word eventually ended with Tuttle. At first, those persons contacted denied anything was planned. I then wrote out exactly what I had been told, without telling them who told me. The next word I received was no denial, but they were looking for the leaks. Reportedly, the probe stopped at some congressional offices, including a Congressman on the POW Task Force with connections to one of the persons I had been contacted by earlier.

This is one reason for a "rescue" mission being downgraded to a "reconnaissance" mission. Another theory is that the reconnaissance mission was the prelude to the rescue mission. That too, however, was compromised. I learned, through Miller, that several days before the reconnaissance forces returned, the news media had been told about their mission. To the credit of the media, however, they sat on the story, as I sat my information, until the day that Ron Miller called me and asked me that question. Who leaked here?

Looking at news items, *The Sentinel Star* wrote about Velvet Hammer. On hand were media representatives along with "self-proclaimed mission organizer" Ann Griffiths, with her government clearance. The *Washington Post* also named Griffiths as "mission organizer." *The Sentinel Star* said a reporter from the *Washington Post* was at the training grounds. Gritz declared having media personnel there was not his idea, but they agreed to keep quiet. In the aftermath, Gritz was condemned by Griffiths, George Brooks of the League, and the **Soldier of Fortune** Magazine. All three were directly or indirectly involved in this 1981 operation. Griffiths was at the training camp "supplying information." Brooks contributed thousands of dollars to the effort. In the case of **Soldier of Fortune**, the person associated with them and prominently mentioned in news articles was also later involved in a botched effort in Laos.

On May 22, 1981, The *Washington Post* Wire service said Griffiths and other League members were supportive of a twenty-six man private rescue mission that trained in Florida. The article identified Gritz as the mission leader saying their goal was to rescue prisoners at a location separate from the government sponsored one. The *Washington Post*, itself, however, on May 21, said, Ann Griffiths, mission organizer, made several trips to Florida passing along intelligence and target data gleaned from government sources. She said she would "bet my life" Americans were captive in Southeast Asia. Griffiths also claimed knowledge about spy satellite photos with the word "B-52."

On **April 6, 1981**, the League Newsletter said, "Some media coverage has recently been given to private rescue operations. Articles appeared ... alleging that the League's Executive Director was the organizer of one such project. On an individual basis, Ann Griffiths was aware of this particular project ... met with the participants, subsequently determining that the proposed operation was not presently feasible." The letter said it was imperative the League be made aware of rescue missions planned or contemplated (note 1 month before real operation).

At this time, Griffiths served on the Inter-Agency Group for POWs, supposedly bound by a "DIA Secrecy Agreement - DIAR 50-2" which states, "by virtue of my ... association with the Defense Intelligence Agency, I may be granted access to information, material, plans, and intelligence ... classified ... I will never divulge ... classified information ... without the prior consent of the Director ... I agree to submit for review ... all manuscripts, articles, speeches ... which contain or are derived from information obtained by ... association with the Defense Intelligence Agency ... **I will report ... to my superior ... an unauthorized person has obtained or is attempting to obtain classified information** ... or ... such information ... is being disclosed ..." (**Emphasis added**)

Did Gritz have government connections? I talked with him and examined an affidavit filed in a court case by MAJ Clarence Johnson, stating that Johnson was aware of Gritz' activities and that Gritz was acting at the request of General Harold Aaron, former DIA Deputy Director. Johnson claimed Gritz discovered camp "52" in 1980 and had found Giang. Gritz also told me he had interviewed Giang.

In *Smith v. Reagan*, a memorandum from Aaron to Gritz was entered as evidence. Aaron said "... have mixed emotions about your ... pursue this PW/MIA matter, but frankly I don't know any other way... Understand the Hughes arrangement is satisfactory ... Keep your government contacts limited to those with ... need to know ... too bad we have to proceed this way but the Administration will not face ... the problem. General Tighe is well aware of the situation ... so sensitive it could result in a real inquisition if word leaked ... proceeding unofficially... a real hot potato... Keep the press and government offices out ... I am confident that once you prove ... our men are still captive, the system will do the rest..."

I examined Gritz's testimony on this issue given in 1983 to the Solarz committee. He was accurate in details touching on what I knew. Johnson's affidavit, Gritz' testimony, and what I know, point to the involvement of Aaron and Admiral Jerry Tuttle in the rescue/reconnaissance mission on the "52" camp. Sources that I trust told me that "Bo's on our side." On a nationwide *CBS* news program in 1985, Congressman Dornan stated that Bo was asked to do a job by the government then he had his legs cut out from under him. If Griffiths passed classified information to Gritz on an **unsanctioned** operation why wasn't she or Gritz or both, tried in court?

Now for some independent confirmation. Johnson wrote in his affidavit, "Bo reported that his Asian recon units had located **30 US POWs** at (redacted) Laos in April, 1980. **CIA was to confirm by (redacted) overflights. Target confirmation was received in November**, making the (redacted) report "A-1" intelligence. Affiant maintained liaison while Bo was in Florida preparing for a private sector rescue mission. Admiral Jerry Tuttle, DIA, caused Bo to stand down after White House decision to use 'Delta' Force ... " The House report reads, "In **November, 1980,** a 'sensitive source' reported that **30 US POWs** were being held near Muong Nhom Marrot ... **Source** who passed information from original source evaluated as '**very high in reliability.**'"

The dates match. The number of POWs match. The (redacted) overflight fits the number of letters for SR-71. The redacted locations fit the number of letters for Nhom Marrot. A-1 intelligence means confirmed from highest reliable source, meaning overflights. If Gritz had Aaron's blessing, he would be rated as "very high in reliability" and would of course be "sensitive source" as he was operating in a gray area of legal responsibility. Tighe knew about Gritz' mission.

Gritz had access to classified photos. When I asked Colonel Grahowski how Gritz got the photos. He said the information could have come from the League or his own sources in government. DIA operatives tried persuading me that Aaron's letter was phony. However, they don't explain a second letter filed in *Smith*. Dated 27 December, 1979, it says, "Dear Bo: I received the material that you sent me and I was overwhelmed with what you had done ... From the accounts you sent me, there can be no doubt about live Americans. I always suspected it but, at the same time hoped it wasn't so... De oppresso liber: Sincerely, Harold Aaron."

DIA vs. DIA

Before we leave the "52" camp and the March 1981 events surrounding the May 1981 operation, I want to point out why deceit and cover-up pertain here. In July 1981, I was again at the League's Inter-Agency Forum. In attendance was Admiral Paulson of DIA. I questioned him about the reconnaissance operation. Incredibly, he took the "party line" there was no proof any operation took place. Even when I laid out hard evidence, his main comment was the news media was too nosy. He never conceded any operation took place. (Remarkable considering his attendance at the closed session on June 25,1981)

Yes, the media did some checking. On June 25, 1981, the same day General Tighe testified, the *New York Daily News* ran an **UPI** article "Jailed GIs' in Laos shifted, US believes." The article reads "United States intelligence ... believe ... prisoners ... American servicemen were transferred from a jungle stockade in Laos ... because of publicity ... administration sources said ... Laotian mercenaries paid by the CIA went into Laos from Thailand in January and May to confirm evidence from US reconnaissance photographs that Americans were held in the stockade-like encampment but they found none."

In 1992, the government declassified some new material. Among those items released were two from the NSA concerning this camp. In December, 1979, a COL Picinich, DIA, determined that there needed to be "closer coordination between NSA and DIA" on the POW issue. The reason was that his department, and him specifically, had just returned from a meeting with LTG Tighe. "COL Picinich was visibly excited about recent events. It is the opinion of that office that US POWs are in fact still alive in SEA..."

An internal NSA memorandum on **December 30, 1980**, reiterated a meeting presided over by RADM Tuttle. Attending the meeting were representatives of DIA, CIA, and NSA. "... Tuttle reviewed DIA photo and report chronology (March 1979-Dec 80) on American PW facilities and sightings in Laos. RADM Tuttle has strong suspicion that American POWs remain in Laos." In light of these two new documents, I reiterate a point made by Congressman Dornan on June 25, 1981, "Dornan interjected at this point that he was briefed by Tuttle, while still at DIA, that 'prior to November 1980, but about the same time area, a broadcast ... referring to 27 American POWs moving from a camp up north to this camp ... prepared for occupancy, some time around this period.'" In addition, the notes show, "in the file folder in which this transcript ... kept, ... the conversation regarding the **radio intercept** ... It was noted ... that every mention of 'radio broadcast' or 'intercept' was lined through and **replaced** with the word 'information' or 'intelligence.'** It is probable... the final transcript has no reference to a 'radio broadcast.'"

One further note. In discussing the meaning of the "52" or "B-52" at the camp, I noted the intelligence speculation about it standing for "Baron 52." In late 1996, I received another possible meaning. One of the Special Ops code names for a Special Forces Mike Strike Force was "B-52."

In **Kiss the Boys Goodbye**, the Stevensons found persons who had seen the famous photos. Here, you'll see a Committee version of that photo. Like Loc before, DIA could not agree with DIA because despite official policy, "None were alive." (On page 25 of their book, you'll find my name supporting the theory of the 1981 rescue mission. Now, you know why)

The "Gun Runner" and live POWs

In checking proof that Americans were being held captive in Laos, I became aware of an IRA gunrunner named Sean O'Toolis (one of his many aliases). O'Toolis told of being in a American POW camp in Laos where he talked with the men. He named those with whom he talked. I sat on those names for over a year before **Soldier of Fortune** made them public. O'Toolis had fingerprints of alleged POWs. Prints were turned over to DIA for identification. I was furnished a set by Foley. He confirmed the IRA ties of O'Toolis. My set went to Congressman LeBoutillier who was told by the FBI and I was told by LTC Venanzi that the fingerprints were "too fuzzy" or "too indistinct" to identify. Pure hogwash. Several police officials examined the fingerprints. One affirmed he could find six to eight points of comparison on the "fuzzy" print. This is good enough for a tentative identification. With proper equipment, he could add two more points for positive identification.

On the clear print, he could see ten points without any problem, a positive identification. Another police official said he could find, without difficulty, some sixteen points. Since DIA has the same set of prints and the names attached to them, it should be simple to match the prints with the names or discredit the source. This is cover-up, pure and simple.

Our government has trouble with MIA fingerprints. In 1992, I got a family to ask for their son's fingerprints. I remembered Foley's comments to me. "Larry, they've changed my brother's fingerprint records. I've made preparations, however, to preserve his originals." They asked. One of the first things that happens to a man in service is that he is fingerprinted. The FBI files contain records in their civil file of "fingerprints of individuals fingerprinted as a result of ... military service." The FBI was given the man's name, rank, Social Security number, date of birth, place of birth, Service number, date of entry on active duty, and the place of enlistment. A search of the civil file said, "No FBI record, name search only ..." meaning there was no record. Further, "No fingerprints found, Army - Navy - Marine Corps indicates that a name search for the ID Civil File did not locate a military fingerprint card for ————. Although not indicated by the stamped notation, this name search included a search of all branches ..." **(Official FBI reply)**

Scott Barnes and "liquidate the merchandise"

Scott Barnes swears he saw live Americans in a prison compound in Southeast Asia. In an affidavit in *Smith v. Reagan*, he expounded upon his background. An army veteran, he has expertise in the area of intelligence and organized crime investigations. He was engaged in that type of work when contacted in April 1981 by Hughes Aircraft "on behalf of ... Bo Gritz." Later, Gritz talked with him.

Gritz wanted to be introduced to Vang Pao, whom Barnes knew. Gritz also sent Barnes a package of materials, which "contained intelligence documents pertaining to living American Prisoners of War in Laos ... as well as a defense intelligence letter from General Aaron addressed to LTC James G. Gritz."

Gritz wanted Barnes to "conduct an operation ... its purpose the identification and extraction of ... Prisoners of War in ... Laos." Barnes said he confirmed who Gritz was through "two officials of the Defense Intelligence Agency... who confirmed to me that Col. Gritz's operation was 'a chartered activity.'"

Barnes said that while meeting with American officials in Thailand, he was given "four specific files" and was told "these are the people we are concerned with on this mission." He was also told efforts would be made to discredit Garwood and that Gritz' previous operation was responsible for the ground reconnaissance confirmation. (Barnes would later tell me the same thing in a phone conversation)

Later, Barnes met Gritz. The Thailand trip was to test his reliability in following instructions. Gritz again asked to meet Vang Pao. The meeting occurred in Dornan's Los Angeles office. There, Vang Pao was assured, by Gritz, his operation was privately funded and not a US government operation. Vang Pao was previously burned by the CIA on POW information.

Barnes affirmed: "I crossed into Laos with another American ... identified ... as Mike J. Baldwin and approximately thirty indigenous individuals. The purpose... was ... to confirm or deny ... intelligence ... of ... American POWs in Laos.... we traveled ... east into Laos into the Mahaksi region (probably Mahaxy).... arrived at a triangular shaped prison camp on approximately the 21st of October, 1981." Continuing, "... we were able to look down ... to ... the prison camp. We remained ... for approximately fifteen to thirty minutes ... observed ... guards in towers, and two men ... clearly Caucasian.... ... through the photographic and telephoto lenses ... The approximate distance ... from these individuals was 600 feet..."

Barnes said he was told if Americans were confirmed here the "merchandise was to be liquidated." "The support operations... previously arranged to make an extraction had been canceled without explanation... I refused to participate ... mailed the photographs ... to ... a pre- designated address. I immediately returned ..."

Even US officials get stymied

In March 1982, two Congressmen, Hendon and LeBoutillier, traveled covertly to Southeast Asia seeking the "ultimate POW proof." A million dollars was transferred to a bank in Southeast Asia releasable once the POWs crossed the border (put up by Ross Perot). Admiral Paulson traveled from the United States to Hawaii, using a cover story to mask his absence from Washington. In addition, two news crews from competing networks (**ABC** and **CBS**), one on the spot and one looking for it, were available to record the event. None of this would have taken place without the assurance a transfer could take place. This assurance would be credible only from the highest levels of government. None of these men were new to the issue and none were ignorant of current intelligence. (**Details from Hendon, LeBoutillier, Ron Miller and Perot**)

What happened? Two groups of POWs were involved totaling up to seven men. Originally, they were located near the Lao/Vietnam border. These men were negotiated for; moved from their prison camps; and further moved to a transfer point near the Lao/Thai border where they were then segregated into smaller groups. Reportedly, one POW made it to the border well ahead of the other groups. The Americans on the Thai side of the border wanted absolute proof of who the Americans were before they would accept delivery. Somehow, communications broke down. The Vietnamese got wind of what was up and sealed off the border. The lead POW reportedly got within one hundred yards of the border when this occurred. He was transported back to his detention compound. Our negotiators came back empty handed. Neither major network recorded the story of the decade.

There may be another even more tragic ending. In 1983, a report said that in April or May of 1982, an American POW was executed for attempting to escape his captors. The location of this attempt was in the same geographic location as the transfer point. Open to speculation is if the executed POW was the same one who came within one hundred yards of freedom just one to two months earlier.

Close only counts in horseshoes

On July 14, 1983, DIA came the closest, outside General Tighe, to saying Americans were being held. Congressman Solarz asked the question: "But ... you had **five** live sightings ... who were polygraphed and where the results ... indicated that they were telling the truth...." GEN Williams answered:" ... the most recent report was in August 1982..." **Solarz asked**: " .... did the individual see one ... or a group ?" ADM Paulson replied: ...the August 1982 sighting... The numbers were several Americans and the location was ... specific." Solarz inquired: "It was several ... being held against their will?" **Paulson answered**: "... correct.... The reported conditions ... indicated ... **captivity**.... The August 1982 report ... is about several ... other cases ... singular sightings and... multiple sightings."

In 1984, the CIA, not wanting to be left out, submitted "The **first believable story** on the possibility of live American POWs in Laos... A Prisoner of War CAMP located at the foot of Ngoua Mountain (NCA) ... There were 23 American POWs detained..." Of these six reports, two of which was also "very specific" in location, none passed muster. Of fourteen hundred reports, not one has passed muster. **Cover-up, incompetence, mind-set to debunk?** Give Solarz credit for gall. He also forgot his own classified briefing on June 25, 1981.

Bobby Garwood - a casualty of the war

Early in the book, I asked the reader to evaluate Garwood's story carefully before rendering a final judgment. That is how I left him and his predicament in

1979 and in the 1986 update. Now, I will finish his story which is interwoven with that of Loc the Mortician..

For background, I was at home in early 1979, and received a phone call from Dermot Foley. "Larry, what do you know about Bobby Garwood?" Answering, "all I know about him is that in the book **POW,** he's described as a traitor. He seems to fit the description. From day one in Vietnam, I heard about the American up north 'who was fighting for the VC.'" I told Foley, "Now, I know his name."

"Find out all can about him. I received a request to represent him in a court martial. Do the research 'yesterday.'" I said, "Thanks, Dermot," thinking, however, "couldn't you find someone else to research? A traitor!" I knew men had been left behind. For the first to return to be a collaborator, however, really took the cake. That is what I thought then. When I finished the book in 1979, I had changed my mind a little. The statement about Garwood was also advice to myself. Now, I'll fill in the details on why I fully changed my mind.

In 1965, Bobby Garwood was captured by the VC. There is little argument that for two years, he was a prisoner of war. In 1967, it is alleged that he chose to collaborate with his captors. He said he cut the best deal he could to survive. Captured documents from that time and that geographic area show the VC were having a terrible time keeping their prisoners alive because of a food shortage.

Books about the camp Garwood was held in gave a perspective significantly different from what Garwood's prosecutors presented. They were written not expecting him to reappear. It is alleged Garwood struck a fellow prisoner. Former captives wrote he pushed a fellow prisoner in a manner telling him to shut up since he broke camp rules. Garwood shoved to keep him from messing up more. He was a survivor, street wise, able to adapt to a changed environment.

One report alleges Garwood was killed. A Marine patrol leader positively identified Garwood being killed in a fire-fight; wearing a sash. Captured documents from that time showed the sash **identified a prisoner** being returned from captivity. If Garwood was shot at, obviously he survived. That incident, could have lead, however, to an extended tour of captivity.

I contrasted the prison system in North Vietnam with the south where Garwood was held. The prisons in the North were structured. There was no POW support structure in Garwood's camp. There was a POW "Peace Committee" in the North. Some POWs cut out model airplanes for the Vietnamese to target practice with. Aircraft were lost to small arms fire due to the low flying altitude the missions required. Before the prisoner return, the POWs in the North were offered a deal. Those returning under the Senior POW leadership would have certain actions "forgotten." Garwood had no such opportunity. Those choosing not to recognize the authority of the senior POW had charges filed against them, later not prosecuted under a ridiculous theory that a prisoner of one branch did not have to obey a senior officer from another branch. That theory was approved by President Nixon.

I felt the Marine commissioned officers charged with collaboration should have been prosecuted, along with commissioned officers in any other service. The ultimate irony is that a "distinguished" member of the few, the proud, and the Marines, accused of collaboration, later served on a Presidential Amnesty Board under President Carter. The same President Carter who allowed the prosecution of a Marine PFC with information on POWs.

I know Foley intended to use a defense including selective prosecution. I know he told Garwood to keep quiet from the beginning. Foley knew anything Garwood said would be used to fill in blanks on what the government already knew. I recognized, from the beginning, Garwood knew about POW locations and POWs left behind. Garwood told Foley and Foley told me. I also knew that Garwood had not been debriefed because of these restrictions.

I felt that some "uncorrelated reports," released before Garwood returned pertained to him. These, I fed to Foley as he untangled what Garwood knew. Of the two hundred thirty-one refugee reports referred to earlier, at least two pertained to Garwood. I also read the report of a Vietnamese general who had seen Garwood as a prisoner. The government said the general was "wrong."

While Garwood was on trial, I received calls from wire service reporters about Garwood. I was quoted nationwide in some reports. Hours of conversations, however, did not make the news articles. Some reporters not so secretly hoped Garwood would get the max penalty. Some probed my relationship with Foley. Garwood, for his own reasons, changed attorneys and Foley and I decided to keep our working relationship quiet. There is no reason to now.

Before Garwood's verdict was handed down, one of the wire service reporters told me that he overheard a conversation of the judges speculating about the sentence Garwood was going to get; before he had been found guilty. Garwood got what the speculators thought. A coincidence? A rigged trial? I did not think it a coincidence then and I do not now.

Garwood and live POWs

The government, in 1977, officially decided he was dead. Refugee reports, from Yen Bai, were correlated to him. I knew the "debriefing" alleged by the government was phony. Garwood went public with his POW locations: *1973 Bat Bat prison camp: 15-20 POWs *1975 Bat Bat : about 20 POWs *1975 Gia Lam : about 6 POWs *1977 17 Ly Nam De: 1 person * 1977 Yen Bai (Thuoc Ba Island) about 30 POWs *1977 Yen Bai (Thuoc Ba) : 20 - 30 POWs *1978 17 Ly Nam De: about 7 POWs. He was also told about Americans with Vietnamese wives who moved into Son Tay Province, the same type of information I received at that time.

What was the reaction to this disclosure by PFC Garwood? Skepticism, dismay, and in some quarters, hostility. On June 19, 1985, Congressman Solarz said on the House Floor: "We now... have ... someone who betrayed his nation, ... worked for the enemy, ... deserted the institution which he was pledged to support... making all sorts of allegations,... who deserted his country. He has been convicted of desertion... refuses to take polygraph tests ... to cooperate with the Defense Agency ... under such circumstances, this gentlemen's credibility is not very high."

This is the same Stephen Solarz of whom Senator Barry Goldwater wrote he knew of no one in Congress with more contempt for his colleagues and the concept of trust than Solarz. His push for self publicity was only exceeded by his speed to disclose confidential information damaging to the GOP. Goldwater charged Solarz violated the confidentiality of secret testimony and he may have leaked extensive parts of secret testimony to the **Washington Post**. Goldwater countered this was the same Solarz who regularly lectured Reagan on his foreign policy morality. "He has a strange notion of ethics and honor" (**Goldwater, pg. 315-16**)

Solarz' response to Garwood's allegations was typical of many in Congress. Most preferred keeping themselves in the dark. Intelligence professionals, however, tell a different story.

General Tighe declared some of Garwood's information was consistent with known facts. Congressman Hendon proclaimed on *60 Minutes* (December 15, 1985) that Garwood's reports fit like a glove with other reports. On the same program, SFC McIntire and MAJ Smith revealed that Garwood's reports dovetailed with some of their intelligence. What Garwood said is consistent with material developed by me independent of all these others.

In July 1985, I spent numerous hours talking with and observing him. Many times, I listened in on conversations with others comparing what he said to what I knew. This was my first face-to-face meeting with him. I previously talked with him indirectly through Foley. I also "knew" him through research. Answers to certain questions would determine my estimate of his credibility.

I was intrigued by acceptance he gained from vets after going public with his knowledge. I knew that reported DIA operatives were attempting to discredit him. I was unaware of the total depth of his POW knowledge. I asked him, through an intermediary, about a certain prison and was impressed with his answer.

There is nothing to compare with an eye-to-eye encounter. You can read faces and observe reactions to questions. Congressman Solarz was disturbed by Garwood not taking a polygraph examination. DIA insisted the emphasis on establishing credibility is by weighing the evidence given. Then, the new information is subject to verification by technical means. This information is cross-checked as to currency (time), specificity (place), and circumstances of sighting. Then and only then do they say that "hopefully, at least one source's credibility will be **enhanced** by polygraph examination." DIA asserts the polygraph is a tool, not an end. The taker of the polygraph, if he believes in POWs, is in a no-win situation.

I feel Garwood is a living contradiction. He was specific in his information. I used techniques I learned in my interrogations of Viet Cong prisoners and skills learned as an investigator. I did not use a polygraph. I did not need one to accomplish what I needed. My questions were specific as to geographic locations he should know intimately. I used various forms of observation during the hours I was with and around him. I was looking for the little details that would trip him up if he was not telling the truth.

When I asked him about a specific geographic location, he not only told me what I wanted to know about it; he filled in details that only a person intimately familiar with or thoroughly briefed on would know. He put every "camp" into their proper location. His descriptions fit to a tee what declassified information showed. I inquired about a "bad boy's camp." (A western term for a camp to which POWs were threatened to be sent and from which they may never emerge.) He said he had not heard that specific term, but he knew about a camp for "non-progressives." I asked him where that was. He told me Thuoc Ba, Yen Bai. I knew, from declassified reports, that Yen Bai had been listed as a camp for the "bad boys" or the "non-progressives."

In 1986, I wrote, "With just a small reservation, evidently he is telling the truth." My small reservation was I could find nothing on which to attack him on his credibility. I get nervous with stories and descriptions that fit perfectly. However, since reading **Kiss the Boys Goodbye** with the description of the debriefing he was given by Tighe and the endorsement Rowe gave him, I feel comfortable with my own assessment. I don't mistrust my instincts or data bank. I am not General Tighe with thirty-nine years of intelligence work. I am not COL Rowe with his knowledge of a POW environment and his intelligence experience. I am pleased that my analysis dovetailed with theirs.

I felt he could not pass a polygraph because of certain personality characteristics. He was debriefed by General Tighe in 1987 and passed. COL Rowe said that the government knew all along he had been a prisoner.

Let's look now at his information. He gave specific information about specific geographic locations. His data on Bat Bat coincided with material given to a Congressional delegation in 1979. His information on the locations I asked about coincided with declassified intelligence. Information he gave to others that I overheard fit declassified material I had seen. Rowe confirmed the government knew he was a prisoner. The material I read for Foley suggested the same. Barnes told me of the plan to discredit him. Garwood's facts fits the definition of confirmed information.

A final thought. What Garwood went through by the government, Solarz, League officials, was certainly played long and often in Vietnam Gulags and elsewhere. Our unreturned POWs must have long thoughts about coming back after seeing what he went through. Returnees will ponder his experience to determine if they want to emerge. A CIA contact told me in 1993, "The POWs were told they were not wanted; Americans don't want them back. They had the Garwood example."

The Bible says the criteria you use to judge others by will be the criteria by which you will be judged. When government agents lead the charge against Garwood, it is a sure sign what he did not do in prison. Make no mistake, government agents attempted to get veterans to disown Garwood.

DIA tried one more time to discredit Garwood. In Early 1985, before I met with him and while DIA had never yet debriefed him, someone there prepared a memorandum on him. "... Garwood held a press conference ... live sighting claims. The news conference was sponsored by the National Vietnam Veteran's Coalition (NVVC)... The group has... had access to documents sanitized in response to (FOIA)... These documents were released over five years ago and... apparently are the basis for many of Garwood's reported live sightings. Additionally, several NVVC members have access to privy PW/MIA related information known only to selected Congressmen and / or their staff assistants. ... It is interesting to note that NVVC officials have either had access to or knowledge of variations of Garwood's claimed sightings for over five years. Thus, Garwood's allegations may have been tainted by his known association with the NVVC or with several Congressman, and he may have, in fact, been coached regarding these stories..."

In answer to DIA, the number of declassified pages were in excess of 10,000. The number of pages involving these locations were less than 50 pages total, scattered in 15 volumes. It took three years and three readings of the total pages to find my first information you'll read later. I did not find all the information used in questioning Garwood until six years had passed.

Another event intertwined with Garwood. At the 1985 League Meeting, Garwood was a special target of the government. How does this tie in with Deceit and Cover-up? Earlier, we covered Mr. McFarlane's off the record acknowledgment of POWs. The 1985 Inter-agency Forum was the first year where the media was barred. The following is from that "off the record meeting." (I was barred from later League forums and events because of this appearing in print in 1986.)

The IAG forum began with a prepared briefing for the audience. The floor would be opened for questions. This freewheeling exchange often provides an alert newsman untold opportunities for POW stories. The openings disappeared with a "no newsmen" format. I will present a couple of the more interesting questions before divulging what got me into trouble.

Dave Dimas, author of a booklet on POWs asked LTG Williams if there was not irrefutable evidence that MIAs were alive in Southeast Asia. Williams replied that in all his years in intelligence, he never saw irrefutable evidence on an intelligence subject. This is quite an admission considering Williams' reply to Congressman Moore that if a report of an MIA in captivity could be verified (i.e., irrefutable evidence), then "... we will notify the U.S. Government decision makers ... that the next and more critical phase of action may be initiated." This "next phase" could be anything from negotiations to "black helicopters in the night." Word games!

Jerry Kiley, a leader in Vietnam Veterans groups, asked the League leadership what it would take to ease the tension between the League and support groups; to jointly work towards solving the POW question. He was told Viet Vets could join the lead of the League and follow their "leadership" in working towards a solution.

George Brooks was asked a question about the identity of the "yellow journalists" referred to in League publications. He denied the term was used. When informed two published authors were present who had written about a cover-up and the term was definitely used, he turned the question over to Griffiths. She stated that those who used "unsubstantiated" material to grab a headline for sensationalism were examples of "yellow journalists." It was clear from the context that she had the *Wall Street Journal* and other papers who dared challenge government denials in mind as "yellow journalists".

Bill Hendon and the battle of the chairs

Fireworks began when Hendon appeared. He was denied permission to address the League membership concerning his wanting to create an independent permanent commission to solve the POW question. The Reagan administration and some League leadership opposed it. Hendon was *persona non grata* as far as addressing the membership.

Hendon now sat on the front row, opposite his governmental adversaries. Reluctantly, Brooks allowed Hendon to speak. After his pitch, there followed the battle of the chairs. A chair for Hendon was put up on the dais. It disappeared (apparently with the help of Richard Childress). The chair reappeared. It disappeared again. Finally, the chair and the Congressman arrived together on the dais for the balance of the program. The description of the battle of the chairs is necessary to set the stage for the most important happening in the forum. In a Congressional Hearing on June 27, 1985, Hendon asked administration officials if a certain refugee had not twice passed a polygraph test showing he saw live Americans at a specific location and had not Bobby Garwood seen live Americans at the exact same location. At the hearing, the answer was yes, the refugee twice passed polygraph tests. No, Bobby Garwood did not see Americans at the exact same location. The government did not believe the refugee, in spite of his passing the polygraph, because other refugees had not seen live POWs at this particular location.

These same questions were posed at the forum. Hendon asked if there was not a refugee who twice passed a polygraph, had knowledge of the area, and saw live POWs at this particular location. He further questioned if Garwood did not also possess an intimate knowledge of the area, and saw live POWs at the exact same location. Childress denied they were at exactly the same location. Hendon again asked if they were not seen at exactly the same location. Childress again denied it was exactly at the same location. Hendon then asked if it was exactly the same address. Childress muttered no comment. **No Comment** on a yes or no question? This waltz around the truth is an example of "deceit" at the highest levels.

Later, Hendon and other congressmen traveled to Hanoi. *ABC News* is there. Hendon and Congressman Smith make their way to the compound in question, recorded on film all the way. DIA expressed doubts about the compound because their "technological spies" said that this compound lacked a cistern described by one of the witnesses. Hendon and crew got into the compound by knocking on the door. The startled Vietnamese, seeing a camera crew, allowed the Americans in. They looked around while other Congressmen were keeping the Vietnamese hosts busy, allowing Hendon the time to accomplish this project.

The world saw the cistern with a roof over it so the satellite could not look under the roof to see the cistern. The film was shown on an *ABC 20/20* program I watched. **This was the exact same address, 17 Ly Nam De, Hendon referred to in his questioning**. DIA did not change their opinion.

Even without the cistern, this particular location is a large compound. It should have been acceptable that one person could see POWs in one part of the compound and another person sees POWs in another part of the compound and their stories not match up. Debunkers take the smallest "discrepancy" to make a "federal case" by saying "no evidence" exists POWs were left behind. There can be no deviation from this party line. Hendon, in his League talk, provided an example of a refugee arriving with knowledge of POWs being kept in a specific location who brought out the "telephone number" of the field phone where the POWs were kept. Only half jokingly, he said why didn't someone call up and ask to talk with the POWs being kept there. More seriously, after the "no comment" from Childress, Hendon said, "This is what we have to put up with in Congress." (In my files, I have that report with the telephone number)

A final note. Garnett "Bill" Bell suggested that the POWs seen at this location were Kit Mark, Charles Duke Jr., Jimmy Malone, and Robert Garwood. The refugee seeing the POWs and passing the polygraph tests was Loc, the mortician. (**Testimony before the Senate POW / MIA Committee**)

In 1989, Yoshida, a Japanese monk claimed being held prisoner with POWs. DIA said yes, we know he knew about the Americans. They were not prisoners, however. The question was asked if that is true, then you must know, by name, who those people were that he saw. DIA said yes, but would not tell. Also in 1989, a question came up about a Laotian report on five (or so) POWs seen. The official DIA answer was that the men seen were "albino Laotians." (**From people allowed at the IAG forum where I was barred**) In April, 1997, the story of the five Laotian "albinos" was still used.

No matter who saw POWs; under what circumstances; how solid the case; DIA argues a way out through "words." Properly phrased, you can deny the truth and not tell a lie. If the POWs were not at exactly the same spot in the compound, technically, they were not at exactly the same location.

Ba Vi - the prison - the area - the POWs

A probable POW prison exists known to DIA analysts. In describing this location 13 years ago, I did not reveal it's name. After consulting many experts, that will change. DIA specifically denied to me any POWs were here. Quang suggested they were and so did Sejna.

In 1986, I called a location "prisoner highway" because this geographic location had more than one probable prison location within a twenty-five kilometer radius. Garwood, in his debriefing with General Tighe, said it covered a hundred square mile radius. This report on BA VI or site N-13 is built upon the reports of several sources over a multi-year year period who never met each other.

West of Hanoi is countryside described as gently rolling hills containing a dense conifer cover. A prison compound once described as having "tens" of American prisoners was there. It is an agricultural area growing everything from opium (poppies) to edible vegetables. It also has a dairy farm. French prisoners were held there. One main prison, known as Trai-Giam Au Phi or African Prison was suspected by DIA of holding Americans. First a French prison, the Vietnamese turned it into a prison for the Legionnaires. In 1964 or 1965, the Legionnaires were moved to make room for new inhabitants, the Americans (perhaps CIA or SOG).

New prisons were added as more Americans were captured. By 1967, several encampments, some permanent and some temporary, were in place. One facility was described as being under a double canopy jungle. Another was described as being on a river. A third near a man-made lake built by the Chinese. Another, built by Cubans, was in the "foothills." Garwood knew all these locations.

Au Phi or C3QP is one compound consistently described. Two reports from different individuals in 1970, put it on the same corner of road going towards Ba Vi Mountain. In 1985, Bobby Garwood identified the same road junction when I placed the map in front of him. I sprang the question on him, no preparation, and he responded, no hesitation. There are numerous military installations around the area, though none of a strategic bombing nature. It was safe for Vietnamese training purposes, and enough military installations to discourage escape attempts.

Au Phi (Ba Vi) was described as a high-security detention center, staffed by officers. It was subordinate to the Secret Security Department (Intelligence Division) of the Ministry of Public Security. The CIA had at least one controlled American source in this area for several years. By 1970, several sources emerged with consistent descriptions of this compound. The only major discrepancy was the "pond" seen was put on different sides of the road by a couple of sources. Each source gave a consistent description of the gates to the compound. They differed in what was inscribed on the gate. Each source saw American captives.

One reported that several of his friends knew of the camp. Another was related to the camp commander. There were other indirect reports. Aerial photography showed the camp was "active" and "was found to be as described, a possible POW camp. All available photography of the area was screened, but we are not able to confirm the area as a PW camp." Why? "Due to scale of photography, no fences, gates, or guard towers were discernible to indicate the existence of a PW camp."

One "source was cooperative and highly consistent throughout the interrogation .... above average intelligence. No attempts at deception, evasion, or exaggeration ... source responded favorably to control questions." The information provided was verified and complemented by another unrelated source. A third source knew of American prisoners being kept in some PW camps that the USAF interrogator was familiar with. These camps were in the same general location as "Au Phi." The entire geographic area was a series of possible "high security" POW camps, a fact verified by Garwood over a year after I first wrote this.

DIA agreed. Several of these sub-camps, along with the "Au Phi" camp were listed as part of eighteen camps designated "possible POW camps." DIA expected returnees from them. There were none.

Sightings from this general geographic area continued, however. At least one first hand sighting reported several Americans being hauled by truck to the center of this geographic area in 1976. Garwood reported that in July, 1976, American vehicles brought in American and Vietnamese prisoners to this area. First and second hand sightings continued through 1979. The reports are consistent. No one appears to be giving deceitful information. Bobby Garwood reported seeing Americans in this geographic area. His description of the area, when debriefed by General Tighe in 1987, was consistent with information from declassified reports. As I read it in **Kiss the Boys Goodbye,** I could map trace in my mind the reports I had studied. I was chilled! His knowledge of the sub-camps was superb.

When I questioned Garwood in 1985, I asked first only about Ba Vi. He answered by putting it in it's proper location. Then, he went on and described several other camps in the immediate vicinity with identifying information corresponding to known information from declassified documents.

The government knew more about the location sooner than I did. DIA even corrected my pronunciation on this location as they told me and some of my contacts that they knew nothing about it. DIA flat out lied to me about its knowledge of a location that it did several reports on. Deception? Cover-up? Incompetence? Mind-set to debunk? When DIA and I talked about Ba Vi, they only wanted to know what Garwood knew. They said they had no information about Americans being held there. Yet, Ba Vi had a DIA designation. Some persons working for DIA had developed a profile on it during the war. They are now top POW analysts.

The May 1991 Minority report said "Robert Garwood... (in) the mid-1970's, he saw French prisoners used as forced laborers in a North Vietnamese dairy farm not far from Hanoi." (**SFR pg. 9-3**) Across from Au Phi is a dairy cooperative where it was reported that French Legionnaires were working.

In 1986, LTC Keith Schneider, of DIA public relations, told me, DIA had "no knowledge of American POWs" at Ba Vi. The next paragraph holds the key to DIA's non-knowledge of Ba Vi and why Joseph V. Heller Jr., called me and we agreed to a working relationship on exchanging information. I wanted know why all these positive signs were discounted by DIA. The call was pleasant and cordial. In writing, however, he stated that all information had to go through Schneider's office. He also looked forward to whatever I could give to them on Garwood. What I did not know then was that Sejna and his friends were also attempting to get DIA to focus official attention on the chemical interrogation done on American POWs. Thus, they may have suspected that I knew more than I did **then.**

Chemical Interrogation of our POWs

One chilling aspect comes from the source related to the camp commander, who saw "three of them undergoing interrogation, 'softening', in the 'Chemical Interrogation Room' of the Headquarters building. All ... looked ill and tired, and appeared to have been severely beaten... had plastic tubes running into their nasal passages, leading from bottles of unknown chemicals. The chemicals were reportedly made at the nearby dairy farms... and were ... refined from the urine of cattle."

In September, 1996, Sejna, said chemical experiments were done on POWs in Korea and Vietnam. In the case of the Vietnam vets, he said he personally witnessed as many as 200 Americans in 1965 to 1967 being shipped to the USSR from Vietnam through Czechoslovakia. This would coincide with the opening of this area to POWs in 1964. Terry Minarcin described the area as being part of a group of super secret prisons involving transshipments to the Soviet Union. The numbers being in the Soviet Union and the opening of this prison in 1964 would not make sense unless the inhabitants were parts of Covert Operations. It would account for Foley's 2000 off - line MIAs and the 1205 document, however. Veterans from these covert operations told me American losses took place before 1964.

GEN Quang, coordinator of the abuse of POWs said, "... We are continuing to collect and study materials from POW interrogations..." In 1970, this area was penetrated by American ground forces gathering information on the "sub-camps" outside Son Tay, just five kilometers from "Au Phi." In the area were poppies.

This sadistic type of treatment would explain the remains of Edwin Tucker. Prior to their return in 1987, they were used in Vietnamese medical circles as we use plastic **skeletons** today. Several years prior, refugees reported details exactly like what happened to Tucker. Their reports were discounted. A Frenchman was believed. His report led to Tucker's remains being repatriated. The refugees, also saw live Americans, thus they were not believed.

Drugs and the Super CIA

Besides evidence of live Americans emerging from Vietnam came a pattern of possible corruption in the intelligence agencies supposedly looking for our POWs. The cover was "POWs". The real object — drug trafficking and a "Super-CIA" responsible to no one. Briefly, as it was adequately covered in **Kiss the Boys Goodbye,** I'll cover aspects I found independent of their research. A column on November 15, 1985, in the *Midland* (Texas) *Reporter-Telegram* said "Missing men may be next Watergate." A key paragraph read "an even more shocking story involving the CIA is under investigation by the British Broadcasting Corp.... and by *ABC* Television. The BBC correspondent... (said) he ... does not yet feel secure enough ... to go on the air. ... if it can be proven, **it will shake Washington to the roots."** (**Emphasis** added) This is where I left the subject in 1986.

Later, I found out about the poppies being grown around "Au Phi." Contacting my sources, we came to the suggestion that possibly drug lords were holding Americans. In 1989, I was given information gathered by LTC Gritz. He released two letters on the subject of drugs, trafficking, and the drug lord Khun Sa. The letters were addressed to Vice President Bush and to the US Justice Department. In October 1990, I met with Gritz in Phoenix. I watched a video tape of his meeting with Khun Sa, lasting for over two hours. I saw other documentation listed in the video.

Letter To Bush

Gritz' letter to Vice-President Bush on 1 February, 1988 listed several serious charges. He went to see Khun Sa because of allegations Khun Sa "had access to US POWs." Gritz wrote, "Unfortunately, Khun Sa knew nothing about US POWs. He did, however, offer to trade his nation's poppy dependence for a legitimate economy." Gritz returned to Khun Sa and video taped another interview with him. This second interview was turned over to "the Chairman of the Select Committee on Intelligence; Chairman of the House on Foreign Affairs Task Force on Narcotics Control; Co-Chairman, Senate Narcotics Committee; Senator Harry Reid (D-NV); Representative James Bilbray (NV); and other Congressional members."

What made this meeting special?

Khun Sa stated in the video tapes (including the ones I watched) he wanted to get out of the narcotics trade. High level American officials had been in the trade with him for twenty years. Gritz sent the information to the government. He was indicted for false use of a passport. Gritz did not quit. He charged (in his letter to Bush) that "Lance Trimmer and I submitted a 'Citizen Complaint of Wrongdoing ...' to Attorney General Edwin Meese III on 17 September, 1987. ... inquiries to date indicate that the Attorney General's Office ... 'lost' the document."

Khun Sa makes his charges

Khun Sa is an acknowledged drug lord. He was indicted for drug trafficking in 1989. His June 28, 1987 communiqué to the Justice Department said he wanted "...to make it clear about our... wishing to help eradicate drugs and for all the American people ... to know ... they have been misled to look upon us as the main source of all the drug problems."

Khun Sa claimed he first asked to get out of the drug trade in 1977. He presented a "Six year drug eradication plan" to Congressman Wolff. He continued that further writings to Presidents Carter and Reagan brought no response. " ... the US Government refuses our participation and help to make a success of the drugs eradication program." He wondered why "the world ... accuse(s) us as the main culprit for all the drug trades... when ... we are ... willing to help solve the drug problems in South East Asia." He added, "... our own secret investigation... found... some high officials in the US Government's ... with the influence of corrupted persons objected to our active participation in the drugs eradication program ... to ... retain their profitable self-interest from the continuation of the drug problems...."

Charging, "During the period 1965 - 1975, CIA Chief in Laos, Theodore Shackley was in the drug business, having contacts with the opium warlord Lor Sing Han ... Santo Trafficante acted as his buying and transporting agent... Richard Armitage handled the financial section with the banks in Australia. ...after the Vietnam War ended, when ... Armitage was being posted to ... Thailand, his dealings in the drug business continued ... After 1979 ... Armitage resigned from the US Embassy's posting and set up the 'Far East Trading Company' as a front for his continuation in the drug trade and to bribe CIA agents in Laos ..."

Khun Sa continued, "Soon after, Daniel Arnold was made to handle the drug business as well as the transportation of arms sales. Jerry Daniels then took over the drug trade from Richard Armitage. For over ten years, Armitage supported his men in Laos and Thailand with the profits from his drug trade and most of the cash were deposited ... in Australia ...." Included in his letter was reference to a July 1980 article in the **Bangkok Post**, an English Language newspaper. It charged CIA agents used Australia "as a transit-base for their drug business and the banks in Australia for depositing, transferring, the large sums of money involved."

Gritz, in January 1987, turned over to Tom Harvey, the Vice-President's National Security Staff Assistant, a video tape of Khun Sa offering to stop some nine-hundred tons of heroin/opium from entering the free world. According to Gritz, Harvey said "... there is not interest here in doing that." Harvey earlier told Gritz that Bush received a letter from Arthur Suchesk, alleging Khun Sa had access to American POWs. Gritz was then instructed to seek Khun Sa.

Gritz took Scott Weekly. They arrived in November 1986. The CIA reported Khun Sa had been assassinated some months before. Gritz, armed with "language under White House and NSC letterhead" found Khun Sa. They brought back Khun Sa's offer. As Gritz accused, "Instead of receiving an 'Atta Boy' for bringing back video tape showing Khun Sa's offer to stop 900 tons of illegal narcotics and expose dirty USG officials, Scott was jailed and I was threatened... if I didn't 'erase and forget' all that we had discovered, I would, 'hurt the government'. Further, I was promised a prison sentence of '15 years.'"

Instead of cowering, Gritz returned to Burma with two more witnesses, Lance Trimmer and Barry Flynn. There, Khun Sa again reiterated his charges on videotape. After this, Gritz was charged with "misuse of a passport." Still, Gritz did not stop. At a Breakfast Club in Houston on January 20, 1988, Gritz implored Bush to "seriously look into the **possibility** that political appointees ... are guilty of bypassing our Constitutional process, ... promoting illegal covert operation, conspired in the trafficking of narcotics and arms."

Gritz charged that several years prior, a secretary working for Armitage, asked him, "Why would he have us expunge his official record of ... past POW/MIA assignments and activities?" Gritz laughed "maybe he was considering running for public office and didn't feel the POW/Vietnam association would be a plus in his resume.... It was about the same time a CIA agent named by Khun Sa (Jerry Daniels) turned up dead in Bangkok under 'mysterious circumstances' (gassed to death in his apartment)." Gritz further opined it was "also about this time, as an agent of NSC's Intelligence Support Activity, I was told by ISA Chief Jerry King, '...there are still too many bureaucrats ... who don't want to see POWs returned alive.' I failed to realize the fullness of his meaning, ... until ... General Khun Sa, ... named (Armitage) as a key connection in a ring of heroin trafficking mobsters and US government officials."

Gritz also said a "US agent I have known for many years ... remarked that he had worked for those CIA chiefs named by Khun Sa ... by his own personal knowledge, he knew that what Khun Sa said was true..." Gritz asked why Ross Perot, when he gave Bush documentation on Armitage and others was ordered by Bush (**Time** May 4, 1988 pg. 18) and Secretary of Defense Frank Carlucci to "stop pursuing Mr. Armitage."

Then, Gritz gave Khun Sa's fantastic offer. "On 28 January, 1988, General Khun Sa tendered an offer to turn over to me one metric ton (2,200 pounds), of heroin. ... a good faith gesture ... that he is serious about stopping all drugs .... I challenge you... to arrange to receive this token offer, worth over four billion on the streets ... the largest 'legal' seizure of heroin on record. You can personally torch it, dump it in the ocean, or turn it into legal medication; ... "

Gritz ended, "If you say 'yes' then the ever increasing flow of heroin from Southeast Asia (600 tons '86; 900 tons '87; 1200 tons '88; 2000 tons '90) may dry up — not good for business in the parallel government and Super CIA circles Oliver North mentioned..." Khun Sa was arrested by Burmese authorities in early 1996. They refused to turn him over to American authorities. Gritz was acquitted of his "illegal passport" charges in April, 1989. No drugs were confiscated.

SUPER CIA — fiction or fact?

Gritz mentioned the Super CIA in his letter to Bush and to me in our meeting in October 1990. I was intrigued. I knew LTC Shinkle charged the CIA with interfering with military efforts in Laos seeking POWs. CHECO said Shackley was in charge of CIA operations at Site 85 and with him was Richard Secord. In nosing around the POW issue, I kept coming up with the same names that were emerging in the Iran - Contra scandal. In fact, I was informed by one source I called that he had accidentally become involved in a phone trap involving the Iran-Contra scandal and congratulations, I was now being added to the list. In addition, there was a classified reference to the EC-47 use, in 1973, in keeping track of smugglers.

As a former intelligence officer, I knew how the system was supposed to work; the checks and the balances. During my research on POWs, however, I came across more secret operations than I had ever wanted to know about. Was there more to the "off-line" operations than I wanted to admit? In 1988, Barry Goldwater, in his book **Goldwater**, mentioned he was particularly upset about the CIA mining of the harbors in Nicaragua. CIA Director Casey was supposed to brief the Senate Intelligence Committee, which Goldwater headed. Casey didn't. Goldwater added some things that are relevant, although not conclusive, about a possible super CIA.

Goldwater charged that Casey was uncomfortable talking with Congress because of his distrust for some members. When convenient, he made errors of omission in testifying. Casey disliked Congressional "meddling" in intelligence operations because Washington leaked like a sieve. Goldwater wrote, "I knew he was going to march his own way." (**Goldwater pg. 302**)

Another insider knew what makes Casey tick. In his book **Revolution**, Martin Anderson described the Super CIA, as he saw it. Anderson served on the Foreign Intelligence Advisory Board until he was purged just prior to the Iran-Contra scandal. He wrote the Super-CIA "never did get a full-scale test before it was exposed and killed." (**Revolution, pg. 403**) As described by Anderson, private businessmen would make money selling weapons to Iran, funnel the money to the Contras, and the administration had its way at no taxpayer cost. Anderson said, "Bill Casey was entranced by the idea" of private money funding covert operations, with Congress out of the loop. Those controlling the fund-raising would determine the use of the funds. "It was the ultimate fantasy of the old master spy... the ultimate covert activity..." Casey saw it as the invoking of the glory of the United States for whatever purposes that the CIA deemed appropriate. (**Ibid. pg. 402-403**)

Casey had no problem with it morally. It was a copy of how a group of industrialists in Europe used their power, money, and influence to keep England alive before World War II. Leading the group was the spy-master, Sir William Stephenson, or **Intrepid who** kept his sovereign, King George VI, and his mentor, Winston Churchill, informed of what was going on. Casey, however, was not the first CIA director to do this. In 1940, at President Roosevelt's urging, General "Wild Bill" Donovan studied British intelligence for ways of centralizing American intelligence. In 1948, the CIA leadership "passed the hat," at the New York Brooks Club, among their wealthy intelligence "graduates," to fund covert operations in peacetime, thereby skirting Congressional oversight. The CIA used companies of these "graduates" as conduits for CIA secret funds. Included were Sarah T. Hughes, the judge who swore Johnson in after Kennedy's assassination, and Leon Jaworski of Watergate fame. (**The Espionage Establishment**, pgs. 124 - 127)

I was also told that Iran - Contra, if it had come off as planned, would be a prelude to some offering of the same sort on POWs. In other words, if we could get hostages out of Iran, for weapons, then we could get POWs out of Vietnam and elsewhere for an exchange of who knows what. If true, that would put a whole new perspective on why various people did not answer questions during the Iran - Contra hearings. They could not without jeopardizing other initiatives being put forward. As I later found out, perhaps it worked. Perhaps the shutdown of Iran-Contra also shut down the return of POWs.

The officials named by Khun Sa are adamant that they had nothing to do with drugs or the charges listed. Some did, however, refuse to undergo any examination of their record on MIAs or the drug charges. I was told by reporters at the *Washington Post,* when it appeared that Armitage might be appointed Secretary of the Army, he had his name withdrawn for consideration because he did not want to answer questions on those two subjects. He was high in covert activity, working as the assistant to Eric Von Marbod in Vietnam. Both arranged for the movement of military supplies to Thailand as Vietnam fell. Von Marbod oversaw weapons sales from the Pentagon to Iran in 1975-77. (**The Palace File**, **pgs. on Von Marbod**)

Did they do what has been charged? Their names have surfaced in many places and in many reports. All have denied all involvement. Khun Sa said that his "investigation" uncovered their involvement. None have been charged with violating or found guilty of violating any law. Thus, they stand innocent.

Did a Super CIA exist? My personal opinion was yes, it did and it does. That does not mean that a Super CIA did all that has been charged. It does mean, however, that there should be a full investigation of the charges leveled. That is the only way to clear the air about the drug connection and it's association with POWs. It might also answer the political questions about Khun Sa's "Shan State;" his ties to Communist China; and Chinese influence in this mess (drug smuggling).

Vietnam and campaign contributions

Besides the Super CIA, other items have emerged as reasons to forget MIAs and unreturned POWs. OIL is one! I'll explore the subject more thoroughly in another chapter. Here, however, I want to focus on another subject as it pertains to this chapter on Deceit and Cover-up.

Originally writing about the trade embargo being lifted by President Clinton, I did not know the deceit behind the move. I originally believed it was the usual political sellout of the POWs. As I probed, however, I found that the Clinton Administration sold the POWs out for campaign contributions. This charge is harsh, but the next few pages, I believe, will adequately support the claim. To sell them out, there have to be prisoners alive in 1993. As will be demonstrated in Chapter 13, the Senate POW Committee staff found adequate documentation to say that POWs were alive in 1989 and further evidence shows their survival through 1992. This report went to President Clinton in January, 1993.

In February 1993, an Australian researcher, Stephen Morris, found in the Soviet Union the famous 1205 document. This shows, as will be demonstrated later, that over 670 POWs never made it home. The document is the first "smoking gun" direct from Hanoi validation of previous estimates of significant numbers of POW survivors. This report went to President Clinton soon after it's discovery.

On March 9, 1993, Mochtar Riady, head of the Lippo Group, wrote to President Clinton in what the *Wall Street Journal* described as Riady asking for normalized relations with Vietnam. He frankly admitted that two of his managers were in Vietnam attempting to do business. The *Journal* reported that in August, 1993, Lippo opened a trade office in Vietnam. For normalized relations, the Trade Embargo would have to be lifted. Ann Coulter, in **High Crimes and Misdemeanors**, wrote that Riady asked for at least two other things in this letter; one was to give

China Most Favored Nation (MFN) status and to meet with President Suharto of Indonesia. Clinton did all three. These are foreign policy requests from a foreign national with unusual ties to the President and Chinese intelligence. Riady also had business ties in the United States.

The upshot is that by 1997, with no visible signs of progress on POWs and with no follow-up on leads provided by the POW staff on live prisoners, the Clinton foreign policy on Vietnam dropped the trade embargo, normalized relations, dropped POWs from public policy discussions and ignored evidence of POW transfers to Russia and China. No President deep-sixed the POWs as quick and as neatly as this draft-evading President. He did it simply for the need of money.

For the love of money is....

None of this could have happened without Clinton becoming President. He might not have without a huge influx of cash from the Riady family. Before exploring this cash flow, however, one has to know the Riady family. The Thompson Committee on Governmental Affairs (Senate Report 105-167) reported (pg. 2507) that government officials told them that James and Mochtar Riady have a long term relationship with a Chinese intelligence agency. The Riady family gets assistance in finding business opportunities and the intelligence agencies receive large sums of money. As always in such a relationship, the intelligence agency seeks to locate and develop relationships with information collectors (read agents), particularly persons with close connections to the U.S. Government.

With Bill Clinton, they hit a grand slam! Not only did the Riady family know Clinton from the mid-80's, their "man in the government," John Huang secured a job at the Commerce Department which helped overturn the Trade Embargo against Vietnam. John Huang not only worked for the Riady family, but was described in a June 11, 1997 press release from Congressman Solomon as one who "committed economic espionage and breached our national security by passing classified information to his former employer, the Lippo Group." That group is, of course, the Riady family. The source of this most serious charge was "government sources" using "electronic intercepts." (Thompson Hearings Vol. II, pg. 157)

John Huang raised money for Clinton with the help of Maria Hsia, Ted Sioeng, and Yah Lin "Charlie" Trie. Sioeng "worked and perhaps still works on behalf of the Chinese government." He purchased a Chinese language newspaper in California and turned it from a pro-Taiwan to a pro-Beijing paper. Sioeng, in Beijing, "reported to and was briefed by Chinese communist officials." He also heavily funded PRC projects. (Thompson 2505-2506)

Hsia "has been an agent of the Chinese government... acted knowingly in support of it... attempted to conceal her relationship with the Chinese government... and ... has worked in direct support of a PRC diplomatic post in the U.S." (Thompson 2506). Hsia worked with Sioeng and Huang to solicit contributions from Chinese nationals in the U.S. and abroad along with targeting non U.S. citizens overseas who might contribute to Democratic causes.

Trie has ties to the PRC through his financial mentor, Ng Lap Seng, "a Macao businessman with alleged ties to the PRC." Trie also escorted Wang Jun, an alleged PRC gun runner, to a meeting with President Clinton and Secretary of Commerce Brown. (Thompson 2507) Trie's contributions (from Ng and others) bought him access to Clinton and an appointment, otherwise unwarranted, to the Commission on US-Pacific Trade and Investment Policy. (Thompson 2519)

None of this would matter except that Clinton became President. It was alleged that Brown had been bribed by the Vietnamese for a few hundred thousand dollars to help lift the Trade Embargo. That investigation died with Brown. The following sequence of events will establish a prima facie case for possible bribery to change foreign policy.

In early 1992, Clinton was out of steam and nearly out of money. He survived the Gennifer Flowers sex scandal, which he lied about, and according to *Businessweek* (November 4, 1996), he received a much needed $3.5 million line of credit from the Worthen Bank, controlled by the Riady family. In August, 1992, Clinton and his running mate, Senator Al Gore, needed money again. Almost $500,000 came from James and Aileen Riady to the DNC and the state parties of Louisiana, North Carolina, Georgia, Arkansas, Michigan, Ohio, and California. Clinton owed Riady twice more

When Clinton won, Riady came to collect. James Riady described John Huang as "his man in the U.S. government." He came with the blessings of the Riady family and Democratic heavyweights. Included in the latter group were Senators Paul Simon, Kent Conrad, and Tom Daschle (on the Senate POW Committee). Others included California Treasurer Kathleen Brown, Lt. Governor Leo McCarthy, and activist Maeley Tom (a Lippo consultant). Tom described Huang as "the political power that advises the Riady family on issues and where to make contributions." (Thompson 1222-1235)

To drive home a point, Tom continued, "They (the Riady family) invested heavily in the Clinton campaign. John is the Riady Family's top priority for placement because he is like one of their own... a good friend of Ron Brown..." Huang, in his resume, said, "Cold War is over. Trade will take more dominant role in our coming foreign policy... United States cannot be and cannot afford to be the policeman of the world anymore... Vietnam - we really need to wrap up this historical tragedy in this administration..." (Thompson pg. 1218-1219)

Huang received his appointment to the Commerce Department in 1993, as assistant to Brown's principal deputy, Charles Meissner. The record is mixed as to his authority. Those who testified, both Brown and Meissner being dead, said he had no policy clout. However, the facts say he ignored his so-called walling off from policy matters. He received regular classified briefings on areas including Vietnam and China. Some of his briefings were of a nature including the identification of "sensitive sources." This means that the information came from a source that could be immediately identified and compromised if the information leaked. He received information on business investment policies in Vietnam. His log book showed several policy meetings and briefings on Vietnam.

Huang's tenure at Commerce lasted 18 months. He was assured of a position in January, 1994. The trade embargo was lifted in February. This was a shift from the July 1993 position of President Clinton emphasizing that no change would be made without a significant change in MIA policy on the Vietnamese part. On this point, Press Secretary McCurry said Clinton was "unbudgeable." By the time he left, we had diplomatic relations with Vietnam. With the Solomon revelation, one wonders about Huang's habit of secretly going across the street from Commerce to a Riady affiliated company office and making probable calls to Riady personnel and using fax machines and copiers. Other questions arose about his access to PRC diplomatic personnel and his overseas contacts.

Both Scott Kaminski and Paul Buskirk, security personnel familiar with Huang, had problems in these areas. Kaminski learned about Huang's travels, his contacts abroad, and a foreign bank account. That earned for Huang an "E" or potential security problem that no one acted on. (Thompson 1169). Buskirk became worried about the lack of an overseas security check on Huang and once the scandal broke, he wanted to know "Was Huang an agent for Chinese intelligence?" He never received a satisfactory answer for himself. (Thompson 1170)

Besides his classified briefings, Huang had access to classified material sent to Meissner and others. He had a clearance for material months before his appointment and months after he left. Although the Thompson Committee wrote that his official duties were insignificant, policy wise, one has to wonder about it from a common sense view. Huang was a Riady man with unusual access to both Brown and Clinton. His unusual access to classified materials and simultaneous communication with the Riadys and their access to Chinese intelligence should have never happened. The Chinese do not like wall flowers. They expect collectors to collect and disseminate information. As the Riadys had a man in the government (thereby giving the Chinese one more foothold) having the Riadys in Vietnam gave Chinese intelligence a foothold in Vietnam.

The Chinese connection to the Riadys, China Resources, is reported to be a "corporate agent of economic and political espionage serving the government of China. Intelligence officials have confirmed... the Chinese intelligence establishment is heavily involved in the operation of China Resources and that China Resources selects overseas business partners in part on the basis of their value as potential intelligence gatherers." (Thompson 1120) "Reliable but unconfirmed" FBI reports say that Huang passed a classified document to the Chinese government while at Commerce. (Thompson 1180 quoting Bob Woodward, *Washington Post*, 11/14/97, pg. A1) The fact is policy changed while Huang had input.

Of significant note, the Riady family did little work in election efforts prior to 1992. That changed when Clinton ran. By 1996, our intelligence came across evidence that China was heavily involved in an effort to keep from being surprised on U.S. political, economic, and diplomatic initiatives through various overt and covert schemes. At least one scheme involved an attempt to corrupt the presidential election process. One DIA operative wrote that the PRC and it's business affiliates have used overseas Chinese to gather intelligence as part of their economic espionage effort. (Thompson 2509-2511fn)

As this book is being finished in 1999, the front page story for months has been the continuing discovery of Chinese success in penetrating virtually every type of missile program we have had for years. Many of these initiatives can probably be traced back to Clinton and his affair with China. As seen in other parts of the book, the POWs are inextricably tied to political and economic concerns. As Clinton spent more bargaining chips, we received little back on the POW question.

Another way to show the probable policy shift in exchange for campaign contributions is to examine a couple more examples. The first involves Charlie Trie. On March 21, 1996, he sent Clinton a "rather provocative letter about U.S. actions taken prior to the Presidential election on Taiwan." (letter to NSC adviser Anthony Lake 4/22/96) concerning the "US carriers and cruisers involvement":

- **"Any negative outcomes of the U.S. decision in the China issue will affect your administration position especially in this campaign year"**

- "Why US has to send the aircraft carriers and cruisers to give China a possible excuse of foreign intervention and hence launch a real war?... don't such conduct will cause a conflict for 'intervening China's internal affairs'... cause problems for the U.S. policy of not interference of China's internal affairs?"

- "Has the U.S. government considered if China starts to occupy the two small outer islands (Wu Chiu and Ma Tzu) (possibly flash points Quemoy and Matsu), will the U.S. proclaim war against China? or just withdraw its ships?"

- "Once the hard parties of the Chinese military incline to grasp the U.S. involvement as foreign intervention, is U.S. ready to face such challenge?"

- "It is highly possible for China to launch **real war**, based on its past behavior in Sino-Vietnam war and Zhen Bao Tao war with Russia."

- "I hope the president will carefully consider these issues..."

These quotes from the letter (I supplied the emphasis) along with the reply will, I believe show several things. First, this received a personal reply on April 26, a relatively quick response under the best of circumstances. The recommended reply was that Trie be reassured the "US has no hostile intentions toward the PRC." Clinton's reply said, "It was not intended as a threat to the PRC." In neither, was there any mention of policy towards Taiwan. Since all knew Trie, one obvious conclusion is that it was recognized that Trie was a messenger from the PRC.

Further, this letter was faxed to the White House by Mark Middleton, a former aide to Clinton. Trie's reply was sent through Middleton, although Trie had a Washington, D.C. address in the Watergate complex. Middleton had ties to Riady. This puts him in the same class as Webster Hubbell, Joseph Giroir (both law partners of Hillary), Mark Grobmyer, Paul Berry, and Maeley Tom, as being Friends of Bill and employees or paid consultants to the Riady family.

The reference to war ties in with stories, reported in April 1998 by the *Washington Times* and *New York Times*, that during this period, a Chinese official threatened the United States with an attack on Los Angeles if the "United States interfered in China's campaign of intimidation against Taiwan." These warnings also dove-tail with Senator Fred Thompson's revelations on July 8, 1997 of a PRC plan of influencing U.S. policy towards Taiwan. His revelations were edited and approved for release by both the CIA and FBI. (Thompson 2508 fn)

Trie probably did not write the letter. It was too stiff and formal for one who knew Clinton as well as he did. His capacity for strategic thinking is lacking and was described (in a similar foreign policy context) as being "superficial, gramatically deficient, completely incomprehensible" and found to be drafted by another person entirely. (Thompson 2535) This letter, although fitting part of the description, uses precise wording and communist wordings like "intervention in internal affairs" and "hard party" threats of war and cutting off of campaign contributions. Trie is connected to Chinese Triad gangs (**Year of the Rat**, pg. 107). His financial benefactor, Ng Lap Seng is similarly described and identified as being tied to the PRC and criminal activity in Macao. Ng is "a member of the Chinese People's Political Consultative Conference, an advisory board for the Chinese government and ruling Communist Party." (Thompson 2524)

In the cover letter to Trie's fax, he is described as a personal friend of Clinton from Little Rock and a "major supporter." This came about because of his $1.5 million in contributions from foreign sources, including $1.1 million from Ng. On the day he faxed the letter, he contributed almost a half million to the Presidential

Defense Fund (later to increase to almost a million). The source of the half million is described as a Vietnamese lady leader of a Buddhist cult residing in Taiwan but who was preparing to move the cult to Cambodia, base of Sioeng, Hun Sen, and a mutual friend of both, Theng Bunma, a reputed Cambodian drug trafficker. (*Wall Street Journal* editorial 1/13/98) Not much else is known of the woman except that in getting the money together, it is alleged she used "coercive" methods in getting "voluntary" contributions and in some cases reimbursed people for "their" contributions. Trie was a reported disciple of hers. Many of her followers had Vietnamese names. A known fact is that after the several warnings, including that of Trie, Clinton changed his Taiwan policy.

One further example will show how money speaks with Clinton. The *Wall Street Journal* carried a column by John F. Fund in 1996 dealing with Guam and Saipan and their being able to chart their own political course. After a visit by Hillary Clinton in September 1995 and $892,000 going to DNC coffers, it took only three weeks to allow Guam to receive a shift of policy towards island autonomy. Saipan, only able to raise $70,000, and only 150 miles away, was rewarded with less autonomy than before. The $892,000 represents about $10 per person on the island, including children.

One policy shift could be called accidental. Two might be coincidental. Three (and there are more including Indian tribes) smacks of buying foreign policy shifts with campaign contributions and causes one to think in terms of bribery. The White House had it's own spin. Mike McCurry said that it was not credible to believe that **one piece** of correspondence took precedence over the decision making process the President was already involved in. Clinton told *AP* that the Riady letter was like tens of thousands of others he gets on other subjects. Hundreds every day suggest what White House policy ought to be. Coulter reported that Clinton also said that reporters could find no evidence that he had changed foreign policy **solely** because of campaign contributions. Well, maybe a combination of campaign contributions, private letters from friends of the Chinese, contributions from the Chinese will be revealed later. It is a matter of record the POWs suffered.

McCurry said normalization took place when it did, and not before, because Clinton was "unbudgeable" on his insistence that normalization could not take place until unreturned POWs and MIAs were accounted for. RIGHT.

A further piece of evidence occurred in March, 1998. Clinton waived a major restriction on American trade with Vietnam. The easing allows American companies access to help from the Export-Import Bank, headed by a Clinton crony and friend of Huang (*Wall Street Journal*). Virginia Foote, head of the U.S.-Vietnam Trade Council, a business group, said, "We're very pleased." Also associated with the Trade Council, described by Bill Bell in a September 17, 1996 testimony before Bob Dornan's Committee, as a "front organization headed by former Ambassador to Laos, William Sullivan;" is Frances Zwenig, a former POW staff assistant to Senator John Kerry.

To show how tempting it is to sweep the MIAs under the economic rug, consider that in the same hearings, Bell revealed that three people involved in the MIA accounting, including "the team chief of the discrepancy case team" and two others from DPMO, successor to JCRC, went to work for Catepillar and Nations Books, in Indochina. They went to work shortly after the shutdown of the POW Senate Committee, headed by Kerry. They were recruited for their jobs by the U.S.

- Vietnam Trade Council. Dornan pointed out that this was an obvious conflict of interest which he abhorred. (pg. 115)

Kerry, for his part in this sordid mess, received a $10,000 contribution from Johnny Chung which ensured a trip for Chung and his guest, Chinese communist intelligence LTC Liu Chao Ying, to study from the Securities and Exchange Commission how to get involved in the US economy through the listing of Chinese businesses on the US Stock Exchange. (**Rat**, pg. 206-207) Ying is also the daughter of GEN Liu Hauqing, China's top uniformed military soldier and proponent of China's acquisition of satellite technology to enhance China's military capabilities. Also, Kerry's cousin reportedly received, after the shutdown of the POW Committee, preferential treatment for real estate ventures in Vietnam.

That trip must have paid off since in May 1999, it was revealed in the *Arizona Republic* that COFCO, described as "a corporate giant owned by the Bejiing government," invested $35 million in a "Chinese Cultural Center" in Phoenix, near the airport. Listed as principals in the deal were Wang Jun, son of a former Chinese Vice-President and reputed gun runner; and Robert Ma, a former Colonel in the Chinese People's Liberation Army who was indicted on gun-running charges. Jun is also head of CITIC, charitably called "China's most powerful financial and industrial conglomerate," by the *Republic*. In **Year of the Rat**, CITIC is identified as one whose "business is satellites, a prime focus of China's military buildup." (pg. 212) In Chapter 11, you'll discover that COFCO, China National Cereals, Oils, and Foodstuff's Export and Import Company, was heavily involved in a proposed POW switch. Their head of Economy was described as "the main leader of China's intelligence office, specializing in Soviet affairs." COFCO was also listed as being involved in auto financing, real estate promotions, land developments, shoe factories in China, among numerous other holdings plus those proposed. The Chinese profits go towards modernizing their military might whose main purpose is to gain a strategic military advantage over the United States.

Is this all a coincidence or a deliberate pattern to deep six POWs for "pieces of silver" and lots of them? There exists more to this pattern of behavior including outright bribery involving Indian lands and the attempted intimidation of a United States Senator who opposed the transfer and who was definitely no Friend of Bill. Now, we return to the first question of Riady money and the POW situation.

The Vietnam normalization process obviously now was deceitful, having more to do with money that with our POWs and MIAs. How many of those hundreds of letters, referred to as the President receiving, come from "friends of Bill?" How many of the writers of the tens of thousands of letters ever see the President himself? I know that when I wrote just to a White House Press Secretary, I received a letter back from the Pentagon.

How much influence did this one tiny three page letter have? Riady's son made it to the White House 20 times at least. Six times, he met with the President personally. Riady met with Clinton at a private meeting during the inauguration. The White House said it was in a more public room associated with MTV's coverage of the inauguration. Outside of big donors who rent the Lincoln bedroom, how many of those "hundreds" of people each day get to see the President even once, let alone tens of times? How many of the letter writers get their "own man in the U.S. government?" How many of the letter writers and their associated friends are involved with Chinese intelligence?

To further prove the point, in May, 1998, it was revealed from a succession of media articles from the *New York Times* to *Newsweek* to the *Wall Street Journal* that the President waived Commerce Department procedures, over State Department and Pentagon objections, to allow the export of superior technology to China for missile guidance use. Prior to this, the Democratic National Committee received hundreds of thousands of dollars in campaign donations, all illegal, from Clinton fund-raiser Johnny Chung, who received it from the Communist Chinese military intelligence. Chung is cooperating in a criminal investigation of these donations. The donor, LTC Liu Chao-Ying, made it to the White House also, posing with the President for a photo. You met her earlier in this chapter.

Cover-up. Would releasing this letter of questionable ethics have switched votes from the draft evader to the war hero? **The donations from China took place prior to the 1996 election. What would voters have thought? Deceit.** Now we know why the rush for normalization - money, money, money. Lippo is a banking and real estate conglomerate. There is money to be made in Vietnam in oil. Investors in Vietnam need money. Banks lend money. Besides, Lippo is very active in China besides Vietnam.

Our POWs? As I wrote in 1979 and 1986, they are right in the middle once again. The accounting that Clinton, the war evader, was "unbudgeable" on never occurred. Normalization did, however. The negotiated peace in Cambodia fell apart and we received no POWs . Normalization worked only for the Vietnamese.

The government stands charged with willful suppression of information concerning the fate of MIAs / POWs. A corollary charge is willful deceit on obtaining an accounting. The government pleads innocent. In view of the evidence in this chapter, how can a jury find it but guilty?

After the technology transfer was revealed, the world was next treated to a round of nuclear detonations from India and Pakistan. India claimed it needed to test to protect itself from the new technology China had. Pakistan declared it needed to protect itself from the new tests India conducted. Pakistan received part of it's technology from China. Also unfolding was the revelation that China had stolen technology to simulate nuclear explosions and to detonate neutron weapons. All occured on the watch of President Clinton and his party that benefited from the campaign donations of the Chinese.

In early March, 1999, the world woke up to the fact that China had advanced a generation in missile technology, including guidance systems that included advanced multiple, independently targetable rockets. The threat made by "Trie" was now almost ready to be fulfilled since China had about 650 rockets aimed at Taiwan, the southern most leg of our Pacific rim defense. And people think this story is just about POWs. Connect the dots and find out the real story.

The Families Fight Back

The families realized immediately after January 1973 the government would not account for the MIAs and unreturned POWs. Status changes began with death declarations without proof. A way was found to eliminate the problem of 4400 men unreturned from war. This chapter deals with several subjects. First is status changes. Second, is the legal challenge to the government's accounting raised in the *Smith* case. Third is a remedy provided by a new set of laws. Finally, is the specter of governmental interference in the internal affairs of the League.

Status changes were "delayed time bombs." Men were "killed off" by a presumptive finding of death (PFOD). Under law, for a man missing over a year, this PFOD could be issued with proof of the death by eyewitness reports, intelligence reports, or debriefings of returnees. The presumption used most often, however, was the lack of information from the enemy.

The case of David Hrdlicka shows how the system worked. This system might have been good with absolute control of the battlefields and fighting to win wars. With defeatist Congresses and wars fought for vaguely defined goals, the laws were woefully inadequate. Until we regain our stature in international affairs, we have no right to declare men dead on the mere basis of time lapse. Our enemies are unconcerned about our "legal" status of the men. They are either alive or dead.

Early fighting by the families

Colonel Earl Hopper testified why the families fought status changes. "We felt strongly ... the law under which status changes were being made was unconstitutional." (**House Select Committee, Vol. 4 pgs. 55-75**) The first court challenge was *McDonald v. McLucas*. The court ultimately ruled the law unconstitutional on its face and as administered. The only remedies the court directed, however, was to notify the MIA next of kin of status hearings and afford an opportunity for relatives to have counsel present.

The services then rewrote their regulations and status changes resumed. Mandatory changes were halted with the help of Rep. John Rhodes (R-AZ) and Goldwater who persuaded President Nixon to help.

Why worry about status changes? The Paris Peace Accords provided parties would only "take any ... measures ... required ... about those **still considered missing in action.**" (**Emphasis added**) An affidavit filed in *McDonald* showed the Vietnamese considered it a responsibility to only account for missing men. (**Appendix H**) This affidavit was used in two court cases and the Montgomery Hearings. It was never challenged. Frank Sieverts, was asked under oath what effect a determination of death would have on the Vietnamese in accounting for our men. He answered, the Vietnamese **made no response whatsoever**.

How have the Vietnamese perceived our MIA delegations? In 1979, the Vietnamese were puzzled by the fuss over the MIAs. They told officials they "didn't know that you cared" about the issue. (**Congressman Dornan in a talk with author.**) In 1987, Vessey told Congress the protocol was "correct" for his reception. Executive departments continually ignore the law. In *Hopper*, one argument presented by the government was that they were not obligated by statute to seek an accounting for our missing men. This, in spite of plain language contained in two public laws stating, "The President **shall** continue to take all possible steps to obtain a final accounting of all Americans missing in action in Vietnam."

The law v. the Executive Department

Even more significant is a law passed in 1868 (Section 1732 of 22 United States Code) which was used in the *Smith v. Reagan* case: "Whenever it is... known to the President that any citizen... has been unjustly deprived of his liberty by... any foreign government, it **shall** be the duty of the President forthwith to demand... the reasons of such imprisonment and if... wrongful... the President **shall** forthwith demand the release of such citizen, and if... unreasonably delayed... the President **shall** use such means, not amounting to acts of war... to ... effectuate the release; and... be communicated by the President to Congress."

Here, in black and white, is the Presidential requirement towards the rights of all American citizens. Prompt action by the executive to release POWs, using all means short of war. A further commitment was to involve Congress in the oversight of the actions taken. The reply to this plain language filed by Richard K. Williard, Acting Assistant US Attorney General and Samuel T. Currin, United States Attorney, stated:

"This action seeks to have this court direct the manner in which the President ... deal with foreign governments on ... the return of any POW's/MIA's alive... a nonjusticiable political question... (does not) make this court the appropriate forum for the resolution of the political questions ... They have submitted twenty-six affidavits in support of this allegation (there are living American POWs in captivity)... (**footnote to this point reads ... defendants' official position as to ... live POWs is not necessarily at odds with plaintiff's allegations**)... the court must accept as true all well-pleaded factual allegations... plaintiffs assert that... POWs' constitutional rights... are... violated by the actions ... of the defendants... the rights of ... POWs **are inextricably bound up with the conduct of foreign relations**... The Paris Peace Accords... reflect an effort... to ascertain the existence... and return of... POW's.... the threshold duty of inquiry... has been met... (Even assuming POWs are alive) the court still should not interfere with ... the executive and legislative branches to gain an accounting of ... POWs and to obtain their ... repatriation. " (**Emphasis added**)

The administration attempted to have it both ways. They plead that only the executive department has the say on the conduct of foreign affairs. They say that the issue is a nonjusticiable political question. They concede, for the arguments of dismissal of the suit, that the allegation of POWs being alive and held captive must be assumed to be true. Yet, they assert that their threshold responsibility was met by the Paris Peace Accords. Further they said that because Smith and McIntire were allowed to testify before the Senate in early 1986, their further obligations were met. It was not pleaded, however, that the best case received a full hearing. The government could not plead that because it would be a bald-faced lie.

The families, supporting vets, and other witnesses came close to presenting a full case for the existence of live POWs in Dornan's 1996 hearings. Normally, the government hides behind secrecy, information suppression, and outright lies to keep the best case against them from being put before the American public. There have been threats, coercion, intimidation, and interference in private affairs to prevent this from happening. That was brought out in Dornan's hearings (chapter 13).

In the 1991-92 public Senate hearings, early on, American governmental officials testified that American POWs had been left behind (first ever public admission). The Senate Committee then did not know what to do with that information. (We'll look at some behind the scenes findings in Chap. 13) In *Hopper*, the lame excuse presented that the government met its obligations by holding the Montgomery Hearings. Now, the government uses the Montgomery Report, the Paris Talks, and the Senate POW Hearing. None denied POWs were alive.

Defects in the law on status changes

The status change laws had defects. Many have now been corrected. The late Dermot Foley outlined these defects before the Montgomery Committee (**vol. 4 pgs. 63-64**). These are the defects he found.

There was no provision for notifying the MIA representative of a status hearing with no provisions for the MIA representative to attend. The notices mandated in *McDonald* were only for beneficiaries of government payments whose interests may conflict with the MIA. No one is specifically authorized to represent the interests of the MIA. There were no guidelines dictating under what circumstances hearings should be held or determinations of death made. Hearings were held while search efforts were in progress. The case of Russell Bott is an example.

A man may be declared dead despite evidence that he is alive. Ron Dodge and David Hrdlicka were both were declared dead despite pictures of them in captivity. Dodge's remains were returned. No determination was made how long after capture he survived. In September 1991, Colonel Peck told an American Legion Convention in Phoenix that even if no Americans were alive, he wanted their remains back to determine when they died.

Those determining the status of the MIA often don't have all available information. Data has been deliberately withheld from some panels, including classified. Hearing witnesses were not subject to cross-examination. The government presents its case in a summary form, not subject to scrutiny. The family member was supposed to see this case beforehand, although the government couldn't be forced to supply all the information in its possession. There were no rules of evidence commonly found in the lowest court rooms. Finally, only the wealthy could afford to contest the government. Was the MIA protected?

Married or not? Only the government knows

MAJ Brent E. Davis was an MIA when his wife decided to remarry. The Davis' had no children. Davis' parents were still alive. When Mrs. Davis remarried, the Marine Corps deciding she was no longer Davis' dependent, stopped her allotment. His full salary was put into a special trust fund, payable upon his return or to beneficiaries with a PFOD. Davis' beneficiary was his wife.

Mrs. Davis (then Mrs. Herman) sought a PFOD in court. The action was dismissed on the government's motion due to the judge's belief the PFOD would take place soon. The judge was unaware that Mrs. Herman could not ask for a hearing. Later, Mrs. Herman filed her second action in the same court. The parents of Davis and the League retained Dermot Foley to protect the rights of the MIA.

During the second action, Mrs. Herman obtained an annulment of her marriage in California. In the eyes of the military, she became the wife of MAJ Davis again. As Mrs. Davis, she asked to be reinstated as the recipient of his pay. Simultaneously, she requested, as an MIA wife, a status review. Both her lawyers and the government counsel moved to suspend the intervention of Davis' parents. Without notice to anyone, the requests were granted and a PFOD was issued. The case became moot. As Foley later recounted, "... the rights of the MIA were trammeled and that arbitrary definitions ... were part and parcel of ... the injustice ...." The remains of Davis were returned in December, 1997.

The Fanning Case - how the system works

A second case reveals the inequity of the "status review" system. On October 31, 1967, MAJ Hugh Fanning was shot down near Haiphong. The report sent to Mrs. Fanning said, "all available information ... has been carefully reviewed ... It is conceivable ... that the occupants of the aircraft ejected ... were captured before ... use their survival radio.... your husband will ... be listed as missing in action.... he will be carried in this status for a substantial... length of time... We know... they **are holding prisoners that have not been acknowledged.**" (**Emphasis added**)

Katherine Fanning recounted in her affidavit in the *Smith* case, "My husband was carried in a 'missing in action' status until the 24th of September 1976... his status was changed from 'MIA' to 'presumed dead'... about the 17th of July, 1984, his alleged remains were returned... and on the 8th of August, 1984, his alleged remains were buried in... Oklahoma City..." Continuing, "Approximately one year later, I filed an application for an exhumation ... because of the information which I saw in my husband's ... file... in July, 1985. This information generally provided or reported that my husband had been captured alive."

An NVA rallier on July 19, 1971, identified MAJ Fanning's picture as resembling a man he saw captured. He later "received $150 for the identification ... of Major Fanning. The **source identified Major Fanning** from an assortment of 20 photographs **and provided circumstances of capture which correlated to official records.**" (**COMUSMACV Message 070750c August 1971. Emphasis added**)

On August 5, 1971, "Supra," the source, was re-interviewed and authorities believed the details then more closely resembled a Navy pilot shot down and returned probably in 1969. On May 19, 1972, another NVA rallier reported a shootdown where the man died. The report said the "description of the POW resembled ... Fanning." There is a time conflict in this report and no correlation made.

Mrs. Fanning continues, "By... (July 1985), no ... government representative informed me of these intelligence reports ... I was horrified ... this had not been brought to my attention ... I had always been assured that any information ... surrounding my husband's status would be ... and this obviously did not happen." She affirmed, "None ... was brought to my attention in 1971 ... or in 1976 when my husband was listed as 'presumed dead' or in 1984 when I buried the remains ..."

"After exhuming the remains on August 23, 1985, I requested Dr. Clyde Collins Snow, a Forensic Anthropology Consultant to the Oklahoma State Medical Examiner, to evaluate the alleged remains... he concluded... the available evidence was not sufficient to positively identify the remains ..." Dr. Michael Charney, at Mrs. Fanning's request, reviewed the work of CIL-HI. He reported, "It is not possible to positively, individually, make an identification of the skeletal remains as ... that of Major Fanning... One can say that these bones are those of a person over the age of 19 or 20." Charney charged none of the papers showed how a determination of identification was made; noting that all necessary skeletal remains were not present.

Any old explanation will do

On September 21, 1990, DOD announced that "Remains recovered during January 5-10, 1990 joint excavation efforts by the US and Lao governments have resulted in accounting for four servicemen...;" Sp4 Joel C. Hatley, CPT David L. Nelson, WO Ralph Moreira, and Sp4 Michael E. King. Senator Jesse Helms, said "Almost anyone ... might well conclude that U.S. experts have made positive identification of the remains... Unfortunately, that is not the case."

Helms shockingly revealed "There are no remains whatsoever for ... Hatley or for ... Nelson. For ... Moreira and ... King, there are minuscule fragments of bone and a tooth .... four coffins will be buried... Why does the Department of Defense put the families through this kind of charade?"

In 1986, a member of the Royal Laotian Army reported being imprisoned with Nelson and another Westerner in 1978. He nursed a badly burned Nelson who later died. (The helicopter crash occurred in 1971) He buried Nelson in the camp. This eyewitness gave specific locations, geographical names, a hand drawn map and the site of the grave. Helms continued "Press reports ... stated ... instead of treating the Laotian eyewitness' information seriously, DOD sought to discredit him... administered lie detector tests on him... claimed that he was lying... the information on his map checked out with other sources... some reports say that he was threatened with deportation ... if he did not retract his story." Helms challenged, "I hope ... these reports are inaccurate... the conduct of the interrogation team was questionable ... no native language statement was taken ... his testimony should be reexamined... Meanwhile, DOD insists that the empty casket ... is the true 'remains' of Captain Nelson." (**Congressional Record, October 5, 1990**)

About this "mock burial," Helms discussed the press guidance to the local media where the "men" were buried. Some pertinent points from the "general guidance" are: "The serious cooperation of the Lao government was instrumental in achieving productive results ... Address the possibility of live Americans being held against their will **using only the official USA position** ... answer four below ... Discussion with media should emphasize that POW/MIA accounting is a separate humanitarian issue ... emphasize that the USA is deeply committed to ... fullest possible accounting ... We have complete confidence in our identification and review process. ... these cases were reviewed by forensic consultants who agreed with the laboratory's findings. All information has been made available to the next of kin..."

The *New York Times* reported in June, 1996 that declassified documents prove the United States sent hundreds of Vietnamese commandos into North Vietnam, declared them dead, lied and buried their story under a shroud of secrecy. Almost 200 survived and live in the United States. Eighty eight are believed captive in North Vietnam. One document shows that 10 of 13 men declared dead are alive. Some were declared dead after Radio Hanoi reported them captured. The government opposes efforts to pay the men for their years of captivity because secret contracts for covert operations are unenforceable. Now substitute American for Vietnamese in light of GEN Quang in the 1205 document saying, "Among the other 47 prisoners captured in North Vietnam, ... 36 advisors of diversionary detachments ... inserted in the border region between the DRV and Laos; lone diversionists ... conducting reconnaissance of our main transportation routes from helicopters and reconnaissance ships; and several seamen who abandoned their ships that we damaged and whom we picked up..."

The "care" that goes into a status review

If LTC Hart, MAJ Fanning, or SGT Cressman, were found, the government said that their military pay and benefits could be restored. Dr. Shields swore in his deposition in *Hopper* that only military assets could be restored. As Garwood found out, if declared a "collaborator," he loses his military assets as well.

The government attempted to show they tried to find evidence of live MIAs / PWs. In *Hopper*, the government filed an undated, unsworn declaration stating debriefings of returning POWs "indicated that many... listed in the MIA status did not enter into the captivity environment." Sieverts testified before the Subcommittee on National Security on May 23, 1973: "... each POW returned ...was carefully debriefed for any information ... (on) US military personnel, ... a nickname, or a glimpse ... across a prison compound. No matter how small ... it was logged ... carefully analyzed... a stockpile of information ... already helped resolve the cases of some ... All American prisoners **known** ... have either been released or been listed ... as having died in captivity...Returnees ... are clear in their belief that no US prisoners continue to be held." **(pg. 69)** These debriefings, however, are not available even to the men who gave them with the "political" exception of Senator John McCain. (**Ted Guy**, Laos POW and other POWs to author.)

In contrast, former POW Red McDaniel told an audience in July 1985 that he believed in 1973 no Americans were left behind. Since then, however, in his work with DIA, he now believes Americans were left behind. Further, one picture recovered by our intelligence agencies was shown to all returnees in their debriefings. It remained unidentified, "uncorrelated." In 1979, it was shown to Garwood. He recognized it as a picture of him, in captivity, head bowed, obviously a prisoner.

Let's look at carefully logged information. In an Arizona case (Thomas Beyer), in reviewing the "uncorrelated" documents, one report said JPRC determined a prisoner seen in captivity in 1968 appeared to be Beyer. The Beyer family never saw this document until I informed them. Twenty-three years after the document's creation, the Beyers saw it. As of December 1999, they still don't know why JPRC thought Tom was captive. This is the careful governmental examination.

In July 1992, several thousand photos and negatives of POWs and MIAs, were obtained from the Vietnamese government by a DIA operative. Some ended up in the custody of a POW activist. (Our government had their own copies) Some photos are of POWs, alive and in captivity, who have not been returned. The government's reaction? They said that the photos should not be in the private sphere because of "privacy" considerations.

The find was hailed as a "significant breakthrough," declaring there were no quid pro quos for the information. The analyst, hired by DIA, however paid from $5 to $250 a frame for photos available to the public from the Vietnam News Agency for about $1.70 a frame. (***Washington Post*, Feb. 14, 1993**) In February, 1993, The League said **most** photos pertains to MIAs already accounted for.

In 1976, Dermot Foley charged MIA files held by the Montgomery committee were incomplete; MIA fates could not be determined without access to withheld information and prophetically added, "I hope that none of us will be in a position to regret the damage we have caused by having reached conclusions without really examining the evidence." (**HSC, Vol. 5, pg. 106**) One POW who believes others were left behind told me the following story illustrating how the government handled POW debriefing information. Two prisoners were held together when the guard took one for interrogation. The first POW did not return. When the guard returned, he told the other POW, "You are lucky because you are still alive." That is all the knowledge gathered about the MIA in POW debriefings. As a result of this one statement, it was determined the unreturned POW died in captivity. Was the unreturned POW was part of the 670 claimed by Quang or transferred elsewhere?

The plant false info by the enemy ruse

Similar reports were used to break prisoner morale. An earlier example bears repeating. CPT Rocky Versace was confined to a hut near COL Nick Rowe. One day Rowe noticed the hut was empty. Hanging inside was a pair of bloody pajamas. The obvious conclusion was Versace had been killed. Understanding Vietnamese, Rowe learned the blood belonged to an unfortunate eel. On a later occasion, Rowe saw Versace. (Versace was eventually decapitated.)

We know many MIAs died in captivity, in their loss incident, or attempting to avoid capture. The uncorrelated documents, despite "official" claims are verifiable in some cases. One MIA was declared dead because of a document in the uncorrelated documents. I agree with that finding. The report presented was clear, concise, containing verifiable information. This eyewitness to the accidental killing of the POW was sharp and relayed other credible information.

In the case of Larry Allan Bullock, the computer runs listed him as one we felt the enemy knew little about him. BUNK! I found no less than five separate reports concerning a pamphlet, written by a POW. The Vietnamese could not remember the full name, but at least three said the name was "L A ———". All stated the prisoner had been captured on a certain date, in a certain battle. Those fit Bullock.

I estimate that at least thirty to fifty cases can be correlated. Some men are alive and some are dead. How many families have these documents? Why are they in the "uncorrelated files?" Some "sanitized" special intelligence reports, probably radio intercepts, shows the fate of some POWs. Some are captive and some are dead. Why they are called uncorrelated is beyond reason. These documents are like the refugee reports. Some are good and some are worthless. The government, however, wrote off all the "uncorrelated" documents just as they wrote off every one of the **14,000+** reports received on POW/MIAs.

No place to go to find the truth?

Forty-four hundred men are either missing or unreturned POWs. The government never recognizes this figure. Earl Hopper Jr. is on a secret CIA list. The EC - 47 crew was not on the list given to the Vietnamese in 1973. The Minority Report raises an interesting question: "Who... accounted for their battle casualties... (Referring to so-called "Black Operations") there is ample evidence of Americans participating as civilians in covert operations... outside of the Republic of Vietnam (e.g., Air America, Continental Air Services, CIA paramilitary operations), ... US ... losses... must be reviewed for accuracy, ... providing information to the next of kin ... DIA ... asserted... all American casualties are accounted for in its lists... Without cross-checking... this ... (is an) open question." (**Staff Report pg. 7-5**)

I believe that Quang answered that question. Chapter 11 will explain covert activities. A short synopsis first. I was in the classified Phoenix Program, a legal nightmare. I was a lieutenant in army intelligence. One boss, the District Senior Advisor, was sometimes military. My Phoenix boss was military. Our Phoenix boss in Province, however was OSA or CIA. We were in the "civilian" CORDS program. We flew Air America to our destinations. We stayed in civilian CORDS hotels while in Saigon. On occasion, we could wear civilian clothing.

I had at my disposal, a Vietnamese "army" unit and the Vietnamese "civilian" army, the PRU's (Provincial Reconnaissance Units — run by the local OSA man). Near the end of my tour, the "OSA" tie to the PRU's was "officially" over; the PRU's reporting directly to me in my "military" capacity. I advised the military intelligence chief, the local Police chief, his assistant for security (FBI equivalent), the Military Security Service (military counterintelligence), and numerous civilian agencies we tapped for intelligence.

I did not run cross-border operations at my location. I wrote earlier of the deliberate napalming of our men on such operations. I examined the computer runs for casualties from these early missions. Here and there appeared a Laos SOG MIA. There are not enough men, however, to make up the totality of the men lost on such incursions. The late Dermot Foley was the first to peg that number at an additional two thousand. Knowing Foley and his sources, I used his figures.

In October 1990, we were vindicated by the Minority Staff. On page 6 they listed the usual 2383 MIAs. Then they added: "In addition, **there could well be an equal number** of ... personnel missing ... from ... covert actions ... Since DOD files ...have not been opened...participants ... never publicly identified... could not establish any number for covert POW/MIAs. However, public source books and interviews with participants suggest ... covert operations adds a substantial... dimension to the MIA question ..." (**Emphasis added**)

I know tactical and strategic deception. If you don't want something to exist, develop cover stories, keep knowledge in tight circles, and never admit anything. Soon it will disappear. The deception can last for decades. Quang bragged about prisoners from special operations we never acknowledged.

Forcing the government to disclose

In *Hopper*, the families needed disclosure of documents and evidence. That was denied. The families knew of governmental misconduct. During the deposition of Dr. Roger Shields, Foley made clear his need for discovery. Shields often told Foley the information was available elsewhere. Exasperated, Foley said: "I am not allowed to ask anybody... that's my problem. I am only allowed to ask you. I have a great need for... discovery ... and the only place I can get it is from you ..."

In 1986, discovery was needed in *Smith*. In dismissing the case in 1988, the Court of Appeals said, "Accountability lies in oversight by Congress or in criticism from the electorate, but not in the judgment of the courts."

That Foley spoke the truth is now painfully obvious. Continual roadblocks are thrown up blocking the truth as in this exchange between Foley and Shields:

Foley: Do you know any place ... to get documentation if it exists on this?

Dr. Shields: I would ask Captain Vohden.

Elaine Buck: Do you know whether it exists...

Dr. Shields: I don't know ... I would assume that in the records from the field...

Foley: And you don't know of ... information with respect to eavesdroppers or sensitive ... equipment?

Dr. Shields: I do not.

Foley: Captain Vohden would be the source...

Dr. Shields: Yes....

Dr. Shields: You are asking all these things ... he is going to be very busy ... But you said that you couldn't.

Foley: Yes, by court order.... you gave some testimony ... about the material on pages 310-316. Once again, you do not have information on that?

Dr. Shields: No...

The testimony above could be repeated today. Not only would evidence be found in DIA, but in the primary sources including NSA, the CIA, and the National Reconnaissance Office (NRO). (*Officially, the NRO does not exist. Congressman Applegate (D-OH), found that out when he referred to the NRO in his questioning on information available from the NRO. Official censors lined the reference from his testimony.*) Yes, I know their new building lists the name of the National Reconnaissance Office. However, the NRO is a cover name and the game over its nonexistence is a shell game. (**For the record, try** the name *Joint Star*)

Why the games? Look at the AC-130. The sensitivity of that plane came about because in 1968 it started using the Low Level Television guided weapons; the laser smart bombs; other infrared guided weapons and target acquisition radars. They were state of the art. Not wanting the other side to get this materiel, the command decision was to bomb these downed planes. Vietnam began the use of weather satellites to get clear pictures of target areas over Hanoi and Haiphong. That type of coordination was the beginnings for the integration found in the prototype planes used in Operation Desert Storm called J - Stars. That plane could look over one hundred twenty miles ahead to a target, such as across borders. Vietnam also began an unusual type of reconnaissance — that of microchip injection into human beings traceable by satellites or other devices. Begun about 1967, it enabled us to trace prisoners to prisons by name. It's still in existence.

Colonel Peck stated in his resignation letter he had the authority to process information, but the real handling was done elsewhere. Weaponry, drug trafficking, secret intelligence gathering methods and sources so good we could not use the material gathered. POWs lost in the middle.

The history of World War II is becoming declassified. The secrets of the code-breaking forced historians to rethink the strategic battles of World War II. Coventry England was sacrificed to a German bombing raid to keep the Germans from knowing about this leak in their communications system. Saving Coventry could have compromised the "Ultra Secret" advantage we possessed. Deception stories developed "plausible explanations" on how things were known in advance. Intercepts from "Ultra" were paraphrased so that if copies were captured by the Germans, there was no word for word translation, a dead give away of the source.

In Vietnam, the government adopted a policy of not acknowledging POW existence, in part, to protect our most secret intelligence gathering programs. Like the "Ultra Secret," examination of one program would lead to discovery of others. Saying POWs exist leads to "how do you know?" Explanations would reveal other "spooky" programs. The proof lies hidden in the vaults of some of the most sophisticated programs imaginable. The POW cover-up may lead to the unnecessary unmasking of these programs, unless the validity of the 1205 document and Russian prisoner transfers are acknowledged.

While not buying the cover-up rationale, I understand from a purely security stand point what was done. What I don't understand is why we allowed Vietnam to examine what we gathered from them. The explanation is to help them find their MIAs. Some of our covert sources probably died from this exercise and they never found their unwanted MIAs either.

Truth is a rare commodity. Refugees tell of live prisoners. Their reports were classified. Smith and McIntire were shut down by "security" concerns. If barriers are not broken, future soldiers will face the combat question of "**What happened to private John Doe?**" I predicted if the men were declared dead, we would get little cooperation from the Vietnamese in an accounting. I also forecast the Vietnamese using every trick to get money for MIA information. That has happened.

Over time, people die, people retire, memories fade. Senator Bob Smith recalled one incident. DIA's Deputy Director testified in June 1990 about Loc, the Mortician: "... remember the Vietnamese mortician who ... provided reliable evidence concerning the ... **warehouse** ... that held US remains. He personally prepared **over 260 remains** ... and estimated ... **he saw** exceeded **400**. ... forensic experts ... found ... a substantial number of the remains repatriated ... show ... **long-term storage**." (**Emphasis added**) Smith believes actions delaying an accounting should not be tolerated. (October 1990 issue of *US Veteran News and Report*)

This is a fight for human rights. Covering up their weaknesses, some officials have participated in a fraud on the American people. This MIA situation is a cover-up of massive proportions. The issue is simple: The truth. Are there any POWs left alive? If so, where and how many. The corollary is when do we get them back?

Negotiations for the sake of negotiations

Government agencies participated in a numbers game muddying the question by lowering the number of MIAs showing "progress" on the problem. That is not uncommon to Washington, D.C. Angelo Codevilla and Senator Malcolm Wallop wrote in **The Arms Control Delusion,** their thesis the United States negotiates for the sake of achieving a negotiated settlement. Regardless of the real outcome, it is called "progress." The "progress" is measured by the negotiations taking place. With no definable end result, POW "progress" is shown, even if none exists.

Dermot Foley truthfully said: "Manifestly, 4400 men did not disappear from the face of the earth without trace. ... **Those seeking an accounting must begin with a clear statement of who and how many are the men ... they seek**... People are tired of cover-ups and paper overs in this country today... everything, should be out in the open ...." (**House Select Committee, vol. 5, pg. 110** *Emphasis added)*

Co-opting the League of Families

Certain levels of the Executive Department have used the League for manipulative purposes on the POW/MIA issue including interfering in League internal affairs. It is yet unclear to what extent the co-opting continues.

In 1983, there was an effort to remove Ann Griffiths, reinstituting an independent League. The Board of Directors were criticized for having an Executive Director making government trips without Board consent and initiating opinions not reflecting board policy. There was criticism of Griffiths' secrecy agreement with the government. As late as 22 March 1982, Griffiths had urged the declassifying of live sighting reports after 1 August, 1979. That changed.

In the 1983 League elections, George Brooks shared two letters that he had received (solicited); pitches from Gilman and Childress asking the membership to accept Ann Griffiths in her new, expanded, role as partner of the government.

The Childress letter, on official letterhead, stated the government was encouraged with the progress being made with the Lao. They had the "**brass ring in**

sight" when Bo Gritz loused everything up. Childress recounted "...the central role that Ann Griffiths has played in all this ... Private meetings with the Lao, letters with specific bait... she is ... **a full partner** in even more sensitive initiatives.... (**Emphasis added**) George, I believe that we have a true partnership.... you, Ann... have seen the charlatans .... know the difference between duplicity ... commitment on the part of the government, ... If we ever have a chance, it is with the current team..." Gilman's letter stressed the need for "stability" in the League, especially in personnel. The letters helped keep Ann in for another year.

Earl Hopper, reinstated as League Chairman, responded to inquiries from State and Regional Coordinators if some remarks made by Griffiths represented Board Policy. In a January 1984, memorandum, he wrote:"... NO. The views expressed are strictly personal and do not represent the official position of the Board.... "

Further, on Veteran's Day, 1983. Hopper appeared in an Asheville, NC ceremony where Hendon charged there was an on-going cover-up in the POW/MIA matter. I called Childress on March 1, 1984, and inquired as to the charges Hendon made. He labeled them "totally false." The League Board invited Hendon to explain his views. Traveling at his own expense, he explained as the Board listened intently. Then, a surprise occurred, engineered by Griffiths. Childress and LeBoutillier. ambushed Hopper and Hendon in what Hopper charged was:"... a concerted effort ... to discredit... Hendon for ... proving American prisoners were alive... information was withheld from ... Carter and Reagan.... A similar effort to discredit me ... undermine my position as Board Chairman ..." Hendon was challenged to his assertion about a cover-up. LeBoutillier had previously supported Hendon just one month earlier saying, "For over ten and a half years, the government has covered up the POW story." In October 1982, he said, "A number of officials ... over the past ten years have known of the existence of these prisoners and have deliberately covered it up." Over the Memorial Day weekend of 1982, he and I discussed his and Hendon's secret trip to Thailand to receive live POWs from Laos. He told me there was a cover-up at mid-level State and Defense Departments on POWs. He also told me of some radio intercepts received in 1981. (**LeBoutillier quoted in Hopper memo, op. cit.**)

I was disturbed. Knowing LeBoutillier, changing his views so radically, was out of character. I called him at home after that League meeting. Hopper was not wrong asserting, "... (I) question whether his presence there with you was voluntary or under duress." (**Ibid.**) I know LeBoutillier's charge of double-cross by administration officials on being given a DEA cover to look for POWs. That was used to control him. Hopper's question is best answered by current actions of LeBoutillier. Today, he has repeated his basic cover-up charges.

Childress contended the House POW Task Force had access to **much** of the information Hendon referred to in his Veteran's Day speech. Hopper wrote, "This confirms Congressman Gilman's and Lagomarsino's affirmation... they had not seen the specific documents brought to their attention by Mr. Hendon."

1984 and another search effort

1984 brought another effort to replace Griffiths. This time, through a full-scale effort including interviews and a grading of candidates in proportion to their abilities. The search narrowed to the final two, Griffiths not being among them. Curiously, however, one applicant told the Board that he wanted to withdraw; he wanted to expand his business. The top applicant also backed out. He told Hopper of meeting with senior military officers; "giving him more insight ." Each advised him to either withdraw or to turn the job down. There was a "bucket of worms" they did not want him exposed to. Finally, Griffiths was who they wanted. Later, this applicant stated his regrets in turning down the job. (**Interview with Hopper**)

In 1984, Hopper received a call from Childress wanting him to fly to Washington to discuss Griffith's rehiring. Childress explained a change in Executive Directors would be harmful to the League's relationship with the government; a lessening of their enthusiasm to pursue the POW-MIA issue. (**Ibid.**) The internal politics of the League is important because of the League's perceived "clout". When I asked my Congressman, Bob Stump, to support a House Resolution establishing an independent POW commission, among his reasons for not supporting it was "the League did not support the Resolution."

The tame lap dog that refuses to bite

The constitutional question raised in *Smith* was, "Accountability lies in oversight by Congress ... criticism from the electorate, ..." (**Court of Appeals, April 20, 1988**) How is accountability accomplished when the "chief advocacy group," the League, blocks efforts to achieve oversight? There have been numerous attempts to declassify live sighting reports. The League opposed these efforts. In September 1987, Griffiths characterized one bill to declassify reports as a danger to live POWs, and a part of the discredited theory of a POW cover-up. Congressman Robert Smith retorted, "I do not advocate, ... releasing sensitive intelligence data on live prisoners. I don't care what Mrs. Griffiths says ... " On August 2, 1991, LTC Peck, on *ABC 20/20*, was asked by interviewer Tom Jarriel, "If the American public saw the data that you've seen on live sightings ... what would be the impact, ... ?" Peck replied "... there would be a grass-roots uprising... "

Griffiths, in her 1987 testimony, acknowledged that "in earlier years" such legislation was "the only option available" to gain government attention. She failed to disclose, in 1982, a full year and a half into the Reagan Administration, a refusal to "release live sighting reports" received after August 1, 1979 when DIA charged "... **By comparing this information to the released documents... would confirm to them the fact that we know the location of these prisoners and show the extent and capability of our collection efforts... Your appeal ... therefore denied.**" (**Letter Burkhalter to Griffiths, April 9, 1982. Emphasis supplied**)

Griffiths is critical of historical undertakings, like this book. In an **October 1988** League document, she charged, "Those long involved are... aware... information was distorted or withheld in years past; however, now is not the time... to undertake... historical investigation... must focus on the present and the future. Our men's lives may ... depend on current negotiations.... not ... on history except in the context of policy negotiations." Here, Griffiths attempts several things. She attempts to intimidate "newly involved" people from thinking differently than the League. Second, she emphatically states, "now is not the time" to look at the issue from a historical perspective because "our men's lives may well depend on current decisions," implying that a major breakthrough is at hand. Countering this in **September 1996**, two former DPMO investigators, Bill Bell and Chip Beck, both argued that only by understanding the history of the subject and investigating from the standpoint that what is happening today is grounded in communist history can we hope to get those men back who are still alive.

A July 21, 1989 League media guide asked, "Why is the League opposed to the activities of some POW/MIA groups?" Their "approved" answer was fund-raising appeals frequently "imply that the rescue of a live POW is imminent." Where is the League's approach different? Year after year, the League told its membership "their approach" was best, implying breakthroughs were imminent. As "Red" McDaniel testified on July 25, 1991, recounting a phone call from Childress, "he told me that he knew Americans were still in captivity and **he said we'd get them home in 'two or three years'.** Do you wonder... Mr. Chairman, how many ....have... died since that phone call — **six years ago?**" (**Emphasis added**)

Keeping Congress uninformed

A brazen attempt to keep Congress from doing oversight responsibility came in 1990. Senator Charles Grassley attempted to gain access to eyewitness accounts on American POWs. He was denied access because they were "classified." On July 31, 1990, Grassley denounced efforts to keep him, other Senators and cleared staff from the reports. The day after the censure, he was granted access with, as he decried, "the most extraordinary of restrictions." In October 1990, he discovered that Griffiths lobbied against his access. A Griffiths memo contended "sensitive information is not subject to... **indiscriminate release** outside ... the respective Select Committees on Intelligence and... staff members with appropriate clearances... (this) authorize(s) access to... members... proclaiming... USG officials are not pursuing... issue with... priority." (**Emphasis added**)

Grassley countered, "This memo... lays out... rationale for ... question(ing)... access to... information by Members... It also provides... explanation of why our access... restricted." He questioned Griffiths opposing his access to reports she had read. "Could it be ... she has become afflicted with .... bureaucratitis?"

Peck said his plan was to "... aggressively pursue innovative... concepts to clear up the live sighting business," however, "I was not really in charge of my own office." Calling Griffiths one of the "many puppet masters playing a... murky role;" "She apparently has access to top secret, code-word message traffic, for which she is supposedly not cleared... receives it... ahead of the DIA... analysts. Her influence ... goes far beyond the 'war and MIA protester gone straight' scenario.... One wonders who she really is and where she came from."

What a web we weave when ......

The League's budget, almost a million dollars, comes from appeals to the public they lock out from their stands. In 1985, the League spent $25,000 attacking other POW/MIA groups through a "Misinformation Book." Some criticism was warranted. Most, however, was an attack upon groups they could not control. A Griffiths memorandum, dated December 18, 1984, attacked the VVA, Garwood, the *Wall Street Journal*, Operation Rescue, **Good Morning America**, Task Force Omega, Congressman Montgomery, "newly involved Americans," but exempting the government. Attacks upon "newly involved Americans" invariably includes Hendon and LeBoutillier; ignoring their expertise on the POW Task Force, or DIA.

The League Book quoted LeBoutillier, "After carefully reviewing secret information ... there is no question ... there are over 200 men held alive ... in Vietnam and Laos." She answered, "Mr. LeBoutillier's opinions are his own..." implying LeBoutillier never had access to classified information.

Did Griffiths sign a secrecy agreement granting clearance to classified material? At times she said that she neither signed the agreement nor had a clearance.

That gives a whole new meaning to Peck's question of "who she really is ..."

The latter point is vital because evidently even League members do not escape wrath. On February 12, 1991, Griffiths wrote a memorandum, marked "Sensitive" to Admiral Mike McDevitt, DOD, on responding to a family member. She asserted this family member "goes back a long way with the League ...1973-74. She became increasingly disaffected, and receptive to Earl Hopper's 'approach' as did her parents who became extremely bitter. **She needs to hear the following:**- Recitation of current policy on normalization ... - You are aware of no 'eliminate the merchandise' orders...- I don't hold individual case file information of sensitivity...- All information... pertains... to her brother has been provided...- If ... his remains... in the hands of SRV... so state - You... are doing your best to resolve this issue...- NOK can help by... portraying unified... support ... to Congress... media... Hanoi... **Note: After... draft... I'll give input."** (**Emphasis added**)

The League will reverse positions to retain political clout. The League attacked the VVA in their 1985 booklet, yet, in October 1985, they prepared a booklet entitled **POW/MIA Special Report: A VVA Update.** in which the attack on VVA was conveniently excised as the rest of the report was reproduced. Griffiths also wrote " ... From 1978-1981, no substantive negotiations ... took place and no accountability resulted through remains ...." Yet, according to a League list in late 1985, 49 sets of remains were repatriated during the Carter Administration, including 12 in 1978. From January 21, 1981, to March 20, 1985, only 27 remains were repatriated. This illustration demonstrates the watchdog becoming the lapdog.

The booklet quoted former National Security Adviser Richard Allen at a 1981 League meeting, "One of the first acts ... President Reagan ... was to charge his National Security Council with keeping him informed on ... POWs/MIAs. ..." I see a photo of Richard Allen and myself shaking hands after his autographing my book at the 1981 CPAC meeting and smile. This photo was autographed at this League meeting. Allen continued, after the above quote, the way to get something done in Washington was to "**Raise Holy Hell**" until the bureaucrats listened.

Many groups attacked by the League were founded by MIA family members. The League's July 1989 media guide says, "Since 1970, the League has been recognized by the USG, the Indochinese governments, and the media as representing the families and our missing relatives." Do they represent families that have repudiated them and formed new organizations? I doubt it.

A December 13, 1984, letter from the Adjutant Quartermaster of the Minnesota VFW stated "The wives, mothers, sisters, daughters... in the... League... have the first right to decide... methods to gain the return of their men!... groups that disagree with the... League... and our Government — it would be better... if those **dissident groups** would find another cause." (**Emphasis added**) However, on August 16, 1990, a Kansas VFW organization questioned the League's $1.1 million budget and Griffith's $75,000 salary. They "voted to **withdraw" support from the League** and pledge it to Our Forgotten Brothers a new organization.

The POW/MIA issue is national in scope and futuristic in concept. It does not belong solely to the families. It concerns the welfare of POWs, alive and dead. All groups have relatives who may be POWs of future wars. All groups have a stake in policy decisions. **To be a good watchdog, you cannot be a lapdog.**

Diplomatic Dilemma

An Overview

The POW - MIA issue remains a thorn in the diplomatic side of the United States with implications for relations with Vietnam, Russia, China, and Cuba. Rhetoric about the issue being a "humanitarian concern," is diplomatic dung ensnared in a new set of problems. Our diplomacy should be based on our best interests, including the morale of our armed forces. Without a well trained and well motivated force, we have no foreign policy of consequence. Selling out prisoners for campaign contributions is reprehensible.

Vietnam is an economic basket case. It could be a burgeoning new economic market. A firm policy could achieve our ends and give Vietnam incentives for reforms. An overview of 1996 will adequately show the problem. The statistics are gleaned from the **Wall Street Journal**. The interpretations are mine.

Our POW policy is based on the argument Vietnam is ready to reform. A democratic market oriented Vietnam will be easier to deal with. Maybe. But, getting it there is easier said than done. Vietnam's Saigon and Haiphong ports needing constant dredging, a known economic weakness since pre - World War II. Although major proposals for multinational lending to allow private enterprise do the job have emerged, Vietnam's bureaucracy keeps it from happening.

Hanoi demanded foreign owned companies give Vietnamese workers a boost in the minimum wage for unskilled workers. (**4/9/96**) This proves the government wants a primary role in the economy. Vietnam's leadership lacks the will to change. Hanoi declines to provide political and economic freedom for the economy to grow. Like the border area of Mexico I visited on a NAFTA tour in May, 1997, political change comes with the economic freedoms.

In July 1996, the Politburo endorsed the aging leadership of Do Muoi, (79), Le Duc Anh (75), and Vo Van Kiet (73). With the leadership being approved every five years, the die is cast into the 21st Century. None are market reformers. Kiet ordered war atrocities against American POWs. They endorse the policy enunciated by Hong Ha that the state sector provides the economic leadership, a cornerstone of the Vietnamese economy. (**6/28/96**)

Foreign investment is not lagging with plants being built for products sold to domestic and foreign markets. Reebok shoes for American consumers are produced in Vietnam (**12/26/96**). 150 foreign projects were announced in the first half of the year. (**7/8/96**). Vietnam merged its state owned companies to form megacompanies giving foreign owned companies competition. (**6/24/96**) Foreign companies faced a new impediment to competition when Vietnam required foreign workers to leave after three years to be replaced with Vietnamese. (**10/10/96**)

Contrarily, Saigon industries attempted to democratize and divest it's state ownership. More market oriented, Saigon may provide impetus for market reforms. In Hanoi, the real government leaders, tired of news of their non-accomplishments circulating, censored domestic economic news and kicked out offending writers. These mixed signals of market reform versus state planning upsets many investment plans. Korea, despite a $600 million portfolio cannot get bureaucratic ears. Government leaders often reverse investment directives. (**6/10, 11/8,& 11/25/96**) Nick Rowe provided a sharp insight into Vietnam's problems. Lower level cadre think only as instructed. Questions outside the "party line" needs an approved answer. Improvisation brings chastisement and possible imprisonment. Garwood exploited that armor's chink to maneuver himself into freedom. The connection to POW - MIAs? Ross Perot almost convinced the Vietnamese to give up POW hostages to get American investment. Antiquated U.S. policies shut him down.

Their diplomatic dilemma is to get rid of the POWs without incurring war crime accusations. There is no one to give the POWs to, officially. In chapter 11, I'll demonstrate some did come home. However POWs are no longer tied to "normalization" problems. For the first time, POW/MIAs were never mentioned (*Wall Street Journal* 6/27/97) by an American Secretary of State. I do agree that better relations with Vietnam is in the best interests of the United States.

Market reforms in Vietnam would presage democratic reforms. Both are inextricably intertwined. If informed, the U.S. public will not allow wholesale investments until the POWs are returned and MIAs accounted for. The problem is no myth as a little known Rutgers Professor argued in 1992. It was not solved in Operation Swamp Ranger as the Pentagon claimed in 1994. It is easy to solve. Admit the problem and ask for the men back.

A historical look

The United States paid war reparations to the SRV. These reparations continue, albeit not in traditional form. Today, it's body ransom. The Paris Accords dictated the United States contributing to the "healing of the wounds of war." Those words were almost identical, in the Vietnamese, to the 1969 Viet Cong Ten Point Program's words healing the wounds of war; understood to mean war reparations. The Viet Cong explicitly said the United States must bear full responsibility for the losses and devastation caused. (<u>The Palace File</u> — appendix F, pg. 447)

Nixon's February 1, 1973 message to Vietnam outlined the aid required. The United States would contribute reconstruction money without political conditions, $3.25 billion over a five year period. Other aid totaled nearly $1.5 billion. Nixon said these estimates were subject to detailed discussion between the two parties. (**Appendix B**) A "laundry list" of wants is in **Appendix I**.

Nixon said recommendations would be implemented by each country "in accordance with its own constitutional provisions." Aid became tied to POWs because Quang said, "**We intend to resolve the American POW issue in the following manner**: ... 3. Nixon must compensate North Vietnam for the great damage inflicted on it ..." Twice before, we attempted to bribe the Vietnamese. Thus, the explicit wording gave the Vietnamese confidence money would come.

Our bribes to have NVN quit the war

On January 22, 1972, Nixon offered a comprehensive peace plan with the United States willing to fund a $2.5 billion reconstruction project in North Vietnam. (*February 9, 1972 Report to Congress from President Nixon, pg. 117-119*) The Nixon bribe was not the first. President Lyndon Johnson tried to bribe Ho Chi Minh to end the conflict, "just an old-fashioned, outright bribe..." It almost worked until Johnson shared it with a foreign leader. The word leaked. (<u>Goldwater</u>, **pg. 244**) Ho Chi Minh wanted to quit fighting in July 1963 for economic ties to Diem's Vietnam. The US messed up that initiative by allowing the murder of Diem.

In April 1975, the SRV applied for membership in multilateral assistance agencies succeeding the RVN. The United States voted against their membership and expressed opposition to their receiving funds. However, a member country cannot prohibit its contributed funds from being used in a particular country.

Vietnamese signal how to be bribed properly

In 1977, the Woodcock Commission was told the Vietnamese expected postwar reconstruction. The Vietnamese were told Congress would not act on war reparations. The Vietnamese indicated flexibility in the form reconstruction aid could take; direct aid, multilateral aid, or bilateral aid, or "humanitarian purposes." An MIA accounting and aid became issues that were "interrelated." We could call this aid any name needed to disguise its purpose. The only stipulation was the Vietnamese got the money. (**Woodcock report**) Vice Foreign Minister Phan Hien was adamant "The United States **contribution to healing the wounds of war and postwar construction ... is an undeniable duty** ... the Paris Agreement ... " (**Wolff Committee, pg. 2**) (*Emphasis added*)

Behind the scenes negotiations

Aid seemed to be doomed. However, the United States was engaged in normalization negotiations with Vietnam. Assistant Secretary of State Richard Holbrooke said multilateral aid was an appropriate way of giving money to Vietnam. On October 1, 1977, Tran Duong, Director of Vietnam's Central Bank, said the $4.75 billion promised by Nixon; reaffirming the Paris Agreements, could be paid through the International Development Association. (**Wolff Committee pg. 75**)

However, there was a Congressional prohibition. The issue became deadlocked in a House-Senate Conference Committee. President Carter personally promised, in writing, that if restrictions on funds were dropped, he would instruct our delegates to vote against any loans to Vietnam. (**"Vietnam: Problems of Normalizing US-Vietnamese Relations."**) The restriction was dropped.

This action came after Vietnam's public affirmation this was considered war reparations. It is inconceivable that President Carter was unaware of this since he called this type of aid as being "non-controversial." (**Wolff Committee, pg. 76**) The administration coming to power after a campaign money laundering scandal became engaged in the "laundering" of war reparations. As we have seen and will see further, money laundering (campaign contributions) can also change policy.

After Carter, DOD asserted no money was promised to Vietnam (**1984 DOD Question and Answer Guide**). The Vietnamese, Cambodians, and Laotians publicly say an MIA accounting is humanitarian. On *CNN Cross-Fire*, Ann Griffiths said there was no linkage of money and all agreed the POW/MIA question was to be resolved on a purely humanitarian basis. (**November 11, 1985**)

On December 9, 1985, Bud McFarlane, National Security Adviser, told the World Affairs Council that apparent improved relations between the United States and Vietnam was deceptive. There would be **no normalization** of relations without a **complete accounting of MIAs and a Vietnamese pull out of Cambodia**. The humanitarian issue became married to a political issue.

General Vessey, on September 30, 1987 testified, "... I stressed ... the talks were to focus on POW/MIA and **other** humanitarian issues ...not linked to broader political questions... our objectives ... the return of ... live Americans... resolution of discrepancy cases ... crash site excavations... repatriation of remains..." Griffiths was asked by Rowland "...are you in favor of ... paying $3.25 billion without interest ... for ... prisoners of war?" She answered, "... what you are proposing is too simple .... They would not simply accept, out-front, publicly, any ... offer such as you have just suggested." (Maybe not publicly.)

She acknowledged, however, in 1987, the family of Robert Schwab got their son released from jail in Vietnam for what Congressman Rowland aptly described as "a lousy $10,000." Schwab, however, had long ties to the League and was a friend of Childress. Griffiths said, "I know exactly how all that took place since Mr. Childress ... negotiated him out." Vietnam took a simplistic bribe in this case.

The following exchange emphasizes how bureaucrats show progress where none exists. Congressman Kostmayer, (D-PA), asked if humanitarian aid from the Reagan Administration represented "a shift in policy." Mr. Lambertson, the State Department, said "No, there has been no shift in policy." Kostmayer believed there was a "shift in policy ... allowing private voluntary organizations ... to aid groups in Vietnam." General Vessey said, "I think that the shift is that we... agreed to ... examine the problem... lay it out in a... more coherent fashion..." Kostmayer replied, "So there is a shift." The General asserted, "there is no policy shift ... but ... a different twist... on the addressal of humanitarian needs."

Kostmayer queried, "so there is a twist, not a shift?" Kostmayer asked Lambertson if "it is a shift or is it somewhere between a skip and a shuffle;" later sputtering, "... I am more confused than when I began." Griffiths added her interpretation by describing "a very important step in ...working separate paths to address these humanitarian concerns." Kostmayer responded, "We have gone from a change to a shift to a step... Thank you very much, Mrs. Griffiths."

By 1987, McFarlane's statement was publicly incorrect. However, someone forgot to clue Solarz in. Lambertson stated the "Essential criteria for normalization is... a Cambodian settlement and a Vietnamese withdrawal..." Just prior, he added that a resolution of the POW/MIA question "would be a factor ... that could then develop." Solarz asked Griffiths: "Is that your opinion...my impression was ... we were asking for ... the withdrawal ... and a satisfactory resolution of the POW/MIA question as a condition for normalization."

She replied, "No, it is not a precondition... not currently linked." Incredulous, Solarz asked "... the League would not object" if normalization happened "in the absence of a prior satisfactory resolution of the MIA question?" After a couple of contradictory answers from Griffiths, Solarz asked Lambertson if, "... a resolution of the POW/MIA question is a precondition for normalization?" Lambertson answered "No, it is not a formal precondition..." Griffiths could envision normalization even if "the POW/MIA issue had not been finally resolved if mechanisms ... developed" *indicating* progress was being made. (**Vessey hearing pg. 126 - 127**)

A June 25, 1991 hearing before Congressman Solarz' committee discussed the lifting of a trade ban on Vietnam. Little about POW/MIAs. Solarz was against lifting the trade ban at that time. Gerald Felix Warburg of the Multinational Business Development Corporation said, "If we want access to aid for POW/MIA families... support increased airline flights, telephone contacts, and opportunities for commercial exchanges of nonstrategic goods. ..." Shephard Lowman, formerly in charge of the Vietnam, Laos, and Cambodia State Department desk said normalization "would begin when the Vietnamese had withdrawn from Cambodia." Senator Frank Murkowski asserted, "American humanitarian workers ... business people

and tourists have a far greater chance of running across valuable (POW) information ... from within Vietnam...."

Nguyen Tinh Hung, author of **The Palace File**, recognized trade embargoes
and the granting of a Most Favored Nation Status as weapons; not given away
without receiving something in return. Hung told of an advantage we lost at the
end of the war. We held Vietnam's gold reserves, valued at $180 million. The State
Department dallied and we lost the opportunity to get the money out before Saigon
fell. Ambassador Graham said the money could have been used as leverage to gain
POW/MIA information. (**Palace File** pg. **334 & 519 fn.**) I asserted in an International Relations graduate class you learn from listening to your adversaries.

What do the Vietnamese say about "aid"

Americans are publicly confused about linkage between POW/MIA progress
and money. There is none on the other side. In 1985, the Laotians allowed excavation of the Pakse crash site after the payment of rice on a "humanitarian" basis.
Yet, in late 1985, the **Wall Street Journal** ran an article, unrelated to the POW
MIA issue, stating that the Laotians did not need rice. This seeming contradiction
was, I believe, answered in the March 4, 1985 edition of **Time**. The Laotians said
continued cooperation on the POW/MIA issue was contingent upon continued
generous US aid. The US answered a pattern of sustained cooperation was needed
to keep aid flowing. In late 1985, the Reagan Administration pushed for a lifting of
this same ban against Laos, the "black hole of POW/MIAs."

Le Duc Tho, in an 1985 interview, said Vietnam made a mistake in keeping the
United States out of Southeast Asia. When they left the money left with them. He
added the Soviets tried to dominate. They, however, had no money. In the January
24, 1985 issue of the **Far Eastern Economic Review**, the Lao Charge' de' Affairs, Bounkeut Sangsomsak, stated the United States should refuse to accept MIA
bones from private individuals like Jack Bailey or Bo Gritz, adding, "Between
states, everything is political." This charge against Bailey and Gritz was followed
by intentional harassment of these two by U.S. officials. Administration sources
said they hoped progress on the MIA front would lead to a granting of aid to Laos.
In a 1984 documentary on Australian MIAs, Nguyen Co Thach said Australia was
granted permission to look for their MIAs because they were more correct in attitude. He decried the lack of "healing the wounds of war."

In September 1987, General Vessey stated the "Vietnamese... acknowledged...
resolving the POW/MIA problem was a humanitarian issue but ... they too had
humanitarian issues... 1.4 million war disabled, 500,000 orphans... destroyed schools
and damaged hospitals... (for) progress on the humanitarian concerns of the US..."

Incredibly, Vessey then asserted, "...any attempt to trade information ... We
cannot agree to this... we will not buy progress through ... The POW/MIA issue ...
linked with broader political issues." Did the Vietnamese get the message? No,
they have their own agenda. In the February 4, 1988 edition of the **Far Eastern
Economic Review**, Thach quoted, "I can accept non-governmental organizational
aid, but there must be some from the (US) government" for help on the MIA question. The Vietnamese tie aid to progress. In the early 1970's, because of domestic
politics, Kissinger sent McFarlane, then his deputy, to the Vietnamese offering
$100 million in medicine to buy out our prisoners and remains. The Vietnamese
refused and as LeBoutillier charged, "Now, ... they were negotiating. Obviously, I
come in with a low bid of $100 million and I've already pledged $3.25 billion,

you'd be stupid to take the $100 million." (**Interview** *NY City Tribune,* **April 3, 1986, pg. 3**)

Past intelligence reports reinforce the statements of Thach, Tho, and others that they expected money for the prisoners. Vietnam offered to let foreign industry into their country with the foreigners holding part of the stock. At one point, they were considering having a Club Med on the coast where GI's used to have in-country R&R. Even Truong Chinh, the Party theoretician, told William Stevenson in 1988 that his country needed capitalistic help. (**KTB pg.** 376)

In 1994, President Clinton lifted the trade embargo and we got nothing. In 1995, he recognized Vietnam and we got nothing. In June 1997, we asked for nothing and got nothing. Irony abounds in POWs being sold out by a draft-evading, communist enemy capitol visiting in wartime President aided by a former POW, McCain and abetted by a decorated veteran, Kerry. Some, however got campaign contributions. More about that in the next chapter.

Other diplomatic problems - on the POWs

Money was just one of the diplomatic problems as it concerned POWs. First, the fighting in Vietnam did not end on April 30, 1975. There was and may still be a sizable resistance movement in South Vietnam. I first became aware of this in late 1975 through refugee sources. I was told the Chinese armed the insurgents.

This insurgent movement was an odd coalition of soldiers from the old Thieu regime; disillusioned VC; Hoa Hao dissidents; and native Cambodians from the Mekong Delta. A fear of the new rulers; suppression of religious beliefs; forced resettlement into "New Economic Zones;" and northern government dominance brought this coalition together. Truong Nhu Tang, in **A Vietcong Memoir**, told of VC cadre who felt betrayed by the Northern dogmatic leaders. Many fled because they could not protect family members from the "reeducation" camps. Some "reeducation" inhabitants and cadres brought POW news.

The 1984 Australian MIA documentary showed in Phuoc Thuy MIA searchers were not allowed to go into the hills to a known crash site because of the "bandits." A mid-June 1984 report in the Czechoslovakia party newspaper, *Rude Pravo*, stated in southern Vietnam, "... there are armed battles with reactionary bands in the mountainous areas ...." The article continued, "Hundreds of thousands of former officers, soldiers, and bureaucrats of the previous regime have been through the reeducation process, but not all ... changed... In Ho Chi Minh City, there are 500,000 Chinese, 400,000 Catholics, and 250,000 families whose parents emigrated to the west.... we know that reactionaries find much support among them." Finally, Hanoi put down armed attacks, "purged the party (and) strengthened discipline...."

Our "humanitarian" negotiations with Hanoi included releasing political prisoners. Hanoi was reluctant to do so as they represented potential resistance members. Letting these people go is the equivalent of "shooting themselves in the foot." (**Jan 24, 1985 Far Eastern Economic Review**) Vietnam accused the United States of being in collusion with China and the resistance groups. This accusation is justifiable as our government overtly aided the Cambodian resistance with **identifiable DIA agents** advertising in foreign papers aiding the Cambodian resistance.

An age old conflict exists between Cambodians and Vietnamese; exacerbated by internal communist feuds. After the Vietnamese invasion of Cambodia came a former Khmer Rouge leader subservient to Hanoi. Prior to this, the Cambodians allowed Vietnamese insurgents use of Cambodian territory to attack the Hanoi regime in the southern part of Vietnam.

In the middle are the Chinese Communists. They backed the late Pol Pot and secretly armed Vietnamese insurgents. The Chinese didn't want a nation of 90 million persons on their southern flank, armed and trained by the then Soviet Union. The Vietnamese want all former French colonies in one federation under Vietnamese control. McCain considers Vietnam as a counterweight to China.

The Chinese did not want the Soviet Union in "their" sphere of influence. They viewed with alarm the port of Cam Ranh and it's Soviet base and the Soviet naval facility in Haiphong, across from strategic Hainan island. Privately, during the war, they rooted for a US backed Vietnam to win. To back their claim of supremacy, the Chinese put their own troops into battle in support of the Cambodians. Refugees reported seeing weapons and supplies being off-loaded from boats along the Camau Peninsula. Refugees and French sources said the insurgents regularly received airdrops of French, Chinese, and American weapons. China has regularly conducted military operations and "invasions" of Vietnamese frontiers.

Where do the MIAs fit? Right in the middle. There are enough problems to enable skilled diplomats to get our POWs and repatriation of MIA remains. There have been "private" attempts to get such concessions. Vietnam pragmatists desire to get rid of their "problem." The Soviet breakup added to the opportunities.

Vietnam craved recognition. An April 21, 1985, story from the *LA Times* said Vietnam wanted recognition prior to the return of MIA remains. This rhetoric was their opening negotiation round. Vietnam did not allow our searching for MIAs because of what Thach called our "wrong attitude." Yet, a few months later, in July 1985, they called for a resolution of the MIA problem in "two years." Perhaps our "attitude" changed. Was it a signal that POWs were ready to be returned?

The Carter administration did nothing to exploit openings. Reagan's China card lead to contacts with the mainland and the signing of a Nuclear Cooperation Agreement on July 23, 1985. This treaty dealt with the exporting of nuclear technology to China. Playing this type of card led Czechoslovakia to denounce a cabal of the United States, the Vatican, and China for the troubles in the insurgency in Vietnam. Clinton blamed the "card" as justification for his outright selling to the Chinese what they could not steal in exchange for power and campaign contributions.

China and Russia can help on the POW matter because both, as we will see later, participated in crimes so heinous that they make Nazis look like angels.

Chinese Communist Advisers in SVN

China plays an important part in Vietnam's history. China left the mandarin and Confucian legacy which may prove crucial in the future battle for a more "democratic" Vietnam. During the war years, there were Chinese advisors to Vietnam. Around the DMZ, "tall Vietnamese" being found decapitated; avoiding the undeniable proof of being Chinese. In my own U-Minh region, I received at least two reports of Chinese advisors in late 1969. Our "Navy UDT personnel." found a Chinese Communist battle flag, coinciding with the reports of the Chinese. ·

The uncorrelated POW material dispels the myth of shoeless peasants fighting with no external fighting allies. They show the participation of Chinese, Soviet, North Korean, and other Communist advisors in the role of combat, combat advisory, and combat support personnel. My sources have added even more details.

Dispelling the shoeless peasant myth

In 1964 near Vung Tau, a Special Forces team found, after a battle, the bodies of Chinese Communist troops. Headquarters ordered the destruction of the Chicom bodies. (**Source: One of the Special Forces personnel in on the operation**)

In 1965, CIA reported American POWs were held in a cave complex near the Pathet Lao Supreme Headquarters. Also present was a contingent of Chinese Communist troops and "diplomatic" personnel supplying logistical support to the Laotians and interrogating our POWs. This complex was dubbed "The Embassy."

In 1967, the Chinese Communists acted as combat advisors to regimental sized units in the "Battle of Chu Lai." Captured VC confirmed the strategy they used from Chinese cadre included how best to lure the American units into ambushes, relying on similar tactics used when they advised the Viet Minh against the French.

Closely paralleling reports of Chinese Communists were those of North Korean advisors. In 1967, in Quang Nam Province, two American POWs, during their interrogation, were shown a large contingent of combat troops, introduced by a guard as "our friends, the North Koreans." By 1971, at Phu Cat Air Force Base, Air Force Intelligence reported Chinese and Korean troops and advisors. Some narratives had our POWs being led away with Chinese and/or Korean advisors present. During a four month period, over twenty such reports were logged. These foreign advisor reports were believed by our security people. A friend of mine spent a two years in Vietnam as a Marine sniper and watched Chinese and Soviet Advisors pass his places of observation.

Soviet Advisors in South Vietnam

In September 1991, the Soviet Union confirmed their involvement in Vietnam. They said that they had some three thousand troops there and in 1965 shot down the first US planes lost in Vietnam. They acknowledged some thirteen advisers were killed. They also admitted indirect help after 1966. (**Associated Press, September 7, 1991**) This first confession leaves much to be desired. In 1967, in the U-Minh Forest, a Navy SEAL team ambushed and killed a bearded Caucasian, later identified as a Soviet Advisor. He was also told to keep his mouth shut. (**A source in the intelligence field**)

In April 1968, in Northern South Vietnam, a Marine Long Range Reconnaissance Patrol captured a Caucasian. Brass aboard a special helicopter sent to pick him up admonished the patrol leader never to tell he captured a Soviet Advisor. (**Source: a member of this patrol**) Sources within the Army Security Agency told me that between 1970 - 1972, they logged numerous intercepts of Soviet Advisors engaged in direct combat related activities in Cambodia. This reinforces information given to me by another intelligence source of a Special Forces sergeant of Polish descent engaging in a radio ruse in Russian. He spoke fluent Russian but with a distinct accent, thus the Russians in Cambodia quickly broke radio contact.

A Vietnamese reported Soviet Advisors engaged in road construction in Northern South Vietnam in 1974. Asked if they might be Americans, he said that he had seen both and knew the difference. Years later, a Vietnamese refugee, interviewed in an American newspaper, reported Soviet presence in this same district, in 1974.

Why did our government deny Soviet and Chinese ground combat in South Vietnam? Our leaders lacked the intestinal fortitude to face reality that the Soviets and Chinese were at war with us politically, economically, and militarily. As we will see, they did not want to open to the door to even more nefarious allegations. Our negotiators wanted "progress" and ignored reality. They believed you can artificially separate items into neat little baskets. The Lao are more accurate: "between states, all things are political."

Before looking at North Vietnam, one example will show the believability of Soviets on the ground in South Vietnam. In Korea, we fought the Soviets also. Air Force documents show:"... the North Korean Air Force (NKAF)... was ... basically Chinese with Russian and Polish pilots .... most of the fighter squadrons actively engaging the F-86's were Soviet squadrons ... (**USAF Historical Study No. 72. 1 Nov. 1950 - 30 June 1952 pg. 107**) Dornan added in September 1996, "We have evidence of Soviet participation in the Korean War... General officers... telling how they flew... in Chinese uniforms... MiG 15s... out of North Korean air bases..." We cannot forget role of the Soviets at Phou Pha Thi.

KGB General Oleg Kalugin testified on January 21, 1992 before the Senate POW Committee, "Well, we in intelligence operations, sometimes recall the 'old glorious past' ... George Blake, who was recruited in Korea, in a prisoners camp ... That's the reason why we thought, why not try in Vietnam... Americans who are kept in concentration camps and prisons... in the mid-70s, well after the war was over." He further refined the time frame to 1976 - 78. He said the Soviets were given a choice from a group of "twelve or fifteen" POWs. He could not comment on Soviet activities in Laos or Cambodia, although he was certain of Soviet presence in both countries during the war.

Their purpose? Not only to get "spies," but to extract technical material. The 1205 document provides some information about POWs withheld including men with superb scientific credentials. Mooney and Minarcin recorded intercepts concerning men with "Special Talents." Remember, this term was used by the opposing forces. Our RF-4 pilots flew state of the art reconnaissance planes. The AC-47s contained laser aiming devices. The men on Phou Pha Thi knew the ins and outs of the radar aimed at Moscow. Many pilots previously flew in areas of the world outside of Vietnam. The Soviets asked the Vietnamese to separate men out. The Vietnamese complied and did even more, as we will see later.

The Chinese and Soviets in South Vietnam are the tip of the iceberg about foreign communist advisors there. Another vet friend of mine duties included attempting to capture the Czech and East German antiaircraft advisors operating in his area in the 1970-72 time frame.

More is known about the role of Communist advisers in North Vietnam. On the Son Tay POW rescue mission, approximately four hundred meters south of Son Tay prison was another compound, which was "accidentally" attacked by US forces, the only "mistake" of the rescue mission. Our forces blew a hole in the compound wall and killed 100 to 200 troops before the "mistake" was noted. It is also "coincidental" that these troops provided the only known threat to the raiders. DIA told me in a letter, "**most** of the troops manning the ... facility ... were described as **large Orientals**."

Benjamin Schemmer said in his book **The Raid,** "they were much taller, 5 feet 10 inches to 6 feet, Oriental, not wearing the normal NVA dress." (**see entries under secondary school The Raid**) From intelligence sources of my own, I found that "some" persons killed in the "mistake" could be fairly described as "Caucasian." Others were "Oriental." We "accidentally" killed one hundred to two hundred Soviet and Chinese advisers to the Vietnamese special forces. Some scores got evened at Son Tay, and some SOG casualties in Laos and elsewhere from the

"Special Forces" graduates in Laos were avenged.

In August 1969, we sent CIA operatives into China looking for possible POWs. One mission went five to ten miles inside the border to verify the occupants of a prison camp. They found in this "confirmed" prison camp only Laotian prisoners. Using CIA guidelines, our CIA went at least twice into China to confirm both the location and the occupants of this one prison. If only our CIA had the same gumption in the 1978-79 time frame when it was reported that two hundred of our POWs were located along the Vietnam/China border or in the near recent past when a large number of POWs were reported along the Vietnam/Lao/China border area, near this same Botene check point where this 1969 border incident took place.

The ever present Cubans

Another country could help in the search for our POWs, Cuba. Cuba desires better relations with the United States. In late 1997, the Clinton administration attempted to devise ways of recognizing Castro's regime. Perhaps a Commerce trip for political donations will grease the skids.

In the 70s, we criticized Cuban armed intervention on the African continent. To date, we ignore their role in Vietnam. One participation involved two men from their embassy inflicting some of the most sadistic torture upon our POWs. The books **POW** and **The Raid** refer to these two men as "Cubans" or "Latins". POW Ed Kastler was tortured for a month by one "interrogator." Ed Martin, who had to listen to the torture session, knows they are Cubans. The CIA identified "Fidel" and "Chico" as Eduardo Morjon Esteves and Luis Perez Jaen. (**Human Events, Sept. 3, 1977**) In 1980, at a League meeting, DIA refused to acknowledge the Cubans. A former head of Air Force Intelligence confirmed to me these men were Cubans. In 1996, DPMO and DIA testified there was no proof they were Cubans.

Successive administrations ignored the Cuban role in POW torture. Former POWs were asked to downplay Cuban involvement in torture, including Leo Thorsness. In **1977,** Thorsness charged the State Department did not want comments on the Cubans **because of the possible harm that might be done to POWs who might still be in Vietnam. (Exhibits in Hopper)** Both Chip Beck and Bill Bell, who believe the Cubans were more involved in Vietnam that overtly acknowledged, were eased out of their positions for going against the "party line."

Cuba desires diplomatic recognition and money. I do not advocate giving help to parasites without substantial evidence that such help is warranted. Assistance on our POWs is at the top of my list of demands. Then, DOD can be honest in what they really know about their atrocities.

The changes occurring in the 1989 break up of the European Communist empire and the 1991 disintegration of the former Soviet Union provided dozens of opportunities to exploit on POWs. Resolution of the MIA problem is supposedly the "highest national priority". Yet, every president since Roosevelt ignores the plight of American fighting men "disappearing" into the Communist netherland. But, did they really disappear?

I was informed in late 1991 the fate of the EC-47 included secret intelligence sources tracing the men into Hanoi where they entered one of several sets of prison camps. The men returning in 1973 were part of one set. "Special talents" were in another set. In 1978, it was determined that the EC-47 crew was being removed from Hanoi to Moscow. They were traced and reportedly two unsuccessful attempts at rescue were made. This subset of camps was later verified in the 1205 document where Quang reported; "Currently, we have 11 prisons where American POWs are held. We used to have 4 large prisons, however after ... Son Tay, we expanded this number to 11. Each prison holds approximately 100 POWs... through them, we are attempting to gain an understanding of the current situation which has developed in the American Army, extract the material and information we need, and determine our position toward them."

In a speech before the League in July, 1989, President Bush pledged to seek help from President Gorbachev on our MIAs. The Soviets sought our help on their POWs and MIAs in Afghanistan. This approach was paved by Bill Hendon. The audience read the pledge from Bush as an endorsement of Hendon's initiative. He had just returned from meeting with the Mujahadeen and was present when Bush made his speech. Several persons, including myself, had dinner with him that evening as he told us of his efforts in Afghanistan. In chapter 11, we'll examine what happened to our "disappearing" POWs.

Our pussyfooting diplomats

I did not advocate diplomatic recognition for China, and Vietnam. I don't give away something for nothing. I don't advocate recognition for Cuba. We have what Cuba needs and Vietnam wanted; recognition. Both countries have what we require, POW/MIA information. We've given away much POW diplomacy receiving little in return. This problem lies in Washington, not Hanoi.

A high-ranking official on the Carter National Security Council explained to me that countries were singled out for attacks on human rights violations as they fit into the current concerns of that administration. Vietnam was never singled out. Our State Department lacks the fine art of give and take. Our adversaries have negotiated only with people knowing how to give.

For example, Henry Kissinger was given intelligence by Walter Cronkite about newsmen held captive in Cambodia. Cronkite asked Kissinger to inquire of Chou En Lai about these men. Kissinger told the Chinese "**I told them** (the Cronkite group) **that we had no basis for believing these ... Journalists were alive, or that the DRV was in a position to assist. Nevertheless, ... I would make one further inquiry.**" (House Select Committee, vol. 3 pg. 145) (**Emphasis added**)

Quoting this pitiful inquiry, Cronkite understated, "We in our Committee quite honestly felt ... this was something less than adequate. We ... understand ... diplomatic niceties... But ... to suggest that they had no basis for believing that these American journalists were alive ... seems ... to fly in the face of the evidence we presented to Dr. Kissinger ... a more positive approach would have been more helpful." (**ibid.**) (In late 1994, a civilian returning to Cambodia, was lead to the reported grave sites of Sean Flynn and Dana Stone. The information he developed augmented information given by Cronkite to the Montgomery Committee.)

This is not the only instance where Kissinger showed little interest in MIAs. With his Peace Accords, we fought for an additional four years, lost thousands of KIAs, hundreds of POWs, and billions of dollars forcing the Vietnamese to accept the same terms we rejected in the NLF Ten Points of 1969. (**The Palace File**) He negotiated the terms of the $4.75 billion pledge by President Nixon; authored the $2 billion bribe of 1972; and mislead Congress about the existence of both bribes. He abandoned our POWs in Laos, Vietnam, and elsewhere.

Testifying in September 1973, relative to his nomination as Secretary of State, Kissinger attested Laotian POWs were covered in the Paris agreements; confirmed discussions concerning them in June negotiations; and affirmed a Vietnamese commitment that provisions for an accounting would be observed. (**House Select Committee, vol. 5 pg. 176**) However, on August 20, 1973, a folder was passed to the North Vietnamese about LTC Hrdlicka. Their reply, received before he testified, reiterated they were not responsible for persons lost in Laos. We would have to deal directly with Laos concerning the POWs there. (**ibid., pg. 173**)

Kissinger also knew he received on March 28, 1973, a Top Secret Report from Secretary of Defense Elliot Richardson expressing distress over the return of only 10 POWs from Laos. "As you know, there are over 350 US personnel listed by DIA as missing or captured in Laos. (We have since learned that was short by over a hundred persons) The 1 February list of ten amounts to only a 2.5% accounting; whereas the North Vietnamese have accounted for 45% and the PRG has accounted for 20% ... we have carried as missing or captured in their respective areas."

The memo continued, "I recommend the President consider the following ... to gain some accounting ... in Laos: (A) After the recovery of the last prisoners from NVN, Hanoi should be advised unequivocally that we still hold them responsible for the return of all POWs being held .... further mine sweeping activity as well as all **future US reconstruction assistance** should be described as wholly dependent upon the accounting for and / or release of US prisoners being held in Laos. ... an accounting for 10 men out of ...more than 350 is ... unacceptable."

Richardson added the US would no longer play games in Laos with the POW issue. "The LPF should be told that we know they hold US prisoners... we demand their immediate release as well as an accounting ... on all those who ... died.... failure to provide a satisfactory answer could result in direct United States actions." Richardson acknowledged the denied urging "intensive... obvious tactical air reconnaissance of North and South Laos;" a movement of "a new carrier task force into the waters off Vietnam ... publicly announced;" "the LPF and NVN should be privately advised that Thai Volunteer Forces now in Laos will not be removed until there is a satisfactory resolution of the POW issue."

Kissinger, on May 23, 1973, met with Le Duc Tho, Nguyen Co Thach, and Phan Hien. The Memorandum of Conversation reflects his begging them to declare, "The DRV has been informed that there are no U.S. prisoners being held in Laos — that all ... have been released. It would be very important for us."

A reality check

Vietnam is the home of "reeducation camp" internees. A Congressional estimate placed the number of prisoners between one hundred thousand to three hundred thousand persons. Doan Van Toai, a former internee and anti-Thieu student protest leader, estimated the number at over eight hundred thousand. Truong Nhu Tang confirmed the composition of inmates: former officials of the Thieu regime; former VC who switched sides during the war; and former high-ranking officials of the NLF. (**Vietnam: Problems of Normalizing US-Vietnamese Relations,** pg. 7; *Vietnam News*, July 15, 1978, pg. 10; **A Vietcong Memoir**, chapter 22)

Toai charged the prison conditions were worse than Soviet Gulags. He asserted that torture, starvation, and emotional pressures were customary. Executions, both summary and dragging prisoners behind speeding jeeps, were commonplace. (**Vietnam News, pg. 11**) Tang, though a high cadre, could not help his own family members who worked for the Thieu regime in these camps. They were nonpersons; not dead, but not acknowledged as living. (**Vietcong Memoir**, **pg. 278-79**) The Vietnamese copied the sophisticated Soviet form of disposing of their enemies. They put them into prison and let them rot. When dead, it could be said they died of "natural causes."

Our "policy" on POWs could charitably be called bewildering. One day, the Secretary of State can say that we will use everything from black helicopters in the night to negotiations to get back withheld prisoners. The next day, he says there is no evidence that POWs are captive. Administration spokesmen say the POW issue is divorced from other policy considerations. The next day, the same spokesmen ties them together. Clinton's full recognition of Vietnam was predictable. What was surprising is the full politicization of the intelligence agencies here.

Strange roles in diplomacy

A Frankenstein monster was created in the League which haunts the administration in power. Ann Griffiths, a private citizen, has met with SRV Foreign Minister Thach to clarify statements on MIA linkage with other issues. In December 1983, she again met with SRV officials setting up a government to government meeting. Is Griffiths a *de facto* government employee ostensibly representing a private organization? This unofficial "League Secretary of State" precedent is bad. The families should be heard but only be monitors. The government must be held accountable. On our POW foreign policy, no one is accountable.

There have been diplomatic initiatives, both private and public, but no definable progress. Congressman Robert Dornan urged Solarz in 1987 to subpoena Nixon and Kissinger to find out what they knew and when. He sponsored a multi-million dollar reward for POW returns and wrote the forward to my original book. That never happened, thanks to liberals like Solarz.

Government agencies have been less than honest. Our men are either alive or not. The remains can be returned or not. Like Mr. Cronkite, I understand the need for diplomatic niceties; secrecy at times; however, I cannot comprehend twenty six years of failure on this "highest national priority" issue.

Our intelligence agencies are politicized. When they can say with a straight face that we could not see the Indian and Pakistani bomb tests coming, even though the tell tale signs were there, then they can lie about POWs. When intelligence operatives testify about Cuban involvement in POW matters including the name of a Cuban book on their involvement and DIA, in the person of the same official who wrote me on Ba Vi and Robert DeStatte of the Baron 52 fame deny in official testimony what they know to be true, then it is obvious that intelligence agencies are so politicized as to be almost worthless.

I believe that some POWs were returned to the United States; possibly "detainees" within our own country. I believe that some of our former issue allies are aware of this transfer and have kept quiet. More on this in chapter 11. (Note: I first wrote this in September, 1991. Unbeknownst to me, others in the media field and military circles were getting the same information.)

Here is what I believe needs to be done. First, accept the fact some POWs/ MIAs will never be found. We can estimate who most of them are. We do not name them publicly, but should not expect anything on them. Secondly, we have to add MIAs lost on "Black Operations." Be honest! Let past diplomatic "secrets" come out. Quang told the Politburo that "Among the other 47 prisoners captured

... there are 36 advisors of diversionary detachments ... inserted in the border region between the DRV and Laos; lone diversionists ... conducting reconnaissance of our main transportation routes from helicopters and reconnaissance ships; and several seamen ... whom we picked up ..." Sejna, as you will see, told of POWs being transferred to the Soviet Union in 1961!

Thirdly, we must be forceful in telling the Vietnamese what we expect. Caution them that borders will be no object in returning our men. This enemy is a respecter of firmness and resolve. Be like the Israelis. Hell will freeze over before they give in on a single issue to get back one POW or one set of obtainable remains.

This issue is tearing away at the morale of our fighting men. They know our MIAs were abandoned. Some left the service early because of that knowledge. The Vietnamese are positioned to become more "democratic." We should encourage these trends. Our efforts in Cambodia did nothing to lessen the hold Vietnam has on it. Hun Sen, a Hanoi stooge, is firmly in charge and we have no POWs.

Use of war crimes as leverage

Finally, there is the Ace. In Bosnia and Kosovo, we began war crimes trials. We were poised (June 1997) to try Pol Pot for war crimes, until his **fortuitous** death just prior to the date set for a decision on the matter. We need do the same for Vietnam. Vo Van Kiet was in charge of the deliberate murders of POWs; Rocky Versace, Kenneth Roraback, Harold Bennett, Gerald Kinsman, James Harwood, and Edwin Atterberry. There are hundreds who suffered the same fate being transferred to the former Soviet Union, China, and Korea for medical experimentation. We want our men back. We need to proceed with trials for the truth. Don't do, however, like Clinton, call for war crimes and then not arrest the perpetrators. If a decision is made to go forward with the trials, make sure the perpetrators don't get the opportunity to croak ahead of time. Remember the precedent of General Pinochet in Britain. Charges filed in the United States might make travel for Chinese, Russian, and Vietnamese officials tough where we have treaty rights for war crimes. Use the leverage, either from the government, or as in Spain, privately.

Use secret negotiations, but keep them honest. If we get the men back, we may decide **not** to proceed with war crimes but actually begin the long overdue reconciliation most of us crave. There is a time for toughness and a time for forgiveness. We're still in the toughness state until our men return.

A political cartoon in the *Arizona Republic* about 1986 showed a POW delegation in Vietnam, at the edge of a dark jungle. With a very dim flashlight, they peered into this jungle. The leader timidly asks, "Anyone home?" The very loud answer from the jungle is "Not Yet!" In 1991, the *Fort Worth Star - Telegram* ran a cartoon of persons entering a cave shining a light illuminating a flunky setting at a cobwebbed desk labeled "United States of America MIA Files." The leader of the team questioned, "MIA rescue team. Anybody here?" Perhaps we need to get a note to our POWs that political contributions to the Democratic National Committee and to the Al Gore Election campaign committee might grease the skids for coming home quickly. That thought, by the way, was not in cartoon form!

Covert and Special Operations

Earlier I described a lawsuit filed by Vietnamese former operatives of the CIA caught running a series of covert operations in North Vietnam. **Scorpion** was the name of one of these commando teams. Radio Hanoi announced their capture in 1964. Dang Cong Trinh, the deputy commander of Scorpion, now lives in the United States and survived 15 years of imprisonment and is one of 300 commandos seeking justice.

On February 1 1964, the United States began an "elaborate program of covert military operations" under the code name **Operation Plan 34A**. The purpose was to take "progressively escalating pressures" in clandestine attacks to force North Vietnam to cease support of their troops in South Vietnam and Laos. It was initiated by Secretary of Defense Robert McNamara. On the ocean, it was supported by **Operation Desoto**. In Laos, the operations were code named **Hardnose**. McNamara said, they "represent a wide variety of sabotage and psychological operations against North Vietnam ... we should aid to select those that provide maximum pressure with minimum risk." The overall responsibility for these operations were under SOG and the CIA. (**Pentagon papers**)

SOG

SOG, the "Studies and Observation Group," or Special Operations Group, had many projects assigned to it. Their specialized intelligence collection projects included or assisted: **OAK** - Operated in the 1966 - 67 time frame. Operations included sources in Cambodia and South Vietnam. For example, in March 1967, one source found a POW camp with 2 Americans and 39 ARVN POWs. The "Source helped his cousin, a VC ... cadre, to deliver rice to the ... camp. Source was not allowed to enter the camp... His cousin was permitted to enter .... Source's cousin described the camp... Source is a member of the VC ... Organization in the RUNG SAT Zone... owns a sampan and often carries supplies for the VC... is 28 years old and has been employed by Project OAK for one year."

BLACKBEARD was a Special Forces collection project. It covered Cambodia, at least. Documents show a collection effort from at least 1966 through 1969. It employed agents with free access to POW camps. Some of the agents were "witting of US involvement" and others were "unwitting of US involvement."

NANTUCKET AND VESUVIUS ONE were projects of the B-57 detachment, 5th Special Forces. Operations covered Cambodia from 1967 to at least 1968. Reports with a Nantucket moniker included the 525th and the 149th MI Group. B-57, B-55, and B-52, were Special Forces Mike reaction teams. Associated with Nantucket was **Sunshine Park**, part of Naval Intelligence Operations.

BENT AXLE intelligence collection program was associated with D-7CX - 49018 and D - 7CX - 20000, Special Intelligence Collection Requirements, **BRIGHT LIGHT**, POW intelligence. Bright Light was a SOG reaction program. Bent Axle covered Laos. **GUNBOAT** covered Cambodia. Bent Axle included 1971 and Gunboat went through 1973 . **BIG MACK** covered South Vietnam. Big Mack also worked with the 525th MI Group. In 1970, it ran deep cover operatives in the VC Infrastructure. Some penetration agents had been in place for up to six years.

PINE TREE was an intelligence collection program of MACV and the 525th

MI Group in 1967 in South Vietnam. It was part of Project 26-SV-25. **CORRAL** was a MACV collection program in 1967 and was associated with the 149th MI Group in South Vietnam. It was part of Project 26-SV-24. In addition, Corral was part of **ICEX**, forerunner to the Phoenix program. **RAPID SHAVE** was part of IIR 1464, 525th MI Group and covered part of the 1969 time frame. If PINE continued, it may explain the emergence of the name, LTC Comb in the prison in North Vietnam, found by Arlo Gay in 1975.

The Air Force had the **7602 Air Intelligence Group** and the **6499th Special Activities Group**. LTC Shinkle was "a member of an Air Force clandestine intelligence collection unit ... the 6499th Special Activities Group, later the **1137th Field Activities Group**..." during "my tour of duty in Laos." The 6499th also ran operation **ROBOT**. This operation needed a "No Foreign Dissemination" designation for it's intelligence to protect the "disclosure of it's collection activity." The 6499th conducted sensitive programs with Thai Intelligence sources including in 1968 a "Pathet Lao Junior Officer" with knowledge of Kham Keut's use, on a regular basis, as a detention center.

SACSA was JCS 6116, an action agency who ran the Son Tay POW operation and other POW rescue attempts throughout SE Asia. SACSA stood for Special Assistant Counter Insurgency and Special Activities.

OSA is one acronym for the CIA station chief. The Office of the Special Assistant to the Ambassador, in Vietnam, had representatives operating usually at the Province level. In Laos, OSA was known as **CAS** or **Combined Area Studies**. Our OSA rep in **Phoenix** had, through mid-1969, his own reaction force, the PRUs.

PRU was the Provincial Reconnaissance Units, or Vietnamese units run by the CIA. Prior to being assigned to Phoenix operatives, they were used in many types of operations, including POW rescues. In August 1968, PRUs and their **SEAL** advisor attempted a POW rescue in the U-Minh. The PRUs also ran an operation on 8 December with two Mobile Strike Force Companies from Co. D, 5th Special Forces Group. The target was a POW camp near Song Ong Doc, at the southern tip of the U-Minh. This operation was called **Sage Brush II**. **Sage Brush I**, a POW rescue, ran in October 1966 in the same area. The American POWs were moved only 24 hours earlier. In the latter part of my tour, I was assigned PRUs after their CIA separation, and Phoenix being disconnected from **CORDs** and brought under MACV control. I still had **Kit Carson Scouts**, or former VC working for me.

Daniel Boone operated in Cambodia at least in 1966 - 67 under SICR D - 1E6 - 14883 run by SOG. Their intel reports often went directly to the Joint Chiefs. In many SOG operations, cross border, the operatives were volunteers, able to wear civilian clothing, and were directly tasked by the CIA.

These operations helped launch 119 missions, including 98 "raids" similar to Son Tay. Some operations were run by the **Joint Personnel Recovery Center,** a SOG mission. One POW was recovered, SP4 Larry D. Aiken. Rescued on July 10, 1969, he died in a hospital 15 days later from a wound suffered before the rescue. It's possible the rescue mission was compromised at the last moment. (**The Raid pg. 194 - 95**) Helping, were Phoenix units.

The following operations are also covert.

The Richard Barker affair - bringing POWs home - almost

The following information is from the files of an attorney representing Richard Barker. He found himself on the wrong side of the law in 1986. The files pertain to a plan to return POWs. In October, 1991, I talked with the attorney who agreed the internal documentation appears to be legitimate.

In February, 1985, Richard Barker received a life changing phone call. Douglas Pierce previously contacted Robert Ketcheson, of Wildfire International, located in Hawaii. Pierce lost his son aboard the ship Glomar Java in the South China Sea. The story begins with the Glomar Java incident, but concerns all POWs. Ketcheson informed Barker, also with Wildfire International, of his contact with Pierce. Both agreed to meet with him in April 1985. Pierce gave Barker evidence of his son being alive in Vietnam; kidnapped off the Glomar Java after being sunk.

In August 1985, Barker and Ketcheson went to California and met Jimmey Cillpan, who worked with Vietnamese in the LA area. They further met Ha Krong Boa, who was arranging for the release of John Pierce. Krong and his friend, Vi Han worked with a man, Hoang Van Hoan to get Pierce returned. Hoang also had more grandiose plans. Barker asserted he worked out of the Alberta House, a cover place provided by the Canadian consulate in Los Angeles. He was also sending information to Neil Kingdom, an intelligence officer in Calgary, Alberta; Carla Wicket, FBI; Patty Voltz, CIA; Mr. Jennings, DEA; and other agents.

In September 1985, Barker met with Krong and Vi and learned more details about Pierce and the POW situation. He supplied Krong with a computer list of all known MIAs from DIA. He also provided him with declassified Senate hearings on POWs/MIAs, Soviet tactics, and the Hind 24 helicopter. This was done to show Krong that he was diligent in accomplishing tasks; also an intelligence tactic to see if a person will provide little items before giving him a project of bigger magnitude. These materials were passed to the mainland Chinese having a part of this project. Krong then advised Barker of the overall plan.

Hoang van Hoan was a Vietnamese politburo member who defected to the Chinese in a policy dispute over Vietnam's future. A disciple of Ho Chi Minh, he opposed the pro-Soviet views of Le Duan, Nguyen Co Thach, and Pham Van Dong. He opposed the Sovietization of Vietnam and the invasion of Cambodia. Hoang had influence over military commanders controlling some POWs in Laos and Vietnam. (Trung Nhu Tang, in **Vietcong Memoir**, confirmed this description of Hoang.)

Hoang conceived a plan of overthrowing the Vietnamese government and having a provisional government recognized. China favored the plan. They wanted the Soviets out of Vietnam, but with recognition provided by Western governments. Hoang's offer was the release of 475 American POWs in exchange for recognition of his government in exile, coup support, and removing the Soviets.

Barker and Ketcheson proposed securing the backing of the Canadian government, a political friend of China. They needed absolute proof of the POWs and Hoang's ability to perform. In October 1985, Vi reported from Beijing that Hoang agreed to work with Canada. China welcomed closer ties with Canada, viewing with concern the Soviet expansionism in Southeast Asia.

Ketcheson contacted John Oostrom, a member of Parliament and the Standing Committee on the Defense of Canada. Oostrom approached Mr. Joe Clark, Secretary of State for External Affairs (and later Prime Minister). Both agreed to help if documentation showed that POWs were incarcerated. Barker said he contacted Bill Paul of the *Wall Street Journal* , having met him before, in 1985, while Paul was working on stories on the Glomar Java sinking.

Barker said "I decided, along with Krong Boa, that ... to secure the economic and political aspects of the overall operation, ... a reporter of high caliber be brought into the overall picture... Mr. Paul had been working ... on the POW issue ... abreast of the political ramifications ... if their numbers (of POWs) were confirmed and their release was brought up."

Barker obtained Chinese approval and Hoang Van Hoan's on bringing Paul in. Barker related "China accepted our plan ... the *Wall Street Journal* would reach the international business community ... for increased economic growth for China." Paul's involvement was to "become a condition imposed by the Chinese government. ... I personally contacted Mr. Paul and brought him up-to-date on our information." Barker said that Paul checked his own sources, including General Tighe, Bill Hendon, Pierre Cote, and "others in the State Department and the Defense Intelligence Agency... convinced that our plan was sound and ... very excited about the aspects of this operation." (**Paul ran an article in the Jan. 21, 1987 edition of the** *Wall Street Journal*)

Barker spent the next thirty days awaiting a Canadian response. Hoang told Vi he was willing to release a current two hour film of the live POWs. The POW scheduled for release was Charles Alvin (sic) Dale. He was to be released to the Canadian Embassy. Barker said this information was also passed on to Paul.

Ketcheson told Barker, "... Oostrom had gone to Washington, D.C. to verify our information with Canadian intelligence and sleepers within the United States government... Oostrom ... reported that our information concerning ... the prisoners of war was sound." On December 5, 1985, Barker reviewed a letter from Clark to Ketcheson to the Chinese.

Clark thanked Ketcheson for his letter of November 21, 1985 saying, "The story you relate is an unusual one ... to begin my reply, I might start with the sinking ... of the Glomar Java Sea in October, 1983." Canada followed the Glomar Java story since one seaman was a Canadian. Clark continued, "The government of Canada is in no position to act as liaison between Vietnam and the United States to normalize relations. ... the United States has made clear that normalization is linked to constructive action by Vietnam on the MIA issue and to Vietnamese withdrawal from Cambodia."

Clark asserts, "As for Canada acting as a 'receiving station,' I have no problems ... we need ... to assess ... hard evidence ... there are POWs... I ... authorize the use of diplomatic mail facilities to bring the purported film to Canada, ... to the Canadian Embassy in Peking ... if the film appears genuine, we will ... inform the American authorities ..." Clark ended, "I have made available the Department's facilities ... we cannot afford to second guess ... your information. I have sent a copy of this letter to Mr. Oostrom, M.P, ..."

Barker's general plan included making contact with the Canadian Embassy, the Chinese government, and Hoang. Barker recalled, "The only problem we had ... was financial.... Bob recontacted Douglas Pierce ... and Douglas agreed to ... and cover all plane fares and expenses." Pierce believed people from the Glomar Java were among the general POW population.

Barker, Krong, Vi, and Pierce arrived in China on January 18, 1986. On the 20th, Vi set up a meeting with Hoang and the liaison officer for a China petroleum construction corporation to further brief Mr. Pierce on the sinking and steps China took to search for survivors. Also, meetings were set with Zia Zhang, "... the main leader of China's intelligence office, specializing in Soviet affairs."

Barker met on the 20th with Ambassador Gorham, Canada's Ambassador and they "went over the logistics of the transport of the film" and his ability to arrange transport of the first POW quickly. Returning to the hotel, Barker was informed by Pierce that "he intended to change the plans" and request his son's release first "... because he would be able to identify his son and ... Canada would not be able to ... identify Charles Dale." Barker felt this change compromised the whole plan.

On the 22d, the meeting with Zia Zhang took place. Barker said, "Pierce treated this woman as if she was responsible for holding his son, ..." The Chinese assured Mr. Pierce that the Chinese did not hold his son. Pierce was later quoted as saying that he was only interested in releasing his son and strongly implied "that he represented George Bush and the American government." Barker then said, "although Zia knew what was to happen, this statement scared her and she stated to Vi ... China needed to reevaluate the overall situation before the prearranged transaction was to take place.... they needed more assurances that Canada was on-board."

Barker continued, "I ... debriefed Mr. Gorham, Jeffrey Charlabois, and a representative from Brian Pickford's provincial government. I ... almost begged them to respond to China's request.... They said that Mr. Clark had ... responded in the December 9th letter and it was China's turn."

Barker said he "was informed by the Chinese that we should ... acquire a letter of confirmation from the Canadian government that it ... was still on board. Zia told Mr. Pierce that she personally would try and find out what happened to his son." In the United States, Barker said, "all letters ... between Zia and Vi, ... were given to me to prove China's commitment." Barker received a verbal message from Zia that "China's house was full ... Canada's house was empty and that we must therefore go home and fill Canada's house."

Barker debriefed Ketcheson about events in China. Ketcheson told Barker he "would obtain the letter of confirmation... there was nothing to worry about ... Canada was on-board ... Brian Mulrooney was so confident that he had already made an appointment with President Reagan...." He could arrange "the financial aspects of our next trip as well as obtain the letter of confirmation that "we needed from Mr. John Oostrom, well before March 1."

In the February 13, 1986 letter, Oostrom told Zhang Zia that he was familiar with the "services and operations" of Wildfire International and he personally knew Ketcheson. Oostrom added he was "also aware that ... Barker is active in Wildfire." Continuing, "I can assure you that the Canadian government is also aware of the operations of Wild Fire International, as I ... mentioned its activities to the Honourable Joe Clark, ... some months ago. ... I suggested ... Mr. Ketcheson ... brief Mr. Clark of his activities in writing. This was done on November 21, 1985." Oostrom ended, "I trust that this letter will be of some assistance to you in your work. I look forward to hearing from you."

Barker and Ketcheson went to Thailand to be closer to the action. Barker's information was that Zia and Oostrom were to be in the general area in the immediate future. Barker told Ketcheson, "we still needed an outside source of assistance ... Canada had made mistakes before ...." Mr. Oostrom additionally asked Ketcheson if he and Barker could help the President of the Canadian Buddhist's Association locate four monks missing in Vietnam.

This inquiry led to a "contact man" in Bangkok named John Lasard, Deputy Director of the Catholic Relief Association. Barker planned to leave for Bangkok on April 1, 1986, however "The ... problem was money.... a meeting was tentatively set with Ross Perot in Bangkok during the first week in April. We intended to inform him of what was going on and to use him... to finance the logistical operations ... if the Canadian government backed out."

To get to Bangkok, Barker needed initial financing. Ketcheson informed him that a Dale Peterson in Hawaii "would cover expenses to Bangkok in exchange for my personally transporting a package ... to Great Falls, Montana." Peterson and Barker met in Kona, Hawaii on the 16th of March. Barker declared, "I had a general idea that the contents of the package ... must be sensitive, but I asked ... no questions." He trusted Ketcheson in this secondary type of financing. Barker picked up the package and flew to Great Falls to meet Ketcheson. Instead, Barker was met by DEA agents. He was transporting marijuana. Barker suspected Peterson to be a CIA desk man for Southeast Asia. Ketcheson disappeared and Barker was convicted of drug charges and spent four months in jail. On March 30, 1986, seven days after Barker's arrest, John Lasard was found bludgeoned to death in Bangkok.

Little publicity has been given this case because of Barker's conviction. However, the BBC was set up in this time frame on "drug charges." **(KTB)** Barker's conviction came under what his attorney described to me as unusual circumstances. I remember being told about Lasard's killing from sources unrelated to this case. Finally, DEA involvement is unusual in such a misdemeanor crime, unless a government official told them to get involved. Is it not possible for Barker to be set up by our wonderful, fine, honest government? What if Barker's operation got in the way of or lead to a government sanctioned covert operation? He ran into Perot in February trying to track down a film that John Obassy was supposed to have. Barker insisted Perot's man told Bill Paul that "Bush had better not turn out looking bad over this project." (This was before Bush turned on Perot and Perot decided that Bush was part of the problem.) In July 1986, Mark Smith traveled twice to the Middle East to meet with Obassy to gain further information "concerning the movement locations" of POWs between Laos and China. He was shown a 248 minute film pertaining to POWs in China.

External information confirms the existence of Hoang and his general political characteristics. In the same time-frame, **Rude Pravo** attacked the cabal of the United States, China, and the Vatican (possibly in the person of Lasard of the Catholic Relief Agency). It is possible one of the monks being sought was Yoshida, released in 1989 after seeing American POWs. Further, a DIA study from 1994 showed that "Chinese case officers make extensive use of commercial covers. For example, a vice-president of the China Resources Holding Company... in Hong Kong is traditionally a military case officer... This officer coordinates the collection activities of other personnel operating under the... (Chinese Resources) cover." Zhang Zia, described as Chinese intelligence, headed the economic division of China Food, Cereals, and Oils in Bejiing. In 1996, the Thompson Committee said of such an arrangement, "the increased prestige in commercial and political circles that could be derived from access to US politicians would presumably be of no small value to such an operation." (Thompson pg. 1768) The Chinese insisted upon the including of Bill Paul, the *Wall Street Journal*, for many reasons, including that just shown. This gives increased credibility to the story. Finally, there is the situation of COFCO (China Food Cereals and Oils) itself. In mid 1999, the Cox Committee, studying Chinese espionage, listed COFCO as a Chinese cover for espionage. Only intelligence officers in 1986 would have known this as parts are still classified in 1999. That means Barker had intel connections.

Did China hold POWs? An examination of classified reports show: In 1972, a special liaison cadre from VC MRII reported China agreed to accept custody of American POWs for safekeeping while Hanoi kept "a few tens" for propaganda. This cadre has provided "usually reliable information for over three years," said our intelligence people. A second source confirmed information from BG Tran Minh Duc, "an NVA general in charge of all 'farm camps'" of North Vietnam.

Other sources said POWs were located in the vicinity of Huang - Ni T'i; and Chin - Ma - Chai. The USAF Field Activities Squadron said that the first camp "has been reported previously" and that "The PW camp in the Chin - Ma - Chai area is probably the Yun - nan Provincial No. 1 prison..."

An MI report from 22 September 1971, said that Chou En Lai visited the US POW camp in K'un Ming and the US - Taiwan Defense Command reported construction on the POWs barracks in K'un Ming began in April, 1971. The barracks were to be "Chicom - constructed POWs barracks... to instruct those American military personnel captured in the Vietnam War..."

The special liaison cadre reported once again in **August 1972** that "The North Vietnamese have now moved many of the US POWs held in North Vietnam to secret locations within the People's Republic of China... He elicited the information from visiting cadre from COSVN and the South Vietnamese Liberation Army..."

Victor Louis, a Soviet conduit of information they want out, reported in a February 1, 1973 interview, in London, that American POWs were held in Yunnan, near the Vietnamese border. I was told by a source of mine, with access to the Vietnamese UN Mission, that in the 1985 - 86 time frame the "real POWs" were being held in China after I inquired about Ba Vi prison camp still being active.

In the February 27, 1989 edition of **The New American,** Douglas F. Pierce related evidence that the Glomar Java was sunk by the Vietnamese. An investigation by the US Coast Guard and the National Transportation Safety Board shows that at least nine to eleven SOS signals were received from a lifeboat following the sinking. One signal was traced to an area in or near Vietnamese coastal waters close to Da Nang. Pierce posted a reward of $100,000 for information leading to the return of his son. He received numerous leads and no requests for the reward. He firmly believes his son and others from the Glomar Java survived and that an investigation of the State Department is in order.

We don't want you home yet - Sompongs case

Sometimes an offer comes to you, rather than the other way around. In 1971, in Laos, the U.S. government turned down a COD offer of POWs.

On May 3, 1971, a Dr. Sompongs appeared at the US Embassy in Bangkok. He proposed a Pathet Lao exchange of U.S. POWs for $250,000 per prisoner. These prisoners were held near Sam Neua. Sompongs represented a Pathet Lao Prince unable to negotiate directly because the Pathet Lao did not want the Vietnamese to know about these negotiations.

Sompongs enunciated the Lao were embarrassed because negotiating for human merchandise was not culturally correct. He declared no money was required until the POWs were turned over. Even then, all the money would not have to be paid at that time. Sompongs was told the proper place for the offer was at the Embassy in Laos.

Sompongs persisted by returning on May 12. He maintained the Laotian Prince was still unable to meet with U.S. officials. However, the Prince proposed moving the recovery site to a "neutral area... where US representatives could pick up prisoners and make payment." The Prince would handle the air transportation of thirty POWs to the neutral location. "No money would have to be paid until prisoners were actually delivered."

The Embassy officer again told Sompongs that "he had no authority" to negotiate. He stated it was doubtful that such money was available for the prisoners. Sompongs produced a Thai language newspaper quoting VFW Commander Herbert Rainwater as being willing to pay $200,000 per prisoner returned. The Embassy officer countered he personally could not commit VFW funds. However, he would attempt to determine how much in US government funds could be allocated.

Sompongs agreed that "$250,000 was a little steep ... but ... the Prince would incur considerable expenses in getting the prisoners from Sam Neua to Houa Khong." In this dispatch, the Embassy added, "by refusing to (contact US officials), Prince is able to preserve the air of mystery ... it will be impossible to pin down the elusive Prince until we ... talk cash and therefore solicit the advice of ... JPRC on how much money ... for payment of 'rewards'".

The final known episode occurred on June 16, 1971 when Sompongs returned to the Bangkok Embassy. The American position continued, "difficult to believe that prisoners could be brought out as ... proposed... where North Vietnamese ... unaware of existence of camp and ... would not let American prisoners ... removed without a fight." No one disputed the existence of prisoners. The dispatch argued, "... the danger ... a fight posed for the prisoners themselves ... worried us most about Sompongs proposal..."

Sompongs then revealed General Singkapone would do the actual transfer. Sompongs negotiated for the Prince who represented a ranking PL official whom the Embassy recognized. The Embassy insisted they had no authority to authorize a rescue operation. The Prince had to come forward on his own. Sompongs was apparently never heard from again.

In the war, we offered rewards for returning American prisoners. After COL Nick Rowe escaped, over one hundred thousand reward posters were air dropped over the U-Minh offering six hundred thousand Vietnamese dollars for the safe return of other American POWs. We used a stalling tactic. If this embassy officer lacked the authority to see the deal through, he knew where to go. These messages were sent to everyone with authority to deal on this matter. No POWs were wanted.

Covert dealings for POWs

Dealing for prisoners was not new. The classified, unreleased Pentagon Papers deal with a prisoner swap. Other documents show the following:

A declassified CIA document, dated July 1, 1969, said "In late December, 1968, 27 Americans held prisoner by the Pathet Lao / PL, ... were assembled in Ban Hang Long... before being sent to North Vietnam ... to be used in prisoner exchanges ... For several weeks ... teams of NVA and PL propagandists circulated ... explaining the importance of releasing all American prisoners to the NVA..." (**CIA Cable, TDCS 314 / 09796 - 69, Subject: Pathet Lao Transfer of All American Prisoners from Laos to North Vietnam**)

A second CIA cable amplifies. In late 1969 or early 1970, two Laotian villagers in Ban Nakay, near Sam Neua saw about 20 American POWs in a concealed area. The villagers were threatened with imprisonment for seeing the Americans. A Laotian functionary intervened and the Vietnamese guards severely instructed the villagers not to repeat what they saw. The CIA headquarters comment repeated the transfer of POWs to North Vietnam, specifically citing TDCS 314 / 0976-69.

A third CIA document, dated November, 1969, said 12 Americans, three Thais, and two Filipinos, were transferred from Khammouane Province to Hanoi. The source? A senior Lao Military Officer quoted by a CIA reliable agent source. This document referred to CIA TDCS 314 / 09799 - 69 for back up. That dispatch verified the CIA knew about the camps. Rescued Air America crewmen confirmed the camp locations and occupants. Air reconnaissance showed footpaths leading to the "doors" of the caves housing the American POWs. A third camp with 10 American POWs was part of the "confirmed camps" of "current holdings."

Bobby Garwood told General Tighe in a debriefing that American POWs from Laos were held in the Ba Vi region, specifically in a camp run by Cubans also containing French prisoners. (**KTB** pg. 355) This description dovetails with reports Garwood gave me in 1985 and with declassified reports of POW camps I uncovered in my research.

Frank Snepp wrote in **Decent Interval**, about negotiations involving a high level VC prisoner. They fell through because of American insistence that POWs offered by the VC were not of high enough "stature" to match the VC official being held. Truong Nhu Tang, author of **Vietcong Memoir**, was freed from an RVN prison in 1968 through a CIA exchange. Declassified documents outline numerous attempts at rescues brought about by rewards for American POWs.

The number of prisoners being proposed for the 1968 exchange was much different from those known to have been held. CIA documents show in November of 1970, **forty five confirmed prison camps in Laos**. The largest one holding American POWs was at Ban Nakay Neua. The CIA said, "... American personnel captured in Laos are not believed to be permanently incarcerated in Laos... are escorted to the Ban Nakay Neua prison complex or into North Vietnam."

In November 1970, however, something happened. CIA said, "Until recently, the Ban Nakay Neua (VH 1956) prison complex was the only prison facility in Laos known to contain American POWs.... on a semipermanent basis... however, ... all foreign POWs, ... may have been moved to an undisclosed location north of Ban Nakay Neua." CIA reports show that over twenty prisoners at Ban Nakay Neua **and** an unknown number at Nang Long were moved to this undisclosed location in August and October 1970. The location mentioned by Sompongs is close to Ban Nakay Neua.

Where was the CIA? They tracked the prisoners. They knew about this prisoner movement paralleling Sompongs story. CIA's confirmation process indicates that Sompongs offer was legitimate, but not acted upon.

In November 1988, JCRC received information on American POWs in Laos. Motivated by a two million dollar reward offered by American Congressmen, this person "insisted on knowing the terms of the ... reward..." Incredibly, the JCRC representative said, "the US government ... did not support the private group who is advertising the reward... cautioned source not to be so quick to believe every rumor ... hears... JCRC rep impressed on source ... nothing could be done until the USG had a chance to evaluate the information source claimed to have..."

If captured, the President will disavow any knowledge of you!

Senator Barry Goldwater quoted from a 1967 Preparedness Investigating Sub-committee report saying we were not achieving our objectives in Vietnam because of political limitations discounting JCS advice. (**Goldwater** **pg. 227-8**) Officially, we were not operating in Laos and Cambodia on intelligence gathering missions. Our military actions pinpointed targets, disrupted lines of communication, and harassed the command element of the VC. Several times we almost wiped out COSVN headquarters in Cambodia. Our B-52 strikes caused its occupants and Soviet visitors to unwillingly defecate out of sheer terror. Contrary to mainline press interpretations, COSVN existed.

Air recon located supply dumps. Ground recon located enemy supply lines. Operatives planted the ground sensors monitoring road traffic. Americans flew the planes that dropped covert operators by air. At Phou Pha Thi, we ran the radar guiding our planes over targets in North Vietnam. CIA and DIA ran agent networks verifying POW camps in Laos, Cambodia, North Vietnam, and China. The Special Forces operated in Laos, Cambodia, and North Vietnam. While stationed at Fort Huachuca, I received, as duty officer, reports of some of these activities.

We lost men on these covert operations. For years, we acknowledged only 75% of the losses incurred in Laos. Phou Pha Thi was not acknowledged until the 1980's. In June 1996, Operation Scorpion was discovered. A former SEAL confirmed Scorpion and OPLAN 34A to me as far as U.S. involvement.

Veterans of these cross-border activities acknowledge that if participants came close to being caught, they could be wiped out of existence, literally. DIA operatives tried telling me this one of the myths of Vietnam. Privately, however, they wanted to find out who was leaking information. My Phoenix operations did not require border crossing. I received many intelligence reports inside Cambodia. I did not believe that we got those reports by osmosis.

Officially, all MIAs from these operations are on the POW/MIA lists. I don't believe it. My computer lists don't cover OPLAN 34A activities or those which occurred before. Those men were presumptively ruled dead before the end of the war, thereby "accounted for." Foley estimated two thousand MIAs were "accounted for" in that manner. His sources were usually right on target. Covert operator service records were altered to delete any paper trail of where they operated and when. For example, in April 1976, DOD specifically mislead Congress by telling them only 438 MIAs were carried in Laos. Air Force Intelligence said 227 men were involved in cases where beepers showed life activity after a shootdown. Yet, they only acknowledged 25 men being talked to after their loss incident vice the 138 known survivors shown on AF intelligence rolls. Only after the Montgomery Committee folded did we know that an additional 100 men were lost in Laos.

Many sanitized reports in the "uncorrelated documents" can be correlated to POWs/MIAs. However, some reports detail specific incidents at specific locations not correlated to known operations. These sensitive radio intercepts refer to covert activities proving more men were captured than officially acknowledged.

Asking the Vietnamese for POW returns

During the mid-1980s, our government asked Ross Perot to help determine if MIAs and POWs were still alive. Perot called many people known to have POW / MIA information, including myself.

He opened the way for General Vessey to go to Vietnam as a Presidential envoy. He stepped on someone's toes. The government froze him out of what he accomplished. From March 25 - 27, 1987, Perot, in Hanoi, discussed "all matters of mutual concerns, including the MIA's ... to promote better understandings ... relating to those questions." (**SRV Press Release**) Perot reported Hanoi's concerns were small. They wanted respect. He felt prisoners could be negotiated for without a loss of face to either side. (**KTB pg. 338 - 344**).

Incredibly, someone retroactively almost undid what Perot accomplished. The 30 April 1987 issue of the *Far Eastern Economic Review*, announced that on 17 February, the administration informed Hanoi they wanted to send Vessey to Vietnam. That was a month before Perot went. Vessey's trip was to be preceded by Richard Childress. No mention was made of Perot. Hanoi expressing displeasure, in it's April 27, 1987 Press Release, charged the U.S. was lying, "When Mr. Ross Perot referred to the ... intention to send General John Vessey as... special envoy... the Vietnamese side replied that the question would be considered. It was ... Friday, 17th April, 1987... the U.S. side officially convey the message to the Vietnamese side ... While... being considered, the U.S. side disclosed it to the press. The unilateral disclosure by the U.S. side ... shows the latter's lack of seriousness." Our negotiators could not break the POW logjam. They did not want anyone else to do so. Their integrity is questioned in reporting other issues if they can't be honest on a simple matter of giving credit for a Presidential Envoy's visit.

The Soviets covert mission

One covert mission belongs to the Soviets. From 1965 through the end of the war, the Soviets removed POWs from Vietnam, sending them through Czechoslovakia. Mel Holland, may have been identified as one so removed.

The late Czech General Jan Sejna, former DIA official, testified before the Senate POW committee. He told deposed: He was the first secretary of the (communist) party at the Ministry of Defense from 1964 - 68. He was the Chief of Staff to the Minister of Defense. "Everything would go to (the) Minister from foreign countries, especially (the) Soviet Union, would go through my hand(s). Everything what goes through government, Politburo, Defense Council, I prepare..."

Sejna personally saw in 1965 or 1966 two to three groups of American POWs taken to Czechoslovakia and later to the Soviet Union. The last group he saw was in the spring of 1967. Each group reportedly contained 20 - 25 POWs. Soviet aircraft brought the POWs to Czechoslovakia, where they were interrogated by counterintelligence personnel for 5 - 7 days. A Soviet General, Kuschev, told Sejna some POWs were "used" either for propaganda purposes or to analyze the Vietnam war from the "American side."

Sejna affirmed, "It was the most secret place guarded by military counterintelligence, ... Soviet guards were around the POWs ... They ... took them to the main military hospital for a physical checkup, and the Soviets interrogated them... once ... General Kuschev ... told me some ... American prisoners are very helpful to analyze operation of the United States forces ..."

Sejna knew about drug testing by the Vietnamese on US POWs saying, "Yeah, because they give us the results ..." (Ba Vi was one such location the testing took place) Senja began working for DIA in 1981. In 1990, he was first asked about any knowledge he had of POWs by his own employers.

The transporting of POWs from Vietnam corroborates Garwood's account of an area near Hanoi where Soviets received POWs from the Vietnamese. The Soviet presence in this area is covered in the "Uncorellated Reports." The 1205 report shows a similar use of POWs to analyze the war from the U.S. perspective in camps unknown to U.S. intelligence.

Soviet Covert II

Mooney, Minarcin, Tighe, Garwood, the 1205 document, Smith, and "fictional" books have either testified to or allude to prisoner transfers. What use would the Soviets have for POWs from Vietnam? Plenty, I believe.

Our weapons used in Vietnam knocked the crap out of their best defensive systems. Our planes eluded their best SAMs. True, we lost many planes; but mostly due to restrictions placed on our fliers. Our EW tactics were effective against their radar guided weapons and radar vectored MIGs. We produced "smart" bombs, infrared reconnaissance equipment, and similar systems the Soviets needed in order to produce counters for. At Phou Pha Thi, they failed to get pictures of the phased array of the radar poised against Moscow. Russia needed men trained on that equipment. This is what we did in the Middle East, courtesy of the Israelis. This is covert II. The trained men were available in Vietnam. The prison system was divided to accommodate these needs. This would be an operation of such sensitivity that diplomats cringe thinking of the political fall out if discovered.

These American prisoners provided information about the latest in Air Force tactics; insight into sensitive equipment; information about special infiltration units; and their training. In 1966, CIA agents caught Vietnamese diplomats bragging about American pilots "volunteering" to train Vietnamese pilots. The 1205 document bragged about SOG personnel captured. Defectors to the United States believed such men were readily available to Soviet counterintelligence.

Why would they cooperate? They did not exist. Vietnam hid them, the Soviets grabbed them, the United States denied their existence. Their choice was to go along or die. Mark Smith found two pilots teaching a class in Laos to Soviet bloc personnel in 1988. Earlier, you saw reports of US PWs teaching in China. The papers headlined the kidnapping of Japanese citizens by North Korea in early February, 1997. Their object? To teach Koreans to be Japanese for espionage purposes. North Korea is a Stalinist State, using KGB methods.

After the end of the war, it would be logical for the KGB to use Americans in an attempt to clone spies for espionage in the United States. Enemy radio operators in Vietnam spoke English with "southern" accents. Where did they learn the accents? Dermot Foley told me, from the beginning, about special types of MIAs being "missing" in greater than normal numbers, in particular, EW people. In 1992, US intelligence learned of a former KGB official who bragged of learning his English by "interrogating American prisoners of war" in Vietnam.

In **The Espionage Establishment**, authors David Wise and Thomas B. Ross discuss the "American villages" in the Soviet Union tracing them to the 1950's. KGB agents could learn "Oxford English" or "American English" in their studies. An MI contact floored me with this response, "Yes, we know about these villages. One of the Soviet defectors from the 1950's reported being trained in an American village prior to coming to the United States." In the **Espionage Establishment**, the village was complete with Chevys, Fords, supermarkets, ice cream sodas, and hamburgers. In the "fictional" **Charm School**, they also had 7-11s, a VFW Hall, and one - on - one instructors. More will come in chapter 13.

Special Forces Korea

We covered parts of SFD-K operations earlier. In 1994, MAJ Mark Smith made public more of his operations. Being part of a clandestine operation to track POWs, the rest of his story will be covered here. Smith told Reed Irvine of Accuracy in Media, (AIM) that SFD-K was part of a sensitive worldwide intelligence operation created by the late General Richard G. Stilwell, an Assistant Secretary of Defense from 1981 - 1985. Stilwell used the presence of Special Forces Detachments and conventional military forces as a cover for covert operatives. SFD-K was one of these covers. My sources confirm Korea being part of this program.

The following is a summary of materials presented in 1994 as relates to sensitive materials concerning the unreturned POWs:

* The NSA intercepted a message to the Minister of Defense in Hanoi saying, "This confirms the transfer of 112 USA pilots from Lai Chau to the prison previously used ...." The pilots had been photographed and the pictures sent to the Defense Ministry for "registration." The named prison was Son Tay. **Note**: Lai Chau or N-101, was one of 18 possible POW camps listed by DIA and described as "... operational ... located in a small stream basin on the north side of the Black River... isolated from outside contact, ... located between two hills that precludes a view of Lai Chau City ... an approximate capacity of 250 prisoners.... The physical security barriers, its isolation and the interior containment walls segregating the possible PW quarters indicate **this is a maximum security detention compound**..."

* In November 1973, a radio intercept to the Defense Minister said, "112 USA prisoners now in prison in Son Tay." Ten were having "pain in their hearts and are not in a good way." The governor asked for guidance.

* On June 20, 1977, a US intelligence report said, "General Khamtai, Lao Minister of National Defense maintains extensive highly classified records of Americans captured by the Pathet Lao and Vietnamese in Laos, including the dispatch of captured pilots to POW camps at various locations in Northern Vietnam, including the Son Tay camp."

* In 1984 Smith interviewed a Thai intelligence operative who had escaped from a prison camp in Laos. He saw American POWs in various camps in North Vietnam and Laos. The biggest group was in Son Tay.

* Since 1986, Smith has continued to receive reports of POWs in various camps with the largest still in Son Tay.

* Four US POWs were being utilized in 1980 - 1988 to teach students from the Communist bloc countries at Samoy, Laos. These men got word to agents utilized by Smith and told him of how best to rescue all four of them. This information was passed on to Washington, D.C. and ignored. Included in the informants was a monk who asked, "How can a big country like yours leave these poor men in Samoy and Saleo (the other location where the men were held when not teaching school)?"

* A European, living in Laos, confined to a Pathet Lao prison camp, saw Americans working on a Laotian plantation. Every three months, Smith receives covert assurances they are alive and desire to come home.

* A Taiwanese visiting Laos reported he was on a bus held up by a group of Montagnards and former Vietnamese Rangers along with two Americans. When the Americans learned the man was Taiwanese, the Americans told him to "Tell the army we are still here."

* Smith also had details on the Bai Bang group of Americans.

Son Tay is within 5 km of Ba Vi, Bat Bat, and the area I designated in 1985 as "Prisoner Highway." It is also in the middle of the area where Garwood reported seeing American POWs prior to his return to the United States. This third set of intelligence reports verifies the validity of the Ba Vi prison camp earlier reported.

On July 16, 1986, Smith gave to the Senate Committee on Veteran's Affairs, pictures of three POWs, in captivity, identified to him by his source, as American POWs. He attempted to meet with one of those individuals to see if he knew of other Americans in Laos and if he desired to return to the United States. Smith was instructed to "not approach these people and to leave them alone because there was no interest on the part of the United States Government." The CIA only wanted these three individuals used as "sources of information regarding military intelligence, not as sources on the issue of American POWs and MIAs in Laos."

He also provided to the Committee corroborated probable locations of camps with POWs. Smith said, "none of these locations were reported unless at least two sources reported this information ... there was no cross fertilization between each source." On each reporting, DIA instructed him to "seek additional information."

Smith reported, "we received numerous reports of American POWs being held against their will in a country other than Vietnam, Laos, or Cambodia. This was China... all sources which we had contact with indicated the movement of these personnel back and forth between the border between Laos and China... This general location was further confirmed by one of our principal sources ... John Obassy. This was our motivation in requesting that he procure photographic evidence of the movement of these personnel from China into Laos to participate in the mining and timber operations which were described to this Committee in closed session."

In 1986, Smith traveled to the Middle East to meet with Obassy and view a 248 minute video of POWs described as "an extremely valuable piece of evidence, but only as it relates" to the travel of POWs between Laos and China. In April, both Hendon and Mark Waple saw the film. Obassy agreed to come to the United States to provide further evidence both to Congress and to Waple in the *Smith* case.

However, someone leaked Obassy's real name and sensitive information provided to the Senate Committee in closed session. In a heated exchange between Hendon and Senator Murkowski over who leaked Obassy's name, Murkowski claimed Obassy's identity was leaked in an "internationally available publication;" and in an unclassified document "given to me by the Office of the Secretary of Defense." Smith said, "the unfortunate disclosure of information of our testimony in closed session ... has made it far more difficult for us to remain in contact with those sources who have previously had trust and confidence in both myself and SFC McIntire." Of course China was where Barker said the POWs were.

Spy in the sky keeps track

We have a "spy in the sky" satellite program and an accompanying communications systems. We had an ongoing program, possibly beginning as early as 1967, monitoring places in which our POWs were taken and transferred, accomplished through microchip implants. These chips could emanate or receive signals that could be traced through our satellites.

In 1970, prior to the Son Tay Raid, "Doc" Cataldo, a physician and Green Beret on the actual raid, offered to have himself implanted with a sensor or other device, so that if captured or the raid went awry, prisoners could be traced. (**The Raid - see entries under Cataldo**).

During the war, a satellite was used to take photos on the day of an operation to see how the cloud cover was over a target area. Usually available at 11:00 AM, the photos would help determine if a strike would take place. (**Corona Harvest Reports**) We would use planes like the EC-47 and the SR-71s to help develop special intelligence. Specialized code named operations like **MOTEL, TEABALL, CROWN,** and **COLLEGE EYE**, would sweep the skies for electronic intelligence to support airborne strikes, buffers against intrusion into Chinese airspace, and specialized intelligence operations. Through a combination of these spies in the sky and land listening posts like those at Phu Bai or **WATER BOY** at Dong Ha, we had a good base of intelligence on the enemy and the wherewithal to keep track of selected POWs. Our planners on the Son Tay Mission knew the frequencies, times of operations, and operating patterns of virtually every piece of radar, radio, and electronic equipment known in the DRV.

The civilian equivalent

Perhaps the best way of explaining what has been done is to show what can be accomplished today and then work back to Vietnam. Our government has 24 or so satellites working a system called Global Positioning, run by the Air Force. This system can pinpoint precise locations, one meter or less, by combining the satellite systems with ground based transmitters and triangulation from five satellites. Many US law enforcement agencies use this technology to pinpoint their locations during various types of operations. The technology is so advanced that hunters and boaters can buy equipment to locate themselves for about $200. In farming, equipment can pinpoint land that needs fertilizing and relay it to the farmer. It can also tell him the yield on crops from different areas of his acreage.

Today, federal agents can be found through microchips located on (not in) the official. We have sensor programs to help keep track of military units in various areas of the world, including our subs at sea. These units enable submarines to join in multiunit military battle force operations and share in real time intelligence and communications. A civilian equivalent is the capability to find a truck in downtown Detroit, for example, and locate it to the block and address. This is being done through cooperation with the Russians and their 24 satellite system.

Pictures from satellites are now so good that units as small as one meter in size can be seen in civilian satellites. That means that the military photos and locating devices are much more accurate.

Photos taken in 1992 for the Senate POW Committee came from the KH-11 "keyhole" reconnaissance satellites using television and advanced KH-11's with higher resolution. Their pictures can be radioed back to the National Photo Interpretation Center, at the Washington Naval Yard. Augmenting the KH-11 is the LaCrosse satellite which uses a "cloud piercing radar" with a lesser resolution.

Vortex and Magnum satellites listen in for radio communications. During Desert Storm, their baseball diamond sized antennas were good enough to pick up tactical radio communications at a low wattage. They were tied in to the Defense Satellite Communications System and the Defense Support Program Satellites for good battlefield type communications and control.

Learning the present from the past

During World War II, men volunteered to be "shot down," captured by the Germans where they took into the prison camps devices to let allied intelligence know the locations of prison camps. They also brought in ways to break out. The ways of getting those items inside were publicized after the war and were useless in Vietnam. POWs in the North were stripped to shorts and t-shirts and couldn't hide anything in the conventional way.

Yet, we found some prison locations and names of prisoners inside. Human intelligence accounted for much of this knowledge. Recon photos helped to verify this information. Paid agents on the ground and in the Hanoi government helped, until Johnson and McNamara let many agents "hang in the wind and twist" after cutting off their supplies. Then came the technological processes. It began as mi-cro-transmitters to send signals past "broken backs" allowing patients to function. Our scientists developed a military application. Implants could be used to code the names and other identifying materials to listening posts. My sources tell me that they were utilized, possibly as early as 1967, and that some of our "shoot-downs" were volunteers helping locate men in a more complicated atmosphere than ex-isted in World War II and Korea.

These devices are not the "beepers" going off when a plane went down or the "direction finders" finding radio signals from ground positions. They are activated or shut off by command and inserted with a hypodermic needle. When used as a transponder, it emits a signal giving vital information as well a being a location marker. How accurate? In 1993, the 24 NAVSTAR satellites could track down to 1 centimeter in 1 kilometer. Most of this technology was funded by the CIA. Our earth is becoming "Evergreened."

Of course, there is a program in place to monitor the results. It used to be called the National Reconnaissance Organization (NRO). Until the early 1990s, it "did not exist." When the new NRO facility in Washington in 1994 was dedicated, the existence of NRO become widespread in public knowledge. The NRO has a new name. The tasks are still done and the POWs are still monitored, but under the code word program known as Joint Star (At least that was the last name known). Joint Star prowess was featured in Desert Storm. The J-Stars plane could look 135 miles ahead and produce a 3-dimensional picture. The technology was so new civilians were used to man much of the equipment because the military personnel weren't trained yet. Included in this were the ground personnel using hand held laser devices to guide unmanned rockets to their targets accurately. In Desert Storm, The Joint Star Operational Command played a key role in the technological win.

Joint Star operates in more fields than POWs. Some are indirectly related to the mind warfare field versus the former Soviet Union. We have utilized "mind re-connaissance" to locate our men. When the government said "Project Grillflame" was abandoned, they didn't lie - directly. It continued under another name or agency. Like the former Soviet Union, intelligence programs don't disappear, they just change their cover names.

These are all covert operations - necessary to our national security. I object, however, to their misuse in not being utilized to bring our men home. We can tell the other side we know POWs are in location XX without telling them how. Our POWs are sacrificed for some ill defined purpose.

Bringing the men home

Throughout the book, I made vague references to men being closer to Wash-ington than to Hanoi. Now, I will bring together three different portions of history which may explain why seemingly successful operations like Smith and McIntire may have been cut off at the knees!

The General goes public

BG Thomas Edwin Lacy Sr., was deposed, under oath, on April 22, 1992. During the Vietnam war, he held a variety of senior posts. Prior to that, he was a fighter pilot in the Korean War, and occupied a staff position during the 1962 Cuban missile crisis with the 831st Air Division. In 1965, Lacy was assigned to Vietnam in the Directorate of Operations. There, he allocated "resources of out of country forces ..." He participated in joint strike forces with the Navy and eventually ended up in probably MOTEL, as a Major. After Vietnam, he worked in the Directorate of Operations, PACAF and the Field Command Defense Nuclear Agency.

In Vietnam, he participated in unpublicized bombings in Cambodia and knew of other "secret operations." His deposition was "sanitized." However, he was probably referring to COLLEGE EYE for the command and control in both Laos and Cambodia from March 1969 to sometime in 1970 as his direct knowledge of these code named operations. He was briefed on the Cambodian bombing a couple of days prior to it's inception. Lacy testified that losses in Cambodian and Laotian air operations were handled differently than in operations in North Vietnam. For many operations, there is no "paper trail" because we were not publicly conducting military operations in those countries at that time.

Lacy said men "disappeared" from regular units without military records reflecting that. William Codinha asked, "what do you mean?" Lacy replied, "They were no longer part of your organization ... no gap in my military record, ... I said what happens to me if something happens, if I'm killed, or ...wounded. What happens to my family? Don't worry about that. We'll take care of it...I never got a satisfactory answer... It was a directive." (**Lacy Deposition**)

Lacy confirmed that casualties in Cambodia were often listed as occurring elsewhere. "... we reported people killed or lost... in one location, and they were lost... in some other place due to classifications ... and we never wanted that information to get out... We put US Marines into Mu Gia Pass in North Vietnam... We put special forces into Laos. I don't know how many those numbers were... it is not unreasonable... to think... hundreds, people either killed or captured. We... left people... in Laos when we started withdrawing..." (One source said such operations were handled through HQ, 7th Air Force, Out Country Directorate)

Senator Smith asked, "When you say people are missing, ... do you have direct information that these people were not carried on the missing rolls?" Lacy answered, "yes, sir," adding, "... I will give that in testimony."

Lacy also told a more electric story. On October 5, 1965, he was a mission commander with the overall responsibility for the strike forces attacking Hanoi and Haiphong. He was aboard the Command and Control plane associated with MOTEL. They were monitoring the airwaves, American, Vietnamese, Chinese, and Russian. On that strike, COL Dean Pogreba was shot down. Officially, Pogreba is a category 4 loss in North Vietnam. Lacy tells it differently.

"... he was headed out over the water, and he should have been out over the water in between 8 and 10 minutes... (**Q**) - These are radio calls to you?... (**A**) - Yes, radio calls, mine to him, primarily... Fifteen minutes goes by and he's still showing land ... Then he called and said that I'm being shot at by a MIG. I've been hit. I'm bailing out.... At this same time ... we were listening to an intercept by the Chinese ... shooting at an aircraft that strayed across the border..." Lacy surmised that in the battle confusion, Pogreba's gyrocompass was 180 degrees out of whack. " ... the Chinese MIG reported him ... northwest of Hanoi, over China's mainland ... We talked to him ... by survival radio, ... on the ground, ... he was ... captured."

Lacy was asked, "Was this a concern, that we now have an armed aircraft over China?" Lacy answered absolutely. Lacy's Commander agrees. "The avoidance of a border violation with Communist China was always a factor in our planning .. a buffer zone approximately 25 - 30 miles wide was established ... to warn aircraft approaching the Chinese border. But ... these calls were coupled with numerous MIG and SAM calls, pilots had difficulty determining just who was about to violate the border. **... the situation was complicated ... by reduced visibility and a pilot's temporary disorientation ..., it wasn't surprising for a pilot to come close to violating the border**...there were only a few violations ...." (**General William Momeyer, <u>Airpower in Three Wars</u>, pg. 150-51 Emphasis added**)

Possibly an additional confirmation came in the book, <u>**The Raid**</u>. It was noted on pg. 24 that by 1966, we knew of only a few confirmed POWs in Vietnam, and one in China. Pogreba was shot down in October, 1965. Lacy charged the official report said Pogreba went down over Hanoi. "But you knew that wasn't right? (**A**) That's correct. (**Q**) Did you tell your commanding officer that? (**A**) Yes, I did."

Days later, Lacy was told by a General Simler, "we're in deep trouble." The fear was China might enter the war with a plane shot down and a pilot captured. Then Simler said, "We're going to get him out ... Mr. (redacted) ... a CIA agent, will be contacting you. You're to provide him all the forces that he needs to support this mission, and it may take us awhile."

Over a long period of time Mr. "Black", "White", "Green" (the name changed each time for the same person) ordered support for Pogreba's rescue. Lacy provided Air Force support aircraft, adding, "Five Americans... Special Forces, (redacted) that spoke Chinese and Vietnamese... Asian Americans... were sent in to get Colonel Pogreba... out of the prison camp in China." (Probably **SOG** personnel and maybe **Nationalist Chinese**.)

After about six weeks, Pogreba escaped from China. However, his problems were just beginning. Lacy provided Pogreba and his escorts with supplies as they exited China. Unsuccessful tries were made to extract the men, with some planes heavily damaged. A decision was made to work towards Laos. Efforts to rescue Pogreba lasted for two years. (**Q**) - "You were in communication with them? (**A**) Yes.... The air crew, ... (**Q**) - But they were in communication with Pogreba and these guys on the ground for two years? (**A**) Two years. Yes, Sir."

After retirement in 1977, Lacy worked for an oil company in Jakarta, Indonesia. One of his coworkers had parents in Laos. He saw a live American, about 60 years old, while visiting his parents in 1984. Lacy investigated by crossing the border in Laos with an indigenous group. At Nam Ngun, they find a small prison camp, recently used, where his friend saw the American. There is no one when Lacy arrives, however, buildings with leg manacles attached to the floor were seen. Lacy subsequently left Laos and the POW subject for a few years.

The most electrifying part of the Lacy's sworn statement is he saw an MIA, Tommy Emerson Gist, an RF4C weapons system officer, in the United States, at a Veterans Hospital, in Oklahoma City, OK. in 1989. In describing Gist, he said, "As I'm aware of the situation, Captain Gist, along with 61 others, was extracted out of a prisoner of war camp at Hoa Binh, North Vietnam, in January, 1987." (Gist was listed in 1978 as a category 2 POW and with a hometown in Oklahoma)

Gist told Lacy he did not want his wife (she had remarried) to see him in his condition. "He'd had a drug problem; ... they had given him morphine and he became addicted .... And he was brought back for treatment of the drug addiction..." Lacy said Gist used the name Walter Ray while at the facility.

The second was when he related that in 1989, in North Vietnam, he saw Dean Andrew Pogreba, in a prison. Senator Smith, (NH), recognizing the "bombshell" nature of the information, asked Lacy if he told anyone he had seen a captive American. Lacy replied no. When asked why, Lacy replied simply, "First, who would believe it. ... I certainly would not want to go public ... have him killed. ..."

Smith questioned, "... you have been sworn ... that you saw a live prisoner of war ... you spoke with him... you've identified him... do you stand by that story?... under oath, under penalty of perjury, ... absolutely, without a doubt, clear of mind ... (**A**) Yes, sir. (**Q**) that you spoke to Dean (**A**) To Dean Andrew Pogreba... (**Q**) And you swear that that is the truth? (**A**) Yes ... without any mental, physical, moral reservation ... Dean Pogreba and I were friends in the 1958 - 62 time frame..." The location in North Vietnam was Bao Ninh, 30 miles Northeast of Hanoi.

There are other details in Lacy's deposition. Much more was taken at a very high level of classification. These facts, however, are the gist of what he said. For those who doubt that Vietnamese would allow an American to see POWs and let him go, consider this. William Stevenson, author of **A Man called Intrepid**, saw French POWs after the war, who the Vietnamese denied incarcerating. Authorities officially disbelieved him also. In 1994, two years after this deposition, photos emerged of the ID card of Dean Andrew Pogreba in near pristine condition.

Bringing the men home II

David Hendrix gave a sworn deposition on October 29, 1992. Hendrix is the metro editor for the *Riverside Press Enterprise*, the 70th largest paper in the United States and the 7th largest in California. He became interested in the issue in 1984 after his reporter did a story on Father Charles Shelton Jr., a Catholic priest and a son of the "last" POW. At that time Hendrix did not believe live POWs existed.

Hendrix gave specifics of items he had tracked down, including Duck Soup. Hendrix said that in 1966-68 time frame, Shelton and David Hrdlicka had been rescued by Hmong guerrillas. In the planning was Richard Secord. The first rescue went awry when the rescuers, dressed as Pathet Lao irregulars, were overtaken by North Vietnamese and Pathet Lao forces. "Rather than get into a fight, Hrdlicka and Shelton were returned."

In 1971 or so, another rescue involved US Forces. Once again, Shelton and Hrdlicka were rescued. They "met up with ... a mixed team of Americans and Special Forces and CIA field types... for 8 - 10 days, tried to evade the Pathet Lao ... Shelton and Hrdlicka were slowing people down...It was decided, ... that Shelton and Hrdlicka would be left on the trail and ... Shelton and Hrdlicka, Shelton specifically, ... concurred with the decision ... the others would be able to escape..."

Hendrix also testified about was the introduction of POWs into the United States. In 1989, Hendrix got to know George R. Leard, retired Air Force, who was involved in a new identity program for POWs. At first, Hendrix was told "they are dead." Hendrix replied that the men returned were dead only on paper. The families have the right to know they are alive and back. Leard replied, "whether you're dead on paper or you're dead... you're still dead... to the rest of the country."

Hendrix probed more. He pointed out and Leard agreed that a program like this had "baby-sitters" with the capability of knowing "who is visiting and talking with whom." Then, Hendrix tried another tack. He opined that bringing the men back was correct and patriotic. Those participating should be proud of their part. That worked. Leard said the program of bringing back Americans, to his knowledge began in the 1981 time frame. He warned, "don't get tied up with ... specific dates, because people who were involved in the beginning were not necessarily ... involved at the end... Some might know one part, but not know about the other part."

Hendrix personally believed the program began, accidentally, about 1979 when some late returnees, or deserters, began showing up while the government was court-martialing Garwood. Could they court martial everyone? Obviously, not. "I think that's basically how it started."

Leard said his phase began in 1981, shortly after the alleged ransom offer was made in January, 1981 and the program was "deliberately designed that they not be talked about, or that some were given new identities."

Leard said that the numbers returned were not extensive until the 1984 - 85 time frame. He thought between 100 - 275 were returned. His knowledge of the program was ended in 1986, with the disclosure of Iran Contra.

Hendrix explained Leard knew of the movements due to his being a communications and computer specialist. "The secrets in ... this world are taken care of by clerks ... Generals ... do not do the scheduling. They don't do the crews... you need somebody who knows what they are doing..." Leard said the operation worked with individuals selected for specific tasks. "They were good at what they did." Leard knew about operations at a special place, as yet unnamed by him. Father Charles Shelton heard about it being run out of Clark AFB, the Philippines.

Switching to the Shelton story, Hendrix made it plain he had not written about it and may never do so. It was covered somewhat in **Kiss the Boys Goodbye** . Shelton confirmed it to me sometime in 1991 when we met shortly after his mother died. Shelton was counseling a young man about to get married. During the counseling, the man, noting some of Shelton's POW memorabilia, told this story.

The Air Force sergeant had been on a couple of flights in which "... American POWs were flown out of Haiphong, and I think Hanoi.... they were C-130's, I think — had taken off from Clark Air Force Base, had flown to Thailand, had been refueled, and then flown into Hanoi or Haiphong, were onloaded with Caucasians ... emaciated ... in bad physical shape... 24 ... none of whom were speaking or were permitted to speak ... the crew ... had the patches and unit designator ... removed from their uniforms ... they were his patients ... 3 of this 24 people died because they were in such bad shape before ... their first medical treatment."

This flight happened in 1984. It was Shelton's belief the program stopped in 1985 or 1986. Shelton also told Hendrix of a man named Gordon M. LeBlanc, from Arizona, who had told him of a new identity program in which POWs were gotten out of the way "because of the intense interest to drill for oil off ... Vietnam." Hendrix related, "Another source ... said ... the United States ... provided money, ... tens of millions of dollars to quote improve the living conditions of the American POWs. This source I consider extremely, ... credible. I ... put absolute faith in what he said ... in 1983 a White House Staffer said, we are providing this aid ... to improve the living conditions of the POWs..." Part of the money came from exorbitant amounts paid for the digs in Vietnam, and consistent with previous Vietnamese ways of extorting money from the French. Other ways, Hendrix explored, would be for oil exploration rights or indirectly through World Bank projects.

The questioning got back to where the return program took place. Shelton heard the Philippines. Leard said "The Philippines was not the principal place. ... some might go through the Philippines, ... but there was a principal spot ... for this project... I've checked on Johnson Island, Kwjalein, ... Enwetok.... other places... it's a spot where you ... give ... medical treatment and ... is a reorientation camp also. **And from there, Leard said people were taken to ... mainland US**, and others to Hawaii, ... to Clark, ... Guam or Okinawa." (**Emphasis supplied**)

I checked and found in 1961, COL Edward Lansdale outlined for GEN Maxwell Taylor some CIA run assets in the Pacific. In Okinawa's "paramilitary support station," was a CIA self-contained center, operating under an Army cover. Lansdale said, "Located at Camp Chinen, it comprises a self-contained base ... it can accommodate admirably the holding of black bodies in singleton or small groups, as well as small groups of trainees..."

On Saipan, Lansdale said, "CIA maintains a field training station ... under Navy cover ... the Naval Technical Training Unit ... In addition ... CIA maintains a small ship ... to provide surface transportation between Guam and Saipan ... under the cover of a ... corporation ... offices in Baltimore Maryland ... (with) a potentially wider paramilitary application ... elsewhere." (**Pentagon Papers, pg. 138**)

Hendrix said his research suggested that the people who returned included "several subareas;" defectors like "Greer and Schreckengost." Others "were just outright deserters and who were allowed to come home." Some "were ... bona fide POW's and either under village arrest or under being held in a prison..." (The Official US government position on Greer and Schreckengost is that their remains were negotiated out of Vietnam in 1990)

Some he said, were still in the United States. Others, suffering from culture shock, returned to various parts of Asia. Most were "never reunited with their wife, mother, and children ... except for some, who might have wanted to blow their cover and some may have since then done that." Hendrix is asked why wait so long for his story, which took several years to develop, to come out. Hendrix gives a correct answer. "Something that people need to know, especially about journalists, is that 99.8 percent of us, especially me, ... I do not want to be wrong."

Bringing the men home III

It was 1987. The place is the Philippines, more precisely, a deserted beach near Bagiuo. The guards are specially trained personnel, their normal duty is helping fight the NPA uprising. This is no ordinary assignment.

Marcos was deposed. Aquino had been assassinated. Politics were in a turmoil. The guards, however, were not concerned with these problems. They secured the beach while a ship unloaded its unusual human cargo.

Those unloaded spoke mostly Vietnamese. Their native language, however, was English. They were from another era; one largely forgotten. The men were members of the U.S. Armed Forces; being returned to U.S. custody. There were no brass bands present; no reporters; only those with the unmistakable air of being part of "The Company."

This was not the last time that human cargo emerged under the watchful eye of these guards. The Americans being unloaded were malnourished. There was not a lot said. Strict orders from the "Company" men forbade social intercourse between the guards and the "cargo." For the most part, that was true. The guards knew that these men were former prisoners of war; the "forgotten men" of a by-gone era; a war that diplomats wanted to forget.

More returns took place through 1989. One return was in Cambodia, near the Thai border. Incredibly, the guards "don't exist" either. Like those men on Phou Pha Thi and elsewhere, there is no paper trail establishing that they served in this capacity. There is a big gap in their history; similar to that explained by General Lacy and others in classified programs to me.

However, certain things have emerged. In 1987 or so, I was made aware of a hospital ship that left San Diego Harbor. Contacts within my circle told me that there were doctors, medical personnel, and psychiatrists aboard. A newspaper contact confirmed this particular ship left San Diego at the specified time. It was a military hospital ship bound for the Philippines. The cover story was that it was to participate in "Medcaps" treatment for Philippine citizens with the full media fanfare. Curious. There never was any fanfare. The use of this ship was later verified to me by a source familiar with Joint Star and other programs.

Sources later traced the boat to Diego Garcia, where they lost track of it. There never was enough information at that time to do anything except put it on the shelf. I was told, however, to find out about "Earnest Harbor."

I looked for people or things named Earnest Harbor, Ernest Harbour, and many sound alikes. Everything turned up negative until 1996, when I met "Dutch," one of those guards. Dutch told me Earnest Harbor was Baguio Beach, part of an operation called "Safe Haven." A last leg of the operation, is called "Pumpkin Pie."

After the Philippines part of the operation, these men were transferred, according to Dutch, aboard ship to Diego Garcia and later into safe havens in the Middle East. There, Dutch draws a blank. Perhaps, they landed in Abu Dhabi.

Dutch was not silent, however, on other subjects. He stated that COL Nick Rowe was assassinated because he had come upon this operation and was going public. Rowe was in the Philippines, in 1989 when killed, being posted there in May, 1988. The men used in "Safe Haven" were known to him as were their jobs.

Rowe was a named source of Monika Jensen Stevenson. He was an indirect source of mine, with Dermot Foley being the cut out, for many years. My sources provided me with credible evidence that Rowe was to lead the rescue mission in Laos in 1981. Further, he was ready to quit the military at the time he was killed, disgusted with the way American POW information was being covered up.

The killers? Elements of the US military with strict orders to kill whoever they're told to kill, no questions asked. Do such people exist? Stevenson wrote that a Pentagon Manual named an operation called SLAM or Search, Location, and Annihilation Mission. It's functions included "kidnapping and killing those who helped the enemy in Vietnam..." I've been told that a similar function was performed by C.E.E.A. (the A stands for assassination) (The acronym was "See Ya") The CIA had it's counterpart to SMERSH, the "wet" department of the KGB.

Dutch also said Aquino was killed, not by Marcos, but by his own people. Americans were told not to interfere. Marcos was paid millions to take the fall.

I have been told by a CIA contact, that Americans have been brought back to the United States. They were told that they were not welcome here; being failures in keeping the Military Code. They were further told their families did not want them. Included were the media stories that they were all dead. He had seen one of the POWs in New Mexico, an Air Force Officer. Some of the POWs were in "bad shape." He also told me that the Iran - Contra affair was a prelude to the bringing of POWs out of Vietnam, if it was successful. This source also said that Rowe had been killed probably because of his knowledge of the drug trafficking and the POWs being returned. I pointed out that the bullets that penetrated the armored vehicle and killed Rowe were available only in the police and military circles, he wrote down, "not true, in the Philippines and Mexico." He did not contradict that Rowe was killed by Americans. Aaron alluded to Gritz that trafficking was part of the MIA story. Rowe was also protective of Gritz.

The CIA source told me POWs were in classified wards of military hospitals and out of the way bases. Others reliable sources told me the same. The 1996 meeting with Dutch and knowing who he was allowed me to go public now.

There are many other indicators of the story being true. I had one family trace the fingerprints of their man. "They don't exist" anymore. Foley told me of the changing of the fingerprints in the files of his brother, but he was not sure why. Others have had the same experience. In 1991 it was reported that when live POW photos emerged from Southeast Asia, fingerprints came with them. Like those from Laos years earlier, it would have been easy to credit the photos as being those of the men with the fingerprints. The government "lost" the fingerprints of POWs Albro Lundy II, Larry Stevens and John Robertson. Further, the fingerprints of Stevens also disappeared from the Los Angeles Hall of Records and the hospital where he was born. Robertson's daughter went to the FBI and Motor Vehicle Division with the same results.

On August 29, 1991, the fingerprints of Donald Carr, another "photo POW" disappeared. Dan Borah's fingerprints (a photo POW from Laos) disappeared even from his home town police department. Finally, the fingerprints from the birth certificate of Larry Stevens were determined to be "illegible." Why is this significant? If you want a person to "disappear" and then "reappear," you manipulate the records of his former life. I was told by sources in a position to know that our protected witness program or an equivalent is big enough to absorb live POWs. Missing fingerprints would be one indicator of people entering the program.

While I cannot add anything further to the narrative, covert activities being murky, I will observe, however, that over the years, I have been privy to many possible extraction operations. All seem to have failed at the last second. All seem to have had government baby sitters. Dutch has his. They regularly check in on him to see who he's talked to and what he's been asked. The Company does not like competition in their area of operations.

Other stories

In 1988, there were private negotiations, in Europe, for specific POWs with apparent official sanction. These private negotiations contained the requisite government "baby-sitter." Money was offered and apparently not refused by the Vietnamese side. The Vietnamese official involved became an embarrassment for some reason and got kicked out of Sweden.

One source in the United States wrote to a banker in Sweden asking for funding ($1 million) to ransom POWs out of Vietnam. A specific list of 12 POWs was provided. The correspondence did not escape the attention of the government. The Vietnamese Ambassador to Sweden was recalled.

During the period of this operation, one participant located a woman in contact with Vietnamese refugees. She was suspected of being part of "The Company." An uncle was definitely a company man. This woman said some of the men who returned came home "voluntarily," part of the Federal Witness Protection program. "None were legitimate POWs," she said.

From the documentation I have seen, the persons involved included a very Senior former Democratic Senator with an interest in POW affairs; two private parties doing research; a billionaire putting up the money; a Swedish banker, and two go-betweens. I was told, and documentation appeared to confirm, that the government was aware of this effort - and did not object.

Still more activities

In 1986, private operators went into Laos. After returning, they listed specific places where POWs were seen. The people conducting these operations were not always American, nor not always Asian. There apparently was help in some operations from people sympathetic to the families cause, along with the ever present "eyes of the government" probing to get the fruits of the work. Some even had the nerve to ask for pictures from the operation so that they could be "of some help" in identifying the caves utilized in holding the POWs. By "coincidence," one of those helpful persons was the same one interested in my earlier books. Another writer of fame on POW matters had warned people with these photos of his involvement.

Material presented to the Senate included photos from MAJ Smith's agents that some Senators dismissed as "lightweight." The Senators were informed where the pictures were taken and when. Because there were no verifiable landmarks for our oversight legislators, they dismissed them out of hand. I presume that Smith took the requisite precautions to verify what was coming out, being an intelligence professional. My photocopies of some of those photos show people in captivity.

I have also have photos of Caucasians bathing in a stream in an apparent Laotian location. The naked men are guarded by people in Oriental dress and uniforms. I saw the picture that was taken from a long distance; the blown up version of one part of the original and a blown up version of the significant part of the second picture. There was no doubt in my mind the pictures were of Caucasians being held prisoner. I have also seen satellite photos of Caucasians playing volleyball in a time frame well past when our POWs were supposedly all home, in a location not in the United States.

Now I want to discuss covert operations in general as they pertain to the POW/MIA cases. If we fought World War II with covert operations monitored like Vietnam, we would have lost. If publicity existed about World War II as was in Vietnam, we would have lost. If oversight, in the form demanded today, was in place in World War II, we would have lost. There were slip ups in security early on like the newspaper that wrote that we broke the Japanese code shortly before the battle of Midway. The Japanese fortunately missed the story as did the Germans.

Most people think of World War II in terms of brilliant generalship, outthinking and out-fighting the enemy. True, to a large degree. Covert actions taken during the war, however, gave us the edge. I know from my classes in EW and Tactical Cover and Deception about vast covert activities then. Yet, the bigger story was classified beyond our teaching "need to know." We were researching things perfected in World War II and were not privy to it. It was reinventing the wheel.

That is the second part to the covert equation. If knowledge of covert World

War II activities had come out before it did, the public might have understood the need for security in Vietnam and Korea. They might have supported more covert operations vital to the war. In terms of our POWs and MIAs, let's start an honest accounting for our men. If there are major covert activities going on, take a leaf from WW II and develop cover stories.

The question posed is do we have operations "so secret" that we can afford to dump hundreds of men's lives to protect these activities? If so, develop a cover story as to how you know where the men are and get them out. Three quarters of the people in the country believe in a cover-up. It affects Armed Forces morale.

To get our POWs home, I can overlook the "cover" stories of what would take place if the men are allowed to reunite with their families. You can always invent a cover story and get appropriate parties to agree to it. I once wrote to the Vietnamese at the United Nations. I told them that we could accept stories about men being found in unknown locations, out of the reach of the central government. I then signed the letter, "former Captain, US Army, Phung Hoang Advisor" in Vietnamese. I was told by the messenger that the Vietnamese reading the letter "nearly fell out of his chair" when he read that. Ross Perot told Monika Stevenson and verified to me that he told the Vietnamese much the same when he was there in 1987.

When a man emerges, however, without any such preparation, havoc will be the result. Unfortunately, the fate of the men now rests in the hands of an inept group of politicians who did not even like the war. Our men are in the worst shape; close to home but in perpetual anonymity.

Why am I convinced of the stories of Dutch, Shelton, Hendrix, and Lacy? First, the multiplicity of reports from sources unassociated with each other. I know mine. Hendrix knows his. We are professionals. Lacy and Shelton fit in with a mosaic of other independently developed material.

There are the overt signs accompanying the description of our men from Vietnam. Many were in bad shape - many were disfigured - and many were the "stubborn" types or "Special Talents." Remember, as we discuss special talents. Our educational system, bad as it has become in some areas, was technologically light years ahead of the Soviets and Chinese - who had to copy and back-engineer our equipment in order to produce their own. That was one reason for taking the painful efforts to eliminate the equipment on our EC-47's, AC-47's, and unmanned drones that were shot down. That is why pilots on RF-4s and other high-tech planes were in demand. They knew how to operate the equipment and were privy to the latest operational procedures. The backseaters in the EC-47, ran the equipment and knew first echelon maintenance on the equipment. The Soviets now have satellites which we use in conjunction with our programs. A coincidence?

I recently discovered how much junior officers in the Phoenix Program were worth to the Soviets. I knew reward posters were out for us in Vietnam. I just didn't know how much and by whom. Some of the Vietnamese Phoenix operatives had their addresses listed for kidnappings by VC forces. We also had reward posters out for our targets, the VCI.

Remember the lesson of Garwood. Let me state for the record - clearly, precisely, and unequivocally, Garwood from day one said that he knew of prisoners left behind. I worked closely with his first attorney, Dermot Foley. I knew his claims. That is why I questioned him in 1985. Garwood's information on the location in Hanoi in which the Soviets took over our POWs checks out with declassified files in my possession. His other claims check out with declassified files. Things I asked Foley to verify with Garwood, also checked out. I believe Garwood.

When Israelis conduct negotiations in the Middle East, one stumbling block is the fate of their POWs and MIAs. They refuses to budge until their men are accounted for. Some, they know, are dead. They want them all home before they negotiate on other subjects. Are our men any less important? Is our country so spiritually bankrupt we can write men off so casually as we have in three wars?

Too many "covert" types from the Vietnam war days are doing the same analytical work done almost twenty five years ago. Many diplomatic people from the days that Kissinger gave away our men are still around. Some say drugs are a part of the covert movement and the POWs MIAs are in the way. In December 1993, a CIA type said drug money has been used to "silence" once powerful allies of the families. Perhaps Mena, AR fits into his contention that POWs and South American drugs fit together, along with his contention that "Clinton is an ass."

If a government can make computer records on a known IRA gunrunner "disappear" and "reappear" at will, it can do the same thing to POWs. Only now are covert operation records being declassified, agonizingly slow. They show the "myths" I wrote about in 1979 concerning the napalming of our own men was true. It shows my 1979 discussion of cross border operations of mixed teams of American and indigenous men who were to be disacknowledged if captured was true. The only "myths" were those concocted by the DIA to hide the POW story. Even the Soviet helicopters seen in the uncorrelated documents transporting POWs have been proven. **The message left by Tighe in the uncorrelated documents tell a great reliable story if one knows where to look and what to look for.**

Other evidence to credit or discredit our live POWs is available. To protect the secrets, the "men don't exist." Fine, tell the other side we ran cross-border covert activities. Tell them we hired spies in the Politburo - they'll buy that story as we have done it successfully before. Tell them that we'll admit to finding them in the far countryside where no communist government troops ever ventured. It doesn't matter what the cover story is.

We don't have to believe it and neither does the other side. We had what they wanted - recognition and money. They have what we want - our live men and recovered remains. Hopefully, we still have something to negotiate with since Clinton sold the last candy in the candy store with recognition of Vietnam for campaign donations. The whole thing can be done in order to "heal the wounds of war" and let all of us go forward from here.

After an accounting, black operations will continue. Everyone knows that. Why we pretend that they never happened is beyond rational comprehension. No, we did not operate in Laos, Cambodia, and North Vietnam. No, the other side did not either. See how easy it is to write those things down. In diplomacy, you can accept a lot of crap to get your own way. Nations have done it for centuries. We'll have to do better in our next rounds of black operations. Of course, they'll try harder also. Get the men accounted for and try for once to be what a great power is supposed to be.

Domestic Dilemma

The squeaky wheel gets the grease is what MIA families were told in 1981 by Richard Allen. The families "squeaked" for years, however, soldiers lost in combat is a political losing cause for politicians. MIAs and POWs must be on the front political burner in Washington, D.C. How to get there is the focus of this chapter. President Carter's uncle, Tom Gordy, was declared dead in World War II. He later turned up alive, held in a remote Japanese prison camp. Carter publicized this story to show his concern over the MIA issue. Another story will show how President Carter used the MIA issue simply to win votes.

Carter and the bracelets

In early 1973, Gil Boggs, son of MIA Pascal Boggs, received a congratulatory letter from then Governor Carter for his poem on the problem of missing men. Carter was wearing the MIA bracelet of MAJ Boggs. (*The Voice*, op. cit, pg. 3) Yet, in September 1976, candidate Carter was presented with an MIA bracelet. He was not wearing another bracelet and never mentioned his previous bracelet. What happened to the Boggs bracelet? Taking it off assuming the MIA problem was over was inconsistent with his campaign statements. I believe he no longer wore the bracelet because the political purpose was gone. His flip-flop from Vietnam hawk to draft dodger supporter more likely explained the lack of the bracelet.

Carter and the radical crowd

President Carter's domestic dilemma was his promises concerning an MIA accounting. Keeping those promises would lose the political power base that lead him to the White House. President Carter surrounded himself with radical persons like the following examples.

Sam Brown, a previous advocate of a VC victory, also extracted promises for mobilization of public support for war reparations. In 1975, he was coordinator for a leftist Conference for alternative public policies. The Conference was a "national progressive organization" designed to "strengthen the ... work of the Left... (for) policies for a restructured America." He was also a mentor of **Bill Clinton** in the anti-war Vietnam Moratorium Committee. (*New York Times* article covering Vietnam's entry into the U.N.; *Human Events*, **November 11, 1978**, Alan Brownfield; Covert, pgs. 194, 196 and Unlimited Access, pg.221)

Brown picked **Marge Tabankin** to head the VISTA agency. In 1972, an East German radio broadcast featured her claim POWs believed the bombing of North Vietnam was futile. She also charged we deliberately bombed old persons and civilians who could not run fast enough to bomb shelters, earning her the title, "Axis Sally of Vietnam."

James Fallows served as a speech writer for President Carter. Prior, he wrote how he deliberately avoided the draft by starving himself until he had only about one hundred twenty pounds on a six foot one frame. In addition, he claimed to have suicidal tendencies. The doctors examining him for induction decided he was "unqualified" for military service. (**Brownfield**, *ibid.*)

Closer to the President, we find **Anthony Lake**. He served the President as Director of the Policy Planning Staff for the State Department. Like Kissinger before him, Lake found it easy to find employment both with Republicans and Democrats. With Kissinger on the National Security Staff, in October 1969, he decided that Vietnamization was doomed and would lead to unilateral withdrawal. He and fellow staffer Roger Morris urged Kissinger to propose a "caretaker government" and to "give in" on major points to the North Vietnamese. To enforce our views, he and Morris actively advocated assassination of Thieu. (**Palace**, pg. 81)

Lake became associated with the Washington Cadre School, an offshoot of the Institute for Policy Studies (IPS), a radical leftist think tank used to influence foreign policy and fund anti-CIA and intelligence agencies. In addition, IPS funded anti-war efforts and the "Vietnam Mission to the U.N." On September 13, 1974, Lake chaired, with Morton Halperin, a panel for the Center for Nation Security Studies (CNSS), another IPS spin-off radical organization, entitled "Covert Operations and Decision Making." Lake was then legislative aide to Senator Frank Church, radical from Idaho, who had no love for the CIA, intelligence operations, and particularly covert operations. (**Covert**, pgs. 13, 57)

Under Carter, Lake found employment at State for **Richard Feinberg**, who had ties to the pro-Castro North American Congress on Latin America (NACLA). Lake had ties with Orlando Letelier, identified by the FBI as an "agent of influence" for the Cuban intelligence, DGI, and the Chilean Socialist Party apparatus in East Germany. (*Ibid*, pg. 216) We'll deal with Lake later in this chapter as he appears as the National Security Advisor to Clinton.

How does this relate to the MIAs? These four were representative of many other appointments, like Marian Wright Edelman, of the Woodcock Commission. She was a mentor to Hillary Clinton and a person who believed that children should be able to sue their parents and have counsel provided to do so. A President is fairly judged by his appointments. These appointments proved true to Carter's later actions.

The radical crowd continued

In late 1977, the late Wilfred Burchett arrived in the United States on a speaking tour. (An Australian journalist, many former POWs had a graphic mispronunciation of his name sounding like - **well fed bird** and feces.) Burchett was identified by a Soviet defector as a KGB agent. (*Human Events*, **December 10, 1977 pg. 3**; the *Washington Post*; and a sworn statement given by Yuri Krotov before the Senate Internal Security Committee) He was identified as an interrogator and torturer of American POWs in both Korea and Vietnam (*Human Events*, **November 26, 1977, pg. 4**, also the *Washington Post* and the Australian Magazine **Focus**) He was an apologist for Hanoi and admitted talking to American POWs in South Vietnam. (In North Vietnam, he often used an alias when talking with our POWs. Some told me his opinion carried great weight with the Vietnamese officials.) There was a reason for this action by the Vietnamese. He served on the Soviet payroll since the 1950's. His Australian passport was revoked on grounds of treason. He lived in a luxury apartment in Moscow and traveled on a Cuban passport. By the time of the Vietnam war, he had "been in the employ of the Soviet Union for many years." (Senate Judiciary Committee, SSIS, Nov 3-10, 1969)

Australia was more unforgiving to him. A counterintelligence officer there said, "he would be arrested as a traitor if he ever returned to his homeland... (for) trying to convert Australian prisoners of war to the communist cause while acting as a bona fide war correspondent." (**US News and World Report**, 2/27/67) Burchett also tellingly backed the Vietnamese invasion of Cambodia. (**Covert**, pg. 117)

He urged the POWs to make violent anti-US statements and used them in propaganda films. His questions paralleled those asked by Vietnamese interrogators. His role in beating American POWs from the Korean War was known to the Carter State Department when original entry was denied based upon membership in the Australian Communist party. He was granted a three month "waiver" by a "high ranking" State Department official. That request originated in the White House. Burchett was the guest of honor at a reception hosted by Jane Fonda, Cora Weiss, Mark Lane, Norman Lear, David Dellinger, and William Kuntsler. On the other hand, Giang, who knew about POWs, could not get into the country even with the help of DIA. Perhaps the answer to Burchett lies, like so many other answers in leftist Washington, in the fact that Burchett was an IPS ally.

Carter, beholden to leftists for political support, approved the giving of $150,000 to Vietnam by Friend-shipment, an anti-war group, which helped build a one-hundred bed hospital on the site of the My Lai massacre and allowed the licensing of five million dollars in private aid to Vietnam. This radical group showed a callous attitude towards our POWs. Their value to the Vietnamese came from their influence upon public opinion.

Endless wartime processions to Hanoi and wartime propaganda statements played havoc with troop morale and public support. "Hanoi Jane" is best remembered for grinning up the gunsights of weapons used to shoot down American planes and by calling our POWs "liars and hypocrites" after reporting the torture they suffered as prisoners. Fonda asserted they received kind, humane, and lenient treatment. One trip to an enemy capitol (Moscow) was lead by Bill Clinton, who denounced not only the war, but the United States.

Fonda and others were the subjects of mail covers and "buggings" during the war. This surveillance proved they were conduits for information concerning the names and physical conditions of POWs. (**Schemmer, The Raid, pg.** 174) This surveillance, a repetition of similar actions taken during World War II, was necessary. These people did not always pass POW information in a timely manner. Just prior to the Son Tay raid, Cora Weiss obtained a new version of Hanoi's "complete lists" of captives. That list, discovered through a bugging device, contained the names of some POWs who died in captivity. This information helped speed the Son Tay raid. (*Ibid.*, **pp.** 174-175) Tom Hayden, "former" radical; former husband of "Hanoi Jane;" and establishment politician; was given a letter from a POW to be delivered to his family. The letter was never delivered. (**POW, pg.** 354)

Representative Dornan described some of the radicals: "... a ... story that will live in infamy... over a... sleazy porno shop... Ninth Avenue and 42d Street in New York City, all POW mail was... contaminated by pro-communists ... heroic POWs were tortured to death ... Major Edwin Atterberry. ... was stripped naked and beaten ... He died after eight days of sadistic beatings. Imagine. All of the mail by these brave men ... was manipulated by ... the Committee of Liaison, from above a porno shop ... This disgrace and other disgraces ... made me ... emotionally involved...."

This "emotional involvement" kept Dornan from being picked to travel to Hanoi as a member of a Congressional Delegation until August 1979. However, he was dead on concerning the Committee of Liaison (COL). Formed by Weiss in February 1970, it was a significant reason for the prolongation of the war and was no ordinary organization. Weiss herself is the daughter of Samuel Rubin, founder of Faberge toiletries, a registered communist, and for many years, the chief funder of IPS through the Samuel Rubin Foundation.

COL was formed "at the invitation of the North Vietnamese." Weiss traveled to North Vietnam "at the invitation of the Hanoi government" to begin the release of POW names to influence public opinion "to give in to Hanoi's demands." In January 1970, after the testimony of former POWs Douglas Hegdahl and Robert Frishman, about the torture Hanoi imposed, Weiss countered by saying that as captured war criminals, POWs and Frishman in particular, was "lucky to have an arm at all." (**Covert,** pgs. 38-39)

COL was formed to encourage the families to join the anti-war movement. Hanoi claimed that the "success of" COL would be the "first step" to a POW release. Like other Hanoi statements, they lied to their own also. However, COL was a full partner in the trail of deceit of the releasing of "full POW lists." Like other offshoots of IPS, COL prolonged the war, seriously worked hand in glove with Hanoi, and manipulated the families. Other IPS fronts were the Women's Strike for Peace, Clergy and Laity Concerned, and the Fellowship for Reconciliation. Their concern for the POWs was as phony as their objectives to achieve "peace." (*Ibid.*, pgs. 42, 376. 377)

COL said the POWs were "treated well and housed in 'immaculate' facilities." These parroting statements of the Hanoi line, lead the House Committee on International Security to declare COL as "a propaganda tool of the North Vietnamese government and appeared to be acting as an agent for a foreign power," since COL was formed "at the request of the North Vietnamese" and acted as the "sole conduit for mail and messages between the POWs and their families." (*Ibid*, pgs. 38-39)

Who are these IPS radicals who surrounded Carter and helped turn the President who once denounced the leaking of the **Pentagon Papers,** ironically by IPS personnel and their allies, as necessitating "Federal legislation that would make news organizations criminally liable" for such a release in times of war, to a President who surrounded himself with IPS personnel. (**Covert,** pg. 284-85) It should be remembered that still to be released are the classified portions of the Pentagon Papers which deal with POW matters. It is not certain if Vietnam received any of the **Pentagon Papers,** Top Secret at the time, during the two years from the time of pilfering until the time of publication by newsmen associated with IPS.

IPS is, in the words of a KGB associated agency, who cooperated with IPS, "We know them for a very long time... very good specialists in ... humanitarian and social sciences... some IPS positions... coincide with the perspectives of the Soviet leaders... IPS fellows have pointed out the progressive role that the Soviet Union plays in supporting national liberation movements.... " (*Ibid, pg*. 346-47)

Coincidentally, the KGB decided in 1938 to form and fund organizations to influence public opinion, elect officials to office, define political positions and to help promote the Soviet cause. Their ties to the KGB would be deniable and would not be agents in the classic sense. (**The Haunted Wood** pg. 145)

We've seen how the COL helped the North Vietnamese cause. In other areas, IPS radical organizations leaked the **Pentagon Papers** and information on the My Lai Massacre. Both stories were timed to help the North Vietnamese in their foreign policy objectives.

There are those who are thinking that a lot of this is good information, but how does it tie into the POWs? I guess the best way is to follow the story and see where it leads and how it does tie in. The example I will begin with is the **Pentagon Papers** and how the radical tie in affected our POWs.

The **Pentagon Papers** were copied by Daniel Ellsberg, in 1969, while he worked for the Rand Corporation. Information in the Papers end sometime in 1968. He chose IPS to leak the study. They didn't, however, Neil Sheehan, *New York Times*, learned of the study through the IPS. It is also possible, as the FBI put it, Ellsberg may have obtained "the remainder of the study from IPS for Sheehan to Xerox in the early part of 1971." (**Covert** through FBI, pg. 50) When the case over the printing of the TOP SECRET study went to court, IPS related legal organizations helped defend the printing of the Papers. (Ibid., pg. 51)

The relation to the POWs is this. The radicals intended for the Pentagon Papers to end the war. Henry Kissinger was identified as the one who was even more "alarmed" about the leaking of the study than was Nixon. Kissinger previously worked with Ellsberg on the transition team when Nixon was elected. Ellsberg was privy to more classified material and Kissinger, affirmed on April 29, 1974, through a federal affidavit by Chuck Colson, was determined to stop the leaks "at all costs." (**Watergate**, pg. 282)

Leading conservative activists like Phyllis Schlafly believe Kissinger was worried that the policy he was pursuing, no win in Vietnam, would be exposed through the Papers' leak. (**Kissinger** pg. 158) Ellsberg, IPS, and the anti-war writers on the *New York Times* and *Washington Post*, were fearful that without the publishing of the Papers, the war was being "won."

Concurrent with the leaking of the Papers was a report from an FBI counterspy that the Soviet Union had a full copy of the **Pentagon Papers**. "Fedora," a Soviet double agent, told the FBI this. (**Covert**, pg. 52) This report caused Nixon to fear another Alger Hiss. Ellsberg had knowledge of a Single Integrated Operations Plan, SIOP, in particular, nuclear targeting data, which was then still current. This meant he knew the targets and the means of attacking them. (**Watergate**, pg. 282) The stop the leaks attitude of Kissinger was accompanied by his "literally pounding the President's table." (**Ibid**, pg. 283)

From this, Nixon formed the Plumbers Unit (to stop the leaks) and the rest is history. For the POWs, had not Watergate happened, Nixon may have had enough power and prestige left to have ended the Vietnam War in a different manner and have worked to fulfill his promises. However, there is also an ironic twist. Nixon, the fervent anticommunist, was done in with help from the Soviets. "Fedora" and his information was a Soviet disinformation program designed to deceive and provoke Nixon. (**Covert**, pg. 52) The why remains a mystery. However, a good disinformation plan, like a good deception plan, must resemble "the truth." (**A Man called Intrepid**, pg. 207) That would require detailed planning, detailed knowledge of the intended target, and detailed access to his thinking. This intimate knowledge was needed by the Soviets to pull it off successfully, fooling the recipients; a mole of great influence.

On the other hand, it could have been put together by a network of agents of influence to piece together this information from diverse groups. At this time, Senator Henry "Scoop" Jackson, a liberal of pro-defense tendencies, told Nixon that KGB agents were being welcomed into numerous Senatorial and Congressional offices with impunity. The FBI, our chief counterintelligence defense, was helpless since Director Hoover had agreed to restrictions on Congressional Surveillance. (**Watergate**, pg. 284) By coincidence, the KGB sends agents to many radical meetings, such as IPS. (**Covert**, photos between pgs. 163-167) That Senator Jackson was correct is illustrated best by the 1983 expulsion of KGB agent Aleksandr Mikheyev, for seeking confidential material from a Congressional aide. (**High Tech** pg. 184)

Not that the Soviets haven't succeeded on "the hill." Congressman Samuel Dickstein, D-NY, was actually a spy, code named "Crook." (**Haunted Wood**., pg. xxii) Of course, Nixon was correct in his "Hiss" analogy, in that the Roosevelt White House was full of agents and operatives like Hiss, Lauchlin Currie, Harry Dexter White, Judith Coplon, Andrew Roth, and literally hundreds of others who were either outright covert agents or agents of influence for Russia and the communists in China. One, Guy Burgess, who worked in Truman's War Room, was instrumental in bringing misery to POWs. His assessment to Stalin that Truman would not use the atom bomb in Korea, if the Chinese intervened, was instrumental in Stalin convincing Mao Tse Tung in sending his troops across the border. This set in motion hundreds of POWs and the medical experiments on them. (**Dulles**, pg. 438-439; **Haunted Wood** and **Venona** for the names of the spies)

The Pentagon Papers leak is directly tied to the POW issue. In 1971, at the time of the leak, a new peace initiative was given to Hanoi which Nixon and Kissinger believed "might be accepted." Hanoi rejected it 13 days after publication "without giving any reasons," prolonging the war. (**Watergate**, pg. 284) This prolongation is evidenced by two items. First, the previous incursions into Cambodia in 1970 and other initiatives is believed to have set back the communist timetable by at least two years. The communists were losing on all fronts until their "Ba Be" plan of 1972. The other evidence came from the Chinese themselves, albeit after the war and rarely acknowledged.

On May 20, 1975, Ch'iao Kuan-hue, Chinese Foreign Minister, gave a classified briefing to Chinese Communist cadres, and obtained by friendly intelligence agencies. At this briefing, he said, about the victory in Indochina, "... this victory was granted by Uncle Sam." He awarded "medals" to Nixon, Ford, and Congress for their help. "In the early 1970s... if the war was to continue, it would be too trying and too costly for us to sustain...unexpectedly, the Americans lost patience." He explained that China was looking at Soviet adventurism on it's borders. This adventurism was succinctly outlined by Nguyen Tinh Hung.

In 1969-1970, the Soviets were fighting pitched battles on the Ussuria River border area. This is the area China claims was stolen 100 years ago. Two attacks in early 1969 killed 30 Soviet border guards and hundreds of Chinese. "Victor Louis," a KGB conduit of information, intimated that China could become another "Czechoslovakia," subject to Soviet invasion to aid anti-Mao Chinese communists. Reportedly, there was a request as to the American reaction if the Soviets also took out the Chinese nuclear installations. (**Palace**, pgs. 480-481)

Ch'iao agreed. He said, of this time, in regards to quitting the Vietnam War, "Furthermore, at that time, we were busily occupied in preparing against the Soviet revisionist aggression, and thus could not deal with it wholeheartedly."

This view is important since one of the basic tenets of the fight against NVN was the "containment" of Communist China. Nixon, in 1965 said that the war in

Vietnam was a "confrontation ... between the United States and Communist China..." to keep the Pacific from becoming "a Red Sea... Do we stop Chinese Communist aggression now or wait until ... the risks are much greater?" This promise was one of the ones that kept Thieu banking on American promises. (Ibid., pg. 9)

Dramatically, just weeks after the **Pentagon Papers** were published, Kissinger made his secret trip to China; secret that is to everyone, but China. In 1970, Larry Wu-Tai Chin, a US military and intelligence operative, and long-term Chinese agent, passed to China the "classified documentation" on this trip and its diplomatic ramifications. (**Rat**, pg. 133) In addition, China, in 1994, possibly used John Huang to get at our files on Chin. (Ibid, pg. 31)

This new emphasis on China rightly unsettled Thieu. The visits by Nixon to both China and Russia both emphasized the POW question as fundamental to ending our engagement from Vietnam. In China, Nixon emphasized withdrawal in return for the release of POWs and a cease-fire. (**Nixon Memoirs**, pg. 568-69) This was later reiterated as a prime focus in the 1205 document.

In Russia, Nixon told Kissinger a peace in Vietnam was requisite to resolving other bilateral problems. POWs aside, Kissinger disobeyed and pushed for concessions forming the basis of the Peace Accords. There, he agreed to keep in place the 200,0000 North Vietnamese troops in the South, thus sealing the fate of both the South and the POWs. For the first time, mutual withdrawal became a unilateral withdrawal by the Americans. (**Palace**, pg. 58) As we saw from the Chinese, this "collapse" became their reason for continuing the aid to Vietnam, now seeing a possible Soviet presence on their southern flank if the North won the war.

The North, confused by stiff resistance on the battlefield after their Easter offensive with Americans supplying aggressive air and advisory help. Yet, they were signaling new items at the peace table in Beijing and Moscow. As the 1205 shows, they decided to go with Kissinger as the "pliant one" and use the POW release as a gauge of public and Nixon's reaction. They also made the decision to hold back over 600 POWs to ensure their bargaining position.

Simultaneously, they used their public influencing tools, the IPS offshoot peace groups to pressure the US government and American opinion against continuing the war. The POW issue, highlighted by the "peace delegations" from these groups, solidified the anti-war effort. IPS got it's wish with the **Pentagon Papers** by ending the war earlier although not as quickly as hoped. Unknown to our side, we had been "winning" with China wanting out of their war support. Despite plans not to "win," time and strength were on our side until this "outside intervention" tilted the tables against our position and our helpless POWs.

Minus Watergate, Nixon would have pulled some more help for the South and they could have prevailed. With Watergate and the help of "deep throat," who seemed to know what all the bargaining tools were, the fate of Nixon, South Vietnam, and our POWs were sealed. It was a fate "deep throat" had to be aware of and a full willing participant in.

Fine, but what about this China thing. Well, let's look at it. Many of our POWs became that way through stolen technology. Our planes over Vietnam were being shot down by SA-7s, with our Redeye technology. SA-3s had our Hawk technology. Thus, when our countermeasures worked, POWs were exploited to find out the whys. (**High Tech** through *Janes*, pg. 116). ZIL trucks, with the help of Ford Motor Company, sent continuous supplies down the Ho Chi Minh Trail, despite the promises of the Soviets, they would not do so. (*Ibid*, pg. 117) Similarly, other advances were made by firms wanting profit above security. Legal sales of "non-military" use ball bearing grinders, outlawed since 1961, were okayed by Nixon in light of his "conquests" in Moscow. If we didn't sell it, others would. Despite Pentagon warnings, they were sold and Moscow's missiles became more accurate. (**Ibid**, pg. 111) The Soviet's "NAVSTARski" Global Positioning System was "civilian" registered, but believed to find their subs, had components identical to our GPS system. (**Ibid**, pg. 119) Our KH-11 satellites, which can watch events "live" at receiving stations, used miniaturized computer systems, highly prized by Moscow and Beijing. (*Ibid*, pg. 124) Los Alamos expert, Dr. Lara Baker, emphasized that the Soviets knew what they wanted, asked for it exactly, down to part numbers. The same can be presumed of the Chinese. (*Ibid*. pg. 163)

Now comes the deceit, both at home and abroad. Our politicians and bankers are sold a bill of goods about the backwardness of both Soviet and Chinese industries. They are shown only the worst of the industrial goods. Then, they get money, loans, and the promise of more profits. Western Trade delegations find the Soviets knew all about their companies down to a price per share information. China is probably the same way now with their Western trained analysts. (*Ibid*, pg. 155) For our companies, however, all their information are "State Secrets."

The POW connection? The 1205 showed our POWs being exploited for their knowledge in avionics, science, and then state of the art military weapons. This passion for technology, both by Russia and China, verifies the accuracy of the 1205 and it's accompanying message, POWs were held back.

One further message on the radicals. They spawned both Bill and Hillary Clinton. Both were products of IPS offshoots. Bill's apparent sole purpose at Oxford, in 1969 was to organize anti-US and anti-Vietnam War protests, at the request of Sam Brown. (**Unlimited Access**, pg. 221) Keep in mind the following when you read chapter 15, "Mindset to Debunk," and the testimony of FBI Director Freeh. The security system of the White House was dismantled by Clinton. Secrets were accessible to anyone who wanted to look or take. Classified NSC and CIA materials were read by uncleared persons and transferred to other multinational agencies without proper security arrangements. Security risks have been hired. (*Ibid*, pg. 68, 230-231) What we know about POWs could have been transferred to Russia, Vietnam, China, and God only knows where else. When the 1205 arrived in D.C., it probably soon afterwards arrived in Hanoi, thus priming the Vietnamese for answers to questions before they were even asked. Thus the importance of the radical connection to the POW issue.

Other Security Questions

President Carter overlooked a situation with serious potential internal security implications. Some refugees from Vietnam worked to promote SRV aims by showing propaganda films, lobbying for reparations, urging resident refugees to send money to family members in Vietnam, and urging diplomatic recognition of the SRV. (**A confidential source so lobbied**) Refugees were promised if they supported these aims, they would have no trouble in getting their families out of Vietnam. Some of this activity emerged in the spy trial of David Truong in 1978.

The sending of money to relatives in Vietnam was legalized on January 6, 1978. While "humanitarian," I reported in 1979 that a substantial portion of this money was held "in trust" by the communists. (**From a confidential refugee source**) In

1985, this information was verified by a Senate Committee. This "trust fund" was another ruse used by the Communists to get hard American currency.

This internal security problem may not be big. However, there have been disturbing signs of "murders" of refugees supporting a resistance movement inside Vietnam. Such activity may dampen the amount of information available on MIAs. I wrote in 1979 the largest amount of MIA information comes from refugees. In 1996, after relations were normalized, the security problem became evident. The FBI ran ads in Vietnamese publications asking recent refugees to call an 800 number if Hanoi attempted to recruit them to spy. By March, over 200 calls had been logged. (**New York Times,** March 17, 1996)

Money at all costs - profits before principles

One problem cuts across party lines and administrations, the American business community. To some businesses, profits come ahead of principles. Prior to 1975, there were plans for oil exploration off the coast of Vietnam. These plans continue unabated. This aspect of the domestic dilemma begins with the trade embargo. Businesses looked at Vietnam as a fertile ground for new markets. Since 1975, Hanoi has talked with business interests wanting to open trade negotiations, including oil companies, and not one company brought up the MIA problem. (**House Select Committee, vol. 3, pg. 159**)

In an April 1976 broadcast, Radio Hanoi stressed the "obligation" of the United States to provide postwar aid. It accused the U.S. of sticking to an outmoded, hostile policy where "it still does not want to normalize relations ... counter the aspirations of ... **U.S. political and business circles"** (**House Select Committee, vol. 5 pg. 130 Emphasis added**) The Vietnamese told U.S. oil company executives that if normalization came, within one week, applications to develop Vietnamese oil reserves would be approved. (**Vietnam: Problems of Normalizing US-Vietnamese Relations, pg. 14**)

Leading an effort in Congress to normalize relations was Congressman Sonny Montgomery who said: "**There is oil to be explored.** I would rather have the United States explore the oil than ... Russia or China ... I have voted against any reconstruction aid... I think it will help us in ... an accounting, ... I think (an end) to the MIA issue and **the accounting of the remains** will come much, much faster. (**Wolff Committee, pg. 24 Emphasis added**) In August 1978, concurrent with the congressional delegation, including Montgomery, arriving to recover MIA remains, Vietnam announced an oil discovery in the Mekong Delta; a mighty temptation for businesses to ignore the lack of an accounting for POWs and MIAs.

Oil continues to be a big factor in the MIA problem. Oil can be either a diplomatic or domestic dilemma for a President. In 1983, it presented a diplomatic dilemma with the sinking of the Glomar Java. The Java was undertaking the first American exploratory oil drilling near the Gulf of Tonkin where the Vietnamese asserts exclusive drilling rights. (**Dept. State memo Nov. 22, 1983**) This drilling was done for China. The "Global Marine ... reported ... the ship was frequently harassed by Vietnamese boats, ... was warned... (by China) to look out for frogmen attaching explosive devices, and ... a Vietnamese gunboat standing by... Underwater films of the sunken ship reportedly show massive damage similar to what would be inflicted by an explosion... in addition, *the companies apparently suspect that the Vietnamese hold some survivors*." (**Ibid. Emphasis added**)

While Smith and McIntire were getting information on POWs and presenting

.

their evidence to the Senate, the din for trade grew. The head of the POW hearings, Senator Frank Murkowski, was a leader in the move to lift the trade embargo. The *New York Times International* edition of November 4, 1990 reported that Claiborne Pell (D-RI), Richard Lugar (R-IN), Alan Cranston (D-CA), Joseph Biden (D-DE), John F. Kerry (D-MA), Christopher Dodd (D-CN), Frank Murkowski (R-AK), and Mark Hatfield (R-OR) urged President Bush on October 29, 1990 to open "a new chapter in US-Vietnam relations." They specifically urged President Bush "to act promptly to lift the US trade embargo on Vietnam ...."

The POWs/MIAs got lip support. The Senators lamented the Vietnamese speed, but were encouraged by the "considerable" progress exhibited in resolving the issue. The writer, Clifford Krauss, observed, "The letter should reinforce increasing pressure from ... business executives" wanting to enter the Vietnam market as Vietnam could become a "significant trading partner."

In 1996, the following oil stories emerged. Mobil Oil, with other partners, tested a well in the Con Son Basin, former South Vietnam. (**4/19/96**) China and Vietnam battled over oil rights in the off shore areas. Conoco Oil went with Vietnam. Crestone Energy Corp. went with Beijing. (**4/23/96**) Vietnam Oil and Gas Corp. along with Enron Corp. started a liquefied gas project southeast of Saigon. (**5/13/96**) International Petroleum Corp. found oil, natural gas, and gas condensate in an area between Malaysia and Vietnam. (**6/21/96**) Oxbow International Power Corp. was selected to build a 300 megawatt power station in Quang Ninh Province, NVN. (**6/24/96**) Broken Hill Proprietary Co. wrote off a $119 million investment in an Vietnamese oil field because oil reserves were below estimates. (**7/7/96**) (All *Wall Street Journal*)

This "increasing pressure" and the desire to "open a new chapter" in the Vietnam/US relations worked. On May 16/17 1991, Richard Solomon, State Department, testified before the Senate Foreign Relations Committee that, "New patterns of diplomacy... are... unfolding... the confrontations ... are rapidly giving way to reconciliation ..." It was time to "... seek reconciliation ... with Vietnam." This required attaining "a comprehensive solution to the Cambodian conflict and resolving the POW/MIA issue." The US and Vietnam went over a "road map" of how this could be arranged "quite rapidly" in a four phase program. To solve the POW problem, all we required was "Hanoi's active cooperation." (**I have a copy of that classified "road map." It didn't solve the problem but sold the men out.**)

That cooperation did not come. *The Washington Post* reported on May 31, 1991 that Hanoi objected a plan giving Khmer Rogue insurgents effective veto power. Nguyen Co Thach wanted negotiations to proceed on their own, outside of what happened in Cambodia. In June, Thach stepped down as Foreign Minister and as a member of the Politburo. Vessey, however, felt "Vietnam would stay the course." (**July 17, 1991 hearings Asian and Pacific Affairs Subcommittee**)

Other "heavyweights" wanted to end the trade embargo. Dwight Jasman of AT&T reasoned easing the embargo would eliminate hard currency flow into Vietnam by the black market. (**June 25, 1991 hearings ibid.**) CitiCorp successfully lobbied the Treasury Department to ease the transfer of moneys from Vietnamese families in the United States to their relatives in Vietnam. (*Wall Street Journal*, **April 15, 1991**) Much of what goes on inside Vietnam impinges upon the domestic scene in the States. Thach, a principal proponent of "normalization" while trying to ease out interference from China, argued, "It is time to heal the wounds of war... to ... talk and play and have fun... the people from the State Department, their faces never smile...." (**Time, April 30, 1990**) He added, "... we have met all the requirements of the US — (MIAs, reeducation camps, family reunification, etc.) — But, in the State Department, there is no change."

Purges in Vietnam show that nationalism is emerging. Different factions want different things. Somewhere, there is a way to get an accounting for our missing men. Old walls of hostility are breaking down. There are "free marketers" in Vietnam who insist that socialism can work with free markets.

The Bush administration attempted to exploit the fast moving dynamics in Vietnam without harming the POWs left behind. The "hard intelligence" on POWs had to be exploited while avoiding a "scandal" of "how long have you known and not acted." **Bold imaginative programs were maybe followed**.

We missed many past opportunities. Robert McNamara, as World Bank President, allowed money to go to Vietnam in 1978 to repair irrigation dikes we supposedly bombed. No help for our MIAs in this deal. During the David Truong spy case, Vietnam's Ambassador to the UN, Dinh Ba Thi, was drummed out of the party. On June 17 1978, Hanoi announced his death in an "automobile accident." Refugees insist that he was fleeing from the communists. Thi was one of the top members of the old NLF. In this time frame, Hanoi forcefully eliminated opposition to its consolidation of power. Thi was just one victim. Truong Nhu Tang was another. My Tho, Thi's reported destination, is adjacent to Ben Tre, former base of the NLF and a strong hold of separatist insurgents.

The Washington - Hanoi pipeline

The Vietnamese also scored through what I call the "Washington-Hanoi Pipeline" so named because of what happened to COL Rowe while a prisoner. He spent five years building a cover story of his background. Then, from the United States, came his Green Beret background, infuriating the Vietnamese. They determined to kill him when God intervened with a GVN operation in the U-Minh.

This pipeline provided Hanoi with valuable information on POWs. (**POW, pg. 266**) When returning POWs filed charges against collaborators who refused an amnesty offer, the Vietnamese end of the pipeline sent materials, signed under duress, to "prove" that "all collaborated." Our POWs were threatened this move would happen. Ted Guy was one target. (*ibid.*, **pg. 575**)

Robert Garwood discovered the pipeline when Vietnam said he stayed voluntarily. The Marine Corps, finding no wrong with their officer collaborators, charged him with capital crimes. The League savaged his reputation. DOD refused to reveal his being a legitimate POW and used operatives to trash him to veterans.

Sometimes this pipeline brought torture to POWs. One POW told of his family being approached by a Senior Democratic Senator asking for their signature on anti-war material. The family declined. Within a week, the word was relayed to Hanoi and the prisoner suffered a beating because of the refusal. (**From a confidential source**) A beating came from a visit by the Women's Strike for Peace, an IPS offshoot. Comments made by those "good ladies" concerning the attitude of a POW caused his beating. (**Hubbell, POW, pg. 336-339**)

A look at the domestic Presidential dilemmas

I have been told by national media contacts that sometimes I seem to be too partisan in this issue. I've been accused of being too light on the Reagan and Bush administrations. I am a conservative Republican with the emphasis on conservative. My ties with conservative organizations and personalities go back many years. This led to partisan leadership roles in campaigns and party organizations from local to national. Thus, it may seem that I would protect the most conservative administration in years (Reagan) and his chosen successor (Bush) from embarrassment on this issue. It may seem that way.

The domestic dilemma facing President Carter was his opportunity to start anew with the MIA issue. He botched the job badly by throwing away bargaining chips. His domestic constituencies did not believe the North Vietnamese lied. The MIA problem was swept under the rug and findings of death continued. Finally, when solid evidence emerged on live POWs, he began believing Americans were prisoner (i.e. his 1980 statement in Philadelphia).

By contrast, it took him only one day to set up a program of amnesty for draft dodgers. The amnesty program used as an adviser a man identified to me as a POW collaborator **(From confidential sources)** who retired, "in the best interests of the service." **(Hubbell, POW, p. 603)** This typifies the concern Carter felt for the MIAs and their families.

Carter had no Watergate. Democrats held a two to one majority in Congress to implement an accounting effort. His presidency was welcomed in Hanoi. He knew the trauma of an MIA family. Instead of keeping promises to the MIA families, he answered the call of radical constituencies and fulfilled the prediction all of the MIAs would be declared dead.

President Carter asked to be judged by higher standards, being a born-again Christian and failed miserably by his own standards. Many POWs died in captivity during his presidency because the government ignored solid information.

Dilemma that faced Reagan

President Reagan faced a different predicament. He had fewer alternatives available to him. He had a natural constituency for solving this problem. The "Gipper" wrote to the POW families many years ago that under his administration the problem would be solved. It began that way. The Laotian POW rescue almost came off. He was shot at the end of March and rescue plans were dropped. Soon, "pragmatic" advisers told him to be careful. He did not need a new Iran hostage situation. From a practical viewpoint, many persons working on the MIA problem were holdovers from the Nixon / Kissinger era with roles in writing the Peace Accords. Some survive in their "accounting roles."

One conservative Congressman, Bill Hendon, succinctly outlined the alternatives. He said that the government (on POWs) could 1) **blast them out** 2) **buy them out** or 3) **sell them out;** all bitter alternatives. His Chief of Defense Intelligence testified about persons with a mind-set to debunk POW information. The beginning of live POW awareness came with the riveting testimony of General Tighe. Family members formed new groups. The League and administration minions called them "radical," "militant," and "Rambo." The Reagan administration rode the crest of the work of these organizations. Elements of the Reagan administration allowed people to discredit the new groups and congressmen like Hendon. I say elements because I know personally some high ranking persons in the Reagan administration who did not buy the "party line."

The most serious dilemma facing the Reagan administration and later the Bush administration was a **POWgate** waiting to explode. It came close with the *Smith McIntire* case. Unfortunately, the good guys got snookered by judges in court. In October, 1991, I watched an episode of **LA LAW** having as its theme two brothers inheriting their mother's estate. Their father was an MIA. It featured the drama of live sighting reports, the government saying the father was dead, and even the 1974 "all MIAs are dead" report. One brother wanted to declare the father dead under California law so "he could get on with his life." The other brother wanted him kept "alive" to continue the search his mother began. In this scripted ending, the judge wisely determined that there was sufficient evidence to keep the court from declaring him dead. Only on TV has this happened.

I wrote in 1986 that President Reagan needed a high-level presidential commission, responsible to him, examining refugee reports; intelligence data; electronic intercepts; photo reconnaissance; and other special intelligence that existed. This commission could forge a bipartisan way of getting the men home. That did not happen. In 1989, Reagan's term ended with a report saying there was no evidence of live Americans held prisoner - but the possibility can't be ruled out.

Reagan's congressional oversight committee was headed by a partisan liberal. On February 3, 1986, Congressman Solarz held a Special Order to expose the proof of Marcos owning real estate in the United States. Compare proof he needed there versus what he rejected on the POW / MIA issue. Solarz talked of "strong presumption," "documentary and direct" evidence, and "compelling evidence." He came to the "inescapable conclusion" of Marcos being wrong. He never uttered "irrefutable proof," his standard for live POWs. His conclusions rested on persons who had "testified under oath." He felt that he was correct even without "absolute proof." One standard for an issue of his interest and another standard for an embarrassment to his committee.

The Bush dilemma

President Bush cannot escape the legacy of his Vice-presidency. He stopped Ross Perot's examination of the issue. In 1985, the Presidential Foreign Intelligence Advisory Board was stripped of independent thinkers. One member who was fired said the perpetrator was Bush. The new members were Bush cronies. This was when POWs were being moved. Smith and McIntire were trashed by intelligence operatives. **CBS, ABC, 60 Minutes, 20/20** were focused on the *Smith* case and the invigorated Bobby Garwood.

While President, it was embarrassingly clear Americans were prisoners. He started anew. He made it a point to show concern for POWs during Desert Storm. The Republican staff for the Senate Foreign Relations Committee showed that unacknowledged POWs or MIAs on classified missions, deep into Iraq, were suspected. Governmental scrutiny of the press during the war was high helping the military deceptions and ultimate victory. However, like World War II, the knowledge about the deceptions will be lost to posterity until some censor fifty years from unlocks the files. Fifty years from now, the POWs and MIAs on classified missions might be acknowledged like POWs from World War II. Bush may have begun POW returns, as I suspect happened.

The biggest dilemma facing Bush was shown in 1991. Bush's State Department had a "roadmap" leading to normalization. For the first time, the POWs were not a precondition to normalization. On October 24, 1991, the normalization began. The "road map," with no POW accounting, ultimately lead to the removal of the trade embargo (with help from Clinton's cronies).

The pragmatists lead conservative Reagan away from the POW rescue. Bush pragmatists lead him towards accommodation and oversight in the House lay in the hands of liberal Democrats. The real test came in the Senate POW hearings which started in November 1991. What happened comes in Chapter 13.

LTC Peck supported Tighe's theory of "mind-set to debunk." He was attacked by opponents as being nice, but not in the job long enough to understand the problem. Rumors began he was fired. LTC Sedgwick D. Tourison Jr., a senior analyst with DIA's Special Office for POW/MIA affairs from 1983-1988, came to Colonel Peck's defense. In his July 24, 1991 letter to the *Washington Times*, he said "I resigned ... three years before Colonel Peck and for some of the same reasons. I offered to testify ... My offer was never accepted."

Tourison outlined some problems. "No ... substantive document on what happened to all the MIAs.... * No ... substantive document on holding of ... POWs who returned in 1973, 18 years ago. * A refusal to release the same documents DIA has declassified and released to the next of kin... * Refusal to hire native-born Vietnamese out of fear that they might be working 'for the other side.' * **Collecting information on POW/MIA activists instead of tying to get the truth.** * Maintaining more files filled with disinformation than substantial intelligence. * A fundamental failure of DIA's human intelligence effort ... * A lack of consistent methodologies ... every time a new manager arrives." (**Emphasis supplied**)

The statement on "collecting information on POW/MIA activists" has more meaning than any of us ever knew. We suspect there are "soft files," never provable, which disappear or appear by the whim of the custodian.

A contradiction now exists. If what I believe to be true happened, both Presidents Reagan and Bush brought POWs home. However, no one knows. Why? Are there more left? Did the program stop with Clinton?

The Clinton dilemma

It would be easy to ignore this President. His belief system exists only for the moment. If all the POWs did come home, why isn't he allowing them out of "hiding?" If they did not, then his program of lifting the trade embargo and recognizing Vietnam was ample grounds for impeachment. In 1997, with cynical "symbolism," the first Ambassador to Vietnam was a Democratic Congressman and former POW. A new battle ground has to be found for the POWs.

With Clinton, we got Carter again. This draft evading President who visited Moscow to denounce our government, in the midst of a war, tried amending things by visiting the "Vietnam Wall." Sorry, live men count more than rhetoric. I feel sorry for Bosnian and Kosovo vets under his reign.

Don't forget the "oversight" oversight

I've been somewhat neglectful. I've been so busy in illuminating shortcomings in the Executive Branch, I have shortchanged the Democrats and Republicans who had the opportunity to keep the Executives in line. Since the 1941 debacle at Pearl Harbor, Democrats been reluctant to expose their flanks on shortcomings in national security affairs. They protected Roosevelt on the sneak attack. They protected Roosevelt and Truman on the POWs from World War II and Korea. In 1952, Eisenhower, who knew about POWs from World War II, became President. Neither side wanted to make an issue of it. Korea became a replay of World War II. The House POW Task Force, under nominal "Republican" control, with real power, however, remaining with Congressman Solarz until his election defeat. The pre - 1995 Republican Senate examined Smith and McIntire "under oath." They also protected a Republican President. They did not examine, however, the 1981 rescue mission. "Maverick" Republicans refuse to believe POWs are alive. Murkowski was one and McCain is one. The 1992 Senate POW Committee took testimony by former officials who "believed that Americans had been left behind." That Senate Committee ended in 1993 without any way to get men home. Two of the members, Kerry of Massachusetts and McCain of Arizona, worked to lift the trade embargo and for recognition of Vietnam. McCain said, "in order to maintain and expand further US and Vietnamese efforts to obtain the fullest possible accounting, the President should lift the US trade embargo against Vietnam expeditiously." It was lifted; Cambodia still has a Hanoi stooge in power; and we still have live POWs in captivity. In February 1992, I felt the new Senate POW hearings might be a new beginning. I blew that prediction.

Clean up the agencies

There's a need for a thorough house cleaning in the POW agencies. As was noted by MAJ Smith and Colonels Peck and Tourison, this is necessary to prevent a hardening of the "mind-set to debunk" witnessed by General Tighe. Each has seen compelling evidence of live prisoners. To paraphrase Congressman Solarz, the "inescapable conclusion" of "documentary and direct" evidence presented "under oath" is that American POWs survived. They are somewhere, alive today.

There is one thing readers need to know. Eisenhower, Reagan, and Bush, being military trained, relied on staff reports. Carter and Clinton were "micro-managers," their hands in everything. Tighe's testimony of a hardening in his staff, or the mindset to debunk, existed also in CIA and elsewhere. Hendon and LeBoutillier testified of problems at mid-level State and DOD. Reagan and Bush trusted their staffs, even if the results went against "gut feelings." This is the reason for the house cleaning needed in these agencies.

I understand the phrase, Only Hanoi Knows. However, only Washington can act and ask! Remember, Hanoi spoke in the 1205 document and Washington ignored that straight forward simple admission, "For now, w**e have officially published a list of only 368 POWs. The rest are not acknowledged**. The US government is aware of this, but they do not know the exact number of POWs, or they perhaps only assume an approximate number based on their losses ... we are keeping the number of POWs secret."

I want to point out at this time that governmental reward money works. We had in place, during the war, reward programs that brought forth information on POWs. The basic reason none were ever rescued during the war was the treasonous activity on the part of both American and Vietnamese allies with access to POW rescue information. Read the book **SOG** by John L. Plaster, 1997, Simon and Shuster for full details. It will fully debunk the no known POWs in the U-Minh DIA bull pucky!

Yes, only Hanoi knows. But, Washington forgot to listen!

Deceit Through Public Investigation II

The Senate created a Select Committee on POW / MIAs and held hearings through the end of 1992. A 54 page Executive Summary and over 500 pages of findings was issued. Those findings inquired into previous investigative work and delved into intelligence gathering, covert operations, signal intelligence, public awareness, CIL, and other topics. The final finding was, despite knowing men were left behind, there was no "proof" of captivity.

The overview

I disagree with this finding, but I have less trouble with this Committee than previous ones. There was more probing, more pointed questioning and some sincere agonizing over a final product. Senator John Kerry (D-MA), Committee Chairman, told the *New York Times*, "This report does not close the issue ... There is evidence, tantalizing evidence, that raises questions. But ... not facts ..." **(Jan 14, 1993)** The Vice Chairman, Senator Robert Smith (R-NH), outlined his problem for C-SPAN: "We had ... disagreements on ... evidence.... the committee unanimously agreed that we could not go from evidence to proof that Americans ... are alive. We had evidence ... but ...(not) proof." **(Jan 13, 1993)**

In a letter to me, he was more forthcoming. "... with this letter, I can express my own views... I held several meetings ... with DIA personnel... I did not believe I received complete answers to my questions... and I... became a member of the House POW/MIA Task Force... the Task Force was never properly focused on obtaining information about our POWs and MIAs, despite the sincere efforts of a handful of Congressmen... the more I examined ...the more questions I had, and the more convinced ... American POWs had been left behind... since World War II... This tragic issue needed to be exposed to the American public... in 1991... I introduced legislation to create the Senate Select Committee on POW/MIA Affairs... was subsequently appointed Vice-Chairman .... The Select Committee... attempted to obtain direct answers from Communist governments and ... US officials... We were confronted with an ... difficult task and given limited time and resources... consensus was not always possible... the Committee... reviewed thousands of pages of classified documents... interviewed and deposed several hundred witnesses ... Administration officials, intelligence analysts, and diplomats... the Senate Select Committee... has not closed the book on the POW/MIA issue... our committee has opened the books ... more so than any other previous inquiry... I would like to have deposed the Secret Service agent who claimed knowledge of a 1981 offer from Vietnam concerning POWs which was discussed at the White House" (rejected on a 4-7 vote) "we have left a public trail of Committee documents at the National Archives ... investigative memos, hearing records, and depositions ... these documents would lead most Americans to the conclusion that..."

"1. a number of POWs remained in Communist hands following World War II, the Cold War, the Korean War, and the Vietnam War; and 2) the U.S. Government withheld from the ... people much of what it knew about the fate of these men..."

On the Committee he wrote, "I want to address the issue of whether or not I should have signed the Select Committee's Final Report... My position remains...

This was the most comprehensive investigation ever undertaken ... Senator Grassley
(R-IA) and I believed that certain eyewitness accounts of POWs after the Vietnam
War, along with certain satellite photos and National Security Agency enemy ra-
dio intercepts, represented a strong possibility that American POWs ... survived to
the present. .. I believed Robert Garwood was telling the truth about having seen
... American POWs ... outside of Hanoi long after the Vietnam War. ..."

Continuing, "disagreements among Committee members were clearly noted.
... a careful reading of the report... will show that there are many conclusions on
which you and I would be in complete agreement... I also believe that our own
Government can do much more to investigate the fate of these men... I believe
U.S. efforts have... been flawed and Congress may have been deliberately misled
on facts pertaining to POW/MIA matters... some executive branch personnel had
been 'evasive, unresponsive, and disturbingly incorrect and cavalier.'... General
Dmitri Volkogonov has provided us with dramatic and deeply troubling Vietnam-
era documents concerning the number of American POWs held by Hanoi in the
early 1970s -- a number far greater than those who eventually returned... our own
bureaucracy has been trying to debunk this new information because ... it exposes
the general lack of U.S. knowledge about ... its missing personnel... and calls into
serious question the current ... policy on POW/MIAs... I have no reason to doubt
their accuracy .. the number of reported American POWs held in North Vietnam in
the early 1970s... Volkogonov... says the documents are absolutely genuine..."

Bravely, Smith said, "I am also outraged by President Clinton's actions and his
inaction with respect to the POW/MIA issue. Many of the Committee's most important recommendations have never been seriously acted upon, particularly ...Com-
munist China's complicity in not returning POWs from the Korean Conflict and
Vietnam's complicity in not returning POWs captured in Laos... the President has
not chosen to appoint a new White House negotiator on POW/MIA issues... President Clinton is relaxing the US trade embargo ... when this leverage is critical in
convincing Hanoi to return to the negotiating table... allowing the US Joint Task
Force (Full Accounting) to redefine the measure of Vietnam's progress... as the
level of ... busy work taking place as opposed to the actual return of POWs ... or
their remains... President Clinton believed that this type of "progress," which has
yet to prove an "accounting" for any American POW or MIA in Laos (Sept. 1993),
was sufficient to warrant a further relaxation of the US trade embargo..."

Winding up the problems pointed out by the Committee, Smith said, "With
respect to North Korea... the overwhelming evidence that POWs were not returned
forty years ago... I have traveled to North Korea... to discuss... the fate of our
POW/MIAs... the North Koreans clearly expressed their willingness to research
and provide information and records... I feel my efforts... have been in vain as
**President Clinton is apparently not willing to pursue anything other than the
return of remains**... President Clinton has not directed the US military to vigorously pursue... to learn the fate of American POWs who never returned... With
respect to Russia, the President has taken no discernible steps to personally under-
score ... the importance of receiving full cooperation from their intelligence services... GRU and the KGB... With respect to Communist China, the President has
done little ... to demand answers from Beijing on the American POWs under their
control since the Korean and Vietnam conflicts..."

In another section, we'll see some of Smith's answers to what to do and in this chapter we'll learn more about why Clinton has done little on the issue.

The déjà vu is that a Select Committee presents a newly elected Democratic President with the "proof" that he needs normalize relations with Vietnam. A draft evading President gets the proof that no Americans are alive in Vietnam. That is not what the Committee said, but Clinton read the report the way he wanted to.

What is proof? Definitions are in order. **Proof.** The American Heritage Dictionary's first definition is "1. The evidence or argument that compels the mind to accept an assertion as true;" "3.a. Convincing or persuasive demonstration. b. The state of being convinced or persuaded by consideration of evidence;" "5. Law. The result or effect of evidence; the establishment or denial of a fact by evidence."

Let's look at **assurance**. "2. A statement or indication that inspires confidence; a guarantee or pledge;" "3. Freedom from doubt;" "1. The act of assuring." Which leads us to the word assure; "1. To inform positively, as to remove doubt."

The purpose of this exercise is to set the stage for the coming debate in front of the Committee. LTG Williams and LTG Tighe did not disagree in principle. Williams stuck to a supervised script; there is no "irrefutable **proof**" on any subject. However, the more literal LTG Tighe's "personal opinion and stated **assurance**" was there was at least one American captive. With there being no such thing as "irrefutable proof," that proved the point that there was no "proof of live Americans." Tighe also said he could not "prove" the fact of live Americans, but, true to his personal opinion, told the Committee that I am giving you my best professional advice that they are there. That is what military intelligence professionals are paid to do. Here, I throw myself into that category.

Cross-trained as an infantry officer, I wanted often to set out to bring home the "proof" of my convictions as an intelligence officer. Lacking that authority in many instances, I had to wait for the "operations officer" or other authority to act. Once for example, I was convinced from intelligence reports that a certain group of VCI were operating in a certain section of the forest on the eastern edge of our District. Previously, I plotted intelligence reports on my "situation map." Soon, that map had numerous dots covering a certain area. I had the "proof" I needed that an operation should be conducted, having cross confirmed my information with personal ground reconnaissance and aerial reconnaissance. I urged my counterpart to run the operation. The result was the killing of two VCI; the capturing of one; and the near miss of eliminating the rest of the District VCI.

How can so much evidence be routinely dismissed? It is easy. Intelligence becomes so politicized as to become meaningless. Many diplomatic moves in the past would never be pulled off today. We are spoiling for another Pearl Harbor.

Let me explain. Prior to December 7, we had the classic signals of war:

* The burning of the code books by the Japanese at their embassies * Intercepted radio communications ordering a break in diplomatic relations at a precise time and date * Japan's precedence of not preceding war with a formal declaration * The submarine found inside Pearl Harbor hours prior to the attack * The agent report from "Tricycle" stating Pearl Harbor was being targeted - including reports as to how torpedo bombing would be used * Prior American intelligence estimates showing that Japan would likely strike on a Sunday, just after dawn, with no warning * The all intelligence summaries, never correlated, showing military intelligence gathered inside secretive Japan having named Pearl Harbor several times as a primary target and never passed on by State Department "professionals" wanting

their place in history as peacemakers * The "evidence, tantalizing evidence," clear to military intelligence professionals, that Pearl Harbor would be a main target. In fact, a warning from them went out one week early, just missing the exact day.

There was no "proof" as defined today. They did not have the spy inside Tojo's cabinet authoritatively telling them the exact time and date of the strike that they knew was coming. Contrarily, the politicians offset this professional advice with the clear calm assurance of the Japanese government that peace could be negotiated. Our "spy" in Hanoi, the "1205" document, and "Spy" from Russia, Sejna, were not found until after the POW hearings were over.

The Joint Chiefs of Staff, aware of the clear intelligence, sent ambiguously worded warnings to commanders in the field. These commanders, unaware of the full extent for the warnings and lacking clearance to see the intercepts, did what they could with what they had. Unfortunately, like the radar operator with planes "seen" almost an hour early, their "proof" came with the bombs.

Proof is in the eye of the beholder. COL Joseph Schlatter, DIA, in July 1989, testified, "If we look at everything we collected during the war and everything we've collected since the war, we don't find any evidence that Americans are captive." Not proof, mind you, but "evidence." Contrast that statement with the Minority Staff Interim Report statement, "... classified and unclassified information all **confirm** one startling fact: That DOD in 1974, concluded ... **several hundred** living American POWs remained ... in Southeast Asia. This was a full year after DOD spokesmen were saying publicly that no prisoners remained alive."

POWs held until at least 1989

The staff of the POW Select Committee said, "The intelligence indicates that American Prisoners of War have been held... and remain in captivity in Vietnam and Laos as late as 1989... no American Prisoners of War have survived in Cambodia." (Senator Smith asserted most define "proof" as being a live POW, and of course we don't have that "proof" yet. *Washington Times*, July 1993)

In June, 1992, Staff member Bill Hendon polled the staff investigators on their live POW beliefs, based upon the evidence before them. The results were: Le Gro, 200; Hendon, 650; Nicklas, under 100; Holstine, 650; and McCreary, 850. The 1205 document shows 671 POWs held in Vietnam were not returned. In 1994, Major Mark Smith told a TV audience that 572 POWs were alive in Laos. Neither the 1205 document nor the Smith estimate covers any POWs returned to the United States nor transferred to the former USSR during or after the war.

How did we get from the staff views to the published views? The mystery lies in what General Tighe described as that "great and unknown distance." In 1985, he declared, "*Judge a report — phony for any reason — it's not (to) be used to cross-check others* nor is its author likely to be interrogated." (**Emphasis added**)

There were deep differences on the Committee. In an overview, the Committee report declared, "The Central Intelligence Agency retained no formal responsibility for POW / MIA collection and analysis and has deferred completely to the Department of Defense..." Continuing, "CIA field officers knew to report information on POW - MIAs ... The National Security Agency and it's military service components that support it largely dismantled their collection efforts in Southeast Asia ... Vietnam and Laos developed secure landline communications to replace the radio networks during time of war ... The Committee met significant resistance from certain agencies of the U.S. government in the declassification of the requested materials ... The Committee relied on the good faith compliance of the agencies and departments to its subpoenas and requests."

POW rescue raid discounted

We'll pull an all intelligence review of Nhom Marrot, or "Fort Apache," seeking that elusive word, "proof:" * Rowe told Monika Stevenson that the camp commander's name was known * The USAID employee in January, 1976 knew of POWs * Previously, the USAF located a Thai who saw Americans in 1974 nearby in Kham Keut * Prior, in 1972, CIA had confirmed sightings of POWs in an unnamed cave near Kham Keut * In 1979 a guerrilla source wrote to Vang Pao that Americans were moved to Nhom Marrot and held near Kham Keut * In November, 1979, the guerrilla source reported the name of a POW — similar to a known MIA. The guerrilla leader "passed polygraph test (s) in ...1980." * Bo Gritz, in November, 1980 was told that U.S. prisoners were now at Muong Nhom Marrot.

Confirming is the technical intelligence: * Photography from satellites and SR-71s - shows the previously reported cave site "generally correlates with description of detention area." * In December, 1980, the imagery indicated a secure detention facility built after 1978 with a man made "52" stomped in the ground and with "people continuously observed."

Here is intelligence describing American prisoners in the same area over a long period of time. Individual reports confirm each other once analyzed. Eyewitness testimony is augmented by technological means — both imagery and polygraph. This is the corroboration leading to General Tighe's "personal opinion and stated assurance" on live POWs following a "fast moving train of evidence."

What did the Committee say about Nhom Marrot? "The intelligence community's actions to confirm the presence of American POWs ... were inconclusive ..." The "efforts taken by the intelligence community and the US military to investigate and prepare for ... a rescue of live American prisoners were extensive. President Reagan and his National Security Advisor, Richard Allen, were aware of this intelligence and the actions taken. ... Steps were underway to resume efforts to obtain a conclusive answer **when a press leak killed any further efforts.**" (**Senate report pgs. 273, 278, Emphasis added**) In this closely held operation, who risked the lives of the POWs by leaking to the press?

Satellite photography discounted

Let's examine satellite photography. There is an extensive amount of photography suggesting the presence of POWs. Pilots were taught to scratch into the ground or build with man-made materials, characters, which when seen from the air, would signal the presence of a prisoner or prisoners. Further, each pilot had a unique "authenticator number." Together, they would "confirm" other intelligence about the presence of a prisoner, at least in wartime and sometimes peacetime "theory."

For those with the view that all men were dead, there had to be a way of ignoring the unmistakable. An "obviously man-made symbol" was a USA and a "walking K" image found on Jan 22, **1988** in a rice paddy near Sam Neua. The CIA discovered the symbols and "investigative steps were promptly taken." (**Senate Report pgs 261 - 63**) That prompt action was taken in November, **1992**; an investigation team was dispatched to the field after Laos gave permission to go. "... it was the DIA that 'sat on' the investigation for four years ..." (**Ibid. pg. 253**)

The Committee asked DIA why it waited 4 years for an investigation by JSSA (specialists in evasion symbols and techniques). Mr. Robert Sheetz, DIA, responded 23 July; "... the judgment of DIA... the possible K ... is most likely not an evader symbol, but ... merely the spoil created when the USA letters were constructed by scraping away harvested rice stubble to expose bare earth..." (**Ibid. pg. 261 - 63**)

Yet, DIA analyst Chuck Knapper swore the original 1988 analysis was that the "K" was ground scarring. Not until 1992 was it his opinion the "K" was formed by the rice stubble. Thus, a 1992 opinion, overruling a 1988 decision, was used to lamely explain the 4 year wait. That 1992 investigation consisted of questioning the farmer and his son who tilled the land about the symbols. They said they made the USA. They did it to imitate the USA they saw on an envelope they received from relatives in the United States. **So they made the 12 foot high letters, perfectly made, and consistently wide, out of rice stubble, to imitate letters on an envelope, which was never produced or verified as ever existing.**

The "K" and "USA" case was then dismissed because "USA" was not a recognized distress symbol. DIA said that the case is not closed and that no one said the "symbol was fraudulent." (***Ibid.***) DIA had intimated, however, that the "USA" was formed by a POW activist based in Thailand. (***Ibid.***) Not noted is the fact that the "52" or "B52" at Nhom Marrot was not a recognized distress symbol either.

Even if the "USA" had been a recognized distress symbol, the case would have been dismissed. Illustrating this point; symbols near Dong Vai Prison, Vietnam were discovered in **June, 1992** photography. Revealed were an authenticator symbol, GX2527 located 415 feet southeast of Dong Vai Prison, in an open field. JSSA experts matched it to a known MIA. In the same vicinity were letters forming a name. The analyst gave a 70% confidence call of them being man-made.

In December, 1992, two Committee analysts reviewed the symbols. One analyst reaffirmed his original call of their authenticity. The other declared them "to be a natural shadings in the field ... not man-made intentional symbols. I can only state coincidence with the possible match with an authenticator symbols."

Nineteen correlated authenticator numbers were reviewed by panels. None passed muster. The Committee wrote, "Accepting ... that intentional symbols may be scarcely visible or a clever mixture of natural and man-made objects has contributed to the extremely difficult task of confirming the presence of several symbols ..." (**Ibid. pg. 255**) The Committee asked the CIA, DIA, and National Photographic Interpretation Center for another review. This panel said, "The consensus of the team was that although portions of what could be interpreted as letters / numbers were observed in the field, they appeared to be too haphazard and ill-defined to be a man-made distress symbol." (**Ibid. pg. 267**)

Let's look at this situation from another view. Consider the haphazardly formed argument. To regard it seriously, you must overcome the following. For six symbols to be arranged in a particular order, the chances are 1 in 720 for that to randomly happen. Given the various sides to each symbol, for the symbols to be formed at all and then to appear in the order listed (considering only 11 separate sides), the odds are 1 in almost 40 million. Now, the odds of that symbol matching a randomly given number of an MIA are too great to calculate.

This is why authenticator numbers were designed. It takes the odds out of guessing. But, when one is determined to say that no one is alive, a haphazard explanation is good enough. That is why Bill Hendon said on ***Larry King Live*** on April 15, 1994 that the symbol, GX 2527 belonged to Peter Matthes, MIA 11/24/69. He also charged the nearby words SEREX and the code 72 TA 88, belonged to MAJ Henry M. Serex, MIA 4/2/72 were found in 1992 and did not pass muster either.

The cluster theory discounted

Since we're examining behind the scenes fights, let's look at a good one. The Senate Committee was briefed on April 9, 1992 about a theory roughly corresponding to the approach I used in developing intelligence information, map plots. I'll present their opinions, the reaction to it, and what I found.

John McCreary, DIA, and Hendon developed a "cluster analysis" or a "measles map." They combined radio intercepts, distress symbols, and sighting reports. They weeded out "clearly outrageous, inflated, exaggerated, or impossible reports;" "several hundred reports equating to Robert Garwood" or other known returnees; reports that could plausibly equate to foreign nationals; reports of people not living in confinement; reports of yachtsmen, adventurers, or smugglers; and sightings equating to Americans detained in Saigon and later returned.

What was left? DIA continuously implied nothing was left. Incredibly, there were "928 flags representing 215 eyewitness accounts and 484 and 229 hearsay accounts..." (**McCreary Working Papers**) Senator John McCain, aware of this briefing, told his staff member, Mark Salter, to contact DOD because "... McCain felt it was critical that DIA be present at this briefing to rebut the assertions ..." (**MFR. Charles Wells and Mark Bitterman, Staff, on 9 April Briefing**) After a debate concerning the propriety of DIA presence, the Committee voted 7 - 2 to allow DOD to attend. Again, this is equivalent to the General looking over the shoulder of the junior officer investigating him. Highly irregular. What happened?

McCreary began by pointing out that the staff did not accept DIA's position of fabrication on many reports: "the minority could not accept at face value many of DIA's final evaluations of sources ... DIA's resolution that a live sighting was not credible when the source passed multiple polygraphs and every item in his account had been verified .... it is reasonable to draw a conclusion that a source of this quality provided credible information ..." (**Senate Report ppg. 231 - 2**)

McCain strongly criticized the use of "fabrications" in the analysis. Senator Smith protested McCain's criticisms. Chairman Kerry then said the McCreary analysis "was ... an alternative approach which deserved a fair hearing..." (**MFR., op cit.**) This charitable stance by Kerry masked his later sabotaging of this effort.

General Tighe's dictum, " ... *Judge a report - phony for any reason - it's not likely that report would be used to cross-check others ...*" is shown in it's conclusion while DIA forgot the testimony of. Robert Sheetz, DIA, who was asked about mistakes in judging a report phony or fabricated. He said, "the conclusions were reached by human beings and human beings make mistakes."

The Minority Report of the Committee said: "In every instance that DIA found the source of a live sighting to be credible, ... analysts left the resolution of the sighting 'open-ended' or ... the source ... mistaken ... In the former case, no additional analysis was evident. In the latter, none was needed. The minority assessed that credible sources produced believable reports and credible information. Additional analysis could lead to additional results." (**Senate Report pgs. 231 - 232**)

Here, we need to look at several things. First, there is a minority report to examine only because Smith insisted on there being one. (**Memo of Senator Kerry, October 6, 1992**) Second, these open-ended sightings are the so-called "unresolved" ones or the ones where the source cannot be discredited. Analysts can't call it a fabrication, but it goes against the party line. This finding validates the Senate Minority report in 1991 and what I have been writing since 1979. Tighe's testimony, "Some people have been disclaiming good reports for so long that it's become habit forming," a "mind-set to debunk" takes on new meaning. Jon Holstine questioned, the open-ended sightings, "Why does DIA continue to carry 87 of these 117 reports as 'unresolved?' ..." (**Holstine memo dated July 31, 1992**) No one has answered that question. The Minority Staff in 1991 predicted they too will disappear as has every single sighting report. It just takes time and effort to find a reason, even inventive ones like "albino Laotians."

This new approach lead to the McCreary briefing. In preparation, he wrote, "This is a long-standing and proven method of analysis used by the U.S. Intelligence Community ... the same method ... used ... to track SCUD Missile firings by Iraq during the Gulf War ... a similar process also is used in tracking SS-25 mobile missile units in the Commonwealth of Independent States ..." (**McCreary Working Papers, op. cit.**) This cluster system is what I described at the beginning of this chapter. I used it to trace VC local force units, VC main units, and VCI in the U-Minh Forest. The report analysis, dot locations, and photo recon reports would tell me the relative dispositions of each target. I determined that if unit X was located at one place, unit Y was at another specific location.

The Rand Corporation used this same type of analysis to develop a mainstay of the Phoenix Program, the *Modus Operandi* of selected VCI cadre. By analyzing many reports over a long period of years, the VCI were found to have a well-defined method of doing things. By studying their habits, we could predict their future operations. I used this *Modus Operandi* to my advantage many times.

The Senate Minority determined the cluster method showed: * The existence of logistical and administrative relationships among camps in northwestern Laos and in northwestern Vietnam not reflected in DIA documents * **Evidence of a second set of camps in Vietnam from which no prisoners returned** * Differences in the policies, the patterns, and the characteristics of POW incarceration in Vietnam and Laos * Most importantly, the cluster map analysis created a context for interpreting and understanding the limited amounts of signal intelligence of POW movements in Laos and Vietnam, and for the photography of alleged distress signals. In every instance, the signal intercepts and the alleged distress signals coincided with a cluster of live sighting reports posted to the map. This integration had never been done before. (**Senate Report pgs. 231-2**)

The Committee Majority decided against this approach, saying, "The analysis is meaningless. Plotting ten or twenty flags representing individual reports in the close proximity on a map means very little if the reports themselves are not valid. While it may raise questions ..., it cannot in and of itself be taken as evidence of someone being alive ..." (**Ibid.**)

The Majority deferred to a DIA report alleging the map plot included first hand live-sighting reports, 70 percent of which "an inter-agency review board has approved as being complete fabrications." DIA then reverted to form; "In addition, DIA emphasized that the other plotted reports, many of which have only limited analytic value because they lack specifics on the time and / or place of sighting. (**Ibid.**) This was the printed report. What is printed is not necessarily exactly the way that it happened. This cluster theory analysis left out items. McCain urged the presence of DOD at the briefing Here's what happened behind the scenes.

That morning, April 9, Salter provided a summary of the McCreary profile with supporting documents to DOD. McCreary's outline utilized a large map of Indochina and his color coated pins. Kerry stated that the McCreary report "was a good starting point, but that anyone who drew conclusions from such (a) briefing, 'ought to have his head examined.' ... a great deal of work needed to be done before Senators ... consider(ed) the analysis ..." (**MFR., Wells, etc. op. cit.**)

Near the end, only Smith remained. During this time, Hendon joined McCreary. On one point, DIA challenged Hendon saying his rendering of a live sighting report was out of context. Hendon and Smith both challenged DIA's assertion. The charges grew "contentious." Frances Zwenig, staff Director for Kerry, approached Mark Bitterman saying, "Senator Kerry had not intended the briefing to be carried on after he left. DOD should not continue to answer the questions..." DIA dutifully left over Smith's protests and the briefing adjourned. (**Ibid.**)

In review, it is not unusual for a committee briefing to continue after a chairman leaves. This was supposed to be a bipartisan committee, however, as with the Solarz POW Task Force, real power under Democrats resides in a Democratic Chairman, Mr. Kerry. I doubt he intended to find evidence of POWs. His leanings lie with Vietnamese Communists since his days as the leader of Vietnam Vets Against the War. Additionally, Kerry wanted McCain as his Vice-Chair. POW activists persisted in keeping McCain out and putting Smith in.

Regarding Kerry's statement on drawing conclusions from the cluster theory; during the war, Kerry earned his medals by acting upon the conclusions of intelligence professionals. As McCreary asserted, "I am an intelligence expert on detail from DIA... paid to come to these conclusions. ... about the 'intelligence.'" (**Memo to Kerry from Codinha, April 16, 1992**) Codinha opined, "as long as McCreary worked for the Committee, he was a staffer ..." and that only the Committee's writings were a final product. (**Ibid.**) McCreary was correct. Staff members were instructed by the Senate in the case of the aerial photography and the distress signals to reach a conclusion. The Senators wanted a consensus. However, a conclusion could not be reached on some points. Where no consensus exists, there is doubt. Where there is doubt, there is no "proof." Where there is no "proof," the politicians say, "there is evidence, tantalizing evidence," about POW survival.

Kerry orders study destroyed

Where the staffers were united and their professional conclusions provided "proof" to themselves of the existence, in great numbers, of POWs at least to 1989; that evidence got suppressed and destroyed. Kerry instructed that the McCreary proceedings were to be "closely held" and not released. Why? He was afraid that release would cause someone in the public domain to conclude that the Committee had reached a conclusion. He was specific and adamant that the briefing contents were not to leave the room. (**MFR. Jon Holstine Apr. 21, 1992**)

In agreement with Holstine, McCreary noted in his April 21, 1992 MFR., that on April 8, Staff Director Zwenig, ordered all copies of the briefing to be accounted for. At least two were missing. One turned up the next day in the hands of McCain. Following the briefing, copies were again counted. At least one still remained unaccounted for. The others were bundled for destruction.

On April 15, Hendon and McCreary met with the Committee Chief Counsel Codinha. The purpose was to discuss both the cluster theory and the destruction of the documents. The discussion led off with Codinha telling both McCreary and Hendon that their effort was only the beginning of the examination of the possibility of Americans being in captivity. The duo "took umbrage" at that suggestion, arguing their efforts reflected a finished product. They contended the correlation proved their point with McCreary reasoning the "total was greater that the sum of the reports." In other words, the way to see the whole picture was to piece together the individual parts. By just looking at the individual parts, DIA missed the relevance of the so-called discredited reports. McCreary also felt his DIA posting added a dimension of legitimacy to the study. In 1996, Dornan urged a similar type of approach to the POW morass.

Codinha then explained the political facts of life: "Unless and until the Senators understand and **agree** with your findings, there are no findings or conclusions." Hendon and McCreary dissented vehemently from that logic. At this point, McCreary reiterated he was a professional paid to arrive at conclusions. Hendon concurred. Being a former Congressman and wise to the ways of Washington, Hendon then pulled one out of his hat declaring since their final work product had been destroyed, he felt that destruction constituted a crime.

To this point, Codinha referred to the finished briefing as a "draft" copy. Both McCreary and Hendon avowed their work product was a finished document, subject to protection. They bluntly maintained that this project represented their conclusions and opinions. Codinha said, well, the Senators voted to destroy the documents. Hendon boldly proclaimed such a vote was proof of a cover-up. By destroying the work and backup, the "evidence" supporting the conclusions was also destroyed. Codinha countered, "your opinions and writings are evidence of absolutely nothing." (**Memo, Codinha to Kerry, April 16, 1992**)

Here, a substantial work, heretofore never undertaken, is ordered destroyed. This product of intelligence professionals; examining files from various intelligence agencies and correlating reports; weeding out extraneous, outrageous, and correlated items. Yet, Kerry orders it destroyed. The authors are assured the work will continue, but how can you build on items no longer in existence? It's easier to expand a model than to recreate it.

Hendon's attack worked. It got people rattled. Kerry admitted the order to destroy came from him but it was only meant to cover "extraneous copies of the document." No vote was taken on the destruction. Kerry asserted, "no one objected." Then, Kerry pulled his political rabbit. The issue was "moot," he charged, because the original copy had remained in the Senate Security Office all along.

McCreary checked that assertion. The copy referred to by Kerry was checked into the Security Office at 1:07 PM on the 15th, the day of the meeting with Codinha, and Hendon discussed felony destruction. The stamp proved Codinha, Kerry, and Zwenig's assertion of the document being there since the 9th false. (**McCreary memo, April 27, 1992**) Senator Smith saved the briefing documents. His expression of concern about the destruction and the purging of computer files to Kerry caused Zwenig to obtain a copy of the briefing from McCain's office and deposit it in the Security Office. Security personnel told McCreary that it was marked "eyes only" and deposited in her personal file. (**Memo to Smith, May 3, 1992**)

"Classifying" the document with a security caveat of "eyes only," showed further contempt for the cluster theory and the accompanying correlation. Codinha questioned McCreary and Hendon, "who's the injured party ... How are they going to find out, ... it's classified ..." (**Memo McCreary to Smith, April 27, 1992**)

Proving the cluster theory

How correct was the cluster? Hendon, in 1989, told me the Ba Vi area was crawling with POWs. Mark Smith told me that Ba Vi was identified in his work. Garwood described to me in 1985 the camps that he saw around Ba Vi. Minarcin told me Ba Vi was a parallel camp for high security prisoners. Tighe testified that Garwood's reports dovetailed with reports he knew about. I called Ba Vi and it's environs "Prisoner Highway" in 1986. DIA denied Ba Vi's importance.

Let's examine DIA's position on the cluster theory. LTG Williams, testified on August 8, 1984, "Last year, ... I alluded ... our live sighting reports sort of look like a **measle sheet** when the reported locations are plotted on a map ... when we get an agglomeration of reports like that, then our interest in the information increases ..." LTG Tighe, on June 25, 1981, backed his "stated assurance" of live POWs with a series of reports, clusters if you will, in the same general area over a long period of time. Those clusters included technological intelligence backing the human intelligence; the same approach used by McCreary and Hendon and the same approach I was taught to use in the US Army Intelligence School.

Now, let's look at Codinha's theory that Hendon and McCreary only had produced a "draft." Well, Codinha was both right and wrong. Huh? The testimony of Williams on August 8, 1984 emphasizes a dilemma reiterated by Tighe. Williams said on page 35: "The committee asked a question ... what actions the U.S. government would take to effect the release of an American if confirmed to be in captivity ... my answer ... is beyond the purview of DIA. Our charter is to provide the military intelligence ... We are the information gatherers and intelligence analysts, not the policy makers... Should our research develop information ... that warrants activities beyond the charter of DIA, action would be transferred to the appropriate organization or agency for whatever response is deemed necessary."

The General agrees the work product of Hendon and McCreary was final. They took the next step of bringing it before the decision makers, the Senators. There, the politicians fluffed it. It was not "proof;" emphasizing Tighe's point, "From there to a U.S. effort to recover... is a great and unknown distance."

Now, I'll bring up a personal point. In 1984, Williams testified about what he called "dog tag" reports. These are reports relating to "the claimed recovery of a dog tag or other identifying information from crash or grave sites.... We believe this is part of a managed misinformation effort ... We devote our primary effort to live sighting reports." (**August 8 hearing, op. cit. pg. 33-34**) I received one of the first dog tag reports in **1980** while attending a League Meeting. I received a message to call a certain person, "It was urgent." I called. The person on the other end was also an intelligence professional. He responded to a Vietnamese he sponsored, now living in Virginia. She received a letter about her father, a prisoner in Nam Ha, Vietnam. He observed about 30 Americans in captivity, in **early 1980**. The father sent out the name, social security number, blood type, and religion of one of the prisoners or "dog tag" information.

The information also provides a little more. By having a social security number for identification, it shows that the person probably entered active duty around 1969 or 1970. That is when the army, at least, switched from military numbers for identification. Immediately, I looked at a list of MIAs. That name is not on the list. The person passing the report to me first turned the information over to Ann Griffiths and DIA. The Vietnamese receiving the letter lives virtually across the highway from DIA. Griffiths reportedly avoided the person turning in the information.

I still have the name, address, and telephone number of the woman who received the report, and the name, address and telephone number of the brother to whom the letter was forwarded after DIA showed no interest in it. By now, the letter is probably destroyed. There is no official interest.

The information is turned over to a friend on Dornan's staff. He investigates. He gets the run around. He smells a rat. A further investigation shows that the Social Security number originated in a certain state. We are told also that person to whom the number belongs served in Vietnam, was wounded, returning in 1970. No one has seen that person. On the MIA list is a person with the same last name. He was lost in Vietnam in 1970. His remains have never been sent back.

In the mid 1990s, after reports of "dog tags" became routine, I went to the office of Senator Dennis DeConcini, AZ. He was on the Senate Intelligence Committee. His aide, Judy Leiby and I discussed this case. She asked for the name on the "dog tag" report. I told her. She immediately recognized it. I believe she told me that it was surfacing with regularity.

Let's look at the facts. The report was dog tag information, but in a private letter. The Vietnamese gave it to an intelligence professional. We are to believe that dog tags from a wounded American, who safely returns to the United States, finds it's way to a North Vietnamese prison camp, 10 years later, and is turned over to a South Vietnamese inmate by a POW, one of about 30, and then that information comes to the United States in a private letter. When I see this person, in the flesh, I will ask to see his dog tags. I also want to meet the analyst who came up with this explanation. I have a bridge in Brooklyn to sell. Nam Ha prison surfaced several times in refugee reports as being a place holding POWs.

The point to this? McCreary is not the first to see good solid evidence of live POWs explained away. Many suffered personal agony over their finding out that no one wanted to travel that "great and unknown distance." Tighe, Smith, McIntire, Howard, Peck, Hendon and LeBoutillier all paid a price. McCreary? In an April 21, 1992 MFR., he recounted a phone call he received from Chuck Wells, a liaison officer for DIA. McCreary was "urged" to make an appointment with Dennis Nagy, DIA, to discuss his position. Both Nagy and General Clapper, DIA, were "receiving reports that I was disloyal to DIA and that I might find that I did not have a job when I returned... (Wells) ended, 'This conversation did not happen.'"

Neal Kravitz wrote in a May 7, 1993 memo, "Wells responded ... he gave ... McCreary some 'advice' ... McCreary ... misinterpreted this advice."

I have been asked why didn't I go and testify. Well, it's not quite that easy. You have to be invited. I gave a lot of information to minority staffers on the Senate Foreign Relations Committee. In exchange, I got their interim and final reports. I recognized some of my handiwork. I turned over to Senator McCain's office my affidavit on the 1981 Nhom Marrot raid, filling in the names you see in this book. I put off finishing this edition awaiting the results of the Senate Panel. I had high hopes for it. The Interim Report looked like everyone was on the right track.

I received contemporaneous reports of who was testifying and what they said. The good guys got five minutes and the bad ones got all the time in the world. McCain took regular pot shots at the good guys. He never once asked about my information, all 50 - 100 pages of it. To testify in Washington, D.C., you have to pay your own way. I saw the direction of the results. Good guys on staff were getting fired. I did not have the money to go to Washington for five minutes testimony. I had a lot to say and it was going to come out my way, not the way some spin doctor would do it. I know how to turn things rightside up when necessary.

Thus, this edition of the book. Besides, I discovered I was not finished anyway. 1996 provided information on why 1989 might have been a cut off point for good intelligence on some of the POWs.

So, at least one copy of the briefing survived, helped by Hendon, McCreary, Smith and team. Those in charge of the investigation at this time are real anxious to see the whole problem disappear since there is money to be made in Vietnam.

How many POWs survived?

Three areas need to be explored. Those are A) How many POWs; B) Signal Intelligence; and C) Cover-up. The obvious question is how many POWs survived. Professional analysts ventured their opinions from less than 100 to 850. Could these evaluations be correct?

In Laos, in 1992, an American oil worker saw a POW in captivity. In his sworn deposition, he said that for almost a minute he saw a prisoner, head bowed, guarded by military personnel with AK-47's; at least six foot tall; with a hangman's noose around his neck. The oil worker said, "No one wants to talk about Americans ... (I)f you see a POW, you're going to jail forever ... the Lao will tell you ... when our POW / MIA team was over there, about transferring this one prisoner around."

For large numbers to exist, there had to be large numbers to begin with. Five hundred ninety-one (591) men came home. How many did we expect?

CINCPAC was tasked by JCS to estimate the number of POWs we could reasonably expect to return. No one believed Vietnam's "complete lists." In charge of the estimating was LTG Tighe. This effort was crucial because DIA was putting together documents listing known and suspected POW camps for use by trained debriefers. If, for example, you expect only 600 POWs and 591 return; if you know of 8 POW locations and 13 are found; the evidence points to an intelligence mission well done. Although the actual list was never found, a reconstruction of events showed that Tighe's efforts produced a list of between 900 - 1000 men. Tighe told Senate investigators this number was a "realistic list" including only those men for whom there was "solid, reliable information showing they were alive in a situation in which capture was likely. Evidence of an actual capture was not a requirement ...." (**Memo to Codinha from Neal Kravitz, March 2, 1992**)

The Army Times, July 6, 1992, reported that Admiral Thomas Moorer, then JCS Chairman, wrote to President Nixon's top aides that the exchange of prisoners was incomplete. He urged the halt of troop withdrawals until Laos accounted for their POWs. (Earlier estimates were that at least 244 more POWs should have come home in Operation Homecoming) Moorer told the Senate Committee on June 25, "I was overruled by my superiors." Kerry publicly charged that at least 133 US POWs were probably left alive after Operation Homecoming. (*Times Leader, AP* **story, June 24, 1992**) Tighe testified the US had "irrefutable evidence" American prisoners were held in Vietnam long after the war ended in 1975. "I think they ... disregarded the evidence because they knew there was no way they were going to be able to prove it and we weren't about to undertake hostile activities against Vietnam," he added. (**Ibid.**)

Tighe's estimate dovetails with the top secret 1205 report from Hanoi. Prepared by General Tran Van Quang, it lay hidden until January, 1993, when Harvard Researcher Stephen J. Morris dug it out of dusty Russian archives. An accompanying cover sheet was signed by Pyotr Ivashutin, Chief, Soviet Military Intelligence. Authenticating the document was Konstantin Katuschev, Secretary, Central Committee of the Communist Party. This document, written in Russian, transcribes a report to the Vietnamese Politburo saying 1205 American POWs were held while publicly acknowledging only 368.

Immediately, spin doctors went to work. First, they tried silence. Discovered in January, the White House was informed in February. By April, there was no reaction. Morris released the document on April 11. What you can't ignore, you explain away. DIA questioned the document's accuracy. Media spokesman said the document listed 16 American Colonels as being held when only 10 were reported missing. Quang asserted three prisoners had already passed the basic training to be cosmonauts. GEN Vessey, while not doubting the document was authentic, asked if the document was properly translated. Was the document an original Vietnamese document to begin with? Give enough doubts and people start to wonder.

I want to begin my own interpretation before I look for help from other experts. First, the sixteen Colonels. DIA is once again literally truthful and wonderfully misleading. There are less than 10 Colonels on the missing list (included are those returned). However, the total number of personnel in the rank of O-5 and above (LTC and above) at the time of capture numbers just under 175. In the film **"Pilots in Pyjamas"**, LTC Robinson Risner is interviewed. At the time, he was the highest ranking POW acknowledged. The interviewer stated, dubbed for the audience, that he had just been promoted to Colonel and did not know it. The Vietnamese knew the POWs were being promoted while in captivity. For 16 Colonels to be alive in 1972 out of 175 would not be extraordinary.

On the matter of cosmonauts. In reading POW documents and books from returnees, they claimed extraordinary deeds, to mislead the enemy. Once again in **"Pilots in Pyjamas,"** one POW, LCDR Robert Harper Shumaker, captured 2/11/65, is listed by the propagandists as a "backup man in the astronaut program." POW John McCain told his captors he flew over 4000 hours (another point in the 1205 document) and wanted to be in the astronaut program. Two of three.

The 1205 document backs up my assertions that men were held back for reparations. This corroborates captured documents examined earlier in the book. It also explains the secret aid agreement from Nixon and Kissinger. Let's look at other authenticators: (sources: contemporaneous news accounts of the releasing of the document and subsequent interviews)

* Le Dinh, a Ministry of Defense defector told DIA that Hanoi had retained about 700 POWs. Interrogators said Le Dinh had "access to PW/MIA information within" his ministry position. In addition, a January 25, 1980 DIA summary on Le Dinh said he "reported having personal access to information about U.S. POWs in Vietnam... demonstrated accurate knowledge about his department ... its staff... of former US PW detention facilities, and events associated with the US PWs who were released from northern Vietnam... source is ... former Intelligence official who defected in October, 1979"

* Zbigniew Brzezinski, former National Security Adviser, said 1205 was about the number of POWs expected back; he was impressed by the "Katyn-like classification system" of POWs; and he was impressed with the style of writing which corresponded to documents of a similar nature

* Henry Kissinger said, "Those parts that I know something about have an authentic ring to them ...;" referring to specific negotiating items listed in the document which actually occurred. He added, "About three weeks after this document, they changed their positions ... and they certainly wouldn't have told anybody ... That ... could have only been known to a very few people."

* Senator Robert Smith said, one passage stood out. Hanoi said they would soon "free several prisoners of war from here, in order to put pressure on the Nixon government ... (ten days later) Hanoi released three pilots..."

Quang said he was not in the position listed in the document. The "intelligence service that made this report was a very bad intelligence service...." (Soviet GRU made it) He lied! USJSPAO listed Quang as a "Central Military Affairs Party Committee Deputy Chief of Staff" in September, 1972. Douglas Pike listed Quang as a member of North Vietnam's central military party committee since 1961.

This number of prisoners had to be housed somewhere. DIA, as we previously saw, had a list of 18 possible prisons. Three positively responded to the Son Tay Raid. The significance is two known POW camps also responded to the Son Tay Raid. These two were within 5 miles of some of the suspected camps. Those camps which responded, Coc Mi, Cam Chu, and Xom Giong, held no known returnees. One, near Yen Bai, is described as a "maximum security detention compound."

We looked at another possible camp, Ba Vi or C3QP. One other sign was in the compound, 24CCPS, described as saying **24th US Prison camp**. It was also described as a high-security detention center; staffed by officers; subordinate to the Secret Security Department (Intelligence Division) of the Ministry of Public Security; and directly subordinate to the Ministry of National Defense. I wrote this description in 1985. Quang described part of the Ba Be plan involving, "Intelligence Directorate of the Ministry of National Defense and the Ministry of State Security" which is also known in Soviet circles as public security.

In April 1993, an SRV oral history states in part, "When asked for his opinion concerning cadre who may be able to provide information on US personnel still accounted for, source was able to recall the following ... Mr. 'Van,' commander of the B-22 intelligence camp... Sr. Col. Van Duy was involved in the exploitation of US POWs for aviation / avionics technology ..." Le Dinh recalled that camps "C-23, B-22, and B-17" housed POWs kept back along with some camps Southwest of Hanoi. Ba Vi is located to the Southwest of Hanoi. B-17 is referred to in the uncorrelated documents the POW Branch of the COSVN Security Section, responsible for US, ARVN, and other POWs.

Further, in 1992, ground signals, containing emergency authenticators of American pilots known to have been captured were located at some of these locations. (**US Senate Armed Services Committee, April 8, 1993**) Terry Minarcin told me that NSA had indicators also of this separate POW system that I detected and that Robert Garwood reported. FBIS reported on 23 April, 1993 that "Over the year we were able to clear up the fate of 22,000 Americans who found themselves on the territory of the former Soviet Union. Among them is a large group of **former Americans** mainly of Slavic descent who while in the Soviet Union were taken repressive actions against (sic) by the Stalinist regime and spent many years in concentration camps. Now those who remained alive feel themselves like native Russians, have been married and do not want to return to the United States."

We turn to my liking, Signal Intelligence, (Sigint). The POW Report, pgs. 277-8, verified listings from ADI and included: * December 1979, a third party intercept showed 3 US prisoners being moved from Muong Vieng Sai to Muong Attopeu to work in the mines * December, 1980, a third party intercept had 20 American POWs moved from Oudom Sai Province to Vientiane * In **1984**, an intercept referred to the movement of 23 unidentified prisoners from Muong Sepone prison to Tha Vang Center in Laos. **NSA noted that this number corresponded with collateral information** concerning the presence of **23 American POWs** at a camp in Southern Laos * 1986, an intercept referring to moving "prisoners of war" to Nong Tha, Laos perked up the ears of NSA because "the Lao do not normally refer to captured Thai soldiers or Lao expatriates as 'prisoners of war.'"

The Committee noted that these and other reports raised questions concerning POWs present in Laos after 1973. The Committee cautioned, however, that none of the reports were judged to be accurate by either NSA or DIA. Also known are the intercepts at Nhom Marrot; those in 1981 I was told about by Hendon and LeBoutillier; and the EC-47 intercepts.

The intercepts, like the refugee reports, got explained away. Despite the caveats that all the sigint reports looked authentic, we get the caution crap from the "Committee." Well, bully. My training tells me sigint reports are good, unless proof exists otherwise. My training in TC&D tells me that reports going through review committees will emerge as not opposing the party line.

So, does a cover-up exist? Our friend Loc, the Mortician, was examined by the Committee. He "testified ... he had processed 452 sets of remains ... he believed were those of U.S. servicemen, during 1975-76 ... the Vietnamese had 'warehoused' them ... Witnesses familiar with current Vietnamese approaches testified that any warehouse now is empty, and that remains are probably in private hands." (**POW Report pgs. 359-60**) The day the Vietnamese government turns remains over to "private hands" will be the day the tooth fairy becomes real.

Senator John Kerry, in an October 7, 1992 memorandum said, "We need to do at the next hearing ... what we did at the last meeting ... Show that the 'K' is not a K and does not have walking feet ... Come on **Very Strong**..." Frances Zwenig, in a handwritten note, October 6, said, "**I am working on the script with DIA.**"

Jon Holstine, speaking to the National Vietnam Veterans Coalition, November 7, 1992, said certain assistant secretaries of defense, etc., while testifying under oath in their depositions had "fleeting" memories and could not remember a thing.

One finding with insidious implications took place in March 1993. It involved the destruction of documents held by Detachment 1 Joint Task Force - Full Accounting (JTFFA), Thailand. This organization is the successor to the Joint Casualty Resolution Center (JCRC). (The following is from several sources including a letter from Michael D. Janich, a participant in the destruction story from day 1 (**USV July / August, 1995**) (used with the permission of Ted Sampley, editor))

The order began as a move to declassify documents pertaining to POW / MIAs issued by President Bush. With bureaucratic efficiency, the order became longer, more complicated, and sinister. By February, 1993, MG Thomas Needham, Commander of JTFFA, ordered: "review all classified holdings ... declassify all JCRC/ JTF-FA originated documents ... those absolutely necessary to perform assigned tasks should be retained, all others will be destroyed or returned ... for retention or disposition..." The deadline was March, 1993 and as Janich recalled, "the memo

clearly stated that no extensions were to be considered."
Janich correctly stated, the deadline was unrealistic. Only an originating unit can declassify a document. Many in JTF-FA's possession originated elsewhere. Strict guidelines govern declassification. To be done correctly, many months were needed. On documents originating in JTF-FA, the officers in charge, from Needham down, went about their task with an obvious relish. The question boiled down to what was needed to accomplish a mission and what documents were duplicated elsewhere. The rest could, after appropriate review, be destroyed. The guidelines were unrealistic, perhaps deliberately so and, disaster was courted. Janich said he sought to preserve papers not known to be anywhere else. He attempted to bring investigators like Garnett Bell, a Vietnamese linguist, to examine records containing written notes to preserve the "institutional memory."

Let me explain. When I first started my tour in Vietnam, I was it. My predecessors left no notes, no guidelines. In the files were items from higher headquarters, but no one remembered seeing them. I found them by accident many months later in cabinets not belonging to me. After Phoenix schooling, things clicked. I took notes for myself. As my knowledge of the area grew, I could instinctively respond to many reports. I left these notes for my successors. Over the 30 years of working on the POW issue, I have many resources to draw on. This ranges from computer files to declassified documents and interviews. In addition, I have the research and accumulations of documents from people who have submitted items to me. I also have my memory of details and work done by me and my associates. All this constitutes the "institutional memory" of my "POW office."

At JTF-FA, the files and Garnett Bell were it's main institutional memory. Others preceding Bell were determined to prove POWs did not exist. Bell attempted to get at the truth. Janich was the JTF-FA Security Officer wanting to preserve necessary files without covering-up ineptitude. He would not participate in a wholesale document destruction. The situation was chaos. MAJ George Petrie, a former Special Forces Officer, described the files as "... informal notes and memoranda - the meat of actual investigations ... field reports ... not duplicated in other files.." (*Washington Times*, **April 8, 1993**) They also contained refugee reports, and side notes written by investigators. While classified duplicates existed at other headquarters, the side notes did not. Janich asserted, "the document holdings ... represented over a decade of critical information ... the detachment's efforts ... Due to the sensitive nature of the MIA mission, the destruction of ... documents could be considered very controversial and tantamount to a government cover-up." Unless done properly, Janich threatened resignation.

Eventually, some documents were destroyed. Command emphasis from Needham forced needless hurry in complying. Much was alleviated by the efforts of Bell and Janich. How much institutional memory was lost?

As this incident was probed, other examples of document destruction were found. Sedgwick Tourison wrote to Zwenig on May 31, 1992, that the initial cover-up of cross border covert actions coupled with reported destruction of operation files in Vietnam in 1972 posed "significant problems..." By 1977, DIA collection operations in Southeast Asia ground to a complete halt. He later wrote to Codinha on May 26, 1992, "Everyone wanted the POW / MIA issue to be done away with..."

In 1974, DIA discovered that 60 personnel lost in Laos were officially listed as being lost in South Vietnam. In 1977, Tourison estimates that "no one in the Ad-

ministration could have asked the Vietnamese the right questions about ...a number of KIA / BNR or MIA ... The ...exchange of negotiation folders in 1973 - 75
now must be viewed as giving information ... sufficiently inaccurate as to have
been meaningless in perhaps half of ... the MIAs (1118 PFODs)..." Ominously, he
added the "likelihood that DIOR deleted a large number of history / current files ...
should raise questions regarding the credibility of the entire Southeast Asia casualty data base ... one incredible nightmare regarding the reliability of DOD casualty data and the fact that it can be manipulated at whim." (*Ibid.*)

Janich recommended the destruction of only two sets of files; those known to
be duplicated elsewhere at JTF-FA. Three sets were urged to be retained. The
others were recommended for shipment to Hawaii for further review. The destruction, however, took place. A resulting investigation was the cover the butt of the
commander type. Janich charged that 173 refugee reports were missing from
holdings. The total destruction could not be evaluated until a laborious comparison of document to document and file by file be completed. That was never done.
His evaluation of single copy destruction? "We'll never know for sure..."

Janich never believed before in a MIA cover-up. However, "... the way this
press release distorted the facts, I was convinced that JTF-FA and CINCPAC ...
had the capacity ... to cover-up the facts, ... the full sanctioning of the government
to do so... (they) subsequently conspired to cover this up ... by obtaining copies of
the missing reports and replacing them in JTF's files ... The results' of the CINCPAC
investigation, ... the complete endorsement they received ... are clear evidence of
a blatant disregard for the truth and willingness to distort the facts ... the documented efforts ... to quietly replace the missing documents, while making absolutely
no mention of their absence to the public, can only be described as 'cover-up' ..."

"... doing the job quickly (of declassifying or destroying the documents) force(d)
others to ... to create the illusion of progress ... through intimidation ... appointed
individuals ... (who) ... but actively supported these methods ... 'mission' ... took
precedence over compassion and integrity. Nothing ... would be allowed to detract
from the illusion of progress ... The solution ... a deliberate cover-up effort to
replace missing documents, and a liberal dose of lying and misinformation..."

The National Vietnam Veterans Coalition found a document whose citation
was omitted which shed some light on one further aspect of the Senate Committee
and other investigations. It reads: "Few are aware of the letters (alleged to have
been received from MIAs recently), or that they were evaluated for coded messages ... by JSSA ... They were not able to break the messages because (their)
folder ... had been destroyed by DIA in the mid - 70s in a purge of a number of
folders ... JSSA, without the folder, attempted to interpret the letters using whatever background information available on each individual, primarily from personal records. A number of striking correlations and interpretations were made,
resulting in JSSA's conclusion that the letters could very likely be the work of
POWs attempting to communicate ... When this analysis was submitted to DIA in
late 1991, ... , DIA believed the letters to be ... fraudulent."

An explanation shows the significance of this find. During the war, monitored
and censored letters were allowed from the POWs to family members to lessen the
possibility of critical POW intelligence leaving the prisons. However, ADM James
Stockdale, in one letter, told Naval Intelligence the names of three men held captive. In return, Naval Intelligence sent him a specially prepared letter from his

wife desiring information. The desired information had special meaning known only to the POWs. Destroying the files with these unique signals was inexcusable.

One further destruction, found in Codinha's box, was, "The detailed reports of Search and Rescue (SAR) missions were discarded by the Air Force several years ago despite their potential use in identifying and distinguishing between loss incidents." The value of this can be seen in the EC-47 case. There, Colonel Blau examined existing photos and identified one crash site as being "new" and belonging to Baron 52 while others believed it to be old. The importance of institutional memory is proved. The "good guys" with the institutional memory and the desire to work get forced out. Those remaining often have a "mind-set to debunk."

In reflecting on this book, I have probably left out many details I would later wish were inserted. However, my 100 percent experience is nothing has occurred changing my mind on "deceit" being the principal word in this book. As this book was being put together, many things came to light. I put together the basic text by the end of 1991. Only one thing has emerged which potentially challenges my thesis. A book concerning the opening of Hanoi's archives to DIA investigators was printed saying Vietnam's dirty secret was the MIAs never acknowledged were killed. The 1205 document disproves that theory. In fact the book itself acknowledges there is no proof. It admits not seeing many of the best reports Hanoi has to offer. The book receives the acclaim of the "they are all dead crowd."

The going into Hanoi's files was inspired by Richard Armitage. The people giving glowing reviews on the dust cover **almost** to a person have never acknowledged the possibility of men being alive. On the other hand, the 1205 document substantiates my work and those of the minority on the POW Committee. It too is from Hanoi's archives and was dug out by hard work.

Newsweek, in their November 2, 1992 edition, reported Hanoi may have withheld from investigators records of Americans transferred to Laos in the late 1970s In addition, their sources, reported to be close to Vietnamese officials, also said a B-52 crashed almost intact. The plane, along with it's crew, was supposed to have been shipped to the Soviet Union. A high DOD official, commenting on this said to me, "it would be much better, for the Russians, if the pilots were transferred."

Finally, McCreary, in a June 9, 1992 memo to Kerry and Smith said that his team believed that only 30 of DIA's "unresolved" cases are genuinely unresolved. On the other hand, he added, "over 200 other firsthand live-sightings assessed as resolved ... are in fact, not resolved."

The legacy of Kerry - McCain is more doubts were left than were solved. Typical politics by the golden boy of the Anti-War effort. An unexplainable hostility by a former POW I remember as starting in sympathy with the families. Back door deals to keep Senator Smith from assuming a leadership role as Kerry's aide tried to get the State Department to block his nomination as Vice-Chairman. (*Tacoma News - Tribune*, **November 24, 1992**) Robert Codinha complained that Dino Carluccio, Smith's aide, "controls the B-78 boys and they take no direction from" me. (**Codinha and Zwenig to Kerry, September, 2, 1992**) The B-78 boys are Holstine, McCreary, Hendon, LeGro, and Nicklas. Codinha apparently wanted only the usual follow the company line. Now you know why I listed this chapter Deceit through Investigation II.

HOWEVER, on September 17, 1996, one of the most masterful hearings took place that I have had the privilege to write about. It took place before the Military

Personnel Subcommittee of the then House National Security Committee. Chaired by Dornan, it set the standard for future hearings. For that reason, I have decided to treat that particular hearing in it's own section and have that section called:

No deceit through investigation: I

The forces supporting the theory that Americans are alive were treated with respect. In addition, another horrifying story emerged. In an era where public sensitivities are rubbed raw with obscenities like beheadings, chainsaw massacres, and other equally revulsive topics in movies; it is "understandable" that what was covered in this hearing created little public outcry. The "slaughter" portrayed in the testimony was political in nature and was a carnage that continued the length of the Soviet system. The slaughter is being ignored for equally political reasons - we haven't learned to deal with reality. Politicians who cannot deal with a political crime of "lying under oath" and "obstruction of justice" sure can't handle the systematic extermination of mere military men used as "cannon fodder" in war - either that of a "noble cause" like World War II or "underexplained" reasons like Korea and Vietnam. It is well past time to bring to light these atrocities.

Killing of innocence

The official beginning lies in the Korean War. I believe, however, that near the end of World War II is the origins of what happened. I believe there are survivors of treatment similar to what will be described. They were in "hospitals" located in the border region of Czechoslovakia and Poland and were rescued by "guerillas" of an undetermined origin. There are not many. What will be described, however, may explain the demise of hundreds, if not thousands, of GIs abandoned because the most powerful nation on earth was paralyzed morally. The political moral compass of this nation was so askew that it allowed the slaughter of it's military men by moral midgets hiding in the coat of political lions. Communism never had the power we possessed; we propped it up for decades. If the writing of this causes political embarrassment to anyone - so be it!

The Soviet system authored what will be described, regardless of the nation it occurred in. A system designed to protect the party officials, enrich party officials, and rule through party officials takes advantage of the human weakness of wanting a "king" to rule over us. People do not want to make hard decisions; be responsible for the choices they make. They want "security." There are always thugs to fill the void. When thugs have reign in the world political system, however, the following story takes place - regardless of what it is called, Shintoism, Nazism or Communism.

GEN MAJ Jan Sejna was part of that system until he came to freedom in 1968. He was a member of the Czech Communist Party Central Committee, the Presidium, the Czech Defense Council, First Secretary of the Communist Party, and one of the top 10 people in the government. Sejna gave an example of how little knowledge there is in intelligence about how the communist system works. It shows a mindset on gathering information that borders on the ridiculous.

Sejna said, "... I'm talking about people who interrogate me... there were some people who ... were the smartest people... and then there were some idiots... Can you imagine... I will remember how many rifles are in a ... platoon?... they were probably shocked because they had never had such a high defector... They told me... we have a question... about chemical weapons. ... I can discuss the general question on how to use chemical weapons in the war... but they asked me the technology... I was not a ... chemist... they told me... you was general; how do you know about the system? They don't know that in Czechoslovakia or Russia, the general officers are in Central Committee. They are in the Parliament, as I was. If you are not politically involved, you were never a general. It's that simple."

Sejna explained, "...policy is the major strategy of deception. I didn't agree with the policy... In Soviet planning, two wars dominate the planning. First, there was the general nuclear war... Second, there was a political and intelligence war, the revolutionary war... infiltration of the government, the press, sabotage, subversion, deception, narcotic traffic, organized crime, the training of terrorists, terrorism ... and *compromise political and business leaders*... I heard personally from Khruschev... he said, the United States was the major rock in the way to communism..." Sejna said that he likewise misunderstood us. He thought all the network anchors and politicians "are KGB agents;" not understanding freedom of expression. He admitted, "I was wrong. I think some of them didn't understand what's going on between the Soviet Union and the United States. I think the part of the deception strategy was also how to use POWs from Korea, and Vietnam and Laos..."

Pointedly, he said, "I don't say any fantasy. I was there.... I was in charge of some operations ... I think one day the truth will come out... Some people who call me liar, and even ask the Defense Department to fire me..." (referring to former Ambassador to Russia, Malcolm Toon) Continuing, "When the war was over in Korea, there were still a hundred prisoners in Korea... Czechoslovakia built a military hospital in Korea... a 'gift to the Korean people.' The major purpose ... was to train Czech doctors and Russians .... But... deception. The top secret purpose ...was to experiment on Americans and South Koreans... to test the effects of chemical and biological warfare agents and ... atomic radiation. The Soviets also used the American ... to test the psychological and physiological endurance of American soldiers... to test various mind-control drugs. Czechoslovakia also built close to the hospital a crematorium..."

Continuing, "The Americans... were very important to the Soviet plans because... the United States was their worst enemy... they want to be sure they understand the mental and physical condition of American soldiers. The Soviets were deadly serious in ... their development of various drugs and chemicals... detailed tests on the people from the United States. At the end of the war, it was made a decision of the Soviet Defense Council to do everything possible to cover any operation in Korea ... prepared by Soviets and other satellites... to cover the tests which were performed on American soldiers... I learned about these things ...from the documents... from the doctors and my friends who were in Korea. They participated in the tests..."

In his prepared statement, Sejna elaborated on a couple of points, "...At the end of the Korean War, there were about 100 POWs who were still considered useful for further experiments. I believe all others had been killed ...because I do not recall ever reading any report that indicated any of the POW patients at the hospital left the hospital alive -- except the 100 ... at the end of the war. These 100 were flown in four groups first to Czechoslovakia, ... given physical exams... then onto the Soviet Union. I learned about all this from the Czech doctors... Czech military intelligence officers in charge... Soviet advisors, and from official documentation... I also reviewed reports ... results of autopsies of the POWs and received briefings on various aspects of the experiments..."

Sejna continued, "I want to point out that the same things happened in Vietnam and Laos .... The only difference is ... Vietnam was better planned and more American POWs were used, both in Vietnam and Laos and in the Soviet Union... I believe there were others who were shipped to the Soviet Union through North Korea and East Germany, although I have no first hand knowledge of those transfers. I know that many were given to the Chinese for experiments during the Korean War, and Czech intelligence reported that the North Vietnamese also provided American POWs to the Chinese... this operation was conducted at the highest level of secrecy. Information ... was labeled State Secret... higher than Top Secret... my estimate is that fewer than 15 people in all of Czechoslovakia were aware of the transfer of American POWs to the Soviet Union. ... the written directions on the original Soviet order ... **in 1951**. ... the operation was to be conducted in such a way that 'no one would ever know about it.'" In 1999, it was pointed out in **The Haunted Wood**, that on **March 1, 1951**, the Soviets called the United States their "main adversary." This is the earliest Soviet document from their intelligence files to say this. Probably not a coincidence. (**Haunted** pg. 300)

The rest of the story will be a combination of testimony by Sejna, his affidavit (this testimony is sworn), and that of others who have relevant material. Before we get to the "official" start of the program, perhaps the insidious beginnings came from unit 731 at Harbin, Manchuria, part of Japan's experiments, still classified. The Japanese ran medical experiments on US POWs and some of the material tracks well with the Soviets use. Dornan, who saw the records begins:

"One thing comes to mind. I tried to get the records for the Japanese demonic medical facility, unit 731 at Harbin... it was a disgraceful cover-up, because some of the Japanese who had amputated limbs, trained their medical doctors to amputate first one limb, then another, and finally a torso is lying there... Then they would operate on their intestines and kill them. It seems unbelievable, but it happened... The records were all up at Fort Meade... I had a hell of a time getting them in 1977... They're still classified... the Japanese tests at Harbin, ... 'How would anthrax react on a blond or a redheaded American, Brit, or Australian soldier? How would it react on Koreans, and is there a difference between Koreans and Chinese.' They would work different medical experiments on different racial types... General Sejna. Did I not read in some of your statements that there seemed to be some interest on how American officers responded to drugs, higher educated people, mind control drugs, how enlisted men acted, and how people of different races reacted, South Vietnamese prisoners, ..."

Sejna replied, "Yes. As I said, they had an interest in different races. For example, how do drugs react on black and white... Afro-Americans or Asians... When they shipped these prisoners to the Soviet Union, they ... separated American officers on how to use the drugs which controlled the mind and chemical weapons. ...these things were scientifically orchestrated, and with different groups ... different ranks... in the testimony from the Soviet Union, they came to the conclusion, which I remember right today, when they checked these soldiers, 20 percent of the American soldiers already passed many heart attacks, as they called it."

Dornan interrupted, "... induced heart attacks?"

Sejna responded, "Yes. The Koreans, just 1 percent. So they came to the conclusion that it is necessary to do something to even make the rate higher in case the World War starts, to use chemical weapons or drugs or whatever... As an example ... especially about the officers, they came to the conclusion, as more intelligent was the human being, they are better targets for the drugs to control his mind. If you were... so primitive, it was a different approach... how to control your mind, how to make you not fight and simply give up. Different things were approached to the officers and staffs... very scientific planning for all this stuff..."

COL Phil Corso, a former head of Special Projects, Intelligence for GEN Douglas MacArthur, and former military aide to President Eisenhower, added details, necessary for understanding what follows. He was charged with developing information on enemy POW activities on captive soldiers. He found, as I have written often in the book, that in the operation of treatment and handling of our POWs; all acts were part of "conscious acts of Soviet policy." The Soviets taught their allies, the North Koreans and Chinese a "detailed scientific process aimed at molding" POWs into exploitable objects. Continuing, "I got my hands on a film at CIA... titled 'Silvery Dust'... made by the Soviet Union. It showed the exact experiments that they did on human beings to condition the reflexes... In Korea... prisoners of war told me that, once a prisoner came under this treatment... they could almost time the time he was going to die... The man would just give up... This was a result of these experiments on mind control... If fact, Congressman, if you see pictures of prisoners, at times they have a blindfold... The purpose of the blindfold is not to break the conditioning... This was actually practiced by the Soviets..."

A beginning in Korea

While I believe that some of the experiments, especially on combat wounds and amputations, began in the ending days of World War II or just after, we'll begin here in Korea because of the documentation that exists. Joseph D. Douglass, Jr., was a friend of Sejna and debriefed him. Douglass is a defense analyst and author with 35 years of experience in the national security field. He provided Dornan's committee much of the information from Sejna, having spent 18 years in "picking his brain." Their collaboration on **Red Cocaine, Dealing with Russian Narcotics Trafficking**, brought out first the brutality exhibited towards our men.

Czech participation in the Soviet run medical intelligence operation began early in the Korean War. The cover story was the experimental hospital in North Korea was built to test new medical procedures for treating battlefield casualties and training new doctors. Douglass said, "It also served as a special, highly secure medical intelligence facility in which captured American and South Korean servicemen were used as guinea pigs in the types of medical experiments" enumerated by Sejna. "The Czech's also built a crematorium in North Korea to dispose of the remains of those GIs who did not survive the experiments." For those who did survive, there is no record that Sejna is aware. However, Douglass testified, "... in light of the sensitive nature of the facility, it is doubtful that any were ever returned to the regular POW compounds..." and Sejna never saw any information that they were returned to the North Koreans.

Douglass made two points, both DIA and CIA "were both surprised" with Sejna's allegations. However, "the existence of this hospital has been confirmed by Czech authorities." They denied the experimental use. But, as Douglass pointed out, the doctors who ran the hospital regularly briefed Sejna on it's operation. He was also present when they briefed the Kollegium, the "highest decision making body in intelligence, counterintelligence, defense, and anything of a national security or internal security issue." Sejna was a member of the Kollegium until 1968.

Continuing, the Soviets "terminated" the hospital's part of the experiments in

1954, after the armistice. POWs of no further use because of mental or physical impairment "were killed and their remains cremated." The remaining 100 or so POWs were transferred to the Soviet Union for further experimentation. One such experiment was the determination of "long term effects of sublethal doses of atomic radiation." Long term meant, decades long and included the effects of radiation on "the soldiers' reproductive organs and on their subsequent children and grandchildren." These POWs were shipped to Russia, via Czechoslovakia, to "break the trail" and make "correct" the deception that no POWs were shipped to Russia from North Korea. That also is why the hospital was Czech and the Russians did not "run it." As I have pointed out several times, the POW issue has been and continues to be one of deception practiced in the highest form by many parties.

In 1956, Sejna became Chief of Staff to the Minister of Defense. He received a briefing from General Major Kalashnik of the Soviet Main Political Administration about several subjects including deception and "a new view about drugs and other chemicals that can affect the minds and behavior of millions of people" in a military context. This briefing was to "justify" the participation of Czechoslovakia in providing medical support for the experiments being run in the Soviet Union on the American POWs. In preparation, Sejna personally "reviewed the files and decision documents" for the Korean operation, including the "original Soviet Defense Council instruction that initiated the operation and those that terminated it."

The experimentation continued in the Soviet Union with the research victims changed, however. In 1960, plans were made with the Vietnamese Chief of the General Staff (CoGS) and about ten senior officers came seeking military assistance. "This was when the Soviets first agreed to supply the North Vietnamese with weapons. As head of the Defense Council Secretariat, Sejna was their host and focal point for scheduling meetings and discussions."

In one meeting, with five participants including Sejna, Soviet Advisor General Alexsandr Kuschev told " the Vietnamese General how American POWs had been used ... during the Korean War and how valuable this use had been. One ... cooperation the Soviets would like to receive in return for providing military technology... was more American POWs for medical experimentation. The Vietnamese CoGS ... used the opportunity to press for even more military assistance. Kuschev then stressed the need to begin organizing ... to use the captured American servicemen to avoid the ... delays encountered at the beginning of the Korean War."

Vietnam - a continuation of the Korean experimentation

The suggestion of the North Vietnamese General was "it would be a good idea to keep any Americans ... captured and selected to be sent to the Soviet Union separate from other POWs." Kuschev agreed and the deception program was on. Continuing, "Soviet, Czech and Vietnamese military counterintelligence officers would ... draw up plans for secure management of American POWs ...sent to the Soviet Union from the instant of their capture ...."

This segregation of prisoners is what Quang referred to and the DIA dismissed as "contrary to precedent." Our public pronouncements ignored the guiding factor, "... the determining factor in the espionage activity of the KGB is the foreign policy of the Soviet government..." (*KGB manual - Organization of KGB Counter-Espionage Work* - **KGB,** Myagkov, pg. 22) Since Sejna was Soviet trained, he emphasized in his debriefing, "... the overall operation was the responsibility of Soviet ... GRU... the security plan specified ...which POWs were to be used for medical experimentation would be made as soon as they were captured... a Soviet request ...would identify the number of specimens required... specify race requirements and rank... the Soviets were interested in older officers as well as younger officers because they wanted to test the effects of mind-control drugs on people from different age and rank categories. The older officers were... regarded as the more 'reactionary'... especially important subjects to test. Based on Soviet 'requirements,' the North Vietnamese military counterintelligence would ... begin collecting appropriate new American POWs as candidates... the POW had received a one-way ticket to oblivion or to death... the next action was a joint Soviet-North Vietnamese psychological debriefing ... If the POW was considered psychologically dangerous, he was to be immediately liquidated...not ...placed in normal POWs compounds because that would risk security ... better to simply kill him..."

The pilot plan began in 1961. While DIA would object that the date was way too early to be true, let's examine it from a true perspective. The "first" MIAs are from Laos in January and March 1961 and only 10 of 17 MIAs in 1961 were accounted for through 1996. Sejna said the first shipment arrived in August and consisted of about four or five South Vietnamese, six or seven Americans and one American separated from the rest who Sejna personally observed. We saw covert activities in 1964 under OPLAN 34A. How about covert operations earlier?

The *Pentagon Papers* declare on April 29, 1961, the President approved the expansion of "present operations in the field of intelligence, unconventional warfare, and political psychological activities... expand current ... counterintelligence operations... in South Vietnam and... North Vietnam... dispatch of agents to North Vietnam... overflights of North Vietnam for photographic intelligence... using American or Nationalist Chinese crews... Expand ... the First Observation Battalion... in Laos, infiltrate teams under light civilian cover... training ... combined CIA... and US Special Forces... in North Vietnam, using the foundation established by intelligence operations from... covert bases ...for light sabotage and harassment... .. in North Vietnam as ... appropriate... additional 40 personnel for CIA..."

BG Edward Lansdale, in July 1961, specified the First Observation Battalion had "... the mission of operation in denied (enemy) areas. It currently has some limited operations in North Vietnam and some shallow penetrations in Laos... Operations require the approval of President Diem... (for US operations) ... There are 9 CIA officers ... in addition to one MAAG advisor... there are three 4-man intelligence training teams... Foreign Operations Intelligence (clandestine collection)... (in Laos Thai Forces) ... Police Aerial Resupply (PARU)... has a mission of undertaking clandestine operations in denied areas... covertly to assist the Meos in operations in Laos, where their combat performance has been outstanding..." The CIA had two advisers to the PARU and three to the Thai Border Patrol. In addition, they had nine CIA officers working "in the field" with Vang Pao's Meos "backstopped" by two additional officers in Vientiane and 154 Special Forces personnel providing "tactical advice" to Lao Armed Forces commanders.

In addition, the **C**ivil **A**ir **T**ransport (nominally Chinese Nationalist), a CIA proprietary operation, ran missions in North Vietnam. and Lansdale said, "CAT supports covert and clandestine air operations ... (including) extensive air support in Laos during the current crisis..." By November, 1961, the die was cast, as outlined by GEN Maxwell Taylor, to radically increase US support to clandestine, cross-border, and intelligence gathering operations, including the increase of US personnel to the operation. These are just some of the programs begun in this era. As Douglass wrote about the "first" POW being in 1964, "This is more word games by US officials... deliberately ignores the civilians, CIA agents and military involved in so-called black operations... who were lost. The US government policy is clearly revealed in the book, **President Kennedy: Profiles in Power** by Richard Reeves. Military pilots ... recruited... in 1961.. were asked to ... sign a statement ... they would be wearing civilian clothes and that their 'government would disclaim any knowledge' of them if they were captured..."

Douglass said that Sejna had reason to believe that the first shipment of POWs was accompanied by the Vietnamese deputy chief for military intelligence, likely our friend, General Quang of 1205 fame. He and his staff and KGB military counterintelligence escorts "went along with the POWs to make certain the operation was secure... to quickly resolve any problems... Sejna hosted the entourage..."

US pilots were a priority item for research. In one conversation, Czech Defense Minister General Lomsky stressed the pilot's ability to handle stress. General Quong (Quang?) responded that "if you do not think the US pilots are nervous, just wait until we finish with them. General Lomsky countered... that what he was referring to was the ability to handle natural stress, not unnatural stress. Over the next couple of years, less than thirty POWs were taken over this route from Vietnam to Russia. The largest came in 1963."

At this time, Sejna became aware of shipments from Vietnam to North Korea and then on to Russia. The Koreans said that experiments could have been done directly in Korea, avoiding the shipment. Soviet General A.I. Antonov, "declined the invitation, saying that such a practice would constitute an unnecessary security risk. If the experiments were run in North Korea, the Chinese were likely to learn about the tests and this was unacceptable..." Sejna suspects the East Germans were involved in chemical experiments and he "knew the East Germans were involved in interrogations of American POWs using experimental drugs... which he knew because of data sharing agreements the Czechs had negotiated with the Germans."

The end of 1963 and early 1964 began the full scale operations. Khruschev informed his Warsaw Pact allies that "the American soldiers had been useful in the past ... there were many new drugs and chemical and biological warfare agents under development that needed testing... negotiations between Hanoi and Prague for Czech military assistance were completed in early 1964... provisions for using American POWs for 'medical research' in North Vietnam and ... exporting selected POWs to the Soviet Union via Czechoslovakia for research and for intelligence cooperation..." Ba Vi opened in 1964, as previously stated in declassified documents. Problems arose in that the North Vietnamese were more "independent" as opposed to the Koreans. The Soviets and Czechs wanted to deploy "volunteer" officers, such as pilots, to gain combat experience. The Vietnamese resisted since they were "secretly sharing Soviet technology with the Chinese."

Sejna personally negotiated with Laotian commander General Sinkapo, of the communists and Kong Lee of the "neutralist" forces for use of POWs from that country. Douglass said, "In Laos, both Soviet and Czech doctors worked directly on the patients. There were two 'hospital' facilities where experiments were performed... conditions at these facilities... 'primitive'... not bad reasoned the Soviets, because combat was often conducted in primitive conditions... operating under such conditions was good experience..."

In 1964, Sejna was told by the East German Minister of Defense that "the new drugs tested on the Americans were 'one thousand percent more effective than physical means of persuasion...'" These tests were conducted in Laos, North Vietnam and North Korea, using drugs for 'interrogation' and involved American POWs. "Experimental drugs were used in interrogations." At Ba Vi, they had the chemical interrogation room with Americans being "softened," sometimes with beatings.

As is usual, those being spied upon do their own research. The Czechs identified the movement of American POWs from Vietnam to China. The Czech attaché monitoring the movement was asked by the Chinese why China and Russia could not share information. "There is no reason to keep your program secret," he was told, "We know the American POWs are being sent to the Soviet Union for research. Information exchange... would be of use to both our countries."

While Sejna mentioned that through 1968 he was knowledgeable about POWs being experimented on in Laos and North Vietnam, he also added that to "complement the experiments run" in those countries, "each year during the Vietnam war, scores of selected GIs - those who were the most healthy- were shipped back to the Soviet Union for use in more highly classified, sophisticated, and long-term experiments, again through Czechoslovakia" and other countries, "to break the trail."

Since Sejna "personally supervised" parts of the operation, he also knew some of the small nuances of the transfers. For example, at Zatek Airbase, outside Prague, the prisoners were under the control of military counterintelligence. From there, they were bused to a "highly secret military counterintelligence barracks at Pohorele, in Prague." Normal loads of POWs were 20 - 25. In the fall of 1966, however, there was a large shipment of 60 POWs. In that large shipment were 6 - 7 "special" POWs. Douglass defined the "special" ones as those who "usually" decided to cooperate with the Soviets, "progressive" or those who were sick and needed isolation. There were others, usually 2 - 3 in other groups that were also "special." Included in the shipments through Czechoslovakia were at least two Australians.

Without going into too many more graphic and excruciating details, let it suffice to say that the experiments did not end at death. Between 1959 and 1966, autopsies were conducted on those not surviving. Those were conducted to find out how the experiments went and the "effects and improvements in special destructive weapons for use in preparation for war and during war..." The focus of the study was the "physical destruction of organs such as the heart, brain, nervous system," etc. The report was on a data base of between two hundred to two hundred fifty POWs, an unknown amount of whom were "cadavers." "The principal recommendations" of the report was "directed to the development of drugs and biological organisms that would destroy specific organs at a faster rate."

In testing, it is of importance to notice that two test groups were used, basically officers and enlisted. The officer group was selected to "gently degrade" an individual's ability to function, but not destroy it. The Soviets referred to operations, "experimental data that had been collected in operations run against the U.S. military forces based in Germany and in Okinawa," but without any elaborating details. The importance is the existence of the further experiments and the separation of the officers from the enlisted, something that DIA insisted went against "precedent." Further details on some of the experiments, especially those involving the Soviet testing of "new narcotic drugs" are included in the book, **Red Cocaine: The Drugging of America** (Clairion House, 1990) by Douglass and Sejna.

For the purposes here, there are a few more points. By 1968, the Soviets, realizing that someday the war would end, started to send the effort to the Soviet Union exclusively and encouraged North Vietnam to cooperate. The Vietnamese resisted, having their own agenda. Part of that was to make POWs spies or witting agents in the future. The Soviets said they had their own operations in Australia and other locations where GIs were on R&R. What won some cooperation from the Vietnamese was the argument "stay-behind" agents might blow the operation. What the Vietnamese did agree to was the continuation of the program until the end of the war, a Vietnamese decision. Guiding the operation was the Soviet decision, first elaborated in 1951, that *no one was to ever know about the operation*. Deception, putting out the cover stories and making it plausible or deniable.

Douglass emphasized that "there is a great deal of information available on what happened to missing American servicemen. That presented... appears to be extensive, which may be why it tends to frighten people, yet it is less than half of what I learned from Gen. Sejna, and my debriefings were only preliminary. The problem is how to track down information... and what to do with it and when..." He continued that preliminary to the 1991 Senate minority staff report, the 1986 interagency Task Force found "serious shortcoming in every important area: attitudes, management, procedure, organization, and leadership... unhealthy attitudes... deeply defensive mindset which promotes a rigid inflexibility toward criticism and an adversarial approach to those with strong dissenting views... strong moralistic bias... which manifests as a preoccupation with everybody's motives and unrealistic expectations with regard to source accuracy... also could be termed the 'Mindset to debunk'... and attitude of resignation toward outside events... contributes to a noticeable lack of persistence in problem solving and initiative generation. Management... is preoccupied with minutia and preservation of the status-quo and forward thinking is a rarity..." Douglass added that in 1992, when he presented Sejna and his facts he determined that "the people in charge want it to persist." That in a program now estimated to cost $100 million a year.

The minority are frustrated, like Peck. The command emphasis, in my opinion, is why. No one in authority wants an answer, because it would force them to come up with a solution. The same problem found in other programs like missile deterrence. Progress is defined as having a program, not achieving results. That was defined in the "roadmap" discussed in other sections of the book. As long as you had a way of achieving the desired end result, that being improved relations, small problems, like POWs, medical experiments, covert operations, could be overlooked by debunking the source bringing the problem forward, even if was unimpeachable like Sejna. Those you can't impeach, you ignore with faint praise.

On the enemy front, we discovered our efforts to give Vietnamese ways of silencing those with information, through the CDEC declassification. Douglass then briefly referred to the Soviet initiatives, including our sharing information with them, and other information known to him of "Russian efforts to silence witnesses and destroy evidence." Douglass asked, years ago, MG Bernard Loeffke, head of DIA Task Force Russia, why "would anyone with information of value give it to your task force?" Douglass said the short answer was "I wouldn't."

Indications of policy decision

Those readers recoiling in horror from the story just presented must think that "this cannot be. Someone knew, I would have heard about it. You can't keep something like this secret." Think about that statement. The government uses a variation of that to justify their position that there is and can be no "cover-up" or variation to that word. Yet, you have the statements of Tighe, Peck, Smith, and others on living POWs and their reasons for it. In this hearing, 1996, you have more people coming forward. Common sense tells you that something is amiss. Now to the medical experimentation. Dornan asked Corso if "you ever had a clue, until you heard General Sejna about these medical experiments?" Corso replied, "Yes...."

Dornan asked, "You did hear that?... Please tell us." Corso said, "I was getting reports ... in Korea ... they had some sort of a hospital ...where General Kamil, the Soviet, was heading all the interrogation and brainwashing... a hospital there where they were actually experimenting on our prisoners Nazi style... We sent out agents to try to get the information ... I did keep receiving... reports that this was happening... the main reports... was how they were conducting their brainwashing technique... there were other medical experiments that I was getting information on..."

There is also the indirect evidence. Corso testified that in Korea, there were no amputees, mentally walking wounded, soldiers with crutches, or normal war wounds. "... Senator Grassley asked me that question... I was there from the beginning when the first men, the sick and wounded first came over... I didn't see one soldier with crutches, which wasn't - which couldn't be." The question is one that dogged the Vietnam war also - as examined earlier in the book. Earlier in the book I gave the answer on this question, the lack of amputees etc., as being evidence of live Americans and who they might be, as given by CIA informants. As writing this section, the real answer struck me with an electric force. This was the indirect evidence of the medical experiments and perhaps the survivors of some of those described as being long term experiments, perhaps the real truth about the amputees and emotional cripples. Also of interest is the 230 POWs listed as being in Bat Bat by a Vietnamese physician doing treatment on them. So it would seem that plenty of evidence was available, from Sejna in 1968, Dr. Tan in 1969, and the cousin of the camp commander in 1970, if someone was really interested in finding the truth and acting on it.

More about covert activities

The truth about what we have witnessed can be understood only in terms of long term programs aimed at the destruction of the United States. As I have argued since 1979, this program is futuristic in scope and can only be understood from history. Being on the outside, i.e. lack of access to still classified materials, hampered specific arguments over the years. Yet, reading the testimony of those on the "inside" and who agree with my perspective only amplifies what I wrote before.

Testifying before the Dornan Committee was Commander William "Chip" Beck, a special research and investigations assistant on the DPMO. He stated, in a prepared paper for the record, "As a retired member of the Clandestine Service, and a Special Operations Officer with more than 33 years experience, I have participated in many of the Cold War's 'shadow conflict' ... I have witnessed many things that supposedly 'never happened.'... For over half a century, the Soviet Union master minded an elaborate exploitation of foreign prisoners of war... the pool of foreign prisoners included hundreds, if not thousands, of Americans ... The transfer of Americans into the Gulag was intentional. If it were a 'mistake,' the Soviets would have corrected it ...decades ago. The very nature of clandestine operations means they are not accidents. Nor are they acknowledged or willingly revealed.

The greater the magnitude of the covert operation, the great is the secrecy that surrounds it. The transfer of American POWs to the USSR is one big secret..."

From the bowels of secrecy, the Soviet Union, comes a confirmation of some of this. Sejna testified that the security provided during the transfer was the province of counterintelligence. One top defector from the KGB was a counterintelligence captain who brought with him top secret materials. One manual, *"Organisation of KGB Counter-Espionage Work"* states very plainly, "... the determining factor in the espionage activity of the KGB is the foreign policy of the Soviet government..." The governing statute stated "... the KGB is a political working organisation of the CPSU (communist party Soviet Union)... carry out their work ... the fulfillment of party directives... laws, decrees and instructions of the government... All important questions relative to KGB activity are previously decided by the Central Committee of the CPSU and are enforced by KGB orders..."

The tasks are laid out by the **Statute of the Committee of State Security attached to the Council of Ministers of the USSR**, a top secret document which emphasizes " Duties of KGB organs... to supply documentary information on the latest scientific technical achievements... to give the enemy misinformation for political and operational purposes... they ensure the security of state and military secrets (note the priority listed)... KGB organs carry out individual tasks entrusted to them by the Central Committee of the CPSU and Soviet Government..."

Perhaps coincidentally, perhaps not, in 1961, the functions of KGB counterintelligence were stated as including disinformation to camouflage especially important military objectives; to carry out "special missions" for the Central Committee; to begin counterintelligence work on "special and particularly important targets"; to identify intelligence officers in the opponent's military structure; and to begin the work for preparing "active" counterintelligence work at "special times."

Targets for counterintelligence officers, both from a practical viewpoint and from a recruitment viewpoint in the Soviet structure included, staff officers; missile, radar personnel, pilots; ordnance officers, and those responsible for bringing military forces to a "heightened state of battle readiness." KGB regulations from 1966 and 1967 stressed that counterintelligence tasks are determined by "Committee regulations." Intelligence functions and counterintelligence functions must begin to not limit themselves to "separate spheres of action." Active offensives were to be launched; the dispatching of "agents is not to be delayed;" and facilities of the different state security organs were to be "fully utilized."

To emphasize there is no contradiction to what Sejna said, Aleksei Myagkov, wrote that the USSR "indirectly" participated in many "local" wars including Vietnam. Perhaps he did not know the extent of the participation, perhaps he was not allowed to tell what he knew in all areas. What he did write about, in one area, so resonates with Sejna as to be eery. In talking about what happens to citizens of the Soviet Union, Myagkov mentioned the hundreds of secret camps in the Soviet Union into which people just "disappeared" without trace. Then he wrote that others end up in lunatic asylums or psychiatric hospitals. One such person, GEN Peter Grigorenko, became a dissident in 1964, and also became a KGB counterintelligence problem. The solution, psychiatric care. First came the use of "repression" and "persecution." Then, there was the "compulsory treatment" including "various medical preparations which destroyed his nervous system." He was freed, only after his case came to the attention of the free world and he showed all the signs of "madness" to which KGB doctors could attest. Myagkov was present, however, when the KGB case officer for Grigorenko stated plainly that he never suffered from mental illness but was anti-Soviet and did not agree with Politburo policies. Myagkov also emphasized the case of Pyotr Yakir, son of a "disgraced" Soviet. Doggedly defying the Soviets, Yakir eventually ended up in the mental hospitals with a permanent nervous disorder. That lead to his increased drinking and the Soviet initiative to get him hooked on morphine. The Yakir case was emphasized to the KGB crowd as use what you have and improvise.

Thus is Beck and Sejna verified. Beck was also right on target when he said that secrecy on the part of the Russians necessary, even today, because of the "Soviet orchestrated" program which exploited "foreign POW ranks as high as it's nuclear secrets, perhaps higher." Beck emphasized the difficulty in uncovering the secrets of this operation by noting that communism is not dead. This fact was emphasized to me by a high ranking person still vulnerable in Russia who said that the relative freedom allowed there was possibly short lived. His ability to travel and do what he needed to do to keep freedom alive in Russia could come to an end "any day or any year." He meant the resurgence of communism. Beck said that as its doctrine decrees, "it is only underground." The former KGB is now the SVR and a "dozen other services in Russia" and there were "no purges in the communist intelligence services." They kept the records on this operation.

Ham handed operations of asking the new keepers of the records overtly for POW-MIA information will not work without guarantees to those providing information that there will be no retaliation, not only from us but from those who may someday once again hold power. Today, the government of Yeltsin has a communist tinge to it and the Duma is communist controlled. Freedom is on a thin string. As Beck wrote, "...one former KGB officer told me, 'journalists and businessmen are being killed in Moscow and St. Petersburg for trying to break secrets far less sensitive than the POWs...'"

However, Beck is optimistic that "the US has a chance of solving this issue, but only if it employs and applies, the proper resources, and most dedicated people it can muster." He added that we need to take a new approach toward solving the "key POW mystery." He urged the leaving the effort focused on "individual loss cases" and work more on the "strategic aspects" of the communist operations and policies toward foreign POWs; in particular that group being treated as "assets." He affirmed, "such an understanding is fundamental to finding out what happened to unrepatriated POWs who were transferred to the USSR." With disdain, he wrote that "If we continue the habit of acting as 'bone-hunters and archeologists,' it makes it far easier for the Vietnamese and Lao Communists, Khmer Rouge, North Koreans, Chinese, and 'Soviets,' to hide the existence of the broad based and long-term clandestine programs they coordinated and executed against the POWs."

I want to interject a deduction of mine based upon what I feel is an interpolation injected for common use by not so common enemies. I was bothered for a long time by a book that stated the POW hunt was over. There were none. We were allowed access to files showing none survived. They were all killed and that was the big secret. The Vietnamese military, for reasons of their own, allowed us surreptitious entry into the files to copy what we needed. That was the story portrayed to the world in the book reviews. As I have often stated, that is the public portrait.

"Swamp Ranger," as it was called, came at a curious time. This is my deduction and those opposing it will have to prove differently to me. It came about near the time that those who had the most to hide, the Vietnamese and their apologists in the government, wanted to divert attention away from a new round of interest in POWs. In particular, the book drew rave reviews as having the "solution" to the nagging POW problem. Surprise, they were all dead and the Vietnamese may have killed them. My deduction is that the story was a high tech form of deception formed to draw attention away from the realities of the hearings, men like Peck and Sejna, and focus on the moving ball while ignoring the freight train of evidence overlooked. It served the needs of men like Armitage well and of course took pressure off the Vietnamese to answer unwelcome questions about POW transfers. Swamp Ranger, while interesting, never answered real questions.

Most importantly, it portrayed POW families as distraught, willing victims of shysters, not willing to accept the truth. Veteran supporters of POWs were crazy and unable to move on with their lives. The cover-up specialists were portrayed as having no foundation on which to base their claims. Now, those books are having the truth fall in on them and leaving them with the well deserved egg on the face.

Beck had it right when he wrote, "Investigators must understand that, in terms of the POWs, WWII, Korea, the Cold War, and Vietnam, were linked. Soviet policy perspectives, intelligence requirements, and covert operational needs were coordinated with their allies. Just as Soviet political doctrine was taught to emerging communist states, so were more practical issues, which included the handling and exploitation of foreign POWs. Americans must understand the connection between those conflicts before it can solve the mystery of unrepatriated prisoners."

Beck, with his advantage of covert operations for so many years offered an answer to an often asked question - why were they kept and he offered that the solutions he came up with were in consultation with others he worked with. Beck said that in WWII, "perhaps 6000 - 7000 American POWs... went to the Gulag. This was partially because the Western Allies would not forcibly return Russian POWs who had fought for Germany against Stalin. (Operation Keelhaul) Stalin could not exact revenge on those he considered traitors, so he took a measure of revenge against the soldiers of countries... who denied him his will." Continuing, he said, "In Korea, American POWs were sent to Siberia... while others were sent to Moscow for atomic radiation experiments, drug experiments, and medical testing... Additionally, they were exploited for intelligence, the use of their identities, espionage support, technical information, avionics, skilled labor, propaganda insights, and forced labor. In the Cold War, the US did not admit to violations of Soviet air space, so the Soviets conveniently did not have to acknowledge the presence of live airmen it may have captured in this clandestine war."

Wrapping up, Beck said, "The Vietnam War was not isolated from the rest of the communist world... Too many credible people have stepped forward, in private situations... General Sejna's testimony that transfers took place... have been supported in conversations I had with other reliable defectors... We cannot afford to continue to be arrogant ...and think we have answered all the questions concerning the POWs in Indochina or elsewhere... The communist strategists who brought the West such surprises as Dien Bien Phu... the Ho Chi Minh Trail, vast tunnel systems... are very capable of planning, executing, and covering up an elaborate, secret, second-tier, POW system. These programs were guided and supported by the Soviets, who are masters of 'maskirovka,' or deception... The Soviets never expected to lose the Cold War or to answer for human rights abuses of its own people or foreigners. So they acted with impunity. They still are..."

Supporting a solution of mine, Beck wrote, "The facts may turn out to be ugly, but they must be revealed. What to do with the facts when they become known is also a major consideration. Mr. Douglass brought up the specter of war crimes. Since America's record on prosecuting war crimes after Nuremberg is virtually zero, the question of amnesty may have to be considered as an option for the truth to be revealed. Resettlement for those who come forth with the facts may also be in order. I know from my own investigations that other western nations, who had POWs transferred to the USSR in WWII and Korea, faced these same issues and enacted their own solutions. The British response in Korea was mentioned... what was missed in the hustle of the hearings was that the British got their POWs back from the Soviets, not the Koreans... If we determine, as some of us in JSCD have, that the really hard questions have not been effectively addressed, much less answered, then new methods, new approaches, and fresh minds, need to be applied toward the lingering POW/MIA mystery."

Roger DeStatte, that great tactician from the EC-47 case, wrote to Beck in July, 1996, on the Cuban issue, and said about this transfer program, "The Vietnamese explanation is plausible and fully consistent with what we know about... Vietnamese practices granting outsiders access to American POWs. I don't know what you have in mind when you refer to a 'Soviet POW program during the Vietnam War era.' I do know that we can state with complete confidence that the Vietnamese did not permit Soviet persons to interrogate American POWs, nor did they send American POWs to the Soviet Union...." There are those who wonder why I still like the title, "**Trails of Deceit**."

Finally, Beck pointed out in testimony a point I had made earlier in the book about the air attack on Phou Pha Thi. "When I was a paramilitary advisor out in Laos, it was common forklore among the case officers out there that that attack on Phou Pha Thi included Cuban advisors flying the AN-2 Colts... They were the third world brigade. They were the internationalists that were the surrogates for the Soviets... the Russians have a reputation of being condescending and a bit racist to the third worlders so the Cubans were used to ... fill the gap... What the Cubans were involved in in Vietnam was long term. It was intelligence related..."

Whether Russians or Cubans were in the plane, it was all for the benefit of the Soviets. One more mystery deepens just a bit or solved just a bit. And folks just think the issue is about missing men. The trails of deceit run long, hard, and deep.

Only Washington and Hanoi Can Act!

A true accounting is not possible if the Communists cannot provide accurate information. Washington's central theme is only Hanoi knows. Hanoi apologists say they can't do more. What constitutes a satisfactory accounting? We've seen a gamut of estimates from zero to over 800 POWs and 500 additional remains that can be returned. What should the public demand from their government?

Authenticating 1205

Sometimes one turns to the obvious to find the estimate of POWs. The 1205 document provides the most authentic estimate of men for whom Hanoi owes an accounting. The document is controversial, although nothing indicates it is phony. Indeed, the document provides it's own authenticity. For example, the political report assessing the war and peace negotiations states, "our victories gained over the period from 30 March, 1972 to present is given." The Vietnam Easter Offensive began on 30 March, 1972.

Quang referred to secret meetings in Paris as "drawing up a solution to the Vietnam problem." Trung Nhu Tang wrote that Le Duc Tho sprang a political trap coinciding with the Spring Offensive; the dictum of negotiate and fight. From insolence in early 1972, the Vietnamese, in July turned "reasonable," according to our diplomats. The reason? Kissinger decided to allow North Vietnam to keep their troops in the South in exchange for the POWs. (**Vietcong Memoir, pg. 214.**)

Quang refers to a "Ba Be" plan to hasten the end of the war. He explains it in detail and tells of meeting with Vietnamese "neutralists" in Paris, including several former generals and the former Vietnamese Emperor, Bao Dai. He also referred to a new plan that would begin in October. On October 8 and 12, North Vietnam backed off the previously intractable demands that Thieu be gotten rid of and began plans on a National Council of Reconciliation to include neutralists. (**ibid.**) Of note is the fact that "uncorrelated" documents show that a major plan of the PRG was to bring from exile two of the same neutralists Quang had mentioned by name. On October 6, 1972, President Nixon sent a "Top Secret / Sensitive" memorandum to President Thieu. He said that Kissinger was about to explore "what concrete security guarantees the other side is willing to give us ... on the political points ..." He urged Thieu to go along. The attitude was cooperate or the CIA will assassinate you. (**Palace File** Letter 8 pg. 376)

On October 16, Nixon wrote that Kissinger's meetings with the North showed that Hanoi was prepared to agree to a cease-fire prior to the resolution of the political problem, a reverse in doctrine. (**Palace File** pg. 377)

Quang said, "we must attract the neutralists to our side." One was the Bao Dai, hereditary monarch of Vietnam. This approach was identical to one used in 1945 when Ho Chi Minh forced him to abdicate. However, to preserve his monarchist followers, Ho conferred on him the title of "Supreme Adviser." (**Vietnam Crisis, pg. 67**) In the 1954 era, Bao Dai was revered in the countryside, considered the leader, and had many followers. Nguyen Tinh Hung, working for Diem's election, found that out. (**Palace File**, pg. 177)

The Ba Be Plan referred to activation of agents in South Vietnam to begin the influencing of politics from within. Tang identified Comrade "Ba" as Le Duan. In a 1966 letter, Duan said, "... to rally and organize a large mass of people, we must develop... transitional organizations, operating overtly or semi-overtly under many disguised forms... designed ... to cover our core elements, ... to operate success-fully." (**Vietcong Memoir** pg. 104) In addition, both Quang and Tang made spe-cific reference to the August 1945 Revolution as using a similar method to precipi-tate the First Indochina War. (**op. cit. pg. 105**)

Quang described Ba Be as "elimination of all people: ... who occupy leader-ship positions ... a full paralyzation of the wills of these people..." Louis Fanning, a former intelligence analyst, wrote that in the Easter Offensive, the Vietnamese sent in their "killer teams," known as Dich Van who took as prisoner personnel identified by regular military units as the "policemen, spies, pacification agents and security agents." They would then hold a mock trial and execute them. He estimated up to ten thousand met this fate. In a footnote, Fanning described Dich Van as similar to SS men whose sole purpose was to "serve as executioners for the politically or socially undesirable." (**Betrayal in Vietnam**, pg. 106)

Quang said, "... conduct of activities for ... disruption in the Saigon govern-ment apparatus ... the people who oppose us... our decision ...must be ... firm. ... an important place in ... the Ba Be plan. We must have ... full dossiers on them before-hand ... to quickly do away with them and ruin their order..."

On the political side. Quang said, "... in the private meetings with ... Kissinger, we understood that Nixon... is being stubborn ..." This referred to Nixon not agreeing to all concessions Kissinger made. In October, Kissinger wanted a settlement signed even saying, "Peace is at hand." From his viewpoint, it was. Nixon, how-ever rejected some points as did Thieu. Only an informed Quang could understand Kissinger telling the Vietnamese, "deal with me and I'll take care of Nixon."

Having shown the authenticity of the political part of the 1205 document, let's look at the POW estimate. Quang said to test the effectiveness of the POW issue in the United States, he would free a few POWs to see the public reaction. Less than a week later, three POWs were freed. Earlier he told of Politburo decisions to exploit POWs made in March 1971 and April, 1972. In 1972, parades of "celebri-ties" went to Vietnam like Jane Fonda to tell how "leniently" the POWs were treated. Although Quang and the Politburo would not admit a mistake, that exploi-tation backfired and stiffened the resolve of the American public to hang tough until the POWs were all returned.

Quang said among the prisoners were "scientists in other technical areas," pre-viously identified "from our interrogations of American aviators... shot down over North Vietnam and **American scientists** captured in this war, **particularly Air Force specialists** ..." Some were examined to look at the war from the American side. We saw that in 1993 a source revealed that Sr. Col. Van Duy, commander of the B-22 intelligence camp was involved in the exploitation of US POWs for avia-tion / avionics technology.

Mooney, Garwood, Minarcin, and Sejna all told of Americans being sought out for their special talents. Sejna said some were transferred to the Soviet Union to examine the war from the American side. Quang said some were exploited for "material on how to use different types of weaponry, tactical / technical character-istics of aircraft, Air Force Directives, as well as materials about other types of armament of the US Army." Many specialists from the AC-130 to the EC-47 were highly suspected to be captured and never returned, including EW officers. You can't keep them all or you might as well put up a neon sign about your intentions.

Commander Chip Beck, testified, "I think there was... big, clandestine, covert operation aimed at exploiting out prisoners from World War II... Korea, the cold war... Vietnam" He was asked by Dornan, "But Victor Blenko... told you that, as a Soviet fighter pilot during the Vietnam period, they were getting information of air battle tactics that were so accurate and so timely, that he just assumed it came from the interrogation by the Soviet Army military of our pilots..." Beck answered, "he said... I was an instructor pilot ... we used to get requirements. We would send our requirements on air combat maneuvering... We would get back incredible briefing ... within two weeks... I know how the system works..."

The Secret KGB training document, "Counterintelligence work of the State Security Organs of the USSR," talked in its outline about scientific intelligence. Socialist intelligence services divided intelligence activity into several fields. One was scientific - technical intelligence. "Science makes the transition from super-structure to basics, Military intelligence." It also included basic educational work. Dialectical materialism formed the basis for scientific knowledge from the Socialist standpoint. KGB Directive No. 43, 1967, directed the counterintelligence services to take active measures for discovering and foiling enemy schemes.

Of importance was the KGB Secret Report on "Ways, methods, and devices used by agents of western intelligence services for the collection of intelligence information ..." from the same time period. Counterintelligence officers were alert for attempts by "imperialist forces" to gather intelligence on missile forces, anti-aircraft units, radio relay networks, radar stations, infrared devices, etc. One way to gather the information is to conduct interrogation of specialists who battle these devices on a daily basis. Again, using socialist terminology, these air force specialists were "scientists." (**KGB** Appendices)

For the Easter Offensive, the Vietnamese used Marshal Pavel F. Batitsky; LTG A. N. Sevchenko; LTG of Artillery F. M. Boldarenko; and LTG M.T. Beregaroy, as advisers to the Offensive. (**Betrayal**, pg. 105 and *Hanoi's International News Service*, March 29, 1972.) This also coincides with Sejna's report saying, "General Kushchev ... told me some ... American prisoners are very helpful to analyze operation of the United States forces ..." The American prisoners were interrogated by KGB counterintelligence personnel to discover how we were doing so well against their best weapons.

Quang specifically said, "We are continuing to collect and study materials from POW interrogations... to have a basis in specific circumstances to expose US designs ... Collections and study of these materials has provided us great assistance in studying the scientific discoveries... in developing methods to counter contemporary weapons, including chemical..."

Do the numbers of the 1205 document fit? DOD told me in April, 1997 that the 1205 figure refers to both allied and American POWs. Bull pucky. From the beginning, Quang said, "In addition... I will also report to you today on **American POWs** captured ..." Continuing, he said, "The work with **American prisoners of war** ... the issues of exploiting these **American POWs** captured during the war."

Only American POWs were mentioned. In fact, Quang correctly reported, "The number of **American POWs** in the DRV has not been made public ... We have kept this figure secret... I will report to you, comrades, the exact number of **Ameri-**

can POWs." The implication of the correctness of 1205 American POWs held, versus 591 actually returned, is serious. It shows the incompetence, cover-up, or mindset to debunk for a domestic political scandal of catastrophic proportions..

How good are the figures in the 1205 document? Laos, 47 prisoners. CIA documents show that at least 28 were moved to Vietnam at one time. There were "36 advisors of diversionary detachments ... inserted in the border region between the DRV and Laos; lone diversionists ... conducting reconnaissance ... from helicopters and reconnaissance ships; and several seamen who abandoned their ships that we damaged.." OP PLAN 34A, De Soto, and Hardnose operations, both overt and covert, suffered losses.. SOG special operations included troops inserted, like Lacy said, into the MuGia border region.

Taking the known prisoners in Laos (about 200), adding in 1205 in North Vietnam, the 200 or so POWs / MIAs lost after the 1205 document, the transfers to the Soviet Union (about 200), and subtracting 591 POWs returned, and about 300 returned through a new identity program, minus the various deaths reported, leaves plenty of room for 572 POWs to be alive in Laos in 1994 as reported by Smith.

Working another way, using the 368 prisoners Quang said would be returned first; adding in 220 in Dogpatch, 9 returned from captivity in Laos, subtracting the three returned early and adding in 57 known returnees after the 1205 documents is only 60 above the actual number returned. Any number of reasons would reverse a decision on returning 60 of the 368 prisoners Quang referred to as "progressive." For example, some of the known POW camps housed those considered to be "troublemakers." These men were moved en masse for being bothersome to their Vietnamese captors.

A third way of evaluating Quang is this. He said prior to Son Tay, there were four major prisons. US intelligence says POWs were consolidated in this time frame into "five major camps" including Dogpatch which did not open until after May, 1972. Quang added that number (4) was expanded to 11 after Son Tay. Our POWs came back from four prisons opened after Son Tay and two were opened specifically to respond to the Son Tay raid. Some prisons were used exclusively to house high ranking prisoners (as described by Quang); some for troublemakers (again confirming Quang); and others had sections to prevent communications between the sections, thus facilitating transfers as North Vietnam perceived a need.

The numbers fit

While an exact numerical correlation to the 1205 document is very difficult due to the differences between what Quang knew and what returned POWs reported, the gist of the 1205 document fits known Vietnamese operating habits. While one could play with numbers all day, every scenario fits well with 1205 prisoners held in North Vietnamese prisons in September, 1972. The "Katyn-like" breakdown of prisoners fit both known returnees and reports of suspected POW prisons. Ba Vi reportedly was called the 24th US POW camp. Some of the camps holding known returnees were not described as major POW camps, again making a direct numerical tie in to Quang difficult.

We can say, however, the numbers in 1205 document fit the numbers we expected, but did not receive. The second system of POWs fits what Minarcin and Mooney predicted and I discovered in declassified documents. The "special talents" described by POW activists early on as being missing; those described by Mooney and Minarcin and Sejna; fit the descriptions provided by Quang. Captured documents describing POWs being held back all back Quang's assertion this happened. Some described "farm camps" under the direction of a top North Vietnamese general, implying a second set of camps. The minority on the Senate POW Committee found (a) the existence of logistical and administrative relationships among camps in northwestern Laos and in northwestern Vietnam not reflected in DIA documents; and (b) evidence of a second set of camps from which no prisoners returned. A coincidence or evidence of 1205 authenticity?

The Vietnamese as seriously misread the American government as Kissinger did the Vietnamese. Once "all the POWs" returned and reparations were turned down, the POWs became a liability. The Vietnamese made many efforts to refer to POWs being held back. We ignored or missed their overtures. We offered to ransom some out, offering $100 million instead of the promised $4.75 billion. Smith says the Vietnamese army personnel now holding the men are fearful of war crime trials if they execute those they hold; a legitimate fear on their part.

How good is Hanoi on remains? Loc testified to processing nearly five hundred sets of remains. He also testified to secondary information about several hundred other remains in another location in Vietnam. If correct, these verify serious deficiencies in the Pentagon accounting numbers. On November 13, 1995, the Pentagon revealed that they considered only 567 of the remaining 2170 "official" cases to be hopeless in pursuing an accounting. Of course, the Pentagon did not reference the additional 2000 plus cases they have yet to acknowledge.

Of the 567 cases, 366 were aviators lost far enough at sea to make it virtually impossible to resolve the case, the Pentagon said. Inexplicably however, some aviators "lost at sea" have been "officially" accounted for. Taking the new number of 2170 and subtracting 567 cases "nonrecoverable" and additionally subtracting 572 reported alive in Laos leaves 1031 cases to be accounted for. Loc reported processing and seeing about 500 remains at Ly Nam De and knowing of several hundred more at another location. The numbers leave plenty for Soviet transfers.

Confirming what 1205 says II

In 1994, the Pentagon was "blindsided" by one of their own operatives. Photos bought from the Vietnamese at premium prices emerged in POW activist hands. DOD was shocked. The families were shocked. Hundreds of photos including images of ID cards in pristine condition emerged. The graphic history recorded Vietnamese officials scouring crash sites. KGB agents are shown with POWs. A Hanoi newspaper detailed the death of a category 1 POW, Navy Lt. Edward Dickson. Incontrovertible evidence emerged of some MIAs being captured. This find came years after General Vessey detailed Hanoi's problem with "worm eaten" and "water damaged" records. Some of the crash sites shown were later searched by our JTF-FA teams. The Vietnamese charged exorbitant prices for the privilege of finding what remaining pieces of plexiglass they chose not to take. The Vietnamese never revealed their earlier excavations.

A DOD spokeswoman confirmed that copies of the photos had been in DOD hands for 2 years. They "resolved the fate of 14 missing Americans and provided clues about 15 others, all believed dead." Some families did not know the photos existed until the activist made them public. (*Riverside Press - Enterprise*, **July 14, 1994**) Former Assistant Secretary of Defense Frank McGaffney Jr. said: "The explanation for this stunning withholding of information ... may lie in ... that these photos represent damning new evidence of ... the American and Vietnamese governments have covered up critical information on missing U.S. servicemen... the great lengths... North Vietnam went to document its inventory of ... prisoners and their equipment ..." (*Washington Times*, **July 26, 1994**)

The photos validate information presented to the Montgomery Committee about the Vietnamese meticulousness. The government's excuses about the Vietnamese inability to account for POWs disappeared with the emergence of this previously suppressed stockpile of information. The tragedy is that Quang reported, "When the American government resolves the political and military issues on all three fronts of Indochina, **we will set free all American POWs**. We consider this a very correct course." It is possible had we not declared those POWs, not returned, dead and made that an official policy in 1974; the victory of North Vietnam in 1975 would have freed our POWs, their purpose fulfilled.

The corruption of a system

I want now to present information showing what has been done to corrupt the accounting system. This is a generic study, using fictional names in a real case to protect the privacy of families involved. "Bob Bartle" and "Harry James" were shot down over North Vietnam. An intelligence report from a captured Vietnamese surfaced four years after their loss incident showing two fliers captured. This report was called "uncorrelated." By accident, the families discovered the report.

The report was specific, occurring within days of the known loss of the two men. The aircraft shot down corresponded generally to their plane. The prisoner ranks matched Bartle and James. The heights and weights of the prisoners were close to the men's actual heights and weights. A noticeable gap in one man's front teeth matched his dental records. The eye color of the younger man was correct. The older man's eye color was unknown, being closed at the time of observation. The target location was within the "route package" flown by Bartle and James.

The families asked DIA for comments. The intelligence community estimated that Bartle and James were not involved because the shootdown was beyond the outer limits of their planes fuel capacities. Yet, just two months earlier, both men earned a DFC for flying into the support area for this target. DIA knew that.

The intelligence community said the men would not have been diverted from their "primary" mission to take reconnaissance photos of this new target. Their "official" target was a radio antenna. The "new" target was a strategic target. Photos demanded by Washington on bombing runs of this target were of highest priority. Other reconnaissance planes attempting to get those photos were lost. The plane flown by Bartle and James was preferred for this type of mission. Two MIA planes fit the target date designated by the witness. One contained Bartle and James

To the intelligence analysis of the "new" report showed it could pertain to some twenty some other cases. Prior efforts on this fourteen year old report were unable to find one case to correlate the report to. Now, twenty cases jumped at the analysts. The unnamed POW returnees said that the details provided by the eyewitness corresponded to happenings in their shootdown. Neither returnee, however, said he was involved in the bombing of this strategic target. The corresponding information that "happened to them" were they were stripped to their skivvies; the villagers gathered around them; and one of the men was offered a glass of water. Big deal. In "**Pilots in Pyjamas,**" that happened to many people. In declassified documents, that happened all the time. One said he "faked" unconsciousness. In the report, the unconscious man moaned, apparently near death.

DIA informed the family they ignored the specific items matching Bartle and James to "expand the search" of potential matches. They did not even contradict the compatible information. The "correlated" POWs were shot down in 1965. On October 14, 1966, the Joint Chiefs of Staff were still pleading for permission to bomb the strategic target. (**Pentagon Papers**, **pg. 553**) DIA did not blink at this impossibility. The source was precise on how he knew the date of the shootdown. It coincided with the bombing of the strategic target and near Tet. Official records show this strategic target was bombed near Tet in that year.

The analysts next resorted to their rabbit out of the hat trick. They claimed the original eyewitness "just happened" to enter the country as a refugee precisely a few months before the intelligence report was found. Now, eighteen years after witnessing the incident, his recollection "more nearly fits" the analysis provided by DIA. After surviving a POW status with US forces and becoming a refugee, his mind is "razor sharp." Eighteen years later, his remembrance is more correct than only four years after the incident. The bombing now occurred before we were allowed to strike the target, according to DIA.

A photo was given to DIA to see if it matched "James." That photo had been identified before as being "James." At that time, DIA said, no, but perhaps with improved technology a "match" could be made in the future. This being the future, another analysis was attempted. DIA said that there were "numerous similarities" between the photo and "James." Even more intriguing is the fact that this photo came from "**Pilots in Pyjamas**" and the year more nearly fits Bartle and James than the DIA "match." DIA took the photo, a multi-generation photocopy, and attempted to analyze it to see if it matched either Bartle or James. DIA said the attempt was difficult because of the "poor quality of the photo." Not once did they confirm their possession of a first or second generation "negative" to do an analysis. Evidently, DIA decided to hide from whence the original came.

In February, 1992, personnel from JTF-FA were in Vietnam to "account" for Bartle and James. They gathered first hand evidence to the pilots' demise. The people witnessing the shootdown reported, unanimously, it happened four to six months after Bartle and James had been lost. The date more nearly corresponds to another case, being investigated, with the same type of basic aircraft. One set of remains was returned from that case three years prior to the field trip. The investigators were stymied why the other set of remains was not found. The returned remains matched neither Bartle nor James.

Investigators found, "Prior to interviewing witnesses at the Provincial Military Command, (redacted) asked Mr. (redacted) of the VNOSMP to present witnesses separately... to isolate them from hearing each other's statements.... In ...isolated interviews ... the statements of the witnesses were clearly more contradictory than previous interview sessions. VNOSMP representatives ... tried ... to correct discrepancies in witness statements ... by prompting or leading the witness ... After (one) interview, Mr. (redacted) led him away to another room ... and was overheard chastising him severely. The interview of the next witness was then delayed over 30 minutes while he was 'in conference' with Mr. (redacted)... When the next witness was presented for interview, the U.S. Team Chief opened the questioning by asking him if he any information to add to the statements of the first two witnesses. Although ... supposedly ... isolated from hearing the earlier interviews, he ... responded ... without hesitation and showed no signs of confusion ... He was quickly cut off ... who realized the ... intentions. (Redacted) explained that (redacted) could not answer such a question since he was not present for the previous interviews ... Incidents such as this cast great doubt upon the truthfulness and spontaneity of witnesses ... confirm that they are coached extensively ...."

The plane was also shot down in the wrong location to belong to Bartle and James. Vietnam was split up into "route packages," each the exclusive flying province of an armed force. Bartle and James flew in route package VIA, belonging to the Air Force. This shootdown occurred in the Navy sector, Route Package VIB; 100 kilometers from their "official" loss location. The Vietnamese produced parts from the supposed wreckage including those common to both an RF-4 and an F-4. Most belonged only to an F-4, and Bartle and James flew an RF-4.

In this attempted match, we have a) the shootdown date is unanimously wrong by up to six months; the shootdown location was inaccurate by at least 100 kilometers; the plane belonged to the wrong service; the plane was the wrong type; and the witnesses were coached and coerced.

The verdict? Investigators determine they have a probable "Correlation."

This is only one example of on-site investigations. Nothing matches, yet the government is ready to write off two flyers at a time when DIA had information these two men survived their loss incident. In 1993, investigators tried matching Bartle and James to another shoot down site. They had pictures of an aircraft this time. To date, Bartle and James have been shot down four or five times, in four or five locations (at least) and DIA and other intelligence agencies can find witnesses to all these facts. They have even been buried in a sixth location. In April, 1997, when informed of all this, General Wold, said, "I hope this case is just a aberration and not part of what has happened in the past." Right!

A wealth of information on POWs/MIAs

DIA possess a computerized data bank on our MIAs. They can pull names out of a hat to either prove or disprove a point. This legitimate information includes the "wealth of information" that was published in the Vietnamese press. (**House Select Committee vol. 3, pg. 125**) Walters reported that a central office in the DRV Ministry of Defense stored all of the personal effects, documents, dog tags, and other items carried by prisoners or those whose remains were sent to Hanoi. (*Ibid.*) They then supplied some materials observed in Hanoi's "War Crimes Museum." The testimony of Loc the mortician shows Vietnam can resolve hundreds of cases. One of the photos released in 1994 showed a Zippo lighter as an example of their meticulous work.

One further point. Prior to the raid on Son Tay, we had a source deep in the Vietnam hierarchy supplying our side with detailed intelligence on prisoners incarcerated in Son Tay prison. He was not our only source. Another source was compromised by our own intelligence, not too long ago, because of some harebrained scheme. (**Dornan hearing**)

A deceitful position gained a foothold in our bureaucracy early. On October 27, 1977, Frank Sieverts was questioned about the State Department's estimate of information held by the Vietnamese. Congressmen were attempting to define an achievable accounting. He said, "Withheld implies ... that they have a stack of information.... a very difficult question to answer.... our speculation ... versus what they ... have.... we do not know what they have over ... what they have given us already." (**Wolff Committee, pg. 112**) Congressman Gilman reminded Sieverts of the DOD estimate. Sieverts conceded he knew of that estimate. Gilman asked if a reasonable conclusion was the Vietnamese could provide information on about 1339 cases. Sieverts replied, "We are... trying to guess what the Vietnamese know... I do not personally find it useful to speculate ... except ... when we get information from them." (*Ibid.* **pg. 114**) Gilman retorted, "I am frank to say that I fail to understand the Department's attitude ... towards this important issue." (*Ibid.* **pg. 115**)

Congress and diplomatic recognition

There is another area of oversight. This area is in the realm of money and diplomatic recognition. The Clinton Administration recognized Vietnam with no MIA accounting. Further, getting Vietnam out of Cambodia failed. Hun Sen, a protégé of Pol Pot and Hanoi stooge, in mid- 1997 threw out the results of an election and kept power for himself. Now, we have no accounting, POWs in captivity, Hanoi in charge of Cambodia, and campaign money funneled to Clinton, a war protester and draft dodger, by allies of Vietnam to keep this "nation's highest priority" from being resolved.

Congress faltered in their oversight responsibility. What ever the name, mindset to debunk or cover-up; it is alive and well. In 1978, an affidavit filed by Dermot Foley called for honesty in accounting. It is even more relevant today.

"No one appears to be disposed to make a statement like that under oath, subject to cross-examination. ... we now know that there was credible evidence (of live POWs) and that it was being ignored." (**Dermot Foley,** *Hopper v. Carter*)

Dornan, in 1996, said," ... it has gotten very confrontational now... your whole senior team... should have had their tails in this room during the testimony of a two-star Czech defector, General Sejna, and Philip Corso... for the testimony of Bill Bell, who ... was eased out of his job because he testified truthfully and openly to a closed Senate Committee... I learn more from these people outside the system than I ever do inside. I'm learning now how people are prepared... to give canned answers from DPMO to questions... We need a whole new team at DPMO, gentlemen, It is confrontational now, I'm very sorry." (Hearings Sept. 17, 1996 House National Security Committee, Military Personnel Subcommittee, pg. 124, 125)

Dornan verified my "Party Line" theory I first brought it up in 1979. Out intelligence agencies knew about the "chemical interrogation room" at Ba Vi in 1970, two years after knowing from Sejna that chemical interrogation of our POWs was taking place. Why didn't it correlate - if indeed it didn't? The reason given was CIA, in debriefing Sejna, did not care about the information.

Let's put all the cards on the table and have everyone come forward with their best case, under oath, and see who is and who is not telling the truth. I want the men home and accounted for. I bring out what I knew and when only for the purpose of demonstrating that the truth was out there for the paid analysts to find. It also demonstrates the weakness of the "he doesn't know the classified material" argument that may be used to debunk this book.

The POW bumper sticker that says "**Only Hanoi Knows**" used to mean something. Yes, they know. However, so does **Washington.** I follow the dictum of former National Security Adviser Richard Allen and **raise** that "**Holy Hell**" to get the wheel greased. That is the ultimate purpose of this series of books.

Mindset to Debunk

The U.S. Government, under liberal leaders, has been a willing or unwilling dupe. Policy makers look obvious facts straight on and then proceed as if they did not exist. In the last forty years, policy advisers exhibited the same propensity and seemingly lacked the moral courage to tell policy makers they may be wrong. With few exceptions, GEN John Singlaub, GEN Daniel Graham, GEN Eugene Tighe, and MAJ Scott Ritter, being among the exceptions, no one wants to buck the system. The result has been disastrous for the security of our nation. In the context of this book, it is similarly disastrous for the lives of our unreturned POWs.

Hanson W. Baldwin, former military editor for the *New York Times* anticipated this type of development in his 1970 book, **Strategy for Tomorrow**. This look at defense needs up to the year 2000, accurately depicted many problems in this area. Baldwin wrote that since the beginning of the century, Americans are like liberals. By not learning from history, we win wars and lose the peace.

For military advice, he wrote that the professionalism our Joint Chiefs possess should be factored into decisions Presidents make and not manipulated for PR purposes. Government fails, he added, unless the military viewpoint, even if fragmented among the services, is reflected "comprehensively and honestly and in detail" to the President. Since World War II, Baldwin argued, military chiefs while not "yes men," were not the "pound the table" tough chiefs like those serving previously. They were split in loyalty to both their commander in chief and to the Congress and the people. Part of the problem, he wrote, and is still visible, is that Congress refused to live up to it's defense and foreign policy obligations; preferring to defer to the executive department. (**Strategy**, pgs. 13-17)

The Defense and other Executive Departments, especially under liberals who cannot comprehend the military, have tended to dilute or contradict military advice. In the field of intelligence, this has been exacerbated by the prevalence of CIA interpretations vice NSA or DIA interpretations even in pure military fields. Thus, politics causes the United States to be "surprised" time again militarily even when the military estimates are right on. Lyman Kirkpatrick Jr., in **Captains Without Eyes**, wrote, "... where civilian authorities dominate the decision making process in matters exclusively military... then national catastrophe may result..."

That Baldwin and Kirkpatrick were correct became abundantly apparent in 1998 when the entire intelligence and diplomatic fields were "surprised" by the explosion of an atomic device in India. That of course lead to a round of explosions by their enemy, Pakistan. In May 1998, retired ADM David Jeremiah was appointed to examine how this major intelligence catastrophe came about. The results are all too familiar to those working in the intelligence fields, especially on the POW issue. Jeremiah reported that this "miss" was not an "isolated incident," but was part of a system wide weakness in collection, analysis, and management. Jeremiah said, like I did 20 years ago on POW matters, there is an "everybody thinks like us mindset" in both intelligence and foreign policy makers decision process. He challenged the intelligence management to become creative thinkers and to increase contact with outside experts so the "conventional wisdom" could be challenged, a confirmation of Tighe's "mindset to debunk." (*Wall Street Journal* 6/3/98)

To illustrate this in the POW field, I'll use examples as analogies for what happened to our POWs. Traditional mythology tells us that Ngo Dinh Diem was overthrown because of his repressive policies towards the Buddhist majority. The reality is that liberal policy makers at mid-level State Department decided he had to go because he was too independent minded and was bucking what the "best and the brightest" decided was best for Vietnam.

The war effort in mid-1963 was not affected by the "Buddhist crisis." First, the Buddhists, a significant portion of the populace, were not the majority. Second, the war effort was progressing for our side. A special National Intelligence Estimate, 10 July 1963, said, "... the Buddhist issue has not been effectively exploited by the communists, nor does it appear to have had any appreciable effect in the counterinsurgency effort..." (**Pentagon Papers**, pg. 193) Agreeing, MAJ Nick Rowe wrote of a major battle won by his local Vietnamese forces in the U-Minh area. Marguerite Higgins, a war correspondent, examined the countryside from Hue to Bac Lieu and interviewed the American advisers. Triumphs were evident in all areas. The resident CIA agent and GEN Harkins agreed that the war was progressing in the correct direction. GEN Victor Krulak and his boss Robert Kennedy, who oversaw the counterinsurgency effort in Vietnam, also were positive about the war effort. (**Our Vietnam Nightmare** by Higgins)

Opposing this view was Roger Hilsman and W. Averell Harriman and their State Department group. Ironically, the Viet Cong agreed they were not winning. Their internal documents showed they were meeting "unexpected resistance" from the populace. They feared the strategic hamlet program, albeit unpopular, would fatally injure their whole insurgency effort. (**Vietcong**, pg. 158) The strategic hamlet program was what Krulak, Harkins, and the American advisers were crediting with the progress being shown.

Supporting the State Department "rogues" was the Saigon press corps. Their dispatches often determined State Department policy. (**Nightmare**, pg. 124-125) In time, the State Department policy was "facts became irrelevant" and "the rights and wrongs don't matter, it's what people believe." (*Ibid.* pg. 186)

Thus, even though Ho Chi Minh was seeking a rapprochement with Diem in July 1963 (*Ibid.* pg 176); even though North Vietnam and South Vietnam were beginning a process of quitting the war in 1963 (Rev. DeJaegher to author); and the VC thought they were losing; the State Department view won out and Diem was murdered. The mindset to debunk the obvious and provable became the accepted norm and the road to over 95% of our POWs and MIAs was set in stone.

Unfortunately, also set in stone was the dictum, first established by a genuine friend of free Vietnam, and who would probably have cringed at the outcome of his remark, "who pays, commands." (John Wilson O'Daniel, **Palace File**, pg. 39) In 1964, this became a Top Secret policy which dictated, "The U.S. would seek to control any negotiations and would oppose any independent South Vietnamese efforts to negotiate..." (**Pentagon Papers**, pg. 375)

This was no doubt put into effect by the near success of the Ngo brothers of ending the fighting by early 1964. The liberals in Washington were furious as things were going on outside their control. Tran Van Dinh, the go between for the

Ngo brothers was instructed to seek a "cease fire with Hanoi"; the "departure of all US forces"; and the acceptance of the Vietcong both in Diem's government and in an election to be called sometime in 1964. The U.S sponsored murder of the Ngo brothers ended this chance for peace. Father DeJaegher told me in no uncertain terms that while these stories were true, Diem would never let communism reign in Vietnam. He wanted a peace that best fit an independent, "democratic" Vietnam.

The second instance of a mindset to debunk comes in very recent history. In fact, much of it is still unknown and unwritten because it is still classified. The story involves China and our foreign policy. What happens in China will inevitably involve the well-being of our POWs. To the degree that we kowtow to them, our POWs suffer. They suffer because for a multiplicity of reasons, our policy makers deny the obvious about POW survival.

On July 8, 1997, in a carefully crafted statement, Senator Fred Thompson (R-TN), outlined a plot by Beijing to secretly "increase China's influence over the U.S. political process;" illegally contribute money to favored candidates; and to "buy access and influence in furtherance of Chinese Government interests." The aim is to bend our foreign policy to match their desired results. (**Thompson Committee** Part 1, pg. 1-2) The one thing to remember about communist foreign policy is that the strategy may be economic; political; scientific; involve spies; or involve POWs; the end result is that all the aspects are tied together. Their strategy is unified towards the goal of our destruction or their dominance over us. Unlike our liberal diplomats, they do not compartmentalize strategy. All is integrated. With enough information, an analyst can connect the dots. The result then becomes obvious, unless there is a mindset to debunk.

The Chinese are patient. In 1989, they told a spy, Bin Wu, "You will patiently ... work your way up into the United States power structure. You will come to know congressmen... and perhaps one day even be able to report information from the White House." This is just a collateral policy to what was attempted with POWs by the Chinese in the Korean War. The idea was to attempt to bend their minds to become useful to the Chinese cause after the war was over. Bin Wu was allowed to leave China after he "agreed" to the Chinese plans for him.

The Chinese aim is to become the big player in Southeast Asia; North Asia; and even in Russian Asia. One aim is to isolate Vietnam and bend it to China's foreign policy will. Vietnam is attempting to keep Chinese influence out and therefore will tolerate the United States back in. In fact, one theory is that the United States, in attempting to use Vietnam as a "counterweight" to China, may even some day have another military tie to Vietnam, like we did with Diem.

How is China attempting this power broker play? Up through a few years ago, it has been a big bluff in military terms. Chinese military officials found in Korea that human wave attacks against a technologically superior military foe will not work. In Vietnam, the Chinese observed first hand the Soviet SAMs being outfoxed by technologically superior counter- weapons. The Chinese did, however, gain direct insight in how to exploit what the enemy had through prisoners of war.

After the fall of the Soviet Union, the Chinese began a big move. They had already made a decision to steal, buy, or otherwise acquire technology to bypass years of experimental work. Being experts in reverse engineering, they wanted to compress decades of scientific work into years. In recent years, China began their covert plan against the United States. The Thompson Committee examined primarily campaign contributions to the Clinton-Gore, DNC, and other Democratic campaigns, generally in the 1996 election cycle, with origins in China or with Chinese agents of influence. Chinese money probably helped the Clinton and later the Clinton-Gore campaigns at crucial times in 1992. Earlier, we saw how one agent of influence impacted the recognition of Vietnam to the detriment of POWs.

What did China want? A compendium of "well-placed" "surreptitiously monitored" conversations of "top Chinese officials suggested that Beijing was ready to illegally funnel money" to American politicians "through front companies for the Chinese government" "to buy influence with American politicians." Seven named PRC agents of influence were tied into President Clinton and Vice-President Gore through fund-raisers; many of which involved PRC intelligence agents.

Some of the same persons were tied to money going to two members of the POW Senate Committee. One of these agents of influence, John Huang, was well placed during the period of time that crucial decisions were made about Vietnam normalization. The Thompson Committee found a "broad array of Chinese efforts to influence U.S. policies... most of which are classified at the Top Secret compartmented level." (**Thompson** ibid) How extensive is this effort? The author is aware of a multimillion dollar effort in the capitol of his home state through an agency identified in the covert plans section of this book which is well placed to "make extensive use of commercial covers" to gain access to politicians through "American" companies and gain access to policy makers.

The Thompson Committee only scratched the surface. Liberal Democrats made full use of "national security" to suppress the extent of Chinese penetration of American policy making decisions. However, in early 1999, another committee, the Cox Committee, released a "unanimous and bipartisan report" from this "Select Committee on ... the People's Republic of China" which exposed the liberal cover for the smoke and mirrors it was. Closely preceding the Cox Report, also mostly classified at the Top Secret compartmented level, was a book, **Betrayal**, by Bill Gertz, a National Security writer for the *Washington Times*. **Betrayal** made use of leaked Secret, classified, Top Secret and compartmented documents which has a bearing, I believe, on the POW matter. None of the documents, however, directly mention the issue. Connecting the dots, however, is revealing.

What is shown in the documents Gertz has is a mindset to debunk obvious facts and a mindset to create an atmosphere in which American military capacity and security is undermined by pure lying to both Congress and the American people by officials in the Clinton Administration. Ominously for the POWs, this debunking in other areas shows the mindset of an Administration and it's military and intelligence functionaries who can look at the 1205 document and the POW Select Committee minority findings along with the testimony of a Jan Sejna and say the facts there do not exist.

To illustrate this in a more graphic way, we'll examine another facet of the Clinton Administration. In 1992, GEN Sejna presented his politically explosive testimony on live POW medical experimentation to the Senate POW Committee. Later, it became more public in September 1996 in the Dornan Committee hearings. We've already seen where there were efforts in 1996 to obtain documentation on the POWs from officials in former European Communist countries in exchange for help in getting into NATO. Nothing came of that effort and the countries slid into NATO with no problem. Simultaneously, our policy makers dropped POWs from their official lexicon on problems to be solved. The question arises as to how this golden opportunity passed with no action. President Yeltsin and other top Russian officials were helping. Of course, there was not general knowledge of the extent of this new problem and the potential difficulty it could create. I believe I found part of the answer in two places.

First, it is known that having Yeltsin in power has been a central stone of our foreign policy for many years. We now know the lengths to which bureaucrats will go to keep him there, regardless of the costs to our POW hostages. Malcolm Toon, Ambassador to Russia, was so upset with the revelations of Sejna that he attempted to get Sejna fired from his DIA job for daring to reveal the fate of some of the POWs (**Dornan** pg. 8). Yet, that sordid action could not explain the policy of Clinton in light of all the corroborating material that has come to light.

What does, however, is a classified memorandum between Clinton and Yeltsin on 3/13/96. This memorandum discussed the Presidential elections in both the United States and Russia. Clinton said, in the elections, he wanted to make sure that everything the United States did would have a positive impact and *"nothing* would have a negative impact..." (Gertz, **Betrayal**, pg. 276) This would also help explain other similar "unexplainable" military and foreign policy debacles in which the United States looked the other way with Russia.

In attendance at this meeting was Russian Foreign Minister, until his recent firing in August, 1999, Yevgeni Primakov, also the former intelligence chief. Clinton emphasized that Primakov and then Secretary of State Warren Christopher would be the primary ones to ensure that the "two sides would not do anything ... which could cause conflicts..." We know Russian security forces were used to keep the secrets of POW experimentation. The memorandum would also help explain the sudden shift from help to no help on the POW issue in Russia. Clinton valued his election and power over any other issue, including our POWs.

This last point can best be illustrated by the recent release of the Cox Report. Although the public portion deals with non POW material, again, connecting the dots will tell a lot. J. Edgar Hoover, former head of the FBI, warned Congress on March 4, 1965 that Chinese intelligence would become one of the biggest internal security problems of the future. On February 10, 1966, he continued the warning that problems with Chinese intelligence had doubled and they increased their efforts to acquire unclassified technical data and it was logical to assume that the espionage would pick up. (**Espionage**, pg. 177) These early efforts concentrated mainly on the collection of unclassified material from publishers and where there was no diplomatic mission, like the United States, they would use commercial enterprises as covers for their espionage. When I worked for IEEE (Institute of Electrical and Electronics Engineers), I discovered that one of our biggest and earliest subscribers to our technical publications was the Chinese Embassy.

In the covert operations chapter, it was established that China was using POWs to experiment on and gather technical data they had. They were as ruthless and thorough as the Russians and Vietnamese. However, their aim has been to be the biggest power broker in Asia. That, they consider, is their sphere of influence. From their earliest days of collaboration with the Soviets, the aim has been to ease out the Soviets and ease in the Chinese. Of course, they found that a Soviet economic modeled economy was no more efficient in China than in Russia. When the Soviet Union disintegrated, the security needs of the United States to "play" Russia off against China disintegrated. Instead of helping a "free" Russia, the same people then looked for another "counterweight" to China. That was Vietnam. That meant the POWs got the short end of the stick once again.

ADM Arthur W. Radford, then Chairman of the Joint Chiefs of Staff, stressed that a unified China, either free or communist, would represent a potential threat to the United States. Even Lenin wrote that the way to Paris lay through Peking. (**Strategy** pg. 233) The Soviets saw the absolute ruthless way that the Chinese used the POWs in their experimentations in order to perfect their weapons of mass destruction, nuclear, chemical and biological. These weapons the Chinese will use to pass the United States as a superpower or to dominate it in diplomatic and economic areas.

The key to our Pacific defense has been the assumption that China would be hemmed in by a chain of islands from the Kuriles to the Philippines with Taiwan as a major anchor. Under this assumption, China could not move with naval or other forces undetected as long as the United States had access to that chain. This was most succinctly addressed by GEN Douglas MacArthur in his address to the Joint Session of Congress after his dismissal by then President Harry S. Truman.

This assumption has been challenged since the fall of the USSR and the flexing of Chinese Communist muscles. China today is poised to either take over or at a minimum dominate Asian Russia. China has claimed this territory since it's annexation by Russia over a hundred years ago. Some estimate China will be ready to move in the early decades of the 21st Century (**WSJ** 4/25/96) This 800, 000 square miles would place Chinese territory thousands of miles closer to the United States and give China the ability to strike from within it's territorial waters or from land and not require the longer ranged missiles needed today. In the past, this area has been difficult for Russia to defend because of the extremely long distances from Moscow and the sparseness of the Russian and Caucasian populations vice the Chinese. This area is the direct cause of much of today's conflict. In 1936, Chiang Kai-shek was a prisoner of Mao Tse Tung's allies. He was under orders to be executed by a "People's Court" when the Soviets intervened. Stalin feared that the spreading war in Asia would engulf his Asian provinces. He was not prepared to defend them and the Chiang Kai-shek forces provided the only real deterrent to Japan. Stalin ordered the General's release and the rest is history. (Introduction *Amerasian Papers*, pg. 12 and Russian admission to this fact of history)

Should this area be lost to China, and parts of the island defense chain are already being "chipped away" by Chinese occupation of small and seemingly "insignificant" islands claimed by Japan and the Philippines, then our defense posture, vice China would need to be redrawn. China would be able to strike from within it's territorial waters and land area. In addition, our soft underbelly, the Panama Canal, may be similarly affected..

Taiwan, a key island link, is used as an intelligence gathering center. Agents from their government gather advance information on economic, commercial, and foreign policy initiatives of China. While liberals have long ridiculed this bastion, in the Korean War, the Nationalists had advance accurate knowledge of the makeup of Chinese armed forces before they were committed to battle. (**Strategy**, pg. 254)

Taiwan, a thorn in the side of China, is a key to our relations with China today. For the POWs, if we knuckle under on our relations with the country I prefer to know as the Republic of China, then we will have no leverage to recover either

POWs or remains from China. I believe that under President Clinton, nothing will happen. This Commander in Chief will do nothing to rescue subordinates in China. We know why this is with Russia. We'll now look at the issue with the Chinese.

In 1986, China adopted their 863 program to advance the PRC's "economy and ... national defense construction." Part of the 863 program was a new plan for gene research that "could have biological warfare applications." In 1997, part of the codification of the program included combine the military and civil; combine war and peace; give priority to military products; and let the civil support the military. The was the extension of the philosophy espoused by Deng Xiaoping first in 1978. (**Cox Report**, pg. 45, 46) In practice, this means the burgeoning commercial economy, instead of easing the plight of the Chinese people, actually is funding "a number of advanced weapons systems." (**Cox**, pg. 48)

Now, the People's Liberation Army has a way to provide "civilian cover for military industrial companies" for spying and other purposes. (**Cox**, pg. 49) Li Peng, second ranking member of the Chinese Politburo outlined the aim in 1996 when he said the army had to be strengthened, defense science enhanced, and a priority given to fight a high tech war and defend against the same. (**Cox**, pg. 51)

To help do this, China placed an emphasis on using "princelings" or family members of high Communist Party members and military officials to "exploit their military, commercial and political connections" to buy, illegally acquire, or pressure U.S. companies to legally or otherwise transfer high tech information to China, (*Ibid*, pg. 54) for further transfer to the Chinese Army. One of these princelings was Wang Jun, also involved in legal and illegal arms trading and who also became involved in COFCO, the company involved in the Barker affair in Chapter 11. In 1996, he also met President Clinton and Commerce Secretary Brown.

Another Princeling is LTC Liu Chaoying, Chinese Military Intelligence and connected to the Chinese missile program through her father. In 1996, she got to know how to get "foreign companies listed on the U.S. Stock Exchange," definitely a help to implement the Chinese program, courtesy of a $10,000 donation to the campaign kitty of Senator John Kerry, Chairman of the Senate POW Committee. Kerry's office said the meeting was just a "tour," although a spokesman for the Security and Exchange Commission (SEC) said it was definitely to gather the listing information. (**Rat**, pg. 206)

It is possible the $10,000 came from the Chinese Communists as Johnny Chung met with LTC Liu in Hong Kong, received $300,000 in order to help "establish reputable ties and financing for her acquisition of technology." She later, with Chung, founded Marswell Investment, Inc. The tour paid off. (**Cox**, pg. 58)

One of the potential tie-ins to the POW situation, is that the Chinese, during the Clinton watch, stole a theoretical code useful in determining the survivability of systems to electronic and dose penetrations in humans. In addition, the PRC is continuing their chemical, biological, and nuclear programs, which we have seen, use POW guinea pigs. To brass tacks on the POWs. For China, some are believed alive or at least under the influence of Chinese Vietnamese allies. If so, we have huge problems. We saw earlier the ambitious program of China to displace the United States in Asia. That was reaffirmed in the Cox Report and a 1997 book, **The Coming Conflict with China**, by specialists Richard Bernstein and Ross H. Munro. (**Betrayal**, pg. 100)

More to the point, in 1985, Naval Intelligence determined that China sought to infiltrate, take over, or otherwise acquire or control parts of our outward chain of island defenses, including Taiwan. (*Ibid*, pgs 100-101) Our resources under President Clinton to defuse or contravene the Chinese intentions has dried up including previously used assets in determining that POWs were alive.

Also, the mindset to debunk is shown conclusively in another setting. In 1996, China sold missiles to Pakistan. We had conclusive proof, yet a Clinton NSC staff director raised the intelligence bar for "proof" so high that the irrefutable became refutable, much like the 1205 document. More tellingly for our captive POWs, our NSA capabilities, unrivaled in the world, have been slashed 90% in funding for future research and development under Clinton. (*Ibid*, pgs. 158, 212)

The key to why the POW issue, despite the smoking guns, will not be resolved under Clinton or his designated successor, with the Chinese is simple. Clinton will lie and his subordinates, military and civilian, will back up his lies. In 1998, Clinton admitted that to keep the Chinese trade going, for his friends and political contributors both internally and externally, he had to "fudge" the facts to avoid automatic congressional sanctions against the repression China practices. (*Ibid*, pg. 136) However, fudging is minor compared to what we're about to discuss.

In the POW realm, we've seen where permission to inspect camps and advance notice is required. This is standard procedure with the Clinton Administration. Even in areas where we suspect our "adversaries" have committed a provocative act of war against our armed forces and we have the means to inspect to confirm our suspicions, we seek advance permission to inspect. (*Ibid*, pg. 20) We have seen where POW investigators, seeking the truth, have had their "loyalty" questioned when they go against the "party line." Clinton operatives continue this even in Congressional investigations of provocative acts of war. (*Ibid*, pg. 26)

In the POW area, we have seen where business interests come first and the POW concerns come second. This is standard operating procedure for Clinton especially where big contributors are concerned. For China, as was emphasized time after time in the Cox Report, profits come first and security concerns come later, if at all. That was part of the problem with Hughes Electronics in their stance to China (**Cox** pg. 244-45) and to President Clinton in regards to improper technology transfers (**Betrayal**, pgs. 273-74) However, DOD summarized differently in 1998 when they found that in this area we can't allow "industry to police itself when it comes to National Security... History is filled with unnecessary shortcuts in safeguards resulting in the loss of American lives... by major corporations in an effort to increase their profits..." (**Cox**, pg. 292)

Former Secretary of Defense Caspar Weinberger asked why did this happen in relation to the PRC problem as outlined in the Cox Report. Why would a President and Vice-President "so cavalierly endanger American Security?" Then he asked, "Is it really a matter so simple, so sordid, so base as campaign contributions?" (**Cox Report**, Regnery Edition, Foreward)

I say perhaps. However, as a former security officer trained in counterintelligence, I find a disturbing pattern. One that has not gone unnoticed, but most assuredly has been under reported. Because human nature does not change, what emerges in "Chinagate" impinges on the POWs. This pattern is disturbing. Reality kicked in and old training said, "look hard; as hard as if this were John Jones and not the President and Vice-President."

One part comes in a section of the Thompson Committee Report. Senators

Arlen Specter and Robert Bennett discuss a problem with identifying Ted Sieong as being used or being linked to China. The question was asked of the CIA and FBI Chiefs. They replied that the information was not in their files. Senator Bennett provided a "road map" on how to find the information. The information was later found and an FBI shake-up was reported. (**Rat** pg. 100)

Senator Specter, on October 7, 1997, revealed that the information connecting Sieong to China had been in the FBI files for two years. In an understatement he said, "incompetency goes only so far." (Pg. 9-14 **Thompson Hearings**) Earlier on the Senate Floor, he questioned if the information had been deliberately withheld. (**Rat**, pg. 100) Senator Bennett added that both the CIA and the FBI had the requested information. He asked for both a classified and unclassified version. Weeks later, the classified version showed up in the Senate classified reading room. The unclassified answer? "Oh, the fellow who handled that is on vacation..." Again understated is Bennett's remarks, "I find it distressing that once more the incompetence defense has been raised..." (9-26, 27 **Thompson Hearings**)

The Thompson Committee was on the track of what the Cox Committee verified. However, the Thompson Committee was stonewalled, delayed, and denied information as crucial witnesses fled the country in such droves that an FBI witness once testified that only in a mob trial had he seen so many witnesses disappear. Incompetence is raised on China as a defense and by extension on the POWs..

I believe, however, the answer lies elsewhere. That elsewhere is still classified, what is known is disturbing. Most has been found by *Human Events* newspaper in a series of articles and interviews with competent sources. Those interviews tie into an early 1999 report that Attorney General Janet Reno and FBI Director Louis Freeh were investigating ways of determining if Chinagate leads would be briefed to the National Security Council and the President. (The original testimony was given to the Burton Committee in August, 1998) The reason, as testified to on August 4, 1998 was that the FBI was investigating the President and Vice-President in a criminal matter. At that time, Freeh said he and Reno had determined, no, certain aspects would not be briefed, even to the President. As a follow-up, David Shippers, a Democrat who worked as lead prosecutor for the House Impeachment effort, told *Human Events* in their May 28, 1999 edition that while gagged on what classified and privileged material he had seen, he did not disbelieve that the FBI sought to go around the President on Chinagate matters.

When asked if he would have pursued the question of *quid pro quo* for the Chinese money in an impeachment trial, Shippers replied yes. When asked if the Attorney General was covering for the President in Chinagate and numerous other China related questions, Shippers again replied yes. He added that the "conspiracy" to cover-up so as to not embarrass the President on Chinagate and other related issues, went so far as to cut the FBI and Congress out of what has already been found out from an independent investigation done in the Justice Department. Rep. Chris Cannon, R-UT, said, "It's absolutely absurd to have the FBI not brief the President because it's concerned about security leaks. The enormity of that statement... it's just mind boggling... You have Louis Freeh essentially saying, 'I can't trust my President and I'm gonna keep this information from him.'" (HE 7/2/99)

Then Shippers unloaded the revelation that all of this could have come out in the impeachment trial had not liberals and all the Democrats held firm for the President. Then corroborating what I was told about the POWs by my CIA contact, Shippers said that Filegate was the foundation for Chinagate, "the big move" and that the files could have been used for "intimidation," "blackmail," or "other purposes." His purpose was to find out what. "I would play hardball like nobody's ever played hardball."

The hardball, a memorandum from FBI Director Louis Freeh and one from Charles LaBella, former director of the Justice Department Chinagate Investigative Task Force. On June 7, 1999 Rep. Curt Weldon (R-PA), a member of the Cox Committee, charged that the memorandums suggested criminal behavior by both Executive Officials and warranted independent criminal investigations. The implications here are staggering. They suggest even more forcefully than the classified memorandum that the Commander In Chief is compromised and either cannot or will not do anything to free POW hostages. Backing this assertion is the sworn testimony from one of those who originally decided not to cooperate. On August 11, 1996, Johnny Chung met with GEN Ji, the military intelligence director to the People's Liberation Army. (Testimony is from the May 11, 1999 House Government Reform and Oversight Committee) The meeting took place in China across from Macao. The upshot of this and subsequent meetings is that General Ji and LTC Liu Chaoying offered, through Chung, $300,000 to the DNC or President Clinton's reelection campaign. Why? Ji said, "We like your President very much... We hope to see him reelected..."

China's big move was to not be surprised, as it was by the 1994 vote for support to Taiwan, after spending money in the 1992 campaign. It would not be embarrassed as it was by the 1995 trip of Taiwan President Lee to the United States, after their bellicose protest of that trip.

Among some of the more important points of that meeting were: A) Chung said that Liu told him he was a "much more impressive prospect than Charlie Trie because 'I had better connections...;'" B) Liu mentioned money being sent through Mark Middleton; and C) a middle man for China both threatened Chung if he were to cooperate with the FBI and also suggested a Presidential pardon if he kept quiet.

A second item in this scenario on why POWs will not be negotiated for is that Strobe Talbott, a senior member of the administration, wrote for *Time* Magazine that the Cold War was a "paranoid fantasy" of "threat mongers" whose policy was "based on a grotesque exaggeration of what the USSR could do if it wanted." I presume with the kowtowing to China they were still, in Talbott's mind, the "agrarian reformers" who sometimes got a little out of hand like the ranch boys who went into town on Saturday night to blow off steam.

Since the Cold War was this "fantasy;" the President cannot bring up "negative things" about Russia; and Chinese intelligence "like" our President; it is small wonder that the mindset to debunk on verifiable information on POWs is spawned by a "grotesque exaggeration" of what China, Vietnam, and Russia did to our men. To get the men back will demand a housecleaning in Washington.

Finally, the ultimate question. Since we've had GEN Tighe, DIA, GEN Graham, DIA, COL Peck, DIA, MAJ Smith, DIA, COL Howard, DIA, GEN Aaron, DIA, Congressmen Dornan, Hendon, LeBoutillier, and Solomon (all on the POW Task Force), Senator Bob Smith (POW Task Force) and Senators Grassley and Helms, Bill Bell and Chip Beck from the DOD official accounting team, all say in one forum or another that POWs are alive; how is it that nothing has been done since the convictions of these men were verified by GEN Sejna (DIA and former communist official) and the 1205 document?

Now we look at the compromised angle by examining him like we would John Doe. Communists look for people who are A) dissatisfied with their jobs; B) Overindulging in alcoholic drinks (or drugs); C) greedy for money (or for power); D) promiscuous; E) have excessive ambition; F) have a breakdown in a marriage or family life; G) "leads" provided by intelligence agents; H) have amoral behavior; I) indulge in speculative deals; J) engage in commercial deals either in the Soviet Union or abroad with Soviet enterprises (can also substitute China for Soviet Union); and K) those who journey to Socialist (communist) countries. (Counterintelligence guide for the KGB; **KGB** pgs. 128-129)

We know the Chinese want to operate their covert war by gaining access to "economic, military and political" targets of opportunity. (**Cox**, pg. 329) In the case of Bin Wu, the Chinese took an internal dissident and "turned" (KGB style) him into an agent. Basically, he was told, "you cooperate and you can leave. Don't and you'll stay." He was expressly told to work over a long period of time; find a way to the White House; and meet congressmen. "Don't worry," they added, "we have our own people there..." (FBI report in **Rat**, pgs. 125-127)

Johnny Chung was told by Chinese intelligence that Charlie Trie was one of theirs. He said that Mark Middleton, formerly of the White House, "got half a million" to do good things for or to benefit China." (**Human Events**, 5/21/99 pg. 7) Charlie Trie was described by Senator Tom Daschle (POW Committee) as a big player in Washington (Thompson Committee). Trie also gave just under a million dollars to the Clinton Defense Fund. Trie delivered a letter, through Middleton, to the President laying out a basic ultimatum on Taiwan. This also was in line with a threat from a Chinese General that we would not exchange Los Angeles for Taiwan in war. Further in 1994, China squared off against the US navy in the Yellow Sea while Chinese officials promised a US DIA attaché that force would be used the next time. (**USV** through press sources, Dec 1994, pg.4)

Next, with Chinese military intelligence agents and agents of influence constantly in the White House, hundreds of times, you develop a "red flag" of concern. In addition, people who developed Chinese policy worked, prior to government service, for a company described as a tool for Chinese intelligence; another flag of concern. Additionally, the Chief of Chinese Army Intelligence expresses an interest in seeing an incumbent President and his Vice-President reelected after intelligence agencies uncover a very real plot to influence our elections. We've been told multiple times that the public has only seen "one percent" of what the FBI has. Finally, the head counsel for impeachment proceedings and the head of the FBI are worried about a *quid pro quo* for campaign contributions. It took only a foreign bank account on John Huang for security officials to be concerned.

No, there will be no POW progress under this President or his chosen successor. Has he been compromised? Taking the progress made on the POW issue, the backsliding of support for Taiwan, and the kowtowing to Russia, Vietnam, and China on multitudes of issues, there is a void of logical reasons for the actions. It's your call on what you believe. For me, I agree with former Presidential candidate, Alan Keyes that "If nobody else in this country and nobody else in this party will call it by its right name, I will. He (President Clinton and his chosen successor Mr. Gore) has assaulted the security of this country by his treasonous betrayal of our national security." (Iowa GOP Straw Poll Presidential event, 8/14/99)

The Public Must Act!

Vociferous public outcries helped POWs before. Only in movies like "Rambo" and "Uncommon Valor" have POWs been "officially" rescued. Certain elements of the media have been helpful. Over the years, I have cooperated with numerous network officials, talk show hosts, network programs, and newspaper reporters. There are too many to name all of them but Bill Paul of the *Wall Street Journal*, Ron Miller of *ABC National News*, columnist Jack Anderson, and the Stevensons of **Kiss the Boys Goodbye** helped tremendously in informing the public. In various ways, we worked together in sharing information; each doing the story their own way. That is the way it should be done. That is the **Phoenix concept**.

War crimes

Here is what I advocate. We need to plan for war crime trials for the leadership in Hanoi and other countries if we do not get back, now, our unreturned POWs and MIA remains. There is precedent. We proceeded in July, 1997 against butchers in Bosnia. We planned the same for Pol Pot in Kampuchea. Vo Van Kiet and his Soviet masters deserve the same tender mercies. For Clinton, the Commander in Chief when the 1205 document was discovered supporting the Minority findings of the Senate POW Committee, let history decide his fate.

The Trial Judge in *Smith* ruled "... The court has reviewed all ... factual material submitted ... and concludes that there is subject matter jurisdiction ... to determine the issues of fact ... At the heart ... is the question of whether living American servicemen ... continue to be held ... The Plaintiffs allege that such a class exists ... The Defendants argue that the political ... doctrine ... The Defendants ... become the sole judges of the facts ...The Hostage Act ... creates a class of citizens, i.e., American citizens held captive ... this class has certain rights ... The act mandates that it shall be the duty of the President and that the President shall use such means to obtain or effectuate the release of the hostages... Accordingly, the Court finds that there is an implied cause of action under the Hostage Act..."

Judge Terrence W. Boyle further disagreed that the administration of foreign policy was the sole domain of the Executive Department, making it, in the words of Boyle, "the sole judges of the facts involved in executing the law merely because the contested facts involved a question of foreign affairs. This claim of power is in excess of the constitutional authority vested in the executive branch."

Boyle argued that the **political process** which is the public's only recourse in a ideal situation failed to afford relief. "Indeed, this is precisely the core of the plaintiffs' claim: that despite ... hearings and investigation of this issue by Congress and ... petitions to the President ... there has been a deliberate strategy on the part of the Executive Branch, the defense agencies and the government intelligence agencies to conceal what plaintiffs allege to be the true facts....To read the Article II powers of the executive branch as vesting the exclusive authority to determine the facts that it will use in administering the government and executing the laws of the United States as it applies to the alleged class of persons in this case 'would upset the constitutional balance of a workable government and gravely impair the role of the courts under Article III' ... The Supreme Court, in considering the Hostage Act, stated that 'the enactment of legislation closely related to the question of the President's authority in a particular case which evinces legislative intent to accord the President broad discretion may be considered to invite measures on independent presidential responsibility.'" Boyle further found ,"the language and legislative history of the Hostage Act convince us that Congress placed a judicially enforceable duty on the Executive to inquire into the circumstances of an American citizen's extended detention abroad." Likewise, since the Congress has joint powers with the Executive over the military in terms of rules of conduct, how the armed forces are constituted, they have an enforceable duty to determine if he has been negligent towards his subordinates. Congress needs to exercise vigorously this responsibility.

To get this ruling into the Court of Appeals and nullified, the Executive Department argued that "the evidence necessary to decide the factual issue of ... live prisoners of war would ... involve classified intelligence and military information ..."; the old bugaboo, National Security. Clinton refused to act when confronted with the 1205 document. It was the first "smoking gun on the issue." The document explains many historical happenings and why refugees have reported seeing POWs. Instead, he upheld activities of Lippo, a foreign company involved in Vietnam. Possibly, Clinton even bottled up huge coal deposits in southern Utah to give world commercial advantage to Indonesia, home of Lippo.

Numerous press accounts detail Chinese agents accessing President Clinton directly via Huang's influence; posing severe internal security questions. Combine this with the reported bribes given to the late Secretary of Commerce Ron Brown from Vietnam totaling $700,000 for the Clinton administration's dropping the trade embargo and other concessions. Since the POWs could not provide campaign money, they apparently were abandoned by their Commander in Chief.

James Iredell, in his writings on the Presidency, Spies, the Pardoning Power, and Impeachment (North Carolina Convention debate, 7/28/1788), observed that "If the President had received a bribe without the privity or knowledge of the Senate, from a foreign power, and had, under the influence of that bribe, had address enough with the Senate by artifices and misrepresentation, to seduce their consent to a pernicious treaty - if it appeared afterwards that this was the case, would not the Senate ... exclaim against his villainy? Would they not feel a particular resentment against him for their being made the instrument of his treacherous purposes?" Unfortunately for us, this was predicated upon honest politicians.

Coincidentally, Senator John Kerry is related to C. Stewart Forbes, Chief Executive Officer of the Boston based Colliers International. In December, 1992, Vietnam granted Colliers a contract designating them the "exclusive real estate agent representing Vietnam." They have written contracts since then worth billions and are possibly involved with Lippo. (**USV**, Jan-Feb 1997, pg. 5)

A further coincidence shows Senator McCain approving Anheuser - Busch planned investments in Vietnam while openly opposing reforms in the POW - MIA accountability act, and benefitting from his father-in-law's Busch distributorship. Both deny "proof" of POWs held in captivity.

McCain retired as a Captain in the Navy. Were his promotions with his contemporaries, as with most other POWs, or did he receive the benefit of mentoring from the late Senator John Tower? I presume he was what is described as a "late bloomer" in showing his military mettle. <u>Only an informed and enraged public can bring this last sad chapter to the Vietnam experience to a conclusion</u>.

Contradicting Clinton's spin doctors

In looking at the 1205 document, let's examine why you should take it seriously. This TOP SECRET document from the Kremlin and Vietnamese archives belies the cover stories of the Vietnamese and their American apologists. This "secret" of the Vietnamese is a keystone of this book. Let's examine it a little further for authenticity. One section says, "368 POWs holding progressive views can be released first; — 372 POWs hold neutral positions; — 465 hold reactionary views ... All the POWs among the senior officers hold reactionary views ... " This categorization of POWs by political views was crucial to who could be sent home. Le Dinh, in a summary I received about him years before the finding of this 1205 document said, "Dinh also has intelligence information on the categorizing of US POWs during and after the war which apparently has a determining affect on who of the POWs was returned and who was not." He estimated 700 POWs were held.

One argument read that there was no evidence of senior POWs being segregated in captivity. Yet, DIA, in 1976 said of Alcatraz, it "became operational in October 1967 when 12 prisoners captured in North Vietnam were moved into this facility. These men were either high ranking PWs or PWs known to North Vietnamese as 'trouble makers.'" This would be equivalent to POWs of "reactionary views" or as Garwood's "non-progressives." Other readings of the DIA submission to Congress shows a segregation by country captured, by being troublemakers, or to become a showplace for the outside world of acknowledged prisoners..

Quang said that among the prisoners were those from diversionary detachments inserted into the border region between the DRV and Laos and on other special operations. Op Plan 34A shows this happened. Quang claimed increasing the number of prisons after Son Tay. The classified DIA study of the "possible" 18 other prisons shows the reaction of some of those prisons to Son Tay along with other proven POW locations. This document proves the second tier of POW prisons asserted by intelligence officers and elements of the Senate POW Committee.

The 368 POWs acknowledged by Quang by no means infers that they were all "progressive." Some were "obstinate" by Vietnamese standards. However, some POWs had to be released. Further, almost 200 more POWs and MIAs were later lost in Southeast Asia and only fifty seven of those returned. Quang described those holding "neutral positions" as their "political outlook is not fully progressive, yet not too reactionary.... they still do not clearly understand the role of the American administration in unleashing the aggressive war in Indochina."

Quang confirms a reason for holding men back. Besides compensation, the POWs were political pawns for the "successful resolution of the Vietnam problem ... when the American government resolves the political and military issues on all three fronts of Indochina, we will set free all American POWs. We consider this a very correct course." Earlier Quang said, "This is not political horse trading but rather an but rather an important condition ... for successful resolution of the Vietnam problem. That is why the matter of the American POWs has great significance in exposing Nixon's designs." What the Vietnamese did not count on was the abandonment of our military men, leaving them with several hundred POWs.

Dirty little secrets of the U.S.

The Public Must Act!

Liberal policies in Vietnam have been shortsighted, irrelevant to the real world, and disastrous. Liberals have miscalculated the politics and policies of the Vietnamese enemies. The end result has been the deceits described in this book. Elements of the U.S. government forced Diem to accept Duong Van Minh into his government in order to be "democratic." (Unpublished elements of the **Pentagon Papers**). Minh eventually orchestrated the murdering of Diem and the surrendering of free Vietnam after being invited back into the political process by the North Vietnamese Politburo. He had relatives in the enemy hierarchy. These same liberal elements never forced a communist government to accept "democrats" into their government. Senator Kerry, over the Memorial Day weekend, 1997, argued that such a course in China would be unworkable. Quite a switch from his positions vis a vis free Vietnam.

Elements of our government helped assassinate the leadership of a free Vietnam because they dared negotiate on their own with the Communist leaders of the North. Had policies begun under Diem been allowed to flower, perhaps hundreds of thousands of casualties could have been averted. Had Diem been allowed to live and govern, Vietnam would probably be free today. On the day of his overthrow, Diem met with a general of free China exploring the receiving of money keeping his security forces intact after liberals cut off their funds. Other security arrangements were also explored. (**Father Raymond DeJaegher to author**)

After the assassination of Diem, liberal policy makers lacked the guts to follow through to win the war. They started covert actions like OP Plan 34A, DeSoto, and Hardnose knowing inevitably it would lead to full American involvement. For political reasons, they used just enough effort to keep Vietnam from falling to the stupidity of their own moves, but not allowing it to survive as an independent nation. They kept the plans secret to elect Johnson in 1964.

Liberals likewise forced President Thieu to "reach out" to subversive elements to show how democratic he was. Twice, in 1968 and in 1972, he was threatened with assassination if he did not comply. (Letter, October 6, 1972 from Nixon to Thieu, **Palace File** pg. 376) Thieu had to accept hundreds of thousands of enemy troops in his country for the "privilege" of remaining in office. Kissinger arranged for that and guaranteed the eventual overthrow of free Vietnam.

Far more importantly, the wording of the Paris Peace Accords, in the Vietnamese, were word for word liftings from the 1969 10 point program of the Viet Cong. (Appendix F Analysis for President Thieu by Hung, **Palace File, pgs. 446 - 8**) We fought for 4 years, lost billions in equipment, suffered thousands of dead, thousands of wounded, hundreds of POWs and MIAs, to force the Vietnamese to accept the terms we refused in 1969. Kissinger was no conservative and no friend of the military, thinking them to be dumb appendages to his foreign policy schemes.

In 1963, 1968, and 1972, we lost opportunities to guarantee a free Vietnam. We now have had hundreds of POWs from Vietnam, successors to thousands from Korea and WWII, because liberal politicians lack political courage. On March 12, 1999, we accepted into NATO, the Czech, Polish, and Hungarian Republics. Yet, in all the hoopla surrounding this momentous occasion, the POWs/MIAs became lost. Remember the words of Beck, "... the transfer of American POWs was more or less an 'open secret' in the government hierarchies of Hungary, Czechoslovakia, East Germany, and Poland during the Cold War. Officials of the present day governments... are aware of the clandestine Soviet transfer operations and experimental programs for which the POWs were used..." Madeline Albright, proud of her Czechoslovakia, forgot her American allegiance.

The end or a new beginning?

Why did I write this book? I will say only once, I have to tell this story. I have no choice. I hope this is the final version. What you are reading is the end of a thirty six year project on Vietnam and this subject. God has been gracious and allowed me to meet the late Father DeJaegher; heads of Air Force Intelligence, Defense Intelligence; officials in the CIA, NSA, ASA, Joint Star, CEEA, and other intelligence agencies; and those with White House privileges.

I trained for seven years to become an Army officer. After commissioning in 1968, I trained at the Infantry School, the Intelligence School and directly entered the Phoenix program. Later, I received training in Electronic Warfare and Tactical Cover and Deception. The book contains some of what I did there. I was the first full time Phoenix advisor in each of my districts. Earlier I told of my interest in LTG John Wilson "Iron Mike" O'Daniel. I recently learned that he also worked as an intelligence officer in the Soviet Union. Prior to going to Vietnam, I read most of the books available on Vietnam, including classified studies. Arizona State was a government repository and contained a fine Asian Studies Department. My knowledge of Vietnam grew as I honed debating skills backing our being there. All that "cerebral knowledge" however, is nothing compared to looking at a Viet Cong across an interrogation table. Your senses race as you climb into the back seat of an OV-1 Bird-dog and fly over areas known to harbor VC forces. You then fit written reports received with the reality of what you observe on the ground.

You feel elated when your agent network brings information on a POW camp and you put together a full description of where it is and what type of forces might be protecting it. Discouragement sets in when you realize your area is on the bottom of the list to get reaction forces for any rescue. Vindication comes when you read Nick Rowe's book showing the areas you knew about all along held POWs. That compensates until you hear the government tell people that you and Rowe were wrong, the U-Minh never held "confirmed" POWs after Rowe escaped.

The binding tie of combat

There is no better way to gain information than to go on recon and examine an area firsthand. You can then formulate plans using what you know about the enemy's tactics to capture or eliminate him. It is especially rewarding when your ideas work and forge a lasting working relationship with your Vietnamese counterpart.

Sometimes your ideas concerning combat and the risks you face change when you carry battlefield casualties to a helicopter for their final journey anywhere. I've had to get up at three in the morning to go identify dead VCI turned in by villagers who were tired of being intimidated. I had to also identify the body of a poor American soldier who drowned while swimming in a river. His body was recovered a week later. I also remember patrolling the deep mire of rice paddies enveloping my body well past my knees.

I recall vividly a Vietnamese civil servant showing me a long ugly scar left by a VC during interrogation. I think of the Vietnamese officer who laughed when we told him how long it would be before we returned home. He said I've got many years before my duty ends and I'm already home. These experiences prepared me mentally for two realities. First, no human institution binds together people tighter than those links forged in combat. That is why Vietnam vets are assertive about bringing their "brothers" home. The second is mortality and your obligations to your Creator. This book is the result of dual obligations to God and fellow vets.

Every fiber of my being tells me POWs are alive. Specifically, I researched tens of family reports on unreturned POWs. I talked with tens of other families. For the late Dermot Foley, I investigated all known material on Bobby Garwood. I interviewed Garwood and talked with Tighe. Many intelligence analysts told me of POWs they tracked over the years. I found Dutch and his corroboration for Hendrix and Lacy. I read Sejna's testimony.

Our government brings forth "documents" from inside the archives of Hanoi to prove no Americans survived. These received great play in the media. Let's look at what the reviews did not say. The Vietnamese dirty little secret of killing American POWs was passed on verbally with no documentation. Evidence was arranged for by "leaks" inside Hanoi's government. However, this program was instituted by mid-level American personnel who always proclaimed all Americans were dead. In my estimation, the whole program was incredulous. However, such a "program" is a good cover story for denying POW existence.

My contention is at the end of the war, U.S. internal politics and "security" considerations dictated "hiding" the knowledge of our men. We had a Cold War to fight and knowledge of what happened to some of the men might trigger something no one wanted. Simultaneously, a problem occurred. Documents and witnesses swore knowledge of Americans being left behind, including those that could not be discredited easily. What to do?

As any good Cover and Deception man will say, the answer is simple. Deny! Look the protagonists square in the eye and say "your information is wrong." Infiltrate the main groups opposing you with people who emerge first as heroes and then slowly and subtly become agents provocateurs. Using your own security forces, discredit the agents provocateurs. Slowly, sympathy for the POW / MIA cause falls because no "proof" emerges. People you cannot convince by denials, you ignore. Walter Cronkite is a case in point. Eventually, even the best quit.

The $4.75 billion offered to Vietnam, via Nixon and Kissinger, takes on a new meaning courtesy of the 1205 document. The men left behind posed a problem. The Vietnamese at any time could emerge them and cause internal political problems. Vietnamese negotiators gave subtle messages they could do it all along. The Vietnamese were embarrassed when Garwood came home. A legitimate prisoner, he became, for both sides, an issue. The result was Garwood's trial.

However, the message sank home that other "Garwoods" were out there. Who were they? Part of the answer stared us in the face all these years. We said that no one with disfigurements, severe burns, amputations, or severe mental problems came home. That leaves the proposition many unreturned POWs have these conditions. Witness the testimony of Sejna. Many others were the "technical" people useful to Hanoi and the Soviets in their projects. "Hard core" prisoners were other men left behind. Quang covered both situations. Still others were held by local "drug lords" or local power brokers.

How to get POWs home. Some are home already, in protected witness type programs and classified government hospital wards. Families have quietly been approached and scenarios laid out assuring them that their men were home and OK if only they would not disrupt the program and quietly disappear politically.

Not doing so would jeopardize POWs still unreturned. Subtle family pressures can keep people quiet. As God is my witness, I cannot believe some of the pure bull droppings shoved my way as explanations of why we cannot get our men home or why we do not know they are there.

As an analyst, you reach a decision to do something. In your guts, you know the truth. Mooney, Minarcin, Peck, Smith, Howard, McIntire, Aaron, Gritz, Hendon, Sejna, Bell and Tighe all reached that point; they acted. I decided to keep this book alive. Battling to get the publishing rights took several years. In the meantime, I forged new relationships, friendships, and sources.

One constant guides me. I can forgive leaderships who decide to break with the past and "find" our men. I can forgive "enemies" who change. I cannot forget American wimps turning their backs on our fighting men, abandoning them as yesterday's problems. How do we explain the years of neglect? The Israelis do not abandon their men. Each man is valuable. Their soldiers realize that they will not be forgotten. Without that standard, we are lost as a civilized nation. Until we return to the Teddy Roosevelt pronouncement of our men returned or your civilization destroyed, we cannot be seriously taken as a "superpower."

Fortunately, Congress changed the MIA rules alleviating the weaknesses I pointed out in 1979 and 1986. They even are trying to open up a little bit for POWs / MIAs from prior wars. That law passed in 1996. Of course, they had to undo some of Senator McCain's 1996 chicanery in 1997.

Let me state clearly for the record. I am proud to be a Vietnam vet and proud of my intelligence background. We did the right thing in helping Vietnam try to stay free of communist domination. Unfortunately, like Phyllis Schlafly wrote in her book on Kissinger, they did not stand a chance because our liberal policies, set in TOP SECRET stone in the Pentagon Papers, would not allow them the opportunity to fight for their own freedom.

Will you support the call for war crimes trials? I will forget that call if many POWs and MIAs come home "immediately." Otherwise, I go ahead. In prior duties as an associate publisher for a newspaper, I have been called provocative, irritating, and pointed in my assessments. I have never been called boring. I hope this book fills that billing. I will end this book with the label I tagged several hundred columns (as a nod to my unabashed conservatism). This book is being brought to you from **The Starboard Side....**

Epilogue

This is the part of the book where the author gets to wrap up loose ends. As I wrote earlier, things usually happen when you write a book like this. They have. I have run across a few things that will strengthen my case and answer some questions that are probably lingering in people's minds. And then, I met a good friend named "Fred," who is very knowledgeable about the POW/MIA issue and whose insight helped focus some of my thinking.

First of all, as of December 31, 1999, the "official" number of "unaccounted for POWs/MIAs" from Southeast Asia is 2031. That figure is courtesy of the National League of Families. While I have been harsh on that organization, the last few things I have seen have shown that while we do not agree on methodologies and probably on little else, they seem to be pointed at least in the direction that maybe they got themselves unfocused. It must have come as a shock to everyone that the government has picked 2004 as the year for "ending" the charade they call "accounting." The National Alliance of Families (and several e mails through POW activist groups) gave me that information. After that date, the intention is to focus on rapidly closing cases in the future. Kind of like going back to Korea again. Those bureaucrats will never learn that closing early means you're doing your job and forcing the other side to be honest.

In the cases of Thomas Hart and George Macdonald, the AC-130 shot down on December 21, 1972, I pinned down some dates that I knew, but couldn't find. The DOD rescinded the findings that the remains found at Pakse were of Thomas Hart and George Macdonald in 1987. Further at the site run by Jennifer Martinez, referred to earlier with the E&E photo, two of the men Mark Smith had knowledge of were Hart and Macdonald. Martinez is one of thousands of people running POW/MIA sites on the Web remind a new generation, not to mention prod the older ones, that POWs and MIAs were abandoned by a government who will say one thing and do the opposite.

In early 2000, I met some remarkable people at CPAC 2000, including Frank Gaffney Jr., and Gary Aldrich. Gaffney runs the Center for Security Policy. In one of his policy statements, he ran across some very interesting material. It seems that predictably, after the recognition of Hanoi, the Clinton Administration has found that the reciprocity policy, advocated by Dermot Foley and so many others long ago, was best after all. The more we give in to Hanoi, "the less forthcoming the Vietnamese actually become." Gaffney reiterated a finding in a June 28, 1995 Dornan hearing that most of the remains returned by Vietnam are eventually established as "animal or non-American individuals."

Gaffney spotlighted the testimony of Michael Janich, described earlier in the book, who said that while he was a Laos team leader he reported regularly the occurrences of "witness coaching, prompting, and intimidation;" along with withholding of information and documents that would amount to "obstructions of our investigation efforts." In addition, Major Sandra Coughlin, who evaluated the field investigations of live sighting incidents (LSI), swore "the results of these investigations are not credible." She continued, "We must question the validity of all the live sighting investigations" in Laos because "the investigations are going to be hindered by the government" in Laos. She determined it may be "impossible" to establish a credible live sighting mechanism.

The same can be said of Vietnam, given the facts you read earlier in the book about the "cooperation" they rendered. A February 1994 article in the **American Spectator** magazine reinforces some points I made earlier in the book. In 1971, A Vietnamese doctor said American POWs were being held in numbers greater than were being acknowledged. No surprise there. What is surprising is that a CIA declassified document said, "the possibility of a second prison system for the detention of American POWs cannot be disregarded." They said this as they disregarded it publicly.

More chillingly, in light of Sejna's revelations, is that South Vietnamese prisoners reported to the government that at Tan Lap, Quyet Tien, Yen Bai, Ha Son Binh and Thanh Hoa, they buried in cemeteries, POWs in the late 1970s and 1980s, some of whom might have been murdered.

Finally, John Kerry, it is charged, told one investigator that if the report of POWs alive to 1989 ever leaked out, "you'll wish you've never been born."

Gary Aldrich helped me form more closely what I feel about the Clinton/Gore team on the issue. I wrote I agreed with Alan Keyes. Let me add this postscript. I also agree with the analysis Aldrich provided that the ideological stance of the Clintons and Gore form the basis to explain what they did. To me, it would also logically explain the flow of Chinese money to them and why the Chinese "liked" the team. Their ideological stance, rather than a simple term, compromised, means that a true passionate believer is more effective for the other side than one who had been compromised. A look at the Venona intercepts from the World War II era will adequately back that up. We got hurt more by believers in the Soviet system who actively, passionately, believed they were working for the betterment of mankind than by ones who the Soviets compromised.

Of course, the end result, the damaging of the United States, it's security posture, and the harm done to POW/MIAs is all the same, regardless of why they did it. The record still stands.

Before I get to "Fred," let me say that I have also made contact with Joe Douglass Jr, the source for Sejna; Bill Bell; Chip Beck; and Mark Smith. That will enable me to keep abreast of things. The drug connection is one that is evolving and I have made more contemporaneous contacts with people who shall remain in the background. The ones I have made convince me even more about the existence of the rogue element in our intelligence agencies that need to be checked. Our system is set up to be exploited by these elements and they have rushed in to fill the void. As I was told, the POW-MIAs became problems to other issues and were exploited for their value to hide other exploits. Let me make explicit one more time, the material covering Shackley, Armitage, etc. are charges made by others. I have covered those charges. My personal opinion is that these allegations must be investigated fully and completely to lay to rest all suspicions surrounding them.

"Fred" is a career bureaucrat. He's been around for decades and has seen a lot of material. He was helpful on some things and silent on others. For example, on the Richard Barker affair, Fred said that DIA knew of the plans, as Barker believed. They even knew of the film, including material on Charles A. Dale. Further, our agencies knew of the reported transfer of David Demmon to Cambodia, after being seen in the U-Minh.

Epilogue

Backing up BG Lacy, Fred said that despite the official stance of the government, our intelligence agencies received several reports that Pogreba had indeed been downed over China, as Lacy said. It appears that he may have been downed over Hainan Island.

Team Scorpio was not the only OP PlAN 34A commandos to leave Vietnam, Fred said. As early as 1985, DIA knew of the release of people from Team Hadley, captured in 1962. They informed DIA of the escape of "others." In a play on words, Fred made mention of an 1994 Air Force study about POWs and Laos. Often called the "Black Hole," Fred said the study would shed some light on that black hole and confirm that "505" U.S. citizens, at least, were lost during the war years.

Fred was very familiar with my "dog tag" report. Contrary to the popular rumors spread to me and others on the case, this particular person was independently reported by persons other than those I knew, at times other than when I knew of him. However, the reports were unanimous that he was imprisoned in Nam Ha prison. One refugee even claimed he may have died there. This is strange considering that officially, he made it back from Vietnam in 1970, very much alive.

Fred said that those who are interested should look up reports on Project X and Project 400. These reports carried conclusions that in 1976, during the time of the Montgomery Hearings, conclusions were reached by JCRC and others that at least 57 men could be alive at that time. Quite a contrast from the Findings of that Committee and their erstwhile staff.

Where Fred shed some more light was the correlation that existed in the mind of LTG Tighe when he testified on June 25, 1981, in classified session, on the connection between Paul W. Bannon and Paul Mercland. Fred said there was a deeper connection than what the record of the meeting shows. From 1969 on, DIA was receiving information on Mercland and or Bannon. The reports were all concentrating on the Mahaxy / Kham Keut region. Fred even raised the heretofore unknown possibility that the other person in Bannon's plane, Peter Pike survived. Even the infamous JTFFA, Fred said, could not put to "official rest" information on Bannon or Mercland. In 1998, they could not "resolve" the case by death because of "insufficient" evidence.

Fred knew about Sejna's case also. He pointed out that for years our intelligence agencies were receiving collateral information about "high security" hospital sites in Vietnam and elsewhere. Native specialists received training in specialized forms of medicine including chemical and biological warfare. Some of the reports mentioned the treatment of American POWs. A former CIA source also told me that Sejna was right on concerning his allegations.

Citing his precarious position, Fred would not comment on Clinton and the POWs. However, others were not silent. To understand their actions, as confirmed to me by Aldrich, one has to understand their politics. In August 1999, Sidney Blumenthal was characterized by the American Conservative Union as the "White House 'smear man.'" While they attributed this to his efforts to aid the impeached President, the title was probably earned years ago. He had a decade long association with the IPS before being hired by the Washington Post in 1984. His job there was described as being mainly attack pieces on President Reagan and conservative policies. In 1986, he attempted to sabotage funding for democratic forces in Nicaragua. Congressional investigation into his lead story found his charges "baseless." (**Covert** pg. 112)

President Clinton has an affinity for people associated with the Communist Chinese. Samuel R. "Sandy" Berger, is the National Security Advisor. He was associated with a legal firm, identified by a liberal Democrat, as a "point man' for the Chinese Trade Office. A McGovernite, who met the Clintons in 1972, Berger has been particularly effective in arguing for reduced restrictions for high technology transfers to China. He also helped blunt the criminal investigation into a technology transfer by a big Democratic campaign contributor. (**Rat**, pg. 184-85)

Berger also headed the National Security Staff during the time when William Safire charged, accurately according to the FBI, that the FBI was worried that "secret intelligence" both from agents and intercepts, would, if shared with the National Security Staff, make it to Chinese "operatives" close White House policy makers. The additional fear was that the Chinese investigation would then be "shut down." (Safire, *NY Times*, 7/16/98, Freeh testimony August 1998 Burton Committee). Given the fact that the head of the CIA under Clinton, John Deutch, was known for years to have taken home for use on an unclassified computer, top secret code word covert programs, among others, and then type reports on it and someone used the same computer to go to pornographic sites and correspond on e mail to Russia, lends credence to FBI misgivings. In the correct circumstances, whatever Deutch typed out could be intercepted with proper equipment. Since Russia blatantly was caught recently eavesdropping in our own State Department, it is likely that Deutch's home was likewise targeted.

Like Aldrich said, to know the workings of the Clinton Administration, one has to know Bill and Hillary. So I looked again. Both are "radical" or to be kind, like to associate with "radical" money. They were staffers on the McGovern campaign. Hillary Rodham was a legal staffer for the House impeachment panel of President Nixon. Bill was a draft evader and demonstrator in Moscow and later Asia. That would have drawn the attention of the KGB.

In the 1970s, Clinton came to the attention of alleged China intelligence operator Charlie Trie and the Riady family. Trie was one Bill confided in that he would run for President. Hillary was law partners with Riady targets Webster Hubbell and Joe Giroir. Clinton has appointed many persons with ties to Chinese operatives or intelligence agencies there or elsewhere. Hillary was a Director in the 1980s of The New World Foundation which gave $15,000 to the National Lawyers Guild (a reputed communist front) and CISPES, also strongly affiliated with international communist groups. (**Covert** pg. 239) The Foundation also contributed to IPS, one of whose founders, Robert Borosage, was a classmate of Hillary. Her apparent devotion to IPS and it's objectives contributed to her involvement with the Black Panthers and the antiwar movement, both special IPS projects.

None of this has phased Democrat supporters, like Tom Daschle, POW Committee fame, who in writing a recommendation for John Huang said on 1/8/93, "I have known John Huang for four years... I can personally attest to John's strong background in trade and Pacific Rim issues..." Left unsaid was Huang's feelings about Vietnam, trade, and the eventual abandonment of POWs.

President Clinton, in late 1999, allowed to go free FALN terrorists if they would renounce terrorism. He did, and they didn't. Between 1974 and 1983, FALN carried out 130 bombings. While his wife's Senate campaign might explain some of his motives or provide political cover, it has to be remembered that IPS was, through Orlando Letelier, an IPS Fellow, in contact with the FALN, Weathermen,

PLO, and other terrorist organizations. Hillary's organizations had ties with the FALN and their political beliefs provided the affinity to explain Clinton's action and the First Lady's fascination with a "Palestinian" State. (**Covert** pg. 218)

Finally, in this line, The *Los Angeles Times* featured on February 6, 2000, a rendering of some of Charlie Trie's debriefing by the FBI. Trie raised $200,000 from a Jakarta businessman, Tomy Winata, a billionaire, and an aide to the Chief of Chinese Intelligence. Funds were to be used for DNC contributions and to reimburse donors to the Clinton Defense Fund. Trie, despite all the evidence presented here and elsewhere, denied ties to China's intelligence but said that he did form a business arrangement with apparently LTC Liu Chaoying, who had close ties to General Ji Shenada, chief of PLA intelligence. And in a humorous line, Vice President Gore went the incompetence defense one better. In an interview early in February 2000, he said he wasn't really paying attention to facts about the Buddhist Temple "fund-raiser" and other things because he was drinking too much tea and the real good stuff was discussed while he was in the toilet. (Drudge Report)

For those who disbelieve the injection theory of positioning finding, as relates to the POWs, then you'll want to see Joseph Farah's column on 2/14/2000 on World Net Daily. There he discussed exactly what I talked about. It seems like the military aspect has been converted into a "nonmilitary" aspect. It took several years for the mainline press to discuss the microchip "bypass the broken spine" that I found out about in mid 1987.

The thought that occurred to me and others on Sejna's testimony was did our government want to dismiss him so as to not expose some of our own experimentation along the same lines? Did we not want to acknowledge either the Soviet experimentation on our own men and thus risk exposure of our own programs? Briefly, we had our own program, MKULTRA. Others have explained it (John Marks, **The Search for the "Manchurian Candidate" : The CIA and Mind Control**) Although written from a liberal standpoint, it does show what we did and how. Where he went wrong was to blithely accept the government's contention that the Soviets did not engage in the same programs (pg. 31). If he thought what was given to him really represented what the Soviets and Chinese did and they did not engage in mind control experimentation, (pg. 136, 138), then his liberal eyes needed adjusting. As you read the next section, think about Sejna's testimony and then remember that according to an early veteran of MKULTRA, it stands for Making Killers Utilizing Lethal Tradecraft Requiring Assassinations. One project involved the attempted assassination of Prince Norodom Sihanouk, Cambodia, (Project Cherry) and another probably helped in the assassination of Diem.

Marks missed evidence on pages xvi, xvii, 220 and 227 plus the footnote on page 10 on what the CIA knew about Russian projects.. Our POWs from North Korea coming from Russia, through a special zone in Manchuria, had a "blank period of disorientation." A Russian defector described the secret laboratories, off limits to all but those in on the program, and variously described as *Spets Byuro #1* or the *Kamera*. The experimentation Marks found done by our side included a "drug program" including human control, radiation, electro - shock, and harassment substances. Project OFTEN helped develop a drug to simulate a "heart attack or stroke" and one wonders if also stimulate the same type of heart attack or stroke. All similar to what Sejna said the Russians had. One has to be naive to believe only we did this type of testing and not the other side.

Finally, in fairness to Clinton and his policies, in September 1999, Albright said the opening of the new consulate in Saigon, next door to the old embassy building, was made possible, because of the "excellent cooperation," the Vietnamese had displayed on the POW/MIA issue. What type of cooperation did they exhibit? From her own words, expressed in **Far Eastern Economic Review**, it was the return of a "few" remains in September, just in coincidental timing for the occasion, that "paved the way" for consulate ties in Saigon.

Even more telling is the March, 2000, arrival of Secretary of Defense William Cohen in Vietnam, just in time for the 25th Anniversary of the ending of the war in Vietnam, or as the communists call it, the defeat of the American Imperialists. He said, that the timing was coincidental and that he had no intention of apologizing for the war. However, in the Orient, "face" is important. The timing is just like the "defeated foe" arriving at the celebration of the "conqueror" to do tribute to those who conquered him. Hanoi announced last year, twice putting off a similar trip, the timing was not right. What changed their mind, other than the scenario I outlined here? Cohen did not come to ask about unresolved cases of those last known alive, or to ask about information of those suspected to be alive. He did, however, go to a crash site to resolve a case of two MIAs. That is their priority, no emphasis on live Americans, but use any excuse to advance the political aims of Hanoi. A spokesman for one affected family strongly protestested Cohen using his father's case to show "progress." I said I could be fair, but sometimes the truth is not "fair." But then, I never said I would be a PR flack for their side, did I?

Finally, on February 26,2000, the *Associated Press* reported about a diary kept by a Soviet citizen who asserts that servicemen from the 1940's and 1950's were "silently swallowed up in the" USSR, "never to be heard from again." This time, a US official said, "There has to be something to this... the memoir is exceptional because it provides names of individual servicemen..." On March 10, 2000, the LaBella memorandum was "leaked" to the *L.A. Times* in an apparent attempt to blunt the June publication of the allegations of Impeachment Counsel David Schippers book, said to be a "barn burner." Regnery is the publisher. In Early 2000, DPMO announced they would not seek funding for inspection sites past the year 2004. There is no way, at the present pace, to adequately close the books with any sort of accuracy by that time, even with the known deficiencies up to this time. The die is finally cast - a cut off time to "close the books." And, consider the case of young Elian Gonzales. Found floating in the ocean, attempting to flee Cuba, Attorney General Janet Reno, with concurrence of the Clintons, wants to return him to his father, who did not have custody, in Cuba, where Castro government officials vow to keep custody of Elian, away from his father, and bring him up as a good communist. That says legions about political inclinations and what type of "village" it takes to "raise a child" as per Clinton and his chosen successor.

I believe this closes all the loose ends. I hope this adds to your understanding of the complexity of the POW issue and that it's just not a simple account for the remains problem. Unfortunately, those in charge believe the opposite and their lack of progress over a quarter century or more proves that it's not how long you've been on a job that counts; it's how long it takes to recognize the problem and arrive at a solution that really matters. I believe I've outlined the problem, a potential solution, and succinctly argued my position. Now, we get to work on the solution.

Excerpts from the DOD Presentation to the Woodcock Commission, Col. C.M. Matthews, USA, March 15, 1977.

... Today, I would like to tell you ... how we know the communists can account for them... any accounting we may get will be less than a full one.

The Vietnam cease-fire agreement contained the most comprehensive provisions to account for the missing ... Had these provisions been implemented, we would have had our accounting...We have no evidence ... any American servicemen are being held as prisoners ....There is a great deal of information that we can reasonably expect ... After the cease-fire, the Vietnamese gave us information about some we did not expect them to know about. On the other hand, they denied knowledge of some Americans who were known to have been in their custody .... Our five categories and the criteria for placing an individual in a certain group are ....

CATEGORY 1 CONFIRMED KNOWLEDGE: This category includes all personnel who were: **a.** Identified by the enemy by name; **b.** Identified by reliable information received from releases/ escapes, or; **c.** Reported by highly reliable intelligence sources; and **d.** Identified through analysis of all-source intelligence...

CATEGORY 2 - SUSPECT KNOWLEDGE: This category includes personnel who were: **a.** Involved in the same incidents as individuals reported in category 1; **b.** Lost in areas or under such conditions that they may reasonably be expected to be known by the enemy; **c.** connected with an incident which was discussed but not identified by name in the enemy news media; or **d.** probably identified through analysis of all-source intelligence....

CATEGORY 3 - DOUBTFUL KNOWLEDGE: This category includes personnel whose loss incident is such that it is doubtful that the enemy would have knowledge of the specific individuals:

CATEGORY 4 - UNKNOWN KNOWLEDGE: ... the unknown category, are those we simply don't know about...(or) what the enemy might have ...

CATEGORY 5 - CATEGORY UNRELATED TO DEGREE OF ENEMY KNOWLEDGE: This category includes those personnel whose remains have been determined to be non-recoverable... The men in category 5 are known dead but not recoverable.... (**Note: Some have been**)

The categories were developed to determine what we should reasonably expect from the other side. The numbers of men currently listed in the various categories (1977) are 179 in category 1; 1160 in category 2; 344 in category 3; 428 in category 4; and 436 in category 5... We simply cannot accept the other side's denial of knowledge of any of these men.... We want that information... Accounting for our men and recovering remains have always been a strictly humanitarian issue ..... An earlier denial of information by the North Vietnamese appears to be no barrier to later release of that same information. ... we are inevitably asked how many ... the other side should account for. ...we would say it would be reasonable to expect an accounting for those in categories 1 and 2 - a total of 1339 men....

APPENDIX B
Message from President Richard M. Nixon to the Prime Minister of the Democratic Republic of Vietnam, February 1, 1973.

The President wishes to inform the Democratic Republic of Vietnam of the principles which govern the United States participation in the postwar reconstruction of North Vietnam...., (1) The government of the United States of America will contribute to postwar reconstruction of North Vietnam without any political conditions. (2) Preliminary ... contribution ... will fall in the range of $3.25 billion of grant aid over five years. Other forms of aid will be agreed upon ... studies indicate the appropriate programs could fall in range of 1 to 1.5 billion dollars...

APPENDIX C

Edited Conclusions and Recommendations of the House Select Committee on Missing Persons ... 'FINAL REPORT', December 13, 1976.

That the results of the investigations ... have led this committee to the belief that no Americans are still being held alive as prisoners .... That were one or more missing Americans alive ... repeated statements since 1973 by Indochinese officials ... militate against any returning alive from captivity.... That at least one deserter and one defector the latter currently listed as a POW (Bobby Garwood), were alive in Indochina in the early 1970's and may still be alive, and that a small number of other deserters and civilians may still reside in Vietnam... no reliable evidence ... represents a careful studied assessments of all acquisitions ... the national intelligence community demonstrated an impressive ability to produce reliable information on POWs held ....

...the Department of State policy of quiet diplomacy prior to 1969 was ineffective in improving the treatment of American prisoners, whereas the go public campaign after 1969 produced favorable results.... the Socialist Republic of Vietnam has called for selective implementation of the Paris Agreement ... dealing with American reconstruction aid to Vietnam, in exchange for POW/MIA information ... the Department of State failed to inform the select committee fully... of ... the correspondence between the ... United States and Vietnam (**Note: Nixon letter**)

... the governments of Indochina may be capable of returning the remains of more than 150 Americans ... the Congress and the administration will not agree to any conditions even faintly resembling blackmail in order to gain an accounting...

APPENDIX D

Additional Views Congressman John J. Moakley, Jim Lloyd, and Richard Ottinger, December 13, 1976.

The report is an excellent one.... Nevertheless, I feel compelled to express a few thoughts of my own. ... we have found no evidence to support either the contention that all the missing are dead nor that they are alive.... I do not believe that this report intends to argue for an assumption that there are no Americans alive in Indochina. .... I wish to state as clearly as possible ... as floor manager of the resolution, that it neither obliges nor even authorizes the Committee to deal with the issue of status reviews. There is substantial reason to believe that then President Richard M. Nixon, in a letter to Hanoi, named a specific dollar amount of reparations which would be paid after the war as ransom for information on the missing .... the Nixon-Kissinger secret diplomacy is producing the stalemate in which we now find ourselves....

John Joseph Moakley, M.C.
Jim Lloyd, M.C.

The Honorable **Richard L. Ottinger** *wishes to associate himself with the additional remarks of the Honorable John Joseph Moakley. His name was inadvertently omitted.*

I received your letter dated January 5, 1977. I asked to be included with Congressman Moakley's separate opinion but for some reason the printer did not get my word. I still support Mr. Moakley's views....

APPENDIX E

Separate views Congressman Benjamin A. Gilman and Tennyson Guyer, December 13, 1976.

Our mutual concern that certain conclusions and recommendations in the final report may serve to reduce the momentum attained by the Select Committee.... There are certain conclusions and recommendations... with which we respectfully disagree and herein voice separate views and opposition. ... First, we disagree with the conclusion ... that governments of Indochina may be capable of returning the remains of more than 150 Americans.'... To limit arbitrarily the amount and type of information we demand could result in discouraging Hanoi, Vientiane, and Phonm Penh from providing all the information they have available....

Second, we disagree ... that the moratorium on individual case reviews by the military secretaries be lifted ... We believe that individual case reviews would generally result in reduced congressional and administration concern... A third ... concern is that early termination of ... Select Committee would de-emphasize the importance of the POW/MIA issue.... A fourth area ... is that the administration should take prompt and appropriate steps to guarantee the most favorable atmosphere ... for an accounting .... a positive gesture on the part of the United States will help bridge the vast gap ... between the United States and Vietnam...

Finally we believe the committee should not consider that all POW/MIAs are dead until the United States has received as full and exhaustive an accounting as it is possible. ... There is no justification for erecting a POW/MIA tombstone.

Benjamin Gilman, M.C. Tennyson Guyer, M.C.

APPENDIX F

Letter, Congressman Moakley to President Carter, February 1, 1977,

... The Committee's final report presents two findings and recommendations which go to the heart of the controversy. The Committee concluded that there are no Americans alive in Indochina and recommended that the administration proceed with immediate status reviews. I think it is important to note that outright dissent ... were expressed ... by two members ... I filed ... a far more cautious position... supported by two other members. **This even split must be seen as representing the true views of the Committee** ... it would be most unfortunate if ... (the final report) ... were used as a basis for foreign policy and DOD status decisions.... We have seen clearly the willingness of the Vietnamese to exploit our anguish over the MIA issue ...

John Joseph Moakley, M.C.

APPENDIX G

Brief of Congressman Benjamin Gilman as AMICUS CURIAE, HOPPER V. CARTER, FEBRUARY 6, 1978

I am submitting this brief ... because ... a supposed final report of a Congressional Committee, ... have been offered to the court ... the documents so provided are not complete but are missing material that goes to their weight and credibility ... is of dubious validity and its defects should be pointed out. Missing from the copies of the Final report ... is an addendum written by representative Ottinger, ... any indication that Rep. Lloyd was also a dissenter. .... Of the ten members ... no more than five supported the Final report ... a majority of those voting is necessary to adopt a report. ... no record of any vote having been taken. That half of the Committee dissented is clear. The Final Report is then but a statement of one side of an unresolved dispute ... to adopt a report, the committee must act together... in a situation where the committee is was equally divided, the committee may ... transmit the evidence, ... the committee may not transmit a 'report'....

...there was no sworn testimony given by any of the witnesses at any hearings ... It was nothing more than a succession of expressions of views by a series of individuals of varying expertise. I believe that it would not be proper to consider any of this material on the same probative level as sworn testimony of witnesses subject to cross-examination.... *Benjamin A. Gilman   4 February 1978.*

APPENDIX H
Affidavit of Stephen Frank, HOPPER v. CARTER, March 13, 1974

... On or about July 23, 1973, a meeting was arranged whereby the undersigned and three colleagues would meet with Colonel Nguyen Do ... responsible for any accounting relating to the 1300+ Americans still listed as Missing in Action or unidentified Prisoners of War.... Colonel Do was asked as to certain individuals comprising the 1300+ list. He stated "We do not know why you are here because your government considers all these men dead.".... his government felt is was inappropriate for any Americans to discuss with the North Vietnamese anything dealing with Americans who had already been classified as dead ...

Stephen R. Frank signed and sworn March 13, 1974

APPENDIX I
Extracts from the first-year Program for Reconstruction and Healing the Wounds of War (Final Report)

Prefabricated housing ...150,000 - 200,000 square meters; Building Steel, shaped and plated, 200,000 metric tons; Pharmaceutical raw materials, $2 million; Working Tools, $3 million; Bulldozers: 140 HP, 250 - 500 ea., 75 HP, 200 ea.; Industrial Chemicals, $10 million; Synthetic Rubber 15,000 metric tons; Steel Alloy, 5,000 metric tons; Telephone cable, 500 kilometers; Thermal Power station and 400 kilometers of transmission line; Oil storage, 150,000 cubic meters; Floating dock, capacity 1 million metric tons a year; Tugs, 100 ea.; Road-building equipment, 30 teams; Rail, complete, 70,000 metric tons; Industrial chemicals $50 million; Industrial machinery, $100 million

APPENDIX J
TOP SECRET

TFR 136 - 4 GENERAL STAFF OF THE ARMED FORCES OF THE USSR MAIN INTELLIGENCE DIRECTORATE (GRU)
REPORT of the Deputy Chief of the General Staff of the VNA General - Lieutenant Tran Van Quang at the Politburo Meeting 12 September, 1972
(Translated from Vietnamese into Russian - Moscow - 1972 (edited)

Dear Comrades: I reported to you earlier about the ... fundamental characteristics of the past stage of our people's conflict against the American Imperialists...

These tasks once again confirm our resoluteness to attain victory. This is a very correct course ... We will also dwell on a number of the Supreme Command's ... in which an evaluation of our victories gained over the period from 30 Mar 72 to the present is given ... Several meetings between us and the US aimed at developing measures on resolving the Vietnam issue have already taken place. We have decisively rejected a number of proposals ... we have maintained our position ... If the US truly wants to resolve the Vietnam issue ... it must refuse to support the Nguyen Van Thieu regime ... We organized meetings with South Vietnamese representatives aimed at preparing a solution of the military and political issues in South Vietnam ...we are affiliating several of our plans with them ... we have succeeded in winning their sympathy at these meetings ... we have conducted 8 similar meetings with representatives of the Saigon authorities ...

meetings with General Ngo Dinh Dzu... a candidate for president of South Vietnam and battled with Nguyen Van Thieu and Nguyen Cao Ky ... during the Ngo Din Diem government, he was a senator in the upper chamber ... he is characterized as a reactionary, an enemy of communism ... He spoke against American troops on South Vietnamese territory ... This is why we tried to attract this person to our side ... our meetings with him have allowed him to see the nature of the Americans and the present face of the Saigon Government... agreed to enter into a future coalition government and spoke out against the policy of "Vietnamization" ...

Significant changes have taken place in General Dzu's ... way of thinking. He is already not the same ardent anti communist ...General Dzu is for the expansion of democracy and freedom over the entire territory of South Vietnam... we understood what kind of major changes took place in his way of thinking ... these meetings and contacts with General Dzu had very good results... requested to meet with one of the prominent leaders of the NLF ... This meeting will be conducted secretly ... he is among those in the Saigon Government whose number is growing every day.

The second person is Nguyen Khanh, who earlier occupied the Prime Minister post ... after the overthrow of Ngo Dinh Diem ... a representative of the new trend ... These contacts took place in Paris, where we conducted 5 meetings ... periodically returns to Saigon where he engages in political activities ... he believes Nguyen Van Thieu is a dictator and fascist ... he is against the bombing of North Vietnam ... speaks for the establishment of a new government which would ... carry out a nationalist policy, while receiving foreign aid ... we are not striving to directly attract him to our side ...

The third person is Duong Van Minh ... he occupied the Prime Minister post after Nguyen Khanh... The political views of Duong Van Minh differ ... This is first expressed in ... the independent solution of internal problems by the Vietnamese with out US interference... He subjects the Vietnamese policy of Nixon to sharp criticism and also the policy carried out by the current Saigon Government. These are very good political views ... we have attained an important victory, forcing him to reflect. He also met with Nguyen Thi Binh several times in Paris ... he began to conduct this great work with us and with the intelligentsia ... with the aim of entering into a coalition government ...

The fourth person is the former Emperor Bao Dai. At one time, the possibility existed that the former emperor would have been with us ... he was forced to emigrate to France... holds great influence amongst the political figures in Quang Tri and Thua Thien Provinces and also in the city of Hue ... This is why we moved to make contact with Bao Dai ... to attract him to our side to attract his supporters in the regions where he has influence ... will come out against the presence of American troops ... calling for all of the political factions to create a free, neutral, peaceloving government ...

The fifth person is General Nguyen Van Vi ... which allowed us to understand his political position. He thinks the US will certainly suffer defeat in this war ... coming out for the creation of a coalition government ... We scored a great victory at the meeting with him ... his agreement to take part in a coalition government ... officially recognized the **victories won by the National Liberation Front of South Vietnam, i.e., our victories**... It is fitting to mention here the letter from Nguyen Cao Ky ... he lays out his views on the route to a resolution of the Vietnam problem...

you would know how the Politburo's **instructions on the recruitment** of these people to our side is being carried out ... **the agreement of these people to enter into a coalition government will precisely go in our favor** ... we have gained an understanding of the political views of these people ... **They also think that if the US withdraws its troops from South Vietnam and stops aiding the regime, the government would instantly fall to pieces** ...

In the provinces and in many towns ... we also tried to win over this category of people to our side ... we see we have chosen the correct course ... In other words, we should recruit these people to our side, and bring them into the coalition government so that we can use them to our favor in the diplomatic and political plan ... Thanks to these meetings, we are able to know who supports us and who is against us in South Vietnam...

With the goal of realizing these aims, The Supreme Command ... has developed directives for ... **the "Ba Be" plan, which is scheduled to be executed in October** ...Four hundred and six individuals were sent to execute the plan in South Vietnam. These individuals had gone through sufficient preparation and are well armed . Earlier, these people worked in the South Vietnam government apparatus. After the August Revolution, ... these people were left behind by us to active work with the enemy and therefore enter into the staff of various organs of the Saigon government ... we prepared and armed them well ...

The basic tasks for the "Ba Be" plan are: **elimination of all people who are stubborn and oppose our course**; who occupy leadership positions in the realm of the prince and above... conduct of activities for carrying out disruption in the Saigon government apparatus in the realm of province and lower with the goal being the installation of new people at the next shift of this apparatus. **We are attentively observing the people who oppose us** and our decision with regards to this group must be very serious and firm... **We have lists of these people and full dossiers** ... **to quickly do away with them** and ruin their order ... search and acquire materials testifying to the crimes of the Americans and their puppets ... we may accuse them of the perpetration of these crimes ... These are the three basic missions of the people **for carrying out the Ba Be plan ... in the month of October ... to influence the course of the Paris Peace Talks** ... the "Ba Be" plan is already being implemented ... **the elimination of all traitors, reactionaries, and counter-revolutionaries**, ... is an important task of the "Ba Be" plan. **We must** attract the neutral forces to our side ... to successfully carry out the "Ba Be" Plan ...

The political views of puppet army officers captain and above are very reactionary ... we should likewise search for ways to establish connections with officers and officials of the Saigon government ... the preparation of Plan "Ba Be" is developing well ... The goal of plan "Ba Be" is introduction of division into the ranks of the enemy and lowering of his will to resist ... to attain successes at the Paris negotiations ... a great step in the resolution of many issues in the current situation... For successful realization of this plan, we should as soon as possible deploy our forces, in order to approach implementation of this plan in the month of October ...

In the Paris negotiation ... Nixon being stubborn as before and is trying above all to achieve a military solution of the issue ... As a result of the exchange of opinions in the private meetings with Nixon's advisor, Kissinger, we understood that Nixon as before is being stubborn on settling the situation ... to attain settlement, we should conduct careful preparation to counter Nixon's designs... Nixon is being stubborn in continuing aggressive war ...

That is why we are filled with resolution to carry out Plan "Ba Be," the realization of which will be a turning point in the settlement of the situation on the front ... The intelligence directorate of the Ministry of National Defense and the Ministry of State Security conducted the training of these people ... the thorough training which is now going on ... it can be said that its successful realization will assist us to attain new large victories at the Paris negotiations on Vietnam ... this plan is being carried out. We have already succeeded in inserting a portion of our comrades into South Vietnamese territory ... and now our people are occupying stable positions in the puppet governing apparatus...

In addition to these issues ... **I will also report to you today on American POWs captured** on the various fronts of Indochina. The work with American prisoners of war has always been within the field of vision of the Politburo and has been reflected in its decisions ... Both of these decisions concern the issues of exploiting these **American POWs** ... This disturbs the public opinion of the whole world and of the US... The American POW issue is very complex. The peoples of the world ... want to know the exact number of POWs located in North Vietnam. Allow me to inform you specifically on this matter. **We have captured a very large number of American POWs** on the fronts of Indochina since the time that the US introduced their troops into Vietnam ... The number of American POWs has not been public to this day. we have kept this figure secret. **At today's Politburo session, I will report to you, Comrades, the exact number of American POWs. The total number of American POWs captured to date on the fronts of Indochina, i.e. in North Vietnam, South Vietnam, Laos, and Cambodia, comprises 1205 people.**... the total number of aviators, and saboteurs (special operations) (American advisors on diversionary ships and divers), captured on the territories of North and South Vietnam comprises 814 people. In addition, from other categories of American servicemen in Indochina, we have captured 391 people, including 283 in South Vietnam, 65 in Cambodia and 43 in Laos; **814 and 391 comprise 1205 people**...

We have captured 624 American aviators in North Vietnam... the 624 American aviators include 3 astronauts, i.e. three people who have completed the necessary training for space flight ... This figure also includes 15 US Air Force aces having more than 4000 flight hours each:... Among the other 47 prisoners captured in North Vietnam, there are 36 advisors of diversionary detachments who were inserted in the border region between the DRV and Laos; lone diversionists who were conducting reconnaissance of our main transportation routes from helicopters and reconnaissance ships; and several seamen who abandoned their ships that we damaged and whom we picked up...

In South Vietnam we have captured 143 US air crew members ... Among the 391 American POWs captured in South Vietnam, Laos and Cambodia ... Thus in summary I want to remind you again that **the 1205 American POWs presently in prisons of North Vietnam** include: 624 aviators captured in North Vietnam; 143 aviators captured in South Vietnam; 47 diversionists and other American servicemen captured in North Vietnam; 391 American servicemen of other categories, which includes 283 captured in South Vietnam, 65 in Cambodia, and 43 in Laos.

All of them are presently in prisons in North Vietnam. Currently, we have 11 prisons where American POWs are held. We used to have 4 large prisons, however after the American attempt to free their POWs from Son Tay, we expanded this number to 11. Each prison holds approximately 100 POWs... through them, we are attempting to gain an understanding of the current situation which has developed in the American Army, extract the material and information we need, and determine our position toward them.

We are also holding 104 American lieutenant colonels in one location and are attempting to extract information - secret information about troop dispositions and information concerning the US Defense Department from them. We have 235 majors concentrated in two locations.

Thus, we have dedicated special prisons for senior officers of the American Army: one for colonels, one for lieutenant colonels; and two for majors. The rest of the POWs, captains and below, were placed in other prisons...

There are 368 POWs who have progressive attitudes. They understand well that this war is unjust and unpopular on their part ... We will be able to release these 368 prisoners first ... There are 372 of the POWs who hold neutral views, i.e. their political outlook is not fully progressive, yet not too reactionary ... The remainder of the POWs hold reactionary views. In spite of the work carried out to explain to them the real state of things, they have not changed their reactionary views... All the POWs among the senior officers hold reactionary views, i.e. they do not condemn Nixon, they do not protest his policies, and they distort our course of action. **We understand that these officers come from rich families** ... We well understand that the American POW issue has great significance for the resolution of the South Vietnamese problem...

Soon, we will free several POWs in order to put pressure on the Nixon administration, observe his reaction, and the reaction the American public, as well as to demonstrate our good intentions in this matter. Thus, **the 1205 American POWs ... presently kept in prisons in North Vietnam** ... should cause the US government and Nixon himself to reflect. **We intend to resolve the American POW issue in the following manner**:

1. The US government must demonstrate compliance, i.e. a cease fire and the removal of Nguyen Van Thieu ... 2. While the American side is resolving the above mentioned problems, we can free several more aviators from the number who are

progressively inclined ... 3. Nixon must compensate North Vietnam for the great damage inflicted on it by this destructive war ... However, Nixon continues to resist resolving the Vietnamese question, thereby delaying the resolution of the American POW problem... we also have these comrades who do not understand this problem correctly... If we take a path of concession toward Americans and release POWs, then we would lose much ... this issue must be resolved on the basis of military and political aspects of settlement.

Holding 1205 POWs creates certain difficulties for us ... we were able to collect data about American weapons and also valuable scientific materials about the US Army, for instance, material on how to use different types of weaponry, tactical / technical characteristics of aircraft, Air Force directives, as well as materials about other types of armament of the US Army. We have been able to uncover US intentions in the international arena and on a number of other issues which are related to war in Indochina.

That is why we are convinced that our position concerning POWs has and continues to be correct... That is why we are now concentrating on the successful resolution of this problem on the collection and study of materials from interrogations of American aviators who were shot down over North Vietnam and American scientists captured in this war, particularly Air Force specialists, as well as scientists in other technical areas...

The 1205 American POWs kept in the prisons of North Vietnam represent a large number. For now, we **have officially published a list of only 368 POWs. The rest are not acknowledged.** The US government is aware of this, but they do not know the exact number of POWs, or they perhaps only assume an approximate number based on their losses ... we are keeping the number of POWs secret. We are continuing to collect and study materials from POW interrogations ...

Collection and study of these materials has provided us great assistance in studying the scientific discoveries of the USA, in developing methods to counter contemporary weapons, including chemical, which have inflicted great harm upon us in this war.

We still have among us Comrades who think: why do we keep these POWs and not take advantage of the Nixon proposals? ... This is not political horse trading, but rather an important condition and serious argument for successful resolution of the Vietnam problem. That is why the matter of the American POWs has great significance in exposing Nixon's designs ... when the American government resolves the political and military issues on all three fronts of Indochina, we will set free all American POWs. We consider this a very correct course...

At the present time these plans are being worked out with the goal of preparing the necessary forces for their implementation... We should mobilize 250,000 men, 200,000 of which would be sent to South Vietnam, and 50,000 to Laos and Cambodia... We hold high the invincible banner of Marxism - Leninism. We are carrying out the precepts of Ho Chi Minh... The course of our party is assuredly correct... I have completed the presentation of the report.

TOP SECRET

(DEFENSE INTELLIGENCE AGENCY
WASHINGTON, D.C. 20301

LTC James G. Gritz
Chief, Congressional Relations
OSD/DSAA

Bo:

Received your retirement notice. I have mixed emotions about
your hanging it up to pursue this PW/MIA matter but, frankly I
don't know anyother way of getting to the bottom of it all.
Understand the Hughes arrangement is satisfactory. You should
enjoy spending the winter in California. Your desire to put
your career on hold is appreciated. Your experience in special
operations can be used to best advantage. When this matter is
concluded there will be strong support for your return to active
duty. Depending on politics that should not be a problem.

Keep your government contacts limited to those with an absolute
need to know. The word spreads fast here in Washington. I'll
do what I can before checking out of the net myself. I trust
you will have no problem developing a flow of information. It
is too bad we have to proceed this way but the Administration
will not face up to the problem. Gen Tighe is well aware of the
situation but, his hands are tied. He is a true soldier in a
blue suit.

Because of the politics involved, contact me only if you get in
a spot with no way out. This thing is so sensitive it could
result in a real inquisition if word leaked out that we were
proceeding unofficially. . This is a real hot potato so watch your
back trail carefully. We will arrange to meet as time and
circumstances allow. Of course if you uncover something critical
contact me immediately. Keep the press and government offices
out of it.

So, you have the experience and background to confirm this thing
one way or another. Don't do anything to endanger your life or
the lives of those we left behind. I am confident that once you
prove beyond a doubt that our men are still captive the system
will do the rest. Your task is not to be a one-man show but,
to pull together evidence to convince political skeptics of PW
existence. You will be free to do whatever is required on the
outside.

So, destroy this and all other written communication between us.

De oppresso liber!

EXHIBIT 2, P. 1 of 1

7722 Kalorama Road
Annandale, Va., 22003
27 December 1979

LTC James G. Gritz (USA Ret)
8107 Delgany Avenue
Playa Del Rey, CA, 90291

Dear Bo:

I received the material that you sent me
and I was overwhelmed with what you had done. It
must have taken a great deal of time and energy.
But, you have done that before.

From the accounts you sent me, there can
be no doubt about live Americans. I always suspected
it but, at the same time hoped it wasn't so. I
remember our talk about the affair in Panama. I
knew it must be true even then but I didn't realize
the scope of it until I got all your material.

Keep after it Bo and if I can be of help,
let me know. You deserve a great deal of credit
for what you have done. I am sure you will be
appropriately rewarded.

De oppresso liber!

Sincerely,

The Rt. Hon. Joe Clark, P.C., M.P.
Secretary of State for External Affairs

Canada

Le très hon. Joe Clark, C.P., député
Secrétaire d'État aux Affaires extérieures

OTTAWA, ONTARIO
K1A 0G2

December 9, 1985

Dear Mr. Ketcheson,

Thank you for your letter of November 21, 1985.

The story you relate is an unusual one and perhaps in order to begin my reply I might start with the sinking during Typhoon Lex of the Glomar Java Sea in October 1983.

My Department is aware of the article carried in the HOUSTON CHRONICLE of June 1984 reporting that a Vietnamese citizen claimed to have sat in prison next to six Americans and that one of them matched the description of John Pierce, a member of the crew of the Glomar Java Sea and whose photograph he had seen in a magazine. It was uncertain at the time and, I think, remains so today how much credence should be given to this story in light of the efforts undertaken to locate survivors. Immediately following the sinking of the drilling ship, American aircraft searched the area. Similarly, the Chinese authorities launched an extensive search involving 22 ships over an area of 63,000 square kilometers. These efforts by two countries met with no results. As there was, however, also a possibility that survivors in lifeboats could have drifted into Vietnamese waters, the Vietnamese themselves conducted a search of their territorial waters and coastline. No survivors, bodies or debris or lifeboats were found. Later in the Spring of 1984, the owners of the Glomar Java Sea recovered 31 bodies from the wreck. The remaining 50 crew members were presumed dead.

Mr. Robert D. Ketcheson
General Manager
Wild Fire International
Emergency Services
Box 181
Blackfalds, Alberta
T0M 0J0

-2-

As a victim of the disaster was a Canadian citizen, our Embassy in Bangkok which is also accredited to Vietnam, was instructed in November 1983 to raise the matter with the Vietnamese authorities. Two separate demarches were made, one in Bangkok in November of that year and again in December in Hanoi. In response, the Vietnamese authorities re-confirmed that they had conducted a thorough search for survivors, bodies or other signs of the tragedy but that they had found nothing. There is no evidence that the Vietnamese authorities would have misused the results of their search for survivors. It is likely, I think, that if survivors had been found, the authorities would have produced them as a sign of their goodwill.

The combination of survivors of the Glomar Java Sea disaster and POWs from the Vietnam war hardly seems believable, since I must ask myself what would the Government of Vietnam hope to gain today that it could not have achieved two years or even longer ago. If the answer lies in the conditions attached to the POW's release, then the situation is indeed bizarre. The Government of Canada is in no position to act as liaison between Vietnam and the United States to normalize relations. This is for those two countries to work out themselves, and I might add that the United States has made clear that normalization is linked to constructive action by Vietnam on the MIA issue and to Vietnamese withdrawal from Cambodia. To date while there have been some recent signs of cooperation on recovering MIA remains, Vietnam appears to have no intention to effect an early withdrawal of its forces from Cambodia. Again, in regard to the condition for Vietnam's political and economic realignment, this strikes me as more wishful thinking on the part of Vietnamese refugees than any real desire by the Government of Vietnam. There is nothing to prevent Vietnam from taking steps to shed itself of Soviet influence and control. Unfortunately the Vietnamese authorities have reiterated on several occasions their satisfaction with the close relationship they hold with the Soviet Union.

As for Canada acting as a "receiving station", I have no problems with this in principle, but before taking any steps, I think we need an opportunity to assess first whatever hard evidence is available that there are POWs alive in Vietnam. I am prepared to authorize the use of diplomatic mail facilities to bring the purported film to Canada, and you should inform your contacts that the film can be delivered to the Canadian Embassy in Peking for forwarding to the Bureau of East Asia Affairs in Ottawa. That Bureau will let you know when the film arrives and what action it will plan to take to assess and to verify or to disprove its contents. I might caution you that if the film appears genuine, we will need immediately to inform the American authorities since I suspect they alone would be in a position to make positive identification of any POWs.

-3-

In closing, I would like to offer my hope that there
may be some basis for the reports your organization has received.
I have made available the Department's facilities in the belief
that we cannot afford to second guess the accuracy of your
information.

I have sent a copy of this letter to Mr. Oostrom, M.P.,
as well as copies of our exchange to the Embassy in Peking.

Yours sincerely,

MEMORANDUM

NATIONAL SECURITY COUNCIL

ACTION

January 21, 1980

MEMORANDUM FOR: ZBIGNIEW BRZEZINSKI

FROM: MICHEL OKSENBERG

SUBJECT: Renewed League of MIA Families Request
for Appointment

Once again, the National League of Families of American
Prisoners and Missing in Southeast Asia seeks to meet
you (Tab B).

They have nothing new to say, and I am capable of summarizing
any developments for you. So I recommend turning down the
request, and I will call Ann Griffiths separately to say
you have instructed me to see her.

However, a letter from you is important to indicate that
you take recent refugee reports of sighting of live Americans
"seriously." This is simply good politics; DIA and State
are playing this game, and you should not be the whistle
blower. The idea is to say that the President is determined
to pursue any lead concerning possible live MIAs.

Do not offer an opinion as to whether these leads are realistic.
Apparently you revealed skepticism to Congressman Gilman, and
my recommended letter to the League walks you back from that.

RECOMMENDATION:

That you sign the letter at Tab A to Ann Griffiths.

COMMITTEE CONFIDENTIAL

From the files of the Solarz Subcommittee;

Stenographic Transcript of Hearings before the Subcommittee on
Asian and Pacific Affairs of the Committee on Foreign Affairs
(and hard copy Briefing Slides).

The transcript was in typed draft, with pencil editing changes.

Thursday, June 25, 1981

Statement of:

LTG Eugene Tighe, DIA
Rear Admiral Jerry Paulson, DIA
Lt Col Jack Kennedy, DIA
Fred Brown, Deputy Assistant Secretary of State, East Asia and
Pacific Affairs

SUBJECT: Nhom Marrot

1.   -- As an employee of USAID, reported sighting 5
caucasian prisoners in Jan 1976 in Laos. A first hand sighting.
Passed polygraph. USAID employment verified.

2.   -- wrote letter to Vang Pao on April 19 1979
saying 18 US POWs and 25 Lao Prisoners were being held in a cave
near Nhom Marrot. The information was relayed to   by a
resistance leader named   . The prisoners were moved into
the Nhom Marrot area on 10 March 1975. The letter said they were
being held in a cave near Kham Keut (Note: not clear if it was
referring to a previous detention site or the same one.) It also
said 2 US POWs, 1 Australian and 1 Japanese prisoner were held in
an adjacent cave. (NOTE: Briefer noted that it took some time
before this letter reached US government hands.)

3. Photography -- Cave area apparently identified. Imagery of
October 1979 through 1980 "generally correlates with description
of detention area." One cave located. Foliage heavy - other
cave entrances possibly concealed.

4.   -- In November 1979, reported the detention of a
Lt Col. Paul W. Mercland, near Moung Nhom Marrot. DIA found no
correlation for a Mercland. However, a Major Paul W. Bannon was
lost in Laos in 1969. Briefer noted it was not uncommon for POWs
to assume they had been promoted while in captivity and would use
new rank designations - hence the Lt Col. Tighe commented that
Mercland sounds like "American" and made the supposition that
source may have dropped or mistakenly supplanted "American" for
last name. It was noted that   passed polygraph
test(s) in "Sep/Oct 1980."   not given polygraph.

5. "Sensitive Source" -- In November 1980, a "sensitive source" reported that 30 US POWs were being held near Muong Nhom Marrot. The information reportedly provided to source by LPDR officials, reliability unknown. However source who passed information from original source evaluated as "very high in reliability."

6. Photography -- Imagery from 4 December, 1980 indicated secure detention facility near Nhom Marrot. The facility was not constructed in Imagery of April 1978. The number "52" was detected stomped in the row crop area of the camp on 30 December, 1980 imagery. Group of people continuously observed.

Adm Paulson comment, " It was based on that evidence, Mr. Chairman, that the recommendation was made that we had enough significant evidence to attempt verification."

It was mentioned that "by this time (Dec 1980) Dick Allen, Jim Buckley and Secretary Haig" had been briefed on this information.

Congressman Dornan interjected at this point that he was briefed by Tuttle while he was still at DIA that "prior to November 1980, but about the same time area, a broadcast was picked up referring to 27 American POWs moving from a camp up north to this camp when it was prepared for occupancy, some time around this period."
"Remember Admiral, you (NOTE: referring to a previous briefing presumably in May or June 1981 after Paulson replaced Tuttle) had not heard of this and one of the other Colonels with us at the briefing said that is right."

Paulson did not respond. Tighe said he was not aware of the message.

(NOTE: It was noted, that in the file folder in which this transcript and briefing slides were kept, the two pages on which the conversation regarding the radio intercept were transcribed had been copied and paper clipped together. It was noted that on this copy, of that part of the discussion, that every mention of "radio broadcast" or "intercept" was lined through and replaced with the word "information" or "intelligence." It is probable, therefore, that the final transcript has no reference to a "radio broadcast." It is not clear why this was done, but it may have been to allow storage at a lower level of classification.)

CONCURRENCES

U-56,245/DB-4   1 0 AUG 1979

MEMORANDUM FOR THE SECRETARY OF DEFENSE

SUBJECT: Prompt entry into the United States, of a Vietnamese refugee
          reporting American Prisoners of War in Vietnam as late as
          1978 - ACTION MEMORANDUM

A Vietnamese refugee, ▮▮▮▮▮▮▮▮▮▮▮ who is presently in a Vietnamese
refugee camp in Indonesia, has reported that he was captured in 1971 while
serving as an ARVN soldier, held in various Vietnamese prison camps, and
just prior to his release was detained in a camp from December 1977 to
July 1978 with 49 Americans.

If the substance of ▮▮▮▮▮▮▮▮ information is true, then its importance
goes without saying. However, if ▮▮▮▮▮▮ is not telling the truth -- if
for some reason it is a fabrication -- it raises cruel false hopes for the
families of those men still missing in Southeast Asia.

There are some difficulties with ▮▮▮▮▮▮▮▮ coming to this country in that
he made material misstatement of facts during his application for entry to
the United States. Additionally, during his initial interviews, he denied
to State Department officials any knowledge of U.S. prisoners or having had
any military service. Although initiatives have been taken with State
Department to have ▮▮▮▮▮▮▮ brought to this country for thorough interrogation, his status remains as "ineligible" at this time.

As reported, ▮▮▮▮▮▮▮ story of capture and confinement with Americans is
plausible. His report agrees in some instances with confirmed information
and yet there are some important discrepancies.

I feel there is an obligation on the U.S. Government to make every effort to
confirm or deny ▮▮▮▮▮▮ report and that this can best be done through
interrogating him in this country.

Recommend you sign the enclosed letter requesting Mr. Vance's assistance
in this matter.

                                         SIGNED

Enclosure   EUGENE F. TIGHE, JR.
                                         Lieutenant General, USAF
                                         Director
Coordination:

OASD/ISA Brig Gen TC Pinckney, USAF

Prepared by Mr. CF Trowbridge, Jr., x25928

CFTrowbridge:bp:3 Aug 79:DIA/DB-4H:25928:WPE

OSD Record Copy   DIA CAO Comeback
Signer's Copy   DIA File Copy

THE SECRETARY OF DEFENSE
WASHINGTON, D.C. 20301

AUG 17 1973

Honorable Cyrus Vance
Secretary of State
Washington, D.C. 20520

Dear Cy:

   I have received a report of a Vietnamese refugee in
Indonesia who claims to have been detained in the northern
part of Vietnam with 49 American prisoners of war as late
as July 1973. This former ARVN soldier, ▇▇▇▇▇▇▇▇▇▇
▇▇▇▇▇, has been interviewed and relates a consistent and
plausible story, although there are some significant discrepancies.

   If his story is true, it provides important information, and if it is not it cruelly raises false hope for
the families of those still missing in Southeast Asia. I
therefore believe there is an obligation on the part of the
U.S. Government to make every effort to confirm or deny
▇▇▇▇▇▇▇▇ report.

   However, I understand that there are apparently some
difficulties associated with ▇▇▇▇▇▇▇▇ entry into this
country--he is reported to have made material misstatements
of fact to U.S. immigration officials during his processing
for entry. Although approaches have been made to the State
Department concerning the desirability of interrogating ▇▇
▇▇▇▇ in this country, his status continues to be categorized
by State as ineligible.

   Could you help?

                          Sincerely,

                          Hand

EXHIBIT 9, P. 2 of 3 (9B)

O · 7

THE SECRETARY OF STATE

WASHINGTON

RECEIVED IN H/S   SEP 1 8 1979

9/21/79

September 17, 1979

Dear Harold:

Thank you for bringing to my attention the case of Nguyen Dac Giang, the Vietnamese refugee who claimed to have information about US prisoners of war in Vietnam. I share fully your desire to check the veracity of Mr. Giang's story, and to this end our staff in Indonesia would welcome a visit by Defense Department officials as soon as possible. We are fully prepared to cooperate in helping you determine, as quickly as possible, the accuracy of Mr. Giang's statement.

In view of the decision of the Immigration and Naturalization Service not to admit Mr. Giang to the United States, you might wish to consider approaching the Commissioner of Immigration to have the decision changed. For the moment, however, I believe the necessary interviews could be conducted in Indonesia, with the advantage that officials who previously interviewed Mr. Giang would be available.

Whatever venue is finally arranged for further questioning of Mr. Giang, you have our full support in your efforts.

With warm regards,

Sincerely,

April 23, 1980

Mr. Larry O'Daniel
1080 Bandon Road
Toms River, N.J.   08753

Dear Larry:

        Enclosed, as discussed on the telephone today,
is a copy of a letter dated 6 August 1979 from Charles
F. Trowbridge, Jr. from DIA to the National League of Families.
I also attach the various enclosures which were included
with that letter, including "enclosure 2" consisting of "Six
case files providing information from Southeast Asian refugees regarding U.S. prisoners in SEA" - this was, as you
will recall, the one page enclosure identifying six particular cases of refugees reports which were regarded as
very creditable.

        To appreciate the significance of this letter,
it should be borne in mind that this is the material which
was given to Congressman Wolff and others prior to their
trip to Hanoi last year. It was material that was available for them to discuss when they went there and quite
obviously, if it was weak, it would have done nothing but detract from rather than enhance any arguments that might be
made to the Vietnamese urging them to provide an accounting.
These six cases, as you know, are the mere tip of the iceberg. We now have literally hundred's of DIA reports and
DIA candidly admits that they are withholding many hundred's
more.

        I trust you will find this information useful.

                            Sincerely yours,

                            Dermot G. Foley

DGF:gf
Enclosure.

CUMBERLAND COUNTY

NORTH CAROLINA   AFFIDAVIT OF ROBERT GARWOOD

NOW COMES Robert Garwood, and hereby swears and affirms the following.

1. As a Prisoner of War of the Vietnamese in Vietnam between the approximate time frame of 1973 and 1979, I personally saw United States Prisoners and heard about others from Vietnamese prison guards. I learned that in the late 1970's that

Page Two

me about United States Prisoners of War in Vietnam. I speak Vietnamese and was given a standing order by the Vietnamese not to talk with other American Prisoners.

3. To the best of my recollection I believe there were forty to sixty American Prisoners at Yen Bay, approximately twenty in the Bat Bat district of Sante Province, six American Prisoners of war at Gia Lam and approximately six or seven at Ly Nam De. Also, in approximately the summer of 1977 I personally observed approximately thirty to forty Americans climb down from a box car in a train directly in front of me. All of these men were speaking American English. There is no doubt in my mind

American Prisoners of War remain in Vietnam. I provide this information under oath and under penalty of perjury.

Subscribed and sworn this 23ʳᵈ day of August, 1985.

ROBERT GARWOOD

STATE OF Virginia

COUNTY OF Arlington

November 19, 1984

The Honorable
Former Congressman John LeBoutillier
P. O. Box 230
Old Westbury, NY 11568

Dear Congressman LeBoutillier:

During my career in the military, including many
years in military intelligence, the cause of Prisoner-Of-War
and the Missing In Action has been of great concern to me.
I have kept a close eye on the evidence available on this
matter, and believe that some of our men are still alive
and imprisoned. As long as there is the possibility of our

Sincerely,

Daniel O. Graham
Lt. Gen., USA (Ret.)

November 12, 1984

Congressman John LeBoutillier
P.O. Box 22683
Dallas, Texas 75222-6683

Dear Congressman LeBoutillier:

I have been deeply involved in the POW/MIA issue during the three wars in which
I have been privileged to serve my country.

At the end of World War II I parachuted onto Hainan Island to rescue some
prisoners of war held there by the Japanese. During the Korean conflict,
as deputy chief of station for CIA, I worked on evasion and escape operations.
Again, in Vietnam, the joint organization which I commanded had the responsibility for the evasion and escape operations in Southeast Asia including
rescue operations into North Vietnam. Many of the names on the current MIA/POW
lists are familiar to me from those days.

I feel very strongly about the men left behind in Vietnam. The Sky Hook II
Project is the best hope to recover these men. I am proud to be a part of it
and I look forward to seeing these heroes finally come home to America.

Sincerely,

JOHN K. SINGLAUB
Major General, USA (Ret)

In November 1979, DIA interviewed a former junior officer who had
served in the North Vietnamese Ministry of Defense and who reported
having personal access to information about U.S. PWs in Vietnam. He
demonstrated accurate knowledge about his department and its staff. He
also demonstrated accurate knowledge of former U.S. PW detention facilities,
and events associated with the U.S. PWs who were released from northern
Vietnam.

DIA is following-up on this case.
(Source is Le Dinh, former Intelligence official,who defected
in October, 1979)

received 1/25/80
vt

In November 1979, DIA interviewed a refugee, a former low level civil
servant in communist Vietnam, who provided apparently accurate information
about U.S. remains deposited at a military facility in Hanoi City,
Vietnam. This refugee exhibited some apparently authentic documents
which support his claimed direct access to information relating to
U.S. remains. This claim was reinforced by statements made by other
refugees who professed to have been acquainted with this person's background. · Furthermore, this refugee gave knowledgeable answers to test
questions designed to evaluate his familiarity with topics associated
with the handling of U.S. remains. DIA believes the refugee source to
be credible and will continue to pursue initiatives to confirm the
reported information.

Source also reported seeing 3 causcasions in 1978 and
1979 at the facility where he was processing the American
remains. He was told by the guards the three were American
prisoners and he heard them speaking English with an
American accent. The 3 drank bear and were "loosely
guarded" while they were in the compound. DIA rates the
source as credible.

received 1/25/80
vt

(Source is a Mr. Loc, a mortician who defected in
October 1979.)

DETENTION CAMP EAST OF THANKHEK, LAOS
DECEMBER 1980

DAM

ROW CROPS

M

Dear Ms. Griffiths:

This is in response to your letter of 22 March 1982, in which you appeal DIA's decision not to release live sighting reports of U.S. personnel in Southeast Asia received after 1 August 1979.

It is the policy of this Agency that all live sighting reports of U.S. personnel in Southeast Asia received after 1 August 1979 are properly classified in their entirety and are exempt from release under provisions of 5 U.S.C. 552 (b) (1), Freedom of Information Act.

Release of the information in the form you requested would enable the Vietnamese and Lao Governments to equate this released information to that which may exist. Obviously, these governments know the location of any American prisoners they might hold. By comparing this information to the released documents, even though they may be sanitized, would confirm to them the fact that we know the location of these prisoners and show the extent and capability of our collection efforts. Thus release of the information in the form you requested would be counterproductive to our intelligence efforts in this vital area. Your appeal for release of these documents is therefore denied.

Sincerely,

E. A. BURKHALTER, JR.
Rear Admiral, USN
Acting Director

I could not resist this juxtaposition of a document telling about POWs they knew they had from DIA and a slide print from the 6/25/81 testimony of DIA Director Tighe of "Fort Apache" or Nhom Marrot
Larry O'Daniel

MAJ Charles A. Dale was lost on 6/9/1965 with SSG David S. Demmon. Dale was part of a reported prisoner swap from China in 1986.

SSG David S. Demmon, lost with MAJ Charles A. Dale on 6/9/1965, was seen in captivity in the U-Minh Forest. Subsequent reanalysis said the captivity "never took place."
Part of <u>Trails of Deceit</u>

NORTHERN LAOS NEAR SAM NEUA

JANUARY 1988

POSSIBLE "K"

"USA" CLEARLY VISIBLE

This is the "Walking K" that Senator Kerry (MA) tried to make go away and this his Staff Director Zwenig had DOD working on a script to do just that. This is also the one that the farmer and his son made the "USA" 12 foot high to emulate the "USA" on the envelope from the USA that no one ever saw.

HOUSE OF COMMONS
CHAMBRE DES COMMUNES
OTTAWA CANADA
K1A 0A6

HOUSE OF COMMONS
Room 404 West Block
Ottawa, Ontario
K1A 0A6
(613) 952-2722

JOHN M. OOSTROM, M.P.
WILLOWDALE

CONSTITUENCY OFFICE
4950 Yonge St. S. 610
Willowdale, Ontario
M2N 6K1
(416) 223-9910

OTTAWA
February 13, 1986

Miss Zhang Xia
Head of Economy
China Food Cereals and Oils
82 Dong-An Men Street
Beiging
China

Dear Miss Zhang Xia:

This is to inform you that I am familiar with the
services and operations of Wild Fire International
Emergency Services in Blackfalds, Alberta and that I
personally know Mr. Robert Ketcheson, the general
manager of that organization. I have been in contact
with Bob since the autumn of 1985. I am also aware
that Mr. Robert Barker is active in Wildfire.

I can assure you that the Canadian government is also
aware of the operations of Wild Fire International, as
I have verbally mentioned its activities to the
Honourable Joe Clark, our Minister of External Affairs,
some months ago.

Subsequent to my conversations with Mr. Clark and
several of his departmental officials, I suggested to
Mr. Ketcheson to brief Mr. Clark of his activities in
writing. This was done on November 21, 1985.

I trust that this letter will be of some assistance to
you in your work. I look forward to hearing from you.

Best wishes.

Sincerely yours,

John Oostrom, M.P.
Willowdale

LCDR Ronald Dodge was a classic case of North Vietnamese gall. Captured on film in, Pilots in Pyjamas, the Vietnamese never acknowledged his capture until after they returned his remains in July, 1981. His story is onpage 31.

Xom Giong top secret camp.

They don't know what happened to him?

CPT David L. Hrdlicka, lost over Laos, the black hole of Asia, on 5/18/1965, was often seen in captivity with CPT Charles Shelton. On one occasin, the two were rescued, and then returned to captivity because of circumstances beyond their control. Obviously, he was alive as this picture amply demonstrates.

Lost in the Black Hole of Laos - Known Captured

POWS never have a nice day

COL Charles E. Shelton, Captured in Laos on 4/29/1965, was known as the symbolic "Last POW" until his status was changed at the request of the family. Held in captivity with CPT David Hrdlicka, the two were rescued at one point and returned to captivity due to battlefield conditions.

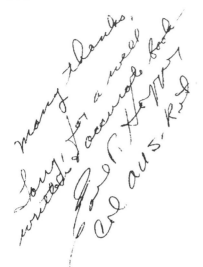

LTC Earl P. Hopper Jr., shot down over North Vietnam on January 10, 1968. He flew his crippled plane towards Laos and ejected. He has been carried on a CIA list as captured. He was the last POW from North Vietnam to be declared dead with no evidence of that death.

POW or MIA Let Hanoi know we care

COL Robert D. Anderson, USAF, shot down over North Vietnam October 6, 1972. Hanoi announced his capture. He was officially described by DOD as one on "whom there is 'hard evidence'" that he was "captured or detained by communist forces. Hanoi chooses not to account for him.

Note: The pages listed are not necessarily the only pages you will find these men referred to